Biblical Arc

Volume 2

Famous Discoveries that Support the Reliability of the Bible

SECOND EDITION

DAVID E. GRAVES

Electronic Christian Media
Toronto, Canada
2018

Biblical Archaeology Vol 2: Famous Discoveries that Support the Reliability of the Bible: Second Editon.
Includes bibliographic references and indexes.

Revision April 2018; May 2018; October 2018
Published by Electronic Christian Media
Toronto, Ontario, Canada M2J 4T4

ISBN-13: 978-1987754049
ISBN-10: 1987754042
1. Bible–Evidences, authority, etc. 2. Bible–Antiquities 3. Bible-Archaeology. I. Graves, David E. II. Title

Interior Book Design: David E. Graves
Cover Design: David E. Graves

Front Page Background - Dead Sea Scroll Messianic Testimony (4Q175) located in the Amman Museum, Jordan. God's Name, Yahweh is represented by four dots. Ammon Museum, Jordan. Photo by David E. Graves
Center – Reproduction of the bronze cast of the so-called "Prima Porta" statue of Augustus, Rome, Italy, Via dei Fori Imperiali, erected in the 1930's. Photo by David E. Graves.
Top Left – Merenptah Stele also known as the Israel stela, and is the earliest extrabiblical record of a people group called Israel. Egyptian Museum in Cairo (JE 31408). Courtesy of Greg Gulbrandsen.
Bottom Right – Reproduction of the Judaea Capta coin. David E. Graves.
Top and bottom boarder - Drawing of the Shema Seal depicting the roaring lion as the symbol of Judah. The inscriptions reads "(Belonging) to Shema [top line] (the) Servant (of) Jeroboam [bottom line]." Replica in the Israel Museum, Jerusalem, Israel (Cast 230). Drawing by David E. Graves.
Back Page Background – Assyrian Court scene (ca. 865-860 BC), from Nimrud, North-West Palace, Room G, panels 2-4 portraying King Ashurnasirpal II (883-859BC) with attendants. Original is in the British Museum, London, copy from Pushkin Museum, Moscow, Russia. Photo by David E. Graves.

Picture Acknowledgements

Maps and charts
David E. Graves all maps and charts

Printed in the United States of America.

To my loving wife
and archaeology companion
Irina

Acknowlegements

This book owes a great debt of gratitude to many friends and family whose profession and passion for the Bible and archaeology have contributed to its completion. First, I would like to acknowledge Glen Ruffle my good friend and editor. He has tirelessly laboured on the initial manuscript through its several revisions and provided helpful comments and suggestions along the way. His eye to detail and prompt attention to editorial issues is much appreciated. This work has benefitted greatly from your expertise.

I wish to thank Kimberly Day, the resource sharing librarian, at the Jerry Falwell Library, Liberty University, and her staff for their help in locating journal articles and books for my research. It is not always easy to do research from a distance so it is with gratitude that I wish to thank the Library department at Liberty for their quick response to my endless requests for obscure articles and books.

I also wish to express my gratitude to Todd Bolen, Leen Ritmeyer, Greg Gulbrandsen, Ferrell Jenkins, Peter J. Gentry, and Rex Geisler for their permission to use their professional work in photographs, and images to enhance the reader's experience.

Lastly, I wish to express my thankfulness to my loving wife Irina for her helpful comments, deep love, care, and patience during the long hours of writing and editing this work. Her editing skills and keen eye to detail were deeply appreciated.

Sola Deo Gloria

Intentionally left blank

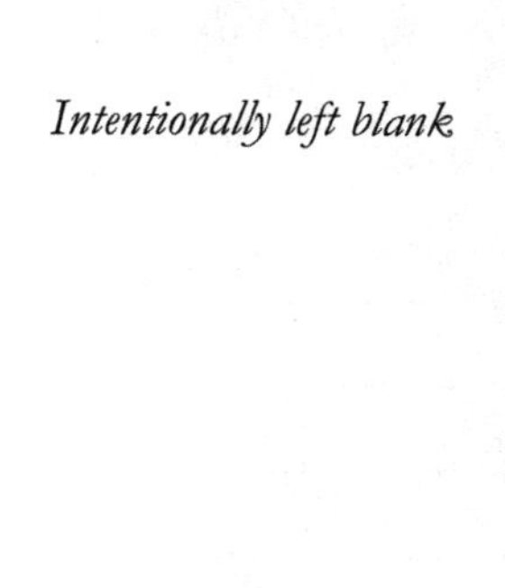

TABLE OF CONTENTS

Index of Images

Abbreviations

This work will conform to the abbreviations and general format conventions set out by *The SBL Handbook of Style: for Ancient Near Eastern, Biblical and Early Christian Studies* by Patrick H. Alexander, *et al.* eds. second printing (Peabody, Mass.: Hendrickson, 2002) for general literary conventions, Bible translations, biblical books, Dead Sea scrolls, pseudepigraphical, early patristic books, targumic material, *Mishnah*, Talmud, other Rabbinic works, *Nag Hammadi* tractates, commonly used periodicals, reference works and serials. Unless otherwise indicated the references to the works of ancient sources reflect the Loeb Classical Library numbering system and Latin abbreviations. Note that there are several spelling variations for most sites especially as used by early explorers, since they spell the Arabic words as they sound.

OLD TESTAMENT

Gen	Genesis
Exod	Exodus
Lev	Leviticus
Num	Numbers
Deut	Deuteronomy
Judg	Judges
Josh	Joshua
1–2 Sam	1–2 Samuel
1–2 Kgs	1–2 Kings
1–2 Chr	1–2 Chronicles
Neh	Nehemiah
Esth	Esther
Job	Job
Ps/Pss	Psalms
Prov	Proverbs
Eccl	Ecclesiastes
Isa	Isaiah
Jer	Jeremiah
Lam	Lamentations
Ezek	Ezekiel
Dan	Daniel
Obad	Obadiah
Jonah	Jonah
Mic	Micah
Nah	Nahum
Hab	Habakkuk
Zeph	Zephaniah
Mal	Malachi

NEW TESTAMENT

Matt	Matthew
Rom	Romans
1–2 Cor	1–2 Corinthians
Gal	Galatians
Eph	Ephesians
Phil	Philippians
Col	Colossians
1–2 Thess	1–2 Thessalonians
1–2 Tim	1–2 Timothy
Phlm	Philemon
Heb	Hebrews
Jas	James
1–2 Pet	1–2 Peter
1–2–3 John	1–2–3 John
Rev	Revelation

DEAD SEA SCROLLS

11Q5	Psalms, 11QPs[a] Sanders, *The Psalms Scroll of Qumran Cave 11*. DJD 4. (1965).
1QIsa[a]	*The Great Isaiah Scroll.* Kutscher, *The Language and Linguistic Background of the Isaiah Scroll: I QIsaa.* (1974).

1QIsa[b]	Isaiah[b] Scroll. Kutscher, *The Language and Linguistic Background of the Isaiah Scroll: I QIsaa.* (1974).
IQIsa[d]	Isaiah[d] Scroll. Kutscher, *The Language and Linguistic Background of the Isaiah Scroll: I QIsaa.* (1974).
3Q15	*The Copper Scroll.* Milik, de Vaux, and Baillet eds. *Les "petites grottes" de Qumrân.* DJD 3. (1962)
4Q175	4QTest; *Testimonia* from Qumran Cave 4. Allegro, and Anderson. *Qumrân Cave 4: I (4Q 158 - 4Q 186).* DJD 5 (1968)
4Q41	Ulrich, Cross, and Crawford, eds. *Qumran Cave 4: IX. Deuteronomy, Joshua, Judges, Kings.* DJD 14 (1999).
4Q242	4QPrNab, Collins, et al. *Qumran Cave 4: XVII, Parabiblical Texts, Part 3.* DJD 22 (1997)
DJD	Discoveries in the Judaean Desert
DSS	Dead SeaScrolls
Mur	Dead Sea Scrolls from Murabbaʿat, (eds Benoit, Milik, and de Vaux, DJD 2, 1961)

ANCIENT SOURCES

1 Clem.	*1 Clement*
3 Bar.	*3 Baruch* (Greek Apocalypse) *APOT*
Acts of John	*ANF* 8
Aen.	Virgil, *Aeneid,* LCL 63
Ag. Ap.	Josephus, *Contra Apionem, Against Apion,* LCL 186
Alex.	Lucian of Samosata, *Alexander (Pseudomantis), Alexander the False Prophet,* LCL 162
Ann.	Tacitus, *Annales, Annals,* LCL 249, 312, 322
Ant.	Josephus, *Antiquitates judaicae, Jewish Antiquities,* LCL 242, 410, 433, 456, 489
Anth. pal.	Lucian of Samosata, *Anthologia Palatina, Palatine Anthology, part of The Greek Anthology,* LCL 86 (trans. Paton).
Apol.	Tertullian, *Apologeticus, Apology, ANF* 3
Att.	Cicero, *Epistulae ad Atticum, Letters to Atticus,* LCL 7
b.	(before rabb. txt.) Babylonian Talmud, Rodkinson, ed. *New Edition of the Babylonian Talmud: Original Text* (1918)
b. Hul.	Babylonian Talmud tractate *Hullin*
b. Pesaḥ.	Babylonian Talmud tractate, *Pesaḥim, Pesahim,* Rodkinson 1918
Balb.	Cicero, *Pro Balbo,* LCL 447
Barn.	*Barnabas*
Bell. Cat.	Sallust, *Bellum catalinae, War with Catiline,* LCL 116
Bell. civ.	Appian, *Bella civilia, Civil Wars,* LCL 4
Bell. Van.	Procopius, *de bello Vandalio, Vandal War,* LCL 81
Bell. civ.	Julius Caesar, *Bellum civile, Civil War,* LCL 39
Build.	Procopius, *On Buildings,* LCL 343
Caecin.	Cicero, *Pro Caecina,* LCL 198
Cels.	Origen of Alexandria, *Contra Celsum, Against Celsus, ANF* 4
Chron.	Pamphilus Eusebius, *Chronicon, Chronicle,* Fotheringham, ed. *The Bodleian Manuscript of Jerome's Version of the Chronicles of Eusebius* (2012)
Civ.	Augustine, *De civitate Dei, The City of God* (ed. Dyson, 1998)
Claud.	Suetonius, *Lives of the Caesars, Divus Claudius, The Deified Claudius,* LCL 38

Comm. in Ep. Paul Jerome, *Commentary on Epistles of Paul, APNF* 2
Comm. Apoc. Victorinus of Pettau, *Commentary on the Apocalypse,* Weinrich (2012); *ANF* 7
Comm. Matt. Origen of Alexandria, *Commentary on Matthew, ANF* 9

Declam.	Calpurnius Flaccus, *Declamations,* Sussman (1994)
De or.	Cicero, *De oratore, On the Orator,* LCL 348
Descr.	Pausanias, *Description of Greece*, LCL 172, 188
Dom.	Suetonius, *Lives of the Caesars, Domitianus, Domitian*, LCL 38
Ep.	Cyprian of Carthage, *Epistulae, Letters, ANF* 5
Ep.	Pliny the Younger, *Epistulae, Letters*, LCL 59
Ep.	Seneca, *Ad Lucilium Epistulae Morales, Moral Essays,* LCL 214
Epict. diss.	Arrian, *Epictetus Discourses,* LCL 218
Epig.	Marcus Valerius Martial, *Epigrams*, LCL 94
Flac.	Cicero, *Pro Flacco, Valerius Flaccus, In Defense of Lucius,* LCL 324
Flacc.	Philo, *In Flaccum, Against Flaccus,* LCL 363
Geogr.	Strabo, *Geographica, Geography,* LCL 50, 223
Gr. Ant.	Antipater of Sidon, *Greek Anthology* (LCL 67, ed. Tueller, 2014
Haer.	Irenaeus, *Adversus haereses, Against Heresies, ANF* 1
Her.	Philo, *Quis rerum divinarum heres sit, Who Is the Heir?,* LCL 261
Hist.	Herodotus, *Historiae, The Histories of the Persian Wars,* LCL 117, 119
Hist.	Tacitus, *Historiae, Histories*, LCL 111, 249
Hist. eccl.	Pamphilus Eusebius, *Historia ecclesiastica, Ecclesiastical History, NPNF*[2]; LCL 153
Hist. Rom.	Cassius Dio, *Historia Romana, Roman History,* LCL 32, 175, 176
Hist. Rom.	Livy, *Ab Urbe Condita Libri, History of Rome,* LCL 133, 191
Hist. Sac.	Sulpicius Severus, *Historia sacra, Sacred History,* or *Chronica, Chronicorum Libri duo, Chronicle, NPNF*[11]
Il.	Homer, *Iliad,* LCL 171
Inst.	Commodianus, *The Instructions of Commodianus in Favour of Christian Discipline, Against the Gods of the Heathens, ANF* 3
J.W.	Josephus, *Bellum judaicum, Jewish War,* LCL 203, 210, 487
Jub.	*Jubilees ca.* 200–150 BC *APOT*
Jul.	Suetonius, *The Lives of the Caesars: Divus Julius, Deified Julius,* LCL 31
Laps.	Cyprian of Carthage, *De lapsis, Concerning the Lapsed, ANF* 5
Leg.	Cicero, *De legibus, On the Laws,* LCL 213
Legat.	Philo, *Legatio ad Gaium, On the Embassy to Gaius,* LCL 379
Lib. Mem.	Lucius Ampelius, *liber memorialis, Notebook,* ed. Assmann, 1935.
m.	*The Mishnah* (ed. Eugene J. Lipman)
Mart. Isa.	*Martyrdom of Isaiah* (Knibb 1983)
MasDeut	Masada Deuteronomy Scroll, (eds, Talmon and Yadin 1999)
MasEzek	Masada Ezekiel Scroll, (eds, Talmon and Yadin 1999)
MasGen	Masada Genesis Scroll, (eds, Talmon and Yadin 1999)
MasLev	Masada Leviticus Scroll, (eds, Talmon and Yadin 1999)
MasPs	Masada Psalm Scroll, (eds, Talmon and Yadin 1999)
MasSir	Masada Sirach Scroll, (eds, Talmon and Yadin 1999)
Metam.	Ovid, *Metamorphoses,* LCL 42

Mid.	*Talmud* tractate, *Middot*
Midr.	Rabbinic writing, *Midrash*
Mort.	Lactantius, *De morte persecutorum, The Deaths of the Persecutors, ANF* 7
Mos.	Philo, *De vita Mosis I, II, On the Life of Moses 1, 2,* LCL 289.
Nero	Suetonius, *Lives of the Caesars, Nero,* LCL 38
Nat.	Pliny the Elder, *Naturalis historia, Natural History,* LCL 352, 370, 419
Nat.	Tertullian, *Nat. Ad nations, To the Heathen, ANF* 3
Oct.	Marcus Minucius Felix, *Octavius,* LCL 250
On.	Eusebius, *Onomasticon, On the Place-Names in the Holy Scripture,* Wolf trans. (1971)
Or.	Dio Chrysostom, *Orations Discourses,* LCL 257, 339, 358, 376
Orat.	Aelius Aristides, *Orations,* Behr trans. (1981)
P.Mich.	Michigan University Papyri
P.Oxy.	Oxyrhynchus Papyri, Grenfell and Hunt, trans. 75 vols. (2009)
Pan.	Epiphanius of Salamis, *Panarion (Adversus haereses), Refutation of All Heresies,* Williams, trans. (1993)
Pesiq. Rab.	*Pesiqta Rabbati* (ed. Ulmer 2002)
Phil.	Cicero, *Orationes philippicae, The Philippic Speeches,* LCL 189
Praescr.	Tertullian, *De praescriptione haereticorum, Prescription against Heretics, ANF* 3
QE	Philo, *Quaestiones et solutiones in Exodum I, II, Questions and Answers on Exodus 1, 2,* LCL 401
Rab. Post.	Cicero, *Pro Rabirio Postumo, Speech in Defence of Gaius Rabirius Charged with High Treason,* LCL 198
Rab.	*Rabbah,* rabbinic writing usually on one of the books of the Pentateuch (i.e., *Genesis Rabbah*)
Sat.	Macrobius Ambrosius Theodosius, *Saturnalia,* LCL 510
Schol. ad Juv.	*Scholia on Juvenal* (ed. Wessner 1931)
SH	Procopius of Caesarea, *The Anecdota, Secret History,* LCL 290
Sib. Or.	*Sibylline Oracles APOT*
Strom.	Clement of Alexandria, *Stromata, Miscellanies or Patchwork, ANF* 2, *ANF* 1
t.	The *Talmudic* tractates of the *Tosefta,* Goldwurm and Scherman, eds. *Talmud.* 73 vols. Schottenstein Edition (1990)
t. Menaḥ.	The *Talmudic* tractates of *Menaḥot, Menahot*
Targ. Pal.	The *Palestine Targum*
Tib.	Suetonius, *The Lives of the Caesars: Tiberius,* LCL 31
Verr.	Cicero, *In Verrem, Against Verres,* LCL 221
Vir. ill.	Jerome, *De viris illustribus, On Illustrious Men* (ed. Halton, 1999)
Vit. Apoll.	Flavius Philostratus, *De Vita Apollonii, Life of Apollonius of Tyana,* LCL 16

MODERN SOURCES

§	section
AB	The Anchor Bible
abbr.	abbreviation
ABD	*The Anchor Yale Bible Dictionary* (eds. Freedman *et al.*, 1996)
AEL	*Ancient Egyptian Literature: The Old and Middle Kingdoms* (Lichtheim 2nd ed., 2006)
AF	*Apostolic Fathers*

AfO	*Archiv für Orientforschung*
AJA	*American Journal of Archaeology*
AJSL	*The American Journal of Semitic Languages and Literatures*
Akk.	Akkadian
ANE	ancient Near East (Eastern)
ANET	*The Ancient Near Eastern Texts Relating to the Old Testament* (ed. Pritchard, 1969)
ANF	*The Ante-Nicene Fathers* (eds. Roberts *et al.*, 10 vols, 1994)
ANRW	*Aufstieg und Niedergang der römischen Welt: Geschichte und Kultur Roms im Spiegel der neueren Forschung* (ed. Haase and Temporini)
APOT	*The Apocrypha and Pseudepigrapha of the Old Testament.* 2 vols. (ed. Charles, 1913).
ASOR	American Schools of Oriental Research
AUSS	*Andrews University Seminary Studies*
BA	*The Biblical Archaeologist*
BAR	*Biblical Archaeology Review*
BASOR	*Bulletin of the American Schools of Oriental Research*
BHK	*Biblica Hebraica*
BHS	*Biblia Hebraica Stuttgartensia*
BJRL	*Bulletin of the John Rylands University Library of Manchester*
BMCRE	*Coins of the Roman Empire in the British Museum* (6 vols. Mattingly, 1965)
BN	*Biblische Notizen*
BS	*Bible and Spade*
BSac	*Bibliotheca sacra*
Byz.	Byzantine
BZAW	Beihefte zur Zeitschrift für die alttestamentliche Wissenschaft
ca.	Lat. *circa,* "around, about."
cent.	century
ch.	chapter (s)
CBQ	*Catholic Biblical Quarterly*
CIG	*Corpus inscriptionum graecarum* (eds. Böeckh et al., 4 vols. 1877)
CJ	*The Classical Journal*
CNG	Classical Numismatic Group, Inc. www.cngcoins.com
COS	*The Context of Scripture* (eds. Hallo and Younger, 3 vols. 1997–2002)
CSNTM	The Center for the Study of New Testament Manuscripts
DBib	*A Dictionary of the Bible: Dealing with Its Language, Literature and Contents Including the Biblical Theology* (eds. Hastings and Selbie, 5 vols. 1911)
DJD	Discoveries in the Judaean Desert
DNTB	*Dictionary of New Testament Background* (eds. Evans and Porter, 2000)
DSS	Dead Sea Scrolls
e.g.	*exempli gratia*, for example
EB	Early Bronze
EBA	Early Bronze Age
ed(s).	editor(s), edited by
EJ	*Encyclopedia Judaica* (eds., Berenbaum and Skolnik, 2nd ed., 22 vols., 2006)
ESV	English Standard Version

et al.	*et alii,* and others
etc.	et cetera, and the rest
ExpTim	*The Expository Times*
Fr.	French
ft.	feet
Ger.	German
Gr.	Greek
Gr.P.	Rylands Papyrus
Heb.	Hebrew
HTR	*Harvard Theological Review*
IAA	Israel Antiquities Authority
IDB	*The Interpreter's Dictionary of the Bible* (ed. Buttrick. 4 vols. 1962)
i.e.	*id est,* that is
IEJ	*Israel Exploration Journal*
I.Eph.	*Die Inschriften von Ephesos* (ed. Wankel et al., 8 vols. 1979–1984)
Int	*Interpretation*
IOMS	International Organization for Masoretic Studies
ISBE2	*The International Standard Bible Encyclopedia* (ed. Bromiley, 4 vols., 1995)
IVP	Inter-Varsity Press
JAOS	*Journal of the American Oriental Society*
JBL	*Journal of Biblical Literature*
JCS	*Journal of Cuneiform Studies*
JE	*The Jewish Encyclopedia* (ed. Singer, 12 vols. 1906)
JEA	*The Journal of Egyptian Archaeology*
JETS	*Journal of the Evangelical Theological Society*
JJS	*Journal of Jewish Studies*
JNES	*Journal of Near Eastern Studies*
JÖAI	Jahreshefte des Österreichischen archäologischen Instituts
JQR	*The Jewish Quarterly Review*
JRS	*The Journal of Roman Studies*
JSNT	*Journal for the Study of the New Testament*
JSOT	*Journal for the Study of the Old Testament*
JSOTsup	*Journal for the Study of the Old Testament Supplement*
JTS	*Journal of Theological Studies*
Kh.	Khirbet
KJV	King James Version
km	kilometer
LAE	*The Literature of Ancient Egypt : An Anthology of Stories, Instructions, Stelae, Autobiographies, and Poetry* (ed. Simpson, 2003)
Lat.	Latin
LB	Late Bronze
LBA	Late Bronze Age
LCL	Loeb Classical Library
loc. cit.	*loco citato,* in the place cited

LXX The Septuagint (the Greek OT)
m meter
MB Middle Bronze
MBA Middle Bronze Age
MS Or. Codex Orientales
MT Masoretic Text
NBD *New Bible Dictionary* (eds. Marshall et al., 3rd ed. 1996)
NDT *New Dictionary of Theology* (eds. Wright, and Ferguson, 1988)
NEA *Near Eastern Archaeology*
NEAEHL *The New Encyclopedia of Archaeological Excavations in the Holy Land* (eds. Stern, Levinson-Gilboa, and Aviram, 5 vols. 1993)
NICOT New International Commentary of the Old Testament
NIV New International Version
NovT *Novum Testamentum*
NPNF *Nicene and Post-Nicene Fathers, Series II* (eds. Roberts et al. 14 vols. 1994)
NT New Testament
NTS *New Testament Studies*
OEANE *The Oxford Encyclopedia of Archaeology in the Near East* (ed. Meyers, 5 vols. 1997)
OGIS *Orientis graeci inscriptiones selectae,* (eds. Dittenberger et al. 2 vols. 1905)
OIM Oriental Institute Museum, University of Chicago
OT Old Testament
OtSt *Oudtestamentische Studiën*
p papyrus
PD Public Domain
PEFSt. *Palestine Exploration Fund: Quarterly Statement*
PEQ *Palestine Exploration Quarterly*
pls. plates
P.Magd.Gr. Magdalen Greek Papyrus
PSBA *Proceedings of the Society of Biblical Archaeology*
P.Oxy. Oxyrhynchus Papyri
r. ruled
RA *Revue d'Assyriologie et d'archéologie orientale*
rabb. rabbinic
RB *Revue Biblique*
RE Supp *Realencyklopädie für protestantische Theologie und Kirche Supplement*
RIC *Roman Imperial Coinage* (13 Vols. ed. Mattingly et al. 1923)
SB *Sammelbuch Griechischer Urkunden aus Ägypten* (ed. Preisigke, 5 vols. 1915-1955)
SBL Society for Biblical Literature
SEG *Supplementum epigraphicum graecum* (eds. Chaniotis, Corsten, Papazarkadas, and Tybout, 1923–)
sic "so, thus, in this manner" meaning the error was in the original
SIG *Sylloges insciptionum graecarum* (ed. Dittenberger, 4 vols., 1915–1924).
SJOT *Scandinavian Journal of the Old Testament*
ST *Studia Theologica*

TCL — *Textes cunéiformes* (Musée du Louvre, 1910)
TOTC — Tyndale Old Testament Commentaries
TynBul — *Tyndale Bulletin*
UF — *Ugarit Forschungen*
VT — *Vetus Testamentum*
WBC — Word Biblical Commentary
WDBA — *Wycliffe Dictionary of Biblical Archaeology* (ed. Pfeiffer, 2000)
WUNT — Wissenschaftliche Untersuchungen Zum Neuen Testament
ZAW — *Zeitschrift für die alttestamentliche Wissenschaft*
ZPE — *Zeitschrift für Papyrologie und Epigraphik*
ZPEB — *Zondervan Pictorial Encyclopedia of the Bible* (eds. Tenney and Silva, 5 vols. 2009)

Preface

There is an ever growing number of discoveries that shed light on the Bible. In volume one of *Biblical Archaeology: An Introduction with Recent Discoveries That Support the Reliability of the Bible* I presented the discoveries which have surfaced in recent years that directly relate to the biblical text, and only mentioned the older discoveries in charts at the start of each chapter. However there are a number of notable discoveries from the past that deserve fresh examination and it has been some time since a scholarly resource has been produced to deal with the exciting discoveries made in the past by famous archaeologists such as Petrie, Rawlinson, Layard, Woolley, Kenyon, and others.

Two hardcover works, with excellent footnotes, were produced by Alfred Hoerth (1999) and John McRay (1991) in their *Archaeology of the Old Testament* and *Archaeology of the New Testament*, published by Baker House. When they were condensed into a single volume in 2006, entitled *Bible Archaeology: An Exploration of the History and Culture of Early Civilizations*, they were published without any footnotes or bibliography.

A recent work by Clyde E. Fant and Mitchell G. Reddish, titled *Lost Treasures of the Bible: Understanding the Bible Through Archaeological Artifacts in World Museums* published by Eerdmans in 2008, is an excellent work for use if one is visiting one of the world's museums, but it contains very little resource material for students to explore further study. In addition, *Biblical Archaeology* Vol. 2 approaches the biblical significance of the discoveries from a maximalist perspective, while Fant and Reddish approach their conclusion from more of a minimalist stance.

A recent work by Joseph Holden and Norman Geisler, titled *The Popular Handbook of Archaeology and the Bible* was recently published in 2013. This is an excellent work with a few endnotes and small, select bibliography on archaeology, but almost half of the book is on manuscripts (13 chapters). There was a need for an easily accessible, single volume dealing with famous archaeological discoveries, with suitable references and a bibliography for students, to enable them to carry out further research.

While there is a certain level of duplication in this volume of the famous artifacts featured in other works, this work has a number of items that they do not consider and provides the resources for further research and study. The notable discoveries from the past, presented in this work, are not meant to be an exhaustive treatment of the subject, nor presented as a technical discussion and the final conclusion of archaeological research. As with all archaeological investigations, many of the conclusions are ongoing. In addition, some of the artifacts presented here are still considered by many to be forgeries (i.e., Pomegranate Inscription, Jehoash Inscription and the "3 Shekel" Ostraca from Shlomo Moussaieff and Oded Golan), but many others are clearly provenanced and remain genuine examples of high quality. The removal of some artifacts from the collection of over 135 famous discoveries does not nullify the value of the remaining examples.

The term "famous" has been chosen instead of notable because many of these discoveries have risen to a certain level of fame in the field of biblical archaeology. Students may not be familiar with them all as famous, but by presenting them here, their importance in the field of biblical studies can hopefully be raised.

These "famous" discoveries have been selected to provide undergraduate students with a cross-section of relevant artifacts and sites to assist them in interpreting the biblical text. Some of the most significant and promising finds have been selected to demonstrate the historical reliability of the people and events of the Bible. This work, combined with *Biblical Archaeology Vol. 1,* is intended to help fill the void in providing an accessible and collective work on the subject of biblical archaeology, that will demonstrate that the Bible is reliable as a historical ancient document.

While only a few sites have been mentioned in this work, such as Ephesus and Pergamum, many of the cities of the biblical world have been excavated and many lesser known finds have come to light, which are beyond the scope of this work. Most good recent Bible Dictionaries have a good discussion of the discoveries and their biblical implications.

The advantage of such a text is that it provides a collected source of materials for students that would otherwise take a long time to assemble or be inaccessible. Of help for the student are more than 160 photographs, charts, timelines, maps, and a glossary, which will facilitate the difficult task of understanding the unfamiliar lands of the Bible. Numerous footnotes and an academic bibliography are provided to give students the tools for doing further research. It is my hope that those who use this work will find it useful and develop a love and passion, like the author, for the fascinating field of biblical archaeology. Students can read the Bible with confidence that the details of its geography and facts are accurate and be encouraged in their faith that the Bible is reliable.

The online *Biblical Archaeology: Vol. 1* companion website is free for everyone and accessible through this link http://biblicalarchaeologygraves.blogspot.com/2014/12/chapter-one.html. The website provides material from both Vol. 1 and Vol. 2, enlarged in color photos, external web links, and an extended bibliography for research, along with additional bonus material that could not be put into both books due to space limitations.

David E. Graves, PhD
Toronto, Canada
October 1, 2015

Preface to Second Edition

While the Bible does not change, the same cannot be said for archaeological finds. There is a continual release of archaeolgical information each year that demands the need to update the discoveries for the public in a format that is both informative and understandable. Thus, this second edition was completed to provide the most up-to-date archaeological material and also make the material available in both black and white and color. The layout has been refreshed using a single column and many new images were added. It is the hope and prayer of the author that those who read these discoveries would be blessed and encouraged in their faith and that know that the Bible is historically accurate so they can better understand what is being said.

David E. Graves, PhD
Toronto, Canada
January 17, 2018

Archaeology and the Text

1. A photographic reproduction of part of the Isaiah Scroll discovered among the Dead Sea Scrolls from cave one. It is the best preserved of the biblical scrolls found at Qumran and contains the entire Book of Isaiah in Hebrew (second cent. BC).

The Bible contains 66 books written by around 24 authors over a period of 2000–3500 years. The Old Testament (OT) consists of 39 books, while the New Testament (NT) contains 27 books. But of all the books collected none of the original documents have survived. Scholars base the transcript of the Bibles that we all use on thousands of copies of different manuscripts, comparing and analysing them, in order to determine the most accurate text. There are more manuscripts to support the text of the Bible than any other ancient document, with over 5,686 NT Greek manuscripts in existence today and 19,000 Syriac, Latin, Coptic, and Aramaic copies (see the chart below).[2] If the Bible is unrealiable on the basis of available manuscripts, then one must dismiss all other ancient documents as unreliable, since their manuscript numbers are far less.

With so many documents useful for consideration it is surprising that so little discussion

Author and Work[1]	Date Written	Time Span between Original and Copy	Oldest Copy	Number of Copies
Pliny's *Natural History*	61–113 AD	750 yrs	850 AD	7
Plato's *Dialogues*	427–347 BC	1,200 yrs	900 AD	7
Herodotus' *Histories*	480–425 BC	1,300 yrs	900 AD	8
Thucydides' *History*	460–400 BC	1,300 yrs	900 AD	8
Suetonius' *The Twelve Caesars*	75–160 AD	800 yrs	950 AD	8
Julius Caesar's *Gallic Wars*	100–44 BC	1,000 yrs	900 AD	10
Tacitus' *Histories* & *Annals*	*ca.* 100 AD	1,000 yrs	1,100 AD	20
Aristotle's Works	384–322 BC	1,400 yrs	1,100 AD	49
Sophocles' *Plays*	496–406 BC	1,400 yrs	1,000 AD	193
Homer's *Iliad*	900 BC	500 yrs	400 BC	643
New Testament	45–100 AD	less than 100 yrs	130 AD	5,600

[1] This chart was adapted from three sources: 1. Norman Geisler, *Christian Apologetics* (1976), 307; 2. Josh Mcdowell, *A Ready Defense*, (1993), 45; and 3. the article *"Archaeology and History attest to the Reliability of the Bible," by* Richard M. Fales, in *The Evidence Bible*, Edited by Ray Comfort (Gainesville, Flor.: Bridge-Logos, 2001), 163.

[2] Norman L. Geisler and Peter Bocchino, *Unshakeable Foundations* (Minneapolis: Bethany House, 2001), 256.

is provided in biblical archaeology textbooks to biblical texts and manuscripts.[3] This chapter will introduce the major manuscripts that have provided the basis for the English Bible.

IMPORTANT BIBLICAL MANUSCRIPTS

The study of ancient documents is called paleography. Biblical manuscripts were produced in the form of either scrolls or books (Latin *codex* meaning "block of wood;" plural *codices*). The apostles and prophets wrote God's message on parchments, which no longer exist. However, there are over 7,000 NT manuscripts and between 30,000–35,000 Latin copies. Compare this with Plato, who died (348/347 BC) over 2300 years ago, but only one copy of his work has survived.

From the thousands of available manuscripts, translators are now able to provide more accurate translations of the text by correcting uncertain words through the discipline of Textual (lower) Criticism.[4] The following are several groups of manuscripts which stand out for their importance to biblical research.

OLD TESTAMENT MANUSCRIPTS

The OT text relies on two main traditions to provide the English Bible with the OT: the Hebrew Masoretic Text and the Dead Sea Scrolls. However, several other manuscripts have been dated as even earlier witnesses to the events in the OT text. The manuscripts presented here, although not an exhaustive list, represent some of the earliest texts of Scripture.

The *Silver Scroll* (*ca.* 600 BC)

Perhaps the earliest biblical text is the *Silver Scroll* (*KH2*), which is actually two small (4 cm long) scroll fragments made out of silver (IAA 1980-1495; IAA 1980–1496) that date to *ca.* 600 BC, discovered by Gabriele Barkay and Gordon Franz in 1979 at the Ketef Hinnom (Heb. "shoulder of Hinnom") burial chambers, cut out of the rock just southwest of the Old City of Jerusalem (see Fig. 2).[5]

2. The Silver Scroll (KH2; IAA 1980-1495) found in Ketef Hinom.

Photograph, drawing, and transliteration by Tamar Hayardeni / Wikimedia Commons

---

[3] For an extensive list of NT manuscripts see *The Center for the Study of New Testament Manuscripts*. http://www.csntm.org/

[4] Kurt Aland and Barbara Aland, *The Text of the New Testament an Introduction to the Critical Editions and to the Theory and Practice of Modern Textual Criticism*, trans. Erroll F. Rhodes, 2nd ed. (Grand Rapids: Eerdmans, 1995); Keith Elliott and Ian Moir, *Manuscripts and the Text of the New Testament: An Introduction for English Readers* (Edinburgh, U.K.: T&T Clark, 1996); Emanuel Tov, *Textual Criticism of the Hebrew Bible* (Minneapolis: Augsburg Fortress, 2001); Philip Comfort, *Encountering the Manuscripts: An Introduction to New Testament Paleography & Textual Criticism* (Nashville, Tenn.: Broadman & Holman Academic, 2005).

[5] S. Ben Arieh, "A Burial Cave on Mount Scopus," *Atiqôt* 8 (1982): 59–60; Gabriele Barkay, "News From the Field: The Divine Name Found in Jerusalem," *BAR* 9, no. 2 (1983): 14–19; *Ketef Hinnom: A Treasure Facing Jerusalem's Walls* (Jerusalem, Israel: The Israel Museum, 1986); Ada Yardeni, "Remarks on the Priestly Blessing on Two Ancient Amulets from Jerusalem," *VT* 41, no. 2 (1991): 176–85; Gabriele Barkay, "The Priestly Benediction on Silver Plaques from Ketef Hinnon in Jerusalam," *Tel Aviv* 19 (1992): 139–92; Jeremy Daniel Smoak, *The Priestly Blessing in Inscription and Scripture: The Early History of Numbers 6:24-26* (Oxford: Oxford University Press, 2015).

Although the silver amulets were difficult to unroll, a process was developed by the Israel Museum to preserve them over the next three years.[6] Once unrolled, scholars were able to date them to before the Babylonian captivity.[7] The treasure inside contained a portion of the Priestly Blessing from the Book of Numbers (6:24-26) and other portions of the Pentateuch (Exod 20:6; Deut 5:10; 7:9;[8] Num 6:24–26) written in proto-Hebrew script.[9] The text in Fig. 2 translates as: "May h[e]/sh[e] be blessed by Yahweh, the warrior [or: helper] and the rebuker of [E]vil: May Yahweh bless you, keep you. May Yahweh make his face shine upon you and grant you p[ea]ce."[10]

The authors of a revised edition of the Ketef Hinnom scrolls believe that they were used as amulets to ward off evil spirits. They conclude:

> While neither inscription makes specific reference to Satan, demons, or other agents of wickedness, they do offer God's protection from Evil through the invocation of his holy name and the text of his most solemn of protective blessings. Given that context, it is safe to conclude that these artifacts both served as amulets and that their function falls in line with similar amulets whose inscriptions invoke divine protection for the wearer through the use of one of the tradition's most famous prayers.[11]

This is possibly the oldest surviving text from the Hebrew Bible. The text of the *Silver Scrolls* are identical to the later Masoretic text and Dead Sea Scrolls, which attest to the accuracy of the methods used by the scribes for 400 years in transmitting the biblical text. The discovery of this text also supports the belief that the Pentateuch was written prior to 600 BC, and certainly prior to the Babylonian Exile, when some minimalists suggest the OT was written. They also contain the earliest record of the name of YHWH, indicating that it was not a late development in Israelite history as some have suggested.[12]

3. The *Nash Papyrus*.

Stanley A. Cook, "A Pre-Massoretic Biblical Papyrus." *PSBA* 25 (1903), 56. The British Museum Library (MS Or.233). Wikimedia Commons.

The *Nash Papyrus* (150–100 BC)

The *Nash Papyrus* (MS Or.233) contains a collection of four Papyrus fragments purchased by Walter Llewellyn

[6] Gabriele Barkay et al., "The Amulets from Ketef Hinnom: A New Edition and Evaluation," *BASOR* 334 (2004): 41–70; Gabriele Barkay et al., "Using Advanced Technologies to Recover the Earliest Biblical Texts and Their Context," *NEA*, Using Advanced Technologies, 66, no. 4 (2003): 162–71.

[7] Goldie Feinsilver, "How the Silver Amulet Inscribed with the Divine Name Was Unrolled," *BAR* 9, no. 2 (1983): 19.

[8] In 1990, Bruce Zuckerman used special photography and computer software to reconstruct another biblical verse from Deuteronomy 7:9; Gabriele Barkay et al., "The Challenges of Ketef Hinnom: Using Advanced Technologies to Reclaim the Earliest Biblical Texts and Their Context," *NEA* 66, no. 4 (2003): 162–71.

[9] Barkay et al., "The Amulets from Ketef Hinnom," 41–70; Gabriele Barkay, "The Riches of Ketef Hinnom: Jerusalem Tomb Yields Biblical Text Four Centuries Older than Dead Sea Scrolls," *BAR* 35, no. 4 (2009): 23–35; Erik Waaler, "A Reconstruction of Ketef Hinnom I," *Maarav* 16, no. 2 (2011): 225–63.

[10] Barkay et al., "The Challenges of Ketef Hinnom," 170; Graham I. Davies et al., *Ancient Hebrew Inscriptions: Corpus and Concordance*, vol. 1 (Cambridge University Press, 1991), 4:301–302. See also COS 2.18: 221

[11] Barkay et al., "The Amulets from Ketef Hinnom," 68.

[12] Ibid., 41–70; Barkay et al., "Using Advanced Technologies to Recover the Earliest Biblical Texts and Their Context," 162–71; Barkay, "The Riches of Ketef Hinnom," 23–35.

Nash in Fayyum, Egypt in 1902 (see Fig. 3).[13] In 1903 it was given to Cambridge University Library where today it is part of the Treasures of the Library Collection.[14] The fragments were identified from the Decalogue (Exod 20 and Deut 5) including the *Šema'* (from Deut 6:4–5) leading scholars to speculate that they may have been used as part of a lectionary for liturgical purposes[15] or private prayers (phylactery). The text displays close similarities with the Septuagint Greek translation of the OT and differs significantly from the Masoretic text.

Although originally Cook argued to date it in the second cent. AD,[16] Albright dated the document to the second cent. BC (*ca.* 150–100 BC).[17] Until the discovery of the Dead Sea Scrolls it was considered the oldest copy of the Hebrew Bible in existence.[18]

4. A photographic reproduction of part of the Isaiah Scroll discovered among the Dead Sea Scrolls from cave one. It is the best preserved of the biblical scrolls found at Qumran and contains the entire Book of Isaiah in Hebrew (second cent. BC). There is no break between chapters 39 and 40 in the scroll.

The Dead Sea Scrolls (AD 70)

The accidental discovery of the Dead Sea Scroll (DSS) manuscripts (see Fig. 4) by shepherds in the caves around Khirbet Qumran in 1946 and 1947 has revolutionised biblical studies.[19] Portions of approximately 1100 manuscripts were recovered[20] dating from ca. 300 BC to AD 40, with the majority of them identified as Zealot correspondence from the Second Jewish Revolt[21] and the Essene monastic community.[22] About 220 are scrolls from biblical texts[23] with copies of all of the Hebrew Bible.[24] Up until the discovery of the DSS no substantial

[13] Stanley A. Cook, "A Pre-Massoretic Biblical Papyrus," *PSBA* 25 (1903): 34–56.

[14] Stefan C. Reif et al., *Hebrew Manuscripts at Cambridge University Library: A Description and Introduction*, University of Cambridge Oriental Publications 52 (New York, N.Y.: Cambridge University Press, 1997).

[15] F. C. Burkitt, "The Hebrew Papyrus of the Ten Commandments," *JQR* 15 (1903): 392–408.

[16] Cook, "A Pre-Massoretic Biblical Papyrus," 34–56.

[17] William F. Albright, "A Biblical Fragment from the Maccabean Age: The Nash Papyrus," *JBL* 56 (1937): 145–76.

[18] Bleddyn J. Roberts, "Recent Discoveries of Hebrew Manuscripts," *ExpTim* 60, no. 11 (1949): 305–308.

[19] Angel Sáenz-Badillos, *A History of the Hebrew Language*, trans. John Elwolde (Cambridge, U.K.: Cambridge University Press, 1996), 112–46; James C. VanderKam, *The Dead Sea Scrolls Today*, 2nd ed. (Grand Rapids: Eerdmans, 2010), 2–28.

[20] For an extended bibliography of individual texts see: Craig A. Evans, *Ancient Texts for New Testament Studies: A Guide to the Background Literature* (Grand Rapids: Baker Academic, 2005), 76–154.

[21] J. Randall Price, *The Dead Sea Scrolls Pamphlet: The Discovery Heard around the World* (Torrance, Calif.: Rose, 2005), 2.

[22] VanderKam, *The Dead Sea Scrolls Today*, 99–120.

[23] Stephen A. Reed, *The Dead Sea Scrolls Catalogue: Documents, Photographs, and Museum Inventory Numbers*, ed. Marilyn J. Lundberg and Michael B. Phelps, SBL Resources for Biblical Study 32 (Atlanta, Ga.: Scholars Press, 1994); Emanuel Tov, "A List of the Texts from the Judean Desert," in *The Dead Sea Scrolls After Fifty Years: A Comprehensive Assessment*, ed. Peter W. Flint and James C. VanderKam, vol. 2 (Leiden: Brill, 1999), 2:669–717.

[24] Florentino García Martínez and W. G. E. Watson, *The Dead Sea Scrolls Translated: The Qumran Texts in English*, 2nd ed. (Leiden: Brill Academic, 1997); James H. Charlesworth, *The Dead Sea Scrolls: Hebrew, Aramaic, and Greek Texts With English Translations* (Louisville, Ky.: Westminster/Knox, 2000); Martin G.Abegg, Jr., Michael O. Wise, and Edward M. Cook, *The Dead Sea Scrolls: A New Translation*, Rev. ed. (New York, N.Y.: HarperCollins, 2005); Eibert J. C. Tigchelaar and Florentino García Martínez,

copies of any of the Hebrew Scriptures were known from before the tenth cent. AD (i.e., *Aleppo Codex* AD 935).[25] The dates have been confirmed by archaeology,[26] paleography, and radiocarbon dating.[27]

There were twenty-one scroll fragments from Isaiah recovered. The most famous, *The Great Isaiah Scroll* (1QIsa^a^), is the only OT book ever recovered intact (see Fig. 4).[28] It was written on 17 sheets of leather stitched together, and measured 7.16 m (23.5 ft.) long with 54 columns which orthographers date to between 125 and 100 BC.[29] The scrolls of Isaiah were over 1,000 years older than any previous copy and confirm the scrolls as the oldest example of Hebrew writing on papyrus. This scroll strongly confirmed the accuracy of the copies. The text of the scroll differs very little (1%) from the newer Masoretic (*Textus Receptus*) Hebrew text.[30]

Until their discovery it was believed that such perishable materials as parchment and papyrus could not have survived for two millennia. Since the discovery of the initial scrolls several others were discovered in eleven other caves north and south of Qumran along the west scarp of the Jordan River Valley. A twelfth cave (53)[31], that once contained DSS, was identified in January 2017 by a team of which the author was a member. A small unmarked leather scroll was found among broken Qumran pottery.[32]

The discovery of the Dead Sea Scrolls was likely the greatest archaeological discovery of the twentieth century.[33]

MASORETIC TEXT (MT)

There are no vowels in the early forms of Hebrew, with vowels only being added later by the *Masorite* (from Heb. *Masora,* "tradition") scribes.[34] The complex work of adding vowel points (Heb. *niqqud*) and cantillation marks, called *Masora,* to the manuscripts was carried out by two independent schools (the Babylonian and Palestinian). The most famous group were led by the Palestinian families of Moses ben Asher (AD 895), and Moses ben Naphtali (AD 890–940),

---

The Dead Sea Scrolls, Study Edition, 2 vols. (Grand Rapids: Eerdmans, 1999); Robert H. Eisenman and James M. Robinson, *A Facsimile Edition of the Dead Sea Scrolls* (Washington, D.C.: Biblical Archaeology Society, 1992); Robert H Eisenman and Michael Owen Wise, *The Dead Sea Scrolls Uncovered: The First Complete Translation and Interpretation of 50 Key Documents Withheld for Over 35 Years* (Rockport, Mass.: Element, 1992).

[25] Price, *Dead Sea Scrolls Pamphlet*, 8; *The Stones Cry Out: What Archaeology Reveals About the Truth of the Bible* (Eugene, Oreg.: Harvest House, 1997), 280.

[26] Lawrence H. Schiffman, ed., *Archaeology and History in the Dead Sea Scrolls: The New York University Conference in Memory of Yigael Yadin*, vol. JSOT/ASOR Monographs 2, Journal for the Study of the Pseudepigrapha Supplement Series 8 (Sheffield, U.K.: JSOT Press, 1990); Jodi Magness, *The Archaeology of Qumran and the Dead Sea Scrolls* (Grand Rapids: Eerdmans, 2003).

[27] James C. VanderKam and Peter W. Flint, *The Meaning of the Dead Sea Scrolls: Their Significance for Understanding the Bible, Judaism, Jesus, and Christianity* (San Francisco, Calf.: Harper, 2002), 27–32; Georges Bonani et al., "Radiocarbon Dating of the Dead Sea Scrolls," *Tigot* 20 (1991): 27–32; Georges Bonani et al., "Radiocarbon Dating of Fourteen Dead Sea Scrolls," *Radiocarbon* 34, no. 3 (2006): 843–49; G. Doudna, "Dating the Scrolls on the Basis of Radiocarbon Analysis," in *Dead Sea Scrolls After Fifity Years*, ed. Peter W. Flint and James C. VanderKam, vol. 1 (Leiden: Brill Academic, 1999), 1:430–71.

[28] VanderKam, *The Dead Sea Scrolls Today*, 126–27.

[29] VanderKam and Flint, *Meaning of the Dead Sea Scrolls*, 131; R. K. Harrison and Martin G. Abegg, Jr., "Dead Sea Scrolls," ed. Merrill C. Tenney and Moises Silva, *ZPEB* (Grand Rapids: Zondervan, 2009), 2:64.

[30] VanderKam, *The Dead Sea Scrolls Today*, 127–29.

[31] Rudolf Cohen and Yigal Yisraeli, "The Excavations of Rock Shelter XII/50 and in Caves XII/52-53," *Atiqot* 41, no. 2 (2002): 207–13.

[32] Oren Gutfeld and J. Randall Price, "Hebrew University Archaeologists Find 12th Dead Sea Scrolls Cave," *The Hebrew University of Jerusalem,* February 8, 2017, https://new.huji.ac.il/en/article/33424.

[33] Keith N. Schoville, "Top Ten Archaeological Discoveries of the Twentieth Century Relating to the Biblical World," *Stone Campbell Journal* 4, no. 1 (2001): 29.

[34] F. F. Bruce, Philip W. Comfort, and James I. Packer, *The Origin of the Bible* (Wheaton, Ill.: Tyndale, 2003), 158.

working from Tiberias.[35] Until that time the only way to determine the exact pronunciation and meaning of the words was by their context. Thus the Masoretes became famous for developing and standardizing the vowel notation (diacritic) system used for the pronunciation of Hebrew.

The Masorite also added a series of critical notes to ensure the accuracy of the text. According to the *New Jewish Encyclopedia* they also "counted the letters and the words of the text; they discussed grammatical rules, vowels, and accents."[36] The Massoretic apparatus was designed to protect the copies from error.

The Russian National Library in Saint Petersburg, Russia, houses the largest collection of Hebrew OT manuscripts in their Second Firkovitch Collection.

5. Facsimile of the *Codex Orientales*, showing Lev. 11:4–21.

The British Museum Library; MS Or.4445. Image from Christian D. Ginsburg, *Introduction to the Masoretico-Critical Edition of the Hebrew Bible*, vol. 2 (New York, N.Y.: KTAV, 1897), 468.

The *Codex Orientales* (AD 820–950)

The manuscript known as the *Codex Orientales* (See Fig. 5; Or. 4445) contains most of the Five Books of Moses (i.e., Pentateuch; Gen 39:20–Deut 1:33 with Num 7 and 9 added in AD 1540).[37] It has been dated to the early ninth cent. (*ca.* AD 820–950)[38] and represents the Ben Asher family of scribes.[39] It covers the text of the OT that is missing in the *Aleppo Codex*. Ginsburg points out that "in the ten chapters of Genesis, in Exodus, Leviticus and Numbers exhibit no fewer than 116 variations between this MS. and the *Textus Receptus*."[40] It was acquired in 1891 by the British Museum.[41]

The Cairo Geniza Collection (AD 870–1880)

The *Cairo Geniza* collection of some 300,000 documents (see Fig. 6)[42] was noticed by several individuals (Archibald Saucy in 1892 and E. N. Adler in 1896 but some were collected by twin sisters, Agnes S. Lewis and Margaret D. Gibson), in a storeroom (Heb. *genizah* which is a repository for old defective manuscripts)[43] in the Ben Ezra Synagogue in Fustat (Cairo), Egypt

[35] Hayim Tawil and Bernard Schneider, *Crown of Aleppo: The Mystery of the Oldest Hebrew Bible Codex* (Philadelphia, PA: Jewish Publication Society, 2010).

[36] David Bridger and Samuel Wolk, *The New Jewish Encyclopedia* (Springfield, NJ: Behrman, 1962), 309.

[37] Aron Dotan, "Reflections Towards a Critical Edition of Pentateuch Codex Or. 4445," in *Estudios Masoreticos: Proceedings of the 10th Congress of IOMS* (Madrid: Instituto de Filogogia, CSIC, Departamento de Filologia Biblica y de Oriente Antiquo, 1993), 39–51.

[38] Christian D. Ginsburg, *Introduction to the Masoretico-Critical Edition of the Hebrew Bible*, vol. 2 (New York, N.Y.: KTAV, 1897), 469.

[39] Page H. Kelley, Timothy G. Crawford, and Daniel S. Mynatt, *The Masorah of Biblia Hebraica Stuttgartensia: Introduction and Annotated Glossary* (Grand Rapids: Eerdmans, 1998), xi, 18.

[40] Ginsburg, *Introduction to the Masoretico-Critical Edition of the Hebrew Bible*, 2:472.

[41] http://www.bl.uk/manuscripts /FullDisplay.aspx?ref=Or_4445

[42] Malcolm C. Davis and Ben Outhwaite, *Hebrew Bible Manuscripts in the Cambridge Genizah Collections*, 4 vols., Cambridge University Library Genizah (Cambridge, Mass.: Cambridge University Press, 2003).

[43] Adina Hoffman and Peter Cole, *Sacred Trash: The Lost and Found World of the Cairo Geniza* (New York, N.Y.: Schocken, 2011), 12.

in 1896.[44] The twins brought the documents to the attention of Cambridge University scholar Solomon Schechter who acquired the remaining collection of 140,000 fragments in the same year. Today many of these texts are in the Firkovitch collection and Antonian Collection in the Russian National Library in St. Petersburg, with others scattered around the world in various collections, such as the Enelow Memorial Collection in the Jewish Theological Seminary in New York, and in the universities of Cambridge and Manchester in the United Kingdom.[45]

6. The *Cairo Geniza.*

Paul Ernst Kahle, The Cairo Geniza, 2nd ed. (Oxford, U.K.: Basil Blackwell, 1959), plate 3.

The *Codex Cairensis* (AD 896)

The *Codex Cairensis* (symbolized as "C", also called *Codex Prophetarum Cairensis* or the *Cairo Codex of the Prophets.* See Fig. 7)[46] is the oldest dated Masoretic manuscript of the complete writings of the Prophets (Heb. *Nevi'im*),[47] and according to the notes in the manuscript was written by Moses Ben Asher in Tiberias, Israel, in AD 896.[48]

In the Hebrew Bible the Former Prophets included the books of Joshua, Judges, Kings and Samuel, and the Latter Prophets included Isaiah, Ezekiel, Jeremiah, and the Minor Prophets, excluding Daniel. It forms the basis of today's Hebrew Bible.[49]

The *Codex Cairensis* was also discovered in the storeroom (Heb. *genizah* which is a repository for old defective manuscripts)[50] of the Ben Ezra Synagogue in Fustat (Cairo), Egypt in 1896.[51]

7. The *Codex Cairensis* of the Prophets from an old fascimile edition.

Wikimedia Commons.

The *Babylonian Codex* (AD 916)

The *Babylonian Codex* (*MS Heb. B3;* symbolized as "V(ar)P" in the *Biblia Hebraica Stuttgartensia.* Also called *St. Petersburg Codex* [*Codex Babylonicus*

[44] Paul Ernst Kahle, *The Cairo Geniza*, 2nd ed. (Oxford: Blackwell, 1959); Hoffman and Cole, *Sacred Trash*, 3.

[45] Rebecca J. W. Jefferson and Erica C. D. Hunter, *Published Material from the Cambridge Genizah Collections. A Bibliography 1980-1997*, 4 vols., Cambridge University Library Genizah 13 (Cambridge, Mass.: Cambridge University Press, 2004).

[46] D. S. Loewinger, ed., *Codex Cairo of the Bible from the Karaite Synagogue at Abbasiya*, Facsimile Edition (Jerusalem, Israel: Makor, 1971); Federico Pérez Castro, *El Codice de Profetas de El Cairo*, 9 vols. (Madrid: Instituto Arias Montano, 1979).

[47] Tov, *Textual Criticism of the Hebrew Bible*, 47.

[48] Aron Dotan, "Ben-Asher, Moses," ed. Fred Skolnik and Michael Berenbaum, *EJ* (New York, N.Y.: MacMillan, 2006), 3:321.

[49] Norman L. Geisler and William E. Nix, *A General Introduction to the Bible*, New and Revised (Chicago, Ill.: Moody, 1986), 358–59; Ernst Würthwein and Alexander Achilles Fischer, *The Text of the Old Testament: An Introduction to the Biblia Hebraica*, trans. Erroll F. Rhodes, 2nd ed. (Grand Rapids: Eerdmans, 2014).

[50] Hoffman and Cole, *Sacred Trash*, 12.

[51] Kahle, *The Cairo Geniza*; Hoffman and Cole, *Sacred Trash*, 3.

Petropolitanus][52] or the *Leningrad Codex of the Prophets*)[53] dates to *ca.* AD 916. This document supports the Babylonian school of Masoretic scribes.

The *Aleppo Codex* (AD 925)

8. Page from the *Aleppo Codex* (IMJ 96.85/221A) displaying a portion of Deuteronomy with the pointing and marginal notes of Aaron Ben Asher.

Photo by Ardon Bar Hama © 2007 The Yad Yitzhak Ben Zvi Institute. www.aleppocodex.org. Wikimedia Commons

The *Aleppo Codex* (Heb. *Keter Aram Tzova* "Crown of Aleppo"; see Fig. 8) is a medieval (tenth cent. AD) bound manuscript that originally contained the entire OT. Today of the 487 pages[54] it originally contained, only 294 parchment pages remain.[55] Most of the Torah section and many other pages have been lost.[56] It was copied in Israel in *ca.* AD 925 by Shelomo ben Baya'a, but later Moses ben Asher (*ca.* AD 930) added the vowel markings (dots and lines around the letters).[57] It is considered the oldest Hebrew manuscript of the complete OT and earliest text of the Ben Asher masoretic tradition. The travels of the manuscript from Jerusalem, Egypt and Syria is both interesting and mysterious.[58] It is currently on display at the Shrine of the Book Museum in Jerusalem, but now also available online.[59]

The value of the text is due to the accuracy of the scribes who knew the OT by heart and took great care in preserving it for over a thousand years.

The *Leningrad Codex* (AD 1008)

The *Leningrad Codex* B19A (also called the *Codex Leningradensis* and symbolized as "L"; see Fig. 9)[60] is the earliest complete Hebrew manuscript of the OT dating to AD 1008 according to the colophon notes.[61] While the *Aleppo Codex* is older it is missing pages, so the *Leningrad Codex* has been used to correct the missing portions. It represents the Ben Asher tradition of the Hebrew scribes from Tiberias, Israel, and forms the basis for both the *Biblica Hebraica* (BHK 1937) and the *Biblia Hebraica Stuttgartensia* (BHS 1977). The manuscript is presently housed in the Leningrad Public Library in St. Petersburg, Russia.

---

[52] Würthwein and Fischer, *The Text of the Old Testament*, 26; Hermann Leberecht Strack, *Prophetarum posteriorum codex Babylonicus petropolitanus* (Petropoli: Editio Bibliothecae Publicae Imperialis, 1876).

[53] Frederic G. Kenyon, *Our Bible and the Ancient Manuscripts* (New York, N.Y.: Harper, 1958), 85.

[54] Izhak calculates the number of original pages at 380. Izhak Ben-Zvi, "The Codex of Ben Asher," *Textus* 1 (1960): 2. The Aleppo Codex website cites 491 original pages http://www.aleppocodex.org /links/9.html.

[55] Hayim Tawil and Bernard Schneider, *Crown of Aleppo: The Mystery of the Oldest Hebrew Bible Codex* (Philadelphia, Pa.: Jewish Publication Society, 2010), 110; Norman L. Geisler and Joseph M. Holden, *The Popular Handbook of Archaeology and the Bible* (Eugene, Oreg.: Harvest House, 2013), 28.

[56] Kenyon, *Our Bible and the Ancient Manuscripts*, 359.

[57] Matti Friedman, *The Aleppo Codex: In Pursuit of One of the World's Most Coveted, Sacred, and Mysterious Books* (Chapel Hill, N.C.: Algonquin, 2013), 32.

[58] Tawil and Schneider, *Crown of Aleppo*; Friedman, *The Aleppo Codex*.

[59] www.aleppocodex.org

[60] David Noel Freedman et al., eds., *The Leningrad Codex*, Facsimile edition (Grand Rapids: Eerdmans, 1998).

[61] Foreword by Gérard E. Weil to K. Ellige and Rudolph, eds., *Biblia Hebraica Stuttgartensia* (Stuttgart, Germany: Deutsche Bibelstiftung, 1977).

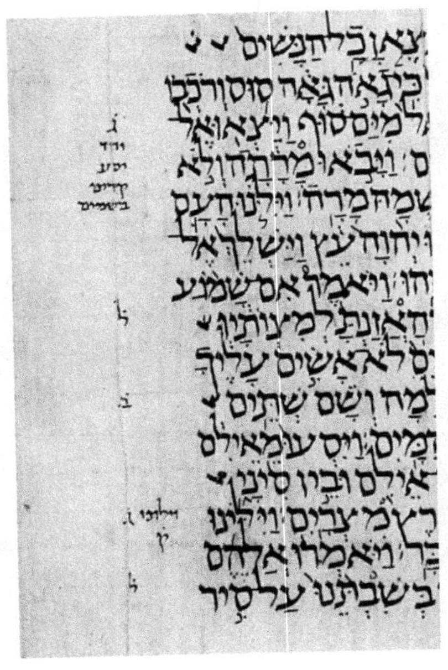

9. The *Leningrad Codex* showing portions of Exodus 15:21–16:3.
Wikimedia Commons

NEW TESTAMENT PAPYRUS

The NT Papyri are a series of over one hundred and twenty fragments mostly discovered in Egypt between 1895 and 1897.[62] In 1900 only 9 papyri manuscripts were known, but by 2008 there were 124 papyri. According to Daniel B. Wallace, director of "The Center for the Study of New Testament Manuscripts", in 2012:

> seven New Testament papyri had recently been discovered—six of them probably from the second century and one of them probably from the first. These fragments will be published in about a year. These manuscripts now increase our holdings as follows: we have as many as eighteen New Testament manuscripts (all fragmentary, more or less) from the second century and one from the first. Altogether, about 33% of all New Testament verses are found in these manuscripts. But the most interesting thing is the first-century fragment…if this Mark fragment is confirmed as from the first century, what a thrill it will be to have a manuscript that is dated within the lifetime of many of the original followers of Jesus! Not only this, but this manuscript would have been written before the New Testament was completed.[63]

These papyri are identified by the gothic letter $\mathfrak{p}$ with the number of the papyri in superscript (ex. $\mathfrak{p}^{52}$).

Mummy Mask Texts

A controversial process of harvesting ancient texts from mummy masks (see Fig. 10) has been around since the 1960's. It uses a chemical process to dissolve the glue that holds the ancient paper (*cartonnage*) together, while preserving the ink, text and painting. Craig Evans, of Acadia Divinity School, states in an interview the types of manuscripts harvested: "We're [papyrologists are] recovering ancient documents from the first, second and third centuries. Not just Christian documents, not just biblical documents, but classical Greek texts, business papers, various mundane papers, personal letters."[64] This was in response to claims that some scholars (Scott Carroll, Josh McDowell and Dan Wallace)[65] have used the method to preserve biblical texts, and in so doing apparently destroying the mask. Carroll claimed that he "has found a portion of the Old Testament book of 1 Samuel in a mummy mask, but he has never claimed that he was involved in the discovery of an ancient portion of the Gospel of Mark."[66] Billington maintains that Carroll knows the person who discovered the fragment of Mark and has seen it and that it did not come from a mommy mask, but came from an ancient item that made secondary use of this old papyrus of the Gospel of Mark.[67] Carroll and others, have been sworn to secrecy by the European owner—who is not an evangelical—until it is sold and

---

[62] For a list of significant NT Manuscript Papyri see Geisler and Holden, *Popular Handbook of Archaeology and the Bible*, 111–22, 373–82.

[63] Daniel B. Wallace, "Earliest Manuscript of the New Testament Discovered?," *The Center for the Study of New Testament Manuscripts*, February 10, 2012, http://www.csntm.org/.

[64] Owen Jarus, "Mummy Mask May Reveal Oldest Known Gospel," *Live Science*, January 18, 2015, http://www.livescience.com/49489-oldest-known-gospel-mummy-mask.html. For documents recovered using this method see Erja Salmenkivi, *Cartonnage Papyri in Context: New Ptolemaic Documents from Abū Ṣīr Al-Malaq* (Helsinki: The Finish Society of Sciences and Letters, 2002).

[65] The sample was provided by the Green family of the Museum of the Bible in Washington, D.C.

[66] Clyde E. Billington, "Christian Century Attacks Document Seekers," *Artifax* 33, no. 2 (Spring 2018): 12.

[67] Billington, "Christian Century," 12–13.

published.

Papyrologist, Jaakko Frösén, states that the practice of destroying masks to harvest the papyrus "has been abandoned for obvious reasons as unethical."[68] However, first it must be recognized that archaeology is an inherently destructive science by definition. Second, the painted cartonnage mask does not need to be destroyed to remove the inside layer of papryus. Frösén, reports that "the new techniques of papyrus restoration, combined with methods of conserving wall paintings, have made it possible to extract papyrus successfully while safeguarding the mummy portraits and other paintings made on papyrus cartonnage."[69] And, third, is not a fragment of the NT of more value than any mummy mask, if the mask must be destroyed?

The implications for biblical studies were announced in 2012, during a debate between professor of New Testament at Dallas Theological Seminary, Daniel B. Wallace, and agnostic Bart D. Ehrman. Wallace announced that one of the ancient documents processed using this method was from the Gospel of Mark.[70] The small fragment (4.4 x 4 cm) from the foot of a well-preserved papyrus codex leaf has been published as Oxyrhynchus Papyrus LXXXIII 5345 (inventory # 104/14(b),[71] and contains Mark 1:7–9, 16–18. Although originally believed to date to the first century, a second/third cent. date is confirmed by the Oxford papyrologist Dirk Obbink.[72] In Mark 1:17 instead of αυτοις ο Ιησους the papyrus does not have ο Ιησους. This further supports an early date for the writing of the Gospel of Mark.

10. Egpytian mummy masks of the Hellenistic and Roman periods(50 BC-AD 50) often had gilded faces that reflected the association of the deceased with the gods. This mask has been molded over a core, with layers of mud and linen, while others used ancient documents such as old copies of the Bible.

Walters Art Museum no. 78.3. Wikimedia Commons

The Magdalen Papyrus

The *Magdalen Papyrus* (𝔭[64]) consists of three small fragments of a papyrus of the gospel of Matthew discovered in Luxor, Egypt, in 1901 (see Fig. 11). Roberts dates the papyrus to the late AD 200's.[73] Based on comparisons with other known papyri from the first century, Thiede concluded that 𝔭[64] should be dated as early as AD 70–100,[74] though several scholars

[68] For a detailed description of the recovery process, see Jaakko Frösén, "Conservation of Ancient Papyrus Materials," in *The Oxford Handbook of Papyrology*, ed. Roger S. Bagnall, Oxford Handbooks (Oxford: Oxford University Press, 2011), 87.

[69] Ibid. 87. Frösén describes the twenty steps for conserving the paintings and the Papyri. 88–70

[70] Candida R. Moss and Joel S. Baden, "Why Did the Museum of the Bible's Scholars Destroy Ancient Egyptian Artifacts?," *The Christian Century*, November 29, 2017, https://www.christiancentury.org/article/features/why-did-museum-bible-s-scholars-destroy-ancient-egyptian-artifacts.

[71] Peter John Parsons and N. Gonis, eds., *The Oxyrhynchus Papyri*, vol. 83, Graeco-Roman Memoirs (London, UK: Egypt Exploration Society, 2018), 5345.

[72] https://www.classics.ox.ac.uk/publications-2017.

[73] C. H. Roberts, "An Early Papyrus of the First Gospel," *HTR* 46 (1953): 233.

[74] Carsten P. Thiede, "Papyrus Magdalen Greek 17 (Gregory-Aland P64): A Reappraisal," *TynBul* 46 (1995): 13–20; Ibid., 29–42; Matthew D'Ancona and Carsten Thiede, *The Jesus Papyrus* (New York, N.Y.: Doubleday, 2000).

have challenged Thiede's conclusions.[75] Most scholars consider the *Magdalen Papyrus* to be one of the oldest copies of Matthew in existence.[76]

11. The *Magdalen Papyrus* $\mathfrak{p}^{64}$ (P. Magdalen Greek 17).

http://chrles.multiply.com. Wikimedia Commons

The Martin Bodmer Papyri

The *Martin Bodmer Papyri* are a group[77] of ancient Greek and Coptic manuscripts[78] discovered in 1952 at Pabau, Egypt and purchased by Swiss collector Martin Bodmer in 1955–1956. But as Robinson points out, in reality "there is no clear picture as to the size of the collection."[79] Bodmer's private collection was set up as the Foundation Martin Bodmer, and housed at the Bibliotheca Bodmeriana, in Cologny, Switzerland.[80] Some of the Bodmer collection are also housed in the Sir Chester Beatty collection, the Universities of Mississippi and Cologne, and the Fundacio "Sant Lluc Evangelista" in Barcelona[81] $\mathfrak{p}^{74}$ and $\mathfrak{p}^{75}$ are now in the Vatican Library in Rome. They have been in the process of publication in the *Papyrus Bodmer Series* since 1954.[82]

The oldest papyri from the Gospel of John ($\mathfrak{p}^{66}$) dates to *ca.* AD 200 (see Fig. 12).[83] Other significant papyri in the Bodmer collection are $\mathfrak{p}^{72}$ (the earliest known copy of Jude along with 1 and 2 Peter), $\mathfrak{p}^{73}$ (Matt 25:43; 26:2–3), $\mathfrak{p}^{74}$ (Acts 1:2–28:31; Jas 1:1–5:20; 1 Pet 1:1–3:5; 2 Pet 2:21–3:16; 1 John 1:1–5:17; 2 John 1–13; 3 John 6, 12; Jude 3–25), and $\mathfrak{p}^{75}$ (contains a portion of John and portions of the oldest known written fragment from the Gospel of Luke, now in the Vatican Library).[84]

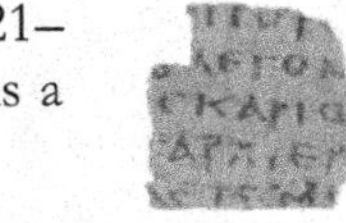

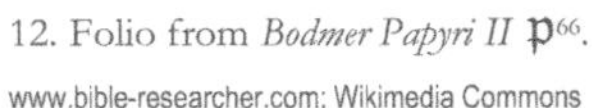

12. Folio from *Bodmer Papyri II* $\mathfrak{p}^{66}$.

www.bible-researcher.com; Wikimedia Commons

[75] Peter M. Head, "The Date Of The Magdalen Papyrus Of Matthew (P. Magd. Gr. 17 = P64): A Response To C. P. Thiede," *TynBul* 46 (1995): 251–85; J. K. Elliott, "Review of the Jesus Papyrus by Carsten Peter Thiede; Matthew d'Ancona; Gospel Truth? New Light on Jesus and the Gospels by Graham Stanton," *NovT* 38, no. 4 (1996): 393–99; David C. Parker, "Was Matthew Written Before 50 CE? The Magdalen Papyrus Of Matthew," *ExpTim* 107 (1996): 40–43.

[76] Roberts, "An Early Papyrus of the First Gospel," 233; Theodore C. Skeat, "The Oldest Manuscript Of The Four Gospels?," *NTS* 43 (1997): 1–34; Stanley E. Porter, *How We Got the New Testament: Text, Transmission, Translation*, ed. Craig Evans and Lee McDonald, Acadia Studies in Bible and Theology (Grand Rapids: Baker Academic, 2013).

[77] Robinson records that there are "fifteen ancient books containing thirty-one ancient texts" and the numbering of the series is misleading as they do not correspond to the texts they contain. James M. Robinson, *The Story of the Bodmer Papyri, the First Christian Monastic Library The Story of the Bodmer Papyri: From the First Monaster's Library in Upper Egypt to Geneva and Dublin* (Nashville, Tenn.: James Clarke & Co., 2013), 12. Appendix 2 of Robinson lists the published manuscripts and the remaining unpublished manuscripts. Robinson, *Story of the Bodmer Papyri*, 185-196.

[78] Not all manuscripts are papyri such as $\mathfrak{p}$16, $\mathfrak{p}$19, $\mathfrak{p}$22. Albert Pietersma, "Bodmer Papyri," ed. David Noel Freedman et al., *ABD* (New York, N.Y.: Doubleday, 1996), 766.

[79] Robinson, *Story of the Bodmer Papyri*, 10.

[80] Pietersma, "Bodmer Papyri," 766.

[81] Ibid.

[82] Ibid.

[83] John 1:1-6:11, 6:35b-14:26 and fragments of forty other pages of John 14-21.

[84] James Neville Birdsall, *The Bodmer Papyrus of the Gospel of John* (Wheaton, Ill.: Tyndale, 1960).

NEW TESTAMENT CODICES

First-century Christians appear to preferred their Bibles in the form of a codex (bound book) than a scroll. Virtually all manuscripts we have from the third and fourth cent. AD are found as codices. The important manuscripts include:

Codex Vaticanus (B)

The *Codex Vaticanus* (B)[85] is perhaps one of the oldest Greek manuscripts and one of the great uncial codices of the Bible (see Fig. 13). It was originally written in either Rome, Alexandria, or Caesarea in uncial letters (capitals) on 759 pages of vellum and dates to the fourth cent. AD (*ca.* 325–350).[86] The codex has been preserved in the Vatican Library since the fifteenth cent. and thus acquired its name.[87] Along with the *Codex Sinaiticus* it is considered to be one of the best Greek texts and the widely available editions of the Greek NT are based on it.[88]

13. Page from *Codex Vaticanus* B showing 2 Thess. 3,11–18, Heb. 1:1–2, fourth cent. AD.

Bibl. Vat., Vat. gr. 1209; Gregory-Aland no. B or 03; Wikimedia Commons

Codex Alexandrinus (A)

The *Codex Alexandrianus* (no. A or 02)[89] is a mid 5th cent. (*ca.* 400–440 AD) uncial Greek manuscript that contains the OT (Septuagint including Psalm 151), the Apocrypha, and most of the NT (some 773 leaves out of 820; see Fig. 14).[90] It also contains the First and Second Epistle of Clement to the Corinthians, along with other non-canonical works.[91]

It is one of the earliest mostly complete copies of the entire Bible in existence. It bears the marks of the Alexandrian scribes in Egypt from which it thus acquired

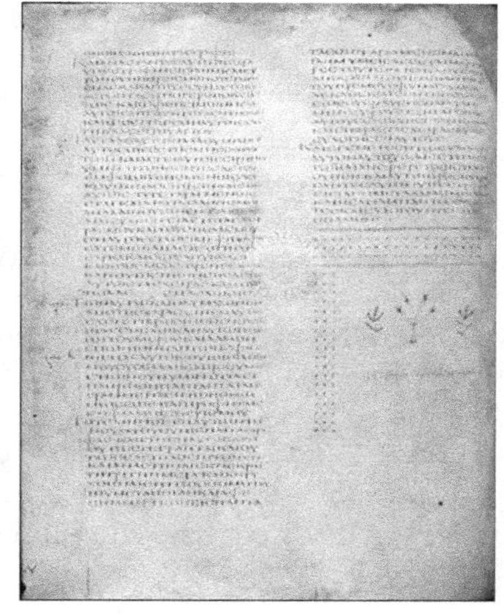

14. Folio 41v from the *Codex Alexandrinus* (MS Royal 1 D. VIII) contains the end of the Gospel of Luke with the decorative tailpiece found at the end of each book.

Wikimedia Commons

---

[85] Constantine Tischendorf, *Novum Testamentum Vaticanum* (Lipsiae: Giesecke & Devrient, 1867).

[86] Aland and Aland, *The Text of the New Testament*, 109.

[87] Theodore C. Skeat, "The Codex Vaticanus in the Fifteenth Century," *JTS* 35, no. 2 (n.d.): 454–65; Bruce M. Metzger and Bart D. Ehrman, *The Text of the New Testament: Its Transmission, Corruption, and Restoration*, 4th ed. (Oxford: Oxford University Press, 2005), 67; Bruce M. Metzger, *Manuscripts of the Greek Bible: An Introduction to Greek Palaeography* (Oxford: Oxford University Press, 1981); Theodore C. Skeat, "The Codex Sinaiticus, the Codex Vaticanus and Constantine," *JTS* 50, no. 2 (1999): 583–625.

[88] Aland and Aland, *The Text of the New Testament*, 26–30; James W. Voelz, "The Greek of Codex Vaticanus in the Second Gospel and Marcan Greek," *NovT* 47, no. 3 (2005): 209–49.

[89] Frederic G. Kenyon, *The Codex Alexandrinus*, Facsimile edition, 4 vols. (London: Trustee of the British Museum, 1915).

[90] Theodore C. Skeat and H. J. M. Milne, *The Codex Sinaiticus and the Codex Alexandrinus* (London: Trustee of the British Museum, 1963), 31.

[91] Philip W. Comfort and David P. Barrett, eds., *The Text of the Earliest New Testament Greek Manuscripts*, Corrected and Enlarged ed. (Wheaton, Ill.: Tyndale, 2001), 79; Joel C. Slayton, "Codex: Codex Alexandrinus," ed. David Noel Freedman et al., *ABD* (New York, N.Y.: Doubleday, 1996), 1:1069; Juan Hernández, *Scribal Habits and Theological Influences in the Apocalypse: The Singular Readings of Sinaiticus, Alexandrinus, and Ephraemi* (Leiden: Mohr Siebeck, 2006), 96–131.

its name.[92] It was delivered to Constantinople by the Eastern Orthodox Patriarch Cyril of Lucaris in 1616 and then later given to Charles I of England.[93] Today it is displayed along with the *Codex Sinaiticus*, in the Ritblat Gallery of the British Library.[94]

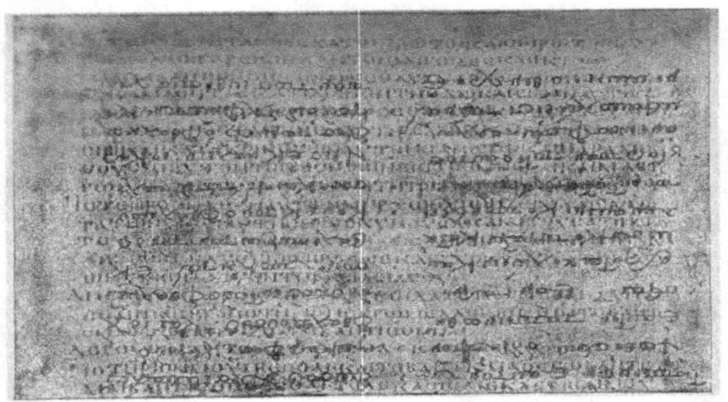

15. *Codex Ephraemi Rescriptus*, at the Bibliothèque Nationale, Paris, Département des manuscrits (Grec 9, fol. 60r rotated; Plate 24.

The S.S. Teacher's Edition: The Holy Bible. New York: Henry Frowde, Publisher to the University of Oxford, 1896

Codex Ephraemi Rescriptus (C)

The biblical text of the *Codex Ephraemi* (C; see Fig. 15),[95] which dates to *ca.* 450 AD, was recovered from underneath the later text of a twelfth cent. monk who copied the discourses of Ephraim Syrus overtop the earlier biblical manuscript. This practice is called a *palimpset rescriptus* and was common due to the limited availability of writing material.[96] The text was written on top of the earlier erased text. Metzger describes it as follows: "An important palimpsest of the Scriptures is the fifth-century copy of the Greek Bible known as the Codex Ephraemi, which was erased in the twelfth century to receive the homilies of Saint Ephraem, a Syrian church father of the fourth century."[97]

Modern chemical processes were able to restore the erased text and reveal the biblical text underneath the older manuscript. It revealed the entire NT except 2 Thessalonians and 2 John together with parts of the OT. Parker records that "There are 63 OT leaves extant (containing parts of Proverbs, Ecclesiastes, Canticles, Job, Wisdom, and Sirach) and 145 of the NT (in which every canonical book is represented)."[98] It has been identified as an Alexandrian text and dates to the fifth century AD. Based on the hand writing, the OT and NT were copied by different scribes.[99] Parker states that: "In the early 16th century the codex was brought to Italy, and passed into the possession of Catherine de Medici, with whom it went to Paris [Bibliothèque nationale], where it has remained ever since."[100] Due to its careless calligraphy it is believed that it was copied for private use.[101]

---

[92] Jack Finegan, *Encountering New Testament Manuscripts: A Working Introduction to Textual Criticism* (Grand Rapids: Eerdmans, 1974), 150; Scot McKendrick, "The Codex Alexandrinus or The Dangers of Being A Named Manuscript," in *The Bible as Book: The Transmission of the Greek Text*, ed. Scot McKendrick and Orlaith A. O'Sullivan (New Castle, Del.: Oak Knoll, 2003), 1–16.

[93] Matthew Spinka, "Acquisition of the Codex Alexandrinus by England," *The Journal of Religion* 16, no. 1 (1936): 10–29.

[94] Metzger and Ehrman, *The Text of the New Testament*, 67.

[95] Constantine Tischendorf, *Codex Ephraemi Syri Rescriptus, Sive Fragmenta Veteris Testamenti* (Lipsiae: Tauchnitz Jr., 1845); Harold H. Oliver, "A Textual Transposition in Codex C (Ephraemi Syri Rescriptus)," *JBL* 76, no. 3 (1957): 233–36.

[96] David C. Parker, "Codex: Codex Ephraimi Rescriptus," ed. David Noel Freedman et al., *ABD* (New York, N.Y.: Doubleday, 1996), 1:1073; Hernández, *Scribal Habits and Theological Influences in the Apocalypse*, 132–55.

[97] Metzger, *Manuscripts of the Greek Bible*, 325.

[98] Parker, "Codex: Codex Ephraimi Rescriptus," 1:1073.

[99] R. W. A. Lyon, "Re-Examination of Codex Ephraemi Rescriptus," *NTS* 5 (1959): 266–72; R. B. Stone, "The Life and Hard Times of Ephraimi Rescriptus," *The Bible Today* 24 (1986): 112–18.

[100] Parker, "Codex: Codex Ephraimi Rescriptus," 1:1073.

[101] M. R. Dunn, "An Examination of the Textual Character of Codex Ephraimi Syri Rescriptus (C 04) in the Four Gospels" (Ph.D. diss., South Western Baptist Seminary, 1990); Parker, "Codex: Codex Ephraimi Rescriptus," 1:1074.

THE *NAG HAMMADI* PAPYRI

This collection of fifty-two Gnostic papyri (1,200 pages; see Fig. 16),[102] written in Coptic, was discovered in a sealed jar by a local farmer (Muhammed al-Samman) at Jabal al-Tarif near *Nag Hammadi* in Egypt in December 1945.[103] Of the thirteen leather-bound papyrus codices, one was burned but not destroyed by the farmer's wife.[104]

While they date to the fourth cent. AD, they are based on earlier Greek manuscripts from the first to third cent. AD.[105] They are important for understanding the religious beliefs of the Gnostics, some of whom Paul dealt with in his NT letters (Col 2:8–23; 1 Tim 1:4; 2 Tim 2:16–19; Titus 1:10–16, etc.). Today they are stored in the Coptic Museum of Cairo[106] and are available online.[107] They deal with a reinterpretation of the biblical accounts of creation and include various visions that pertain to Gnostic beliefs as proposed by Marcion, Cerinthus, and Basilides.[108]

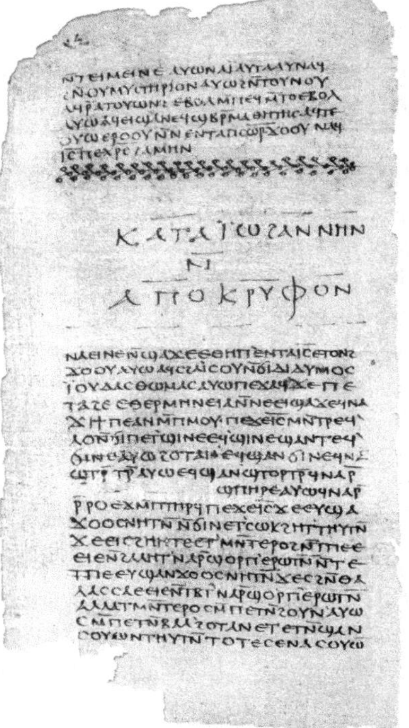

16. Folio 32 of Nag Hammadi Codex II, with the ending of *The Apocryphon of John*, and the beginning of the *Gospel of Thomas* (fourth cent. AD).

Wikimedia Commons

Gnostic Creation and Salvation

These works include: *The Apocryphon of John; The Hypostasis of the Archons; On the Origin of the World; The Apocalypse of Adam;* and *The Paraphrase of Shem.*

The Gnostic Nature of Reality

These works include: *The Gospel of Truth; The Treatise on the Resurrection; The Tripartite Tractate; Eugnostos the Blessed; The Second Treatise of the Great Seth; The Teachings of Silvanus;* and *The Testimony of Truth.*

Gnostic Liturgical Rites

These works include: *The Discourse on the Eighth and Ninth; The Prayer of Thanksgiving; A Valentinian Exposition; The Three Steles of Seth;* and *The Prayer of the Apostle Paul.*

---

[102] John W. B. Barns, Gerald M. Browne, and John C. Shelton, eds., *Nag Hammadi Codices: Greek and Coptic Papyri from the Cartonnage of the Covers* (Leiden: Brill, 1981); James M. Robinson, ed., *The Nag Hammadi Library: A Translation of the Gnostic Scriptures* (London: HarperCollins, 1990); Marvin Meyer and James M. Robinson, eds., *The Nag Hammadi Scriptures: The Revised and Updated Translation of Sacred Gnostic Texts Complete in One Volume* (New York, N.Y.: HarperCollins, 2009).

[103] For a detailed description of their discovery see Roger Pearse, "The Nag Hammadi Discovery of Manuscripts," *A Survey of the Manuscripts of Some Ancient Authors*, July 31, 2003, http://www.tertullian.org/rpearse/manuscripts/nag_hammadi.htm; John Dart, *The Jesus of Heresy and History: The Discovery and Meaning of the Nag Hammadi Gnostic Library*, Rev Exp (New York, N.Y.: HarperOne, 1989); Marvin Meyer, *The Gnostic Discoveries: The Impact of the Nag Hammadi Library* (New York, N.Y.: HarperCollins, 2005).

[104] James M. Robinson, "The Discovery of the Nag Hammadi Codices," *BA* 42, no. 4 (October 1, 1979): 206–24; Christoph Markschies, *Gnosis: An Introduction* (New York, N.Y.: T&T Clark, 2003), 48.

[105] Meyer, *The Gnostic Discoveries*; Meyer and Robinson, *Nag Hammadi Scriptures.*

[106] Birger A. Pearson, "Nag Hammadi Codices," ed. David Noel Freedman, *ABD* (New York, N.Y.: Doubleday, 1996), 4:984–93.

[107] www.nag-hammadi.com.

[108] Robinson, *The Nag Hammadi Library*; Meyer and Robinson, *Nag Hammadi Scriptures.*

Gnostic Divine Feminine (Sophia)

These works include: *The Thunder, Perfect Mind; The Thought of Norea; The Sophia of Jesus Christ;* and *The Exegesis on the Soul.*

Gnostic Apostolic Biographies

These works include: *The Apocalypse of Peter, The Letter of Peter to Philip; The Acts of Peter and the Twelve Apostles; The (First) Apocalypse of James; The (Second) Apocalypse of James;* and *The Apocalypse of Paul.*

The Gnostic Jesus

These are called gospels[109] but their form is simply a sequence of unrelated sayings and visions.[110] These works include: *The Dialogue of the Savior; The Book of Thomas the Contender; The Apocryphon of James; The Gospel of Philip;* and *The Gospel of Thomas* (see Fig. 16).

Unclassified

These works include: *The Apocryphon of John Codex II, III, IV;*[111] *The Gospel of the Egyptians Codex III, IV; Fragment of the Perfect Discourse Codex V; Authoritative Teaching Codex VI; The Concept of Our Great Power Codex VI; Plato's Republic 588A–589B Codex VI; The Teachings of Silvanus Codex VI; Zostrianos Codex VIII; Melchizedek Codex IX; Marsanes Codex X; The Interpretation of Knowledge Codex XI; Allogenes Codex XI; Hypsiphrone Codex XI; The Sentences of Sextus Codex XII; Unidentified fragments Codex XII;* and *Trimorphic Protennoia Codex XIII.*

The most controversial document found among the papyri is the Gospel of Thomas, which contains a list of 114 sayings (Gr. *logia*) attributed to Jesus, but dates to *ca.* AD 140–170.[112] B. P. Grenfell and A. S. Hunt in the 1890's identified a number of fragments (P.Oxy. 1, 654, 655) among the Oxyrhynchus Papyri without any title, which they called "Sayings of Our Lord," "New Sayings of Jesus," and a "Fragment of a Lost Gospel" that have since been identified by Henri-Charles Puech as part of the Gospel of Thomas.[113]

Some of the sayings are characterized by a series of questions that the disciples purportedly asked Jesus between the period of his resurrection and the ascension, but do not mention his messianic nature, crucifixion or resurrection.[114] While some similarities with the gospels have been pointed out,[115] the work is not accepted as canonical by the majority of

---

[109] Christopher M. Tuckett, *Nag Hammadi and the Gospel Tradition: Synoptic Tradition in the Nag Hammadi Library* (Edinburgh, U.K.: T&T Clark, 1986); Elaine Pagels, *The Gnostic Gospels* (New York, N.Y.: Random House, 2004); James M. Robinson, *From the Nag Hammadi Codices to the Gospel of Mary and the Gospel of Judas*, Institute for Antiquity and Christianity Occasional Papers 48 (Claremont, Calf.: Institute for Antiquity & Christianity, 2006); Christopher Tuckett, "Thomas and the Synoptics," *NovT* 30, no. 2 (April 1, 1988): 132–57.

[110] Dart, *Jesus of Heresy*; Majella Franzmann, *Jesus in the Nag Hammadi Writings* (Edinburgh, U.K.: T&T Clark, 1996).

[111] Michael Waldstein and Frederik Wisse, eds., *The Apocryphon of John: Synopsis of Nag Hammadi Codices II,1, III,1, and IV,1 with BG 8502,2*, Nag Hammadi and Manichaean Studies: The Coptic Gnostic Library 33 (Leiden: Brill Academic, 1995).

[112] April D. DeConick, *The Original Gospel of Thomas in Translation: With a Commentary and New English Translation of the Complete Gospel*, The Library of New Testament Studies (New York, N.Y.: Bloomsbury, 2006); Darrell L Bock, *The Missing Gospels: Unearthing the Truth Behind Alternative Christianities* (Nashville, Tenn.: Nelson, 2006); Craig A. Evans, *Fabricating Jesus: How Modern Scholars Distort the Gospels* (Downers Grove, Ill.: InterVarsity, 2006), 52–78; Christopher W. Skinner, *What Are They Saying About the Gospel of Thomas?* (New York, N.Y.: Paulist, 2012).

[113] Stephen J. Patterson, Hans-Gebhard Bethge, and James M. Robinson, *The Fifth Gospel: The Gospel of Thomas Comes of Age* (New York, N.Y.: Bloomsbury Academic, 1998), 34 n.2.

[114] Alister E. McGrath, *Christian Theology: An Introduction* (Hoboken, N.J.: Wiley-Blackwell, 2006), 12.

[115] Tuckett, "Thomas and the Synoptics," 132–57.

scholars[116] and is seen as reliant on details found in the Gospels, not the reverse. While Yamauchi acknowledges the non-Christian nature of many of the tractates, based on their later date he argues that they "do not therefore establish a case for a pre-Christian Gnosticism."[117]

17. Lower part of col. 18 (according to the reconstruction by E. Tov) of the Greek (Septuagint) Minor Prophets Scroll from Nahal Hever containing verses from Habakkuk. The arrow points at the *tetragrammaton* [Yahweh] in paleo-Hebrew script rather than writing God's name in Greek out of reverence for God.

Wikimedia Commons

THE SEPTUAGINT (LXX)

The *Septuagint* is the Greek translation of the Hebrew OT (see Fig. 17).[118] The term *Septuagint* comes from the Latin word *septuaginta* meaning "seventy," and is based on the tradition that about 70 Jewish translators were involved in the production of this work. The abbreviation for the Septuagint is thus LXX, the Roman numeral for seventy.[119]

One of the negative influences that came from the spread of Hellenism (Greek culture) was that the Hebrew Scriptures were no longer understandable in the synagogues, as Jews were now speaking Greek. Thus, the Septuagint was the first translation of the Bible (280–200 BC) and was the Bible predominately used by Jesus and the NT writers.

[116] Helmut Koester, *Ancient Christian Gospels: Their History and Development*, 2nd ed. (New York, N.Y.: T&T Clark, 1992), 84–86; Skinner, *What Are They Saying About the Gospel of Thomas?*

[117] Edwin M. Yamauchi, "Pre-Christian Gnosticism in the Nag Hammadi Texts?," *Church History* 48, no. 2 (June 1, 1979): 141.

[118] On the origin of the Septuagint see Graves *Biblical Archaeology* 1:93-94.

[119] Natalio Fernández Marcos and Wilfred G. E. Watson, *The Septuagint in Context: Introduction to the Greek Version of the Bible* (Leiden: Brill, 2000); Jennifer Mary Dines and Michael Anthony Knibb, *The Septuagint* (New York, N.Y.: T&T Clark, 2004); Moisés Silva and Karen Jobes, *Invitation to the Septuagint* (Grand Rapids: Baker Academic & Brazos, 2005).

Genesis

18. The larger and lesser mountains of Ararat, Turkey 16,854 feet (5,137 m). This is the traditional location for the resting of Noah's ark.

Jewish and Christian tradition holds that Genesis was written by Moses, but despite such esteemed authorship, it is still subject to perhaps the most criticism of any section of the Bible. There is little doubt that much of the content sounds mythical, especially considering the mystical descriptions of the creation of the world, the great flood of Noah, the confusion of languages at the tower of Babel, and the destruction of Sodom and Gomorrah.

However, over the years of archaeological excavations, many artifacts have surfaced supporting the more literal historicity of the biblical text. While some scholars have argued that the mythical Mesopotamian accounts of creation and the flood were used to compose the biblical accounts, when the two accounts are carefully analysed it is more likely that the Mesopotamian accounts share the same core historical details as the biblical record, but are independent records. The discoveries of the Ebla and Mari tablets, along with new excavations (i.e., Tall el-Hammam and other sites), have provided a fresh historical approach to Genesis and the patriarchal age.

Creation and Flood

The Epic of Gilgamesh (*ca.* 2100–1600 BC)

In 1853 Hormuzd Rassam, protégé of Austin Henry Layard, uncovered 25,000 inscribed clay tablets from the libraries of the Assyrian king, Ashurbanipal, in Khorsabad and the temple of Nabu in the ancient city of Nineveh.[1] One of the tablets is now known as the *Epic of Gilgamesh,*[2] a famous Mesopotamian account of ancient creation and the flood. The *Epic of Gilgamesh* (see Fig. 19) is a masterpiece of the literary poetry of ancient Mesopotamia composed on twelve clay tablets in the ancient Akkadian language

19. Tablet XI of the Babylonian version of the Epic of Gilgamesh which contains the flood account from the Library of Ashurbanipal. 650 BC.

[1] Brian M. Fagan, *A Brief History of Archaeology: Classical Times to the Twenty-First Century* (Upper Saddle River, N.J.: Prentice Hall, 2004), 84–85.

[2] Various tablets exist today and are displayed in the British Museum (ME K3375), Israel Museum (IAA 1955-2) and Oriental Institute Museum (OIM A29934, A3444, 22007). Simo Parpola, *The Standard Babylonian Epic of Gilgamesh: Cuneiform Text, Transliteration, Glossary, Indices, and Sign List*, SAA Cuneiform Texts 1 (Helsinki: Eisenbrauns, 1997); Benjamin Foster, *The "Epic of Gilgamesh,"* Norton Critical Editions (New York, N.Y.: Norton & Company, 2001); Andrew R. George, *The Babylonian Gilgamesh Epic: Introduction, Critical Edition and Cuneiform Texts*, vol. 1, 2 vols. (Oxford: Oxford University Press, 2003); Morris Jastrow and Albert T. Clay, *An Old Babylonian Version of the Gilgamesh Epic (Illustrated Edition)*, Ill (Dodo Press, 2009).

(lines 55–106 and 108–269).[3] It highlights the earlier exploits of King Gilgamesh, ruler of the Mesopotamian city of Uruk in around 1600 BC. Gilgamesh is described in the story as a great warrior/builder who is part god and part man.[4] While he is not mentioned in the Bible, some scholars (i.e. A. H. Sayce and G. Smith and Jeremias) suggest that he is to be identified with biblical Nimrod (Gen 10:8–12).[5]

George E. Smith,[6] an assistant in the British Museum, was examining the dusty tablets.[7] He later wrote: "The fragments of clay tablets were all sizes, from half an inch to a foot long, and were thickly coated with dirt, so that they had to be cleaned before anything could be seen on the surface."[8] Skilled in reading cuneiform texts, during his examination Smith recognized on one of the tablets (tablet 11) an ancient flood story similar to the biblical story of Noah with the words,[9] "On Mount Nimush [Nisir] the ship ran aground, the mountains held it and would not release it. For six days and seven nights, the mountain would not release it. On the seventh day, I brought out a dove and set it free. The dove flew off, then flew back to the ship, because there was no place to land."[10]

20. Sumerian statue from ancient Mesopotamia (5300 – 2000 BC). Believed to be self portraits, they were presented to temples as votive gifts to honour the gods and represent their donors.

Used with permission of the Oriental Institute Museum of the University of Chicago

Fagan describes the subsequent events:

> On December 3, 1872, George Smith lectured to an overflow audience of the Biblical Archaeological Society. The crowd included Prime Minister William Gladstone. Smith told the story of a prophet named Hasisadra, who survived a great flood sent by the wrathful gods by loading his family and "the beasts of the field" into a large ship. Six days of torrential rain brought a vast inundation. Hasisadra's ark went aground on a high point of land. He sent out a dove, then a raven, in search of dry land. The raven did not return, so Hasisadra released the animals, became a god, and lived happily ever after.[11]

Budge reports the events of that evening as follows:

> Smith took the tablet and began to read over the lines which Ready [the conservator who had cleaned the tablet] had brought to light; and when he saw that they contained the portion of the legend he had hoped to find there, he said, "I am the first man to read that after two thousand years of oblivion." Setting the tablet on the table, he jumped up and rushed about the room in a state of great excitement, and, to the astonishment of those present, began to undress himself.[12]

---

[3] Kenton L. Sparks, *Ancient Texts for the Study of the Hebrew Bible: A Guide to the Background Literature* (Grand Rapids: Hendrickson, 2005), 275–79, 316–17.

[4] Jeffrey H. Tigay, *The Evolution of the Gilgamesh Epic* (Philadelphia, Pa.: University of Pennsylvania Press, 1982); Tzvi Abusch, "The Development and Meaning of the Epic of Gilgamesh: An Interpretive Essay," *JAOS* 121, no. 4 (2001): 614–22.

[5] M. Seligmann, "Nimrod," in *JE*, ed. Isidore Singer et al., vol. 9 (New York, N.Y.: Funk & Wagnalls, 1906), 310; Mark W. Chavalas and K. Lawson Younger, eds., *Mesopotamia and the Bible: Comparative Explorations*, JSOTSup 341 (London: T&T Clark, 2003), 29.

[6] George E. Smith, "The Chaldean Account of the Deluge," *PSBA* 2 (1872): 213–34.

[7] It was translated by George Smith in the early 1870's although more modern translations have been done. George, *The Babylonian Gilgamesh Epic: Introduction, Critical Edition and Cuneiform Texts*; *The Epic of Gilgamesh*, Rev Ed edition (New York, N.Y.: Penguin Classics, 2003).

[8] George E. Smith, *Assyrian Discoveries: An Account of Explorations and Discoveries on the Site on Nineveh, During 1878 and 1874* (New York, N.Y.: Scribner, Armstrong & Co., 1875), 13.

[9] The complete academic translations of the *Epic of Gilgamesh* can be found at: http://king-of-heroes.co.uk/the-epic-of-gilgamesh/

[10] Stephen Mitchell, *Gilgamesh: A New English Version* (New York, N.Y.: Free Press, 2006), 189.

[11] Fagan, *A Brief History of Archaeology*, 84–85.

[12] E. A. Wallis Budge, *The Rise and Progress of Assyriology* (New York, N.Y.: Hopkinson & Co., 1925), 153.

His discovery of the missing lines after only a few days of excavation is one of the great coincidences of archaeology. As he continued translating he found more and more similarities with the biblical account. Carem tells the story best:

> The farther he progressed with the decipherment, the more excited he became and the more anxious to know how the argument would turn out. . . . Indeed, the most essential section of the story was entirely missing — that is, the conclusion. What Smith had read of the Gilgamesh Epic left him no rest. Nor could he keep silent about his discoveries, though to disclose them was sure to rock the Bible-bound England of Victoria's day. Later a powerful newspaper came to George Smith's aid. The *London Daily Telegraph* announced that it was offering the sum of a thousand guineas to anyone who would go to Kuyunjik, find the missing Gilgamesh inscriptions, and bring them back to England.
>
> George Smith himself accepted the offer. He traveled the thousands of miles separating London from Mesopotamia, and there boldly attacked the tremendous pile of rubble that was Kuvunjik — the mound, in respect of the total area, had hardly been scratched in search of the missing tablets. Smith's task was about comparable to finding one particular water-louse in the sea, or the famous needle in the haystack.
>
> And again there occurred one of the almost unbelievable wonders that stunned the history of archaeological excavation. Smith actually found the missing parts of the Gilgamesh Epic.[13]

Smith began work at Nimrud in April 1873. By May 7th he had moved to Koujunjik, where he found "a vast picture of utter confusion and destruction."[14] However, due to the looting of the site by Henry Layard, and its ruthless quarrying by the builders of the Mosul bridge, it was almost impossible to find the missing tablets. Amazingly within the first seven days (May 14) Smith discovered the missing portion of the Deluge Story, with the unfortunate result that the *London Daily Telegraph* declared the excavation a success and cut off funds.[15] However, Smith returned to London with some 384 clay fragments and the all-important missing piece of the Babylonian flood story.

The library of Ashurbanipal revealed a magnificent collection of cuneiform tablets opening the world of Babylonian law, commerce and religion.[16] Among them were several varied copies of the Gilgamesh epic, found in Syria, Canaan and Anatolia. Each version was a retelling or reinterpretation for its particular audience. Heidel concludes:

> The date of the composition of the Gilgamesh Epic can therefore be fixed at about 2000 BC. But the material contained on these tablets is undoubtedly much older, as we can infer from the mere fact that the epic consists of numerous originally independent episodes, which, of course, did not spring into existence at the time of the composition of our poem but must have been current long before they were compiled and woven together to form our epic.[17]

When first published, the *Epic of Gilgamesh* flood narrative on tablet 11 shook the church, as the parallels with the biblical creation and flood account (Gen 5–9) seemed amazingly similar. The hero Ut-Napishtim was seen as the epic's Noah character, leading to the new discovery being used to call into question the uniqueness and authenticity of the Hebrew flood account. The similarities between the Babylonian text and the Hebrew story in Genesis (1–9) are striking, with around twenty items in common.

There appears to be a connection between the Genesis text and Gilgamesh, leading to several possibilities:

---

[13] C. W. Ceram, *Gods, Graves & Scholars: The Story of Archaeology*, trans. E. B. Garside and Sophie Wilkins, 2d Revised Edition (New York, N.Y.: Vintage, 1986), 313.

[14] H. V. Hilprecht, *Explorations in Bible Lands During the 19th Century* (Piscataway, N.J.: Gorgias, 2004), 195.

[15] Fagan, *A Brief History of Archaeology*, 85.

[16] Brian M. Fagan, *Return to Babylon: Travelers, Archaeologists and Monuments in Mesopotamia* (Boulder, Colo.: University Press of Colorado, 2007), 14.

[17] Alexander Heidel, *Gilgamesh Epic and Old Testament Parallels*, 2nd ed. (Chicago, Ill.: University Of Chicago Press, 1970), 15.

Quotes from Antiquity

Epic of Gilgamesh Table XI

A portion of the text of the *Epic of Gilgamesh* reads as follows:

What I had I loaded thereon, the whole harvest of life
I caused to embark within the vessel; all my family and my relations,
The beasts of the field, the cattle of the field, the craftsmen, I made them all embark.
I entered the vessel and closed the door. . . .
When the yound dawn gleamed forth,
From the foundations of heaven a black cloud arose. . . .
All that is bright is turned to darkness,
The brother seeth his brother no more,
The folk of the skies can no longer recognize each other
The gods feared the flood,
They fled, they climbed into the heavens of Anu,
The gods crouched like a dog on the wall, they lay down. . . .
For six days and nights
Wind and flood marched on, the hurricane subdued the land.
When the seventh day dawned, the hurricane was abated, the flood
Which was waged war like an army;
The sea was stilled, the ill wind was calmed, the flood ceased.
I beheld the sea, its voice was silent,
And all mankind was turned into mud!
As high as the roofs reached the swamp! . . .
I beheld the world, the horizon of sea;
Twelve measures away an island emerged;
Unto Mount Nitsir came the vessel,
Mount Nitsir held the vessel and let it not budge. . .
When the seventh day came,
I sent forth a dove, I released it;
It went , the dove, it came back,
As there was no place, it came back,
I sent forth a swallow, I released it;
It went, the swallow, it came back,
As there was not place, it came back.
I sent forth a crow, I released it;
It went, the crow, and behold the subsidence of the waters;
It eats, it splashes about, it caws, it comes not back.

Ceram, *Gods, Graves & Scholars,* 314–15.

- Genesis was copied from an earlier Babylonian account,[18] or
- The Gilgamesh account was copied from an earlier Hebrew story, or
- Both were copied from a common source that was earlier than both of them.[19]

First, it is relevant to point out several areas of common detail between the stories in Genesis and Gilgamesh:[20]

- The Genesis account describes how humanity had become sinful and disobedient and deserved the judgment of God. In the Gilgamesh account, humanity had become too noisy because of their numbers.
- The gods (or God) decide(s) to destroy the earth with a worldwide flood that will drown all humanity, and land animals and birds.
- The gods (or God) knew of only one righteous man, Ut-Napishtim or Noah.
- The gods (or God) instructed the hero to build a wooden ark.
- The ark would be sealed with pitch and contain various internal compartments.
- It would have a single window and door.
- The ark was built and occupied by the hero, members of his family, and a sample of all the animals.
- The rain covered the land and mountains with water.
- The ark landed on a mountain in the ancient Near East (ANE).
- The hero sent out various types of birds at different times to find dry land. The first two birds returned to the ark. The third bird found dry land and did not return to the ark.
- The survivors left the ark, and offered an animal as a sacrifice.
- The gods (or God) smelled the aroma of the sacrifice.
- Noah, or Ut-Napishtim, was blessed.

---

[18] C. W. Ceram, *The March of Archaeology*, trans. Richard Winston and Clara Winston (New York, N.Y.: Random House, 1970), 220, 222; Gordon J. Wenham, "The Coherence of the Flood Narrative," *VT* 28, no. 3 (1978): 336–48.

[19] Izaak Rapaport, *Tablet XI of the Gilgamesh Epic and the Biblical Flood Story: A Refutation of the Generally Held View That Genesis Chapters 6-9 Is Based upon a Babylonian Prototype* (Tel Aviv, Israel: Tel Aviv University Press, 1981).

[20] Ceram, *Gods, Graves & Scholars*, 314–15.

- The Babylonian gods were sorry for the destruction that they had created. Yahweh promised never to destroy the earth with a flood again.

However, while there are many commonalities between the Genesis and Gilgamesh stories there are also significant differences:

- Yahweh spoke directly to Noah while Ut-Napishtim received his instructions indirectly through a dream.
- Noah's ark was a sea worthy rectangular boat (450 x 75 ft.), three stories high. The Babylonian ark was an unfloatable square boat with six stories.
- While Noah only included his family, Ut-Napishtim invited a pilot and additional workmen.
- Noah's ark landed on Mount Ararat; Ut-Napishtim landed on Mount Nisir; these locations are only a few hundred miles apart in Turkey and Iran.
- The rain in the Hebrew flood lasted for forty days and nights and also came from beneath the earth while the Bablylonian flood only lasted six days.
- Noah sent out a raven and two doves while Ut-Napishtim sent a dove, swallow and raven.

On the issue of the possible dependence of the Genesis account on other ANE texts, the similarities between the two accounts could be explained by all of the texts attempting to describe the same worldwide flood. After Lambert and Millard suggest "one possible explanation" of a westward migration of the flood traditions during the Amarna Period (*ca.* 1400 BC), they conclude that "the question is very complex."[21]

As Sasson points out, today a more responsible handling of the two accounts is used by scholars. He states "While scholars still compare the flood accounts in the GE [Gilgamesh Epic] and in Genesis, there is an appreciation that both have adapted traditional narratives to suit their own contexts. Moreover, scholars now generally avoid making judgmental contrasts among the accounts (e.g., which one has a better blueprint for a seaworthy ark or communicates a more spiritual description of the deity)."[22]

The Ziusudra (Eridu Genesis) Epic (*ca.* 1600 CB)

The *Ziusudra Epic* (also known as the *Eridu Genesis*; see Fig. 21) is the fragmentary Sumerian version of the flood epic written in cuneiform.[23] Although it dates to around 1600 BC it is probably a shortened copy of a much older poem that is dependent on an even older account. Kramer concluded that "Ziusudra had become a venerable figure in literary tradition by the middle of the third

21. The Ziusudra or Eridu Genesis flood tablet.

Used with permission courtesy of The University of Pennsylvania Museum of Archaeology and Anthropology (B10673)

[21] Wilfred G. Lambert, Alan R. Millard, and Miguel Civil, *Atra-hasis: The Babylonian Story of the Flood* (Winona Lake, IN: Eisenbrauns, 1999), 24.

[22] Jack M. Sasson, "Gilgamesh Epic," ed. David Noel Freedman et al., *ABD* (New York, N.Y.: Doubleday, 1996), 2:1027.

[23] *COS* 1.158: 513-15; Thorkild Jacobsen, "The Eridu Genesis," *JBL* 100, no. 4 (1981): 513–29.

Quotes from Antiquity

Ziusudra Epic

A portion of the text of the *Ziusudra Epic* reads as follows:

In the name of heaven and earth . . .
. . . the gods in Nippur . . .
Ziusudra stood at the side and listened.
"Stand by the wall at my left . . .
At the wall, I will speak to you, [listen] to my words.
Heed my instructions.
By our [hand] a flood [will sweep] over the capitals
To destroy the seed of mankind . . .
The decision, the word of the assembly, [its final].
By the command spoken by Anu Enlil . . .
. . .
All the destructive winds [and] gales were present.
Then the flood swept over the capitals.
For Seven days and seven nights
the flood covered the country
[And] the wind drove the large boat about on the deep water.
The sun came out, illuminating the earth and sky.
Ziusudra opened a window in the large boat
And sunlight entered the large craft.
King Ziusudra
Prostrated himself before the sun-god.
The king slaughtered an ox and some sheep.
They made the animals come up from the earth.
King Ziusudra
Prostrated himself before Anu Enlil
[He] gave him life like a god [and]
Elevated him to eternal life like a god.
Then king Ziusudra
Who protected the animals and seed of mankind,
They caused to dwell in the land of the country of Dilmun,
the place where the sun rises
{. . . 39 lines missing . . . }

Ziusudra Epic 143–261
Best, *Noah's Ark and the Ziusudra Epic*, 256–58.

millennium BC."[24] The hero Ziusudra ("found long life") is listed as the last king of Sumer in the Old Babylonian Empire in the Sumerian king list. [25] It was discovered by Arno Peobel in 1893–1896.[26]

Its content covers the creation of humanity, animals, and building of the earliest cities of Eridu, Bad-tibira, Larsa, Sippar, and Shuruppak. Following a break in the tablet, the narrative picks up with a decision by the gods to send a deluge to punish humanity.[27]

The narrative records the god Enki directing Ziusudra to build a large boat, followed by a missing section, and picking up with a description of the flood. A seven day storm tosses a huge boat about on the water until the Sun (Utu) appears and the hero Ziusudra worships and offers an animal sacrifice to the gods. Following the flood Ziusudra thanks the gods An (sky-god) and Enlil (captain of the gods), who bless him with "breath eternal" and take him to live in Dilmun.[28] The mention of this place in lines 258–261 is unique in the flood epics. In this version the boat floats down the Euphrates River into the Persian Gulf to come to rest on the island of Dilmun (Bahrain) rather than resting on a mountain.[29] In Sumerian the word *KUR* (line 140) means "country", while in Akkadian (*Epic of Gilgamesh* see. Fig. 23) it is understood to mean "mountain." The remainder of the tablet is missing.

---

[24] Samuel Noah Kramer, "Reflections on the Mesopotamian Flood: The Cuneiform Data New and Old," *Expedition* 9, no. 4 (1967): 18.

[25] Lambert and Millard, *Atra-Hasis*, 138.

[26] Arno Poebel, *Historical and Grammatical Texts*, PBS 5 (Philadelphia, Pa.: University of Pennsylvania Museum, 1914).

[27] Patrick D. Miller, "Eridu, Dunu, and Babel: A Study in Comparative Mythology," *Hebrew Annual Review* 9 (1985): 227–51; Wilfred G. Lambert and Miguel Civil, "The Sumerian Flood Story," in *Atra-Hasis: The Babylonian Story of the Flood*, ed. Alan R. Millard and Miguel Civil (Winona Lake, Ind.: Eisenbrauns, 1999), 138–45.

[28] Lambert and Millard, *Atra-Hasis*, 97; Sparks, *Ancient Texts for the Study of the Hebrew Bible*, 313–14.

[29] Robert M. Best, *Noah's Ark and the Ziusudra Epic: Sumerian Origins of the Flood Myth* (Winona Lake, Ind.: Eisenbrauns, 1999), 30–31.

The Atrahasis Epic (1646–1626 BC)

The *Atrahasis Epic*[30] (also Mesopotamian Flood Story; approximately 405 lines; see Fig. 22) is the Babylonian parallel to Genesis 1–11[31] discovered by Henry Layard in 1872[32] and translated by George Smith in 1876. The flood portion of Tablet III is significantly damaged. Atrahasis (meaning "exceedingly wise") is the nickname of Ut-Napishtim (Gilgamesh XI.187), the Noah of the *Epic of Gilgamesh* (see Fig. 19). The tablet describes the impending flood and instructs Atrahasis to build a cubical boat with six stories and nine sections to save his entire family. The major difference between the *Atrahasis epic* and the *Gilgamesh Epic* is that Atrahasis is about population control while Gilgamesh explains the immortality of humanity.[33] Kikawada describes the general content of the text:

22. Cuneiform tablet from Sippar, southern Iraq with the *Atrahasis Epic* (*ca.* 1646–1626 BC) describing both the Babylonian creation epic as well as the flood.

The Trustees of the British Museum (ME 78941)

Quotes from Antiquity

Atrahasis Epic Tablet III

A portion of the text reads as follows:

Twelve hundred years had not yet passed
When the land extended and the peoples multiplied.
The land was billowing like a bull,
The god got disturbed with their uproar.
Enlil heard their noise and addressed the great gods,
'The noise of mankind has become too intense for me,
With their uproar I am deprived of sleep.
Cut off supplies for the peoples,
Let there be a scarcity of plant-life to satisfy their hunger.
Adid should withhold his rain,
And below, the flood should not come up from the abyss
Atra-hasis opened his mouth . . .
Destroy your house, build a boat,
Spurn property and save life.
The boat which you build . . .] be equal [(. .)]
Roof it over like the Apsu.
So that the sun shall not see inside it
Let it be roofed over above and below.
The tackle should be very strong,
Let the pitch be tough, and so give (the boat) strength.
I will rain down upon you here
An abundance of birds, a profusion of fishes."
He opened the water-clock and filled it;
He announced to him the coming of the flood for the seventh night. . . . What ever he had [. . .]
Clean (animals) . [. . .] Fat (animals) [. . .]
He caught [and put on board]
The winged [birds of] the heavens.
The cattle (?) [. . .]
The wild [creatures (?) [. . .] he put on board [. . .]
. . .] . he sent his family on board,
They ate and they drank. . . .
After he had bolted his door
Adad was roaring in the clouds,
The winds became savage as he arose,
He severed the hawser and set the boat adrift. . . . .
For seven days and seven nights
Came the deluge, the storm, [the flood].

ANET 104-06, 512-14; *COS* 1.130: 450-52
Lambert and Millard, *Atra-Hasis*, 89–101.

---

[30] Jørgen Laessoe, "The Atrahasis Epic, A Babylonian History of Mankind," *Biblioteca Orientalis* 13 (1956): 90–102; Isaac M. Kikawada, "The Double Creation of Mankind in Enki and Ninmah, Atrahasis I 1–351, and Genesis 1–2," *Iraq* 45 (1983): 43–45; Alan Dundes, *The Flood Myth* (Berkeley: University of California Press, 1988); Lambert and Millard, *Atra-Hasis*. Stephanie Dalley, *Myths from Mesopotamia: Creation, the Flood, Gilgamesh, and Others*, Revised, Oxford World's Classics (Oxford: Oxford University Press, 2009), 1–38.

[31] Robert A. Oden, "Divine Aspirations in Atrahasis and in Genesis 1-11," *ZAW* 93 (1981): 197–216.

[32] Daniel Hämmerly-Dupuy, "Some Observations on the Assyro-Babylonian and Sumerian Flood Stories," in *The Flood Myth*, ed. Alan Dundes (Berkeley: University of California Press, 1988), 49.

[33] Isaac M. Kikawada, "Noah and the Ark (The Hero of the Flood)," ed. David Noel Freedman et al., *ABD* (New York, N.Y.: Doubleday, 1996), 4:1124.

The *Atrahasis Epic* begins with the creation of humankind because the labour-class gods are fed up with the heavy tasks imposed on them by the management-class gods, and they make much "noise," especially against the chief god, Enlil. As a result, the mother goddess Mami and magician god Enki create procreating people as a substitute for the labouring gods. The people multiplied so much in 1,200 years that they made a great "noise," to the annoyance of Enlil. Enlil tries to exterminate them first by a famine, then 1,200 years later by a drought, and finally, yet another 1,200 years later, by the flood. Three times Enlil's plans are foiled by Enki and his faithful worshipper Atrahasis. Now the thrice failing and furious Enlil convenes a divine assembly where a post-flood compromise is reached among gods to limit the expanding population. At least three such population control measures are suggested, presumably by Enki and Mami.[34]

23. Upper part of a Neo-Assyrian clay tablet from the library of Ashurbanipal in Kouyunjik (Nineveh). It is part of the creation legend called the Enuma Elish.

The Trustees of the British Museum (ME K3473)

The Enuma Elish (*ca.* 1000 BC)

The *Enuma Elish* (ME K3473; Akk. *Enûma Eliš* incipit "When on high"; see Fig. 23) is one of the early creation myth tablets[35] discovered by Austen Henry Layard in 1848 among the ruins of the royal library in the palace of Ashurbanipal at Kouyunjik (Nineveh, modern Mosul, Iraq) and first published by George E. Smith in 1876 as *The Chaldean Genesis*.[36] It was written in cuneiform on seven clay tablets sometime around 1000 BC, from earlier sources (*ca.* 16th–12th cent. BC).

The *Enuma Elish* is a Mesopotamian (Babylonian) myth of creation that recounts the struggle between cosmic order and chaos.[37] It is named after its opening words "When on High" (Akk. *Enûma Eliš*) and was recited on the fourth day of the ancient Babylonian New Year's (Akk. *Akitu*) festival. Immediately scholars noticed parallels with the Genesis account. Niehaus provides three possible explanations for the parallels: "The Babylonian accounts depended on the Hebrew;[38] the Hebrew depended on the Babylonian;[39] or both the Babylonian and the Hebrew derived from a common source."[40]

The last option appears the most likely as God reveals his revelation in the context of common cultures. Niehaus proposes that "a shared theological structure of ideas existed in the ANE, a structure that finds its most complete and true form in the Old and New Testaments."[41]

---

[34] Lambert and Millard, *Atra-Hasis*, 97; Sparks, *Ancient Texts for the Study of the Hebrew Bible*, 313–14.

[35] Leonard W. King, *Enuma Elish: The Seven Tablets of Creation; the Babylonian and Assyrian Legends Concerning the Creation of the World and of Mankind*, 2 vols. (London: Luzac, 1902); James Bennett Pritchard, *Ancient Near Eastern Texts Relating to the Old Testament with Supplement*, 3rd ed. (Princeton, NJ: Princeton University Press, 1969), 68; Dalley, *Myths from Mesopotamia*, 228–77; King, *Enuma Elish*. See also *COS* 1.111:390-402.

[36] George E. Smith and Andrew Dickson White, *The Chaldean Account of Genesis*, Elibron Classics (Charleston, SC: Nabu, 2010).

[37] Sparks, *Ancient Texts for the Study of the Hebrew Bible*, 314–16.

[38] This option is unlikely due to the early date (1894-1595 BC) for the composition of the Babylonian accounts and the fact that Hebrew was not developed as a language this early.

[39] Bernard F. Batto, "Creation Theology in Geneis," in *Creation in the Biblical Traditions*, ed. Richard J. Clifford and John Joseph Collins (Washington, D.C.: Catholic Biblical Association of America, 1992), 16–38; Hermann Gunkel, *Creation And Chaos in the Primeval Era And the Eschaton: A Religio-Historical Study of Genesis 1 and Revelation 12*, trans. K. William Whitney, Jr. (Grand Rapids: Eerdmans, 2006), xvi; Friedrich Delitzsch, *Babel and Bible: A Lecture on the Significance of Assyriological Research for Religion* (Charleston, SC: BiblioBazaar, 2009), 49–50.

[40] Jeffrey J. Niehaus, *Ancient Near Eastern Themes in Biblical Theology* (Grand Rapids: Kregel, 2008), 21.

[41] Ibid., 30.

The basic creation story existed in various forms in the region. The *Enuma Elish* focuses on Marduk, the patron deity of the city of Babylon.[42]

A similar earlier version, the *Atrahasis Epic* (eighteenth cent. BC see Fig. 22), is written in Akkadian, an old Babylonian dialect. This epic features the Sumerian gods Anu, Enlil and Enki (gods of sky, wind, and water) as the heroes, which suggests that this version was adapted to justify the religious practices in the cult of Enlil in Babylon.[43]

Quotes from Antiquity

***Enuma Elish* 6.1–8**

When Marduk hears the words of the gods, His heart prompts (him) to fashion artful works. Opening his mouth, he addresses Ea. To impart the plan he had conceived in his heart: Blood I will mass and cause bones to be. I will establish a savage, "man" shall be his name. Verily, savage-man I will create. He shall be charged with the service of the gods. That they might be at ease!

ANET 68.

Peter Masters provides a good paraphrase of the Babylonian epic:

> In the Mesopotamian story the two original gods Apsu, the male, and Tiamat, the female, are created from water. They then beget all other gods, but these "children" make so much noise that Apsu is unable to sleep and decides to kill them. However, before he can, one of the offspring puts a spell on him and kills him. Tiamat, to avenge his death, takes up the cudgels, but Marduk (another offspring) eliminates her, splitting her in two, and the two parts of her corpse become the heavens and the Earth. Marduk relieves the other gods of all manual work by creating man (from the blood vessels of a defeated giant god), and Marduk then becomes the chief god. Needless to say, none of this has anything in common with the biblical account of creation.[44]

Lambert observes that there is "no evidence of Hebrew borrowing from Babylon."[45] Hasel argues that the Genesis account of creation functions as an anti-mythological polemic set in opposition to the Babylonian myths which are basically myths portraying the cycle of seasons.[46] Lambert's position is that: "The Epic of Creation is not a norm of Babylonian or Sumerian cosmology. It is a sectarian and aberrant combination of mythological threads woven into an unparalleled compositum."[47] The Babylonian account does, however, demonstrate an intrinsic human instinct that an almighty power created the universe.

The Sumerian King List (*ca.* 2100–1800 BC)

On the importance of the Nuzi Tablets see Graves, *Biblical Archaeology* vol. 1.[48]

PATRIARCHS

Most scholars place the patriarchs during the Middle Bronze period on the basis of the cultural

---

[42] Alexander Heidel, *The Babylonian Genesis: The Story of Creation*, 2nd ed. (Chicago, Ill.: University of Chicago Press, 1963); Thorkild Jacobsen, "The Battle between Marduk and Tiamat," *JAOS* 88, no. 1 (1968): 104–8.

[43] Wilfred G. Lambert, "Babylonien Und Israel," *Theologische Realenzyklopädie* 5 (1980): 71–72.

[44] Peter Masters, *Heritage of Evidence: In the British Museum* (London: Wakeman Trust, 2004), 85–86.

[45] Wilfred G. Lambert, "A New Look at the Babylonian Background of Genesis," *JTS* 16 (1965): 296; Alan R. Millard, "A New Babylonian 'Genesis' Story," *TynBul* 18 (1967): 3–18; Alan R. Millard, "A New Babylonian 'Genesis' Story," in *"I Studied Inscriptions from before the Flood": Ancient Newr Eastern, Literary, and Linguistic Approaches to Genesis 1-11*, ed. Richard S. Hess and D. T. Tsumura (Winona Lake, Ind.: Eisenbrauns, 1994), 114–28; Kenneth A. Kitchen, *On the Reliability of the Old Testament* (Grand Rapids: Eerdmans, 2003), 591 n. 7.

[46] Gerhard F. Hasel, "The Polemic Nature of the Genesis Cosmology," *Evangelical Quarterly* 46 (1974): 81–102.

[47] Lambert, "A New Look at the Babylonian Background of Genesis," 291.

[48] David E. Graves, *Biblical Archaeology Second Edition: An Introduction with Recent Discoveries That Support the Reliability of the Bible,* 2nd ed., vol. 1 (Toronto, Ont.: Electronic Christian Media, 2018), 119–21.

clues mentioned in the biblical text.[49] This is not based on mountains of direct evidence, as it is universally agreed that archaeological evidence is meager. However, this does not mean, as the skeptics have argued, that the historical reliability of the biblical text is questionable.[50] At least eight reasons have been suggested for the lack of archaeological evidence for the patriarchs, including our limited knowledge of the period, the nature of the desert environment, their nomadic lifestyle, the large area to search, looting and looking in the wrong era.[51] However, some of the indirect evidence, supporting the veracity of the biblical accounts, is noted here.

The Ebla Tablets (*ca.* 2500–2250 BC)

In 1974–75 some 1,757 clay tablets (with some 4,875 fragments), now known as the Ebla tablets (see Fig. 24),[52] were discovered under the direction of Paolo Matthiae of the University of Rome, during the excavations of the ancient city of Tell Mardikh (Ebla, Syria). They date to between 2500 BC and the destruction of the city in *ca.* 2250 BC and contain about 3,000 documents made up from some 15,000 tablets and fragments.[53] The majority of the texts were administrative and contained 1,000 place names from the ANE,[54] and help provide the historical

24. Ebla Tablet (*ca.* 2500–*ca.* 2250 BC).
Photo courtesy of Clifford Wilson

[49] John J. Bimson, "Archaeological Data and the Dating of the Patriarchs," in *Essays on the Patriarchal Narratives*, ed. Alan R. Millard and Donald J. Wiseman (Downers Grove, Ill.: InterVarsity, 1980), 59–92; Kitchen, *Reliability of the OT*; Kenneth A. Kitchen and T. C. Mitchell, "Chronology of the Old Testament," ed. I. Howard Marshall et al., *NBD* (Downers Grove, Ill.: InterVarsity, 1996), 190; Alfred J. Hoerth and John McRay, *Bible Archaeology: An Exploration of the History and Culture of Early Civilizations* (Grand Rapids: Baker, 2006), 101; James K. Hoffmeier, ed., *The Archaeology of the Bible: Reassessing Methodologies and Assumptions* (Oxford: Lion Hudson, 2008), 68; Amihai Mazar, *Archaeology of the Land of the Bible: 10,000-586 B.C.E.*, vol. 1, The Anchor Yale Bible Reference Library (New Haven, Conn.: Yale University Press, 1992), 1:225–26.

[50] John Van Seters, *Abraham in History and Tradition* (New Haven, Conn.: Yale University Press, 1975); Thomas L. Thompson, *The Historicity of the Patriarchal Narratives: The Quest for the Historical Abraham* (Valley Forge, PA: Trinity Press International, 2002).

[51] David E. Graves, *Biblical Archaeology: An Introduction with Recent Discoveries That Support the Reliability of the Bible*, vol. 1 (Moncton, N.B.: Electronic Christian Media, 2014), 136–37.

[52] Paolo Matthiae, "Ebla Recovered," in *Ebla to Damascus: Art and Archaeology of Ancient Syria: An Exhibition from the Directorate-General of Antiquities and Museums, Syrian Arab Republic*, ed. Harvey Weiss (Washington, D.C.: Smithsonian Institution Traveling Exhibition Service, 1985), 134–39; "The Archives of the Royal Palace G of Ebla: Distribution and Arrangement of the Tablets according to the Archaeological Evidence," in *Cuneiform Archives and Libraries: Papers Read at the 30e Rencontre Assyriologique Internationale, Leiden, 4-8 1983*, ed. Klaas R. Veenhof, Nederlands Historisch-Archaeologisch Instituut Te İstanbul 57 (Leiden: Nederlands Historisch-Archaeologisch Instituut te İstanbul, 1986), 53–71; "Ebla," in *OEANE*, ed. Eric M. Meyers, vol. 2 (Oxford: Oxford University Press, 1997), 2:180–82; Giovanni Pettinato, "Gli archivi reali di Tell Mardikh-Ebla: riflessioni e prospettive," *Rivista Biblica Italiana* 25, no. 1 (1977): 225–43; *Old Canaanite Cuneiform Texts of the Third Millennium*, vol. 7, Sources and Monographs. Monographs on the Ancient Near East 1 (Malibu, Calf.: Undena, 1979); *The Archives of Ebla: An Empire Inscribed in Clay*, Translation of Ebla: Un Impero Inciso Nell'Argilla (Garden City, N.Y.: Doubleday, 1981); *Ebla, A New Look at History*, trans. C. Faith Richardson, Near Eastern Studies (Baltimore, Md.: Johns Hopkins University Press, 1991); "Ebla and the Bible," *BA* 43 (1980): 203–16.

[53] Scott G. Beld, William W. Hallo, and Piotr Michalowski, *The Tablets of Ebla: Concordance and Bibliography* (Winona Lake, Ind.: Eisenbrauns, 1984).

[54] Alfonso Archi, "The Epigraphic Evidence from Ebla and the Old Testament," *Biblica* 60, no. 4 (1979): 556–66; "The Archives of Ebla," in *Cuneiform Archives and Libraries*, ed. Klaas R. Veenhof, Papers Read at the 30e Rencontre Assyriologique Internationale, Leiden, 4-8 July 1983 (Leiden: Netherlands Institute for the Near East, 1986), 78.

context of Syria in the third millennium BC.[55] Some scholars argue that *si-da-mu*[56] and *è-ma-ra*[57] are the same cities[58] as Sodom and Gomorrah mentioned in the Bible (Gen 19), while others argue they are not.[59] It is difficult to know for sure.

Ur, Hometown of Abraham

25. The "War scene" from the Royal Standard of Ur (*ca.* 2500 BC), discovered in tomb PG 779 at Ur.

The Trustees of the British Museum (ME 121201)

According to the Bible, the city of Ur in Chaldea was the place where Terah's family, including Abraham, lived and from where they left for Haran (Gen 11:31; 15:7; Neh 9:7; Acts 7:2-4). While little more is mentioned in the Bible about this important city it is usually identified with the modern site of *Tell el-Muqayyar* (Arabic "Mount of Pitch") in Iraq. Ur was occupied from about 5000 BC (Ubeid period) to 300 BC, although burned by the Elamites in 2004 BC. Abram was born just after its destruction in about 1952 BC.[60]

Discovered in 1625 by Pietro della Valle, Tell Muqqayyar was first excavated by Sir W. K. Loftus in 1849. Sir Henry C. Rawlinson identified the tell with the city of Ur based on an inscribed brick discovered in 1855. While several archaeologists showed interest in 1918–1919 it was the famous Sir C. Leonard Woolley who directed the joint excavation between the University of Pennsylvania and the British Museum from 1922 to 1934.[61] Unfortunately no research has been completed since that time apart from a partial restoration of the ziggurat.

Several important structures were excavated including temples, a cemetery (known as the royal tombs), and two storied residential houses complete with drainage systems. The largest structure is the ziggurat at the center of the city that was dedicated to the Moon god Nanna (see Fig. 27).

The royal library, containing important tablets, was discovered revealing a commercial system based on written contracts, money, and receipts.[62] Perhaps some of the most spectacular objects came from the burial shaft of the royal tombs of Meskalamdug and the queen Puabi (2600–2500 BC). Her identity is confirmed from an inscription on a cylinder seal found close to her body. In the tomb were found royal chariots with some 80 servants who, no doubt, were executed to accompany the king and queen into the afterlife. Woolley uncovered a

[55] Alfonso Archi, "Ebla Texts," in *OEANE*, ed. Eric M. Meyers, vol. 2 (Oxford: Oxford University Press, 1997), 2:184–86.

[56] Giovanni Pettinato and A. Alberti, *Catalogo Dei Testi Cuneiformi Di Tell Mardikh-Ebla*, Materiali Epigrafici Di Ebla 1 (Naples: Istituto Universitario Orientale di Napoli, 1979), Catalog No. 6522; 76. G. 524; Catalog No. 75. G. 2377, obverse IV.8; Catalog No. 2379 reverse 1.5.

[57] Ibid., Catalog No. 1671; 75. G. 2233; Catalog No. 1008; 75. G. 1570 obverse 111.

[58] Clifford Wilson, *Ebla Tablets: Secrets of a Forgotten City: Revelations of Tell Mardikh, Third, Enlarged and Updated* (San Diego, CA: Creation-Life, 1981).

[59] Chavalas and Younger, *Mesopotamia and the Bible: Comparative Explorations*, 41.

[60] Jean-Claude Margueron, "Ur (place)," ed. David Noel Freedman et al., trans. Stephen Rosoff, *ABD* (New York, N.Y.: Doubleday, 1996), 766–67; Susan Pollock, "Ur," in *OEANE*, ed. Eric M. Meyers, vol. 5 (Oxford: Oxford Biblical Studies Online, 1997), 5:288–91.

[61] C. Leonard Woolley and Peter R. S. Moorey, *Ur "of the Chaldees,"* Revised and Updated (Ithaca, N.Y.: Cornell University Press, 1982).

[62] Olof Pedersen, *Archives and Libraries in the Ancient Near East 1500-300 B.C.* (Bethesda, Md.: CDL, 1998), 116–18, 201–4.

total of some 1,800 graves prompting him to coin the title "The Great Death Pit".[63]

Alongside the royalty in the tomb were golden weapons, helmets, daggers, swords and jewelry. Two beautiful objects that Woolley called the "Ram Caught in the Thicket", although the animal was a goat, reminded him of the Genesis account of the ram caught in the thicket (Gen 22:13; see Fig. 26). Several beautiful gold harps and eleven silver lyres decorated with mother-of-pearl, carnelian, lapis lazuli, and shells were also uncovered along with the famous "standard of Ur".[64] The standard were actually a plague with two beautiful mosaics discovered in the fourth season in tomb PG 779. One panel, called the "war scene," (see Fig. 25) depicted the earliest known representation of an army in a phalanx battle formation with war chariots (see also the Victory Stele of Eannatum or Vulture Stele).[65] The other (not shown) called the "pease scene" depicted life in peaceful times. Woolley called them a standard because they were found overhead one of the bodies in the tomb, as if they were carried overhead as a standard. However, their actual purpose is unknown.

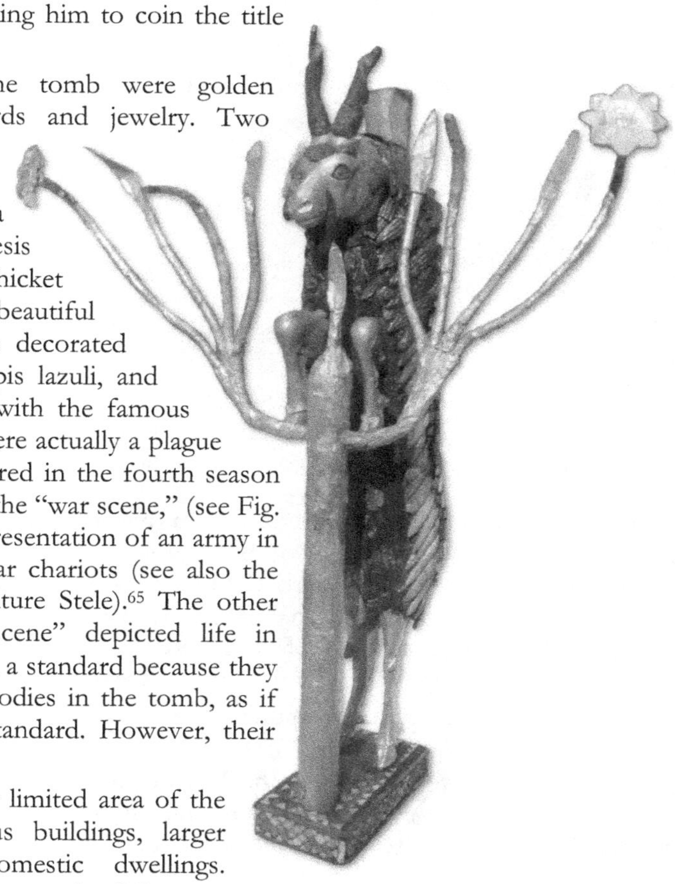

Woolley only excavated a very limited area of the site and focused on the religious buildings, larger structures and two smaller domestic dwellings. Therefore, there is some question as to the full picture of the city and the condition of life in this southern Mesopotamian city (modern Iraq).[66] However, what is not in doubt is the rich culture and well developed society which these discoveries portray. While they predate Abraham they portray the Sumerian people as cultured and operating a powerful city state before its fall.

26. One of two statues of a he-goat, often called the "Ram caught in a Thicket" (Ur, ca. 2600–2350 BC). Daniel's vision in chapter 8 represents the he-goat as "the king of Greece" (8:21).

The British Museum (ME 122200). © Jack1956 / Wikimedia Commons

Sparks points out that the details of Abraham's purchase of the cave of Machpelah for a tomb from Ephron the Hittite in Gen 23, is "strikingly similar to Neo-Babylonian dialogue contracts unearthed at Ur and Uruk, contracts that were used around 700-500 B.C. E. for

[63] C. Leonard Woolley, *Discovering the Royal Tombs at Ur: Joint Expedition of the British Museum and of the Museum of the University of Pennsylvania to Mesopotamia* (New York, N.Y.: Macmillan, 1969), 124; P. R. S. Morrey, "Where Did They Bury the Kings of the IIIrd Dynasty of Ur?," *Iraq* 46, no. 1 (1984): 1–18; Georges Roux, "The Great Enigma of the Cemetery at Ur," in *Everyday Life in Ancient Mesopotamia*, ed. Jean Bottéro, trans. Antonia Nevill (Baltimore, Md.: Johns Hopkins University Press, 2001), 24–40.

[64] Today the objects from the royal tombs are housed in the British Museum in London, the University Museum in Philadelphia, and the Iraq National Museum in Baghdad. Richard L. Zettler and Lee Horne, eds., *Treasures from the Royal Tombs of Ur* (Philadelphia, Pa.: University of Pennsylvania Museum of Archaeology and Anthropology, 1998), 43–174.

[65] Alfred J. Hoerth, *Archaeology and the Old Testament* (Grand Rapids: Baker, 1999), 46–47.

[66] Margueron, "Ur (place)," 766–67.

transferring property and other possessions."[67]

If the decline and fall of Ur came during Abraham's lifetime it may explain why Abraham's father relocated his family to Haran (Gen 11:31; 15:7; Neh 9:7; Acts 7:2–4).

27. The reconstructed facade of the Neo-Sumerian Ziggurat of Ur, near Nasiriyah, Iraq.

© Hardnfast / Wikimedia Commons

The Ziggurat of Ur (*ca.* second mill. BC)

The term "tower of Babel" does not appear in the biblical text, but the citizens of Babylon built a city with a tower, and later the text explains that "Therefore its [city] name was called Babel [that is, Babylon[68]; with a play on the Hebrew verb *bālal* meaning "to mix, confuse"], because there the LORD confused the language of all the earth. And from there the LORD dispersed them over the face of all the earth" (Gen 11:9). Most scholars suggest that the tower of Babel was a ziggurat.[69] There are some 32–34 ziggurat foundations identified in the Tigris-Euphrates basin.[70] Stephen Harris and other OT scholars argue that the ziggurat (Sumerian *u6.nir*) influenced the biblical story of the Tower of Babel during the Babylonian captivity of the Hebrews.[71] Other scholars prefer the Ezida ziggurat in Borsippa (Birs Nimrud), although this option is less likely.[72]

The earliest examples of ziggurats date to the reign of Ur-nammu (r. 2047–2030 BC) in the cities of Ur, Nippur, Eridu, and Uruk (Erech, Gen 10:10). One of the most famous ziggurats (Akk. *ziqqurratu*) dates to the Third Dynasty of Ur (*ca.* second millennium BC),[73] and was called *E-temen-an-ki* (Sumerian: "temple of the foundation of heaven and earth") and dedicated to Marduk at Esagila. This man-made brick[74] structure (62.5 m by 43 m at the base), built by Ur-Nammu, rose to three stories and was accessible by a prominent staircase (see Fig. 27). It was excavated by C. Leonard Woolley in 1924.[75] Parrot believes that this ziggurat was the Tower of Babel.[76]

It contained a temple at its top, built to house and worship the gods of heaven (Akk.

---

[67] Sparks, *Ancient Texts for the Study of the Hebrew Bible*, 44–45; Gene M. Tucker, "The Legal Background of Genesis 23," *JBL* 85, no. 1 (1966): 77–84.

[68] The ancient ruins of the city of Babylon are near Hillah, Babil Governorate, Iraq.

[69] Dale S. DeWitt, "The Historical Background of Gen 11:1–9: Babel or Ur?," *Journal of the Evangelical Theological Society* 22, no. 1 (1979): 20.

[70] Martin A. Beek and Harold Henry Rowley, *Atlas of Mesopotamia* (London: Nelson, 1962), 151; André Parrot, *Abraham and His Times* (Minneapolis: Fortress, 1968), 31.

[71] Stephen L. Harris and Robert Platzner, *The Old Testament: An Introduction to the Hebrew Bible* (New York, N.Y.: McGraw-Hill, 2002), 37.

[72] W. Allinger-Csollich, "Birs Nimrud I. Die Baukörper Der Ziqqurat von Borsippa. Ein Vorbericht," *Baghdader Mitteilungen* 22 (1991): 383–499.

[73] Andrew R. George, "The Tower of Babel: Archaeology, History and Cuneiform Texts, Review of Hansjörg Schmid, Der Tempelturm Etemenanki in Babylon 1995," *AfO* 51 (2007): 75–95.

[74] The Egyptians used bricks as early as 10,000 BC. The Early Egyptian *mastaba* (Arabic "bench") was the standard type of tomb in pre-dynastic (5500 - 3100 BC) and early dynastic (2920 - 2770 BC) Egypt for the Pharaoh. C. L. R. Williams, "A Model of the Mastaba-Tomb of Userkaf-Ankh," *The Metropolitan Museum of Art Bulletin* 8, no. 6 (1913): 125–30. The step pyramid at Saqqara, Egypt was built of brick for Pharaoh Djoser in 2630 BC.

[75] Woolley and Moorey, *Ur' of the Chaldees'*, 88–93.

[76] André Parrot, *The Tower of Babel*, trans. Edwin Hudson, Studies in Biblical Archaeology (London: SCM, 1955), 17.

Ningal, Nanna, or *Sin*).[77] No priest resided in the structure as its only purpose was for the gods.[78] It was rebuilt by Nabopolassar and Nebuchadnezzar II in the 6th cent. BC (Herodotus *Hist.* 1.181:2–5; *Jub.* 10:20–21; Josephus *Ant.* 1:115–117; *3 Bar.* 3:5–8).

Alexander the Great attempted to rebuild the decaying ruins by moving the structure brick by brick. Unfortunately he died before completing the project and all that remains today is the base.

A Sumerian tablet titled *Enmerkar and the Lord of Aratta* (2000 BC)[79] provides a compelling parallel with the Tower of Babel account in Genesis and provides the following background:

> In those days of yore, when the destinies were determined, the great princes allowed Unug Kulaba's E-ana to lift its head high. Plenty, and carp floods-(fish aplenty, barley abundance), and the rain which brings forth dappled barley were then increased in Unug Kulaba. Before the land of Dilmun yet existed, the E-ana of Unug Kulaba was well founded.[80]

E-ana (Sumerian "Temple of Ana" or "house of Ana") was a brick temple or ziggurat in Uruk. The tablet also provides an account of a time when humankind spoke one language. The Sumerian version of the *Babel of Tongues* states that during the "Golden Age" nothing threatened the people: "There was no fear, no terror. . . In those days . . . the land Martu, resting in security, the whole universe, the people in unison (?), to Enlil in one tongue. . . . Enki, the Lord of wisdom. . . . Changed the speech in their mouths, (brought?) contention into it. Into the speech of man that (until then) has been one."[81]

Although there are no other parallels with the Tower of Babel account, the confusion of language by deity is an ancient theme. In the Sumerian text, the confusion of language was the result of rivalry between the gods Enki and Enlil and had nothing to do with a tower. In Genesis 11:1–9 the issue was between God and the people over the building of a tower.[82]

28. Beni Hassan - Tomb of Khnoum-Hotep III - Representing Asiatics.

The Beni-Hasan Tomb Painting (*ca.* 1892 BC)

A mural painting (see Fig. 28) from the tomb (no. 3) of Khnum-Hotep III (governor of Antelope Province, 12th Dynasty) at the Middle Kingdom cemetery of provincial officials at Beni-Hasan, Egypt, depicts a group of "Asiatic" nomads from Canaan traveling to Egypt, and

---

[77] Margueron, "Ur (place)," 6:766.

[78] Larry L. Walker, "Babel," ed. Merrill C. Tenney and Moisés Silva, *ZPEB* (Grand Rapids: Zondervan, 1975), 1:470.

[79] Samuel Noah Kramer, "Man's Golden Age: A Sumerian Parallel to Genesis 11:1," *JAOS* 63 (1943): 191–94; "The 'Babel of Tongues': A Sumerian Version," *JAOS* 88, no. 1 (1968): 108–11; Adele Berlin, *Enmerkar and Ensuhkesdanna: A Sumerian Narrative Poem*, Occasional Publications of the Babylonian Fund 2 (Philadelphia, Pa.: University Museum, University of Pennsylvania, 1979).

[80] *COS* 1.170: 547-50; Samuel Noah Kramer, *Enmerkar and the Lord of Aratta: A Sumerian Epic Tale of Iraq and Iran* (Philadelphia, Pa.: University Museum, University of Pennsylvania, 1952), 1.

[81] Kramer, "The 'Babel of Tongues,'" 111.

[82] Jacob Klein, "The Origin and Development of Languages on Earth: The Sumerian versus the Biblical View," in *A History of Israel From the Bronze Age Through the Jewish Wars*, ed. Moshe Greenberg et al. (Winona Lake, Ind.: Eisenbrauns, 1998), 77–92; Pierre Swiggers, "Babel and the Confusion of Languages (Genesis 1:1-9)," in *Mythos im Alten Testament und seiner Umwelt: Festschrift für Hans-Peter Müller zum 65. Geburtstag*, ed. Armin Lange, Hermann Lichtenberger, and Diethard Römheld, BZAW 278 (Berlin: de Gruyter, 1999), 182–95.

dates to the 6th year of Sesostris II (*ca.* 1892 BC). It was first drawn and published in 1845 by Francois Champollion,[83] although Percy Newberry republished the mural drawings in 1893.[84]

Hoerth describes the scene on the painting best:

> Portion of the Beni Hasan tomb painting that depicts people from Palestine entering Egypt. The men are wearing kilts or long garments that cover the chest and one shoulder. Their clothes are multicolored and fringed on the bottom and they wear sandals on their feet. Each man is shown with a full head of hair, a short beard, but no mustache. The women also wear multicolored garments, but theirs are longer. Their footwear appears to be a type of slipper sock, and headbands decorate their long hair. The painting also depicts some weaponry: spear, bow and arrow, ax, and sword. Two of the men carry water skins(?) on their backs, and another plays the lyre. The donkeys transport two objects, perhaps bellows, which would mean that these people worked with metal.[85]

While the wall painting is not of biblical Joseph and his family, it does depict the world of the semi-nomadic Hebrew patriarchs from Genesis as they traveled to Egypt to sell their wares of eye makeup. The identification of the Asiatics is confirmed by the dress and hieroglyphic inscription identifying the people from this region as "Asiatic" traders.[86]

29. Execration texts written in Hieratic on potsherds (ostraca).
Berlin, SMB-PK, Egyptian Museum Inv. no. P. 14.517. © Naunakhte / Wikimedia Commons

The Egyptian Execration Texts (1878–1630 BC)

The Egyptian *Execration Texts* (also known as *Proscription Lists*)[87] are two groups of about 1,000 Egyptian Hieratic clay bowels and figurines (see Fig. 29) that list curses on the enemies of the Egyptian pharaohs, with these enemies often being the foreign rulers and groups living in Egypt's neighbouring regions. They date from the reign of Sesostris III (1878–1842 BC) to the MB2 (1800–1630 BC), the time of the patriarchs.[88] The curses were commonly written on potsherds and then broken to sever the power of their foreign neighbors. The broken texts were then typically buried near tombs and ritual sites.[89] This was a common practice during the period of conflict with Egypt's Asiatic neighbors during the time of the Patriarchs.[90]

---

[83] William H. Shea, "Artistic Balance Among the Beni Hasan Asiatics," *BA* 44 (1981): 219.

[84] Percy Edward Newberry, "Beni Hasan Part I," in *Archaeological Survey of Egypt*, ed. Fl Griffith (London: Egypt Exploration Fund, 1893), 41–79.

[85] Hoerth, *Archaeology and the Old Testament*, 94.

[86] Shea, "Artistic Balance Among the Beni Hasan Asiatics," 219–28; Kenneth A. Kitchen, "The Joseph Narrative (Genesis 37, 39–50)," *BS* 15, no. 3 (2003): 4–10.

[87] *ANET* 328-29; *COS* 1.32: 50-52; I. E. S. Edwards, C. J. Gadd, and N. G. L. Hammond, *The Cambridge Ancient History: Early History of the Middle East* (Cambridge, U.K.: Cambridge University Press, 1970), 494.

[88] P. Kyle McCarter, *Ancient Inscriptions: Voices from the Biblical World* (Washington, D.C.: Biblical Archaeology Society, 1996), 43.

[89] Geraldine Pinch, *Magic in Ancient Egypt* (Austin, Tex.: University of Texas Press, 1995), 92ff.

[90] Edwards, Gadd, and Hammond, *Cambridge Ancient History: Early History*, 508.

They also mention some of the earliest references to biblical people like Job,[91] Zebulon (*Zabulanu*),[92] Joseph (*Iysipi*) and Jacob[93] along with biblical cities such as Jerusalem (*Rushalimum*), Dan, Ashkelon, Shechem, Hazor, Rehob, Byblos, and others.[94]

Some scholars have suggested that the Egyptian execration texts have inspired the biblical prophets to place curses on their enemies,[95] but as Sparks argues: "the primary problem with this suggestion is that the biblical books contain prophecies against foreign nations rather than simple lists, and there is no evidence that these prophecies were ever attached to ritual ceremonies."[96]

The Mari Tablets (*ca.* 1800–1750 BC)

During the French excavation in 1933 at Mari (Tell Hariri, Syria),[97] led by André Parrot for the Louvre Museum,[98] a palace, ziggurat and royal archive of 23,000 cuneiform tablets was uncovered (see Fig. 30).[99]

30. Tablet of Zimri-Lim, king of Mari, concerning the foundation of an ice-house in Terqa. Baked clay, *ca.* 1780 BC.

Louvre, Department of Oriental Antiquities, Richelieu, ground floor, room 3 (AO 2016). © Jastrow/Wikimedia Commons

The tablets were written primarily in the Akkadian language (Semitic dialect), although a few were bilingual, also written in Hurrian and Sumerian. The tablets were primarily from the second millennium (*ca.* 1800–1750 BC) and contained treaty documents between Iasmah-Adad and Zimri-Lim, as well as between Zimri-Lim and Hammurabi.[100] While the texts deal largely with financial, administrative and business transactions, they mention personal and place names with striking parallels to the patriarchal records in Genesis.

Although LeMaire cautions that: "the biblical texts and the Mari corpus appear, from the first, to be considerably distant from each other geographically and chronologically,"[101] he does go on to highlight the importance of the Mari tablets for our understanding of the linguistic, ethnosociological, and historical parallels with biblical history and customs. The customs,

---

[91] John E. Hartley, *The Book of Job*, NICOT (Grand Rapids: Eerdmans, 1988), 66; Francis I. Andersen, *Job*, TOTC (Downers Grove, Ill.: IVP Academic, 2008), 78.

[92] Pritchard, *ANET OT*, 329 n.6. Zebulon here is probably not the son of Jacob, but a popular name during this period.

[93] The identification of Jacob and Joseph are questioned by Rohl. David M. Rohl, *Pharaohs and Kings: A Biblical Quest* (New York, N.Y.: Three Rivers, 1997), 352.

[94] Yohanan Aharoni, *The Land of the Bible: A Historical Geography*, trans. Anson F. Rainey, 2nd ed. (Louisville, Ky.: Westminster/Knox, 1981), 144–47.

[95] Aage Bentzen, "The Ritual Background of Amos 1.2-2.16," *OtSt* 8 (1950): 85–99.

[96] Sparks, *Ancient Texts for the Study of the Hebrew Bible*, 185; Meir Weiss, "The Pattern of the 'Execration Texts' in the Prophetic Literature," *IEJ* 19, no. 3 (1969): 150–7.

[97] Jean-Claude Margueron, "Mari," in *OEANE*, ed. Eric M. Meyers, vol. 3 (Oxford: Oxford University Press, 1997), 3:413–16.

[98] Edwin M. Yamauchi, "Archaeology of Palestine and Syria," ed. Geoffrey W. Bromiley, *ISBE2* (Grand Rapids: Eerdmans, 1995), 1:272.

[99] Wolfgang Heimpel, *Letters to the King of Mari: A New Translation, With Historical Introduction, Notes, and Commentary*, Mesopotamian Civilizations 12 (Ann Arbor, Mich.: American Oriental Society, 2003); Dennis Pardee and J. T. Glass, "The Mari Archives," *BA* 47 (1984): 88–100; Michaël Guichard, "Mari Texts," in *OEANE*, ed. Eric M. Meyers, vol. 3 (Oxford: Oxford University Press, 1997), 3:419–21.

[100] Abraham M. Malamat, "The Ban in Mari and in the Bible," in *Biblical Essays*, Proceedings of the Ninth Meeting of Die Ou-Testamentiese Werkgemeenskap in Suid-Afrika 1966 (Potchefstroom, South Africa: Society for the Study of the Old Testament, 1967), 40–49.

[101] André LeMaire, "Mari, the Bible, and the Northwest Semitic World," *BA* 47, no. 2 (1984): 104.

practices and names reflected in the Mari texts also illustrate practices during patriarchal times that are similar to those mentioned by Abraham, Isaac, and Jacob.[102]

For example, treaties and covenants were ratified by the killing of an ass, as described in the pact between the Shechemites and Jacob (Gen 33:19; 34:1–3). The name Yahweh appears in the tables, and while it is not likely that Yahweh was worshipped at Mari, it does appear that the name was known among other Yawi names, like the OT name Yawi-El (Joel). The practice of dedication to destruction or the ban (Heb. *ḥêrem*) that was placed on life and property of conquests, proclaimed at Jericho (Josh 6), is also described in the Mari tablets as the *asakkum*. Among the similarities both accounts describe severe penalties for violating the ban.[103]

The discovery of these tablets also greatly increased our understanding of many Biblical words. For example, the Hebrew word *'ed* in Gen 2:6 is translated by the KJV as "mist." From the context within Sumerian and Akkadian languages, the same word is translated as "river" or "river god." The word "river" fits the context of Genesis 2:6.

Again in Proverbs 26:23 the KJV translates the Hebrew word *sîg* "like a potsherd covered with *silver dross*." From Ugaritic the word *spsg* means "glaze." Thus, the ESV translates Proverbs 26:23 "like the *glaze* covering an earthen vessel."[104] While the theological reliability of the text is unaffected, the meaning is clearer.

31. The Famine Stele on Sehel Island, Egypt as found by William M. Flinders Petrie. Some carved sections are missing.

© Morburre/Wikimedia Commons

The Nuzi Tablets (*ca.* 1500–1350 BC)

On the importance of the Nuzi Tablets see Graves, *Biblical Archaeology* vol. 1.[105]

Sodom and Gomorrah

For the most up-to-date research on the locations of Sodom and Gomorrah see Graves, *Biblical Archaoelogy* Vol. 1.[106]

The Famine Stele (332–331 BC)

The *Famine Stele* (see Fig. 31)[107] is an Egyptian hieroglyphic inscription that was excavated by Paul Barguet in 1953[108] and describes a seven-year drought and famine that took place

---

[102] Abraham M. Malamat, *Mari and the Early Israelite Experience* (Oxford: Oxford University Press, 1989); *Mari and the Bible: A Collection of Studies* (Jerusalem: Hebrew University Press, 1977); Daniel E. Fleming, "Mari and the Possibilities of Biblical Memory," *RA* 92, no. 1 (January 1, 1998): 41–78.

[103] Jean-Marie Durand, "Mari (Texts)," ed. David Noel Freedman et al., trans. Jennifer L. Davis, *ABD* (New York, N.Y.: Doubleday, 1996), 4:533.

[104] Charles F. Pfeiffer, ed., *Wycliffe Dictionary of Biblical Archaeology* (Peabody, Mass.: Hendrickson, 2000), 65.

[105] Graves, *Biblical Archaeology Vol 1: An Introduction* 2nd ed 1:130–31.

[106] David E. Graves, *Key Facts for the Location of Sodom Student Edition: Navigating the Maze of Arguments* (Moncton, N.B.: Electronic Christian Media, 2014); *Biblical Archaeology Vol 1: An Introduction*, 2nd ed. 1:121–33.

[107] *ANET* 31-32; *COS* 1.53: 130-34; William Kelly Simpson, ed., *The Literature of Ancient Egypt: An Anthology of Stories, Instructions, Stelae, Autobiographies, and Poetry*, trans. Robert K. Ritner, Vincent A. Tobin, and Edward F. Wente, Jr. (New Haven, Conn.: Yale University Press, 2003), 386–92; Miriam Lichtheim, *Ancient Egyptian Literature: Late Period*, 2nd ed., vol. 3 (Berkeley, Calf.: University of California Press, 2006), 3:94–103.

[108] Paul Barguet, *La stèle de la famine à Séhel* (Cairo: l'institut français d'archéologie orientale, 1953).

during the reign of Pharaoh Djoser (third Dynasty *ca.* 2650–2575 BC). Although dating to well beyond the Genesis account of the seven year famine in Genesis 41, it indicates that seven-year famines were known in Egypt in ancient times. There are also similar motifs to the account of taxation[109] (Gen 41:33–49; 47:13–26), dream omens (41:1–32); and preservation of the priest's land (47:22). A seven-year famine is also mentioned in the *Epic of Gilgamesh* (see Fig. 19) and the "Book of the Temple" under the rule of king Neferkasokar (late second Dynasty).[110]

BIBLICAL COVENANT AND LAW

The term *covenant* is usually the translation given to the Hebrew term *b^erit* [111] however, given the multiple uses of *b^erit*,[112] there is no scholarly consensus regarding its root meaning.[113] While Mendenhall acknowledges that "the etymology of the term is uncertain," he does admit that most embrace the "derivation from Akkadian *birîtu*, 'fetter,' or a cognate root."[114] Thus, in the OT *b^erit* means to fetter, bondage, binding, an intensified oath, where the oath is part of the covenant or contract. In the OT prophets the term covenant is used 32 times (ESV 68 times, NIV 69 times and KJV 75 times). The covenant formula "I will be your God, and you shall be my people" is used in place of the term covenant throughout the OT (Lev 26:12; Jer 7:23; 11:4; 24:7; 30:22; 31:1; 33; 32:28; Eze 11:20; 14:11; 36:28; 37:23, 27; Hos 1:10; Joel 2:27; Zec 2:11; 8:8). In the NT the theological equivalent of the term in Greek is *diatheke* and signifies an agreement, testament, or will.

Despite the uncertainty over the etymology of the term, most scholars agree that *b^erit* "came to signify a binding agreement between two parties."[115] Gräbe defines *b^erit* "as a general comprehensive term for a fellowship enabling relationship. This relationship does not exclude differentiations appropriate to different contexts,"[116] such as contract, agreement, promise and mutual understanding. Wenham points out that "in a secular context *b^erit* is often translated

[109] Miriam Lichtheim, "The Naucratis Stela Once Again," in *Studies in Honor of George R. Hughes*, ed. Janet H. Johnson, Studies in Ancient Oriental Civilizations 39 (Chicago, Ill.: Oriental Institute of the University of Chicago, 1977), 142–44.

[110] Shaul Bar, *A Letter That Has Not Been Read: Dreams in the Hebrew Bible* (Jerusalem, Israel: Hebrew Union College Press, 2001).

[111] Kutsch argues that *berit* does not mean covenant (bund) but rather *Verpflichtung* (obligation). Ernst Kutsch, *Verheißung und Gesetz: Untersuchungen zum sogenannten Bund im Alten Testament* (Beihefte zur Zeitschrift für die alttestamentliche Wissenschaft 13 (Berlin: de Gruyter, 1973), 1; Murray Newman, "Review of Meredith G. Kline, The Structure of Biblical Authority and Ernst Kutsch, Verheißung und Gesetz: Untersuchungen zum sogenannten Bund im Alten Testament," *JBL* 94, no. 1 (1975): 120. Newman challenges Kutsch stating that "although obligation is invariably one element in the meaning of berît, it does not exhaust that meaning. Relationship is also an essential feature." Kutsch argues that *berit* does not mean covenant (bund) but rather *Verpflichtung* (obligation). Ernst Kutsch, *Verheißung und Gesetz: Untersuchungen zum sogenannten Bund im Alten Testament* (Beihefte zur Zeitschrift für die alttestamentliche Wissenschaft 13 (Berlin: de Gruyter, 1973), 1.

[112] Klaus Baltzer, *The Covenant Formulary in Old Testament, Jewish, and Early Christian Writings*, trans. David E. Green (Oxford: Basil Blackwell, 1971), 1-8. For the translation of *berit* in the Septuagint, Vulgate and NT see Petrus J Gräbe, *New Covenant, New Community the Significance of Biblical and Patristic Covenant Theology for Contemporary Understanding* (Milton Keynes: Paternoster, 2006), 12-14.

[113] Cleon L. Rogers, Jr., "The Covenant with Abraham and Its Historical Setting," *BSac* 127 (1970): 242–49; George E. Mendenhall, "Covenant," ed. G. A. Buttrick and Keith R. Crim, *IDB* (Nashville, Tenn.: Abingdon, 1962), 1:714–16; Walther Eichrodt, *Theology of the Old Testament*, Old Testament Library (Louisville, Ky.: Westminster/Knox, 1967), 1:26–45; René A. López, "Israelite Covenants in the Light of Ancient Near Eastern Covenants," *Chafer Theological Seminary Journal* 10 (2004): 95; Dennis J McCarthy, *Treaty and Covenant: A Study in the Ancient Oriental Documents and in the Old Testament*, Analecta Biblica 21 (Rome: Biblical Institute, 1981), 17–24.

[114] Mendenhall, "Covenant," 1:715.

[115] Rogers, Jr., "Covenant with Abraham," 243; McCarthy, *Treaty and Covenant*, 20; Eichrodt, *Theology of the Old Testament*, 1:37.

[116] Gräbe, *New Covenant*, 11–12; Alister I. Wilson and Jamie A. Grant, "Introduction," in *The God of Covenant: Biblical, Theological and Contemporary Perspectives*, ed. Alister I. Wilson and Jamie A. Grant (Leicester, U.K.: Apollos, 2005), 12.

'treaty', . . . but when it refers to God's treaty with Israel it is translated 'covenant'."[117] A covenant then is an agreement between two parties who enter into a working relationship. McCarthy defines a covenant as "a bond established by an oath."[118] Sparks defines covenants and treaties "as agreements enacted between two parties in which one or both make promises under oath to perform certain actions while avoiding others."[119] The covenant is the ground for the relationship between God and man, the context for our response, and the standard by which humanity is judged.

Ancient Near Eastern treaties or covenants can be traced back to the third millennium BC, as well as the second millennium BC from the Old Babylonian period in the Mari tablets, as well as ancient Egyptian, Hittite, and Assyrian treaties (see Fig. 32). Smaller nations depended on these international treaties for protection, rather than suffer the consequences of invasion.[120]

32. Hittite suzerain-vassal treaty on bronze tablet (1235 BC) between Tudhaliya IV (Egyptian) and Kurunta of Tarhuntasa (Hittite). This cuneiform document excavated at Ḫattuša (Boğazköy) in 1986 is the only bronze tablet found in Anatolia. With this treaty Tudhaliya promises the sovereignty of Tarhuntassa and another territory to Kurunta and his sons for the future, although Kurunta is advised to not want to imitate Tudhaliya's "Great Kingdom". "Thousands of Gods" are listed as divine witnesses for the validity of this treaty.

Museum of Anatolian Civilisations, Ankara, Turkey. © Bjørn Christian Tørrissen/Wikimedia Commons

There are basically two types of covenant:

A. *Parity treaties or covenants*: These agreements are made between equals as in two kings or neighbours of equal status.

B. *Suzerainty treaties or covenants:* These agreements are formed by the greater suzerain with a lesser person (vassal) of unequal status and based on certain terms and conditions. The treaties demonstrate five clearly identified elements that form a structure. In fact, Rogers notes that both Balzer and McCarthy believe that one can "rightly speak of a set 'form' which was used in the ancient world."[121] The covenant of God with us is always this second type, the Suzerainty treaty covenant.

Following the exodus from Egypt, the Israelites met at Mount Sinai, where they entered into a covenant with Yahweh and God spoke directly to Moses on the mountain and communicated his law. When the law of God is mentioned, one's mind normally gravitates to the Ten Commandments (Exod 20; Deut 5). While it is appropriate to classify them as *law,* there is much more to law than just the commandments. Law in Israel existed long before the Ten Commandments were given, even though there is no formal account of their occurrence

[117] Gordon J. Wenham, "Grace and Law in the Old Testament," in *Law, Morality and the Bible*, ed. Bruce Kaye and Gordon J. Wenham (Downers Grove, Ill.: InterVarsity, 1978), 5.

[118] McCarthy, *Treaty and Covenant*, 77.

[119] Sparks, *Ancient Texts for the Study of the Hebrew Bible*, 435.

[120] Ibid., 435–36.

[121] Rogers, Jr., "Covenant with Abraham," 246; McCarthy, *Treaty and Covenant*, 7.

in Scripture. However it is clear from the early chapters of Genesis that there were laws and regulations which were binding on God's people. Examples of practices in Genesis which might be considered laws include the practice of offering sacrifices on altars (Gen 35:2), Abraham offering tithes to Melchizedek (Gen 14:20), the practice of circumcision (Gen 17:10), and marriage customs (Gen 25:6). Later Moses writes these laws down for future generations (Exod 20–23; cf. John 1:17).

The Boghaz-Köy Tablets (*ca.* 1570–1200 BC)

When archaeologists found no trace of the Hittite civilization, biblical critics claimed that the Hittite people were imaginary.[122] In 1876 Sayce delivered a lecture to the Society of Biblical Archaeology in London making a startling claim that the Hittites were a vast empire,[123] but the capital was yet to be discovered.[124] In 1906 when the Hittite civilization was discovered in Northeastern Turkey by Hugo Winckler, along with the royal archive library of more than thirty thousand clay tablets (see Fig. 33)[125] during his excavations at Boğazköy (*Ḫattuša*, this established the Hittite empire as an historical reality, just as recorded in the Bible.[126]

33. Fragment of Hittite cuneiform tablet.
Boğazköy Museum, Turkey

The majority of the tablets are written in Hittite and represent most of the ANE gene of literature.[127] Three thousand more unpublished texts have been unearthed at another Hittite sites nearby (Šapinuwa [Ortaköy]).[128] Also, several hundered tablets have been recovered from Tapigga (Masat Höyük), to the east of Ḫattuša.

This new corpus of literature adds to the cultural setting of the Hittites and their interactions with other Mesopotamian neighbours.[129]

---

[122] Francis William Newman, *A History of the Hebrew Monarchy: From the Administration of Samuel to the Babylonish Captivity* (London: Chapman, 1853), 179 n.2. Charles Texier, a French archaeologist, had identified large stone structures as early as 1834 near Bogazkale but they remained unidentified until Sayce.

[123] Trevor Bryce, *The Kingdom of the Hittites* (Oxford: Oxford University Press, 1999).

[124] Trevor Bryce, *Life and Society in the Hittite World* (Oxford: Oxford University Press, 2004), 2; A. H. Sayce, *The Hittites the Story of a Forgotten Empire*, Classic Reprint (Charleston, SC: Forgotten Books, 2012).

[125] Trevor Bryce, *The Major Historical Texts of Early Hittite History* (Sydney, Australia: University of Queensland, 1982).

[126] Bryce, *Life and Society in the Hittite World*, 2; Hans Gustav Güterbock, "Boğazköy," in *OEANE*, ed. Eric M. Meyers, vol. 1 (Oxford: Oxford University Press, 1997), 333–35.

[127] *COS* 3.13-40: 43-72; Pedersen, *Archives and Libraries in the Ancient Near East 1500-300 B.C.*, 44–57. See also the Catalogue of Hittite Texts (CHT) at http://etana.org/node/1546.

[128] Aygül Süel, "Ortaköy: Eine hethitische Stadt mit hethitischen und hurritischen Tontafelentdeckungen," in *Hittite and Other Anatolian and Near Eastern Studies in Honour of Sedat Alp: Sedat Alp'a Armağan*, ed. Heinrich Otten and Sedat Alp (Ankara: Türk Tarih Kurumu Basımevi, 1992), 487–92.

[129] Gary M. Beckman, "Mesopotamians and Mesopotamian Learning at Ḫattuša," *JCS* 35, no. 1/2 (1983): 97–114; *Hittite Diplomatic Texts*, ed. Harry A Hoffner, 2nd ed., Society of Biblical Literature Writings from the Ancient World 7 (Atlanta, Ga.: Scholars Press, 1999); "Hittite Treaties and the Development of Cuneiform Treaty Tradition," in *Die Deuteronomistischen Geschichtswerke: Redaktions– Und Religionsgeschichtliche Perspektiven Zur "Deuteronomismus"–Diskussion in Tora Und Vorderen Propheten*, ed. Marku Witte et al., Beihefte Zur Zeitschrift Für Die Alttestamentliche Wissenschaft 365 (Berlin: de Gruyter, 2006), 279–301.

The Code of Hammurabi (*ca.* 1789–1725 BC)

The Code of Hammurabi is one of the oldest and largest law codes discovered to date and one of the most famous ANE law codes located outside of the Bible.[130] They also resemble other law codes found in the ANE (i.e., Code of Ur-Nammu, king of Ur [*ca.* 2050 BC], the Codex of Lipit-Ishtar of Isin [*ca.* 1870 BC], along with later Hittite, and Assyrian laws).[131] The precise number of laws are not known as there are gaps in the text, but number over three hundred.

Originally the laws were published in public on large stelae, the most famous copy of which is preserved in the Stele of Hammurabi (*ca.* 1789–1725 BC). The stone (diorite) column (2.25 metres by 7.4 ft. high) resembles a black index finger and is inscribed in the Akkadian language (see Fig. 34). The top of the stele has an engraved picture of Shamash (Akk. *Šamaš*), the sun-god of justice, seated on a throne handing a scepter and ring to Hammurabi on a firey mountain like Moses (Exod 19:18; see Fig. 35). This symbolizes the divine origin of the great law code which king Hammurabi received and reinforces the motivation for keeping these laws.[132]

The stele was plundered in 1160 BC by the Elamite king Shutruk-Nahhunte following his conquest of Babylon, and it was taken away to the Elamite capital of Susa (modern Khūzestān, Iran) where it lay until it was discovered in 1901 AD by Egyptologist Gustave Jéquier, a member of an expedition headed by Jacques de Morgan and V. Scheil. Today it is on display in the Louvre Museum (Sb 8).

The code of Hammurabi was a complex, well developed code of law for the period in which it was used. It is phrased in a typical casuistic (Lat. *casus*, meaning "case") style, where each separate law states a hypothetical case followed by the appropriate penalty. This is contrasted with the Mosaic laws, which are not only casuistic (Lev 21:2–22:19), but also formulated as

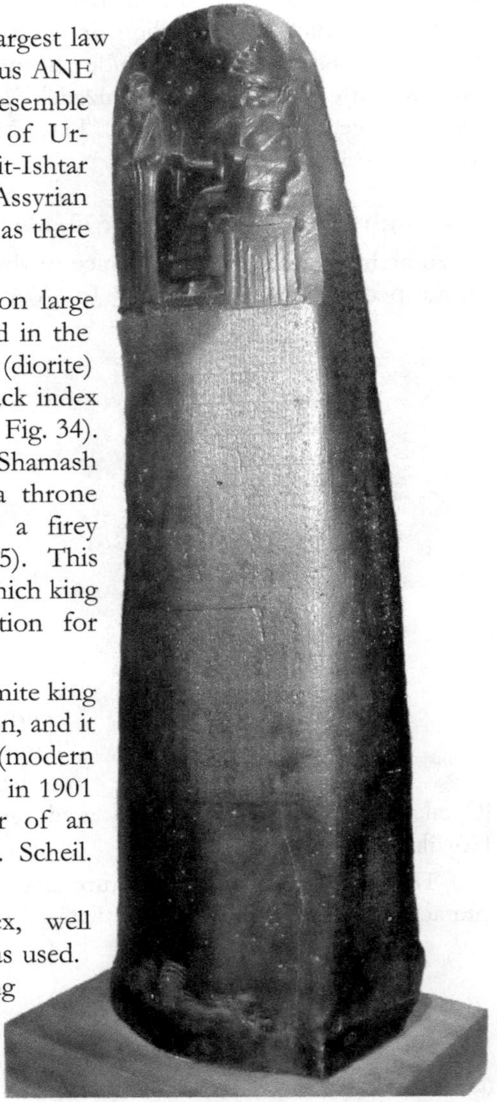

34. Plaster reproduction of the Law Code of Hammurabi showing King Hammurabi before Shamash the sun god. This copy is in the Oriental Institute Museum of the University of Chicago.

Used with permission of Oriental Institute Museum, Chicago. Original on display in the Louvre, Paris (Sb 8)

[130] Hammurabi, *The Oldest Code of Laws in the World: The Code of Laws Promulgated by Hammurabi, King of Babylon, BC 2285-2242*, trans. Claude Hermann Walter Johns (Union, NJ: Lawbook Exchange, 2000); M. E. J. Richardson, *Hammurabi's Laws: Text, Translation and Glossary* (Edinburgh, U.K.: T&T Clark, 2005); Robert Francis Harper, *The Code of Hammurabi* (Union, NJ: Lawbook Exchange, 2010); Leonard W. King, *The Code of Hammurabi* (Calgary, Alberta: Theophania, 2012).

[131] *ANET* 163-80; *COS* 2.131: 335-53; Martha T. Roth, *Law Collections from Mesopotamia and Asia Minor*, 2nd ed. (Atlanta, Ga.: Society of Biblical Literature, 1997), 71–142; G. R. Driver and John C. Miles, eds., *The Babylonian Laws*, 2 vols., Ancient Texts and Translations (Eugene, Oreg.: Wipf & Stock, 2007).

[132] Sparks, *Ancient Texts for the Study of the Hebrew Bible*, 422.

commands (Exod 20).[133]

Similarities between the code of Hammurabi and the Hebrew law code include the principle of *lex talionis* (Exod 21:22–25; Lev 20:10; 24:19–21; Deut 19:16–21; 22:22). The Code of Hammurabi states: "If a man put out the eye of another man, his eye shall be put out" (Hammurabi's code §129). Rather than encouraging revenge, this law safeguarded excessive inequity by maintaining that the punishment must meet the crime. An arm or leg could not be excised for the loss of an eye. Also, the death penalty was prescribed on those who have committed adultery (Hammurabi's code §129; Lev 20:10; Deut 22:22) or in the case of causing death (Hammurabi's code §230).

35. Detail of the top of the stela inscribed with Hammurabi's code, showing the king before the god Shamash; bas-relief from Susa, 18th century BC.

Used with permission of Oriental Institute Museum, Chicago. Original on display in the Louvre, Paris (Sb 8)

Although many people attempt to magnify the similarities between the two codes, the distinctive differences are striking. For example, the biblical law favoured the needs and rights of the poor and underprivileged, while the ANE law favoured the rich. The Code of the Hammurabi observes the class distinctions in the outworking of its law with a lower view of human life, making no distinction between deed and intent, while the Mosaic Law does not.[134]

Also, Hammurabi lived three centuries earlier than Moses, in a different religious background and code of ethics. The mosaic laws were characterized by a distinctly monotheistic (one god) religion which consequently placed a higher value on ethical and moral conduct. For example, the Ten Commandments were basically spiritual in nature and considered universally binding regardless of one's station in life.

There have been four main theories which attempt to harmonize the similarities between the two law codes:

The first, known as the theory of dependence, sets forth the hypothesis that the Hebrew laws were dependent on the Hammurabi code for their content.[135] However, the differences and not the similarities argue against this idea. For example, with regards to justice for the outcast and downtrodden, the Hebrew law is significantly different.

The second is called the theory of intermediate transmission and asserts that the Canaanite culture influenced the Hebrew people at the time of their invasion and their

[133] Chilperic Edwards, *The Hammurabi Code and the Sinaitic Legislation* (London; New York: Watts, 1904); Hans Jochen Boecker, *Law and the Administration of Justice in the Old Testament and Ancient East*, trans. J. Moiser (Minneapolis: Augsburg, 1980), 67–133; W. W. Davies, *Codes of Hammurabi and Moses* (Whitefish, Mont.: Kessinger, 2003); David P. Wright, "The Laws of Hammurabi as a Source for the Covenant Collection," *Maarav* 20 (2003): 11–88.

[134] Donald J. Wiseman, "Hammurabi," ed. Merrill C. Tenney and Moises Silva, *ZPEB* (Grand Rapids: Zondervan, September 19, 2009), 30–32.

[135] Charles Wesley Gethman, *The Code of Hammurabi and the Book of the Covenant* (Evanston, Ill.: Northwestern University, 1911), 5.

settlement in Canaan, and continued to influence them until the two became closely associated.[136]

The third has been called the theory of cognateness, and purports that both codes have been influenced by a common Semitic background during the era of Abraham and Hammurabi.

The final theory is called the theory of independence, and sees the two legal systems as having a common Semitic heritage but not consciously borrowing from one another. This view stresses that the similarities are due to their geographic proximity. Barton, a former professor of Semitic languages at the University of Pennsylvania and proponent of this view, stated: "A comparison of the Code of Hammurabi as a whole with the Pentateuchal laws as a whole, while it reveals certain similarities, convinces the student that the laws of the Old Testament are in no essential way dependent upon the Babylonian laws."[137]

While the Hebrew law code was not based on the code of Hammurabi, the Hebrew legal system was not given in a vacuum. It is clearly evident that Abraham had contact with the law codes in Ur and that the people of Israel had intimate contact with the Canaanites. God's revelation was given in time and space, not removed from the understanding of the Hebrew people. But the Bible clearly declares Israel's laws to be unique and based on a special covenant relationship with God. Morally and ethically the Mosaic Law was superior to the Code of Hammurabi.[138]

The code of Hammurabi is significant in that it is the most comprehensive and well-preserved law code of ancient history apart from the biblical law. The similarities between the Code of Hammurabi and the Israelite legal code attest to the antiquity of biblical law and the pervasive nature of law in the ANE. It also indicates that the writing of the Mosaic laws in a legible script at an early date is not unreasonable and corresponds harmoniously with ancient practices.

The code of Hammurabi provides an historical picture of the society and the civilization of the ANE. It points out the humanitarian structure of ancient society, placing a strong emphasis on family and morals. It was not the barbaric uncivilized culture that we so often think of when discussing ancient people. Rather we have a sophisticated structure of well-ordered law which encompasses all of society.

---

[136] David P. Wright, *Inventing God's Law: How the Covenant Code of the Bible Used and Revised the Laws of Hammurabi* (Oxford: Oxford University Press, 2013), 95–96.

[137] George Aaron Barton, *Archaeology and the Bible*, 7th ed. (Philadelphia, Pa.: American Sunday School Union, 1937), 406.

[138] J. I. Packer, Merrill C. Tenney, and William White, eds., *Illustrated Manners and Customs of the Bible* (Nashville, Tenn.: Nelson, 1997), 379.

The Exodus and Conquest

36. Jordan Valley seen from the Jordanian side. Tall el-Hammam (Abel-shittim) is visible in the center, where Israel camped before entering the promised land.

The archaeological evidence for Israel's 400–430 year stay in Egypt (Exod 12:40–41; Gal 3:15, 17; Acts 13:16–21) and the Exodus is universally acknowledged to be lacking. As a result of the meager archaeological evidence, skeptics have challenged the historical reliability of the biblical narratives. Based on this argument from silence,[1] John Van Seters and Thomas Thompson go as far as to consider the biblical accounts as legends and myths.[2] Hoffmeier observed the impact of the minimalist attack, pointing out that: "once on the slippery slope of historical minimalism, these biblical scholars moved from Genesis to Exodus and marched on Joshua and Judges, and soon even the courts of David and Solomon were under siege."[3]

While there are numerous reasons for the lack of evidence for the Exodus and Conquest,[4] there is sufficient evidence from ancient sources for their historicity.

CANAAN

The Tell el-Amarna Tablets

Tell el-Amarna, the capital of Egypt's controversial Pharaoh Amenhotep IV (Akhenaten), is situated 190 miles south of Cairo along the banks of the Nile.[5] While the present ruins are unimpressive, the primary significance of the site revolves around 382 Akkadian/Canaanite cuneiform clay tablets[6] (fourteenth cent. BC) discovered in 1887 by a bedouin woman (see Fig. 37). The tablets were from the royal Egyptian archives written by Yapahu, the ruler of Gezer, Palestine, to Pharaohs Amenophis III (r. 1391–1353) and his son Akhenaten (r. 1353–1335) in Egypt, to address among other things the problem caused by *'Apiru* (written *habiru* in non-Amarna letters).[7] The term is used over 250 times in the ANE texts.[8] The *'Apiru* were considered disgruntled mercenaries and disturbers of the peace who were traveling throughout the region attacking the established cities.[9]

---

[1] On the Fallacy of Negative Proof, see Graves, *Biblical Archaeology Vol 1: An Introduction* 2nd ed 1:73–74.

[2] Van Seters, *Abraham in History and Tradition*; Thompson, *Historicity of the Patriarchal Narratives.*

[3] James K. Hoffmeier, "The Evangelical Contribution to Understanding the (Early) History of Ancient Israel in Recent Scholarship," *Bulletin for Biblical Research* 7 (1997): 78.

[4] Graves, *Biblical Archaeology Vol 1: An Introduction* 2nd ed 1:148–49.

[5] Nadav Na'aman, "Amarna Letters," ed. David Noel Freedman et al., *ABD* (New York, N.Y.: Doubleday, 1996), 1:174–81.

[6] Tablets are displayed in the Louvre Museum, Paris; Ashmolean Museum, Oxford; British Museum, London and the Egyptian Museum, Cairo. *ANET* 483-90; *COS* 3.92: 237-42; E. A. Wallis Budge and Carl Bezold, *The Tell El-Amarna Tablets in the British Museum with Autotype Facsimiles* (London: British Museum Press, 1892); Jörgen A. Knudtzon, *Die El-Amarna-Tafeln, mit Einleitung und Erläuterungen*, 2 vols. (Leipzig: Hinrichs, 1915); Cyrus H. Gordon, "The New Amarna Tablets," *Orientalia* 16 (1947): 1–21; James Bennett Pritchard, ed., *The Ancient Near East, Volume 1: An Anthology of Texts and Pictures* (Princeton, NJ: Princeton University Press, 1973), 262–77; Anson F. Rainey, *El Amarna Tablets 359-379: Supplement to J. A.. Knudtzon, Die El-Amarna-Tafeln*, Alter Orient Und Altes. Testament 8 (Kevelaer, Germany: Butzon & Bercker, 1978); Shlomo Izreʿel, *The Amarna Scholarly Tablets*, Cuneiform Monographs 9 (Leiden: Brill, 1997).

[7] William L. Moran, *The Amarna Letters* (Baltimore, Md.: Johns Hopkins University Press, 2000).

[8] Niels Peter Lemche, "Habiru/Hapiru," ed. David Noel Freedman et al., *ABD* (New York, N.Y.: Doubleday, 1996), 3:7.

[9] Edward F. Campbell, "The Amarna Letters and the Amarna Period," *BA* 23 (1960): 2–22; Na'aman, "Amarna Letters," 1:174–81; Nadav Na'aman, "Habiru and Hebrews: The Transfer of a Social Term to the Literary Sphere," *JNES* 45 (1986): 271–

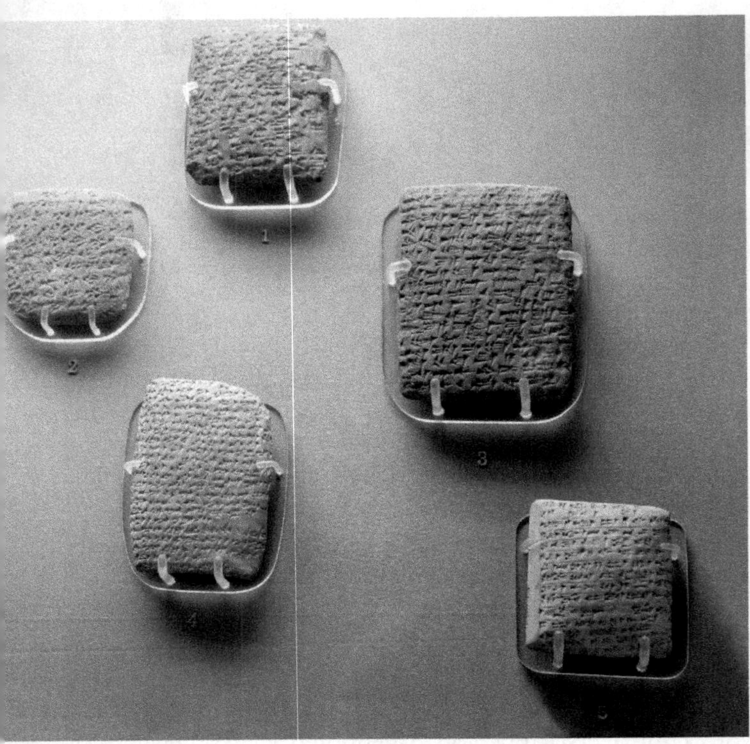

37. Five of the 382 Tell el-Amarna tablets describing the diplomatic relations between rulers of Egypt and her neighbours, such as Shechem, Jerusalem and Byblos.

The Trustees of the British Museum (ME E29836; ME E29832; ME E29844; ME E29855; ME E29831)

Pfeiffer describes their characteristics as follows:

> Originally the Habiru seem to have constituted a stratum of society rather than an ethnic group. While many of their names are Semitic, other names appear as well. According to George E. Mendenhall, the Habiru should be considered a people living outside the bounds of a given legal community, and not controlled by its laws and mores. The term would thus refer to unsettled, nomadic people who continually haunted the civilized communities around the Arabian Desert.[10]

Some scholars have identified the Habiru as the biblical Hebrews based on the similar etymology.[11] However, the Habiru were found as far north as Anatolia in the Hittite region, and it is generally agreed that the terms are not synonymous. However, given the characteristics of the Hebrews Pfeiffer speculates:

> *Quotes from Antiquity*
>
> **One of the Amarna letters states:**
>
> The *'Apiru* plunder all the lands of the king. If there are archers (here) in this year, the lands of the king, my lord, will remain (intact); but if there are no archers (here) the lands of the king, my lord, will be lost!
>
> Pritchard, *ANE*, 1.270

> It is possible however, that the Hebrews were regarded in the same light as the Habiru in the period before the establishment of the Israelite monarchy. Abraham is called "the Hebrew" (Gen 14:13) in a context in which he is involved in the political struggles of the day. Most of the Biblical uses of the term Hebrew appear in contexts in which Israelites identify themselves to other people, or in which other peoples discuss the Israelites (cf. Gen. 39:14, 17; 40:15; 41:12; 43:32). While all Habiru were not Hebrews, the Israelites were regarded as Habiru by the people among whom they lived.[12]

Another biblical connection is found in one of the letters sent by *'Abdu-Heba*, who was

88; Gordon, "The New Amarna Tablets," 1–21; Hugo Winckler, *The Tell-El-Amarna Letters*, trans. J. Metcalf (New York, N.Y.: Metcalf, 1896).

[10] Pfeiffer, *Wycliffe Dictionary of Biblical Archaeology*, 273; Lemche, "Habiru/Hapiru," 6–10.

[11] Oswald Loretz, *Habiru-Hebräer. Eine Sozio-Linguistische Studie über Die Herkunft Des Gentiliziums ‹ibrî Vom Appellativum Habiru*, Beihefte Zur ZAW 160 (Berlin: de Gruyter, 1984), 60.

[12] Charles F. Pfeiffer, "Habiru, Hapiru," *WDBA* (Peabody, Mass.: Hendrickson, 2000), 273; S. Douglas Waterhouse, "Who Were the Habiru of the Amarna Letters?," *Journal of the Adventist Theological Society* 12 (2001): 31–42.

the ruler of Jerusalem.[13] This is one of the earliest non-biblical references to the city of Jerusalem and demonstrates that Jerusalem existed as a city in the fourteenth cent. BC.

Also, many of the towns in Canaan that are mentioned in the Bible associated with Israel in later centuries are mentioned in the Amarna letters. The correspondence also mentions the storm god, Baal (or Hadad) along with the Egyptian sun god when addressing Pharaoh.[14]

The Ras Shamra Tablets

In 1928 a Syrian farmer uncovered a slab of stone while plowing his field at Ras Shamra (Arabic "Fennel Head," identified as the ancient Phoenician city of Ugarit).[15] This was the beginning of the discovery of several libraries with thousands of tablets (see Fig. 38).[16] Under the direction of Claude F. A. Schaeffer from the Musée archéologique in Strasbourg,[17] excavations began in April 1929 and continued for the next eight seasons.[18] Subsequent seasons were directed by Henri de Contenson (1971 to 1974), Jean Margueron (1975 to 1977), and after 1978, by Marguerite Yon.[19]

38. Ugarit (Ras Shamra) clay tablet with the Ugaritic alphabet in cuneiform script (1325–1250 BC).

National Museum, Damascus, Syria. RS 12.063 [=KTU 5.6]

Wright recalls:

> scarcely had a month gone by before one of the most important discoveries of the century was made. This was the uncovering of a scribal school and library, adjoining a temple. Most of the tablets in the library were written in a strange new script; but they were soon deciphered by Semitic scholars, one of whom had been decorated by the French government for brilliant work on an enemy cipher in the First World War.[20]

---

[13] Pritchard, *ANE, Vol 1*, 271; William L. Moran, *Amarna Studies: Collected Writings*, ed. John Huehnergard and Shlomo Izre'el (Winona Lake, Ind.: Eisenbrauns, 2003), 249–73.

[14] Richard S. Hess, "Amarna Proper Names (Egypt)" (Ph.D. diss., Hebrew Union College - Jewish Institute of Religion (Ohio), 1984); "Divine Names in the Amarna Correspondence," *UF* 18 (1986): 149–68; *Amarna Personal Names*, American Schools of Oriental Research Dissertation Series 9 (Winona Lake, Ind.: Eisenbrauns, 1993).

[15] Wayne Jackson, "The Ras Shamra Discovery," *Apologetics Press*, 2013, 1; Aziel Eisenberg, *Voices from the Past: Stories of Great Biblical Discoveries* (London: Abelard-Schuman, 1962), 99; Michael C. Astour, "Ugarit and the Great Powers," in *Ugarit in Retrospect: Fifty Years of Ugarit and Ugaritic*, ed. Gordon Douglas Young (Winona Lake, Ind.: Eisenbrauns, 1981), 3–30; Dennis Pardee, "Ugaritic," in *OEANE*, ed. Eric M. Meyers, vol. 5 (Oxford: Oxford Biblical Studies Online, 1997), 5:262–64.

[16] An additional library of tablets were discovered in 1958, but they were sold on the black market and only partially recovered. They and now displayed at Claremont Graduate University, Claremont, California. Loren R. Fisher, M. C. Astour, and P. D. Miller, *The Claremont Ras Shamra Tablets*, Analecta Orientalia 48 (Rome: Gregorian University Press, 1971); Manfried Dietrich, Oswald Loretz, and Joaquín Sanmartín, eds., *The Cuneiform Alphabetic Texts: From Ugarit, Ras Ibn Hani and Other Places (KTU)*, 2nd ed., Abhandlungen Zur Literatur Alt-Syrien-Palästinas Und Mesopotamiens 8 (Münster: Ugarit, 1995); Dennis Pardee, "Ugaritic Inscriptions," in *OEANE*, ed. Eric M. Meyers, vol. 5 (Oxford: Oxford Biblical Studies Online, 1997), 5:264–66; Wilfred G. E. Watson and Nicolas Wyatt, eds., *Handbook of Ugaritic Studies* (Atlanta, Ga.: SBL, 2015).

[17] *COS* 3.45: 89-14; Claude F. A. Schaeffer, *The Cuneiform Texts of Ras Shamra-Ugarit: The Schweich Lectures of the British Academy 1937* (Munich: Periodicals Service Co, 1986).

[18] Charles F. Pfeiffer, *Ras Shamra and the Bible* (Grand Rapids: Baker, 1962); Loren R. Fisher, *Ras Shamra Parallels: The Texts From Ugarit and the Hebrew Bible*, vol. 1 & 2, Analecta Orientalia 49 & 50 (Rome: Pontificium Institutum Biblicum, 1975); Stan Rummel et al., *Ras Shamra Parallels: The Texts from Ugarit and the Hebrew Bible*, Analecta Orientalia 51 (Rome: Gregorian University Press, 1981).

[19] Marguerite Yon, "Ugarit," ed. David Noel Freedman et al., trans. Stephen Rosoff, *ABD* (New York, N.Y.: Doubleday, 1996), 6:695.

[20] G. Ernest Wright, *Biblical Archaeology*, Abridged (Philadelphia, Pa.: Westminster, 1960), 106–107.

The tablets were dated to *ca.* 1400–1200 BC[21] and indicated that it was possible for Moses to write in *ca.* 1440 to 1400 BC. The importance to biblical studies is in the recovery of literature that described for the first time, outside the Bible, the Canaanite religious practices of the cult of Baal and the pagan religious practice of child sacrifice, prohibited by Yahweh (Lev 20:2–5). Other cultural practices mentioned in the Bible, such as Levirate marriage (Gen 38:8; Deut 25:5–6), were also described in the Ras Shamra tablets.[22]

Also found on the tablets were poems and ancient Hurrian songs, one of which was to the moon goddess Nikkal and is one of the oldest musical notations yet discovered, with both words and music, demonstrating their ability to record and use harmony.[23]

A small fragment of one of the tablets contained an account of the flood story (*Ugaritica* V. 167 = RS 22.421). This account of the flood is unlike the other accounts, which also contained the creation of the world and humanity.[24] This is the only surviving version that has been found outside of Mesopotamia, although a copy of the *Epic of Gilgamesh* (see Fig. 19) was found in Megiddo, Israel, but with only the beginning and the end surviving.[25]

MOSES

The Sargon Birth Legend

During the excavation in *ca.* 1850, at Nineveh (modern Kuyunjik), under the direction of Sir Austen Henry Layard three clay tablets were uncovered, one of which

39. Cuneiform tablet with the legend of Sargon's birth, from the library of King Ashurbanipal (r. 669–631 BC).

The Trustees of the British Museum (ME K3401). © Marie-Lan Nguyen / Wikimedia Commons. Color enhancement and crop by David E. Graves

[21] Dennis Pardee and Pierre Bordreuil, "Ugarit: Texts and Literature," ed. David Noel Freedman et al., *ABD* (New York, N.Y.: Doubleday, 1996), 6:706.

[22] Wayne T. Pitard, "Voices from the Dust: The Tablets from Ugarit and the Bible," in *Mesopotamia and the Bible: Comparative Explorations*, ed. Mark W. Chavalas and K. Lawson Younger, JSOTSup 341 (London: T&T Clark, 2003), 251–75.

[23] Anne D. Kilmer, "World's Oldest Musical Notation Deciphered on Cuneiform Tablet," *BAR* 6, no. 5 (1980): 14–25; "A Music Tablet from Sippar(?): BM 65217 + 66616," *Iraq* 46 (1984): 69–80; "The Musical Instruments from Ur and Ancient Mesopotamian Music," *Expedition* 402 (1998): 12–19.

[24] Lambert and Millard, *Atra-Hasis*, 131–33.

[25] Rivka Gonen, "The Late Bronze Age," in *The Archaeology of Ancient Israel*, ed. Amnon Ben-Tor, trans. R. Greenberg (New Haven, Conn.: Yale University Press, 1994), 249.

spoke of the birth legend of Sargon (ME K3401; see Fig. 39),[26] king of Akkad (or Agade *ca.* 2334–2279 BC).[27] A smaller portion (lower section of Fig. 42; Sm. 2118) of this same tablet was discovered by George Smith in 1874,[28] while working in Ashubanipal's library at Nineveh.[29] Today the largest fragment with a smaller restored piece is displayed in the British Museum (ME K3401+Sm. 2118). Another fragment which originally contained the birth legend is possessed by the Louvre (AO 7673).

Quotes from Antiquity

Sargon Birth Legend

I am Sargon the great king, king of Agade.
My mother was a high priestess, I did not know my father.
My father's brother dwell in the uplands.
My city is Azupiranu, which lies on Euphrates bank.
My mother, the high priestess, conceived me, she bore me in secret.
She place me in a reed basket, she sealed my hatch with pitch.
She left me to the river, whence I could not come up.
The river carried me off, it brought me to Aqqi, drawer of water.
Aqqi, drawer of water, brought me up as he dipped his bucket.
Aqqi, drawer of water, raised me as his adopted son.
Aqqi, drawer of water, set (me) to his orchard work.
During my orchard work, Ishtar loved me
Fifty-five years I ruled as king
I became lord over and ruled the black-headed folk.

Foster, "The Birth Legend of Sargon of Akkad," 819.

It is clear from the Neo-Babylonian dialect used, that this account was written well over a millennium after Sargon lived, and generally accepted by scholar to have been written by the Neo-Assyrian king Sargon II (709–705 BC) to legitimize his reign. Sargon II has a blessing placed inside the text for himself spoken by the older Sargon.[30]

Although only the first ten lines deal with the birth of Sargon,[31] the title has stuck.

The common belief is that because of the obvious similarities between Sargon's Birth Legend and the birth of Moses (Exod 2:1–10), the author of the biblical account used the Sargon tradition to craft Moses' account.[32]

What is clear is that the "rags to riches" motif was a common ANE theme. An earlier tradition of Sargon's birth is refered to in a Sumerian literary fragment from Uruk (*TCL* 16 73). As Childs points out "this is almost the idential pattern[33] found in a series of bilingual Sumerian-Akkadian legal texts known as *ana ittišu.*"[34]

While Childs does argue for a kind of dependence he points out that one cannot dismiss "the fact that two completely different genres of literature are involved, one narrative and one

---

[26] Two other Sargon's are known to rule Mesopotamia: the Assyrian kings Sargon I (r. *ca.* 2000 BC) and Sargon II (721-705 BC).

[27] *ANET* 119; *COS* 1.133: 461; Jerrold S. Cooper and Wolfgang Heimpel, "The Sumerian Sargon Legend," *JAOS* 103, no. 1 (1983): 67–82; Joan Goodnick Westenholz, *Legends of the Kings of Akkade: The Texts* (Winona Lake, Ind.: Eisenbrauns, 1997), 36–49.

[28] George Smith in Henry C. Rawlinson, *The Cuneiform Inscriptions of Western Asia. Vol. III. A Selection from the Miscellaneous Inscriptions of Assyria* (London: Bowler, 1870), 3: pl. 4 n.7; George Smith, "Early History of Babylonia," in *Transactions of the Society of Biblical Archaeology*, vol. 1 (London: Longmans, Green, Reader & Dyer, 1872), 46–51.

[29] Brian Lewis, *The Sargon Legend: A Study of the Akkadian Text and the Tale of the Hero Who Was Exposed at Birth*, ASOR Dissertation Series 4 (Cambridge, Mass.: ASOR, 1980), 1–23.

[30] Ibid., 97ff; Tremper Longman, *Fictional Akkadian Autobiography: A Generic and Comparative Study* (Winona Lake, Ind.: Eisenbrauns, 1991), 57–58.

[31] Benjamin R. Foster, "The Birth Legend of Sargon of Akkad," in *Before the Muses: An Anthology of Akkadian Literature*, trans. Benjamin R. Foster, vol. 2 (Winona Lake, Ind.: Eisenbrauns, 2005), 819.

[32] Hugo Gressmann, *Mose und seine Zeit: ein Kommentar zu den Mose-Sagen* (Göttingen: Vandenhoeck & Ruprecht, 1913); Brevard S. Childs, "The Birth of Moses," *JBL* 84, no. 2 (June 1, 1965): 109–22; John Van Seters, *The Life of Moses: The Yahwist as Historian in Exodus-Numbers* (Louvain, Belgium: Peeters, 1994).

[33] The biblical pattern follows the child is found (Exod 2:5), recognized as a foundling (2:6), delivered to a nurse for a fee (2:9), weaned and returned (2:9-10) and then adopted (2:9).

[34] Childs, "The Birth of Moses," 111.

legal."[35]

As Provan et al. point out: "In both cultures, the idea behind the basket on the water was the commission of the child into the care of the deity who controls the waters (in the case of Exodus, Yahweh himself)."[36]

And while the biblical account is unique in many ways (i.e., a knowledge of Egypt, such as, the papyrus reeds of the Nile, bitumen pitch for the basket, and attendants bathing in the Nile, etc.), there is no doubt that the account of the birth of Moses was described in Exodus similar to the ANE birth legends in order that the audience would understand it as the legitimizing of Moses' divine vocation and identity.

JOSHUA

Two Inscribed Phoenician columns

In the sixth cent., a Greek historian by the name of Procopius of Caesarea (*ca.* AD 500–?), an adviser to Belisarius under emperor Justinian (see Fig. 40), recounts how the Canaanites who had built a fortress at Tigisis (Tangiers) in Numidia, North Africa "had left two columns inscribed in the Phoenician language wherein they claimed that they had fled from Joshua the son of Nun."[37] Procopius reports: "They [the Canaanites] also built a fortress in Numidia, where now is the city called Tigisis [probably Ain el-Bordj in Algeria].[38] In that place are two columns made of white stone near by the great spring, having Phoenician letters cut in them which say in the Phoenician tongue: "We are they who fled from before the face of Joshua, the robber, the son of Nun" (*Bell. Van.* 4.10.21–22)."[39]

However, Millar argues that "the passage of Procopius is set in the very dubious context of a legend about the

40. Detail of a contemporary portrait mosaic of Emperor Justinian I (r. 527 to 565) in the Basilica of San Vitale, Ravenna.

[35] Ibid.

[36] Iain W. Provan et al., *A Biblical History of Israel*, 1st ed. (Louisville, Ky.: Westminster/Knox, 2003), 126.

[37] Anthony J. Frendo, "Two Long-Lost Phoenician Inscriptions and The Emergence of Ancient Israel," *PEQ* 134, no. 1 (January 2002): 37.

[38] Dennis Pringle, *The Defence of Byzantine Africa from Justinian to the Arab Conquest: An Account Of The Military History And Archaeology Of The African Provinces In The Sixth And Seventh Centuries*, BAR. International Series (Oxford: British Archaeological Reports, 1981), 246–48.

[39] Procopius of Caesarea, *History of the Wars: Books 3-4. (Vandalic War)*, trans. H. B. Dewing, vol. 2, LCL 81 (Cambridge, Mass.: Harvard University Press, 1914), 289–91.

settlement of N. Africa."[40] But in addition to Procopius, Moses of Khoren, an earlier Armenian historian (AD 370–386), also mentions the two inscriptions on the Phoenician columns[41] as well as an anonymous Greek historian (AD 630) in the *Chronicon Paschale* who states: "The inhabitants of these islands, [i.e., the Balearic Islands north of Algeria and east of Spain] were Canaanites fleeing from the face of Joshua the son of Nun."[42] However, these witnesses may have repeated the earlier tradition of Procopius.

Schmitz points out,

> In the current state of our knowledge, no archaeological evidence supports the supposition that Canaanites were widely dispersed along the North African littoral before the Iron II period in the Levant. ... In this writer's view, Procopius does not lead us to a forgotten source confirming the biblical conquest narratives. He leads us into the tangles of early Christian oral tradition and its reflexes in chronographic compilations.[43]

Although, as Wood points out: "it is highly unlikely that the Phoenicians of North Africa would have invented such a demeaning tradition to explain how they came to be in North Africa."[44] Nevertheless given the lack of archaeological support it would be wise to approach this testimony with caution.

ISRAEL

The Merenptah Stele

The Merenptah (also spelled Merneptah) Stele (see Fig. 42) dates to the time of the Egyptian Pharaoh Merenptah (1213–1203 BC, *ca.* 1208 BC).[45] It was discovered by Flinders Petrie in 1896 at Thebes[46] and is presently kept in the Cairo Museum in Egypt.[47] One line states: "Israel is laid waste, his seed is no longer; Khor [i.e., Syria] is become a widow because

41. Merenptah Stele also known as the Israel stela, and is the earliest extrabiblical record of a people group called Israel.

Egyptian Museum in Cairo (JE 31408). Courtesy of Greg Gulbrandsen

[40] Fergus Millar, "Local Cultures in the Roman Empire: Libyan, Punic and Latin in Roman Africa," *JRS* 58 (1968): 131; *Rome, the Greek World, and the East: Volume 2: Government, Society, and Culture in the Roman Empire*, Studies in the History of Greece and Rome (Chapel Hill, N.C.: University of North Carolina Press, 2004), 259.

[41] Frendo, "Two Long-Lost Phoenician Inscriptions and The Emergence of Ancient Israel," 40.

[42] Ibid.

[43] Philip C. Schmitz, "Procopius' Phoenician Inscriptions: Never Lost, Not Found," *PEQ* 139, no. 2 (2007): 102.

[44] Bryant G. Wood, "Extra-Biblical Evidence for the Conquest," *BS* 18, no. 4 (2005): 98.

[45] Kenneth A. Kitchen, "The Victories of Merenptah, and the Nature of Their Record," *JSOT* 28, no. 3 (March 1, 2004): 259.

[46] William M. Flinders Petrie, *Six Temples at Thebes in 1896* (London: Quaritch, 1897), 13.

[47] Bryant G. Wood, "Pharaoh Merneptah Meets Israel," *BS* 18, no. 3 (2005): 65.

of Egypt."[48]

This stele is noted for being one of the earliest records to use the name "Israel"[49] outside of the Bible,[50] although it is presently being challenged as the earliest by the Berlin Statue Pedestal Relief.[51] Wood points out: "

> by the end of the 13th century BC [1208–1210 BC], the Israelite tribes had achieved sufficient status to be deemed worthy of being defeated by the king of one of the most powerful nations on earth. This counters the theory being touted by many scholars that the nation of Israel did not come into existence until the 12th century BC.[52]

However, Kitchen and others have pointed out that Israel in the Merenptah Stele bears an Egyptian determinative for a "people" group rather than a "land" (i.e., a formal nation), which corresponds to the way early Israel is depicted in the book of Judges.[53]

The Merenptah's Battle Reliefs, Karnak Temple

In the Karnak Temple (see Fig. 43) complex outside Luxor, Egypt, between the Hypostyle Hall and the seventh pylon, in an area known as the "Cour de la Cachette," Merenptah (1212–1202 BC) carved a relief in the wall in the Temple of his military exploits from his Canaanite campaign in 1210 BC (see Fig. 42). Long believed to be the work of Ramesses II who built the wall earlier to display his peace treaty with the Hittites following the Battle of Kadesh (1275 BC), in the late 1970 Frank Yurco, a young Egyptologist student identified the relief as Merenptah's.[54] Merenptah took space on both sides of this earlier relief to display his Canaanite campaign. Yurco discovered that Seti II (1200–1194 BC) had later obliterated the earlier names by writing his cartouche over theirs.

The Merenptah battle relief (see Fig. 42) also corresponds to the famous Merenptah Stele (see Fig. 41) found in Merenptah's mortuary temple on the west bank of the Nile River. In the Karnak Temple (see Fig. 43), the top panel displays three conquered cities (Ashkelon, Gezer and Yenoam) as they are listed on the Merenptah Stele. The fourth scene to the right of the

---

[48] Edward F. Wente, Jr., "The Israel Stela," in *The Literature of Ancient Egypt: An Anthology of Stories, Instructions, Stelae, Autobiographies, and Poetry*, ed. William Kelly Simpson, trans. Robert K. Ritner, Vincent A. Tobin, and Edward F. Wente, Jr. (New Haven, Conn.: Yale University Press, 2003), 360; Miriam Lichtheim, *Ancient Egyptian Literature: The New Kingdom*, 2nd ed., vol. 2 (Berkeley, Calf.: University of California Press, 2006), 2:73–77. See also *ANET* 376-78; *COS* 2.6: 40-41.

[49] Kenneth A. Kitchen, "The Physical Text of Merenptah's Victory Hymn (The 'Israel Stela')," *The Journal of the Society for the Study of Egyptian Antiquities* 24 (1994): 71–76; Kenneth A. Kitchen, *Ramesside Inscriptions: Merenptah and the Late Nineteenth Dynasty: Translated and Annotated, Translations*, vol. 4 (Oxford: Wiley-Blackwell, 2003), 4:10–15.

[50] Michael G. Hasel, "Israel in the Merneptah Stela," *BASOR*, no. 296 (November 1, 1994): 45–61; James K. Hoffmeier, "The (Israel) Stela of Merneptah (2.6)," in *The Context of Scripture: Monumental Inscriptions from the Biblical World*, ed. William W. Hallo et al., vol. 2 (Leiden: Brill Academic, 2001), 40–41; Michael G. Hasel, "Merenptah's Inscription and Reliefs and the Origin of Israel," in *The Near East in the Southwest: Essays in Honor of William G Dever*, ed. Beth Alpert Nakhai, Annual of ASOR (Boston, Mass.: American Schools of Oriental Research, 2004), 19–44.

[51] Manfred Görg, Peter van der Veen, and Christoffer Theis, "Israel in Canaan (Long) Before Pharaoh Merenptah? A Fresh Look at Berlin Statue Pedestal Relief 21687," *Journal of Ancient Egyptian Interconnections* 2, no. 4 (2010): 15–25; Graves, *Biblical Archaeology Vol 1: An Introduction 2nd ed* 1:153–55.

[52] Wood, "Pharaoh Merneptah Meets Israel," 67.

[53] Kitchen, "The Victories of Merenptah," 272; Lawrence E. Stager, "Merneptah, Israel and Sea Peoples: New Light on an Old Relief," *Eretz Isreal* 18 (1985): 61; Frank J. Yurco, "Mernephtah's Canaanite Campaign and Israel's Origins," in *Exodus: The Egyptian Evidence*, ed. Ernest S. Frerichs, Leonard H. Lesko, and William G. Dever (Winona Lake, Ind.: Eisenbrauns, 1997), 212; John J. Bimson, "Merenptah's Israel and Recent Theories of Israelite Origins," *Journal for the Study of the Old Testament*, no. 49 (1991): 22–24; Hasel, "Israel in the Merneptah Stela," 56 n.12; "Merenptah's Inscription and Reliefs and the Origin of Israel," 37; "The Structure of the Final Hymnic-Poetic Unit of the Merenptah Stela," *ZAW* 116 (2004): 81.

[54] Frank J. Yurco, "Merenptah's Canaanite Campaign," *Journal of the American Research Center in Egypt* 23 (January 1, 1986): 189–215; "3,200-Year-Old Picture of Israelites Found in Egypt," *BAR* 16, no. 5 (1990): 20–38; "Mernephtah's Canaanite Campaign and Israel's Origins," 27–41.

42. Merenptah Battle Relief, on the western wall of the "Cour de la Cachette," depicting a group of soldiers being trampled on the ground under the Egyptian chariots.

peace treaty depicted a defeated people group, also likely described in the Merenptah Stele. The group of soldiers are depicted being trampled on the ground under the Egyptian chariots (*ca.* 1212–1202 BC). The fourth defeated enemy in the Merenptah Stele is listed as Israel. Yurco, supported by Kenneth Kitchen,[55] identified the people group in the Merenptah relief also as Israel, while Rainey suggests the soldiers in this panel are Canaanites and that Isreal is identified on another panel among portrayals of Shasu nomad prisoners.[56] Hoffmeier is skeptical that Israel has been correctly identified as yet and fears the panel bearing the Israelite image may never be recovered.[57]

43. The Karnak temple complex outside Luxor, Egypt. The precinct of Amun-Re was the only part open to the public in antiquity. The rest of the building was a private sanctuary for the priests to carry out their daily routines. It is the largest religious monument in the world.

If Yurco's identification about this relief is correct, this would be the earliest depiction of an Israelite discovered to date. The next visual depiction is *ca.* 370 years later on the black obelisk (see Figs. 59, 60).[58]

[55] James K. Hoffmeier, *Ancient Israel in Sinai: The Evidence for the Authenticity of the Wilderness Tradition*, Illustrated edition (Oxford: Oxford University Press, USA, 2005), 244.

[56] For the debate over the identification with Israel see Stager, "Merneptah, Israel and Sea Peoples: New Light on an Old Relief," 56–64; Donald B. Redford, "The Ashkelon Reliefs at Karnak and the Israel Stela," *IEJ* 36 (1986): 188–200; Anson F. Rainey, "Rainey's Challenge: Can You Name the Panel with the Israelites?," *BAR* 17, no. 6 (1991): 56–60, 93; Frank J. Yurco, "Yurco's Response," *BAR* 17, no. 6 (1991): 61.

[57] Hoffmeier, *Ancient Israel in Sinai*, 245.

[58] Paul L. Maier, "Archaeology—Biblical Ally or Adversary?," *BS* 17, no. 3 (2004): 91.

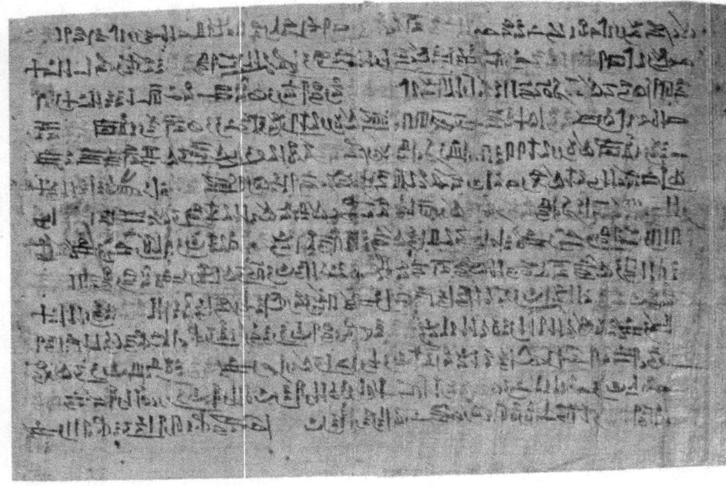

44. The *Ipuwer Papyrus*.

The National Archaeological Museum (Rijksmuseum van Oudheden), Leiden, Netherlands (Papyrus Leiden I 344 recto). Wikimedia Commons

PLAGUES AND THE EXODUS

The *Ipuwer Papyrus*

The *Ipuwer Papyrus* (P Leiden I 344 recto; see Fig. 44)[59] dating to the New Kingdom (*ca.* 1543–1064 BC), contains an ancient Egyptian poem called the *The Admonitions of Ipuwer*[60] or *The Dialogue of Ipuwer and the Lord of All*.[61] The precise date for its composition is unknown (*ca.* 1850–1600 BC),[62] but this singular copy was made during the New Kingdom of Egypt (18th, 19th and 20th Dynasties, *ca.* 1543–1064 BC). It was purchased in 1928 by the Swedish consul to Egypt, Giovanni Anastasi, and is today housed in the Dutch National Museum of Antiquities in Leiden, Netherlands.[63]

The *Ipuwer Papyrus* is a poetic lament over the natural disasters and calamities afflicting Egypt, which have created a state of utter chaos and blamed on an unidentified king (perhaps Pepy II of the Sixth Dynasty *ca.* 2300–2206 BC). It describes an inverted state of affairs where the rich become poor and the poor rich, with war, death and famine afflicting the entire nation. One of the consequences of this lawlessness is the rebellion of servants against their masters.

The description provides remarkable parallels with the story of the Biblical Exodus, and this has led to much debate. Enmarch reports that: "The broadest modern reception of Ipuwer amongst non-Egyptological readers has probably been as a result of the use of the poem as evidence supporting the Biblical account of the Exodus."[64]

Although the *Ipuwer Papyrus* securely dates to after the Exodus events happened, either from an early date or late date, Enmarch notes several striking textual parallels: "particularly the striking statement that "the river is blood and one drinks from it" (*Ipuwer* 2.10), and the frequent references to servants abandoning their subordinate status (e.g. *Ipuwer* 3.14–4.1; 6.7–8;

[59] ANET 441-44; COS 1.45: 93-98; Miriam Lichtheim, *Ancient Egyptian Literature: The Old and Middle Kingdoms*, 2nd ed., vol. 1 (Berkeley, Calf.: University of California Press, 2006), 1:149–63; Simpson, *LAE*, 188–210.

[60] R. O. Faulkner, "The Admonitions of an Egyptian Sage," *JEA* 51 (December 1, 1965): 53–62; Alan H. Gardiner, *The Admonitions of an Egyptian Sage from a Hieratic Papyrus in Leiden* (Hildesheim: Georg Olms Verlag, 1969); R. B. Parkinson, trans., *The Tale of Sinuhe and Other Ancient Egyptian Poems* (Oxford: Oxford World's Classics, 1999).

[61] Roland Enmarch, *Dialogue of Ipuwer and the Lord of All* (Oxford: Griffith Institute, 2005).

[62] John Van Seters, "A Date for the 'Admonitions' in the Second Intermediate Period," *JEA* 50 (1964): 13–23.

[63] http://www.rmo.nl/collectie/zoeken?object =AMS+27+vel+3.

[64] Ronald Enmarch, "The Reception of a Middle Egyptian Poem: The Dialogue of Ipuwer and the Lord of All in the Ramesside Period and beyond," in *Ramesside Studies in Honour of K. A. Kitchen*, ed. Mark Collier and Steven R. Snape (Bolton, U.K.: Rutherford, 2011), 106.

10.2–3). On a literal reading, these are similar to aspects of the Exodus account. (Exod 7–11)"[65] However, he suggests that: "it is more likely that *Ipuwer* is not a piece of historical reportage and that historicising interpretations of it fail to account for the ahistorical, schematic literary nature of some of the poem's laments."[66]

Kenneth Kitchen also suggested that *Ipuwer* and the Exodus account were possibly referring to the same kind of natural phenomenon.[67] Brad C. Sparks claims that some 90 Egyptian papyri[68] demonstrate similar parallels to the Exodus, including the *Ipuwer Papyrus*, *Tale of Two Brothers* (Tomb of Seti II, who ruled from 1200 to 1194, BC),[69] El Arish Stele (305–31 BC),[70] *Speos Artemidos Inscription* (Queen Hatshepsut and Seti I, 1490–1460 BC),[71] *Tempest Stela* (*ca.* 1550 BC),[72] and *Demotic Chronicle* (*ca.* 1550 BC).[73] This implies that the event of the Exodus may still have been part of the Egyptian living memory in either the fifteenth or thirteenth cent. BC.[74]

45. A scene from the *Book of the Heavenly Cow* as depicted in the tomb of Seti I, East Valley of the Kings location KV17. It depicts the sky goddess Nut in her bovine form, being held up by her father Shu, the god of the air. Aiding Shu are the eight gods of the Ogdoad. Across the belly of Nut (representing the visible sky) sails the sun god in his day barque.

The Destruction of Mankind Papyrus

The *Destruction of Mankind* (also called *The Book of the Cow of Heaven*) Papyrus (Turin Cat. 1982; see Fig. 45) is inscribed on four gilded shrines of Tutankhamun, and tomb walls of Seti I, Ramesses II, and Ramesses III.[75] It describes Hathor's divine punishment of Egyptians with

---

[65] Ibid., 174.

[66] Ibid.

[67] Kitchen, *Reliability of the OT*, 250–52.

[68] Brad C. Sparks, "Egyptian Text Parallels to the Exodus: The Egyptology Literature," in *Out of Egypt: Israel's Exodus Between Text and Memory, History and Imagination Conference*, ed. Thomas E. Levy (Qualcomm Institute, University of California, San Diego, 2013), https://www.youtube.com/watch?v=F-Aomm4O794.

[69] Papyrus D'Orbiney (EA10183,10). Lichtheim, *AEL 2*, 2:203.

[70] Barbara J. Sivertsen, *The Parting of the Sea: How Volcanoes, Earthquakes, and Plagues Shaped the Story of Exodus* (Princeton, NJ: Princeton University Press, 2011), 125–29.

[71] Hans Goedicke, "Hatshepsut's Temple Inscription at Speo Artemidos," *BAR* 7, no. 5 (1981): 42; Hershel Shanks, "The Exodus and the Crossing of the Red Sea, According to Hans Goedicke," *BAR* 7, no. 5 (1981): 42–50; Alan H. Gardiner, "Davies's Copy of the Great Speos Artemidos Inscription," *JEA* 32 (1946): 43–56; Sivertsen, *The Parting of the Sea*, 8–9.

[72] Ellen N. Davis, "A Storm in Egypt during the Reign of Ahmose," in *Thera and the Aegean World III*, ed. David A. Hardy and A. C. Renfrew, vol. 3, Proceedings of the Third International Congress, Santorini, Greece, 3–9 September 1989 (London: The Thera Foundation, 1990), 232–35; Donald B. Redford, "Textual Sources for the Hyksos Period," in *The Hyksos: New Historical and Archaeological Perspectives*, ed. Eliezer D. Oren (Philadelphia, Pa.: University of Pennsylvania Museum, 1997), 16; James K. Hoffmeier, *Israel in Egypt: The Evidence for the Authenticity of the Exodus Tradition* (Oxford: Oxford University Press, 1999), 150–51; Kenneth A. Kitchen, "Ancient Egyptian Chronology for Aegeanists," *Mediterranean Archaeology and Archaeometry* 2, no. 2 (2002): 11; Nadine Moeller and Robert K. Ritner, "The Ahmose 'Tempest Stela', Thera and Comparative Chronology," *JNES* 73, no. 1 (April 1, 2014): 2.

[73] Papyrus CPJ 520. Jan Assmann, *The Mind of Egypt: History and Meaning in the Time of the Pharaohs* (Cambridge, Mass.: Harvard University Press, 2003), 406. The dates of these documents would indicate an early date (1445 BC) for the Exodus, although some texts are even earlier than this.

[74] For further views and research see Immanuel Velikovsky, *Ages in Chaos: From the Exodus to King Akhnaton* (New York, N.Y.: Doubleday, 1952); William H. Stiebing, Jr., *Out of the Desert?: Archaeology and the Exodus/Conquest Narratives* (Buffalo, N.Y: Prometheus, 1989); Henry Zecher, "The Papyrus Ipuwer, Egyptian Version of the Plagues - A New Perspective," *The Velikovskian, A Journal of Myth, History and Science* 3, no. 1 (1997): 91–126; Stephen Quirke, *Egyptian Literature 1800 BC: Questions and Readings*, Revised, GHP Egyptology 2 (Golden House, 2004).

[75] Erik Hornung, *The Ancient Egyptian Books of the Afterlife*, trans. David Lorton (Ithaca, N.Y.: Cornell University Press, 1999), 148–51.

the foreigners, who survive the suffering, separated from Ra to live on the back of Nut, the heavenly cow.[76] .The parallels with the Exodus story are striking and Erik Hornung, in his German translation, finds a "startling" name for Ra that has Exodus parallels.

> Evidently [it] means "I am I" or "I am that I am" [Egyptian root *Yawi*]. Since in the given context it must mean: "... as whom I have proven to be" ..., the phrase indeed recalls the Old Testament: see Exodus 3:14 "I am that I am" .... What is here of interest is of course the early [ancient] theology [surrounding] God's name *YHWH*, but not its origin and actual etymology [Trans. Brad Sparks].[77]

Griffiths confirms Hornung's translation of *The Destruction of Mankind* text, declaring:

> since the meaning "I am I" seems the only one possible. Here it is rendered *Ich bin, der ich bin*, with a startling invocation by Fecht (p. 125) of Exodus 3:14 (I AM THAT I AM, or I WILL BE WHAT I WILL BE). The Hebrew is concerned with the meaning of the name Yahweh; the Egyptian context, as Fecht shows, relates to the sun-god's claim: he is what he has shown himself to be – the successful queller of men's mutiny, and so able to say in the following verse, I will not allow them to make (a revolt).[78]

Sparks reports that in addition to the "I am that I am" texts, he also discovered further parallels from the tomb painting of Seti I (1300 BC) including "the parting of the Red Sea and the mass drowning of the Egyptian army."[79]

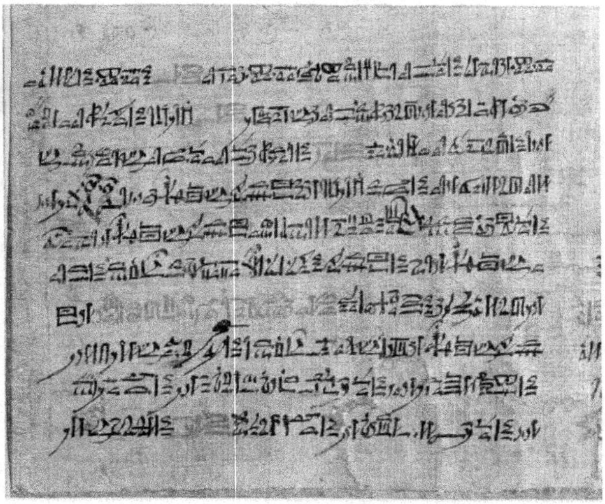

46. Sheet from the *Tale of Two Brothers*, Papyrus D'Orbiney from Egypt. End of the nineteenth Dynasty (1185 BC).

The Tale of Two Brothers Papyrus

The *Tale of Two Brothers Papyrus* (see Fig.46)[80] is an Egyptian style folk tale that became popular in the New Kingdom period (1550–1070 BC) during the reign of Seti II (1200 to 1194 BC).[81] The text is preserved on the D'Orbiney Papyrus[82] and was acquired by the British Museum in 1857 (EA10183,10).[83]

Using human characters the story is told with fantastic details. Two brothers, one called Anpu or Anubis and Bata, grow up in a typical Egyptian household. However, when Anubis' wife tries to seduce Bata, Anubis responds by

---

[76] *ANET* 10–11; *COS* 1.24: 36-37; Erik Hornung, *Der ägyptische Mythos von der Himmelskuh: Eine Ätiologie des Unvollkommenen*, Orbis biblicus et orientalis 46 (Göttingen: Vandenhoeck & Ruprecht, 1982); E. A. Wallis Budge, *Legends of the Gods The Egyptian Texts, Edited with Translations* (London: Kegan Paul, Trench, Trubner & Co., 1912); Simpson, *LAE*, 289–98; Lichtheim, *AEL 2*, 2:2:197–99.

[77] Seti I, KV 17, chamber Je, line 49. Hornung, *Der ägyptische Mythos von der Himmelskuh*, 63 n.121, 125 n.aa.

[78] J. Gwyn Griffiths, "Review of Der ägyptische Mythos von Der Himmelskuh. Eine Ätiologie Des Unvollkommenen by Erik Hornung," *JEA* 74 (January 1, 1988): 276.

[79] Sparks, "The Egyptology Literature"; Erik Hornung, *The Tomb of Pharaoh Seti I* (Zürich: Artemis & Winkler, 1991).

[80] *ANET* 23-25; *COS* 1.40:85–89; Lichtheim, *AEL 2*, 2:2:203–11; Simpson, *LAE*, 80–90; Charles E. Moldenke, ed., *Papyrus D'Orbiney (British Museum): The Hieroglyphic Transcription* (Watchung, N.J.: Elsinore, 1900); Alan H. Gardiner, *Late-Egyptian Stories* (Turnhout, Belgium: Brepols, 1981), 9–29.

[81] Jacobus Van Dilk, "The Amarna Period and the Later New Kingdom," in *The Oxford History of Ancient Egypt*, ed. Ian Shaw (Oxford: Oxford University Press, 2000), 303.

[82] Moldenke, *Papyrus D'Orbiney (British Museum): The Hieroglyphic Transcription.*

[83] Lewis Spence, *An Introduction to Mythology* (Hardpress, 2013), 247.

claiming that Bata had already seduced her, which turns the brothers against each other. Anubis' wife convinces Anubis of his brother's disloyalty and Bata is forced to leave the family. However, later Anubis learns that Bata's wife had schemed the whole plot, and so he kills Bata's wife, leading to a reconciliation between the two brothers. The story continues with the gods providing a wife for Bata followed by more disloyalty. Bata take on a variety of different forms, the last of which is a Persea Tree. While Beta's wife is cutting down the tree, she is impregnated by a splinter that is flung into her mouth, and eventually Bata is reborn as the king of Egypt. He appoints Anubis his brother as his heir.[84]

Susan Hollis states that the story may "contain reflexes of an actual historical situation."[85] The relationship between Beta and his brother's wife is often mentioned as a similar story to Joseph and Potiphar's wife (Gen 39:1–20).[86] Some have seen similarities to the story of Moses and his brother Aaron (Exod 6:16–20), as well as with the death of the Israelite at the hands of Moses (Exod 2:12), believing this to be reflected in the *Tale of Two Brothers*.

Conclusion

While any one of these papyrus accounts may not prove the Egyptians were aware of the Exodus events, the collective body of known literature, with striking parallels to various elements of the biblical story, implies that the event of the Exodus may still have been part of the Egyptian living memory in either the fifteenth or thirteenth cent. BC.

THE CONQUEST

Jericho

For an evaluation of the five excavations of Jericho (Tell es-Sultan) from 1867–2015 and the revaluation by Bryant Wood see *Biblical Archaeology* Vol 1.[87]

Ai

For the debate over the sites of et-Tel, Nisya and Khirbet el-Maqatir as biblical Ai, the second city conquered during the conquest, see *Biblical Archaeology* Vol 1.[88]

Hazor

For a discussion of biblical Hazor (Tel Hatzor), the third city conquered and destroyed during the conquest, see *Biblical Archaeology* Vol 1.[89]

---

[84] Lichtheim, *AEL 2*, 2:203–11; Simpson, *LAE*, 80–90; Susan T. Hollis, *The Ancient Egyptian "Tale of Two Brothers": A Mythological, Religious, Literary, and Historico-Political Study*, Oklahoma Series in Classical Culture (London: Bannerstone, 2008).

[85] Hollis, The Ancient Egyptian "Tale of Two Brothers," 110.

[86] Lichtheim, *AEL 2*, 2:203.

[87] Graves, *Biblical Archaeology Vol 1: An Introduction* 2nd ed 1:159–63.

[88] Ibid., 1:163–66.

[89] Ibid., 1:166–67.

47. Aerial view of the ancient city of Hazor (Tel Hatzor), Israel.

© Javno vlasništvo//Wikimedia Commons

CONCLUSION

Although scholars have claimed for years that there is no evidence for the Exodus and Conquest, and therefore that the events described in the Bible could not have happened, the recent excavations and discoveries listed here and elsewhere indicate that that biblical accounts of the Exodus and Conquest are historically reliable.

United and Divided Monarchy

48. Aerial view of Tel Shiloh (Tell-Seilûn) looking south. The ark of the covenant was located here for 369 years.

The existence of King David and King Solomon in the period of the united monarchy (Iron Age 2, tenth cent. BC), is the next area to be critically debated by archaeologists.[1] The W. F. Albright and G. E. Wright era (1980's) saw most scholars embracing David and Solomon as OT historical figures.[2] But this is no longer the case. Today some minimalist scholars argue, on the basis of the lack of supporting archaeological evidence,[3] that the united monarchy (David and Solomon), and its capital Jerusalem, never existed in the tenth cent. BC and were fabricated as pure fiction.[4] David Ussishkin goes so far as to state: "I am afraid that evidence regarding the magnificent Solomonic capital [Jerusalem] was not discovered because it is nonexistent, not because it is still hidden in the ground."[5] The following evidence refutes this common minimalist position.

Important Inscriptions

Writing was well-established in Palestine while Israel was ruling there, evident from the many inscriptions that have been discovered from that period.[6] Diringer indicated that the Bible has "as many as 429 references to writing or written documents."[7] An early criticism of the Bible was that it could not have been written as early as it stated because extensive literacy was not developed until much later.[8] However, according to Diringer, in 1934 there were "about 300 Early Hebrew inscriptions, ostraca, seals [*ca.* 150+], jar-handle-stamps [*ca.* 600+], weights [*ca.* 100+], and so on."[9] Today there are hundreds more. Three of the most significant inscriptions follow.

---

[1] Steven M. Ortiz, "The Archaeology of David and Solomon: Method or Madness?," in *Do Historical Matters Matter to Faith?: A Critical Appraisal of Modern and Postmodern Approaches to Scripture*, ed. James K. Hoffmeier and Graham A. Magary (Wheaton, Ill.: Crossway Books, 2012), 497–516.

[2] Gary N. Knoppers, "The Vanishing Solomon: The Disappearance of the United Monarchy from Recent Histories of Ancient Israel," *JBL* 116, no. 1 (April 1, 1997): 19–20.

[3] McCarter states "no archaeological discovery can securely be linked to him [David]." P. Kyle McCarter Jr., "The Historical David," *Int* 40, no. 2 (1986): 117; Margreet L. Steiner, "It's Not There: Archaeology Proves a Negative," *BAR* 24, no. 4 (1998): 26–33, 62–63. This is certainly correct in so far as no archaeological evidence can be directly connected to the historical David.

[4] Niels Peter Lemche, *The Israelites in History and Tradition*, Library of Ancient Israel (Louisville, Ky.: Westminster/Knox, 1998); Thomas L. Thompson, *The Mythic Past: Biblical Archaeology And The Myth Of Israel* (New York, N.Y.: Basic Books, 2000); Giovanni Garbini, *Myth and History in the Bible*, The Library of Hebrew Bible/OT Studies (London: Sheffield Academic Press, 2003).

[5] David Ussishkin, "Solomon's Jerusalem: The Text and the Facts on the Ground," in *Jerusalem in Bible and Archaeology: The First Temple Period*, ed. Andrew G. Vaughn and Ann E. Killebrew (Atlanta, Ga.: SBL, 2003), 112.

[6] Alan R. Millard, "An Assessment of the Evidence for Writing in Ancient Israel," in *Biblical Archaeology Today, Proceedings of the International Congress on Biblical Archaeology, Jerusalem*, ed. Avraham Biran (Jerusalem: Israel Exploration Society, 1985), 98.

[7] David Diringer, "The Biblical Scripts," in *The Cambridge History of the Bible*, ed. Peter R. Ackroyd and Craig F. Evans, vol. 1, From the Beginnings to Jerome (Cambridge, U.K.: Cambridge University Press, 1975), 13.

[8] Israel Finkelstein and Neil Asher Silberman, *The Bible Unearthed: Archaeology's New Vision of Ancient Israel* (New York, N.Y.: Touchstone, 2002), 22–23.

[9] Diringer, "The Biblical Scripts," 13; *Le Iscrizioni Antico-Ebraiche Palestinesi* (Florence, Italy: Le Monnier, 1934).

49. The Gezer tablet (tenth cent. BC).
Archaeological Museum, Istanbul. Courtesy of Greg Gulbrandsen

The Gezer Calender

This limestone tablet (tenth cent. BC[10]; Archaeological Museum Istanbul 2089 T), written in archaic biblical Hebrew (Paleo-Hebrew),[11] was discovered at Gezer by R. A. S. Macalister in 1908 (see Fig. 49).[12] It only measures about 4 inches (10 cm) tall and contains a calendar that lists the seasons and their accompanying agricultural activities.[13]

Abijah is a common name in the Bible meaning "Yah (*YHWH*) is my father."[14] This was also the name of one of the kings of Judah (1 Kgs 14:31). Although scholars debate its purpose, most consider it to be either a school exercise or a musical expression of agricultural wisdom.[15] Talmon suggests that it was used to collect taxes from farmers.[16]

The Gezer inscription provides a first-hand account of the agricultural practices in ancient Israel[17] and is one of the earliest examples of the Hebrew script. It dates to the time of Solomon.

Quotes from Antiquity

The Gezer Calender translates as:

Two months of [olive] harvest
Two months of planting [grain]
Two months are late planting
One month of hoeing [up flax]
One month of barley-harvest
One month of harvest and festival
Two months of grape harvesting
One month of summer fruit
Abijah

Albright, "The Gezer Calendar," 16–26.

The Rosetta Stone

For the significance of the Rosetta Stone see Graves, *Biblical Archaoelogy* Vol. 1.[18]

---

[10] Ian Young, "The Style of the Gezer Calendar and Some 'Archaic Biblical Hebrew' Passages," *VT* 42, no. 3 (July 1, 1992): 362–75.

[11] *ANET* 320; *COS* 2.85: 222; John C. L. Gibson, *Textbook of Syrian Semitic Inscriptions: Hebrew and Moabite Inscriptions*, vol. 1 (Oxford: Oxford University Press, 1971), 1:1–4.

[12] Robert Alexander Stewart Macalister, *The Excavation of Gezer, 1902-1905 and 1907-1909* (London: Murray, 1912), 2:24–28.

[13] Daniel Sivan, "The Gezer Calendar and Northwest Semitic Linguistics," *IEJ* 48, no. 1–2 (1998): 101–105; Oded Borowski, *Agriculture in Iron Age Israel* (Winona Lake, Ind.: Eisenbrauns, 2009), 31–44.

[14] William F. Albright, "The Gezer Calendar," *BASOR* 92 (1943): 16–26.

[15] Bustanay Oded, "Gezer Calendar," ed. Fred Skolnik and Michael Berenbaum, *EJ* (New York, N.Y.: MacMillan, December 12, 2006), 569.

[16] Shemaryahu Talmon, "The Gezer Calendar and the Seasonal Cycle of Ancient Canaan," *JAOS* 83, no. 2 (1963): 177.

[17] See also the Sumerian Farmer's Almanac in Miguel Civil, *The Farmer's Instructions: A Sumerian Agricultural Manual*, AuOrSup 5 (Barcelona, Spain: Editorial Ausa, 1994).

[18] Graves, *Biblical Archaeology Vol 1: An Introduction* 2nd ed., 1:44–45.

SEALS AND BULLAE

Seals or signets were made from oval precious or semiprecious stones that contained a distinctive mark or name in mirror-image which identified the owner. The impression, in either wet clay or hot wax, is called a *bulla* (pl. *bullae*), and was made by either rolling the cylinder seal or pressing the ring into the clay or wax.

50. Limestone cylinder seal and impression (*bulla*) on clay of animals overpowered by gods, Early Dynastic III (*ca.* 2500–2400 BCE), found in Mari.

Louvre, Department of Oriental Antiquities, Richelieu (AO 19046). © Jastrow 2006/Wikimedia Commons

Some of the earliest seals discovered have dated to before 3000 BC.[19] In Mesopotamia, cylinder seals were often worn around the neck on a leather cord (Gen 38:18; Isa 8:1), Egypt used scarab seals with a cartouche, while in Israel they were normally worn as rings on the finger (Gen 41:42; 1 Kgs 21:8).

Over two thousand jar handles have been discovered with the impression of *lmlk* (Heb. "belonging to the king") often with the name of the Israelite king.[20] While the seals have been discovered at many sites,[21] the majority of the handles are concentrated in Lachish and likely distributed by King Hezekiah prior to the attack by Sennacherib in 701 BC.[22] The jars were manufactured for liquids (wine) and manufactured at the same location from only twenty different seals.

Papyrus documents were often sealed with clay or wax seal with the name of the owner. About fifty of these seals have been recovered from a private domestic archive in Jerusalem.[23] A few acquired from antiquities markets and unprovenanced have been shown to be forgeries (perhaps the Baruch seal).[24]

The grading schema for determining the identification of people's names on seals and inscriptions is laid out by Lawrence J. Mykytiuk.[25]

---

[19] Chad Brand et al., eds., *Holman Illustrated Bible Dictionary* (Nashville, Tenn.: Broadman & Holman, 2003), 1455.

[20] David Ussishkin, "Royal Judean Storage Jars and Private Seal Impressions," *BASOR*, no. 223 (1976): 1–13; Robert Deutsch, "Lasting Impressions: New Bullae Reveal Egyptian-Style Emblems on Judah's Royal Seals," *BAR* 28, no. 4 (2002): 42–51, 60–62.

[21] Michael Heltzer and Robert Deutsch, *Forty New Ancient West Semitic Inscriptions* (Jerusalem, Israel: Israel Numismatic Society, 1994).

[22] Nadav Na'aman, "Sennacherib's Campaign to Judah and the Date of the Lmlk Stamps," *VT* 29, no. 1 (1979): 61–86; M. Mommsen, I. Perlman, and J. Yellin, "The Provenience of the 'Lmlk' Jars," *IEJ* 34, no. 2/3 (1984): 89–113; Nadav Na'aman, "Hezekiah's Fortified Cities and the 'LMLK' Stamps," *BASOR*, no. 261 (February 1, 1986): 5–21; Andrew G. Vaughn, "Palaeographic Dating of Judaean Seals and Its Significance for Biblical Research," *BASOR*, no. 313 (1999): 43–64.

[23] Robert Deutsch, Shlomo Moussaieff, and André LeMaire, *Biblical Period Personal Seals in the Shlomo Moussaieff Collection*, JNES 62 (Tel Aviv, Israel: Archaeological Center Publications, 2003), 119–25.

[24] Benjamin Sass, "The Pre-Exilic Hebrew Seals: Iconism vs. Aniconism," in *Studies in the Iconography of Northwest Semitic Inscribed Seals: Proceedings of a Symposium Held in Fribourg on April 17-20, 1991*, ed. Benjamin Sass and Christoph Uehlinger, Orbis Biblicus et Orientalis 125 (Gottingen: Vandenhoeck & Ruprecht, 1993), 194–256; Christopher A. Rollston, "Non-Provenanced Epigraphs I: Pillaged Antiquities, Northwest Semitic Forgeries, and Protocols for Laboratory Tests," *Maarav* 10 (2003): 135–93; Christopher A. Rollston and Andrew G. Vaughn, "The Antiquities Market, Sensationalized Textual Data, and Modern Forgeries," *NEA* 68, no. 1–2 (2005): 62, 67.

[25] Lawrence J. Mykytiuk, *Identifying Biblical Persons in Northwest Semitic Inscriptions of 1200-539 B.C.E.*, SBL Academia Biblica 12 (Atlanta, Ga.: Society of Biblical Literature, 2004), 9–89, 212–213; "Corrections and Updates to 'Identifying Biblical Persons in Northwest Semitic Inscriptions of 1200-539 BC,'" *Maarav* 16 (2009): 49–132.

Of the thousands of bullae discovered, most from the 8th to 6th cent. BC, [26] some 34 seal impressions have been identified with the names of OT individuals.[27] But how do scholars know if the names are the same or another person with the same name? The criteria used follows three initial questions, unless there is a clear sense of singularity between the seal and the biblical text (see no. 4). The criteria are listed as:

1. Are the texts reliable (based on solid textual criticism) and not forgeries?
2. Do the two persons on the seal and in the text match the same time and socio-political setting (within 50 years)?
3. How close do the identifying marks (name, title, and patronym) match,[28] or are they different individuals?[29]
4. Do the two persons have "a singular circumstance, such as participation in a particular historical event?"[30]

These criteria are important in determining if the many names listed on the seals are indeed those mentioned in the Bible.

Other biblical individuals identified on seals include Jezebel, Azariah (servant of Jotham), Pekah, Ahaz (see Fig. 68), Hezekiah, Eliakim (Isa 22:20), Amariah, Hoshea, Shebna, Manasseh, Asiah, Joezer, Igdaliah, Azaliah, Meshullam, Nathan-Melech, Ahikam, Shaphan, Baruch (the son of Neriah, Jer 32:1–16; see Fig. 86), Immer,[31] Seriah, Malchiah, Hananiah, Azzur, Jerahmeel (Jer 36:26), Elishama, Jehucal, Shelemiah, Gedaliah (Jer 40:5; 2 Kgs 25:22), Pashhur, Isaiah the prophet, Hilkiah (Isa 22:20), Jehoahaz, Pedaiah, Seraiah, Neriah, Ba'alis (Jer 40:14), Jaazaniah (Jer 40:8), Pelatiah (Ezek 11:1, 13), Shelomith, Elnathan, Shanballat (governor of Samaria), and Darius (see Fig. 97).[32]

KING DAVID

David's journey to kingship began as a lowly shepherd boy, the descendent of Ruth through her husband Boaz (Ruth 4:18–22) and thus in the messianic royal line (Matt 1:3–6; Luke 3:31–33). David was in the fields of Bethlehem tending his father's flocks when Samuel came to find and anoint a king.

When Saul was rejected by God as king of Israel (1 Sam 15:23, 35), God sent Samuel to Bethlehem to anoint a king from the family of Jesse (1 Sam 16:1). While Samuel favoured the

---

[26] John H. Walton, Victor H. Matthews, and Mark W. Chavalas, *The IVP Bible Background Commentary: Old Testament* (Downers Grove, Ill.: InterVarsity, 2000), 666.

[27] For a scholarly treatment and cataloging of West Semitic bulla see Nahman Avigad and Benjamin Sass, *Corpus of West Semitic Stamp Seals*, 2nd ed. (Jerusalem: Israel Academy of Sciences & Humanities, 1997); Larry G. Herr, "The Palaeography of West Semitic Stamp Seals," *BASOR* 312 (1998): 45–77. See also *COS* 2.70: 197–201; 2.77: 202–3.

[28] Names which meet two of the first three criteria and are identified matches are: Hadadezer, king of Aram at Damascus; Ben-hadad, son of Hadadezer, king of Aram at Damascus; Shaphan the scribe, who served Josiah, king of Judah; Gemariah the official, son of Shaphan the scribe; Hilkiah the high priest; and Azariah, son of Hilkiah the high priest. Meir Lubetski and Edith Lubetski, eds., *New Inscriptions and Seals Relating to the Biblical World* (Atlanta, Ga.: SBL, 2012), 47–49.

[29] Ibid., 40.

[30] Ibid, 41. Examples of individuals whose seal matched their historical setting in the text are David, king of Israel; Omri, king of Israel, Mesha, king of Moab; Hazael, king of Aram at Damascus; Ben-hadad, son of Hazael, king of Aram at Damascus; Sennacherib, king of Assyria; Tiglath-pileser III, king of Assyria; Sargon II, king of Assyria; Jeroboam II, king of Israel; and Uzziah, king of Judah. Ibid., 41–47.

[31] Graves, *Biblical Archaeology Vol 1: An Introduction* 2nd ed 1:199.

[32] For a scholarly treatment and cataloging of West Semitic bulla see Avigad and Sass, *Corpus of West Semitic Stamp Seals*; Walton, Matthews, and Chavalas, *IVP Bible Background Commentary: OT*, 666.

oldest son Eliab, David was God's choice for king (1 Sam 16:11–12). And although David was anointed king, he would not rise to the throne for some time.

God's spirit departed from Saul and an evil spirit from God troubled him (1 Sam 16:18). One of Saul's servants had learned of David talents for playing the harp and recommended him to soothe Saul's troubled spirit. This gave David an opportunity to see the life of the court firsthand. David was loved by Saul and was made his armour bearer. This was the period when many of the Psalms were composed (1 Sam 16:14–23).

David grew to prominence by defeating Goliath, the champion of the Philistines (1 Sam 17). He would go on to lead Israel in defeating the Philistines, winning the hearts of the people (1 Sam 18:1–27). Saul's jealousy of David's popularity led to David's rebellion against Saul and to David alluding Saul for many years while he lived among the Moabites.

David captured the Jebusite city of Jerusalem by entering through the tunnel used to supply water to the city during a time of siege. It is still visible today and know as Hezekiah's Tunnel (see Fig. 72).

Jerusalem was made David's capital and he moved the Ark of the Covenant there from Kiriath-jearim, where it had rested since the time of Samuel (2 Sam 6:1–7). David was not content to have the Ark remain in a tent and so made plans to build a temple to house the furniture. But through the prophet Nathan, David was told that it would be his son Solomon who would build the temple (2 Sam 7:1–29). Instead David would build a royal line of eternal significance (2 Sam 7).

Quickly David subdued his enemies. He took the cities of Baal-perazim, Gibeon, Gezer and Gath. The nations he conquered included Moabites, Philistines, Amalekites, the Ammonites, and Syrians at Medeba (2 Sam 5, 8, 10).

The last thing David did as recorded in Scripture was to count the people and prepare for the building of the Temple. For some reason, this was not pleasing to God, perhaps because God had not commanded it and because it showed David's pride to be in numbers rather than in the Lord.

In God's anger, David was given three options by which Israel would be punished for his sin. Seven years of famine, three months of war, or three days of pestilence. David picked the last and seventy thousand Israelites were killed. God stopped the angel of destruction from destroying Jerusalem by standing on the threshing floor of Araunah (2 Sam 24:1–25).

Under the direction of Gad the prophet, David was instructed to go and purchase this land belonging to Araunah and build an altar there. This was to be the location of Solomon's temple. Before his death, David gave Solomon strict orders to follow the directions found in the law of Moses for the building of the temple (1 Chron 22:1–19).

In the closing days of David's life, another of his sons tried to take the throne from him. Adonijah tried to have himself anointed as king outside Jerusalem with the support of Joab and Abiather, but Zadok and Nathan would only support Solomon. Nathan and Bathsheba told David of the plan and Solomon was immediately crowned King of Israel. David ruled for forty years and died and was buried in Jerusalem, the city of David (1 Kgs 1:1–2:12).

The Mesha Stele

The Mesha Stele (or Moabite Stone) is a black basalt slab inscription that was discovered near Dibon (modern Dhiban, Jordan), the ancient region of Moab, in 1868 by Frederick Augustus Klein (see Fig. 51).[33] It is one of the longest monumental stone inscriptions that have survived.[34]

Kleins interest in the stone alerted the local bedouin to its value, and they significantly increased the price from their original agreement. Later, the local tribes refused to let the stone be transported through their territories. Upon hearing of the find, Clermont-Ganneau sent Ya'quµb Karavaca to take paper-mâché impressions (squeeze) of the inscription. Soon the Turkish authorities were prepared to send soldiers into Transjordan to take the stone by force, which led to the local tribes breaking the stone into several fragmented pieces and distributing them among the local tribes as fertility amulets.

51. The Mesha Stela (or Moabite Stone).

Louvre Museum, Departement of Oriental Antiquities, Sully Wing, ground floor, room D (AO 5066). © Mbzt/Wikimedia Commons

Quotes from Antiquity

Mesha Stele

In 34 lines of writing, Mesha, King of Moab states:

I am Mesha, son of KMSYT (Kemosh[-yat]), the king of Moab, the Dibonite. My father was king of Moab thirty years, and I reigned after my father.... Omri king of Israel oppressed Moab for many days, for Kemosh was angry with his land. And his son succeeded him, and he also said, "I will oppress Moab". In my days he spoke this, but I prevailed over him and over his house. Now Israel utterly perished forever. Now Omri had taken possession of the land of Madaba. And he dwelt in it his days and half the days of his son, forty years.... And I took from there [Kemosh in Qiryat] the vessels of YHWH, and I hauled them before Kemosh. Now the king of Israel had built Yahaz and dwelt in it while fighting against me. But Kemosh drove him out from before me and I took from Moab two hundred men, its whole division, and I led it up against Yahaz and I seized it to add it to Dibon.... Now as for Hawronen, the Ho[use of Da]vid dwelt in it and... Kemosh said to me, "Go down, fight against Horonain", so I went down and... Kemosh [retur]ned it in my days.

ANET 320–21; *COS* 2.23: 137–38.

However, Clermont-Ganneau and Charles Warren were successful in purchasing some 57 pieces from the locals, which comprised about two-thirds of the original inscription.[35] With many of the pieces still missing, Karavaca's squeeze cast is an important artifact in its own right in preserving this significant discovery.[36]

The stela dates to 850–840 BC and speaks of Moabite/Israelite relations in the ninth cent. BC, the time of King Ahab and King David.[37] Moab was a vassal state during the time of David and Solomon, but after 930 BC it rebelled against Israel. When King Ahab died in 853 BC, Moab was again under Israel's control, though once

---

[33] John Andrew Dearman, ed., *Studies in the Mesha Inscription and Moab*, SBL Archaeology and Biblical Studies 2 (Atlanta, Ga.: Scholars Press, 1989).

[34] James Maxwell Miller, "The Moabite Stone as a Memorial Stela," *PEQ* 106 (1974): 9–18.

[35] Charles Warren, "The Moabite Stone," *PEFSt.* 1, no. 4 (1869): 169–82.

[36] Siegfried H. Horn, "Why the Moabite Stone Was Blown to Pieces: 9th Century B.C. Inscription Adds New Dimension to Biblical Account of Mesha's Rebellion," *BAR* 12, no. 3 (June 1986): 50–61.

[37] P. M. Michèle Daviau and Paul-Eugène Dion, "Moab Comes to Life," *BAR* 28, no. 1 (2002): 38.

again preparing to rebel.[38] Second Kings states: "Now Mesha king of Moab was a sheep breeder, and he had to deliver to the king of Israel 100,000 lambs and the wool of 100,000 rams. But when Ahab died, the king of Moab rebelled against the king of Israel (2 Kgs 3:4–5 ESV)."[39]

Not only does it contain one of the earliest mentions of Yahweh, the God of Israel, but also mentions the "house of David,"[40] confirming the statement of 2 Kings 3:4–5 as historically accurate. It is presently housed in the Louvre Museum, Department of Oriental Antiquities (AO 5066).

The Tel Dan Stele

With the discovery of the Tel Dan stele in 1993,[41] by Avraham Biran, the extreme minimalist view of Ussishkin and others was challenged, since the phrase "house of David"[42] (Heb. *bytdwd*) was identified as part of an inscription that dates to the time of King David (841 BC; 2 Kgs 8:7–13; 8:28–29; 13:1–3).[43]

While this inscription was widely debated, Grabbe maintains that "it is now widely regarded (a) as genuine and (b) as referring to the Davidic dynasty and the Aramaic kingdom of Damascus."[44] It mentions the biblical names of the "house of David," Ben-hadad II, Hazael, Joram, Ahab, Ahaziah, Jehoram, and Jehu. Deconstructionists have challenged the reading of the Tel Dan Stele, but the accomplished Anson Rainey, Professor Emeritus of Ancient Near Eastern Cultures and Semitic Linguistics at Tel Aviv University, has commented that "[Philip]

52. Tel Dan inscription.
Israel Museum, Jerusalem (IAA 1993-3162; IAA 1996-125)

---

[38] Gary A. Rendsburg, "A Reconstruction of Moabite and Israelite History," *Journal of the Ancient Near Eastern Society of Columbia University* 13 (1981): 67–73; John A. Emerton, "The Value of the Moabite Stone as an Historical Source," *VT* 52, no. 4 (2002): 483–92; André LeMaire, "The Mesha Stele and the Omri Dynasty," in *Ahab Agonistes: The Rise and Fall of the Omri Dynasty*, ed. Lester L. Grabbe, The Library of Hebrew Bible/Old Testament Studies 421 (New York, N.Y.: Continuum International, 2007), 135–44; Brian B. Schmidt, "Neo-Assyrian and Syro-Palestinian Texts I: The Moabite Stone," in *Ancient Near East: Historical Sources in Translation*, ed. Mark W. Chavalas, Blackwell Sourcebooks in Ancient History (Oxford: Wiley & Sons, 2006), 311–12; William F. Albright, "Palestinian Inscriptions: Moabite Stone," in *The Ancient Near East: An Anthology of Texts and Pictures*, ed. James B. Pritchard (Princeton, NJ: Princeton University Press, 2010), 287; Alviero Niccacci, "The Stele of Mesha and the Bible: Verbal System and Narrativity," *Orientalia* 63, no. 3 (1994): 226–48; Gibson, *Textbook of Syrian Semitic Inscriptions*, 1:1:71–84.

[39] Philip D. Stern, "Of Kings and Moabites: History and Theology in 2 Kings 3 and the Mesha Inscription," *Hebrew Union College Annual* 64 (1993): 1–14.

[40] André LeMaire, "'House of David' Restored in Moabite Inscription," *BAR* 20, no. 3 (1994): 30–37.

[41] While this inscription was widely debated, Grabbe maintains that "it is now widely regarded (a) as genuine and (b) as referring to the Davidic dynasty and the Aramaic kingdom of Damascus." Lester L. Grabbe, *Ahab Agonistes: The Rise and Fall of the Omri Dynasty* (New York, N.Y.: Continuum International, 2007), 333; Alan R. Millard, "The Tell Dan Stele," in *The Context of Scripture: Canonical Compositions from the Biblical World*, ed. William W. Hallo and K. Lawson Younger, vol. 2 (Leiden: Brill Academic, 2002), 2:161–62.

[42] Kitchen also points out the possible mention of the "highland/heights of David" in the Sheshonq Relief. Kenneth A. Kitchen, "A Possible Mention of David in the Late Tenth Century BCE, and Deity *Dod as Dead as the Dodo," *JSOT*, no. 76 (1997): 39–41.

[43] Avraham Biran and Joseph Naveh, "An Aramaic Stele Fragment from Tel Dan," *IEJ* 43, no. 2/3 (January 1, 1993): 81–98; "The Tel Dan Inscription: A New Fragment," *IEJ* 45, no. 1 (January 1, 1995): 1–18; Millard, "The Tell Dan Stele," 161–62; George Athas, *The Tel Dan Inscription: A Reappraisal and a New Introduction*, JSOTSup 360 (New York, N.Y.: Bloomsbury, 2006); Hallvard Hagelia, *Tel Dan Inscription: A Critical Investigation of Recent Research on Its Palaeography & Philology*, Studia Semitica Upsaliensia 22 (Uppsala: Uppsala Universitet, 2006); Matthew J. Suriano, "The Apology of Hazael: A Literary and Historical Analysis of the Tel Dan Inscription," *JNES* 66, no. 3 (2007): 163–76. See also *COS* 2.39: 161-62.

[44] Grabbe, *Ahab Agonistes*, 333.

Davies and his 'deconstructionists' [Thomas L. Thompson] can safely be ignored by everyone seriously interested in Biblical and ancient Near Eastern studies."[45]

King Achish (705–701 BC)

Achish, the Philistine king of Gath, was so impressed with David that he gave him Ziklag as his home, which David used as his military base for destroying Israel's Philistine enemies to the south (1 Sam 27). Up until this point in Israel's history they did not have any iron technology and even had to go to the Philitines to get their tools sharpened (1 Sam 13:19–21). The iron technology which appears in the archaeological record of Israel[46] likely was acquired while David was living among the Philistines (2 Sam 5:17–25).[47]

The Ekron Royal Dedicatory Inscription

The Ekron Royal Dedicatory Inscription (705–701 BC; IAA 1997–2912)[48] is a limestone slab discovered in 1996 during the excavations at Tel Miqne,[49] that confirms its identification as Ekron, one of the five Philistine capital cities described in the Bible.[50] Gitin, Dothan and Naveh describe the implications of this important discovery:

53. Ekron Royal Dedicatory Inscription

Israel Museum, Jerusalem (IAA 1997–2912). Courtesy of Greg Gulbrandsen

> The inscription is unique because it contains the name of a biblical city and five of its rulers, two of whom are mentioned as kings in texts other than the Bible. The only such inscription found in situ in a securely defined, datable archaeological context, it has far-reaching implications for our understanding of the history of Ekron and Philistia.[51]

Quotes from Antiquity

Ekron Inscription states:

The temple (which) he built, 'kys [Achish, Ikausu] son of Padi, son of Ysd, son of Ada, son of Ya'ir, ruler of Ekron, for Ptgyh his lady. May she bless him, and prote[ct] him, and prolong his days, and bless his [l]and . . .

Gitin, Dothan, and Naveh, "Royal Dedicatory Inscription," 9.

Scholars generally accept that the name Ikausu (Heb. *'kys*) in the Ekron inscription is the same as Achish, the Philistine king of Gath from the time of Saul and Solomon (1 Sam 21:11–16; 27:2; 1 Kgs 2:39–40; 2 Kgs 18–

[45] Anson F. Rainey, "The 'House of David' and the House of the Deconstructionists," *BAR* 20, no. 6 (1994): 47.

[46] Paula McNutt, *The Forging of Israel: Iron Technology, Symbolism and Tradition in Ancient Society* (London: A&C Black, 1990), 216–18.

[47] Ray Vander Laan, *Faith Lessons on the Promised Land: Crossroads of the World* (Grand Rapids: Zondervan, 1999), 141; Walton, Matthews, and Chavalas, *IVP Bible Background Commentary: OT*, 317.

[48] Peter James, "The Date of the Ekron Temple Inscription: A Note," *IEJ* 55, no. 1 (January 1, 2005): 90–93.

[49] See the official website for up-to-date publications: http://www.aiar.org/tel-miqne-ekron.f. See also *COS* 2.42.

[50] Neal Bierling, *Tel Miqne-Ekron: Report on the 1995–1996 Excavations in Field XNW: Areas 77, 78, 79, 89, 90, 101, 102—Iron Age I*, ed. Seymour Gitin, Tel Miqne-Ekron Limited Edition Series 7 (Jerusalem, Israel: W. F. Albright Institute of Archaeological Research, 1998); Seymour Gitin, Trude Dothan, and Joseph Naveh, "A Royal Dedicatory Inscription from Ekron," *IEJ* 47, no. 1/2 (1997): 9.

[51] Seymour Gitin, Trude Dothan, and Joseph Naveh, "Ekron Identity Confirmed: A Unique Royal Inscription Offers Clues to Early Philistine History," *Archaeology* 51, no. 1 (1998): 30.

19).[52]

> And David rose and fled that day from Saul and went to Achish the king of Gath. And the servants of Achish said to him, "Is not this David the king of the land? Did they not sing to one another of him in dances, 'Saul has struck down his thousands, and David his ten thousands'?" And David took these words to heart and was much afraid of Achish the king of Gath. So he changed his behavior before them and pretended to be insane in their hands and made marks on the doors of the gate and let his spittle run down his beard. Then Achish said to his servants, "Behold, you see the man is mad. Why then have you brought him to me? Do I lack madmen, that you have brought this fellow to behave as a madman in my presence? Shall this fellow come into my house?" (1 Sam. 21:10–15).

Even if the Achish of the Ekron inscription is not the same person as the Achish that lived during David's time, it certainly demonstrates the uniformity of names that survived throughout Philistine culture.

KING SOLOMON

King Solomon (also called Jedidiah; ca. 970 to 931 BC), the son of David, was the third king of the United Monarchy.[53] He is known for his wisdom, wealth and power along with his extensive building projects. For example, he is attributed with the building of the First Temple in Jerusalem during the first seven years of his reign, while Solomon's palace was constructed over the next thirteen years. The furniture for the temple was made while Solomon's house was being built. Then finally, after twenty years, Solomon's temple was dedicated to Yahweh (1 Kgs 8:27).[54]

However, his sin of idolatry and desertion of Yahweh ultimately led to the kingdom splitting in two (Israel under Jeroboam I and Judah under Rehoboam) during the reign of his son Rehoboam (932/931 BC).[55]

The Pomegranate Inscription

Perhaps one of the most famous and controversial artifacts is what is called the "Ivory Pomegranate," (see Fig. 54) which came to the world's attention in 1979 from an antiquities shop in Jerusalem. It was there that it was announced to the world and published by the famous French epigrapher, André LeMaire.[56] Although it is a small artifact (43 mm or 1.68" high) it contains an inscription that is important if authentic, since it is reportedly translated as "Belonging to the Temp[le of Yahwe]h, holy to the priests."[57] From the style of the texts it would date to the eighth cent. BC and would be the only evidence of the Temple of Solomon (1 Kgs 6:1–9) in existence

54. A photo of the re-constructed Ivory Pomegranate as if fully intact. Original on display in the Israel Museum (IMJ 88.80.129). Wikimedia Commons

---

[52] Ibid., 11.

[53] H. G. M. Williamson, "The Accession of Solomon in the Books of Chronicles," *VT* 26, no. 3 (1976): 351–61.

[54] George Aaron Barton, "Temple of Solomon," in *The Jewish Encyclopedia*, ed. Isidore Singer et al. (New York, N.Y.: Funk & Wagnalls, 1906), 98–101.

[55] Peter J. Leithart, *A House for My Name: A Survey of the Old Testament* (Moscow, Idaho: Canon, 2000), 157.

[56] André LeMaire, "Une Inscription Paléo-Hébraïque Sur Grenade En Ivoire," *RB* 88 (1981): 236–39; "Probable Head of Priestly Scepter from Solomon's Temple Surfaces in Jerusalem," *BAR* 10, no. 2 (1984): 24–29.

[57] Hershel Shanks, "The Pomegranate Scepter Head—From the Temple of the Lord or from a Temple of Asherah?," *BAR* 18, no. 3 (1992): 42. See also *COS* 2.48: 173.

if proven authentic,[58] hence the debate over it being a forgery.[59]

It was purchased by the Israel Museum in 1988 for $550,000 and claimed to be authentic by the senior professor of archaeology at Hebrew University, Nahman Avigad and others.[60] However, one of his students, Aharon Kempinski, among others, have challenged his claim and argued that it was a scepter head from the temple of Asherah.[61] The debate over its authenticity is ongoing.[62] If it is found to be authentic, then it would contain the oldest mention of Solomon's Temple.

55. Drawing of one of the Moussaieff "3 Shekel" Ostraca that mentions the House of Yahweh.

The 3 Shekel Ostraca

The Moussaieff[63] or "3 Shekel" Ostraca has been dated to the seventh to ninth cent. BC and mentions a command by king Josiah of Judah (640–609 BC) to deliver three shekels of Tarshish silver to the House of Yahweh,[64] which would make it the earliest mention of the Solomonic Temple.[65]

Quotes from Antiquity

3 Shekel Ostraca

1. As Ashyahu [variant of Josiah] the king has
2. ordered you to give by the hand of
3. [Ze] charyahu silver of Tarshish
4. to the House of YHWH
5. three shekels..

Eph'al and Naveh, "Remarks on the Recently Published Moussaieff Ostraca," 269.

However, its authenticity has been questioned,[66] and Christopher Rollston, an

[58] See Hershel Shanks "Fudging with Forgeries," *BAR*, November/December 2010; Strata, "Accused BAR Editor Replies," *BAR*, May/June 2009; "How an Israeli Forgery Committee Operates," *BAR*, March/April 2009; "Is This Inscription Fake? You Decide," *BAR*, September/October 2007.

[59] Yuval Goren et al., "The Inscribed Ivory Pomegranate from the Israel Museum Examined Again," *IEJ* 57 (2007): 87–95.

[60] Nahman Avigad, "An Inscribed Ivory Pomegranate from the 'House of the Lord' [Hebrew]," *Qadmoniot* 22, no. 3–4 (1989): 95–102; "The Inscribed Pomegranate from the 'House of the Lord,'" *The Israel Museum Journal* 8 (1989): 7–16; "The Inscribed Pomegranate from the 'House of the Lord,'" *BA* 53 (1990): 157–66; "The Inscribed Pomegranate from the 'House of the Lord,'" in *Ancient Jerusalem Revealed*, ed. Hillel Geva (Jerusalem, Israel: Israel Exploration Society, 1994), 128–37; "It Is Indeed a Pomegranate from the 'Temple of Yahweh,' (in Hebrew)," *Qadmoniot* 24 (1991): 60; Yuval Goren et al., "A Re-Examination of the Inscribed Ivory Pomegranate from the Israel Museum," *IEJ* 55, no. 3 (2005): 3–20; Yuval Goren et al., "Authenticity Examination of the Ivory Pomegranate Bearing a Palaeo-Hebrew Dedication Inscription from the Israel Museum," *IEJ* 55, no. 1 (2005): 3–20; Goren et al., "The Inscribed Ivory Pomegranate from the Israel Museum Examined Again," 3–20.

[61] Aharon Kempinski, "Is It Really a Pomegranate from the 'Temple of Yahweh?' (in Hebrew)," *Qadmoniot* 23, no. 3–4 (1991): 126; André LeMaire, "A Re-Examination of the Inscribed Pomegranate: A Rejoinder," *IEJ* 56, no. 2 (2006): 167–74.

[62] Hershel Shanks, "First Person: A New Target," *BAR* 40, no. 6 (2014): n.p.

[63] The ostraca was named after Shlomo Moussaieff, the London antiquities dealer who purchased it from the Israelis antiquities dealer Oded Golan.

[64] *COS* 2.50: 174-75. Pierre Bordreuil, Felice Israel, and Dennis Pardee, "Deux Ostraca Paléo-Hébreux de La Collection Sh. Moussaieff," *Semitica* 46 (1996): 49–76; James M. Lindenberger, *Ancient Aramaic and Hebrew Letters*, 2nd ed., Writings from the Ancient World 14 (Atlanta, Ga.: SBL, 2003), 111.

[65] Hershel Shanks, "Three Shekels for the Lord, Ancient Inscription Records Gift to Solomon's Temple," *BAR* 23, no. 6 (1997): 28–32; Pierre Bordreuil, Felice Israel, and Dennis Pardee, "King's Command and Widow's Plea: Two New Hebrew Ostraca of the Biblical Period," *NEA* 61 (1998): 2–13; Bob Becking, "Does a Recently Published Paleo-Hebrew Inscription Refer to the Solomonic Temple?," *BN* 92 (1998): 5–11.

[66] Ibid., 269–73; H. T. Land and G. Feucht, "Expertise, Sample No. PE 257-1, Sample No. PE 257-5," *Undated and Unpublished Report Submitted by Aventis Research & Technologies*, 2003, 1–15.

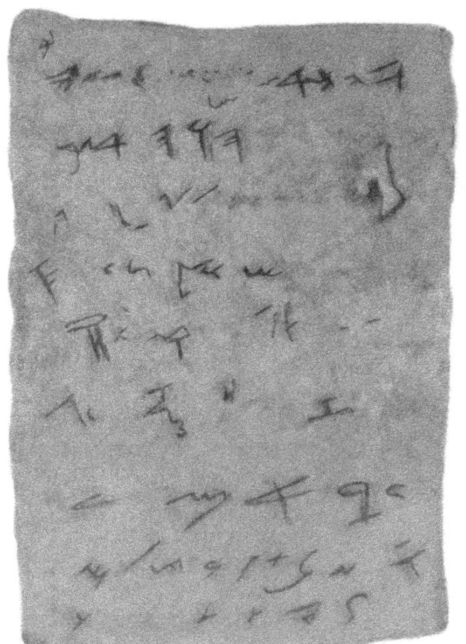

56. The Arad Ostracon (letter 18) from Tel Arad mentioning the "house of Yahweh."

Israel Museum (IAA 1967-669). © Greg Gulbrandsen and enhanced by David E. Graves

authority on Northwest Semitic inscriptions, states: "I am confident beyond a reasonable doubt that both of the Moussaieff Ostraca were indeed written by the same person, and that both are modern forgeries."[67]

However, Shanks reports that other notable palaeographers, such as Frank Cross, P. Kyle McCarter and André LeMaire, all verify it as genuine.[68]

The Arad House of Yahweh Ostracon

Among some 100 Paleo-Hebrew inscriptions found at the excavation of Tel Arad was one that is known as the House of Yahweh ostracon (No. 18; see Fig. 56).[69] It was discovered by Yohanan Aharoni in 1962 in the Israelite Temple at Arad, with the ostracon dating to the sixth cent. BC.[70]

Since the Arad Israelite Temple was destroyed in the eighth cent. BC[71] it is believed that the ostracon refers to the place from where the message was sent, the Temple in Jerusalem.[72] It is now the second oldest mention of Solomon's temple, after the "3 shekel" ostracon, which is the oldest. Presently ostracon 18 is housed in The Israel Museum in Jerusalem.[73]

> *Quotes from Antiquity*
>
> **The Arad Ostracon**
>
> To my lord Eliashib [commander of the Fortress], may Yahweh ask for thy peace. And now: give Shermaryahu [a measure of flour] . . . and to the Kerosite give [a measure of flour]. . . And regarding the matter which thou commandest me - all is well. He dwells in the house [temple] of Yahweh [Ostracon 18, line 1–9]
>
> Aharoni, "Arad: Its Inscriptions and Temple," 16

NORTHERN KINGDOM – ISRAEL

The status of the Northern Kingdom of Israel as a well-established state in the ninth to eight cent. BC (*ca.* 922–721 BC) is

[67] Rollston, "Non-Provenanced Epigraphs I: Pillaged Antiquities, Northwest Semitic Forgeries, and Protocols for Laboratory Tests," 173.

[68] Hershel Shanks, "The Three Shekels and Widow's Plea Ostraca: Real or Fake?," *BAR* 29, no. 3 (June 2003): 40–45; "Three Shekels for the Lord, Ancient Inscription Records Gift to Solomon's Temple," 28–32; Israel Eph'al and Joseph Naveh, "Remarks on the Recently Published Moussaieff Ostraca," *IEJ* 48, no. 3/4 (1998): 269.

[69] Harry M. Orlinksy, *Israel Exploration Journal Reader Selected with a Prolegomenon* (New York, N.Y.: Ktav, 1981), 1:7; Davies et al., *Ancient Hebrew Inscriptions*, 1:17.

[70] Yohanan Aharoni and Joseph Naveh, *Arad Inscriptions [Hebrew]* (Jerusalem, Israel: Israel Exploration Society, 1975); Yohanan Aharoni, *Arad Inscriptions* (Jerusalem, Israel: Israel Exploration Society, 1981); R. B. Lawton, "Arad Ostraca," ed. David Noel Freedman et al., *ABD* (New York, N.Y.: Doubleday, 1996), 336–37.

[71] Dale W. Manor and Gary A. Herion, "Arad (Place)," ed. David Noel Freedman et al., *ABD* (New York, N.Y.: Doubleday, 1996), 334.

[72] Aharoni, "Arad: Its Inscriptions and Temple," 16.

[73] Yohanan Aharoni, "Arad: Its Inscriptions and Temple," *BA* 31, no. 1 (1968): 16; André LeMaire, *Inscriptions Hébraïques. I. Les Ostraca.*, vol. 1, Littératures Anciennes Du Proche-Orient 9 (Paris: Les Éditions du Cerf, 1977), 1:145–253; Aharoni and Naveh, *Arad Inscriptions [Hebrew]*, 32–38, 44; F. W. Dobbs-Allsopp et al., *Hebrew Inscriptions: Texts from the Biblical Period of the Monarchy with Concordance* (New Haven, Conn.: Yale University Press, 2004), 37–41.

accepted by most scholars due to the mention of king Ahab in the Kurkh stele monolithic inscription of Shalmaneser III (853 BC; see Fig. 58), that mentions Ahab's large number of chariots in the battle against the Assyrians at the battle of Qarqar. Inscriptional evidence is also found in the Mesha Stele, that refers to King Ahab's conquest of northern Moab, in the Tel Dan inscription (see Fig. 52), that likely mentions Jehoram, the last king of the Omride dynasty; and on the Black Obelisk of Shalmaneser III (see Figs. 59, 60), on which King Jehu's surrender to the Assyrian king is mentioned.[74]

Mazar also reports on the archaeological evidence for the existence of Israel in the ninth and eighth cent. BC:

> Excavations at a number of other major cities in the Northern Kingdom like Dan, Hazor, Megiddo, Yoqne'am, Taanack, Beth-shean, Reḥōv, Dothan, Tell el-Far'ah (Tirzah), Shechem, Dor, and Gezer as well as surface surveys in the Galilee and Samaria hills and excavations in village sites, farms and citadels, reveal a flourishing kingdom with a complex and dense hierarchical settlement system, immense population growth, expanding international trade relations, a flourishing artistic tradition and the increasing use of writing during the ninth and eighth centuries.[75]

Thus, scholars largely accept the existence of the Northern Kingdom of Israel.

Jeroboam I (930–909 BC)

After Solomon died, the people rebelled and the Nation was divided into the Northern Kingdom (Judah) and the Southern Kingdom (Israel). In the North, Jeroboam I ruled over the ten tribes that rebelled and established his capital in Bethel (1 Kgs 11:26–14:20).

Jeroboam's name means "he who contends for justice for the people" or "may the people multiply." He ruled the Northern Kingdom of Israel from 930–909 BC. He began his career under Solomon's reign as his building manager (1 Kgs 11:28). At this time Ahijah, a prophet from Shiloh, confronted Jeroboam, tore his own coat into twelve pieces, and gave ten of them to Jeroboam. This was to indicate that ten of the twelve tribe were to be ruled by Jeroboam (1 Kgs 11:29–39). Jeroboam tried to take the kingdom at once, but this failed, and he fled to find refuge in Egypt, where Pharaoh Shishak treated him kindly.

After Solomon's death, Jeroboam returned to learn that the tribes would meet at Shechem to make Solomon's son Rehoboam their king. The Southern Kingdom of Judah took Rehoboam as their king, but the ten northern tribes were unhappy with the harsh treatment and high taxes, and Jeroboam used this to sway the people. He promised to lighten the load but never delivered. Callously the ten tribes revolted against the house of David and crowned Jeroboam as their king. He set up his royal residence at Zeredah.

It did not take long for Jeroboam to lead the people astray. It bothered him that the temple in Jerusalem, outside of his territory, was supposed to be the religious centre for his people. So he established a centre of worship of his own at Bethel and Dan, erecting a golden calf to represent God's presence (1 Kgs 15:26, 34; 16:19, 31).

He also appointed men to carry out the cultic activities who were not from the tribe of Levi. He introduced his own calendar of festivals and personally served as High Priest (1 Kgs

---

[74] Brad E. Kelle, "What's in a Name? Neo-Assyrian Designations for the Northern Kingdom and Their Implications for Israelite History and Biblical Interpretation," *JBL* 121, no. 4 (Winter 2002): 636–66; Albert Kirk Grayson, *Assyrian Rulers of the Early First Millennium BC I (858-745 BC)*, vol. 1, The Royal Inscriptions of Mesopotamia: Assyrian Periods 2 (Toronto, Can.: University of Toronto Press, 1991).

[75] Amihai Mazar, "The Divided Monarchy: Comments on Some Archaeological Issues," in *The Quest for the Historical Israel*, ed. Israel Finkelstein and Brian B. Schmidt, Archaeology and Biblical Studies 17 (Atlanta, Ga.: SBL, 2007), 163.

12:25–33). While he was at the altar, he was approached by a prophet from Judah who told him that a future king from David's line, named Josiah, would sacrifice Bethel's priests on that very altar. And a sign was given; the altar split and the ashes fell off it.

Jeroboam fortified Shechem and made it his capital, but later moved it to Tirzah (1 Kgs 14:17). When Egypt's Pharaoh Shishak invaded Judah in the south, they also made inroads into the Northern Kingdom, which is evident from the inscription on the temple at Karnak, which gives a list of the towns captured by him (see Figs. 42, 43).

When the prophet Ahijah was old and blind, Jeroboam sent the queen to inquire about an illness that had taken the king's oldest son. The queen went in disguise but could not fool God, who reported through his prophet that the people whom Jeroboam had seduced into idolatry would be uprooted and taken beyond the river, and that his son would not live. Jeroboam died leaving behind a heritage of idolatry that would affect all of the other kings of Israel.

The Altar of Jeroboam I

A high place podium (Heb. *bamah*) was uncovered at Tel Dan from the time of Jeroboam I (931 BC) by Avraham Biran in 1975.[76] Most archaeologists agree that this was the one Jeroboam constructed to house the Golden Calf altar (1 Kgs 12:28–30 also at Bethel) in order for the Israelites to have their own holy place and no longer keep going to Jerusalem to worship. These high places were forbidden by Hebrew law because they were used for abominable child sacrifice ceremonies. The sites were ordered to be destroyed (Deut 12:2–3), so this site is particularly important. In addition to the four-horned altar[77] other religious artifacts were uncovered, including three iron incense shovels, an iron incense holder, and a small horned altar.[78] Laughlin describes the three periods revealed at the Bamah:

57. Covered High Place of Jeroboam where the golden calf was stored at Dan.

> The Sacred Area or *temenos* at Dan is a large complex over a half-acre in size. The central open-air platform of the Sacred Area went through three phases during the Israelite period. Biran has identified the three phases of the platform as Bamah A, Bamah B, and Bamah C.
>
> Bamah A is probably the one built by Jeroboam in the late tenth century B.C. (This Jeroboam is known as Jeroboam I to distinguish him from a later Israelite king of the same name.) Bamah A consists of an open-air platform approximately 22 feet wide and 60 feet long constructed of dressed limestone blocks on a base of rough stones. Only two courses of Bamah A have survived. It was destroyed by a fierce fire so hot that it turned the edges of the stones red. From this phase of the sanctuary Biran found the remains of incense burners, a decorated incense stand, the heads of two male figurines, and a bowl decorated with a sign resembling a trident. The bowl contained fragmentary bones of sheep, goats

---

[76] Avraham Biran, "Tel Dan," *BA* 37, no. 2 (1974): 26–51; "Two Discoveries at Tel Dan," *IEJ* 30, no. 1–2 (1980): 89–98; Andrew R. Davis, *Tel Dan in Its Northern Cultic Context* (John Hopkins University: UMI Dissertations, 2010).

[77] Avraham Biran, "An Israelite Horned Altar at Dan," *BA* 37, no. 4 (1974): 106–107.

[78] Avraham Biran, "Sacred Spaces: Of Standing Stones, High Places and Cult Objects at Tel Dan," *BAR* 24, no. 5 (1998): 38–41, 44–45, 70.

> and gazelles which had probably been sacrificed at the sanctuary.
>
> During the first half of the ninth century B.C. the open-air platform was rebuilt and expanded into an almost square structure measuring 60 by 62 feet (Bamah B). The masonry of this bamah, including dressed stones with bosses laid in header and stretcher fashion compares well with the royal buildings from the same period found at Megiddo, and similar buildings from Samaria. This masonry is among the finest found in Israel.[79]
>
> A nearly complete horned incense altar was uncovered in an adjacent court which may come from this time period. The altar, with one horn perfectly preserved, is about 16 inches high and shows evidence of long use. We may assume that many of the activities associated with the bamah, including the burning of incense, took place in courtyards surrounding the open-air platform where this incense altar was found.
>
> The third stage of the bamah's history (Bamah C) reflects the period of the first half of the eighth century B.C. At this time a set of monumental steps, about 27 feet long, was built against the southern face of the open-air platform. The upper three courses of these steps were added or repaired in Hellenistic or Roman times, indicating that this Sacred Area continued to be used for cultic purposes perhaps to the turn of the era. Other evidence—additions to walls and new rooms—confirms this conclusion....
>
> In any event it is clear that this entire area at Tel Dan was an important Israelite cultic center. Whether it is the beth bamoth referred to in 1 Kings 12:31, as Biran believes, will no doubt continue to be debated by scholars for years to come. Although the Biblical record is silent concerning the specific cultic acts performed at Dan and does not even specify what use was made of the Golden Calf which Jeroboam made, the archaeological evidence suggests that a large, open-air platform was used, that there were altars, incense offerings, votive offerings involving figurines, and some kind of water purification or libation rituals.[80]

King Ahab (874–853 BC)

Ahab is the compound name for "father and brother". Ahab had married a foreigner, Jezebel, who practiced idolatry. Ahab reigned for twenty-two years from 874–853 BC. He expanded the political and commercial interest of Israel but failed in the spiritual area of Israel's obedience to the covenant (1 Kgs 16:30).

Ahab's wife, Jezebel, was the daughter of the king of Tyre (1 Kgs 16:31). His marriage had been arranged by his father Omri as a political move to strengthen Israel's place in world politics but actually it only served to bring the house of Israel down in idolatry. Jezebel worshipped the Tryian God *Melqart*, and promoted the worship of Baal in Israel by supporting 450 Baal prophets and 400 prophets of the goddess Asherah (1 Kgs 18:19). Baal worship was introduced into the temple at Samaria. Jezebel lived ten years longer than King Ahab, allowing her to exercise a large and negative influence on Israel's spiritual life.

Ahab sought peace with Judah through the marriage of his daughter Athaliah to Joram king of Judah. It produced co-operation between the two Kingdoms, which resulted in the recapturing of Ramoth-gilead, though not before Ahab lost his life (1 Kgs 22:2–40).

Ahab's military campaigns included submitting the Moabite people to his rule, as recorded on the famous Moabite Stone (see Fig. 51). He was also involved in three campaigns with the Syrian king, Ben-hadad. His name is also mentioned on the Kurkh stele Monolith Inscription of Shalmaneser III of Assyria (see Fig. 58).

Despite Israel's idolatry, God did not abandon them. God raised up a "troubler of Israel" in the prophet Elijah. Elijah called Israel back to the service of Yahweh and, after three and a half years of drought, he challenged the prophets of Baal on Mt. Carmel, destroying them as

---

[79] See also - Beersheba Altar

[80] John Charles Hugh Laughlin, "The Remarkable Discoveries at Tel Dan," *BAR* 7, no. 5 (1981): 20–37.

they gathered around the altar. Ahab himself was confronted at Naboth's vineyard, which Ahab had unjustly taken. Elijah placed a curse on the Omri Dynasty, and prophesied that he would be destroyed in battle. So he would not be recognised by the Syrians in battle, Ahab disguised himself, but a stray arrow pierced his armour and he died from his wounds on his way back to Samaria in his own chariot.

The Kurkh Stele Monolith Inscription

The Kurkh Monoliths (879–853 BC) are two Assyrian stelae from the reign of Ashurnasirpal II and his son Shalmaneser III,[81] discovered by John G. Taylor in 1861 at the site of Kurkh (modern Üçtepe, Diyarbakir Turkey).[82] They are now both on display in the British Museum.[83]

Besides a large relief of Ashurnasirpal II and his son, both stelae record the annals of each king.[84] The Shalmaneser III monolith contains a description of the victory (sixth year) of Shalmaneser III at the battle of Qarqar (also Karkar) on the Orontes River (northern Syria) in 853/854 BC over a Syrian allied coalition led by "Adad (ilu IM)–'idri (= Hadadezer) of Damascus, with Ahab of Israel[85] and other kings as vassals."[86]

58. Kurkh Monolith of Ashurnasirpal II
The Trustees of the British Museum (ME 118883)

The battle of Qarqar does not appear in the OT and various explanations have been offered to place it into the narrative. However, according to the OT, Ahab overthrew Ben-hadad, the Syrian leader, with just 7,000 troops when Ben-hadad lay siege to Samaria (under the leadership of thirty-two kings, 1 Kgs 20:1–34).[87] Ahab's base of operation for his troops was likely the city of Jezreel.[88] Luckenbill agrees with this popular view, though he also provides his own explanation: "according to the prevailing interpretation of the Hebrew account in the light of

[81] Shigeo Yamada, *The Construction of the Assyrian Empire: A Historical Study of the Inscriptions of Shalmaneser III (859-824 BC) Relating to His Campaigns to the West* (Leiden: Brill, 2000), 14–15, 359–79, also 161–62; Albert Kirk Grayson, *Assyrian Rulers of the Early First Millennium BC II (858-745 BC)*, vol. 3, The Royal Inscriptions of Mesopotamia: Assyrian Periods 3 (Toronto, Can.: University of Toronto Press, 1987), 11–24; Ada Cohen and Steven E. Kangas, eds., *Assyrian Reliefs from the Palace of Ashurnasirpal II: A Cultural Biography* (Hanover, N.H.: University of New England, 2010).

[82] John George Taylor, "Travels in Kurdistan, with Notices of the Sources of the Eastern and Western Tigris, and Ancient Ruins in Their Neighbourhood," *Journal of the Royal Geographical Society of London* 35 (1865): 21–58.

[83] *Assyrian Sculptures in the British Museum: From Shalmaneser III to Sennacherib* (London: The British Museum, 1938), 5. pl. 1.

[84] Daniel David Luckenbill, *Ancient Records of Assyria and Babylon: Historical Records of Assyria from Sargon to the End*, vol. 2 (Chicago, Ill.: University Of Chicago Press, 1927), 200–52.

[85] Gary A. Rendsburg, "Israel Without the Bible," in *The Hebrew Bible: New Insights and Scholarship*, ed. Frederick E. Greenspahn, Jewish Studies in the Twenty-First Century (New York, N.Y.: New York University Press, 2007), 10; Jonathan M. Golden, *Ancient Canaan and Israel: New Perspectives*, Understanding Ancient Civilizations (Santa Barbara, Calf.: ABC-CLIO, 2004), 275.

[86] Daniel David Luckenbill, "Benhadad and Hadadezer," *AJSL* 27, no. 3 (1911): 267.

[87] Luckenbill, "Benhadad and Hadadezer," 267–83.

[88] David Ussishkin, "Jezreel—Where Jezebel Was Thrown to the Dogs," *BAR* 36, no. 4 (2010): 32–42.

the Assyrian records, the 'two years' truce mentioned in I Kings 22:1 follow immediately upon the defeat of Ben-hadad at Aphek, and leave room for Ahab's presence at Karkar."[89]

As Luckenbill points out, according to the Assyrian account, Ahab was an ally of the king of Damascus. Wiseman provides a possible explanation:

> Aram turned south, perhaps in an attempt to gain new trade routes, since the north had been cut off by the wars of the Assyrian Ashur-naṣirapli II (883–859 BC) and his successor Shalmaneser III (859–829 BC). Some think the wars recorded here took place early in Ahab's reign, to allow time for the mellowing of Israel's relation with Aram when Ahab contributed to the coalition which faced Assyria at the battle of Qarqar in 853 BC (Bright). Yeivin argues that the first war was early but the second followed after Qarqar, but this is unlikely in view of 22:1. The aggression of Ben-hadad II (Hadadezer, Assyr. Adad-'idri) may have aimed to secure his southern flank while he faced the Assyrian drive to the Mediterranean c. 888–885 BC. There is no need to view the prophetic allusions as secondary, for their interpretation of events is consistent with that of the Deuteronomic historian throughout.[90]

Quotes from Antiquity

Portion of the Annals of Shalmaneser III

I destroyed, devastated, and set fire to Karkar, his royal city. <Irhulêni> brought twelve kings to his support; they came against me to offer battle and fight: 1,200 chariots, 1,200 cavalry, and 20,000 soldiers belonging to Hadad-ezer of Damascus; 700 chariots, 700 cavalry, and 10,000 [or 20,000] soldiers belonging to Irhuleni of Hama; 2,000 chariots, and 10,000 soldiers belonging to Ahab, the Israelite[A-ha-ab-bu Sir-ila-a-a]; 500 soldiers belonging to the Gueans; 1,000 soldiers belonging to the Musreans; 10 chariots and 10,000 soldiers belonging to the Irkanateans; 200 soldiers belonging to Matinuba'il the Arvadite; 200 soldiers belonging to the Usanateans; 30 chariots and [ ],000 soldiers belonging to Adunu-ba'il the Shianean; 1,000 camels belonging to Gindibu' the Arabian; and [ ],000 soldiers [belonging to] Ba'sa, son of Ruhubi, the Ammonite. Trusting in the exalted might which the lord Assur had given me, in the mighty weapons, which Nergal, who goes before me, had presented to me, I battled with them. I routed them from Karkar to the city of Cilzau, killing 14,000 of their soldiers, raining destruction on them like Adad. I scattered their bodies far and wide, and covered the face of the desolate plain with their vast armies. Using my weapons, I made their blood to flow down the valleys(?). The plain was too small to let their bodies fall, the wide countryside was used up in burying them. I spanned the Orontes with their bodies like a bridge(?). In that battle I took from them their chariots, cavalry, and tamed horses).

Luckenbill, Ancient Records of Assyria and Babylon, 200–52

The Kurkh stele of Shalmaneser III verifies the historicity of Ahab, king of Israel and the fact that he had a large army. As Ackerman points out: "The size of Ahab's contribution to the anti-Shalmaneser fighting force at Qarqar indicates, for example, that Israel was still a major military power in Syria-Palestine at the end of the first half of the ninth century B. C. E."[91]

King Jehu (841–814 BC)

Jehu (Heb. "Yahweh is He") was the Son of Jehoshaphat and king of Israel, who reigned from 841–814 BC. He rose to the throne via the words of the prophet Elisha and by killing all of Ahab's household, including Joram, Jezebel and seventy more members of Ahab's house.

---

[89] Luckenbill, "Benhadad and Hadadezer," 276.

[90] Donald J. Wiseman, *1 and 2 Kings: An Introduction and Commentary*, TOTC (Downers Grove, Ill.: IVP Academic, 2008), 187.

[91] Susan Ackerman, "Assyria in the Bible," in *Assyrian Reliefs from the Palace of Ashurnasirpal II: A Cultural Biography*, ed. Ada Cohen and Steven E. Kangas (Hanover, N.H.: University of New England, 2010), 127; Wayne T. Pitard, *Ancient Damascus: A Historical Study of the Syrian City-State from Earliest Times Until Its Fall to the Assyrians in 732 B.C.E.*, New edition edition (Winona Lake, Ind.: Eisenbrauns, 1987), 128; Ron E. Tappy, *The Archaeology of Israelite Samaria, Vol. 2: The Eighth Century BCE*, Harvard Semitic Studies 50 (Winona Lake, Ind.: Eisenbrauns, 2007), 509–10.

Jehu showed great craftiness in destroying the worshippers of Baal. Stating that he was a more zealous follower of Baal than even King Ahab, he announced a special festival that only the devoutest followers of Baal should attend. Following the sacrifice in the temple, Jehu's army was sent in and all inside were put to the sword. Although he eliminated the worship of Baal instigated by Jezebel (2 Kgs 10:28), he did nothing about the worship of the golden calf at Bethel.

59. The Black Obelisk.

Used with permission of the Oriental Institute Museum of the University of Chicago. The original is in the British Museum (ME 118885).

The Black Obelisk

Sir Henry Layard discovered this black limestone obelisk in 1846 during his excavations at Kalhu, the ancient Assyrian capital. The obelisk, now on display in the British Museum, celebrates the military achievements of Shalmaneser III (reigned 858–824 BC; see Fig. 59). More importantly, while there are other Assyrian and Babylonian texts that mention Hebrew kings, this obelisk depicts the earliest surviving picture of an Israelite king. One of the panel's depicts the Israelite King Jehu bringing tribute to King Shalmaneser III in around 841 BC (see Fig. 60).

However, while the Black Obelisk states that Jehu is the son of Omri, 2 Kings 9:2, 14 states that Jehu is the son of Jehoshaphat, the son of Nimshi. How does one reconcile this apparent contradiction? There are three possible proposed solutions.

> *Quotes from Antiquity*
>
> **The Black Obelisk**
>
> The tribute of Jehu, son of Omri: I received from him silver, gold, a golden bowl, a golden vase with pointed bottom, golden tumblers, golden buckets, tin, a staff for a king [and] wooden *puruhtu* [javelin].
>
> Pritchard, *ANE* 1:192.

First: that one of the two accounts is inaccurate. Either the Black Obelisk is inaccurate as our modern newspapers are often in error,[92] or, as biblical critics would say, the Bible is inaccurate.

60. One of the panel's of the Black Obelisk depicts the Israelite King Jehu bringing tribute to King Shalmaneser III in around 841 BC.

Used with permission of the Oriental Institute Museum of the University of Chicago.

Second: P. Kyle McCarter challenges the reading of the Black Obelisk, stating that it is not Jehu being referred to, but in fact Jehoram (Joram), the grandson of King Omri whom Jehu killed.[93] However, Galil dismisses this interpretation on linguistic grounds.[94]

Third: Tammi Schneider argues that

---

[92] Hal Flemings, *Examining Criticisms of the Bible* (Bloomington, Ind.: AuthorHouse, 2008), 109.

[93] P. Kyle McCarter Jr., " 'Yaw, Son of 'Omri': A Philological Note on Israelite Chronology," *BASOR*, no. 216 (December 1974): 5–7.

[94] Gershon Galil, *The Chronology of the Kings of Israel and Judah* (Leiden: Brill, 1996), 33 n.2.

Jehu may have been a descendant of Omri.[95]

However, even if the mystery is not resolved, the presence of both Omri and Jehu mentioned in an extrabiblical text lends credibility to the notion that they were real historical individuals.

Jeroboam II (793–753 BC)

Jeroboam II (Heb. "he who contends for justice for the people" or "may the people multiply") was perhaps the most outstanding King in the Northern Kingdom, ruling for forty-one years, twelve of them with his father from 793–753 BC. He regained over much of the territory that had been lost in previous conflicts under Jehu and Jehoahaz (2 Kgs 13:17–25). He was able to conquer the Syrian capital of Damascus, recapturing the eastern boundary of the Kingdom as it was in the days of David (1 Chron 13:5). Wealth and prosperity flowed into Israel like it had never before, not since the days of Solomon. The books of Amos, Hosea and Jonah all recount the peace and prosperity.

There was also religion in the land but not the kind which God wanted. The Israelites continued in the sins into which Jeroboam I had led them (Hosea 8:4–6). There was form and structure but no substance. Amos went to Bethel and spoke out against the golden calves, forecasting that Jehovah would punish the household of Jeroboam (Amos 7:9–17). Jeroboam was succeeded on the throne by his weaker son Zechariah.

The Seal of Shema

While excavating Megiddo (1903–1905), Gottlieb Schumacher uncovered a seal made of jasper in 1904 within courtyard no. 1693, near the northern wall, which was engraved with a roaring lion (the symbol of Judah) and accompanied by an inscription which read "(Belonging) to Shema (the) Servant (of) Jeroboam."[96] Most scholars agree that the inscription refers to Jeroboam II, king of Israel (*ca.* 793–753 BC; 1 Kgs 12–14; 2 Kgs 14:23–29).[97]

61. Drawing of the Shema Seal depicting the roaring lion as the symbol of Judah. The inscriptions read "(Belonging) to Shema [top line] (the) Servant (of) Jeroboam [bottom line]."

Replica in the Israel Museum, Jerusalem (Cast 230)

The seal was first published by E. Kautzsch in 1904 and then again by S. A. Cook (1904) followed by Gottlieb Schumacher

[95] Tammi Schneider, "Did King Jehu Kill His Own Family?," *BAR* 21, no. 1 (1995): 26–33, 80–82.

[96] Gottlieb Schumacher and C. Steuernagel, *Tell El-Mutesellim: Text*, vol. 1, A (Leipzig: Haupt, 1908), 99–100, Fig. 147; Gosta W. Ahlstrom, "The Seal of Shema," *SJOT* 7 (1993): 208–15; David Ussishkin, "Gate 1567 at Megiddo and the Seal of Shema, Servant of Jeroboam," in *Scripture and Other Artifacts: Essays on the Bible and Archaeology in Honor of Philip J. King*, ed. Philip J. King et al. (Louisville, Ky.: Westminster/Knox, 1994), 410–28.

[97] S. Yeivin, "The Date of the Seal 'Belonging to Shema' (The) Servant (Of) Jeroboam,'" *JNES* 19, no. 3 (1960): 205; Carl Watzinger, *Tell El-Mutesellim: Die Funde*, vol. 2 (Leipzig, 1929), 66–67.

(1908)[98] and S. Watzinger (1929).[99] It has gone missing somewhere in Istanbul but thankfully casts were made prior to it disappearance.

Balaam, son of Beor

The Deir 'Alla Inscription

The Deir 'Alla Inscription (also called the Bala'am Son of Be'or Inscription)[100] was discovered during the Deir 'Alla excavations under the direction of Henk J. Franken in Jordan in 1967, written in black and red ink on a plastered wall.[101] There were 119 pieces of plaster recovered, dating to 840–760 BC,[102] and today they are displayed in the Amman Museum. The pieces were carefully reconstructed by Jacob Hoftijzer and G. Van der Kooij, of the State University of Leiden, the Netherlands, into two sections believed to be one continuous narrative. The first translation appeared first in Dutch in 1973.[103] It was then made available in a 1976 article in English.[104] A more recent (1986) translation by McCarter is provided here in *Quotes from Antiquity*.[105]

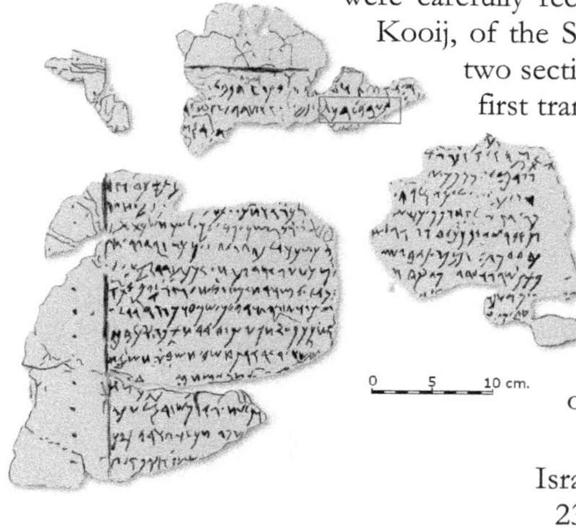

62. Drawing of the opening section of the Balaam text from Tell Deir 'Alla, *ca.* 800 BC. The writing appears to be laid out as a column of a scroll. The name of Balaam is highlighted in the red box.

Original in the Jordan Museum, Amman, Jordan

Millard describes it as "the oldest example of a book in a West Semitic language written with the alphabet, and the oldest piece of Aramaic literature."[106]

Balaam is known from the Bible as a non-Israelite prophet/seer (Num 22–24, 31:8, 16; Deut 23:4, 5; Josh 13:22; 24:9, 10; Neh 13:2; Micah 6:5; 2 Pet 2:15; Jude 11; and Rev 2:14). While some scholars do not believe that this Balaam is the same seer as the one mentioned in the Bible,[107] many scholars consider this "Balaam, son of Beor" to be the same person since the name is stated exactly as

[98] Schumacher and Steuernagel, *Tell El-Mutesellim: Text*, 1, A:99–100.

[99] Watzinger, *Tell El-Mutesellim: Die Funde*, 2:64–67.

[100] Jacob Hoftijzer and G. Van der Kooij, *Aramaic Texts from Deir 'Alla* (Leiden: Brill, 1976); Baruch A. Levine, "The Deir 'Alla Plaster Inscriptions," *JAOS* 101 (1981): 195–205; Jo Ann Hackett, *The Balaam Text from Deir 'Allā*, Harvard Semitic Monographs 31 (Atlanta, Ga.: Scholars Press, 1980); William H. Shea, "The Inscribed Tablets From Tell Deir 'Alla," *AUSS* 27 (1989): 21–37; 97–119; Choon-Leong Seow, "Deir 'Alla Plaster Texts," in *Prophets and Prophecy in the Ancient Near East*, ed. Peter Machinist and Martti Nissinen (Atlanta, GA: Society of Biblical Literature, 2003), 207–12.

[101] For the details of the story of its discovery see André LeMaire, "Fragments from the Book of Balaam Found at Deir Alla: Text Foretells Cosmic Disaster," *BAR* 11, no. 5 (1985): 26–39.

[102] Joseph Naveh, "The Date of the Deir 'Alla Inscription in Aramaic Script," *IEJ* 17 (1967): 236–38.

[103] Jacob Hoftijzer and G. Van der Kooij, eds., *The Balaam Text from Deir 'Alla Re-Evaluated: Proceedings of the International Symposium Held at Leiden, 21–24 August 1989* (Leiden: Brill, 1991).

[104] Jacob Hoftijzer, "The Prophet Balaam in a 6th Century Aramaic Inscription," *BA* 39, no. 1 (1976): 11–17; Hoftijzer and Van der Kooij, *Aramaic Texts from Deir 'Alla.*

[105] P. Kyle McCarter Jr., "The Balaam Texts from Deir 'Alla: The First Combination," *BSOR* 239 (1980): 49–60. See also *COS* 2.27: 140–45.

[106] Alan R. Millard, "Authors, Books and Readers in the Ancient World," in *The Oxford Handbook of Biblical Studies*, ed. J. W. Rogerson and Judith M. Lieu, Oxford Handbooks (Oxford: Oxford University Press, 2008), 554.

[107] Jo Ann Hackett, "Deir Alla, Tell: Texts," ed. David Noel Freedman et al., *ABD* (New York, N.Y.: Doubleday, 1996), 2:130; "Balaam (Person)," ed. David Noel Freedman et al., *ABD* (New York, N.Y.: Doubleday, 1996), 1:571–72.

in the biblical texts.[108] This discovery also presents the first Semitic prophecy to be identified outside the OT forecasting disaster on its own people.

> *Quotes from Antiquity*
>
> **Opening section of the Deir 'Alla Inscription**
>
> (1) [VACAT] The sa]ying[s of Bala]am, [son of Be]or, the man who was a seer of the gods. Lo! Gods came to him in the night [and spoke to] him (2) according to these w[ord]s. Then they said to [Bala]am, son of Beor, thus: Let someone make a [ ] hearafter, so that [what] you have hea[rd may be se]en!" (3) And Balaam rose in the morning [ ] right hand [ ] and could not [eat] and wept (4) aloud. Then his people came in to him [and said] to Balaam, son of Beor, "Do you fast? [ ] Do you weep?" And he (5) said to them, "Si[t] do]wn! I shall inform you what the Shad[dayin have done]. Now come, see the deeds of the g[o]ds!..
>
> McCarter Jr., "The Balaam Texts from Deir 'Alla" 49–60.

King Menahem (752–742 BC)

Menahem (Heb. "comforter") was a military leader who avenged the death of Zechariah by killing Shallum (2 Kgs 15:14–22). He took the vacant throne for himself (2 Kgs 15:10–14). Menahem ruled for ten years (752–742 BC), giving tribute to the Assyrian ruler Tiglath-Pileser III, as did Pekahiah, his son. The Assyrian King may have had a hand in obtaining the throne for Menahem.

Hosea and Amos paint a picture of lawlessness and sin within Israel during this period. He continued to permit worship of the golden calf and even went so far as destroying one of his own cities when it resisted his authority (2 Kgs 15:16). This period led to the fall of the Northern Kingdom, which was taken by the Assyrians, who invaded and conquered the land of Palestine.

Fall of the Northern Kingdom (775 BC)

Until the end of the nineteenth cent. many scholars did not believe that Sargon II, mentioned in the Bible (Isa 20:1), was a real historical character. They claim the biblical writers mistakenly wrote Sargon for one of the other Assyrian kings.[109] Several discoveries have now overturned this notion.

63. King Sargon II's prism commemorating the founding of his capital city, *Dûr-Sharrukên* (mod. Khorsabad;

Used with permission of the Oriental Institute Museum of the University of Chicago

The Annals of Sargon II (738–720 BC)

Prior to 1843 the only reference to Sargon (Akk. "the king is legitimate") appeared in Isaiah 20:1. In the spring of that year Paul-Émile Botta (1802–1870) and Eugène Flandin (1809–1876) excavated Sargon's capital, Khorsabad (Akk. *Dûr-Sharrukên* "Fortress of Sargon"), for the Louvre Museum in Paris[110] and among the inscriptions were the Annals of king Sargon

---

[108] Shea, "The Inscribed Tablets From Tell Deir 'Alla," 21–37, 97–119; Bryant G. Wood, "Balaam Son of Beor," *BS* 8, no. 4 (1995): 114; Seow, "Deir 'Alla Plaster Texts," 207–12; Michael L. Barré, "The Portrait of Balaam in Numbers 22-24," *Int* 51, no. 3 (1997): 254–66.

[109] Steven W. Holloway, "The Quest for Sargon, Pul and Tiglath-Pileser in the Nineteenth Century," in *Mesopotamia and the Bible: Comparative Explorations*, ed. Mark W. Chavalas and K. Lawson Younger, JSOTSup 341 (London: T&T Clark, 2003), 69–71; Johann G. Eichhorn, *Einleitung in Des Alte Testament*, 4th ed. (Göttingen: Rosenbusch, 1924), 387–89.

[110] Victor Harold Matthews, *Old Testament Parallels: Laws and Stories from the Ancient Near East*, 3 Rev Exp (New York, N.Y.: Paulist, 2007), 185–88.

II written in the Akkadian cuneiform dialect. The tablet was first published in 1849[111] with the first translation completed by Hugo Winckler in 1889.[112]

> *Quotes from Antiquity*
>
> **The Sargon Annals state:**
> The city of Samaria I besieged, I took; 27,280 of its inhabitants I carried away; fifty chariots that were among them I collected.
> Ragozin, *The Story of Assyria*, 247
>
> **The Bible states:**
> In the ninth year of Hoshea, the king of Assyria captured Samaria, and he carried the Israelites away to Assyria and placed them in Halah, and on the Habor, the river of Gozan, and in the cities of the Medes (2 Kgs 17:6)

The Sargon Annals chronicle the years when Israel changed from the position of an Assyrian ally (738 BC) to that of an Assyrian colony (732 BC) with the capture of Samaria and fall of the Northern Kingdom in 722 BC.[113] The Israelites were taken into captivity by King Merodach-baladan.[114] They also confirm Isaiah's report concerning the capture of Ashdod, including the title of *Tartan*, Sargon's military commander (Isa 20:1).

The Winged Bull of Sargon II (710–705 BC)

During Paul-Emile Botta's (1802–1870) excavation of the Palace of Sargon II at *Dûr-Sharrukên* (modern Khorsabad), he also discovered two colossal winged bulls (Akk. *lamassu*) with inscriptions.[115] However, because of their size, the French abandoned them at the site and in 1849 the British archaeologist Sir Henry Rawlinson bought them and solved the problem of their size (16 tons) by cutting them into pieces for easy transport back to the British Museum.

King Sargon's achievements and titles are inscribed in a detailed cuneiform inscription that resides between the legs of the winged bull.[116] The inscription also described Sargon's capture of Samaria (Isa 20:6) and the destruction of Ashdod in 711 BC (room 14).[117]

64. Colossal human-headed winged bull (Akk. *lamassu*) from Dûr-Sharrukên (Khorsabad). Neo-Assyrian Period, *ca.* 721–705 BC.

The Trustees of the British Museum (ME 118808, ME 118809)

[111] Paul-Émile Botta and Eugène Flandin, *Les Monuments de Ninive*, 5 vols. (Paris, France: Imprimerie Nationale, 1859).

[112] Hugo Winckler, *Untersuchungen Zur Altorientalischen Geschichte* (Leipzig: Pfeiffer, 1889), 1–46; Albert T. Olmstead, "The Text of Sargon's Annals," *AJSL* 47, no. 4 (1931): 259–80.

[113] Zénaïde Alexeïevna Ragozin, *The Story of Assyria from the Rise of the Empire to the Fall of Nineveh* (New York, N.Y.: Putnam's Sons, 1893), 247.

[114] William Sanford La Sor, "Merodach-Baladan," in *ISBE2*, ed. Geoffrey W. Bromiley, Revised, vol. 3 (Grand Rapids: Eerdmans, 1995), 2:325.

[115] Botta and Flandin, *Les Monuments de Ninive*; C. J. Gadd, "Inscribed Prisms of Sargon II from Nimrud," *Iraq* 16, no. 2 (1954): 180; Luckenbill, *Ancient Records of Assyria and Babylon*, 2:4, 55.

[116] Norma Franklin, "The Room V Reliefs at Dur-Sharrukin and Sargon II's Western Campaigns," *Tel Aviv* 21 (1994): 255–75; "A Room with a View: Images from Room V at Khorsabad, Samaria, Nubians, The Brooks of Egypt and Ashdod," in *Studies in the Archaeology of the Iron Age in Israel and Jordan*, ed. Amihai Mazar, Library Hebrew Bible/Old Testament Studies (Edinburgh, U.K.: T&T Clark, 2001), 257–77.

[117] Bob Becking, *The Fall of Samaria: An Historical and Archaeological Study*, Studies in the History of the Ancient Near East 2 (Leiden: Brill, 1992), 29–30; C. J. Gadd, "Inscribed Prisms of Sargon II from Nimrud," *Iraq* 16, no. 2 (1954): 180; Luckenbill, *Ancient Records of Assyria and Babylon,* 2:4, 55.

Quotes from Antiquity

The Sargon prism inscription states:

I [The man of Sa]maria, who with a king [hostile to] me had consorted together not to do service and not to bring tribute-and they did battle: in the strength of the great gods, my lords I clashed with them 27,280 people with [their] chariots and the gods their trust, as spoil I counted, 200 chariots (as) my [royal] muster. I mustered from among them the rest of them I caused to take their dwelling in the midst of Assyria. The city of Samaria I restored, and greater than before I caused it to become. People of lands conquered by my two hands I brought within it; my officer as prefect over them I placed, and together with the people of Assyria I counted them.

Gadd, *Nimrud Prism IV* 25–41

Although the Bible records Shalmaneser as the Assyrian king when the siege began (2 Kgs 17:3), Sargon may well have been the ruling king when Samaria fell to the Assyrians.[118]

The Jehoash Inscription

The Jehoash inscription is an unprovinanced (not found in its original location) tablet that was brought to light by Oded Golan in 2003.[119] It is reported to have surfaced in a Muslim cemetery or construction site near the Temple Mount in Jerusalem and is currently in the custody of the Israel Antiquities Authority (IAA).[120]

The inscription records the renovation done to the First Temple under King Jehoash (ruled *ca.* ninth cent. BC; see *Quotes from Antiquity*).[121] The Temple repairs are also mentioned in the Bible (2 Kgs 12:1–16 and 2 Chron 24:4–14). If authentic it would be considered the only Judahite royal inscription in existence.

65. Drawing of Jehoash inscription.

Rosenfeld *et al.*, report on the debate in the last few years over the possibility that the Jehoash Inscription is a forgery.

Epigraphic and philologic analyses of the tablet are inconclusive as to its authenticity. Cohen contended that if a forgery, it is a brilliant one, near genius.[122] Freedman advised not to rush to judgment; the Jehoash inscription may be authentic.[123] Sasson noted that the text of this inscription is not a forgery.[124] If it is a forgery, then a combination of some incredible factors must have operated in producing it. Cross,

[118] For a discussion of the chronological and historical difficulties see Becking, *The Fall of Samaria*, 30–32.

[119] Shanks reported that "sources now tell us that partially completed forged seals have been found in Golan's workshop. The IAA also claims it has recovered from Golan drawings of ancient inscriptions intended to be copied onto ancient pottery sherds. The letters appear to have been copied electronically from which an electronic template was made by the forger." Hershel Shanks, "Is Oded Golan a Forger?," *BAR* 29, no. 5 (2003): 37.

[120] Amnon Rosenfeld et al., "Archaeometric Analysis of the 'Jehoash Inscription,'" *Journal of Archaeological Science* 35 (2008): 2966.

[121] Chaim Cohen, "Biblical Hebrew Philology in the Light of the Last Three Lines of the Yeho'ash Royal Building Inscription (YI: Lines 14-16)," in *New Inscriptions and Seals Relating to the Biblical World*, ed. Meir Lubetski and Edith Lubetski (Atlanta, Ga.: SBL, 2012), 243–44.

[122] Meir Lubetski and Chaim Cohen, eds., "Biblical Hebrew Philology in the Light of Research on the New Yeho'ash Royal Building Inscription," in *New Seals and Inscriptions, Hebrew, Idumean and Cuneiform*, Hebrew Bible Monographs 8 (Sheffield: Phoenix, 2007), 222–86.

[123] David N. Freedman, "Don't Rush to Judgment: Jehoash Inscription May Be Authentic," *BAR* 30, no. 2 (2004): 48–51.

[124] Victor Sasson, "Philological and Textural Observations on the Controversial Jehoash Inscription," *UF* 35 (2004): 573–87.

however, maintained that the inscription is a poor forgery.[125] This dispute should not come as a surprise, since no Hebrew royal inscription from the First Temple Period was ever found which could serve for typological comparison. Ilani *et al.*[126] and Rosenfeld *et al.*[127] concluded that it may be authentic based on chemical and petrographic analyses. Following their report on the patina to the IAA, Goren *et al.* claimed that the inscription on the JI tablet was a forgery.[128] New evidence based on microcolonial fungi (MCF) as producers of a black and orange-brown patina, strengthens the view that the inscription was not recently engraved.[129]

> ***Quotes from Antiquity***
>
> **The Jehoash Inscription**
>
> [I am Yeho'ash, son of A]hazyahu, k[ing over Ju]dah, and I executed the re[pai]rs. When people in the (densely populated) land and in the (sparsely populated) steppe, and in all the cities of Judah, enthusiastically volunteered to donate money for the sacred contributions abundantly, in order to purchase quarry stone and juniper wood and Edomite copper/ copper from (the city of) 'Adam, (and) in order to perform the work faithfully (=without corruption), – (then) I renovated the breach(es) of the Temple and of the surrounding walls, and the storied structure, and the mesh-work, and the winding stairs, and the recesses, and the doors. May (this inscribed stone) become this day a witness that the work has succeeded (and) may God (thus) ordain His people with a blessing.
>
> Cohen, "Biblical Hebrew Philology," 243–44.

While the debate continues, one should be cautious about placing too much reliance on this artifact as supporting biblical reliability. As Drinkard has pointed out: "The Jehoash Inscription is also an unprovenanced inscription without context. Since it is almost universally agreed to be a forgery, it is not even a relic and has no value for biblical interpretation."[130] While unprovinanced artifacts need to be examined carefully, many—such as the Dead Sea Scrolls (see Fig. 4)—have provided valuable help in understanding the Biblical text.

SOUTHERN KINGDOM – JUDAH

There is growing archaeological evidence to support the biblical period of the southern kingdom that spans from Iron Age 1 to Iron Age 2.[131]

Mazar describes the issues confusing this debate:

> Unlike its northern sister, Judah did not suffer from any severe military attacks until Sennacherib's invasion in 701 B.C.E., and Jerusalem was not noticeably affected even by that invasion. The lack of destruction layers and the durability of massive stone buildings in the Judean hills and the Shephelah indicate that the same stone buildings were in use for a long period of time. There is also considerable longevity in the pottery production in Judah: the changes were gradual, covering a long period of time. This longevity of the material culture in Judah has blinded the eyes of archaeologists who wish to define in detail the development of Judean material culture in the ninth century as opposed to that of the previous or later centuries. It appears that cities and towns were founded in the late-tenth or ninth century when Sennacherib destroyed many of them. This can be demonstrated in Jerusalem, Beth-

[125] Frank Moore Cross, "Notes on the Forged Plaque Recording Repairs to the Temple," *IEJ* 53 (2003): 119–22.

[126] Shimon Ilani, Amnon Rosenfeld, and M. Dvorachek, "Archaeometry of a Stone Tablet with Hebrew Inscription Referring to Repair of the House," *Israel Geological Survey Current Research* 13 (2002): 109–116.

[127] Amnon Rosenfeld et al., "Archaeometric Analysis of the "Jehoash Inscription"' Stone Describing the Renovation of the First Temple of Jerusalem," in *Geological Society of America Abstracts with Programs*, vol. 7, Annual Meeting: Salt Lake City 37 (Boulder, Colo.: GSA, 2005), 278.

[128] Yuval Goren et al., "Authenticity Examination of Jehoash Inscription," *Journal of the Institute of Archaeology of Tel Aviv University* 31 (2004): 3–16.

[129] Rosenfeld et al., "Archaeometric Analysis of the 'Jehoash Inscription,'" 2966.

[130] Joel F. Drinkard, "North-West Semitic Inscriptions and Biblical Interpretation: Issues of Provenance," in *Israel: Ancient Kingdom or Late Invention?*, ed. Daniel I. Block (Nashville, Tenn.: B&H, 2008), 66.

[131] Mazar, "Divided Monarchy," 164–66.

shemesh, Lachish, Tell Beit Mirsim, and other sites where only few occupation strata are attributed to these centuries.[132]

Rehoboam (*ca.* 928 BC)

After Solomon died the people rebelled and the Nation was divided into the Northern Kingdom–Judah and the Southern Kingdom–Israel. In the south, Rehoboam (Heb. "he enlarges the people"), the son of Solomon retained only the tribes of Judah and Benjamin for his kingdom, continuing to use Jerusalem as his capital (1 Kgs 11:43). He was forty one when he came to the throne, only one year before the death of David, and reigned between 930–913 BC.

Rehoboam's refusal to relieve the tax burdens of the people caused ten tribes to revolt. He prepared to fight against Jeroboam, the king chosen by the revolting tribes, but he was forbidden from doing so. The priesthood was opened to all the people and images of calves were set up in Dan and Bethel, and the date of the feast of tabernacles was changed. Ahijah, a godly prophet, was sent to Bethel to prophesy against the altar. Rehoboam was deceived by another prophet, and killed by a lion for his disobedience (1 Kgs 13:23).

In response to the disobedience of Jeroboam's sons, sickness and death came upon them. The instrument God chose to use in bringing this punishment was Egypt under the rule of Pharaoh Shishak, in the fifth year of his reign. The prophet Shemaiah came to Rehoboam and revealed that this attack was a punishment for forsaking the law of God, but Rehoboam repented. He humbled himself before God, and his life was spared. The remaining years of his reign appear to have been prosperous, but his overall reign is characterized by the words "and he did evil, for he did not set his heart to seek the Lord" (1 Chron 12:14; 1 Kgs 11:43–14:31).

66. The relief of Shishak I's (Shoshenq) campaign listing the cities conquered in Palestine after King Solomon's death. It is located on the southern exterior wall of the temple of Karnak, north of Luxor, Egypt

The Karnak or Shishak I Inscription

In the precinct of Amun-Ra within the Karnak Temple in Luxor, Egypt (see Fig. 43), next to the Bubastite Portal,[133] there is a large relief commemorating the conquests of Shishak I (Shoshenq I; twenty-second Dynasty) that mentions his invasion of Judah and Israel, as is also recounted in 1 Kings

[132] Ibid., 164.

[133] George R. Hughes and The Epigraphic Survey, *The Epigraphic Survey, Reliefs and Inscriptions at Karnak, Volume III: The Bubastite Portal*, Oriental Institute Publications 74 (Chicago, Ill.: The University of Chicago Press, 1954), 21.

14:25–26 and 2 Chronicles 12:1–12 (see Fig. 66).[134]

The OT mentions Shishak (pharaoh of Egypt) seven times (1 Kgs 11:40, 14:25; and 2 Chron 12:2, 5 [twice], 7, and 9) and recounts how Shishak invaded Judah (the region of Benjamin) during the fifth year of the reign of king Rehoboam, plundering the temple. This is further supported by the Shishak stela fragment recovered at Megiddo (Stratum VA/IVB).[135]

> *Quotes from Antiquity*
>
> **2 Chronicles 12:1–4, 9**
>
> When the rule of Rehoboam was established and he was strong, he abandoned the law of the LORD, and all Israel with him. In the fifth year of King Rehoboam, because they had been unfaithful to the LORD, Shishak king of Egypt came up against Jerusalem with 1,200 chariots and 60,000 horsemen. And the people were without number who came with him from Egypt—Libyans, Sukkiim, and Ethiopians. And he took the fortified cities of Judah and came as far as Jerusalem. . . . So Shishak king of Egypt came up against Jerusalem. He took away the treasures of the house of the LORD and the treasures of the king's house. He took away everything. He also took away the shields of gold that Solomon had made.

Although Jerusalem or Judah is not mentioned on the Shishak list, some have explained that Jerusalem, while subdued, was protected from destruction by the payment of the ransom of the Temple treasures, which were given to the Pharaoh at Gibeon (2 Chron 12:9;1 Kgs 14:26; see *Quotes from Antiquity*).[136]

Wiseman describes the archaeological evidence resulting from the invasion of Shishak:

> In the early divided kingdom the raid by Shishak (Sheshonq I) against Rehoboam c. 928 BC (1 Kgs 14:25–26) is shown in his triumphs depicted on the walls of the Karnak temple of Amun in Thebes, which lists 150 towns in Phoenicia, Judah as far as the Esdraelon valley, and into Edom and south Syria. Megiddo was invaded (so a broken stele there) and destruction levels at Beth-shemesh and Tell Beit Mirsim (Debir or Kirjath-Sepher) attest the raid, after which the Egyptians renewed the defences of Sharuhen, Gezer, Tell el-Ajjul and Tell Jemneh to maintain a strong presence against which Rehoboam reacted by strengthening Lachish and Azekah. Meanwhile Jeroboam I reinforced the gate of Dan, built at Shechem, Gibeah, Bethel and Tell en-Nasbeh (Mizpah?) which became the northern boundary of Judah in subsequent clashes with Israel (cf. 1 Kgs 15:15–22). About this time Dan was destroyed (1 Kgs 15:20), but soon thereafter the city gate and fortifications were rebuilt. The massive (4 metre wide) walls and towers and finely preserved city gate at Tell en-Nasbeh appear to be the work of Asa (cf. 1 Kgs 15:22).[137]

King Uzziah (Azariah r. *ca.* 792–740 BC)

Azariah's (Heb. "Yahweh has helped") name may have been changed to Uzziah (Heb. "Yahweh is might") when he took the throne (2 Kgs 15:1–27). He was the son of King Amaziah of Judah. The people brought him to the throne when he was just sixteen years old, following his fathers murder (2 Kgs 14:21; 2 Chron 26:1). He reigned for fifty-two years and was known as a king who feared the Lord and did wisely in the sight of God. The prophet Zechariah was a great help and advisor to him during his reign (2 Chron 26:5). A serious

---

[134] Kenneth A. Kitchen, "The Shoshenqs of Egypt and Palestine," *JSOT* 93 (2001): 3–12; Kevin A. Wilson, *The Campaign of Pharaoh Shoshenq I into Palestine*, Forschungen Zum AltenTestament, 2. Reihe 9 (Tübingen: Mohr Siebeck, 2005); Gary A. Byers, "The Bible According To Karnak," *BS* 17, no. 4 (2004): 98.

[135] Timothy P. Harrison, *Megiddo 3: Final Report on the Stratum VI Excavations*, Oriental Institute Publications 127 (Chicago, Ill.: Oriental Institute of the University of Chicago, 2004), 7–13.

[136] e.g., Siegfried Herrmann, "Operationen Pharao Schoschenks I. Im Ostlichen Ephraim," *Zeitschrift Des Deutscher Palastina-Vereins* 80 (1964): 55–79; Aharoni, *The Land of the Bible*, 326; Kenneth A. Kitchen, *The Third Intermediate Period in Egypt, 1100-650 BC*, 2nd ed., Egyptology (Warminster, U.K.: Aris & Phillips, 1996), 447; Nadav Na'aman, "Israel, Edam and Egypt in the 10th Century B.C.E," *Tel Aviv* 19 (1992): 71–93, 81; Israel Finkelstein, "The Campaign of Shoshenq I to Palestine: A Guide to the 10th Century BCE Polity," *Zeitschrift Des Deutschen Palästina-Vereins* 118 (2002): 111.

[137] Wiseman, *1 and 2 Kings*, 40.

earthquake struck the land of Judah during his reign (Amos 1:1; Zech 14:5).

His first order of business was to deal with his fathers enemies, the Edomites, who revolted against Judah during Jehoram's reign. He conquered the land as far south as Elat (Eloth), the strategic port on the gulf of Aqaba (2 Kgs 14:21; 2 Chron 26:1). His other campaigns included the conquest of Mehunim (people of Maan), and the Arabs of Gurbaal. In the west, Uzziah waged a successful campaign against the Philistines, levelling the walls of some of their most important cities, including Gath, Jabneh, and Ashdod while fortifying other Philistine cities.

He strengthened the walls of Jerusalem and some of its towers (2 Chron 26:9). He provided wells for the herds in the desert, erecting watchtowers for the protection of vineyards and rebuilding the copper and iron mines, which had not been used since the days of Solomon.

Uzziah's downfall came when at the height of his success, he entered the Temple and tried to burn incense on the altar of God. The High Priest Azariah, along with eighty others, confronted Uzziah but as he moved forward to the altar, he was struck with leprosy. As a result of his disease he was banned from his palace, society and the temple, and denied a royal burial (2 Chron 26:23). His son Jotham reigned while Uzziah was banished from society.

The Uzziah Epitaph

In 1931, while Professor Eleazar Sukenik, of the Hebrew University of Jerusalem, was examining a collection of artifacts in a Russian Orthodox monastery on the Mount of Olives, he noticed the Uzziah Tablet, which mentions the burial of King Uzziah in Aramaic (see Fig. 67).[138] The Uzziah Epitaph reads: "To this place were brought the bones of Uzziah, the king of Judah – do not open!"[139]

67. The marble epitaph of Uzziah.
Israel Museum in Jerusalem (IMJ 68.56.38)
© Yoav Dothan / Wikimedia Commons

The plaque is not from the time of Uzziah, evident from the style of the writing, which dated it to the Hasmonean period (early Roman *ca.* 150 BC–AD 50). It is believed that the plaque was created to mark the reburial of the Uzziah, the Judahite king (Josephus *Ant.* 9.10.4).[140] The plaque is presently displayed in the Israel Museum (IMJ 68.56.38).[141]

---

[138] Eleazar Lipa Sukenik, "Funerary Tablet of Uzziah, King of Judah," *PEFSt.* 63, no. 4 (1931): 217–21.

[139] Klaas A. D. Smelik, *Writings from Ancient Israel: A Handbook of Historical and Religious Documents* (Louisville, Ky.: Westminster/Knox, 1991), 78.

[140] Yael Israeli and Ruth Hestrin, *Inscriptions Reveal: Documents from the Time of the Bible, the Mishna and the Talmud* (Jerusalem, Israel: Israel Museum, 1973), (Israel Museum catalogue no. 100), 120, no. 255.

[141] Uzziah is also mentioned in conjunction with the seal of Shebnayau (also Shubnayaw; Louvre AO 6216), the Servant of Uzziah (2 Kgs 15:5; 2 Chron 26:21; Isa 22, 36–37). Avigad and Sass, *Corpus of West Semitic Stamp Seals*, 50; Benjamin Sass and Christoph Uehlinger, eds., *Studies in the Iconography of Northwest Semitic Inscribed Seals: Proceedings of a Symposium Held in Fribourg on April 17-20, 1991*, Orbis Biblicus et Orientalis 125 (Gottingen: Vandenhoeck & Ruprecht, 1993), 199; Lubetski and Lubetski, *New Inscriptions and Seals Relating to the Biblical World*, 46–47.

King Ahaz (*ca.* 732–715 BC)

Ahaz is a short form of Ahaziah (Heb. "Yahweh upholds"). During his reign (732–715 BC) Judah sank to the level of the wicked idolatrous practices of the Assyrians (2 Kgs 16:3). It was during Ahaz's reign that the prophets Isaiah and Micah carried out their ministry. When Rezin, king of Syria and Pekah, king of Israel waged war against Judah, instead of trusting in God, as Isaiah had told him (Isa 7–9), Ahaz took money from the temple treasury to purchase help from the Assyrians (2 Chron 28) and adopted the religion of the Assyrians (2 Kgs 16:10). This resulted in Judah coming under the domination of Tiglath-Pileser III of Assyria. Ahaz made an altar based on and using Syrian patterns and had it placed in the Temple (2 Kgs 16:11). He died in disgrace and was refused burial in the tomb of the kings in Jerusalem (2 Chron 28:15).

The Ahaz Bulla

In 1995 an eighth cent. BC (732–716 BC) clay seal bulla impression was discovered by Robert Deutsch in the possession of an antiquities dealer (see Fig. 68). It was soon discovered to contain the name of King Ahaz of the Bible (Isa 14:28) and his father, Yehotam (Jotham). The bulla also contains a fingerprint which may belong to Ahaz himself.[142]

68. Reproduction of a seal (bulla) with the eighth cent. BC inscription "Belonging to Ahaz (son of) Yotham King of Judah" written in the Paleo-Hebrew script.

Original housed in the Shlomo Moussaieff Collection, London

The seal is currently part of the private London collection of Shlomo Moussaieff, which presently exceeds 60,000 pieces.[143] Deutsch describes its condition and use as: "This lump of clay, called a bulla, was used to seal a papyrus document. We know this because the back of the bulla still bears the imprint of the texture of the papyrus. Also on the back of the bulla, we can see the impression of the double string with which the document was tied."[144] The inscription "*l'ḥz'y / hwtm'mlk' / yhdh*" has been translated as: "Belonging to Ahaz, son of Yehotam, king of Judah."[145]

An additional extra-biblical source, supporting the historicity of Ahaz, comes from Tiglath-Pileser III who is recorded receiving a gold and silver tribute from King Ahaz (2 Kgs 16:5–9).[146]

King Hezekiah (715–686 BC)

Hezekiah (Heb. meaning "Jehovah is strength") reigned over Judah from *ca.* 715–686 BC. The

---

[142] Robert Deutsch, *Messages from the Past: Hebrew Bullea from the Time of Isaiah Through the Destruction of the First Temple-Shlomo Moussaieff Collection and an Up-To-Date Corpus (in Hebrew)* (Tel Aviv, Israel: Archaeological Center Publications, 1997); Hershel Shanks, "Messages from the Past: Hebrew Bullae from the Time of Isaiah Through the Destruction of the First Temple," *Biblical Archaeology Review* 26, no. 2 (April 2000): 64–6; Robert Deutsch, *Biblical Period Hebrew Bullae. The Josef Chaim Kaufman Collection (in Hebrew)* (Tel Aviv, Israel: Archaeological Center Publications, 2003).

[143] Robert Deutsch, "First Impression: What We Learn from King Ahaz's Seal," *BAR* 24, no. 3 (1998): 56.

[144] Ibid.

[145] Mykytiuk, *Identifying Biblical Persons in Northwest Semitic Inscriptions of 1200-539 B.C.E.*; Frank Moore Cross, "King Hezekiah's Seal Bears Phoenician Imagery," *BAR* 25, no. 2 (1999): 42–45.

[146] From a building inscription discovered by Rawlinson on clay preserved in various copies. *ANET*, 282; Rawlinson, *The Cuneiform Inscriptions of Western Asia. Vol. III. A Selection from the Miscellaneous Inscriptions of Assyria*, 67; Luckenbill, *Ancient Records of Assyria and Babylon*, 2:287–88 §§800–801; Luis Robert Siddall, "Tiglath-Pileser III's Aid to Ahaz: A New Look at the Problems of the Biblical Accounts in the Light of the Assyrian Sources," *ANES* 46 (2009): 93–106.

Northern Kingdom had just fallen to the Assyrians in 722 BC. Hezekiah was only twenty-five when he came to the throne, but chose not to follow in his father's footsteps. He set out to reform the religion of Judah and purge the temple of idols. He called upon the Levites to clean up the temple and prepare it for the worship of Yahweh and the sacrifices prescribed in the Laws of Moses. The Passover was reinstituted and an invitation even went out to the Northern Kingdom of Israel to participate in the event at Jerusalem. Even the bronze serpent of Moses, which had been worshipped by the people, was taken down and destroyed (Num 21:4–9; 2 Kgs 18:4).

Quotes from Antiquity

The Bible states:

In the days of Pekah king of Israel, Tiglath-pileser king of Assyria came and captured Ijon, Abel-beth-maacah, Janoah, Kedesh, Hazor, Gilead, and Galilee, all the land of Naphtali, and he carried the people captive to Assyria. Then Hoshea the son of Elah made a conspiracy against Pekah the son of Remaliah and struck him down and put him to death and reigned in his place, in the twentieth year of Jotham the son of Uzziah (2 Kgs 15:29–30).

The Annals of Tiglath-Pileser states:

As for Menahem, I overwhelmed him like a snowstorm and he ... fled like a bird, alone, and bowed at my feet.

ANET, 283–847.

In 711 BC, just a few years after Hezekiah had become king, Sargon II of Assyria captured Ashdod. In response, Hezekiah began a defence program against an Assyrian invasion. He fortified cities and built a 534 metre (1,750 ft.) long tunnel to ensure that Jerusalem had a sufficient water supply in case of a siege (see Figs. 71, 72).

Ten years after taking Israel into captivity, the Assyrians invaded Judah. As the Assyrians invaded city after city, Hezekiah sent word to Sennacherib, King of Assyria, at Lachish, stating that he would pay him a heavy tax if he left them alone (2 Kgs 18:13). The tax was so great that Hezekiah had to strip the temple and palace of its gold to fund the payment.

But it was all to no avail as Sennacherib came back and demanded an unconditional surrender. Against the proud and arrogant boast of the Assyrians, Hezekiah humbly trusted the Lord (2 Kgs 19:21–22). He sent word for Isaiah to intervene and give direction. With both his confidence in the Lord and his well laid preparations, Hezekiah was able to hold off the Assyrians (2 Kgs 19:7). His victory was assisted by God, who sent a plague that killed 185,000 Assyrians in one night. Sennacherib returned home depressed and discouraged, and eventually was killed by two of his own sons. God then caused the Babylonians to revolt against the Assyrians, and as a result, Jerusalem was spared.

69. Drawing of the Incirli Stele of Tiglath-Pileser III (Pul *ca.* 734 BC).

It was around this same time that Hezekiah fell sick, but as a result of Isaiah the prophet's earnest prayer (Isa 38), Hezekiah was granted recovery and another fifteen years to live. He died in 686 BC after leading Judah to one of the greatest revivals in her history.

The Incirli Stele of Tiglath-Pileser III (745–727 BC)

The Incirli Stele was uncovered by Elizabeth Carter of UCLA in 1993 during excavations in the Karamanmarash Valley (Turkey) at a site called

Incirli. It was discovered in a farmer's garden and identified by Bruce Zuckerman and Stephen Kaufman[147] to belong to Tiglath-Pileser III and date to the Assyrian Empire (745–727 BC).[148]

The Incirli stele confirms the existence of Tiglath-Pileser (also called Pul *ca.* 734 BC) in an extra-biblical account. The Bible states that Menahem of Israel (reign *ca.* 745–738 BC) was taken captive by the Assyrian king Tiglath-Pileser (1 Chron 5:26; 2 Chron 26; 2 Kgs 15:19–29).

The Royal Steward Inscription (716–686 BC)

The Royal Steward Inscription (Shebna Inscription) is a Hebrew inscription discovered in

70. An inscription from Silwan (Siloam), from the lintel of a royal steward's tomb. The name is largely obliterated (only the last two letters, "*hw*", survive), but is believed to be Shebna-yahu.

1870 from a lintel over a cave tomb discovered at Siloam (Silwan) in the Kidron Valley in Jerusalem (see Fig. 70).[149] In 1871 the British Museum purchased the limestone inscription from the French archaeologist Charles Simon Clermont-Ganneau, who discovered it. Although severely damaged, two letters of the name (*hw*) were preserved, along with the title of the occupants position which reads "over the house" of the king. With the help of the date of the script, the inscription was finally deciphered in 1953 by the Israeli epigrapher, Nahman Avigad, after Yigal Yadin suggested that the name was Shebna.[150] The inscription is accepted by most scholars as the tomb of Shebna, the royal steward of King Hezekiah (716–686 BC) who is rebuked by Isaiah for having "cut out here a tomb for yourself . . . a tomb on the height and carve a dwelling for yourself in rock (Isa 22:16)".[151]

> *Quotes from Antiquity*
>
> **Royal Steward Inscription states:**
>
> This is [the sepulchre of...] *yahu* [Shebna] who is over the house [royal steward]. There is no silver and no gold here but [his bones] and the bones of his slave-wife with him. Cursed be the man who will open this!
>
> Avigad, "The Epitaph of a Royal Steward," 143.

[147] Steven A. Kaufman, "The Phoenician Inscription of the Incirli Trilingual: A Tentative Reconstruction and Translation," *Maarav* 14, no. 2 (2007): 7–26.

[148] For the most up-to-date treatment of the discovery see: Eric Cherniss et al., "The Incirli Stela Unveiling the Past: The Incirli Trilingual Inscription," 1993, n.p., http://www.usc.edu/dept/LAS/arc /incirli/.

[149] This tomb in the Kidron Valley was among the necropolis tombs of notable people such as Jehoshaphat, Absalom, Zechariah and others. Nahman Avigad, "The Epitaph of a Royal Steward from Siloam Village," *IEJ* 3, no. 3 (1953): 138; Robert M. Good, "The Israelite Royal Steward in the Light of Ugaritic 'L Bt," *RB* 86 (1979): 580–82.

[150] Avigad, "The Epitaph of a Royal Steward from Siloam Village," 137–52; Robert Deutsch, "Tracking Down Shebnayahu, Servant of the King: How an Antiquities Market Find Solved a 42-Year-Old Excavation Puzzle," *BAR* 35, no. 3 (2009): 45; Charles S. Clermont-Ganneau, *Archaeological Researches in Palestine*, trans. John MacFarlane, vol. 1 (London: Palestine Exploration Fund, 1899), 313. Clermont-Ganneau did speculate that the name might be Shebnah.

[151] Avigad, "The Epitaph of a Royal Steward from Siloam Village," 143. See also *COS* 2.54: 180; Deutsch, "Tracking Down Shebnayahu," 45–49, 67.

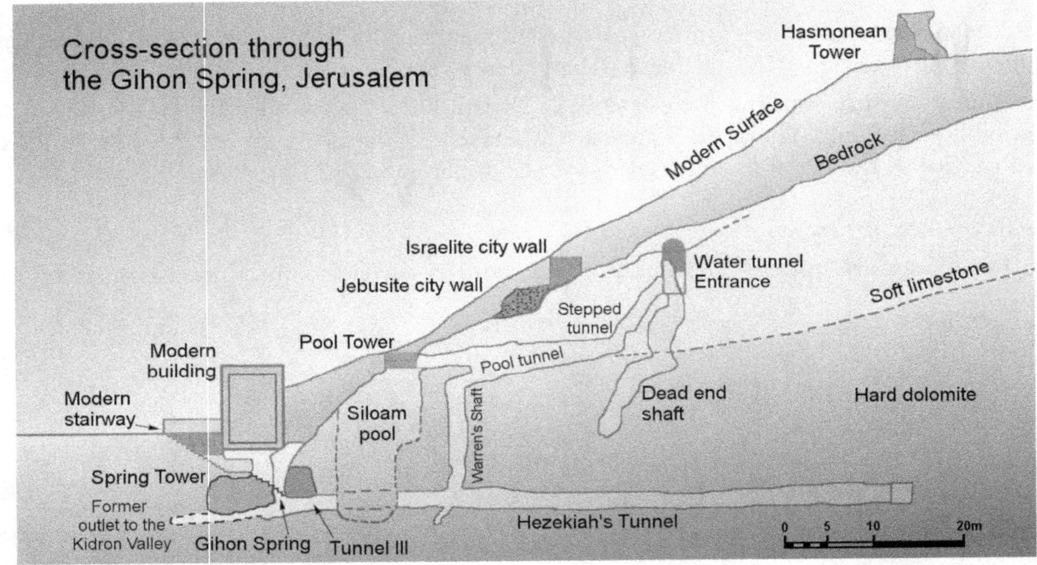

71. A cross-section through the Gihon spring and the pool of Siloam that led to Hezekiah's tunnel into Jerusalem. The Jebusites controlled Jerusalem during David's reign, but David's army entered the city through Hezekiah's tunnel and conquered the city (2 Sam 6:6–8)..

72. The author walking through Hezekiah's Tunnel in 1996.

Hezekiah's Tunnel (ca. 701 BC)

Although Hezekiah's tunnel (also known as the Siloam Tunnel) had been known from ancient times, it was first scientifically surveyed by Edward Robinson in 1838 (see Fig. 72).[152] The tunnel connected the Pool of Siloam (Heb. "sent"), which was discovered in 2004 at the site of *Birket el-Hamra*,[153] with the Gihon (Heb. "gush") spring (see Fig. 71).[154] In 1880 a young boy discovered the "Siloam Inscription" (see Fig. 73) engraved on the inside wall of the tunnel.[155]

The inscription has been used to date the tunnel to *ca.* 700 BC, the time of Hezekiah,[156]

[152] Edward Robinson, *Biblical Researches in Palestine and in the Adjacent Regions*, 2nd ed., vol. 1 (Boston, Mass.: Crocker & Brewster, 1860).

[153] Ronny Reich and Eli Shukron, "The Siloam Pool in the Wake of Recent Discoveries," in *New Studies on Jerusalem*, ed. Eyal Baruch, Ayelet Levy-Reifer, and Avraham Faust, 10 (Jerusalem, Israel: Bar-Ilan University, 2004), 137–39; Hershel Shanks, "The Siloam Pool: Where Jesus Cured the Blind Man," *BAR* 31, no. 5 (2005): 17–23; Ronny Reich, "The Pool of Siloam," in *NEAEHL*, 5:1807; Graves, *Biblical Archaeology Vol 1: An Introduction* 2nd ed 1:218–20. Until 2004 most scholars accepted a small narrow Byzantine pool, called the *Birkeh Silwan*, as the traditional site of the Pool of Siloam and associated it with the healing miracle of Jesus mentioned in John (John 9:1–11).

[154] Graves, *Biblical Archaeology Vol 1: An Introduction* 2nd ed 1:220.

[155] Alan R. Millard, *Discoveries from Bible Times: Archaeological Treasures Throw Light on the Bible* (Oxford: Lion Books, 1997), 126.

[156] Dan Gill, "The Geology of the City of David and its Ancient Subterranean Waterworks," in *Excavations at the City of David 1978-1985 Directed by Yigal Shiloh: Various Reports*, ed. Donald T. Ariel and Alon De Groot, vol. 3, Qedem 35 (Jerusalem, Israel: Institute of Archaeology, Hebrew University, 1992), 1–28; John W. Rogerson and Philip R. Davies, "Was the Siloam Tunnel Built by Hezekiah?," *BA* 59, no. 3 (1996): 138–49; Jane M. Cahill, "A Rejoinder to 'Was the Siloam Tunnel Built by Hezekiah?,'" *BA* 60,

and confirms what the Bible states in 2 Chronicles 32:30: "This same Hezekiah closed the upper outlet of the waters of Gihon and directed them down to the west side of the city of David."

The 534 metre (1,750 ft.) long tunnel was cut through solid rock, 46 metres (150 ft.) deep underground (See Fig. 72).[157] It was a monumental task taking Judean workers through meters of solid rock, attested by the Siloam Inscription which described how two teams of workers, working from opposite ends, carved their way through the rock to meet in the middle. The precise method used to meet underground is not mentioned but theories speculate that it was using a vein in the rock or from the sound of the workers.[158]

73. Reproduction of the Siloam inscription, that records the construction of Hezekiah's tunnel in the eighth cent. BC.
The Istanbul Archaeological Museum (no. 2195 T)

*The Siloam Inscription (*ca. *701 BC)*

The Siloam Inscription was discovered by a peasant boy while exploring Hezekiah's tunnel (see Fig. 73). It records the successful completion of Hezekiah's tunnel in the eighth cent. BC (*ca.* 701 BC;[159] 2 Kgs 20:20; 2 Chron 32:2–8)[160] and contains one of the oldest examples of the ancient Paleo-Hebrew alphabet (see Fig. 73).

In the nineteenth century, it was damaged when thieves cut it from the tunnel wall, but it was recovered and repaired.[161]

> *Quotes from Antiquity*
>
> **The Siloam Inscription**
>
> [. . . when] (the tunnel) was driven through. And this was the way in which it was cut through:–While [. . .] (were) still [. . .] axe(s), each man toward his fellow, and while there were still three cubits to be cut through, [there was heard] the voice of a man calling to his fellow, for there was an overlap in the rock on the right [and on the left]. And when the tunnel was driven through, the quarrymen hewed (the rock), each man toward his fellow, axe against axe; and the water flowed from the spring toward the reservoir for 1,200 cubits, and the height of the rock above the head(s) of the quarrymen was 100 cubits [Albright].

The Bethlehem Bulla (8th –7th cent. BC)

In 2012 the Israel Antiquities Authority (IAA) announced the discovery of a 2,700 year old bulla (clay seal, see Fig. 74) found in the City of David excavation in Jerusalem, that dates to the eighth to seventh cent. BC and contains the earliest mention of the town of Bethlehem[162]

no. 3 (1997): 184–85; Amos E. Frumkin, Aryeh E. Shimron, and Jeff Rosenbaum, "Radiometric Dating of the Siloam Tunnel, Jerusalem," *Nature* 425, no. 6954 (2003): 169; Ronald S. Hendel, "The Date of the Siloam Inscription: A Rejoinder to Rogerson and Davies," *BA* 59, no. 4 (1996): 233–37; Hershel Shanks, "Will King Hezekiah Be Dislodged from His Tunnel?," *BAR* 39, no. 5 (2013): 52–54.

[157] Donald Langmead and Christine Garnaut, *Encyclopedia of Architectural and Engineering Feats* (Santa Barbara, Calf.: ABC-CLIO, 2001), 153–55.

[158] Dan Gill, "How They Met: Geology Solves the Mystery of Hezekiah's Tunnelers," *BAR* 20, no. 4 (1994): 20–33, 64.

[159] Amos Frumkin et al., "Radiocarbon Chronology Of The Holocene Dead Sea: Attempting A Regional Correlation," *Radiocarbon* 43, no. 3 (2001): 169–71.

[160] Dan Gill, "Jerusalem's Underground Water Systems: How They Met: Geology Solves Long-Standing Mystery of Hezekiah's Tunnelers," *BAR* 20, no. 4 (1994): 20–33.

[161] R. I. Altman, "Some Notes on Inscriptional Genres and the Siloam Tunnel Inscription," *Antiquo Oriente* 5 (2007): 35–88; Victor Sasson, "The Siloam Tunnel Inscription," *PEQ* 114 (1982): 111–17.

[162] On the excavations at Bethlehem see Stekelis M. and Avi-Yonah, M., V. Tsajeris. "Bethlehem." *NEAEHL* 1:203–210.

(Micah 5:2).[163] The small (1.5 cm) bulla (seal impression) bears the inscription: "Bishv'at [in the seventh] Bat Lechem [Bethlehem] [Lemel]ekh [for the king][164]

This inscription is the earliest mention of the birthplace of Jesus of Nazareth. The Bulla seal was used to seal a document and identify the sender.[165]

According to Eli Shukron, the director of the excavation on behalf of the Israel Antiquities Authority, it appears that:

> in the seventh year of the reign of a king (it is unclear if the king referred to here is Hezekiah, Manasseh or Josiah), a shipment was dispatched from Bethlehem to the king in Jerusalem. The bulla we found belongs to the group of "fiscal" bullae – administrative bullae used to seal tax shipments remitted to the taxation system of the Kingdom of Judah in the late eighth and seventh centuries BCE. The tax could have been paid in the form of silver or agricultural produce such as wine or wheat". Shukron emphasizes," this is the first time the name Bethlehem appears outside the Bible, in an inscription from the First Temple period, which proves that Bethlehem was indeed a city in the Kingdom of Judah, and possibly also in earlier periods.[166]

74. Drawing of the Bethlehem bulla.

The Sennacherib (Taylor) Prism (705–681 BC)

This hexagonal (six-sided) clay prism (15 inches/38 cm tall), sometimes called the "Annals of Sennacherib", derives its name from Colonel Robert Taylor who acquired it in 1830 among the ruins of Sennacherib's palace in Nineveh (Nebi Yunus). The British Museum purchased it from Taylor in 1855. The British Museum also has at least eight other fragmentary prisms with just a few lines of text.[167]

However, two other copies of the complete prism are known to exist. One, called the Sennacherib Prism (OIM A2793; see Fig. 75) is housed in the Oriental Institute

75. Sennacherib's (Taylor) Prism.

Used with permission of the Oriental Institute Museum of the University of Chicago (OIM A2793)

---

[163] Israel Antiquities Authority, "Earliest Archaeological Evidence of the Existence of the City of Bethlehem Already in the First Temple Period," *Israel Antiquities Authority*, May 23, 2012, n.p., http://www.antiquities.org.il/article_eng.aspx?sec_id=25&subj_id =240&id=1938; Jerome Murphy-O'Connor, "Where Was Jesus Born? Bethlehem… Of Course," *BR*, February 2000, 40–45, 50; Henry B. Smith, "Bethlehem: Seal Uncovered in the City of David," *Associate for Biblical Research*, May 25, 2012, n.p.; Deutsch, *Biblical Period Hebrew Bullae. The Josef Chaim Kaufman Collection (in Hebrew).*

[164] Hershel Shanks, "History of Bethlehem Documented by First Temple Period Bulla from the City of David: Jesus' Birthplace in Ancient Bethlehem Confirmed as an Israelite City Centuries Earlier," *BAR*, May 23, 2012, n.p.

[165] Ibid.

[166] Israel Antiquities Authority, "Earliest Archaeological Evidence of the Existence of the City of Bethlehem," n.p.

[167] Millard, *Discoveries from Bible Times*, 121.

Museum of the University of Chicago.[168] It was purchased for the Museum by James Henry Breasted from a Baghdad antiques dealer in 1919.

A third prism dating to 691 BC, known as the Jerusalem Prism (IMJ 71.72.249), had its text only recently published in 1990.[169] It is held in the Israel Museum in Jerusalem.

The text of all three prisms is virtually identical with only minor variations, although from the dates in the text the Oriental Institute prism was created six months after the other two, in 689 BC. They are inscribed with the Assyrian King Sennacherib's (son of Sargon II) first eight military campaigns (705–681 BC), including his conquest of forty-six cities in Judah and the deportation of 200,150 citizens[170] from his third campaign (701 BC).[171]

Israel had already been conquered when Sennacherib turned his attention to Judah. In true propaganda style, this prism boasts of his siege of Jerusalem and capture of King Hezekiah of Judah (715–687 BC) in 701 BC (see *Quotes from Antiquity*). [172]

This same event is described through the eyes of Judah in 2 Kings 17–19:36 (2 Chron 32; Isa 33, 36–37:37). The prisms silently agree with the biblical account of the mysterious death of the Assyrian army and the siege being called off (2 Kgs 19:35–36; Isa 36–37), but it does not mention the failure to capture Jerusalem nor suggest why.[173] Mitchell explains that it is: "making no claim that Jerusalem was taken, only describing tribute from Hezekiah of gold, silver, precious stones, valuable woods, furniture decorated with ivory …, iron daggers, raw iron, and musicians (cf. 2 Kgs 18:13–16)."[174]

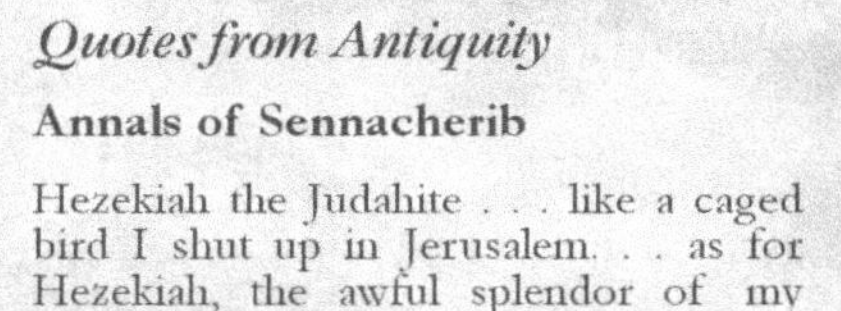

Quotes from Antiquity

Annals of Sennacherib

Hezekiah the Judahite . . . like a caged bird I shut up in Jerusalem. . . as for Hezekiah, the awful splendor of my lordship overwhelmed him.

Thomas, *Documents from OT Times*, 64–69.

The Assyrians claimed complete victory and withdrew from Judah. The Greek historian Herodotus claimed that a plague of field mice entered the camp and gnawed the leather components of their weapons, disarming the military force and leading to many of the soldiers being killed or fleeing (*Hist.* 2.141). The Bible states that it was the angel of death sending plague on the troops, causing many thousands to die (2 Kgs 19:35–37; Isa 37:38).

Strangely the well known siege of Lachish which occurred during this campaign and is depicted on the reliefs in Sennacherib's palace at Nineveh (see Figs. 80, 81) is not mentioned in the annals.[175]

---

[168] Clyde E. Fant and Mitchell Glenn Reddish, *Lost Treasures of the Bible: Understanding the Bible Through Archaeological Artifacts in World Museums* (Grand Rapids: Eerdmans, 2008), 159.

[169] P. Ling-Israel, "The Sennacherib Prism in the Israel Museum—Jerusalem," in *Bar-Ilan: Studies in Assyriology Dedicated to Pinḥas Artzi*, ed. J. Klein and A. Skaist (Jerusalem: Ramat-Gan: Bar-Ilan University Press, 1990), 213–47.

[170] Ziony Zevit, "Implicit Population Figures and Historical Sense: What Happened to 200,150 Judahites in 701 BCE?," in *Confronting the Past: Archaeological and Historical Essays on Ancient Israel in Honor of William G. Dever*, ed. Seymour Gitin, J. Edward Wright, and J. P. Dessel (Winona Lake, Ind.: Eisenbrauns, 2006), 357–65.

[171] Daniel David Luckenbill, *The Annals of Sennacherib* (Eugene, Oreg.: Wipf & Stock, 2005); D. Winston Thomas, ed., *Documents from Old Testament Times,* Ancient Texts and Translations (Eugene, Oreg.: Wipf & Stock, 2005), 64–69.

[172] Thomas, *Documents from Old Testament Times*, 64–69.

[173] R. E. Clements, *Isaiah and the Deliverance of Jerusalem: Study of the Interpretation of Prophecy in the Old Testament,* New edition, JSOT Supplements 13 (New York, N.Y.: Continuum International, 1980).

[174] T. C. Mitchell, *The Bible in the British Museum: Interpreting the Evidence* (Mahwah, N.J.: Paulist, 2004), 66.

[175] David Ussishkin, *The Conquest of Lachish by Sennacherib* (Tel Aviv, Israel: Tel Aviv University/Institute of Archaeology, 1983); William H. Shea, "Sennacherib's Description of Lachish and of Its Conquest," *AUSS* 26, no. 2 (1988): 171–80.

Apart from its biblical importance in confirming the siege of Jerusalem, the prism played an important role in deciphering cuneiform script, since it was one of the first major Assyrian texts to be discovered.

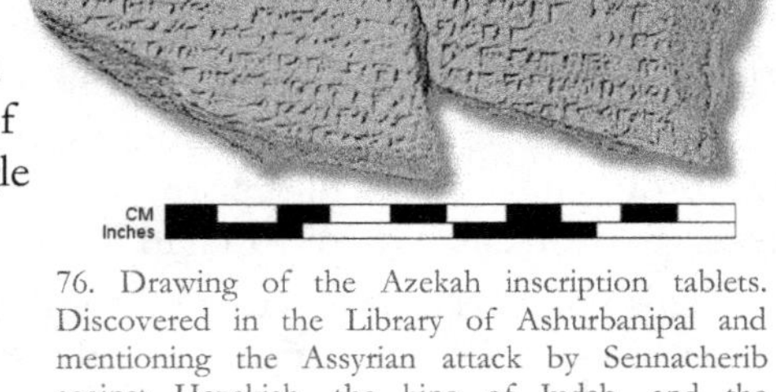

76. Drawing of the Azekah inscription tablets. Discovered in the Library of Ashurbanipal and mentioning the Assyrian attack by Sennacherib against Hezekiah, the king of Judah, and the conquest of Azekah (2 Kgs 18–19, 2 Chr 32).

The Trustees of the British Museum (K.6205 + BM 82-3-23, 131)

The Azekah Inscription (ca. 689 BC)

The Azekah Inscription tablets (see Fig. 76) are several Akkadian cuneiform tablets, discovered in 1903 by Henry Rawlinson in the Library of Ashurbanipal,[176] but identified as belonging to a single tablet by Nadav Na'aman in 1974.[177] Initially scholars believed that the K 6205 tablet belonged to the military campaign of Tiglath-pileser III,[178] while the 81–3–13, 131 tablet[179] belonged to the military campaign of Sargon II.[180] While Shea argues that the joined text now refers to Sennacherib's second campaign in 689 BC,[181] most scholars still maintain that it describes the campaigns of Sargon II.[182]

The relevance for biblical studies is that the tablets mention the Assyrian attack by Sennacherib against Hezekiah, the king of Judah, and the conquest of Azekah (2 Kgs 18–19, 2 Chron 32).[183] Although not the final word on the

Quotes from Antiquity

Azekah Inscription

The inscription on the combined tablet has been translated as follows:

(3) [...Ashur, my lord, encourage]ed me and against the land of Ju[dah I marched. In] the course of my campaign, the tribute of the ki[ng (s)... (4) [...with the mig]ht of Ashur, my lord, the province of [Hezek]iah of Judah like [...(5) [...] the city of Azekah, his stronghold, which is between my [bo]rder and the land of Judah [...(6) [like the nest of the eagle?] located on a mountain ridge, like pointed iron daggers without number reaching high to heaven [...(7) [Its walls] were strong and rivaled the highest mountains, to the (mere) sight, as if from the sky [appears its head? ...(8) [by means of beaten (earth) ra]mps, mighty? Battering rams brought near, the work of [...], with the attack by foot soldiers, [my] wa[rriors...(9) [...] they had seen [the approach of my cav]alry and they had heard the roar of the mighty troops of the god Ashur and [their] he[arts] became afraid [...(10) [The city Azekah I besieged,] I captured, I carried off its spoil, I destroyed, I devastated, [I burned with fire]....

Miano, *Shadow on the Steps*, 235.

[176] Rawlinson, *The Cuneiform Inscriptions of Western Asia. Vol. III. A Selection from the Miscellaneous Inscriptions of Assyria.*

[177] Nadav Na'aman, "Sennacherib's 'Letter to God' on His Campaign to Judah," *BASOR* 214 (1974): 25–39; David Miano and Sarah Miano, eds., *Milk and Honey: Essays on Ancient Israel and the Bible in Appreciation of the Judaic Studies Program at the University of California* (Winona Lake, Ind.: Eisenbrauns, 2007), 126; David Miano, *Shadow on the Steps: Time Measurement in Ancient Israel*, Resources for Biblical Study (Atlanta, Ga.: Society of Biblical Literature, 2010), 235.

[178] Paul Rost, *Die Keilschrifttexte Tiglat-Pilesers III* (Leipzig: Pfeiffer, 1893), 18–20; Hayim Tadmor, "The Campaigns of Sargon II of Assur: A Chronological-Historical Study (Conclusion)," *JCS* 12, no. 3 (1958): 80–84.

[179] Hugo Winckler, *Altorientalische Forschungen* (Leipzig: Pfeiffer, 1902), 2:570–74.

[180] Na'aman, "Sennacherib's 'Letter to God' on His Campaign to Judah," 26–28; "Sennacherib's Campaign to Judah and the Date of the Lmlk Stamps," 61–86.

[181] William H. Shea, "Sennacherib's Second Palestinian Campaign," *JBL* 104, no. 3 (1985): 404–407.

[182] Tadmor, "The Campaigns of Sargon II of Assur," 80–84.

[183] See Shea for the debate over the details. Shea, "Sennacherib's Second Palestinian Campaign," 404–407.

subject, Becking points out: "The joined text forms a part of a "Letter to the deity" written by Sennacherib after his campaign against Juda [*sic* Judah] in 701 BCE. Therefore the Azriyau of the Annals of Tiglath Pileser III is nowadays interpreted as a rebel from the area of Hamath. As a result of this reconsideration of the sources a Judaean or Israelite interference in the coalition of 738 BCE is very unlikely."[184]

Jerusalem Captured (597 BC)

The Babylonian King, Nebuchadnezzar II, defeated Egyptian Pharaoh Neco at the Battle of Carchemish in 605 BC and then invaded Jerusalem. To avoid the conquest of Jerusalem, King Jehoiakim of Jerusalem, made an alliance with Babylon and paid a tribute from the Temple treasury in Jerusalem. As Babylonian strength weakend, Jehoiakim, along with other nations, attempted to break away from the Babylonian alliance, resulting in a Babylonian invasion of Judah and siege of Jerusalem in 597 BC.[185] The Nebuchadnezzar Chronicle describes the capture of Jerusalem and the installation of Zedekiah as the tributary king of Judah.

The Babylonian Chronicles (626–539 BC)

The Babylonian Chronicles are a group of cuneiform tablets[186] describing the exploits of the Babylonian rulers from 626–539 BC.[187] Scholars believe that the chronicles were written in Babylon in "the latest periods of Babylonian antiquity"[188] (*ca.* 550–400 BC). They provide additional details to the biblical accounts of the capture of Jerusalem.

Following the excavations in Babylon in the ninteenth cent., the tablets were taken to the British Museum and stored in the archives. They remained there undeciphered, with translations only appearing in 1887 (Theophilus

77. A Babylonian Chronicle (*ca.* 550-400 BC) describing the first Babylonian capture of Jerusalem (605–595 BC) and Fall of Jerusalem to Nebuchadnezzar in 597 BC and the victories of Nabopolassar mentioned in 2 Kings 24:10–14. The tablet depicted here is presented upside down as it is on display in the British Museum.

The Trustees of the British Museum (ME 21946)

---

[184] Becking, *The Fall of Samaria*, 3.

[185] Walton, Matthews, and Chavalas, *IVP Bible Background Commentary: OT*, 676–77, 689, 792.

[186] *ANET* 301-7 (partial); *COS* 1.137: 467-68 (partial); Albert Kirk Grayson, *Assyrian and Babylonian Chronicles*, Texts from Cuneiform Sources 5 (Locust Valley: Augustin, 1975); Jean-Jacques Glassner, *Mesopotamian Chronicles*, ed. Benjamin R. Foster, Writings from the Ancient World 19 (Atlanta, Ga.: SBL, 2004). A list of the available texts with translations are available online at: http://www.livius.org/cg-cm/chronicles/chron00 .html.

[187] Alan R. Millard, "The Babylonian Chronicle," in *The Context of Scripture: Archival Documents from the Biblical World*, ed. William W. Hallo and K. Lawson Younger, vol. 1 (Leiden: Brill Academic, 2002), 467–68; Caroline Waerzeggers, "The Babylonian Chronicles: Classification and Provenance," *JNES* 71, no. 2 (2012): 285–98; Glassner, *Mesopotamian Chronicles*, 231; A. Leo Oppenheim, "Assyrian and Babylonian Historical Texts," in *The Ancient Near East: An Anthology of Texts and Pictures*, ed. James B. Pritchard (Princeton, NJ: Princeton University Press, 2010), 247–86.

[188] Donald J. Wiseman, *Chronicles of Chaldaean Kings (626-556 BC) in the British Museum* (London: Trustee of the British Museum, 1961), v.

Quotes from Antiquity

The Bible states:

And Nebuchadnezzar king of Babylon came to the city while his servants were besieging it, and Jehoiachin the king of Judah gave himself up to the king of Babylon, himself and his mother and his servants and his officials and his palace officials. The king of Babylon took him prisoner in the eighth year of his reign and carried off all the treasures of the house of the Lord and the treasures of the king's house, and cut in pieces all the vessels of gold in the temple of the Lord, which Solomon king of Israel had made, as the Lord had foretold. He carried away all Jerusalem and all the officials and all the mighty men of valor, 10,000 captives, and all the craftsmen and the smiths. None remained, except the poorest people of the land (2 Kgs 24:10–14).

The Babylonian Chronicle states:

The seventh year [of Nebuchadnezzar's reign 597 BC], in the month of Kislev [Nov/Dec], the king of Akkad [Babylonia] mustered his troops, marched on Hatti [Palestine], and set up his quarters facing the city of Yehud [Jerusalem]. In the month of Adar, the second day, he took the city and captured the king. He installed there a king of his choice. He colle[ected] its massive tribute and went back to Babylon.

Glassner, *Mesopotamian Chronicles*, 231.

G. Pinches), 1923 (Sidney Smith), and the Nebuchadnezzar Chronicles translated by Donald Wiseman in 1956.[189]

Other tablets from the Babylonian Chronicles mention the rebellion which resulted in the murder of Sennacherib, the king of Assyria, by his son (747–668 BC, 2 Kgs 19:36; Isa 37:37); the fall of Nineveh (612 BC, 2 Kgs 23:29; Jer 46:2; 2 Chron 35:20–25); the Battle of Charchemish (605 BC, 2 Kgs 24:7); and the fall of Babylon (539 BC, Isa 13, 21; Jer 50–51).[190]

Siege of Jerusalem (586 BC)

The puppet king, Zedekiah, revolted against Babylon rule and entered into an alliance with the Egyptian Pharaoh Hophra. The offended Babylonian king, Nebuchadnezzar responed by invading Judah and attacking Jerusalem in 589 BC (2 Kgs 25:1–7). The two year siege ended with the conquest of Jerusalem and the capture of Zedekiah, who was blinded and carried off to Babylon as a prisoner (587 BC).

78. Artist recreation of the Assyrian siege of Lachish, based on the assyrian reliefs on display at the British Museum.

Seige of Lachish (701 BC)

Lachish (Tel ed-Duweir) was one of the largest fortified Judean cities and

[189] Wiseman, *Chronicles of Chaldaean Kings (626-556 BC) in the British Museum.*

[190] Pfeiffer, *Wycliffe Dictionary of Biblical Archaeology*, 133–36; Masters, *Heritage of Evidence*, 73–80.

protected the approach to Jerusalem (Jer 34:6–7). The siege and capture of Lachish is mentioned in the Bible (2 Kgs 18; 2 Chron 32; Micah 1:13) as well as recorded in the Annals of Sennacherib (see Fig. 75) and depicted on the reliefs of Sennacherib's palace in Nineveh (see Figs. 80, 81).

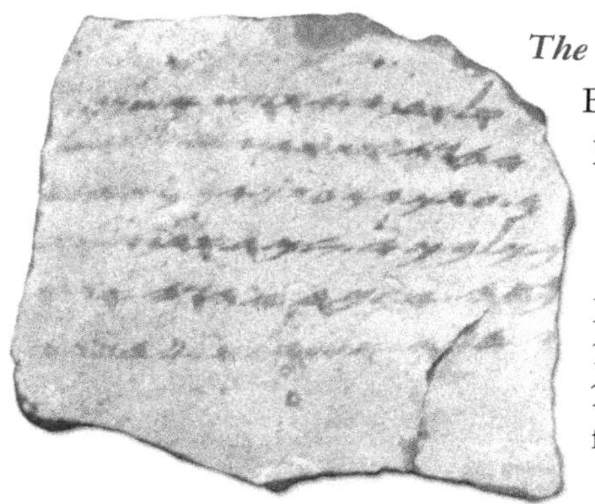

79. Lachish Ostracon II. The word "Yahweh" [yhwh] is used as the first word (on right) of line 2 in this letter.

The Lachish Letters

Between 1935 and 1938, James L. Starkey[191] found 18 pottery sherds (ostraca) written in black ink, in the guardroom of the city gate (stratum III) at the excavations at Tel ed-Duweir (now identified as Lachish),[192] which became known as the Lachish Letters (or Hoshaiah Letters; Israel Museum; IAA 1938.127; IAA 1938.128; British Museum; ME 125701–07, 15a; see Fig. 79).[193] In 1938 Olga Tufnell found 3 more sherds to make a total of 21 ostraca.[194] First deciphered by Harry Torczyner, they were identified as a series of correspondence written in an ancient form of Hebrew, from the time of Jeremiah, describing how there were only three cities remaining under Judean control just prior to the fall of the southern kingdom of Judah to the Babylonians under Nebuchadnezzar.[195] They indicate that the town of Azekah, under the control of Nebuchadnezzar's rebellious puppet king, had just fallen.[196] This is confirmed by Jeremiah and Isaiah (Jer 34:6–7; Isa 36:1–2).

Shortly after the Lachish letters were written (589 or 588 BC),[197] Lachish would also fall, along with the capital of Jerusalem. Mitchell relays that:

> The ostraca belong to this time, and are mostly letters written from outposts to a man named Ya'oah, the military commander at Lachish, reporting on the situation. Most of them use the language of polite formality, rather unexpectedly in view of the critical situation which culminated in total defeat. 'May Yahweh cause my lord to hear news of peace, even now, even now. Who is your servant but a dog that my lord should remember his servant?' [198]

---

[191] After Starkey was murdered in 1938, local Arabs looted all that was left of the temple at Lachish, including the remains of the lowest level.

[192] William F. Albright, "Palestinian Inscriptions: The Lachish Ostraca," in *The Ancient Near East: An Anthology of Texts and Pictures*, ed. James B. Pritchard (Princeton, NJ: Princeton University Press, 2010), 292–93; David Ussishkin, *Biblical Lachish: A Tale of Construction, Destruction, Excavation and Restoration*, trans. Miriam Feinberg Vamosh (Jerusalem, Israel: Israel Exploration Society and Biblical Archaeology Society, 2014). Lachish was also excavated by the Tel Aviv University (1973-87).

[193] Lindenberger, *Ancient Aramaic and Hebrew Letters*, 113–18, 124–31; Charles Marston, "The Lachish Letters," *ExpTim* 46, no. 11 (1935): 502–504; Joseph Reider, "The Lachish Letters," *JQR* 29, no. 3 (1939): 225–39; D. Winston Thomas, "The Lachish Letters," *JTS* 40 (1939): 1–15; G. Ernest Wright, "Judean Lachish," *BA* 18, no. 1 (February 1, 1955): 9–17; Nissim R. Ganor, "The Lachish Letters," *PEQ* 99, no. 2 (74-77): 74–77; LeMaire, *Inscriptions Hébraïques. I. Les Ostraca.*; Albright, "Palestinian Inscriptions: The Lachish Ostraca," 192–93; Gibson, *Textbook of Syrian Semitic Inscriptions*, 1:32–49. See also *ANET* 321-22; *COS* 3.42: 78-81.

[194] Shmuel Ahituv, *Echoes from the Past: Hebrew and Cognate Inscriptions from the Biblical Period* (Jerusalem: Carta, 2008), 63.

[195] Harry Torczyner et al., *Lachish I (Tell Ed Duweir): Lachish Letters* (Oxford: Oxford University Press, 1938).

[196] John W. Adey, "Social and Historical Aspects of the Lachish Letters" (MPhil, University of Cambridge, 2012).

[197] Albright, "Palestinian Inscriptions: The Lachish Ostraca," 292.

[198] T. C. Mitchell, *Biblical Archaeology: Documents from the British Museum* (Cambridge, U.K.: Cambridge University Press, 1988), 78–79.

Quotes from Antiquity

Lachish letter III

Your servant, Hosayahu, sent to inform my lord, Yaush: May YHWH cause my lord to hear tidings of peace and tidings of good. And now, open the ear of your servant concerning the letter which you sent to your servant last evening because the heart of your servant is ill since your sending it to your servant. And inasmuch as my lord said "Don't you know how to read a letter?" As YHWH lives if anyone has ever tried to read me a letter! And as for every letter that comes to me, if I read it. And furthermore, I will grant it as nothing. And to your servant it has been reported saying: The commander of the army Konyahu son of Elnatan, has gone down to go to Egypt and he sent to commandeer Hodawyahu son of Ahiyahu and his men from here. And as for the letter of Tobiyahu, the servant of the king, which came to Sallum, the son of Yaddua, from the prophet, saying, "Be on guard!" your ser[va]nt is sending it to my lord.

Ahituv, *Echoes from the Past,* 63.

Lachish letter IV

And let (my lord) know that we are watching for the signals of Lachish, according to all the indications which my lord hath given, for we cannot see Azekah.

Albright, "Palestinian Inscriptions," 293.

Scholars debate where the letters were written from, and where they were sent to, since the wording is unclear.[199]

Letter IV seems to indicate that it was written just before the account of Jeremiah 34:6, 7 was written, in which Azekah and Lachish are recorded as still being safe.[200] Ostracon IV indicated that Azekah had already fallen and Lachish and Jerusalem were next.[201] Yadin suggests that they are draft documents written in haste on potsherds to be later transcribed to papyrus.[202]

The Lachish letters are important because they confirm ed-Duweir as the ancient city of Lachish. In addition, several biblical names, including Yahweh (the full form of the *Tetragrammaton YHWH* is used 10 times; see Fig. 79), are confirmed recorded on the ostraca.[203] They help to date the period they were written because of the style of the pottery. They confirm the chronological order of the destruction of the remaining cities of ancient Judah.

The Lachish Reliefs

The Lachish reliefs are a group of stone reliefs carved in the walls (12 m. wide and 5.10 m. long) of the Palace of Sennacherib (704–681 BC) that depict the Assyrian victory over the kingdom of Judah in the siege of Lachish (701 BC), one of Judah's major cities. The Palace of Sennacherib was discovered by Austen Henry Layard between 1845–1847, and the large panel reliefs are currently displayed in the British Museum (Room 10b; see Figs. 81, 82).[204]

The Bible mentions the siege of Lachish and Hezekiah offering to pay tribute to Sennacherib to prevent the siege of Jerusalem (2 Kgs 18:13–16; Isa 36:1–2). However, the

---

[199] Oded Borowski, "Scholars' Corner: Yadin Presents New Interpretation of the Famous Lachish Letters," *BAR* 10, no. 2 (1984): 74–77.

[200] Anson F. Rainey, "Watching for the Signal Fires of Lachish," *PEQ* 119 (1987): 149–51.

[201] Albright, "Palestinian Inscriptions: The Lachish Ostraca," 293.

[202] Yigael Yadin, "The Lachish Letters—Originals or Copies and Drafts?," in *Recent Archaeology in the Land of Israel*, ed. Hershel Shanks and Benjamin Mazar, 2nd ed. (Washington, D.C.: Biblical Archaeology Society, 1985), 179–86; Borowski, "Scholars' Corner: Yadin Presents New Interpretation of the Famous Lachish Letters"; John A. Emerton, "Were the Lachish Letters Sent to or from Lachish?," *PEQ* 133 (2001): 2–15.

[203] André LeMaire, "Ostraca and Incised Inscriptions," in *The Renewed Archaeological Excavations at Lachish (1973-1994): Introduction. The Bronze Age Stratigraphy and Architecture*, ed. David Ussishkin (Tel Aviv, Israel: Emery and Claire Yass Publications in Archaeology, 2004), 2099–2132.

[204] David Ussishkin, "The 'Lachish Reliefs' and the City of Lachish," *IEJ* 30, no. 3/4 (1980): 174–95.

80. Relief panel of the siege of Lachish by Sennacherib. Flaming arrows are fired at the city gate during the siege, while Jewish captives are led out of conquered Judea. Time is depicted as static as the captives would have been taken away after the battle of Lachish.

The Trustees of the British Museum (ME 124906)

prophet Isaiah prophecied that Sennacherib:

> shall not come into this city or shoot an arrow there or come before it with a shield or cast up a siege mound against it. . . . And the angel of the Lord went out and struck down 185,000 in the camp of the Assyrians. And when people arose early in the morning, behold, these were all dead bodies. Then Sennacherib king of Assyria departed and returned home and lived at Nineveh (Isa 37:33, 36–37).

Assyrian Kings

The Esarhaddon Chronicle

A clay tablet from a collection called the Babylonian Chronicles (143 texts), and known as the Esarhaddon Chronicles,[205] which contains twenty-one texts of the Babylon Inscriptions recounting the reign of the Neo-Assyrian king, Esarhaddon (681–669 BC).[206] This tablet (ABC

---

[205] A. Kirk Grayson and James Novotny, *The Royal Inscriptions of Sennacherib, King of Assyria: Part 1*, Royal Inscriptions of the Neo-Assyrian Period 3.1 (Winona Lake, IN: Eisenbrauns, 2012), 29–55 nos. 1–3; *The Royal Inscriptions of Sennacherib, King of Assyria: Part 2*, Royal Inscriptions of the Neo-Assyrian Period 3.2 (Winona Lake, IN: Eisenbrauns, 2014), 28–29.

[206] Glassner, *Mesopotamian Chronicles*, 206–10; Grayson, *Assyrian and Babylonian Chronicles*, 30–32, 125–28; Erie Leichty, *Royal Inscriptions of Esarhaddon, King of Assyria 680-699 BC*, The Royal Inscriptions of the Neo-Assyrian Period 4 (Winona Lake, Ind.:

14/CM 18, see Fig. 82) was acquired by the British Museum (BM 25091) in 1898 and stored undeciphered until this tablet was first published in 1924 by Sidney Smith.[207] When found, the tablet was broken in two pieces, and portions of the tablet are missing, but the text was reconstructed from parallel texts (i.e., Akitu Chronicle). This tablet recorded the accounts of the Assyrian military campaigns of King Esarhaddon (Assyr. *Aššur-aḫa-iddina* "the god Ashur has given a brother"; 681–669 BC)[208] and the accessions of his sons *Aššurbanipal* in Assyria and *Šamaš-šuma-ukin* in Babylonia.[209]

81. The only inscription which identifies Lachish on a relief reads: "Sennacherib, the mighty king, king of the country of Assyria, sitting on the throne of judgment, before (or at the entrance of) the city of Lachish (Lakhisha). I give permission for its slaughter."

Austen H. Layard, *Discoveries Among the Ruins of Nineveh and Babylon* (New York: Harper & Sons, 1853), 128.

Although Esarhaddon is briefly mentioned in the biblical text (2 Kings 19:37=Isa 37:38) he was the dominant figure during the reign of Manasseh, King of Judah. On two occasions Esarhaddon ordered the kings of Syria-Palestine and Cyprus to provide building materials (cedars of Lebanon) for the building of a port in Sidon and his palace in Nineveh. Manasseh, King of Judah, is specifically mentioned in the second project.[210]

The value of the Esarhaddon Chronicle, for biblical studies, is in confirming the identity of the Assyrian king Esarhaddon as well as Sennacherib (2 Kgs 18:13–19:37 = Isa 36–37; 2 Chr 32:1–23), Tirhakah (2 Kgs 19:9 = Isa 37:9), Neco (2 Kgs 23:28–30 = 2 Chr 35:20–27) and Manasseh, King of Judah (2 Kgs 21:1–18, 2 Chr 33:1–17), who are all

82. Drawing of the Esarhaddon Chronicle that mentions the reign of Esarhaddon and his son Aššurbanipal in Assyria. It measures 50 mm wide and 76 mm long.

The Trustees of the British Museum (BM 25091)

Eisenbrauns, 2011); Jamie Novotny, "New Proposed Chronological Sequence and Dates of Composition of Esarhaddon's Babylon Inscriptions," *JCS* 67 (January 1, 2015): 147; Irving Finkel and R. J. Van der Spek, *Babylonian Chronicles of the Hellenistic Period*, Forthcoming.

[207] Sidney Smith, *Babylonian Historical Texts Relating to the Capture and Downfall of Babylon* (London: Methuen & Co, 1924), 14; M. Sigrist, R. Zadok, C. B. F. Walker, *Catalogue of the Babylonian Tablets in the British Museum, III* (London, BMP, 2006; Robert Drews, "The Babylonian Chronicles and Berossus," *IRAQ* 37, no. 1 (1975): 39–55.

[208] A. Kirk Grayson, "Esarhaddon (Person)," ed. David Noel Freedman et al., *ABD* (New York, N.Y.: Doubleday, 1996), 2:574.

[209] Grayson, *Assyrian and Babylonian Chronicles*, 30–32, 125–28.

[210] Luckenbill, *Ancient Records of Assyria and Babylon*, 2:690; Pritchard, *ANET OT*, 290–91.

mentioned in the Bible.

Nebuchadnezzar II (r. *ca.* 605–562 BC)

Nebuchadnezzar II (Akk. "O god Nabu, protect my son")[211] was the Assyrian king of the Neo-Babylonian Empire who reigned from *ca.* 605–562 BC. Nebuchadnezzar is famous for several notable building projects including the hanging gardens (Berosus), the Ishtar Gate, the "northern" palace, and the ziggurat. He is also known for destroying the temple in Jerusaelem then carrying the people of Judah off to Babylon in captivity. He is often mentioned in the Bible (Jer 21–52; Dan 1–5; 2 Kgs 24:1–25:22; Ezra 1:7–6:5; Ezek 26:7–30:10), and his existence has been verified by several artifacts.[212]

83. Building brick inscribed with the name of King Nebuchadnezzar II (ca. 600–550 BC) and his title.

Royal Ontario Museum (ROM 912.32)

The Nebuchadnezzar II's Brick

Ancient kings often used inscribed baked bricks[213] in their constructions that would include the name, titles and patronymic names of the King. One such ceramic brick bears the name of Nebuchadnezzar II in cuneiform and was excavated by Robert Koldeway from the south-east corner of the southern citadel (Kasr) in the city of Babylon in 1900–1901.[214] It is one of the earliest stamps of Nebuchadnezzar (604–561 BC), and is now on display in Room 6 of the Museum of the Ancient Near East, Pergamum Museum, Berlin (VA 3862). It is translated as: "King of Babylon, fosterer of Esagilaand Ezida, son of Nabopolassar, King of Babylon."[215]

Similar bricks are on display in the British Museum (ME 90081), the Oriental Institute Museum of the University of Chicago (OIM A2502) and the Royal Ontario Museum (ROM 912.32; see Fig. 83). Other inscribed bricks have been identified for several Babylonian rulers such as Nabopolassar (Hecht Museum, Haifa, NapIB6, NapIB7), Esarhaddon (ME 90248), Sennacherib (ME 90210), Sargon II (Vat. cat. 15025), and Cyrus (ME 118362).[216]

---

[211] Ronald F. Youngblood, F. F. Bruce, and R. K. Harrison, eds., *Unlock the Bible: Keys to Exploring the Culture and Times*, The Best of Nelson's New Illustrated Bible Dictionary to Enrich Your Bible Study (Nashville, Tenn.: Nelson, 2012), 199.

[212] Wiseman, *Chronicles of Chaldaean Kings (626-556 BC) in the British Museum*; Donald J. Wiseman, *Nebuchadnezzar and Babylon*, Schweich Lectures 1983 (Oxford: Oxford University Press, 1985); Ronald H. Sack, "Nebuchadnezzar (Person)," ed. David Noel Freedman et al., *ABD* (New York, N.Y.: Doubleday, 1996), 1058–59.

[213] Koldeway identified three kinds of stamps used to produce the bricks: terracotta pottery, wood moulded in sand to produce a bronze cast and stone cut moulds. Robert Koldewey, *The Excavations at Babylon*, trans. Agnes S. Johns (New York, N.Y.: MacMillan & Co., 1914), 75–76.

[214] Ibid., vi.

[215] Ibid., 75.

[216] Ibid., 79–80.

Jehoiachin (609–598 BC)

Jehoiachin (Heb. "Yahweh establishes" originally Jeconiah or Coniah [Ezek 1:2]) was eighteen when he came to the throne (598 BC) and only reigned for three months and ten days (2 Kgs 24:12, 24:15–24:16, 25:27–25:30; 2 Chron 36:9–36:10). In revenge for his father's alliance with Egypt, Nebuchadnezzar invaded Judah and took many slaves back to Babylon. Nebuchadnezzar stripped the temple of its treasure and carried off the rich, including Jehoiachin, to leave only a poor remnant behind. Jehoiachin was imprisoned, where he spent most of his life until Evil Merodach of Babylon released him after thirty-six years. Although he was given a place of prominence he would never return to Judah to take the throne (2 Kgs 25:27–30).[217] The prophecies of Ezekiel and Jeremiah correspond to this period of biblical history (Jer 22:24–22:6, 29:2, 52:31–52:34; Ezek 17:12).

84. Clay tablet from Babylon mentioning the rations for King Jehoiachin, the exiled king of Judah, and his sons, captives in Babylon.

Pergamum Museum, Berlin, Germany (VAT 16378). © Ferrell Jenkins BiblicalStudies.info.

The Jehoiachin's Ration Tablet

The biblical account of King Jehoiachin states that following his imprisonment "every day of his life he dined regularly at the king's table, and for his allowance, *a regular allowance* was given him by the king, according to his daily needs, as long as he lived." (emphasis added; 2 Kgs 25:29–30).

This was confirmed in 1900 with the discovery by Robert Koldeway, during the excavations of the city of Babylon, of an Akkadian tablet (VAT 16378; see Fig. 84) in cuneiform script that dated to 592–591 BC describing the list of rations set aside for a prisoner of Nebuchadnezzar, who has been identified as Jehoiachin.[218]

Of the thousands of tablets discovered in the city, four were discovered in the vault of King Nebuchadnezzar.[219] These were tablets that set forth the quantity of monthly rations for the prisoners (see *Quotes from Antiqity*).[220]

Quotes from Antiquity

Jehoiachin's Ration Tablet

32 pints (15 liters) (of sesame oil) for Jehoiachin [*Ya'u-kīnu*] king of Judah [*Yahudu*]
5 pints (2.5 liters) (of sesame oil) for [the 5] sons of the king of Judah
8 pints (4 liters) (of sesame oil) for 8 men of Judah: 1 pint (1/2 liter) each.

Studevant-Hickman, Melville, and Noegel, "Neo-Babylonian Period Texts", 386.

---

[217] J. M. Berridge, "Jehoiachin," ed. David Noel Freedman et al., *ABD* (New York, N.Y.: Doubleday, 1996), 3:661–3.

[218] D. Winton Thomas, ed., *Document From Old Testament Times* (Nashville, Tenn.: Nelson, 1961), 84.

[219] Benjamin Studevant-Hickman, Sarah C. Melville, and Scott Noegel, "Neo-Babylonian Period Texts from Babylonia and Syro-Palestine," in *Ancient Near East: Historical Sources in Translation*, ed. Mark W. Chavalas, Blackwell Sourcebooks in Ancient History (Oxford: Wiley & Sons, 2006), 386. See also *ANET* 308.

[220] Ernst F. Weidner, "Johachin, König von Jud, in Babylonischen Keischrifttexten," in *Mélanges syriens: offerts à monsieur René Dussaud, secrétaire perpétuel de l'Académie des Inscriptions et Belles-Lettres*, ed. René Dussaud, vol. 2 (Paris, France: P. Geuthner, 1939), 2:923–35.

The texts not only attest to the reality of the Babylonian exile,[221] but also support the precision of the account recorded in 2 Kings 25 that the king of Babylon provided provisions for Jehoiachin.

CONCLUSION

Although archaeology is indeed limited in what it can prove, and may not (yet) contain full evidence that the United Monarchy of the biblical narrative occurred precisely as described in the Bible, the archaeological evidence laid out in this chapter indicates that the biblical account of David and Solomon is historically plausible. The arifacts, inscriptions and seals listed here in this chapter along with several recent discoveries found in Jerusalem,[222] from the Iron Age occupation, argue for a centralized literate authority in Jerusalem at the time of David and Solomon. This is a cautionary reminder for critical scholars, who place so much weight on negative evidence, to be wary when making unsupported claims, as there is much more evidence available than may at first seem to be the case.

The weight of archaeological discoveries presented here and in other new excavations harmonize with the biblical narrative and indicate that the Bible is a reliable and trustworthy document.

[221] Archival texts from Mesopotamia also mentions Jews living in the region and naming one of their new settlements "city of Judah" (*Al Yaḫudu*) (K.8434). J. Nicholas Postgate, "The Four 'Neo-Assyrian' Tablets from Šēḫ Ḥamad," *State Archives of Assyria Bulletin* 7 (1993): 109–24; F. M. Fales, "West Semitic Names in the Šēḫ Ḥamad Texts," *State Archives of Assyria Bulletin* 7 (1993): 139–50; "A List of Assyrian and West Semitic Women's Names," *Iraq* 41, no. 1 (1979): 55–73; K. Lawson Younger, "Yahweh at Ashkelon and Calaḫ? Yahwistic Names in Neo-Assyrian," *VT* 52, no. 2 (2002): 207–18.

[222] Graves, *Biblical Archaeology Vol 1: An Introduction* 2nd ed 1:198–202.

Babylonian Exile

85. Relief of Assyrian heavy-armed arhers (700–692 BC) from Nineveh, South-West Palace. Nahum prophesied the fall of Nineveh, the Babylonian capital, by the Assyrians (Nah 1) and it is also described in the Babylonian Chronicle.

The period of biblical history that concerns the Babylonian exile involves the region of modern day Iran and Iraq. Due to the recent wars and destruction by the Islamic State of Iraq and Syria (ISIS)[1] humanity is losing many of the artifacts from this period. Fortunately many of the artifacts discovered have been preserved in museums around the world. Many of these have been listed here to help preserve the heritage of the biblical periods.

Jeremiah

Jeremiah (Heb. "Yahweh is lifted up," "throw," or "found")[2] prophesied between the reigns of King Josiah (640–609 BC) and Zedekiah (597–586 BC) during some of the most difficult times for Judah. Jeremiah was the son of Hilkiah, a priest from Anathoth, a small town just northeast of Jerusalem (Jer 1:1). He was called to be a prophet in the thirteenth year of King Josiah (627–626 BC; Jer 1:2). Although he warned his people to repent, he was to witness the destruction of Jerusalem and the Temple (see Lamentations).

Although Jeremiah never married and did not become involved in the festivals of his people (Jer 16:2–8), he did have a close friend in Baruch his scribe. Baruch copied down Jeremiah's prophecies and read them publicly before the people.

The major emphasis of his message and prophecy was the destruction of Jerusalem, which would be accomplished through an enemy from the north (Jer 1:11–16). As a result of his unpopular messages of destruction and judgment, Jeremiah was in constant conflict with the people and leaders, both political and religious (Jer 20:1–6). Jehoiakim destroyed the original scroll of Jeremiah's prophecies, which Baruch had recorded, by cutting it in to pieces and burning it in the fire (Jer 36:9–23), but Jeremiah dictacted it again to Baruch. He was even persecuted in his home town of Anathoth (Jer 11:18–23) and forced to move to Jerusalem,

---

[1] Also known as Islamic State of Iraq and the Levant (ISIL), and Islamic State of Iraq and ash-Sham, (DAESH). They are a self-proclaimed Islamic extremist militant group under the leadership of Sunni Arabs from Iraq and Syria. They have destroyed many of the ancient sites and museums in Iraq and Syria.

[2] These latter meanings are thought to be related to the way that Jeremiah was thrown into the office of prophet or the way the message was thrown as a judgment into the nation of Judah. But whatever the meaning, certainly Yahweh is exalted or lifted up by his message.

where he spent most of his prophetic ministry.

He spoke of Nebuchadnezzar, Judah's hated enemy, as "the servant of the Lord" (Jer 25:9; 27:06), which resulted in a charge of treason for which he was convicted and put in prison (Jer 37:11; 38:1–6). On other occasions he would prophecy of Babylon's destruction (Jer 50–51), which led to his enemies questioning his integrity and the genuiness of his prophecies (Jer 43:1–3; 28:1; 29:24).

Jeremiah also spoke out against the wicked kings of Judah, including Jehoahaz and Jehoiakim (Jer 22:11–17). But while Jeremiah spoke of judgement and doom, he also had words of hope and encouragement in the form of Messianic hope oracles, found scattered throughout his prophecies (Jer 30–31; 32:36; 33:06; 34:4).[3]

Following Jerusalem's destruction by the Babylonians in 586 BC, Jeremiah moved to Mizpah (Jer 40:5). Then after Gedaliah's assassination, he was sent to Egypt by his enemies (Jer 42:1–43:07). There in Egyptian exile, he continued his ministry for a brief period (Jer 43:8–13; 44:1–30). Although the account of his death is not recorded, unsupported tradition records that Jeremiah died in exile in Egypt as a martyr.[4]

The Baruch Seal (Jer 32:1–16)

Two clay bulla have surfaced, from antiquities dealers, which purportedly mention Baruch, the Son of Neriah, Jeremiah's scribe (Jer 32:1–16; 36:4). One surfaced in 1975 (IMJ 76.22.2299) and was published by Nahman Avigad,[5] while the other came to light in 1996, showing the same seal, but with an imprint of a fingerprint (see Fig. 86).[6] Some believe this could be the fingerprint of Baruch himself. The bulla reads:

Line	Transliteration	Translation
1	*lbrkyhw*	[belonging] to Berachyahu
2	*bn nryhw*	son of Neriyahu
3	*hspr*	the scribe

86. Bulla of Berachyahu ben Neriah, the Scribe, with a fingerprint in the upper right corner. It only measures 17 by 16 mm.

Wikimedia Commons

Although N. P. Lemche and others have called into question the authenticity of the Baruch seals,[7] Shmuel Ahituv concludes that the identification with Jeremiah's Baruch is

[3] Jack R. Lundbom, "Jeremiah (Prophet)," ed. David Noel Freedman et al., *ABD* (New York, N.Y.: Doubleday, 1996), 3:685–98.

[4] Philip J. King, *Jeremiah: An Archaeological Companion* (Louisville, Ky.: Westminster/John Knox, 1993), 6; Edward Lipinski and S. David Sperling, "Jeremiah," in *EJ*, ed. Michael Berenbaum and Fred Skolnik, 2nd ed., vol. 11 (New York, N.Y.: MacMillan, 2006), 11:124–33.

[5] Nahman Avigad, "Jerahmeel & Baruch," *BAR* 42, no. 2 (1979): 114–18; Hershel Shanks, "Jeremiah's Scribe and Confidant Speaks from a Hoard of Clay Bullae," *BAR* 13, no. 5 (1987): 58–65.

[6] Tsvi Schneider, "Six Biblical Signatures: Seals and Seal Impressions of Six Biblical Personages Recovered," *BAR* 17, no. 4 (1991): 26–33; Hershel Shanks, "Fingerprint of Jeremiah's Scribe," *BAR* 22, no. 2 (1996): 36–38; King, *Jeremiah*, 85–101.

[7] Hershel Shanks et al., "Face to Face: Biblical Minimalists Meet Their Challenge," *BAR* 23, no. 4 (1997): 37–38; Rollston and Vaughn, "The Antiquities Market, Sensationalized Textual Data, and Modern Forgeries," 62, 67.

almost certain.[8]

However, caution must be exercised in unprovenanced finds (i.e., that have not been located in a sealed excavation square), given the recent forgery charges laid against a number of antiquities dealers.[9] The exact location where this seal was found is also unknown, but is believed to have come from an excavation by Yigal Shiloh.[10]

The Sarsekim Tablet (Jer 39:3)

There are over 130,000 cuneiform tablets in the British Museum archives, and many of them have never been translated.[11] In 2007, while Michael Jursa, associate professor at the University of Vienna, was working in the tablet room deciphering a tablet from Sippar, a Babylonian city where tens of thousands of tablets were discovered,[12] he noticed the Biblical name of Nebo-Sarsekim, the chief officer of Nebuchadnezzar during the siege of Jerusalem (Jer 39:3; see Fig. 87 and *Quotes from Antiquity*).[13] It dates to the tenth year of Nebuchadnezzar (595 BC), just eight years before the fall of Jerusalem.

87. Drawing of the Sarsekim Tablet that mentions Sarsekim, Nebuchadnezzar's chief officer, during the siege of Jerusalem in Jeremiah 39:3–4. It is 2.13 in (5.5 cm) wide.
The Trustees of the British Museum (ME 114789)

Although the tablet was discovered in the 1880's by Hormuzd Rassam it was later brought to the British Museum in the 1920's and remained unread until 2007.

While the name Nebo-Sarsekim is only mentioned once in the OT (Jer 39:3), it demonstrates the detail at which the biblical writers wrote and supports the historical accuracy of the biblical text.

> *Quotes from Antiquity*
>
> **Sarsekim Tablet states:**
>
> 1·5 lb [minas 0.75 kg] of gold belonging to Nabû-šarrussu-(u)kin, Chief of courtiers [eunuch], which he forwarded to the [temple] Esaggil through the agency of Arad-Banitu, Courtier, Arad-Banitu has delivered at the Esaggil. In the presence of Bel-usat son of Aplâ, member of the royal guards, and Nadin son of Marduk-zer-ibni. Shebat 18th, 10th year of Nebuchadrezzar, king of Babylon.
>
> Becking, "The Identity of Nabu-Sharrussu-Ukin," 41.

EZEKIEL

Ezekiel (Heb. "God hardens or strengthens") was among the first Jews to go into exile in Babylon when Nebuchadnezzar captured Jerusalem in 597 BC. Jehoiakim, King of Judah

[8] Shmuel Ahituv, *Handbook of Ancient Hebrew Inscriptions: From the Period of the First Commonwealth and the Beginning of the Second Commonwealth (Hebrew, Philistine, Edomite, Moabite, Ammonite, and the Bileam Inscriptions)*, Biblical Encyclopaedia Library 7 (Jerusalem, Israel: Bialik, 1992), 129 [Hebrew].

[9] Rollston and Vaughn, "The Antiquities Market, Sensationalized Textual Data, and Modern Forgeries," 61–68.

[10] Avigad, "Jerahmeel & Baruch," 118.

[11] Irving Finkel, "Finkel Assistant Keeper Ancient Mesopotamian (i.e. Sumerian, Babylonian and Assyrian) Script, Languages and Cultures Department: Middle East," *The British Museum*, 2015, n.p., http://www.britishmuseum.org/about_us/departments/staff/middle_east/irving_finkel.aspx.

[12] Hermann Gasche and Caroline Janssen, "Sippar," in *OEANE*, ed. Eric M. Meyers, vol. 5 (Oxford: Oxford University Press, 1997), 47–49.

[13] Bob Becking, "The Identity of Nabu-Sharrussu-Ukin, the Chamberlain: An Epigraphic Note on Jeremiah 39,3. With an Appendix on the Nebu(!)sarsekim Tablet by Henry Stadhouders," *BN* 140 (2009): 41; Leichty, *Royal Inscriptions of Esarhaddon, King of Assyria 680-699 BC*, 79–86.

(608–598 BC), died while Nebuchadnezzar was on his way to punish him, so Nebuchadnezzar appointed Jehoiachin puppet king of Judah (Ezek 1:2). He only reigned for three months and ten days. He was only eight when he came to the throne late in 598 BC (2 Chron 36:9). In revenge for his father Jehoiakim's alliance with Egypt (2 Kgs 24:17), Nebuchadnezzar invaded Judah and took many citizens from Judah into exile, including Ezekiel and Jehoiachin in 597 BC (2 Kgs 24:8–12). Ezekiel settled with other exiles in a Jewish colony at Tel Aviv (Ezek 1:1).

Ezekiel 1:3 states that he was a priest and the son of Buzi. However, he was in Babylon, exiled from Jerusalem and could not minister in the temple, so God called him to be a prophet in the period from 598–573 BC (Ezek 24:15–18; 29:17). Ezekiel exercised his ministry during the last years of Jehoiachin (2 Kgs 24:17), King of Judah, and through the reign of Zedekiah into the period of the exile.

Although Ezekiel was isolated from the temple in Jerusalem, he often spoke about the temple and its ceremonies. Like Hosea, he acted out many of his prophecies in his own life, symbolising what would happen to Judah.

Many of the remnant in Jerusalem hoped for a speedy end to the destruction and so false prophets took the opportunity to tell the people what they wanted to hear. Ezekiel's ministry confirmed Jeremiah's message (Jer 29:10). After the final fall of Jerusalem in 586 BC, Ezekiel was given the task of encouraging and comforting the people. While Jeremiah viewed things from Jerusalem, which led him to lament its destruction, Ezekiel's perspective was that of an exile bringing encouragement to the captives.

The Stela of Esarhaddon (Ezek 38:4)

The stela of Esarhaddon (also Dolerite, Zincirli or Senjirli stele)[14] depicts the Assyrian king Esarhaddon holding the rope of two captives attached to a ring through their lip. The captives under submission are believed to be the son of Egypt's Pharaoh Taharqa, and Baal I, king of Tyre (671 BC).[15] Esarhaddon's sons, Shamash-shum-ukin and Ashurbanipal, are depicted on the sides of the stele. Today the stela is displayed in the Pergamum Museum in Berlin (VA 2708; see Fig. 88).

The prophet Amos warned the wealthy people of Israel during the eighth cent. BC with language that is

88. Esarhaddon returned after defeating Taharqa at Memphis; Taharqa's son, the prince, is shown in bondage on this stele. It has the story in cuneiform that has been inscribed over the depicted scene. This victory was the second battle, from 671 BC. The first battle was won by Taharqa in 674 BC.

Pergamum Museum, Berlin (VA 2708). © Miguel Hermoso Cuesta / Wikimedia Commons

[14] Königliche Museen zu Berlin, *Verzeichnis Der in Der Formerei Der Königl. Museen Käuflichen Gipsabgüsse* (Berlin: Herausgegeben von der General-Verwaltung, 1902), 20.

[15] Fant and Reddish, *Lost Treasures of the Bible*, 179; Hoerth, *Archaeology and the Old Testament*, 355.

reminiscent of the images on this stele. Amos states: "The Lord God has sworn by his holiness that, behold, the days are coming upon you, when they shall take you away with hooks, even the last of you with fishhooks" (Amos 4:2).

Ezekiel also describes the fate of Gog, of the land of Magog: "And I will turn you about and put hooks into your jaws, and I will bring you out, and all your army, horses and horsemen, all of them clothed in full armor, a great host, all of them with buckler and shield, wielding swords" (Ezek 38:4).

DANIEL

Daniel (Heb. "God's judge", "God is judge" or "God is my judge") was a man of nobility belonging to the house of David. Nebuchadnezzar was the Babylonian king who attacked Judah in the south three times. The first time was in 605 BC. By this time, the northern kingdom of Israel had already spent a little over 100 years in captivity, having been conquered and taken by the Assyrians.

A second invasion came in 597 BC when Jehoiakim, the King of Judah, surrendered Jerusalem, and Judah was carried off into exile with many of the Jewish leaders. The prophets, Ezekiel and Daniel, were among those taken into captivity to Babylon by King Nebuchadnezzar.

The third invasion came in 586 BC when Jerusalem was completely destroyed and all the people of the land were taken into captivity. Jeremiah was present in Jerusalem when it was taken and finally destroyed.

Daniel served as a high ranking government official under four dynasties of Babylonian power. Daniel governed throughout the reign of Nebuchadnezzar (604–562 BC), though there is no mention of Daniel in the reigns of Evil-Merodach (561–560 BC), Neriglissar (559–555 BC), or Labashi-Marduk (555 BC). Daniel is again mentioned in conjunction with the reign of Nabonidus (555–539 BC; Dan 5). Belshazzar governed the land of Babylon while his father, Nabonidus, was out of the country.

Daniel lived through the entire Babylonian captivity and was 90 years old when Zerubbabel allowed the Jews to return to Jerusalem. Daniel was present in Babylon when the Persian army, commanded by Cyrus, captured and conquered that city. Even here, Daniel rose to power again, becoming a government official in the courts of Cyrus (539–529 BC, see Fig. 92) and Cambyses (529–522 BC). Daniel lived long enough to serve in the court of Darius I, the son of Hystaspes (522–486 BC).

The Nabonidus Chronicle (Dan 5:16)

The badly damaged Nabonidus Chronicle is part of the Babylonian Chronicle Series (Chronicle 7) of tablets (see Fig. 89) that recounts the yearly events of Nabonidus (r. 555–539 BC) from his accession in 556 until the 530's BC. The Chronicle indicates that Nabonidus was absent from Babylon, instead living in

89. Cuneiform tablet of one of the Babylonian Chronicles (no. 7) containing part of the Nabonidus Chronicle (*ca.* 556–530 BC).

The Trustees of the British Museum (ME 35382)

Arabia at Teima, for ten years of his reign, leaving his son, Bel-shar-usur (Belshazzar of the OT), to be co-regent of Babylon in his absence.[16]

Part of the text states: "The king (was) in Tema (while) the prince, the officers, and his army (were) in Akkad [Babylonia]."[17] Babylon was eventually conquered by Cyrus the Persian and Nabonidus was captured (539 BC).[18]

While Nabonidus is not mentioned in the Bible, perhaps because he was absent from Babylon during that time, his son Belshazzar is mentioned in the book of Daniel (4:30–5:1–29). Nabonidus was known to the Jews, as evidenced in the Aramaic text found among the Dead Sea Scrolls called the Prayer of Nabonidus (4Q242=4QPrNab).[19] It also indicates that the Jews were aware that Nabonidus suffered from a mental disease, and chose to leave Babylon and live in Teima.

90. Nabonidus Cylinder.

The details that Daniel records begin to make sense in the light of this information, with Daniel's mention that Belshazzar offered Daniel the chance to be "the third ruler in the kingdom" (Dan 5:16). Daniel also knew that Nebuchadnezzar would rebuild Babylon (Dan 4:30).

The Nabonidus Cylinder (Dan 5:16)

Four clay cylinders were discovered with the same inscription in 1854 at Ur by Hormuzd Rassam and John E. Taylor, in the Temple of Shamash at Sippar (ME 91109; See Fig. 91) and the Temple of Sin at Ur (Mugheir ME 92238; see Fig. 90). They were taken to the British Museum where they are currently on display.[20] One of the cylinders, known as the Nabonidus cylinder (ME 91109; see Fig. 90), was inscribed in Akkadian cuneiform by King Nabonidus (r. 555–539 BC) in the sixth cent. BC.

> *Quotes from Antiquity*
>
> **The Nabonidus Cylinder**
>
> As for me, Nabonidus, King of Babylon, save me from sinning against thy great divinity!...And as regards Belshazzar, the first-born son, my off-spring, do thou implant in his heart the fear of thy great divinity!
>
> Harper, *Assyrian and Babylonian Literature*, 158.

They are significant for biblical studies because, until their discovery, Belshazzar, Nabonidus' son, was only known from the book of Daniel (chapter 5 and 8), and from some

---

[16] *ANET* 312-14; 562-63; Smith, *Babylonian Historical Texts*, 27–97; Grayson, *Assyrian and Babylonian Chronicles*, 104–11.

[17] Grayson, *Assyrian and Babylonian Chronicles*, 108.

[18] Ibid., 21–22.

[19] *COS* 1.89; Frank Moore Cross, "Fragments of the Prayer of Nabonidus," *IEJ* 34 (1984): 260–64; Bastiaan Jongeling, Casper J. Labuschagne, and Adam Simon Van Der Woude, trans., *Aramaic Texts from Qumran*, vol. 1, Semitic Study Series 4 (Leiden: Brill Academic, 1976), 121–31.

[20] Robert Francis Harper, *Assyrian and Babylonian Literature: Selected Translations*, The World's Great Books (New York, N.Y.: Appleton & Company, 1901), 157–58.

other – possibly obscure – texts,[21] leading some skeptics to deny his existence or his kingship.[22] Rowley connected him to one of the Neo-Babylonian kings,[23] while even the Greek historian Herodotus, who wrote the history of Babylon in 450 BC, appears to be unfamiliar with Belshazzar (Josephus *Ant.* 10.11.2). Some have suggested that this reinforces minimalist arguments that Daniel is full of "historical inaccuracies".[24]

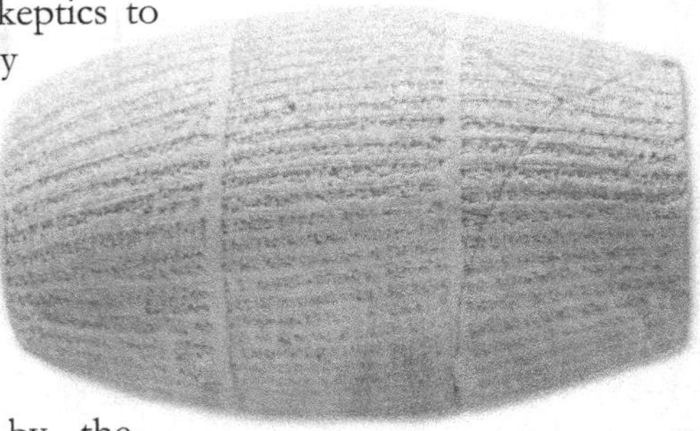

91. Cylinder of Nabonidus.
The Trustees of the British Museum (ME 91109)

Now, based on the evidence produced by the Nabonidus cylinders, it is clear that Nabonidus granted the kingship (co-regency) to his eldest son Belshazzar, while Nabonidus remained in Teima in Arabia (Nabonidus Chronicle).[25]

THE PERSIAN PERIOD

The Cyrus Cylinder (Isa 45:1–3, 13; Ezra 1:1–3)

92. Front panel of the Cyrus Cylinder.
The Trustees of the British Museum (ME 1880)

The Cyrus Cylinder was discovered during excavations by Hormuzd Rassam in the temple of Marduk in Babylon in March of 1879.[26] In 1970 P. R. Berger of Yale University noticed that a clay fragment from the Yale Babylonian Collection (NBC 2504, lines 37–45) was part of the broken section of the cylinder, and it was reunited with the larger section now in the British Museum (ME 1880; see Fig. 92).[27] It is one of the most recognizable clay tablets, given its barrel shape and the fragments that have restored it, inscribed in the Akkadian cuneiform script.

---

[21] Perhaps the first mention of Belshazzar is in a cuneiform text (YBC 3765:2) from the Archaeological Museum in Florence published in 1958–1960 by Karl Oberhuber of the University of Innsbruck. J. A. Brinkman, "Neo-Babylonian Texts in the Archeological Museum at Florence," *JNES* 25, no. 3 (July 1, 1966): 202–3; Raymond P. Dougherty, *Nabonidus and Belshazzar: A Study of the Closing Events of the Neo-Babylonian Empire* (Eugene, Oreg.: Wipf & Stock, 2008), 67–68.

[22] Ferdinand Hitzig, *Das Buch Daniel* (Leipzig: Weidmann, 1850), 77; Carl Heinrich Cornill, *Introduction to the Canonical Books of the Old Testament*, trans. G. H. Box, Theological Translation Library 23 (London: Williams & Norgate, 1907), 384; Robert H. Charles, *A Critical and Exegetical Commentary on the Book of Daniel* (Eugene, Oreg.: Wipf & Stock, 2006), 108–11.

[23] Harold Henry Rowley, *Darius, the Mede and the Four Empires in the Book of Daniel: A Historical Study of Contemporary Theories* (Cardiff: University of Wales Press, 1935), 10.

[24] Fant and Reddish, *Lost Treasures of the Bible*, 234.

[25] William H. Shea, "Nabonidus, Belshazzar, and the Book of Daniel: An Update," *AUSS* 20, no. 2 (1982): 133–49.

[26] Hormuzd Rassam, *Asshur and the Land of Nimrod* (New York, N.Y.: Eaton & Mains, 1807), 259.

[27] *ANET* 315-16; *COS* 2.124: 314-16; C. B. F. Walker, "A Recently Identified Fragment of the Cyrus Cylinder," *Iran* 10 (January 1, 1972): 158–59; Mordechai Cogan, "Cyrus Cylinder," in *The Context of Scripture: Archival Documents from the Biblical World*, ed. William W. Hallo, K. Lawson Younger, and Leo G. Perdue, vol. 2.124 (Leiden: Brill Academic, 2002), 315.

It dates to the Achaemenid period of Persian history (*ca.* 539–530 BC), to the reign of king Cyrus the Great, who was foretold by the prophet Isaiah (45:1–3, 13).[28] The tablet also mentions the capture of Nabonidus, the last Babylonian king (Ezra 1:1–3).[29] Walker states that it was: "a building inscription, in the Babylonian and Assyrian tradition, commemorating Cyrus's restoration of the city of Babylon and the worship of Marduk previously neglected by Nabonidus."[30]

Quotes from Antiquity

The Cyrus Cylinder

From [Ninev]eh (?), Ashur and Susa, Agade, Eshnunna, Zamban, Meturnu, Der, as far as the region of Gutium, I returned the (images of) the gods to the sacred centers [on the other side of] the Tigris whose sanctuaries had been abandoned for a long time, and I let them dwell in eternal abodes. I gathered all their inhabitants and returned (to them) their dwellings.

Cogan, "Cyrus Cylinder," 315.

It is significant for biblical studies because it mentions the repatriation of deported nations and the restoration of their cult sanctuaries.[31] While there is no mention of Jews or Judah, leading some scholars to dispute the Biblical parallels,[32] it supports the repatriation of the Jewish people after the Babylonian captivity as mentioned in the Book of Ezra (1:1–3).[33] Cyrus is also mentioned on an inscription on a clay brick presently displayed in the British Museum (ME 118362).

The Behistun Relief Inscription (Esth 1:21–22)

The Behistun (also Bisitun) Relief is a trilingual inscription[34] (Esth 1:21–22) and relief of King Darius I, the great, on the side of a rock relief (Mount Behistun, Persian for the "Place of God"), that is presently part of an historic site on the famous Silk Road in Iran (see Fig. 93). It is the largest stone relief and inscription in the world.[35] The relief is a striking depiction of king Darius and his soldiers leading his conquered enemies away on a rope.[36]

---

[28] M. A. Dandamaev, *A Political History of the Achaemenid Empire*, trans. W. J. Vogelsang (Leiden: Brill Academic, 1997), 52.

[29] Elias J. Bickerman, "The Edict of Cyrus in Ezra 1," *JBL* 65, no. 3 (1946): 249–75.

[30] Walker, "A Recently Identified Fragment of the Cyrus Cylinder," 159.

[31] Amélie Kuhrt, "The Cyrus Cylinder and Achaemenid Imperial Policy," *JSOT* 25, no. 8 (1983): 83–97.

[32] David Janzen, *Witch-Hunts, Purity, and Social Boundaries: The Expulsion of the Foreign Women in Ezra 9-10* (London: A&C Black, 2002), 157.

[33] Joseph P. Free and Howard F. Vos, *Archaeology and Bible History* (Grand Rapids: Zondervan, 1992), 204; Geisler and Holden, *Popular Handbook of Archaeology and the Bible*, 278–80.

[34] Rüdiger Schmitt, *The Bisitun Inscriptions of Darius the Great: Old Persian Text*, vol. 1 The Old Persian Inscriptions Texts, 5 vols., Corpus Inscriptionum Iranicarum, Part I Inscriptions of Ancient Iran (London: Corpus Inscriptionum Iranicarum, 1991); Elizabeth von Voigtlander, *The Bisitun Inscription of Darius the Great: Babylonian Version*, vol. 2 The Babylonian Versions of the Achaemenian Inscriptions, 5 vols., Corpus Inscriptionum Iranicarum, Part I Inscriptions of Ancient Iran (London: Corpus Inscriptionum Iranicarum, 1978); Jonas C. Greenfield and Bezalel Porten, *The Bisitun Inscription of Darius the Great: Aramaic Version*, vol. 5 The Aramaic Versions of the Achaemenian Inscriptions, etc., 5 vols., Corpus Inscriptionum Iranicarum, Part I Inscriptions of Ancient Iran (London: Corpus Inscriptionum Iranicarum, 1982).

[35] It measures 30.5 by 45.7 meter (100 by 150 ft.) wide on the face of a 609.6 meter (2000 ft.) high cliff. Marian H. Feldman, "Darius I and the Heroes of Akkad: Affect and Agency in the Bisitun Relief," in *Ancient Near Eastern Art in Context: Studies in Honor of Irene J. Winter by Her Students*, ed. Jack Cheng and Marian H. Feldman, Culture and History of the Ancient Near East (Brill, 2007), 268.

[36] Ann Fawkers, "The Behistun Relief," in *The Cambridge History of Iran: The Median and Achaemenian Periods*, ed. Ilya Gershevitch, vol. 2 (Cambridge, Mass.: Cambridge University Press, 1985), 828–31; Chul-Hyun Bae, "Comparative Studies of King Darius's Bisitun Inscription" (Ph.D. diss., Harvard University, 2001).

93. The Behistun Inscription, describing the conquests of Darius the Great in the Old Persian, Elamite and Akkadian languages. These reliefs and texts are engraved in a cliff on Mount Behistun, Iran

© Hara1603 / Wikimedia Commons

The importance of this discovery in deciphering cuneiform is often compared with the discovery of the Rosetta stone in deciphering Egyptian hieroglyphics. Henry Rawlinson, an officer of the British East India Company army, a British diplomat and linguist stationed in Tehran, used the inscriptions that had been gathered by Niebuhr, Le Brun, and C. J. Rich to decipher the then unknown language of Akkadian.[37]

Most of the inscriptions were preserved as paper mache squeezes and displayed in the Royal Asiatic Society's rooms and at the British Museum for over half a century until they were "eventually partially eaten by mice."[38] The actual inscriptions are so inaccessible that Rawlinson had to dangle from a rope to copy the Old Persian inscription, and then had to return some years later to copy the Babylonian version.[39] Ceram comments: "an operation that required enormous ladders, long cables and hooks, equipment hard to come by in the Middle East. Despite these difficulties, in 1846 he laid the first exact copy of the famous inscription before the Royal Asiatic Society, and a complete translation with it. It was the first great British triumph of Assyriological decipherment."[40]

One might question the accuracy of the deciphered text, given the cryptic-look of the cuneiform markings, but as Fagan recounts:

The supreme test came in 1857 when, W. H. Fox Talbot, a mathematician and astronomer who was also

[37] Henry C. Rawlinson, *The Persian Cuneiform Inscription at Behistun, Decyphered and Translated* (London: Parker, 1847); Henry O. Thompson, *Biblical Archaeology: The World, the Mediterranean, the Bible* (New York, N.Y.: Paragon, 1987), 73.

[38] Fagan, *Return to Babylon*, 91.

[39] R. Campbell Thompson, "The Rock of Behistun," in *Wonders of the Past: A World-Wide Survey of the Marvellous Works of Man in Ancient Times*, ed. John Alexander Hammerton, vol. 2 (New York, N.Y.: Wise & Co., 1952), 760–67.

[40] Ceram, *Gods, Graves & Scholars*, 237.

> a pioneer photographer, attempted to translate some Assyrian texts. He took an unpublished 810 line inscription of King Tiglath Pileser I (1115–1077 B.C.) from Assur, translated it, and sent his version to the Royal Asiatic Society in a sealed envelope. Then he suggested that they ask Hincks and Rawlinson to do the same, independently. The three sealed translations could then be compared. An independent committee found that each man had made the same general sense of the inscriptions and that many paragraphs agreed so closely that no one could doubt that Babylonian cuneiform had been deciphered.[41]

The implications for biblical scholarship were enormous, allowing scholars to now have access to a wide range of Babylonian tablets, like the *Epic of Gilgamesh* (see Fig. 19) and the *Enuma Elish* (see Fig. 23), shedding new light on the biblical text. What the Rosetta stone did for Egyptian hieroglyphic literature, the Behistun inscription did for Babylonian Akkadian and the annals of Mesopotamian kings.

Emperors sometimes promoted their military conquests and exploits by producing multiple copies of official documents in different languages.[42] A papyrus copy of the Behistun inscription, now in the Neues Museum in Berlin (P13447), was also found written in Aramaic,[43] at a Jewish military outpost, located at Elephantine Island in Egypt. Wilson points out that it is "noteworthy for spelling Darius with exactly the same consonants that are employed in the Old Testament and in the Persian of the Behistun inscription."[44]

The Silver Bowl of Artaxerxes (Neh 2:1)

Four silver bowls (*ca.* 4.8 cm by 29.5 cm), with an identical inscription mentioning the name of Artaxerxes I (r. 465–424 BC), have been discovered prior to 1935. They are now displayed in the Metropolitan Museum of Art in New York (acquired in 1947; no. 54.3.1; see Fig. 94), Freer Gallery of Art in Washington (F1974.30),[45] the British Museum in London (ME 1994.0127, 1) and the Reza Abbasi Museum in Tehran.[46]

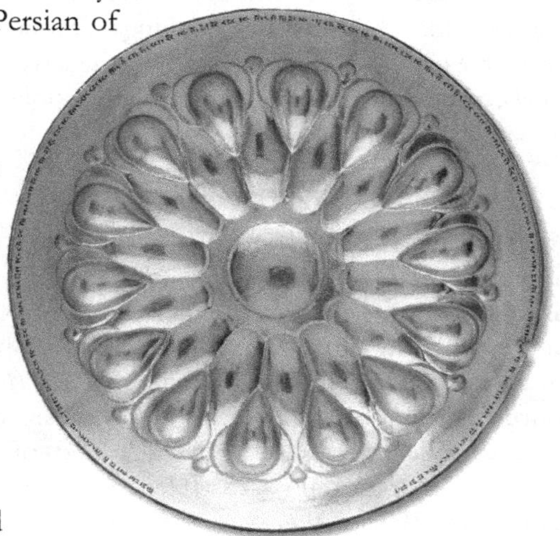

94. Silver Bowl inscribed around the rim with the names of Artaxerxes I Makrocheir, Darius and Xerxes that dates to the fifth cent. BC.

The Metropolitan Museum of Art, New York (no. 54.3.1) / Wikimedia Commons

The bowl was used to drink wine, and Nehemiah was listed as a cup-bearer to Artaxerxes (Neh 2:1). A cup-bearer's job was to test the wine for the king. Artaxerxes is mentioned several times in the books of Ezra and Nehemiah (Ezra 4:7–11, 23, 6:14, 7:1, 8:1; Neh 2:1; 5:14; 13:6). Although the text does not clarify exactly which Artaxerxes is being referred

[41] Fagan, *Return to Babylon*, 93.

[42] Arthur John Booth, *The Discovery and Decipherment of the Trilingual Cuneiform Inscriptions* (London: Longmans, Green & Company, 1902), ix–x.

[43] Greenfield and Porten, *The Bisitun Inscription of Darius the Great: Aramaic Version.*

[44] See Wilson for a translation of the Elephantine Papyrus into English. Robert Dick Wilson, "The Papyrus of Elephantine," *The Princeton Theological Review* 12, no. 3 (1914): 415.

[45] Ann C. Gunter and Paul Jett, *Ancient Iranian Metalwork in the Arthur M. Sackler Gallery and the Freer Gallery of Art* (Mainz: Sackler Art Gallery, 1992), no. 3.

[46] J. E. Curtis, M. R. Cowell, and C. B. F. Walker, "A Silver Bowl of Artaxerxes I," *Iran* 33 (January 1, 1995): 149–53.

95. The northern relief from Persepolis, showing a royal audience before Darius the Great (522–486 BC). Darius's son, Xerxes I, is also depicted behind him, along with a cupbearer. Initially placed at the center of the stairs of the Apadana, it was later moved to the Treasury, where another similar relief is still *in situ*.

National Museum; Tehran, Iran

to, most scholars agree that it is Artaxerxes I (r. 445–432 BC).[47] The importance to biblical studies is that the three Persian kings, Darius, Artaxerxes and Xerxes, inscribed on the silver bowls, played a prominent role in the books of Ezra and Nehemiah.[48]

> *Quotes from Antiquity*
>
> **Silver Bowl of Artaxerxes**
>
> Artaxerxes, the great king, king of kings, king of countries, son of Xerxes the king, of Xerxes (who was) son of Darius the king, the Achaemenian, in whose house this silver drinking-cup (was) made.
>
> Curtis, Cowell, and Walker, "A Silver Bowl of Artaxerxes I," 149–53.

The Persepolis Relief (Ezra 6:6–12)

The "Northern Relief," or as it is sometimes known, "Treasury Relief" (see Fig. 95), was discovered in the Persian capital of Persepolis.[49] It depicts a royal audience before the Persian king, Darius the Great (r. 522–486 BC) with his son Xerxes I standing behind his throne. The royal cupbearer is pictured behind Xerxes (Neh 2:1). On the right in front of the king is a courtier or important official (Pharnaces?) depicted in the conventional attitude of ritual greeting called *proskynesis*. On each end of the limestone relief, the Bearer of the Royal Weapons or immortal guards (Herodotus *Hist.* 7.83)[50] are depicted holding spears and archery equipment. Before the king are these two objects, which have been identified as incense burners.

Initially it was placed at the center of the northern stairs of the *Apadana* (audience hall) at Persepolis, but later moved to the Treasury, where another similar relief is still *in situ,* where it formed part of the eastern stairs. Ernst Herzfeld and Erich Schmidt discovered it in the treasury in 1930,[51] but it is now in the National Archaeological Museum of Tehran, Iran.

This depicts the opulent setting of the Persian court and confirms the picture portrayed in the biblical record (Esth 1:2, Hag 1:1, Zech 1:1 and Ezra 4:6, 6:1). King Darius was directly

---

[47] Fant and Reddish, *Lost Treasures of the Bible*, 282.

[48] A trilingual tablet mentions King Xerxes in Old Persian, Elamite, and Akkadian. *ANET* 316-17; William H. Shea, "Esther and History," *AUSS* 14 (1976): 227–46.

[49] Kim Codlla and David Stronach, "Persepolis," in *OEANE*, ed. Eric M. Meyers, vol. 4 (Oxford: Oxford University Press, 1997), 4:4:273–77.

[50] The soldiers were called immortal because, if one dies he would immediately be replaced with one of the reserves. They are described as Ten Thousand or the *Athanatoi* by Herodotus (*Hist.* 7.83).

[51] Erich F. Schmidt, *The Persepolis Expedition*, Aerial Survey Expedition (Chicago, Ill.: University Of Chicago Press, 1941); *Persepolis II: Contents of the Treasury and Other Discoveries*, Oriental Institute Publications 69 (Chicago, Ill.: University Of Chicago Press, 1957).

involved in encouraging the rebuilding of the Jerusalem temple (Ezra 6:6–12) and subsidizing the project.

The Tiled Archer of Susa (Ezra 5–6)

A beautiful life-size group of four archers (AOD 488) decorated the walls of the winter palace of Susa (Neh 1:1; Esth 1:2; Dan 8:2),[52] that depicts the sophistication of the Persian empire (see Fig. 96).[53] In 1885–1886 Marcel Dieulafoy discovered some 2000 glazed bricks scattered in the area to piece together this amazing relief,[54] which today is displayed in the Department of Oriental Antiquities in the Louvre.[55]

The palace at Susa was built in 490 BC by Darius the Great (r. 521–486 BC; Ezra 5–6) and was decorated with friezes of glazed painted tiles in moulded relief.[56] The picture depicts one of the archers in the emperor's bodyguards of archers (known as Immortals; Herodotus *Hist.* 7.83), holding a spear and dressed in a formal uniform. This

96. Archers frieze from Darius' palace at Susa. Achaemenid era, ca. 510 BC. Detail of the left side of the frieze, made from glazed siliceous bricks.

Department of Oriental Antiquities (AOD 488) © Jebulon / Wikimedia Commons

[52] Ernest Babelon, "Recent Archæological Discoveries in Persia," *The American Journal of Archaeology and of the History of the Fine Arts* 2, no. 1 (1886): 53–60; Schmidt, *The Persepolis Expedition*, vols. 1, pls. 163–65.

[53] John Curtis, *Ancient Persia* (London: Harvard University Press, 1990).

[54] Jane Dieulafoy, *La Perse, La Chaldee and La Susiane* (Paris, France: Hachette, 1887); John P. Peters, "Excavations in Persia," *HTR* 8, no. 1 (1915): 82–93; Jean Perrot, ed., *The Palace of Darius at Susa: The Great Royal Residence of Achaemenid Persia* (London: Tauris, 2013), XVII, 313.

[55] Numerous other reliefs made from glazed siliceous brick are displayed in other museums around the world, including friezes of archers (AOD 488; ME 132525), lions (AOD 489a-c), sphinxes (Sb 3324; Sb3325), winged bulls, and griffins (Sb 3326; Sb 3327).

[56] Annie Caubet and Daucé, "The Fired Arts," in *The Palace of Darius at Susa: The Great Royal Residence of Achaemenid Persia*, ed. Jean Perrot (London: Tauris, 2013), 311–58.

would have been a familiar figure to Esther, the Jewess who in 479 BC became queen to Xerxes I, (Heb. *Ahasuerus*; r. 486–465 BC) king of Persia. Esther would have passed by this tiled archer in Darius' Palace (Ezra 5–6).

The Cylinder Seal of Darius I (Ezra 6:15)

The trilingual cuneiform seal (3.7 cent. high) depicts Darius in his chariot (with a driver) hunting lions with his bow and arrow. The Persian emblam of their winged national god, Ahuramazda, is displayed above them.[57] The inscription includes the three official languages of the Persian empire, old Persian, Elamite and Babylonian, and is translated as "Darius, the Great King".[58] The seal itself is made of agate and currently on display in the British Museum (ME 89132; see Fig. 97).[59]

97. Bullae drawing of the cylinder seal impression bearing the name of Darius I.

The Trustees of the British Museum (ME 89132)

The seal dates to the time of the prophets Haggai and Zechariah (fifth cent. BC) and verifies the existence of the Darius I mentioned in the Bible. The names of king Darius, Xerxes, and Artaxerxes are also mentioned in association with the rebuilding of the temple in papyrus texts from the Jewish community on Elephantine Island, Egypt.[60]

---

[57] Curtis, *Ancient Persia*, 41.

[58] John Boardman, *Persia and the West: An Archaeological Investigation of the Genesis of Achaemenid Art* (London: Thames & Hudson, 2000), 159–61, fig. 5.9; Ada Cohen, *Art in the Era of Alexander the Great: Paradigms of Manhood and Their Cultural Traditions* (Cambridge, U.K.: Cambridge University Press, 2010), 84.

[59] http://www.britishmuseum.org/research/collection_online/collection_object_details/collection_image_gallery.aspx?partid=1&assetid=151651001&objectid=282610. Dominique Collon, *First Impressions: Cylinder Seals in the Ancient Near East* (London: British Museum Press, 2006), 130.

[60] Pritchard, *ANET OT*, 491–92.

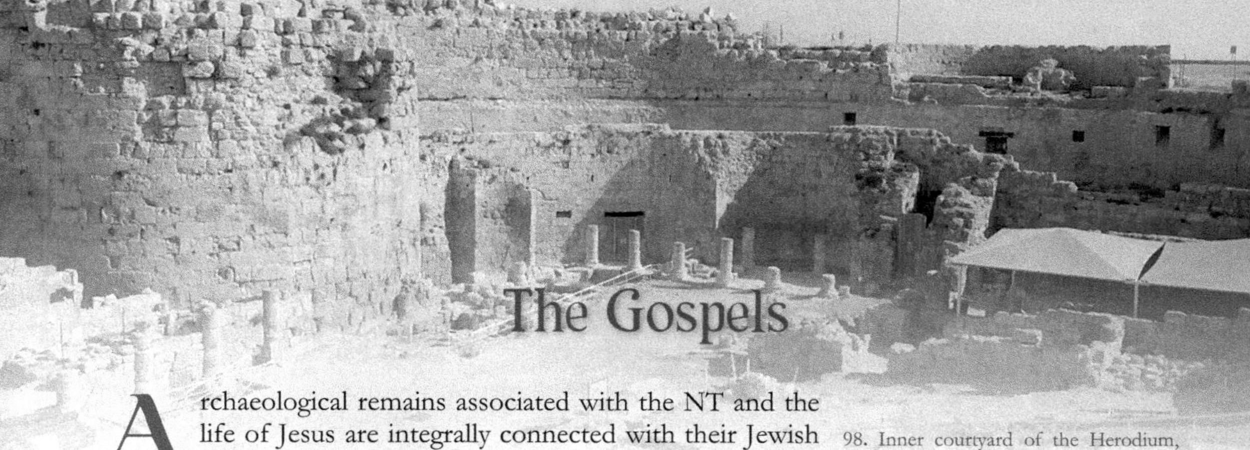

The Gospels

98. Inner courtyard of the Herodium, the winter retreat of Herod the Great.
Lumpeseggl / Wikimedia Commons

Archaeological remains associated with the NT and the life of Jesus are integrally connected with their Jewish and Graeco-Roman cultural settings. These discoveries include hundreds of early ancient biblical texts and manuscripts,[1] numerous inscriptions confirming the historical existence of NT people and places (Herod the Great, Quirinius, Pontius Pilate, Sergius Paulus, Emperor Claudius, Gallio, and Erastus, etc.)[2] and excavations of cities and monuments located in Israel, Jordan, Lebanon, Syria, Cyprus, Greece, Italy, Egypt, and Turkey, that all confirm the accuracy of the geography and history of the NT narrative. Although not all sites and finds can be listed or considered here, what follows are some of the most important discoveries that support the reliability of the Bible.

The Dead Sea Scrolls

In 1947, the Dead Sea Scrolls (DSS),[3] a collection of 931 manuscripts, were discovered in caves near the NW shores of the Dead Sea, near the site of Khirbet Qumran.[4] Up until the discovery of the DSS, no substantial copies of any of the Hebrew Scriptures were known from before the tenth cent. AD (MT, Aharon Ben Asher Leningrad Codex AD 1008).[5] With the historic discovery of the DSS, copies of all of the Hebrew Bible except Esther were found. Portions of approximately 931 manuscripts were recovered dating from *ca.* 300 BC to AD 40, with the majority of them identified as Zealot correspondence from the Second Jewish Revolt.[6] The dates have been confirmed by archaeology, paleography, and radiocarbon dating.[7]

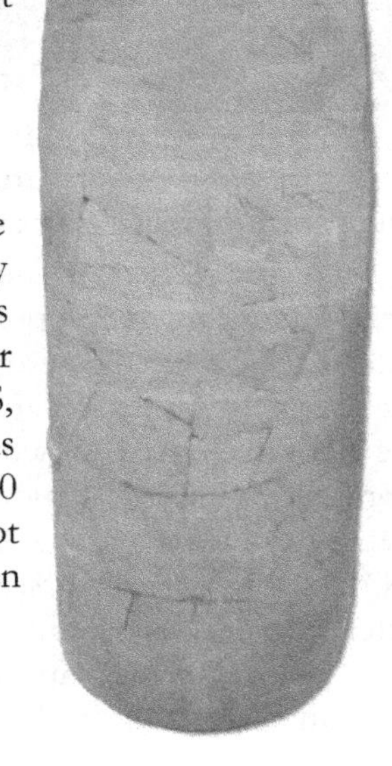

99. Storage Jar in which the Dead Sea Scrolls were stored, along with the jar's unique lid.
Used with permission of the Oriental Institute Museum of the University of Chicago.

---

[1] Wallace, "Earliest Manuscript of the NT Discovered?"

[2] Graves, *Biblical Archaeology Vol 1: An Introduction* 2nd ed 1:234–45.

[3] Peter W. Flint and James C. VanderKam, eds., *The Dead Sea Scrolls After Fifty Years: A Comprehensive Assessment*, vol. 2 (Leiden: Brill, 1999); John J. Collins, *The "Dead Sea Scrolls": A Biography* (Princeton: Princeton University Press, 2012).

[4] G. L. Harding and Roland de Vaux carried out five excavation campaigns between 1951–1956, uncovering an elaborate central building complex that included towers, assembly halls, kitchens, storehouses, and extensive waterway with large cisterns.

[5] Price, *Dead Sea Scrolls Pamphlet*, 8.

[6] Ibid., 2.

[7] VanderKam and Flint, *Meaning of the Dead Sea Scrolls*, 27–32; Bonani et al., "Radiocarbon Dating of the Dead Sea Scrolls"; Bonani et al., "Radiocarbon Dating of Fourteen Dead Sea Scrolls"; Doudna, "Dating the Scrolls on the Basis of Radiocarbon Analysis," 1:430–71.

100. Cave 4 at Qumran.

Discovery of the DSS

In the winter of 1946 or 1947, Muhammad edh-Dhib, a Ta'amireh bedouin boy, was tending his flocks near the NW shore of the Dead Sea. He threw a stone into a cave (see Fig. 100) to scare out his wandering goats and heard pottery shatter. Upon entering the cave he found broken pottery and seven scrolls.

They sold three of the scrolls to Eleazar L. Sukenik of Hebrew University while the other four were sold to Athanasius Yeshue Samuel, a Syrian Orthodox priest at St. Marks Monastery in Jerusalem, who took them to the American School of Oriental Research in Jerusalem where three of the scrolls were photographed. Due to the Arab-Israeli War the scrolls were moved to Syria, and then in 1949 they were moved to the United States where they were placed in a New York bank for several years.

Then on June 1, 1954, Yigael Yadin, the famous Israeli archaeologist, was lecturing in the United States and noticed an advertisement in the *Wall Street Journal*. It read: "The Four Dead Sea Scrolls' biblical manuscripts, dating back to at least 200 BC, are for sale. This would be an ideal gift to an educational or religious institution by an individual or group. Box F 206."[8]

He proceeded to negotiate for the State of Israel and in 1955 purchased the scrolls for $250,000.[9] Today the scrolls from cave 1, including the Great Isaiah scroll, are housed in the Shrine of the Book in Jerusalem, while the non-biblical scrolls from cave 4 (see Fig. 100) have been housed in the Hebrew University since 2003. The Copper Scroll (3Q15), a mysterious scroll with random Greek letters placed throughout the text that some believe is a lost treasure map, is displayed in the new Amman Museum in Jordan.

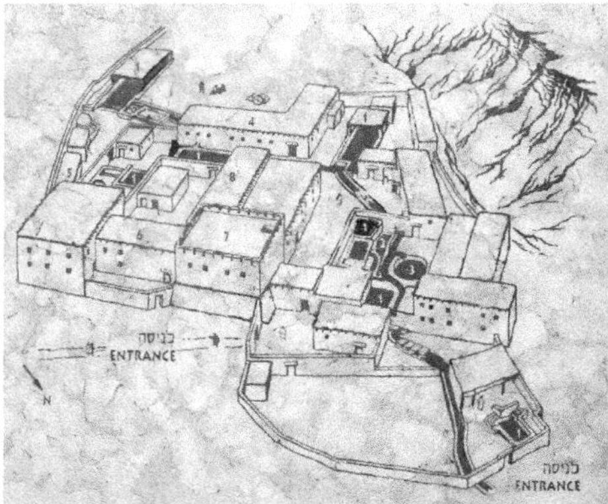

101. A suggested reconstruction map of the Qumran site from the second Temple period. 1. Ritual Bath 2. Aqueduct 3. Cistern 4. Refectory 5. Kiln 6. Kitchen 7. Tower

Qumran display

Content of the DSS

Of the roughly 870 to 889 scrolls, some 220 are portions of biblical books.[10] Due to the fragmentary nature of many of the scrolls the precise number is

[8] VanderKam and Flint, *Meaning of the Dead Sea Scrolls*, 14; VanderKam, *The Dead Sea Scrolls Today*, 12.

[9] Price, *Dead Sea Scrolls Pamphlet*, 5.

[10] Reed, *The Dead Sea Scrolls Catalogue*; Patrick Alexander, John F. Kutsko, and Shirley Decker-Lucke, *The SBL Handbook of Style: For Ancient Near Eastern, Biblical, and Early Christian Studies* (Peabody, Mass.: Hendrickson, 1999), 183–233; Tov, "A List of the Texts from the Judean Desert," 2:699–717. See also http://biblical-studies.ca/dss/critical-editions.html.

not known.[11] Some of the prominent scrolls include the Aramaic *Book of Genesis; The Great Isaiah Scroll* (1QIsa[a]); the oldest copy of the Ten Commandments (Deut 8:5–10; 5:1–6:1; 4Q41); *The Commentary on Habakkuk; The Manual of Discipline; The Thanksgiving Psalms;* canonical psalms (41 scrolls); non-canonical psalms (7 scrolls); Psalm 121 (11Q5 III); *Rule of War; The Damascus* (or Zadokite) *Document; The War Scroll; The Book of Mysteries; The Rule of the Congregation;* and the *Copper Scroll* (99% copper) from Qumran Cave III (3Q15 X, 18) containing a description of hidden treasures.[12]

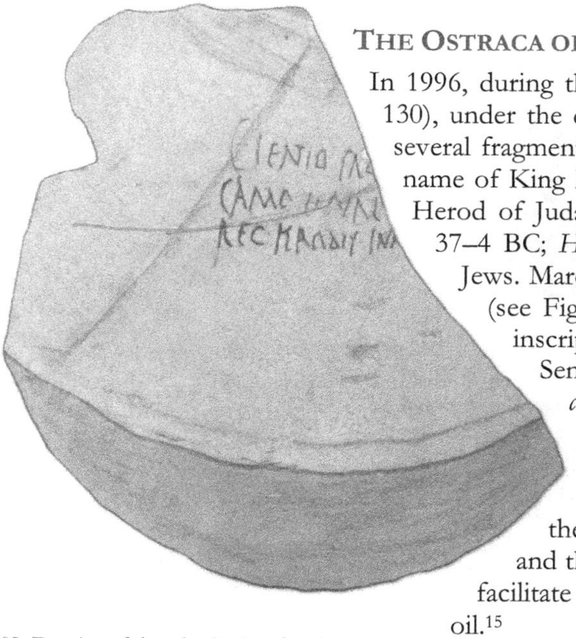

THE OSTRACA OF HEROD THE GREAT (MATT 2:16)

In 1996, during the excavation of Masada (see Figs. 131, 130), under the direction of Ehud Netzer and G. Stibel, several fragments of wine jars were discovered with the name of King Herod (*Regis Herodis Iudaici* i.e., "of King Herod of Judaea" or "of Herod, the Jewish king"; r. 37–4 BC; *Herodes rex Iudaeorum*, Herod, king of the Jews. Marobius *Sat.* 2.4.11)[13] inscribed in black ink (see Fig. 102).[14] The first line of the three-line inscription mentioned the Roman console C. Sentius Saturninus (Lat. *C. Sentio Satur(nino) co(n)sule*), who was in office in the year 19 BC, providing an exact date for the wine jars. One of the storerooms at Masada was believed to be specially designed for the storage of wine with plastered walls and three plastered circular pits in the floor to facilitate the handling of liquids such as wine or oil.[15]

102. Drawing of the wine jar (amphora) ostracon with three lines indicating; (top line) the date the wine was made (AD 19); (middle line) the type of wine produced; and (bottom line) the name and title of the recipient, "Herod, King of Judea."

The products brought to Masada under the name of King Herod included luxury items such as apples, specialty Italian wines, and a select fish sauce identified as garum.[16]

This discovery is important as it identifies the Herod mentioned in the NT as the King of Judea (Matt 2) and as the one who built a winter palace at Masada.

---

[11] The official publication of the Dead Sea Scrolls is by Oxford's Claredon Press and comprises forty volumes by various authors. They are listed under the Discoveries in the Judean Desert series (=DJD; formerly, Discoveries in the Judean Desert of Jordan = DJDJ). For a complete list of volume's in the series see Evans, *Ancient Texts for New Testament Studies*, 83–86. For a list of the scrolls and abbreviations see pages 76-80.

[12] Ben Zion Wacholder and Martin G. Abegg, *A Preliminary Edition of the Unpublished Dead Sea Scrolls: The Hebrew and Aramaic Texts from Cave Four*, 4 vols. (Washington, D.C.: Biblical Archaeology Society, 1996).

[13] Hannah M. Cotton, Omri Lernau, and Yuval Goren, "Fish Sauces from Herodian Masada," *JRA* 9 (1996): 233.

[14] Hannah M. Cotton, Joseph Geiger, and David J. Thomas, *Masada, II: The Yigael Yadin Excavations, 1963–1965. Final Reports; the Latin and Greek Documents*, The Masada Reports 2 (Jerusalem, Israel: Israel Exploration Society and the Hebrew University of Jerusalem, 1989), nos. 804–16, page 141. See *SEG* nos. 804-10, 812-13, and 815-16.

[15] Jo Ann H. Seely, "The Fruit of the Vine: Wine at Masada and in the New Testament," in *Masada & the World of the New Testament*, ed. John W. Welch and John F. Hall, Byu Studies Monographs (Provo, Utah: Friends of the Library, 1997), 208.

[16] Cotton, Lernau, and Goren, "Fish Sauces from Herodian Masada," 233; Piotr Berdowski, "Garum Of Herod The Great (Latin-Greek Inscription On The Amphora From Masada)," *Analecta Archaeologica Ressoviensia* 1 (2006): 239–57; "Garum Of Herod The Great (Latin-Greek Inscription On The Amphora From Masada)," *The Qumran Chronicle* 16, no. 3–4 (December 2008): 107–22.

103. Reproduction of the bronze cast of the so-called "Prima Porta" statue of Augustus, Rome, Italy, Via dei Fori Imperiali, erected in the 1930's.

© David E. Graves

THE STATUE OF AUGUTUS (LUKE 2:10)

The statue of Augustus of "Prima Porta" (Italian: *Augusto di Prima Porta*) is a marble statue (2.03 m. high) of Augustus Caesar (r. 10 BC–AD 14). It was discovered on April 20, 1863, in the Villa of Livia at Prima Porta, near Rome and is now displayed in the Braccio Nuovo of the Vatican Museum (see Fig. 103 and front cover).[17]

Emperor Augustus was 45 years old when Jesus was born (Luke 2:10) and exercised controlling power over Palestine during the life of the Messiah. Jesus would have been a teenager when Augustus died at age 67 (AD 14).[18] The coins of the first century depict the image of Augustus,[19] and would have been familiar to Jesus growing up.

THE LYSANIAS INSCRIPTION (LUKE 3:1)

Lysanias is only mentioned once in the NT, in Luke 3:1, as "tetrarch of Abilene" (*ca.* AD 27–28) as part of Luke setting the historical stage for the beginning of John the Baptist's ministry in AD 27. Because historians could only verify a tetrarch called Lysanias from 36 BC, some scholars claimed Luke was mistaken in his details.[20]

However, an inscription (*CIG* 4521, 4523) bearing the name of tetrarch Lysanias was discovered by Richard Pococke in 1737 in a Doric temple on the hill of Nebi Abel, (Abila) about 15 miles from Damascus.[21] This is also confirmed by Josephus who

> *Quotes from Antiquity*
>
> **The Lysanias inscription states:**
>
> For the salvation of the Au[gust] lords
> and of [all] their household,
> Nymphaeus, free[dman] of Ea[gle]
> Lysanias tetrarch established
> this street and other things.
>
> Hogg, "On the City of Abila," 43.

[17] Paul Zanker, *The Power of Images in the Age of Augustus*, trans. Alan Shapiro (Ann Arbor, Mich.: University of Michigan Press, 1990), 188; Hugh Honour and John Fleming, *A World History of Art*, 7th ed. (London: Laurence King, 2009), 197.

[18] Honour and Fleming, *A World History of Art*, 165.

[19] Adrian Goldsworthy, *Augustus: First Emperor of Rome* (New Haven, Conn.: Yale University Press, 2014), 223, 256.

[20] W. R. F. Browning, *A Dictionary of the Bible*, 2nd ed., Oxford Paperback Reference (Oxford: Oxford University Press, 2011), 241.

[21] Richard Pococke, *A Description of the East and Some Other Countries*, vol. 2, Part 1 (London: Bowyer, 1745), 116; Johann Caspar von Orelli and Wilhelm Henzen, eds., *Inscriptionum Latinarum selectarum amplissima collectio ad illustrandam Romanae antiquitatis*, vol. 2 (Zürich: Fuesslini et Sociorum, 1828), 428–29, No. 4997 and No. 4998; August Böeckh et al., *Corpus inscriptionum graecarum* (Berolini, Italy: Officina academica, 1877), no. 4521, 4523; John Hogg, "On the City of Abila, and the District Called Abilene near Mount Lebanon, and on a Latin Inscription at the River Lycus, in the North of Syria," *Journal of the Royal Geographical Society of London* 20 (1850): 43; Colin J. Hemer and Conrad H. Gempf, eds., *The Book of Acts in the Setting of Hellenistic History*, WUNT 49 (Winona Lake, Ind.: Eisenbrauns, 1990), 149

states: "He added to it the kingdom of Lysanias, and that province of Abilene" (Josephus *J.W.* 2.12.8; *Ant.* 15.4.1).

The inscription can be dated from the reference to "August lords" which was a joint title only given to Emperor Tiberius and his mother Livia.[22] This establishes the date of the inscription to between AD 14 – 29, since the year 14 was the year of Tiberius' accession[23] and the year 29 was the year of Livia's death.[24] This evidence supports the claim of Luke that a Lysanias was tetrarch of the province of Abilene around the year AD 29.

It appears that there were two Lysanias's who ruled in the same area (*CIG* 4521 and 4523), one executed by Anthony in *ca.* 36 BC (Josephus *Ant.* 14.13.3; 15.4.1; *J.W.* 1.13.1), and one who ruled in AD 29 (*Ant.* 14.5.1; *J.W.* 2.11.5).[25] Josephus was unclear in his mention of the rule of Lyasnias, while Luke mentioned the latter one (Luke 3:1).

THE PORTRAIT OF TIBERIUS (LUKE 3:1)

Tiberius (Lat. *Tiberius Caesar Divi Augusti filius Augustus* r. AD 14–37), whose mother was the famous Livia,[26] is only once specifically mentioned in the NT, used to indicate the beginning of John the Baptist's ministry (Luke 3:1), but he was the Caesar mentioned throughout the Gospels and figured prominently in the life of Jesus. In fact the silver denarius coin (Tribute Penny)[27] that Jesus refers to for the payment of taxes was imprinted with the image of Tiberius (Mark 12:13–17; Matt 22:15–22; Luke 20:20–26; see Fig. 104).

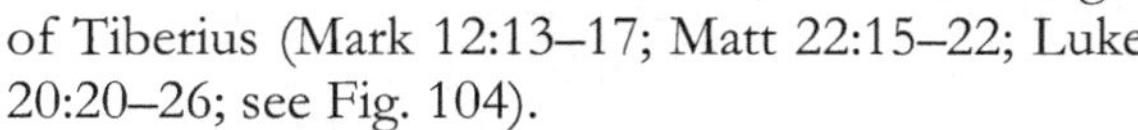

104. Marble portait of Tiberius.
Ephesus Archaeological Museum, Selçuk, Turkey

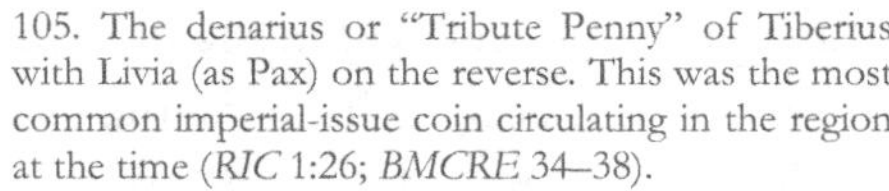

105. The denarius or "Tribute Penny" of Tiberius with Livia (as Pax) on the reverse. This was the most common imperial-issue coin circulating in the region at the time (*RIC* 1:26; *BMCRE* 34–38).

© Classical Numismatic Group, Inc. (CNG). www.cngcoins.com

While Tiberius promoted the Imperial Cult, he suppressed other religions, such as the worship of the Egyptian goddess Isis, the work of astrologers, druidism, and Judaism.[28] As Seager points out "to the Jews at least apostasy

[22] Anthony Barrett, *Livia: First Lady of Imperial Rome* (New Haven, Conn.: Yale University Press, 2004), 209.

[23] Robin Seager, *Tiberius* (Oxford: Blackwell, 2008), 40–42.

[24] John J. Rousseau and Rami Arav, *Jesus and His World: An Archaeological and Cultural Dictionary* (Minneapolis: Fortress, 1995), 67; Barrett, *Livia*, xiv, 191, 221.

[25] Scott T. Carroll, "Lysanias (Person)," ed. David Noel Freedman et al., *ABD* (New York, N.Y.: Doubleday, 1996), 425; Frederick Fyvie Bruce, "Lysanias," ed. I. Howard Marshall et al., *NBD* (Downers Grove, Ill.: InterVarsity, 1996), 708.

[26] Graves, *Biblical Archaeology Vol 1: An Introduction* 2nd ed 1:214–17; David E. Graves and D. Scott Stripling, "Re-Examination of the Location for the Ancient City of Livias," *Levant* 43, no. 2 (2011): 178–200.

[27] The term "penny" is derived from the 1611 King James translation of the Bible, and was adopted since the penny was the standard denomination of the time.

[28] Steven J. Friesen, *Imperial Cults and the Apocalypse of John: Reading Revelation in the Ruins* (Oxford: Oxford University Press, 2001), 122–31.

was offered as an alternative to expulsion."[29] He also drafted four thousand Jewish men into military service and deployed them to the marshes of Sardinia, while deporting all others from Italy (Josephus *Ant.* 18.3.5; Tacitus *Ann.* 2.85; Suetonius *Tib.* 36; Philo *Legat.* 24; Seneca *Ep.* 108.22; Cassius Dio *Hist. Rom.* 57.18).[30]

Also, as Tiberius aged he became more sensitive to any opposition to his power. News of a Jewish peasant from Galilee seeking to establish his own kingdom warranted Romes support for the arrest and trial of Jesus of Nazareth.

Several inscriptions testify to the deification of Tiberius. They state: "Emperor Tiberius Caesar Augustus, son of god" (*SB* no. 8317); "Emperor Tiberius Caesar new Augustus, son of Zeus the liberator" (P.Oxy. 240); "Tiberius Caesar a new Augustus, emperor, son of the god Augustus" (*SB* no. 7174, 8329, 8330; P.Mich. 233).

106. First century fishing boat popularly called the "Jesus Boat." Restored and displayed at the Kibbuz Ginnossar, Yigal Allon Center, Israel.

THE KINNERET BOAT (MARK 1:19–20; 4:36)

There are more than forty-five references to boats and fishing in the Gospels associated with Jesus and his disciples (Matt 4:18–21; 8:18–24; 9:1; 13:2; 14:13–32; 15:39; Mark 1:19–20; 3:9; 4:1, 35–38; 5:2, 18, 21; 16:32–54; 8:10–14; Luke 5:3–7; 8:22, 27, 37; John 6:16–23). Several archaeological discoveries have helped clarify the type of vessels used in Jesus's day.

Following a drought in 1986, the Sea of Galilee dropped to record lows. Two brothers, Moshe and Yuval Lufan, from the Ginnossar Kibbuz, stumbled upon the remains of a first-century boat stuck in the mud. Shelley Wachsmann, an Inspector of Underwater Antiquities for Israel, was contacted to examine the 8.2 meters (27 ft.) long boat remain. She immediately noticed that the boat was ancient, based on its mortise-and-tenon joint construction.[31] The date was subsequently verified to between 120 BC and AD 40 by carbon-14 dating, placing it well within the life time of Jesus.[32]

The material composition of the boat indicated that it had been pieced together from various kinds of wood (oak, cedar, Aleppo pine, hawthorn, willow and redbud), and some of the wood was being used for a second time. It was also apparent that much of the usable material had been stripped from the vessel, including the mast, prior to it being abandoned.[33]

---

[29] Seager, *Tiberius*, 125.

[30] Elmer Truesdell Merrill, "The Expulsion of Jews from Rome under Tiberius," *Classical Philology* 14, no. 4 (1919): 365–72.

[31] Shelley Wachsmann and Kurt Raveh, "The Discovery," in *The Excavations of an Ancient Boat in the Sea of Galilee (Lake Kinneret)*, ed. Shelley Wachsmann, 'Atiquot (English Series) 19 (Jerusalem, Israel: Israel Antiquities Authority, 1990), 1–7; Shelley Wachsmann, *The Sea of Galilee Boat: An Extraordinary 2000 Year Old Discovery* (New York, N.Y.: Springer, 2013).

[32] Israel Carmi, "Radiocarbon Dating of the Boat," in *The Excavations of an Ancient Boat in the Sea of Galilee (Lake Kinneret)*, ed. Shelley Wachsmann, 'Atiquot (English Series) 19 (Jerusalem, Israel: Israel Antiquities Authority, 1990), 127–28; Lea Lofenfeld and Ramit Frenkel, *The Boat and the Sea of Galilee*, trans. Ora Cummings (Jerusalem: Gefen, 2007), 48.

[33] E. Werker, "Identification of the Wood," in *The Excavations of an Ancient Boat in the Sea of Galilee (Lake Kinneret)*, ed. Shelley Wachsmann, 'Atiquot (English Series) 19 (Jerusalem, Israel: Israel Antiquities Authority, 1990), 65–75; J. Richard Steffy, "The

Archaeologists were faced with a serious challenge of how to preserve the wood that was quickly deteriorating, now that it had been exposed to the air. Oma Cohen developed a new technique to preserve the remains. She wrapped the vessel in fiberglass and polyurethane, and then lowered it into a concrete tank filled with water and polyethylene glycol. The theory behind the procedure was that the water would eventually become replaced with the glycol. Although Wachsmann estimated it would take five to seven years to complete the process, in reality it took eleven years before the wood stabilized sufficiently to be placed on display (see Fig. 106).[34]

Experts estimate that such boats could hold from between 5 and 12 adult males (Josephus *J.W.* 3.10.1), and similar vessels can be found pictured on the Migdal mosaic, Beth She'arim catacomb graffito, and various period coins.[35]

While some imagine this to be the very boat used by Jesus, earning it the title the "Jesus Boat", it is highly unlikely that Jesus ever used this exact boat. However, it does provide us with a good example of vessels used during the NT period.

THE SECOND TEMPLE STONE INSCRIPTION (MATT 4:5)

In the mid-seventies, during Benjamin Mazar's excavations at the base of the Herodian wall, at the southwest corner of the Royal Stoa complex in Jerusalem,[36] the parapet that ran along the wall of the Temple complex was discovered (L: 84 cm: H: 31 cm; W 26 cm. Israel Antiquities Authority, IAA 78–1439; see Fig. 107). It contained a Hebrew dedicatory inscription that guided the priest to the place where the Sabbath was announced to the people of Jerusalem and read "to [or for] the place of trumpeting to. . . ."[37]

107. The top stone with the trumpeting inscription on it from the southwest corner of the Temple Mount (IAA 1978-1439).

© Todd Bolen. BiblePlaces.com

Based on its shape, size, and inscription, most scholars suggest that this stone was the exact location where the priests stood to announce the Sabbath and festival days to the citizens of Jerusalem by blowing the silver trumpet.

It is believed that the stone was dislodged and fell 15 meters (50 ft.) to the street below from its original location on the top of the Southwestern corner of the Temple Mount (see Fig. 109) during the Roman destruction of Jerusalem in AD 70. This may be the place where not only the priest stood to blow the trumpet, but where Jesus also stood during his

Boat: A Preliminary Study of Its Construction," in *The Excavations of an Ancient Boat in the Sea of Galilee (Lake Kinneret)*, ed. Shelley Wachsmann, 'Atiquot (English Series) 19 (Jerusalem, Israel: Israel Antiquities Authority, 1990), 29–47.

[34] Oma Cohen, "Conservation of the Boat," in *The Excavations of an Ancient Boat in the Sea of Galilee (Lake Kinneret)*, ed. Shelley Wachsmann, 'Atiquot (English Series) 19 (Jerusalem, Israel: Israel Antiquities Authority, 1990), 15–22.

[35] Rousseau and Arav, *Jesus and His World: An Archaeological and Cultural Dictionary*, 26–27.

[36] This location could be the lintel of the entrance into the Temple, or the pinnacle of the sanctuary itself, but more likely it refers to the southeast corner of the Temple Mount overlooking the Kidron Valley. Robert Horton Gundry, *Matthew, A Commentary on His Literary and Theological Art* (Grand Rapids: Eerdmans, 1982), 56.

[37] Benjamin Mazar, *The Mountain of the Lord: Excavating in Jerusalem* (New York, N.Y.: Doubleday, 1975), 138. A less likely theory is that the inscription was an instruction to the stone cutters indicating the placement of the stone on the wall.

109. Southwest corner of the Herodian temple precinct. This may be the Pinnacle mentioned in Luke 4:9 on which Satan asked Jesus to throw himself down from.

Quotes from Antiquity

Josephus records that this corner was:

Erected above the top of the Pastophoria, where one of the priests stood of course, and gave a signal beforehand with a trumpet, at the beginning of every seventh day, in the evening twilight, as also at the evening when that day was finished, as giving notice to the people when they were to stop work, and when they were to go to work again.

J.W. 4.582 [Whiston]

temptation. If this is the spot, then in the temptation narrative Jesus is not simply standing in a place where he had a panoramic view of the city, but he was standing on the spot where the priests would announce the Sabbath. Satan tempted Jesus on this very spot (Matt 4:5) where Israel was called to rest in God. Josephus described this place as being perilous due to its extreme height. Anyone who fell would, barring direct intervention from God, fall to certain death (see *Quotes from Antiquity*).

Eusebius also recounts the tradition that this was where Jesus' brother James was hurled down to his death (*Hist. eccl.* 2.23). The Jewish *Midrash* claims that the Messiah would announce redemption from the top of the temple (*Pesiq. Rab.* 36).

Quotes from Antiquity

Josephus on the pinacle of the Temple

While the valley was very deep, and its bottom could not be seen, if you looked from above into the depth, this further vastly high elevation of the cloister stood upon that height [corner of the wall], insomuch, that if anyone looked down from the top of the battlements, or down both those heights, he would be giddy, while his sight could not reach to such an immense depth.

Ant. 15.412 [Whiston]

108. The Capernaum synagogue where, in an earlier structure, Jesus gave his sermon on the bread of life (John 6:35–59), healed the centurion's servant (Luke 7:3) and confronted the demoniac (Mark 1:21-27).

THE CAPERNAUM SYNAGOGUE (LUKE 4:33–38; JOHN 6:35–59)

Some of the notable synagogues in Israel that have been excavated are in Capernaum (see Fig. 108),[38] Chorazin (see Fig. 110),[39]

[38] James F. Strange and Hershel Shanks, "Synagogue Where Jesus Preached Found at Capernaum," *BAR* 9, no. 6 (1983): 24–31.

[39] Z. Yeivin, "Has Another Ark Been Found?," *BAR* 9 (1983): 75–76; "Ancient Chorazin Comes Back to Life: A Galilee Town Is Reconstructed from Fragments," *BAR* 13, no. 5 (October 1987): 22–36; "Chorazin." *NEAEHL* 1:301–304.

Herodium, Hamat Tiberias,[40] and Gamla.[41] Perhaps the oldest synagogue is at Masada (see Fig. 130, 131),[42] although Urman doubts that the meeting halls at Masada and Herodium were used for religious purposes and questions their identification as synagogues.[43]

There is also evidence of synagogues outside of Israel during the diaspora in such places as Sardis (Asia Minor; Josephus *Ant.* 14.10, 17),[44] Priene (Asia Minor),[45] Ostia (Italy),[46] and Delos (Greece).[47]

110. The second cent. "Galilean" style synagogue at Chorazin built from basalt stone and characterized by its rectangular shape with three hallways with doors supported by two rows of pillars, and benches around the interior walls.

There were several different architectural styles used for synagogues. There was the early "broadhouse" (rectangular in shape) characterized by the synagogue at Khirbet Shemaʿ,[48] and the later Byzantine basilica style at Capernaum, Israel (Heb. *Kfar Nahum*; Tell Hum).[49]

The synagogue at Capernaum was first connected with Tell Hum by Edward Robinson in 1838, although it was Charles Wilson who made the final identification with Capernaum in 1866 (see Fig. 108).[50] The Franciscans, under the direction of Gaudentius Orfali, carried out excavation at the synagogue from 1921 to 1926.[51] Virgilio C. Corbo and Stanislao Loffreda carried out excavation work at Capernaum from 1968 until 1985, under the direction of Tzaferis Vassilios for the IAA.[52]

While the present structure of the Capernaum synagogue dates to the Byzantine period,

---

[40] Steven Fine, *Art and Judaism in the Greco-Roman World: Toward a New Jewish Archaeology*, Revised (Cambridge, U.K.: Cambridge University Press, 2010), 22–27.

[41] Lee I. Levine, *The Ancient Synagogue: The First Thousand Years*, 2nd ed. (New Haven, Conn.: Yale University Press, 2005), 45–80.

[42] Gideon Foerster, "The Synagogues at Masada and Herodium (Hebrew)," *Eretz Israel* 2 (1973): 224–28.

[43] D. Urman and Paul Virgil McCracken Flesher, *Ancient Synagogues: Historical Analysis and Archaeological Discovery*, SPB 47 (Leiden: Brill, 1998), 37.

[44] A. Thomas Kraabel, "Impact of the Discovery of the Sardis Synagogue," in *Sardis from Prehistoric to Roman Times: Results of the Archaeological Exploration of Sardis, 1958-1975*, ed. George M. A. Hanfmann, William E. Mierse, and Clive Foss (Cambridge, Mass.: Harvard University Press, 1983), 178–90.

[45] Mark W. Wilson, "Letter from the Field: An Ancient Synagogue Comes to Light," *BAR*, 2009.

[46] Levine, *The Ancient Synagogue*, 274 ff.; L. Michael White, "Synagogue and Society in Imperial Ostia: Archaeological and Epigraphic Evidence," *HTR* 90, no. 1 (1997): 23–58.

[47] Monika Trümper, "The Oldest Original Synagogue Building in the Diaspora: The Delos Synagogue Reconsidered," *Hesperia* 73, no. 4 (2004): 513–598; Levine, *The Ancient Synagogue*, 107 ff.

[48] Michael Avi-Yonah and Ephraim Stern, eds., *Encyclopedia of Archaeological Excavations in the Holy Land*, 3rd ed. (New York, N.Y.: Prentice Hall, 1996), 4:1096.

[49] John Charles Hugh Laughlin, "Capernaum: From Jesus' Time and After," *BAR* 19, no. 5 (1993): 54–61; Edwin M. Yamauchi and Bruce Chilton, "Synagogues," ed. Craig A. Evans and Stanley E. Porter, *DNTB* (Downers Grove, Ill.: InterVarsity, 2000), 1147–48.

[50] Laughlin, "Capernaum: From Jesus' Time and After," 54.

[51] Gaudence Orfali, *Capharnaum et Ses Ruines D'après Les Fouilles Accomplies Par La Custodie Franciscaine de Terre Sainte (1905-1921)* (Paris, France: Picard, 1922), 83–84.

[52] Stanislao Loffreda, *A Visit to Capharnaum*, 3rd ed. (Jerusalem: Franciscan, 1975); "Capernaum-Jesus' Own City," *BS* 10, no. 1 (1981): 1–17; *Recovering Capharnaum* (Jerusalem, Israel: Edizioni Custodia Terra Santa, 1985); Vassilios Tzaferis, ed., *Excavations at Capernaum 1978–1982*, vol. 1 (Winona Lake, Ind.: Eisenbrauns, 1989).

111. The octagonal house believed to be the house of the apostle Peter.

excavations have revealed an earlier first cent. basalt stone wall that dates to the time of Jesus.[53] The date was confirmed based on 10,000 bronze coins and pottery found under the basalt walls and floor.[54] Because Capernaum was a small town it is likely that this was the only synagogue in the town and the one used by Jesus to teach and perform miracles (Luke 4:33–38; John 6:35–59).[55]

THE HOUSE OF PETER (MATT 8:14–16)

During excavations at Capernaum in 1968 by Franciscan archaeologists, a single domestic structure stood out from the others.[56] It appeared to be a block of houses surrounded by a courtyard which the excavators called a "holy insula" (*sacra insula*).[57] The house was originally build in the Late Hellenistic period, but they noticed that early Christians had venerated the house with more than one hundred and twenty-five graffiti etchings on the walls (second cent. AD, excavated between 1923–2011),[58] and had converted the residence into a house church (*domus-ecclesia*) in the first cent. AD. McRay reports that:

> These inscriptions have been scratched on the walls in several languages, predominantly Greek, but also Hebrew, Aramaic, Syriac, and Latin, indicating that the room was a place of public attraction. . . . The inscriptions refer to Jesus as the Lord, Christ, the Most High, and God. One inscription says: "Lord Jesus Christ help thy servant." Another reads: "Christ have mercy." Various symbols, such as crosses in various forms and a boat, were also etched on the walls.[59]

During the fourth cent. the house church was enlarged and an enclosure wall was built to separate it from the rest of the town. During the second half of the fifth cent. a church was constructed over the house church in the shape of three co-centric octagons and was used until the seventh cent. AD (see Fig. 111). In 1985 the apse and baptistery were discovered which confirmed that it was used as a church.

The excavators concluded that this house, that was venerated as early as the mid-first cent. AD, among the labyrinth of houses in the village, was the house of Peter the fisherman

---

[53] F. M. Abel, "Notes Complemenaires Sur La Mer Morte," *RB* 38 (1929): 237–60.

[54] Stanislao Loffreda, "The Late Chronology of the Synagogue of Capernaum," *IEJ* 23 (1973): 37–42; Eric M. Meyers, "Ancient Synagogues in Galilee: Their Cultural and Religious Setting," *Biblical Archaeologist* 43 (1980): 97–108; Donald T. Ariel, "Coins From the Synagogue at 'En Nashut,'" *IEJ* 37 (1987): 147–57.

[55] Mark A. Chancey, *The Myth of a Gentile Galilee* (Cambridge, Mass.: Cambridge University Press, 2002), 101–105.

[56] Virgilio C. Corbo, *Cafarnao I: Gli edifici della città*, Studium Biblicum Franciscannum 19 (Jerusalem, Israel: Franciscan Printing Press, 1975); Stanislao Loffreda, *Cafarnao II: La Ceramica*, Studium Biblicum Franciscannum 19 (Jerusalem, Israel: Franciscan Printing Press, 1975); Augusto Spijkerman, *Cafarnao III: Catalogo della monete della città*, Studium Biblicum Franciscannum 19 (Jerusalem, Israel: Franciscan Printing Press, 1975); Loffreda, *A Visit to Capharnaum*; *Recovering Capharnaum.*

[57] Seán Freyne, "A Galilean Messiah?," *ST* 55 (2001): 198–218.

[58] Emmanuele Testa, *Cafarnao IV. I Graffiti Della Casa Di S. Pietro*, Studium Biblicum Franciscannum 19 (Jerusalem, Israel: Franciscan Printing Press, 1972).

[59] Hoerth and McRay, *Bible Archaeology*, 162.

(Matt 8:14–16; Mark 1:29–34; Luke 4:38). The construction of two churches built over the house collaborate the claim.[60]

As Shanks and Strange conclude: "A considerable amount of circumstantial evidence does point to its identification as St. Peter's house."[61] Jerome Murphy-O'Connor also concurs, stating: "The most reasonable assumption is the one attested by the Byzantine pilgrims, namely, that it was the house of Peter in which Jesus lodged (Matt 8:14). Certainly, nothing in the excavations contradicts this identification."[62]

In 1990 a new hexagonal Franciscan Memorial church was built over the excavated remains of the house.

THE POOL OF BETHESDA (JOHN 5:2)

John chapter five describes a pool in Jerusalem that played a central role in Jesus healing a crippled man. John provides a detailed description of the location of the pool, and while some have considered it symbolical,[63] the detailed description that John provides in the narrative indicates otherwise. John states "that there is in Jerusalem by the Sheep Gate[64] a pool, in Aramaic [Heb.] called *Bethesda*,[65] which has five roofed colonnades" (John 5:2).

112. The ruins of the Byzantine Church, adjacent to the site of the Pool of Bethesda.

While some archaeological work had been carried out in the 1800's by Conrad Schick and Charles Warren,[66] the excavations

---

[60] Loffreda, *Recovering Capharnaum*.

[61] Hershel Shanks and James F. Strange, "Has the House Where Jesus Stayed in Capernaum Been Found?," in *Archaeology in the World of Herod, Jesus, and Paul*, ed. Hershel Shanks and Dan P. Cole (Washington, D.C.: Biblical Archaeology Society, 1990), 199.

[62] Jerome Murphy-O'Connor, *The Holy Land: An Oxford Archaeological Guide From Earliest Times to 1700*, 5th ed., Oxford Archaeological Guides (Oxford: Oxford University Press, 2008), 254.

[63] The five porticoes are thought to symbolize the five books of Moses and healing properties of the pool are compared to Jesus's healing power. John Marsh, *The Gospel of Saint John*, The Pelican New Testament Commentaries (Harmondsworth, U.K.: Penguin Books, 1968), 245–46.

[64] Also identified in Nehemiah 3:1, 32; 12:39.

[65] Some manuscripts *Bethsaida, Bethzatha, Belzetha, Bezatha,* and *Betzatha.* John goes out of his way to identify the name as Aramaic or Hebrew and it is found as Bethesda [*Bet 'Eshdatayin*] in the Copper Scroll from Qumran (3Q15 11.12). Józef Tadeusz Milik, Roland de Vaux, and M. Baillet, eds., *Les "petites grottes" de Qumrân*, DJD 3 (Oxford: Clarendon, 1962), 214; Joachim Jeremias, *The Rediscovery of Bethesda: John 5:2*, New Testament Archaeology Monographs 1 (Louisville, Ky.: Southern Baptist Theological Seminary, 1966), 34–36; James H. Charlesworth, "The Dead Sea Scrolls and the Gospel according to John," in *Exploring the Gospel of John: In Honor of D. Moody Smith*, ed. R. Alan Culpepper and C. Clifton Black (Louisville, Ky: Westminster/Knox, 1996), 65.

[66] Warren misidentified the Pool of Bethesda with the *Birket Bani Isra'il* (Arabic for "The Pool of the Children of Israel"), south of the current Pool of Bethesda. Urban C. von Wahlde, "The Nature and History of the Birkat Isra'il and Its Relation to the Pool 'With the Expanse of the Sea' (Sir 50:3): Rereading Charles Warren," *PEQ* 142, no. 3 (2010): 159–81.

at the site, believed to be the Pool of Bethesda (*piscina probaticai*), was renewed between 1957 and 1962 by J. -M. Rousée and R. de Vaux. They uncovered a five sided pool with covered colonnades precisely in the area of the Sheep Gate (see Fig. 112).[67] The pool is located on the grounds of the Church of St Anne belonging to the White Fathers. The first cent. pool was discovered to have two basins situated NS, in a trapezoidal shape, surrounded on four sides by a portico.

The purpose of the pool has been debated for years and has included everything from the cleansing of sacrificial animals (Eusebius *On.* 58.21–26; Pilgrim of Bordeaux), to water reservoirs for use in the Temple[68] as public bathing, and Jewish ritual pools (*mikveh* and *otzer*[69]).[70]

As Von Wahlde concludes:

> The discovery of the pools provided beyond a doubt that the description of this pool was not the creation of the Evangelist [John] but reflected accurate and detailed knowledge of Jerusalem, knowledge that is sufficiently detailed to now be an aid to archaeologists in understanding the site. The Johannine account speaks of (1) its location near the Sheep Gate; (2) the name of the pool as Bethesda; (3) the fact that it has five porticoes; (4) the fact of intermittent turbulence in the water. All these details are corroborated through literary and archaeological evidence of the site.[71]

113. The seat of Moses, synagogue Chorazim.

Israel National Museum, Jerusalem. © אפי ברק / Wikimedia Commons

THE SEAT OF MOSES (MATT 23:2)

The seat of Moses (*Mōuseōs kathedras*) applied to a special chair (*kathedras*) of honor in the synagogue where the leader or ruler of the synagogue (*archisynagogos*) sat. The leader exercised the authority of Moses when teaching from this seat. One such seat made of black basalt stone was

[67] J. -M. Rousée and Roland de Vaux, "Chroniques Archéologiques," *RB* 64 (1957): 226–28; J. -M. Rousée, "Chroniques Archéologiques," *RB* 69 (1962): 107–9; Jeremias, *The Rediscovery of Bethesda.*

[68] Antoine Duprez, *Jésus et les dieux guérisseurs: à propos de Jean*, Cahiers de la Revue biblique 12 (Paris, France: Gabalda, 1970); J. -M. Rousée and M. -J. Pierre, "Sainte-Marie de La Probatique, état et Orientation Des Recherches," *Proche-Orient Chrétien* 33 (1981): 23–42; Rousée, "Chroniques Archéologiques," 107–8.

[69] An *otzer* was a reservoir pool connected to a *Mikveh* by a channel or pipe used to transfer water to the *Mikveh,* keeping the water in the *Mikveh* ceremonial pure through natural flowing "living" water. The disturbance of the water created by the draining of water into the southern pool may be what John describes as the "troubling of the water" that attracted the sick to the pool for healing (John 5:4,7). Herbert Danby, *The Mishnah: Translated from the Hebrew with Introduction and Brief Explanatory Notes* (Oxford: Oxford University Press, 1933), Miqva'ot 732–44.

[70] Shimon Gibson, "The Pool of Bethesda in Jerusalem and Jewish Purification Practices of the Second Temple Period," *Proche-Orient Chrétien* 55, no. 3–4 (2005): 270–93; Urban C. von Wahlde, "Archaeology and John's Gospel," in *Jesus and Archaeology*, ed. James H. Charlesworth (Grand Rapids: Eerdmans, 2006), 560–66; "The 'Upper Pool,' Its 'Conduit,' and 'the Road of the Fuller's Field' in Eighth Century BC Jerusalem and Their Significance for the Pools of Bethesda and Siloam," *RB* 113, no. 2 (2006): 242–62; "The Pool of Siloam: The Importance of the New Discoveries For Our Understanding of Ritual Immersion in Late Second Temple Judaism and the Gospel of John," in *John, Jesus, and History: Aspects of Historicity in the Fourth Gospel*, ed. Paul N. Anderson, Felix Just, and Tom Thatcher (Atlanta, Ga.: SBL, 2009), 40–47; "The Puzzling Pool of Bethesda Where Jesus Cured the Crippled Man," *BAR* 37, no. 5 (2011): 40–47, 65; "The Great Public Miqvaot at Bethesda and Siloam, the Development of Jewish Attitudes toward Ritual Purity in Late Second Temple Judaism, and Their Implications for the Gospel of John," in *Rediscovering John: Essays on the Fourth Gospel in Honour of Frederic Manns*, ed. Leslaw Daniel Chrupcala, Mul (Milano, Italy: Edizioni Terra Santa, 2013), 267–81.

[71] von Wahlde, "Archaeology and John's Gospel," 566.

discovered in 1926[72] during the excavations at the Chorazin synagogue and bears an Aramaic inscription that translates as "Rememered for good be Judan ben Ishmael (Judah ben Ishmael e.g., *b. Hul.* 118b)[73] who made this stoa and its staircase. As his reward may he have a share with the righteous" [Evans; see Fig. 113].[74]

114. Ossuary of the high priest, Joseph Caiaphas, found in Jerusalem in 1990.

Israel Museum, Jerusalem (IAA 1991.468). © deror_avi / Wikimedia Commons

THE CAIAPHAS OSSUARY (MATT 26:3, 57; LUKE 3:2)

Caiaphas was the leader of the Sanhedrin from AD 18–36 and played an integral role in Jesus' conflict with the Jewish leaders in the final week of his life (John 11:49–53; 18:14). Caiaphas was the person who presided over the evening trial in which Jesus confessed to being the Messiah and was ultimately condemned to death (Matt 26:57–68).

In 1990, while workers were working on a water park in the Peace Forest in Jerusalem, Zvi Greenhut uncovered 12 limestone ossuaries when a burial chamber collapsed.[75] One of the ossuaries (Ossuary no. 6) was beautifully decorated with several incised rosettes indicating that it was no ordinary bone box.[76] From the intact tombs, coins and the style of writing, the box was reliably dated to the first century AD (see Fig. 114). On both ends of the box, the Aramaic inscription read: "*Qafa*" and "*Yosef Bar Kayafa*" ("Caiaphas," "Joseph, son of Caiaphas") and dates to AD 36–37).[77] Several scholars argue that this is the Caiaphas of the NT and Josephus (*Ant.* 20.206).[78]

While some debate the Aramaic grammar and construct another name,[79] Evans points out that it is not impossible when translating Jewish names into Greek to lengthen them by a vowel.[80] While the Bible only speaks of him as Caiaphas (Matt 26:3, 57; Luke 3:2; John 11:49; 18:13, 14, 24, 28; Acts 4:6), Josephus mentions his full name as "Joseph Caiaphas" (*Ant.* 18.35; 18.95). Confusion over several accounts of High Priests serving at the same time (Luke 3:2 and Acts 4:6; John 18:12–26; Josephus *J.W.* 2.442; *Ant* 20.205; *Life* 193) is resolved if we accept Josephus' practice of maintaining the title of High Priest while the person is still alive, as a kind of "office for life."[81]

Of the several bodies found inside the ossuary, the one in his eighties is believed by some

[72] J. Ory, "An Inscription Newly Found in the Synagogue of Kerazeh," PEFSt., 1927, 51–52; A. Marmorstein, "About the Inscription of Judah Ben Ishmael," PEFSt., 1927, 101–2. Another seat was discovered in 1920 during excavations at Hammath-Tiberias.

[73] Marmorstein, "About the Inscription of Judah Ben Ishmael," 101–2.

[74] Evans *Jesus and the Ossuaries* 43–45.

[75] Eric H. Cline, *Biblical Archaeology: A Very Short Introduction* (Oxford: Oxford University Press, 2009), 109–110.

[76] Zvi Greenhut, "Burial Cave of the Caiaphas Family," *BAR* 18, no. 5 (1992): 28–44, 76.

[77] Zvi Greenhut, "Caiaphas' Final Resting Place," *Israel Hilton Magazine*, 1993, 16.

[78] W. R. Domeris and S. M. Long, "The Recently Excavated Tomb of Joseph Bar Caipha and the Biblical Caiaphas," *Journal of Theology for Southern Africa* 89 (1994): 50–58; Greenhut, "Burial Cave of the Caiaphas Family." For a full treatment of the research on the Caiaphas ossuary see Evans, *Jesus and the Ossuaries,* 104–112.

[79] Ronny Reich, "Caiaphas Name Inscribed on Bone Boxes," *BAR* 18 (1992): 38–44; William Horbury, "The 'Caiaphas' Ossuaries and Joseph Caiaphas," *PEQ* 126, no. 1 (1994): 32–48.

[80] Evans, "Excavating Caiaphas, Pilate, and Simon of Cyrene: Assessing the Literary and Archaeological Evidence," 323–29; "Caiaphas Ossuary," ed. Craig A. Evans and Stanley E. Porter, *DNTB* (Downers Grove, Ill.: InterVarsity, 2000), 180.

[81] Steve Mason, *Josephus and the New Testament*, 2nd ed. (Peabody, Mass.: Hendrickson, 2003), 188–92.

115. The Alexamenos graffito, presently on display in the Kitcherian Museum in Rome.

Rodolfo Lanciani, Ancient Rome in the Light of Recent Discoveries, 1898 / Wikimedia Commons

to be the remains of Caiaphas.[82] The bones have been buried on the Mount of Olives.

THE ALEXAMENOS GRAFFITO (MATT 27:35)

In 1857, in Palatine Hill, Rome, an unusual piece of graffiti (also called a *graffito*) was discovered, which likely depicts a man named Alexamenos worshipping Jesus as a donkey (see Fig. 115).[83] While the exact location of the discovery is uncertain,[84] its importance is not, as it assists in our understanding of the attitudes of the people towards early Christianity.

The text has been translated: "Alexamenos worships (his) God."[85] The graffiti attests to the fact that early Christians worshipped Jesus as God and by at least the third century adopted the crucifix as an instrument of worship.[86]

Tertullian confirms that: "For, like some others, you are under the delusion that our god is an ass's head. Tertullian confirms that Christians were accused of worshipping a divinity with the head of an ass." (Tertullian *Apol.* 16.1–2 [Lightfoot]) Tertullian traces the roots of this belief back to Tacitus, who believed that the Israelites were led out of Egypt by an ass (Tertullian *Apol.* 16.2).

Tertullian recounts how the early Christians were mocked by a Jew who "carried about in public a caricature of us [Christians] with this label: *Onocoetes* [begotten of a donkey]. This (figure) had ass's ears, and was dressed in a toga with a book, having a hoof on one of his feet. And the crowd believed this infamous Jew." (Tertullian *Nat.* 1.14 [Lightfoot])

Worship of Jesus as God is supported by another discovery in 2005 made at Megiddo. While working on construction of a maximum security prison, workers discovered a third cent.

---

[82] Joseph Zias, "Human Skeletal Remains from the 'Caiaphas' Tomb," *Atiqot* 21 (1992): 78–80; Helen K Bond, *Caiaphas: Friend of Rome and Judge of Jesus* (Louisville, Ky.: Westminster John Knox Press, 2004), 1–8.

[83] Rodolfo Amedeo Lanciani, *Ancient Rome in the Light of Recent Discoveries* (New York, N.Y.: Houghton, Mifflin & Compan, 1898), 106ff.; Augustus John Cuthbert Hare, *Walks in Rome*, vol. 1 (London: Allen, 1897), 186.

[84] Everett Ferguson, *Backgrounds of Early Christianity*, 3rd ed. (Grand Rapids: Eerdmans, 2003), 475; Orazio Marucchi, "Archaeology of the Cross and Crucifix," ed. Condé Bénoist Pallen, Charles George Herbermann, and Edward Aloysius Pace, *CE* (New York, N.Y.: Appleton & Company, 1913); Graydon F Snyder, *Ante Pacem: Archaeological Evidence of Church Life Before Constantine* (Macon, Ga.: Mercer University Press, 2003), 27–28; Geisler and Holden, *Popular Handbook of Archaeology and the Bible*, 308.

[85] Geisler and Holden, *Popular Handbook of Archaeology and the Bible*, 309; Snyder, *Ante Pacem: Archaeological Evidence of Church Life Before Constantine*, 62; Thomas F. Mathews, *The Clash of Gods: A Reinterpretation of Early Christian Art*, Princeton Paperbacks (Princeton, NJ: Princeton University Press, 1999), 50.

[86] Maria Antonietta Tomei, *Museo Palatino* (Rome: Electa, 1997), 104–105; David L. Balch and Carolyn Osiek, *Early Christian Families in Context: An Interdisciplinary Dialogue* (Grand Rapids: Eerdmans, 2003), 103 n. 83; Robin Margaret Jensen, *Understanding Early Christian Art* (New York, N.Y.: Routledge, 2000), 131 n. 2; 134 n. 11.

116. The Church of the Holy Sepulchre, also called the Basilica of the Holy Sepulchre, or the Church of the Resurrection by Eastern Christians, is a church within the Christian Quarter of the walled Old City of Jerusalem.

mosaic floor in what is believed to be the earliest Christian house church (Lat. *Domus ecclesia*) or prayer hall.[87] There are three Greek mosaic inscriptions and one of them reads: "The god-loving Akeptous has offered the table to God Jesus Christ as a memorial."[88] In the oldest mention of Jesus Christ to date in an inscription, Jesus is being worshipped as God while they participate in communion together in a house church in Megiddo.[89]

The Tomb of Jesus (Matt 27:59–60)

Close to Gordon's Calvary is a Garden Tomb that some believe is the "Tomb of Joseph of Arimathea" where Jesus was buried. While the tour guides of the Garden Tomb Association maintain the authenticity of their tomb, which is located on the north side of Jerusalem, just outside the Damascus Gate (see Fig. 117),[90] there is little archeological evidence to support this location. Holden and Geisler point out it is "a First Temple tomb, created hundreds of years before Jesus and part of a quarry containing eighth-century BC tombs; consequently, it

[87] Yotam Tepper and Leah Di Segni, *A Christian Prayer Hall of the Third Century CE at Kefar 'Othnay (Legio): Excavations at the Megiddo Prison 2005* (Jerusalem: Israel Antiquities Authority, 2006); Vassilios Tzaferis, "Oldest Church Found? Inscribed 'To God Jesus Christ' Early Christian Prayer Hall Found in Megiddo Prison," *BAR*, 2006, http://www.bib-arch.org/online-exclusives/oldest-church-02.asp.

[88] Tepper and Segni, *A Christian Prayer Hall of the Third Century*; Edward Adams, "The Ancient Church at Megiddo: The Discovery and an Assessment of Its Significance," *ExpTim* 120, no. 2 (2008): 62–69; Andrew Lawler, "First Churches of the Jesus Cult," *Archaeology* 60, no. 5 (2007): 46.

[89] Cline, *Biblical Archaeology*, 113.

[90] http://www.gardentomb.com.

117. The Garden Tomb, Jerusalem.

© David E. Graves

cannot be the correct tomb, since Jesus was placed in a newly created tomb."[91]

For Protestants, the quiet Garden is a much more serine setting in which to commemorate Jesus' death than the noisy, incense filled church of the Holy Sepulchre (for the Greek Orthodox, this is the Church of the Resurrection).

However, the traditional location of the Church of the Holy Sepulchre (see Fig. 116) appears to be the better option.[92] Several tombs were cut into the ancient quarry on which the Church of the Holy Sepulchre was built. Unfortunately, the original tomb which once was venerated was destroyed in the early eleventh century AD by Muslim caliph Al-Hakim bi-Amr Allah,[93] and now only an Aedicule (from Lat. *aediculum*, small building) stands where the tomb once stood.

There are two types of first-century rock-cut tomb constructions: one is a long narrow niche cut at right angles (Heb. *Kokh,* pl. *kokhim*), while the second is a low bench cut parallel to the wall and into the wall chamber creating a canopy (Lat. *arcosolium,* pl. *arcosolia*).[94] The latter type of tomb was reserved for the wealthy and people of high standing in society and likely the type of tomb that Jesus was buried in, as he was buried in the tomb of a wealthy person (Matt

118. First-century tombs still evident beneath the north wall of the rotunda of the church of the Holy Sepulchre. Typical of first cent. tombs, it has two long recesses or *kokhim* in which a body could be placed. Defaced over the years by pilgrims Unfortunately the tombs have been damaged over the years by tourists, but are classified as *Arcosolium.*

© Courtesy of Peter J. Gentry

[91] Geisler and Holden, *Popular Handbook of Archaeology and the Bible*, 317; Bryant G. Wood, "Jerusalem Report: Israeli Scholars Date Garden Tomb to the Israelite Monarchy," *BS* 11, no. 1 (1982): 30–32; Gabriele Barkay and Amos Kloner, "Burial Caves North of Damascus Gate, Jerusalem," *IEJ* 26 (1976): 55–57.

[92] Virgilio C. Corbo, *Il Santo Sepolcro Di Gerusalemme, Aspetti Arceologici Dalle Origini Al Periodo Crociato. Parts I–III* (Jerusalem: Franciscan, 1982); Dan Bahat, "Does the Holy Sepulchre Church Mark the Burial of Jesus," *BAR* 12, no. 3 (1986): 26–45; Martin Biddle, *The Tomb of Christ* (Stroud, U.K.: Sutton, 1999); W. Harold Mare, "The Place of Christ's Crucifixion And Burial," *BS* 3, no. 2 (1974): 33–39.

[93] Robert Ousterhout, "Rebuilding the Temple: Constantine Monomachus and the Holy Sepulchre," *The Journal of the Society of Architectural Historians* 48, no. 1 (1989): 66–78.

[94] Bahat, "Does the Holy Sepulchre Church Mark the Burial of Jesus," 30; Frank Leslie Cross and Elizabeth A. Livingstone, eds., *The Oxford Dictionary Of The Christian Church* (Oxford: Oxford University Press, 2005), 80.

27:57–60; Isa 53:9). The Garden Tomb does not have either of these type of tombs[95] while the Holy Sepulchre, while eroded from the presents of pilgrims of the centuries, is definitely an *Arcosolium* (see Fig. 118).[96]

THE DESTRUCTION OF JERUSALEM (MATT 24:1–2)

The Roman Emperor Vespasian came from Rome in AD 66 to suppress a Jewish revolt. In AD 69, Emperor Vespasian appointed his son Titus to suppress the Jewish revolt led by the Zealots, John of Gischala and Simon bar Giora (Tacitus *Hist.* 2.1–2; 2.81; 5.1). Using four legions, Titus captured and burned Jerusalem in AD 70, plundering and destroying the temple in the process.[97] This brought an end to the sacrificial system, and institutions of the Sanhedrin and Sadducees. Only the Pharisees with their connection to the synagogue survived and flourished.

The emperor Hadrian rebuilt Jerusalem as *Aelia Capitolina* with its own temple to a Roman god, *Jupiter Capitolinus*, built on the site of the remains of the Jewish temple.[98] It is believed that the Romans attacked Qumran on the way to Masada, but the Essenes hid the Dead Sea Scrolls in the caves (see Fig. 100) along the cliffs before they arrived. Following the fall of the Masada fortress in AD 73, the revolt was finally over.[99]

McLaren points out that there were five key actions undertaken by the Flavian's that demonstrated Rome's subjegation of the Jews and their God. He lists: "Titus' decision to offer sacrifices on the site of the Temple; the dismantling of the Temple, with the site left in ruins; the storage of key utensils associated with the cult in the Temple of Peace; the replacement of the annual tax levied on male Jews with the new *Fiscus Iudaicus*; and the closure of the Temple at Leontopolis."[100]

119. Judaea Capta Bronze Sestertius coin (AD 71) of Vespasian (AD 69–79).

In the NT, Jesus predicted the destruction of the temple in Matthew 24:1–2, Mark 13:1–4, and the destruction of Jerusalem was foretold in Isaiah 3:8, 25–26.

Several artifacts provide evidence of this momentous event in Jewish life.

The Judaea Capta coin

Following the destruction of Jerusalem and the burning of the Temple, for twenty–five years

---

[95] John McRay, "Tomb Typology and the Tomb of Jesus," *Archaeology and the Biblical World* 2, no. 2 (1994): 39.

[96] Bahat, "Does the Holy Sepulchre Church Mark the Burial of Jesus," 30.

[97] Martin Goodman, *Rome and Jerusalem: The Clash of Ancient Civilizations*, Reprint (New York, N.Y.: Vintage, 2008), 449, 452–3; James Carleton Paget, "After 70 and All That: A Response to Martin Goodman's Rome and Jerusalem," *JSNT* 31, no. 3 (March 2009): 350–53.

[98] Jodi Magness, "The Arch of Titus at Rome and the Fate of the God of Israel," *JJS* 59, no. 2 (2008): 201–17; James B. Rives, "Flavian Religious Policy and the Destruction of the Jerusalem Temple," in *Flavius Josephus and Flavian Rome*, ed. Jonathan Edmondson, Steve Mason, and James B. Rives (Oxford: Oxford University Press, 2005), 145–66.

[99] Ehud Netzer, "The Last Days and Hours at Masada," *BAR* 17, no. 6 (1991): 20–32; "Masada," ed. David Noel Freedman et al., *ABD* (New York, N.Y.: Doubleday, 1996), 4:586–87; Robin Ngo, ed., *Masada: The Dead Sea's Desert Fortress* (Washington, D.C.: Biblical Archaeology Society, 2014).

[100] James S. McLaren, "Jews and the Imperial Cult: From Augustus to Domitian," *Antichthon* 47 (2013): 163 n.22.

the Emperors Vespasian, Titus and Domitian issued a series of coins to commemorate the victory over the Jews in denominations of bronze, silver and gold. While most were minted in Rome, some bronze coins were minted in Caesarea in Judea, and other mints. While coins from Rome were in Latin, others minted elsewhere, were enscribed Greek, and stated *Ioudias Ealokuias* (equal to *Judea Capta)*. Various figures were depicted on the coins, but the dominant theme was of a figure morning over the destruction of Jerusalem[101] and the inscription "SC" beneath the figures which was an abbreviation for *S[enatus] C[consulto]*, "by the decree of the senate."[102] Sometimes there was a figure of a captive with bound hands behind his back.

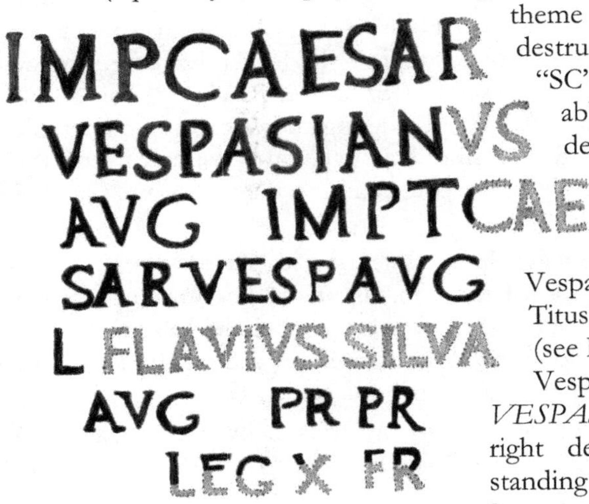

A bronze Sestertius coin of Vespasian (AD 69–79) depicting Vespasian and Titus' victory over the Jews was issued in AD 71 (see Fig. 119). On the left is the laureate head of Vespasian with the words *IMP CAES VESPASIAN AVG P M TR P P P COS III*. The right depicts Vespasian, holding a spear and standing with his left foot on a helmet over a Jewess who is mourning over the destruction of Jerusalem. In Latin it reads *IVDAEA CAPTA,* which translates as "Judea captured".[103] Some coins carried the words "Judaea devicta" meaning "Judea defeated".

IMPCAESAR
VESPASIANVS
AVG IMPTCAE
SARVESPAVG
L FLAVIVS SILVA
AVG PR PR
LEG X FR

120. Drawing of the restored inscription discovered near the Temple Mount in Jerusalem mentioning Vespasian, Titus and Silva.

The Vespasian-Titus Inscription

In 1970, while excavating south of the Temple Mount, Benjamin Mazar uncovered a stone pillar with an inscription that contained the names of Vespasian, Titus[104] and Silva (commander of the Tenth Legion), the leaders responsible for the subjugation of Judea (see Fig. 120).[105]

The excavator comments:

> In the first four lines...the Emperor Caesar Vespasianus Augustus . . . and Titus Caesar Vespasianus Augustus . . . are mentioned. The last three lines mention a commander of the *legio X Fretensis.* It is most plausible that this commander is none other than Lucius Flavius Silva, commander of the legion and governor of the Provincia Iudaea between 73–79/80 A.D. . . .[106]

---

[101] H. Porter, "Money," ed. James Orr and Melvin Grove Kyle, *ISBE2*, 1915, 3:2080; A. Thomas Kraabel, J. Andrew Overman, and Robert S. MacLennan, eds., *Diaspora Jews and Judaism: Essays in Honor Of, and in Dialogue With, A. Thomas Kraabel* (Scholars Press, 1992), 302–303.

[102] Bowman, Champlin, and Lintott, *The Cambridge Ancient History: The Augustan Empire, 44 BC–AD 70*, 10:318.

[103] Ya'aḳov Meshorer, *Jewish Coins of the Second Temple Period* (Tel-Aviv, Israel: Am Hassefer and Masada, 1967), 107–8.

[104] For the early epigraphical evidence for Vespasian and Titus, see Homer Curtis Newton, *The Epigraphical Evidence for the Reigns of Vespasian and Titus*, ed. Charles Edwin Bennett, John Robert Sitlington Sterrett, and George Prentice Bristol (Ithaca, N.Y.: Cornell University Press, 1901).

[105] Benjamin Mazar, "Excavations Near the Temple Mount," *Qadmoniot* 5 (1973): 83–84 [in Hebrew]; W. Harold Mare, *The Archaeology of the Jerusalem Area* (Eugene, Oreg.: Wipf & Stock, 2002), 203.

[106] M. Gichon and Benjamin H. Isaac, "A Flavian Inscription from Jerusalem," in *The Near East under Roman Rule*, ed. Benjamin H. Isaac (Leiden: Brill, 1998), 76.

> *Quotes from Antiquity*
>
> **The Vespasian-Titus Inscription**
>
> Emperor Caesar Vespasian Augustus, Emperor Titus Caesar Vespasian Augustus, his son; Lucius Flavius Silva, Propraetor [Lat. "For Roman military governor"] of Augustus, the Tenth Legion Fretensis.
>
> Mare, *The Archaeology of the Jerusalem Area*, 203.

As Gichon and Isaac argue:

> Mazar's identification of the missing name in 1.5 with L. Flavius Silva is probably correct, though L[ucilius Bassus] could be substituted. Bassus was legatus from the end of 71 until his death in A.D. 73. However, since Bassus' praenomen was probably Sextus, the identification of the missing name as Flavius Silva seems more credible.[107]

The name was either removed as a result of vandalism or following an official condemnation leading to the official name (*damnatio memoriae*) being removed, which was a documented practice.[108] Syme suggests that the name is not Titus but L. Antonius Saturninus,[109] although both proposals are completely hypothetical.

Gichon and Isaac report a second pillar found in Jerusalem with a similar inscription, also with the name of the Legate having been removed. It bears the number I under the title of the Legate, indicating that it was a milestone, something that raises a number of questions about both pillars. Why does a milestone have the Legate inscribed on it in the first place and why was it removed? [110]

What it does indicate is that the Roman leaders are identified in the location where the Temple and Jerusalem were destroyed and burned in 70 AD in accordance with the prophecy of Jesus (Matt 24; Mark 13:1–4).

The Arch of Titus

The honorific Arch of Titus (first cent.) located at the highest point on the *Via Sacra* in Rome (see Fig. 121), was constructed by Titus' younger brother Domitian in AD 81 in commemoration of Titus' victories, including the siege of Jerusalem in 70 AD.[111] This 15m high arch is the oldest surviving example of a Roman arch. This arch has provided the inspiration for many famous arches since the 16th cent. including the famous Arc de Triomphe in Paris, France.[112]

121. Arch of Titus, Rome.

© David E. Graves

The inside of the arch contains two impressive panels with reliefs.[113] The first depicts Titus riding in a chariot accompanied by the

[107] Ibid., 78.

[108] Ibid., 78 n.9.

[109] Ronald Syme, "Antonius Saturninus," *JRS* 68 (1978): 12–21.

[110] M. Gichon and Benjamin H. Isaac, "A Flavian Inscription from Jerusalem," *IEJ* 24, no. 2 (January 1, 1974): 117–23; "A Flavian Inscription from Jerusalem," 1998, 86.

[111] William Knight, *The Arch of Titus and the Spoils of the Temple, an Historical Lecture* (Charleston, SC: BiblioBazaar, 2010), 100.

[112] Fred S. Kleiner, *Gardner's Art Through the Ages: Backpack Edition, Book 1*, 13th ed., vol. 1 (Cengage Learning, 2009), 182–83.

[113] Frothingham identified a drawing of a lost section of the Frieze that portrays other scenes of the plunder of the Temple. A. L. Frothingham, "A Lost Section of the Frieze of the Arch of Titus?," *AJA* 18, no. 4 (1914): 479–83.

122. Relief on the arch of Titus, Rome, depicting the removal of the menorah, table of the presence and silver trumpets from the temple in Jerusalem following its destruction in AD 70 by the Romans.

goddess Victoria and the goddess Roma. The southern relief depicts the Romans' procession carrying the spoils plundered from the Second Temple in Jerusalem (see Fig. 122).

The menorah is portrayed as it was in the Temple in the first century (Matt 24; Mark 13:1–4). Yarden argues that the depiction of the Menorah Stand is the actual Jewish "'carrying frame,' a device serving both as permanent *ferculum* and pedestal,"[114] however, Kleiner and Pfanner are skeptical of this view and prefer to think of it as a specially constructed Roman carrying pedestal, due to the decorations of an eagle and sea creatures that are typical Roman symbols.[115]

Also displayed in relief are the two silver trumpets (which the Israelites called Israel and Jericho) and the table of the presence. These objects were originally gilded with gold, with a blue background.[116] There was a Latin inscription in bronze which read "The Roman Senate and People to Deified Titus, Vespasian Augustus, son of Deified Vespasian."[117]

Procopius of Caesarea provides a brief account of "the treasures of the Jews, which Titus, the son of Vespasian, together with certain others, had brought to Rome after the capture of Jerusalem" (Procopius *Bell. Van.* 4.9.5–7),[118] where Vespasian put them on display in the Temple of Peace (*Templum Pacis*).[119] In AD 455 Genseric, King of the Vandals, took the temple vessels in the sack of Rome.[120] Then in AD 534 Belisarius brought the temple items to Constantinople (Byzantium) from Carthage (Procopius *Bell. Van.* 4.9.5–7),[121] but when Justinian became aware of the items, and when he was informed by one of the emperor's staff of a popular belief that this was the reason for Rome's downfall, he immediately "sent

[114] Leon Yarden, *The Spoils of Jerusalem on the Arch of Titus: A Re-Investigation*, Skrifter Utgivna Av Svenska Institutet I Rom 8 (Göteborg: Astroms, 1991), 48.

[115] Michael Pfanner, *Der Titusbogen*, Beitrage Zur Erschliessung Hellenistischer Und Kaiserzeitlicher Skulptur Und Architektur 2 (Mainz am Rhein: von Zabern, 1983), 73; Fred S. Kleiner, "Review of The Spoils of Jerusalem on the Arch of Titus: A Re-Investigation by Leon Yarden," *AJA* 96, no. 4 (October 1, 1992): 776.

[116] Magness, "The Arch of Titus at Rome and the Fate of the God of Israel," 201–17.

[117] Paul Artus, *Art and Architecture of the Roman Empire* (Bellona Books, 2006), 45–48.

[118] Yarden, *The Spoils of Jerusalem on the Arch of Titus*, 64–65.

[119] Fergus Millar, "Last Year in Jerusalem: Monuments of the Jewish War in Rome," in *Flavius Josephus and Flavian Rome*, ed. Jonathan Edmondson, Steve Mason, and James B. Rives (Oxford: Oxford University Press, 2005), 101–28.

[120] Theophanes, *Chronographia*, ed. Carl de Boer (Leipzig, 1883), 1:109; Edward Gibbon, *Decline and Fall of the Roman Empire*, Wordsworth Classics of World Literature (Ware, Hertfordshire: Wordsworth, 1998), 686.

[121] Theophanes, *Chronographia*, 1:199.

everything to the sanctuaries of the Christians in Jerusalem" (Procopius *Bell. Van.* 4.9.10).[122]

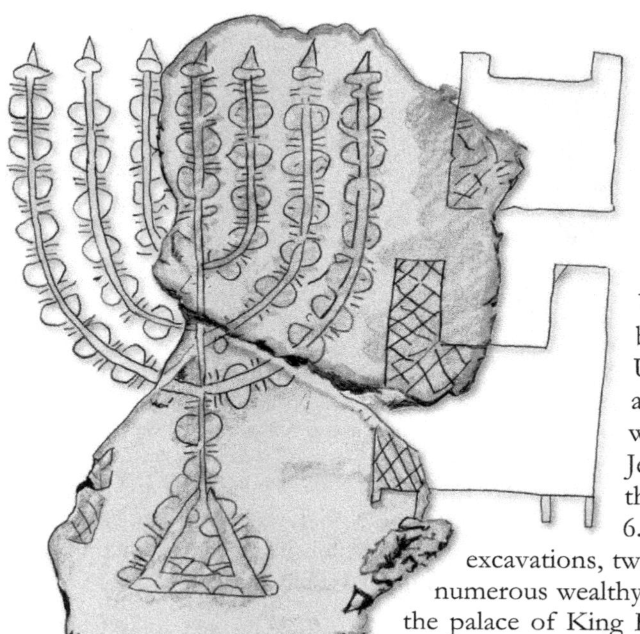

123. Drawing of a menorah inscribed on plaster from a house burnt from the first cent. AD in Jerusaelm.

Israel Museum (IAA 1982–1055)

The Burnt House with a Menorah

Excavations, under the direction of Nahman Avigad of the Hebrew University, were carried out between 1969 and 1983, in the Upper City of Jerusalem,[123] where according to Josephus many of the wealthy Jews lived and where the Jews fled to escape the massacre of the Roman soldiers in 70 AD (*J.W.* 6.404–406). Over the course of the excavations, twenty-two areas were excavated and numerous wealthy homes were discovered, including the palace of King Herod, palaces of the Hasmonean kings, and the residences of high priests and Sadducees.[124]

Inside one of the houses excavated, now known as the *Burnt House*, archaeologists discovered a stone weight with an Aramaic inscription stating: "[of] Bar Kathros."[125]

Reddish and Fant report that "There is no doubt that the Kathos family belonged to one of only a few aristocratic families whose sons occupied the office of high priest under the Romans."[126] (*b. Pesaḥ.* 57:1; *t. Menaḥ.* 13:21). Some have speculated whether this might be the house of the high priest Caiaphas.[127]

In 1990 an inscribed ossuary was discovered in Jerusalem with the inscription of the high priest, *Yosef Bar Kayafa* (trans. Joseph, son of Caiaphas; Josephus *Ant.* 18.35; 18.95).[128] Caiaphas was the leader of the Sanhedrin from AD 18–36 and played an integral role in Jesus' conflict with the Jewish leaders in the final week of his life (John 11:49–53; 18:14). Caiaphas presided over the evening trial in which Jesus confessed to being the Messiah and ultimately condemned

---

[122] Emil Schürer, *The History of the Jewish People in the Age of Jesus Christ (175 BC–AD 135)*, ed. G. Vermes, F. Miller, and M. Black, Rev (Edinburgh, U.K.: T&T Clark, 1979), 510 n. 133.

[123] Nahman Avigad, "Archaeology," in *Sefer Yerushalayim*, ed. Michael Avi-Yonah, vol. 1 (Jerusalem, Israel: Bialik Institute and Dvir, 1956), 145–55 [Hebrew]; *Discovering Jerusalem* (Nashville, Tenn.: Nelson, 1983).

[124] Hillel Geva, "Western Jerusalem at the End of the First Temple Period in Light of the Excavations in the Jewish Quarter," in *Jerusalem in Bible and Archaeology: The First Temple Period*, ed. Andrew G. Vaughn and Ann E. Killebrew, SBL Symposium Series 18 (Atlanta, Ga.: SBL, 2003), 188–208; Hillel Geva, ed., *Jewish Quarter Excavations in the Old City of Jerusalem Conducted by Nahman Avigad: Architecture and Stratigraphy, Areas A, W, and X-2 - Final Report*, vol. 1 (Jerusalem: Israel Exploration Society, 2000).

[125] Nahman Avigad, "How the Wealthy Lived in Herodian Jerusalem," *BAR* 2, no. 4 (1976): 29; Mare, *The Archaeology of the Jerusalem Area*, 174.

[126] Fant and Reddish, *Lost Treasures of the Bible*, 379.

[127] Arthur A. Rupprecht, "The House of Annas-Caiaphas," *Archaeology in the Biblical World* 1, no. 1 (1991): 4–17.

[128] Evans, "Excavating Caiaphas, Pilate, and Simon of Cyrene: Assessing the Literary and Archaeological Evidence," 327–29.

124. Caesarea, Israel: Pontius Pilate (26–37 AD) limestone, inscription (82.0 cm H, 65.0 cm w) Building dedication with 4 lines of writing in Latin (AE 1963 no. 104).

© David E. Graves

him to death (Matt 26:57–68; see above *The Caiaphas Ossuary*).

Also inside the Burnt House, inscribed in plaster on the wall, was a representation of the seven-branched candelabrum or menorah (see Fig. 123).[129] Avigad describes the discovery as follows:

> Perhaps the single most stunning find in the excavation was a menorah, the seven-branched candelabrum, incised on a fragment of plaster. It is about 8 inches high and has tall branches, a short stem and a triangular base—all ornamented in a stylized astragal pattern. This is the earliest depiction of the candelabrum in the Temple ever discovered, and was incised on a wall of a house as a symbolic ornament at a time when the actual Temple Menorah was still in use, only a few hundred yards away.[130]

On the right side of the menorah are two partially preserved boxes which likely represent the incense altar and table of showbread.

THE PONTIUS PILATE INSCRIPTION (MATT 27:2)

During the 1961 excavations of the Roman theatre near Caesarea Maritima, archaeologists led by Antonio Frova uncovered a limestone block with an inscription that read:

[...]S TIBERIÉVM[131]
[...]TIVS PILATVS
[...]ECTVS IVDA[...]E
[...]É[...][132]

It is now on display in the Israel Museum (AE 1963 no. 104; see Fig. 124) in Jerusalem with a replica at Caesarea Maritima. The inscription is believed to be either part of a larger inscription dedicating a temple to the emperor Tiberius in Caesarea[133] or commemorating the restoration of the Caesarea Maritima harbour (Josephus *J.W.* 1.21.5–7; *Ant.* 15.9.6).[134] Recent

[129] Mare, *The Archaeology of the Jerusalem Area*, 174.

[130] Avigad, "How the Wealthy Lived in Herodian Jerusalem," 35.

[131] This word was not known to scholars, but they speculate that it was perhaps a temple (Tiberieum) built to honour the emperor Tiberius.

[132] Antonio Frova, "L'Iscrizione Di Ponzio Pilato a Cesarea," *Rendiconti dell'Istitutio Lombardo* 95 (1961): 419–34; Jerry Vardaman, "A New Inscription Which Mentions Pilate as 'Prefect,'" *JBL* 81, no. 1 (1962): 70–71; Giordano dell' Amore, Virginio Borroni, and Antonio Frova, *Scavi di Caesarea Maritima* (Milano: "L'Erma" di Bretschneider, 1966), 217; Joan E. Taylor, "Pontius Pilate and the Imperial Cult in Roman Judaea," *NTS* 52 (2006): 564–75.

[133] [CAESARIEN]S TIBERIÉVM [PON]TIVS PILATVS [PRAEF]ECTVS IVDA[EA]E [...D]É[DIT...] translated as "[Pon]tius Pilate, [the Pre]fect of Jude[a, has dedicated to the people of Caesarea a temple in honor of] Tiberius". Robert J. Bull, "Caesarea Maritima: The Search for Herod's City," *BAR* 8, no. 3 (1982): 24–40; Robert J. Bull, "Pontius Pilate Inscription," *BAR* 8, no. 5 (1982).

[134] [NAUTI]S TIBERIÉVM [PON]TIVS PILATVS [PRAEF]ECTVS IVDA[EA]E [...REF]É[CIT...] translated as "[Seaman']s Tiberieum "[Pon]tius Pilate, [Pre]fect of Jude[a [restor]e[s..." Géza Alföldy, "Pontius Pilatus Und Das Tiberieum von Caesarea Maritima Scripta," *Scripta Classica Israelica* 18 (1999): 106–7.

archaeological research around the harbour would support Alföldy's proposal.[135]

While Pontius Pilate has been mentioned in ancient texts (John 19:6; Tacitus *Ann.* 15.44; Josephus *J.W.* 2.117–18; *Ant.* 17.55–64; 85–89; 18.3.3 §63; Philo *Legat.* 38.299–305) this was the first physical evidence that Pilate existed. It is known that Pilate lived in Caesarea and only went to Jerusalem on special occasions,[136] so it is not surprising to find an inscription with his name on it in Caesarea.

The mention of Pilate with Tiberius (42 BC–37 AD) puts Pontius Pilate in the same time period as Jesus, in the first century. The inscription also clarifies Pilate's title. The Gospels speak of him as a governor (Gr. *egemon;* Matt 27:2; Luke 3:1) while Tacitus speaks of him as procurator (Gr. *epitropos; Ann.* 15.44). This led to debate over his title and rank[137] until the discovery of the Pilate inscription in 1961 which settled the issue and provided his official title as Prefect (Lat. *Præfectus*).

While this discovery does not prove that Pilate spoke with Jesus or demonstrate that the crucifixion took place, it does support the historical reliability of the gospels in the Bible in corroborating the existence of one of the major characters.[138]

THE LOCATION OF GOLGOTHA (MATT 27:33)

Golgotha (Aramaic *gûlgaltâ*; Heb. *gulgōlāṯ*) is mentioned by all the Gospel writers as the location of Jesus' crucifixion (Matt 27:33; Mark 15:22; Luke 23:33; John 19:17). While Matthew, Mark and John translate the Aramaic term as "Place of the Skull", Luke simply states "Skull." It is often assumed that the place was in the shape of a skull, leading General Charles Gordon, on a visit to Jerusalem in 1883, to identify a small rocky cliff outside the Damascus Gate in Jerusalem, resembling a skull, as the "place of the skull."[139] This location was further verified by an ancient tomb that he located not far from the cliff (see Fig. 125).

125. Rocky escarpment known as Gordon's Calvary resembling a skull, located northwest of the Church of the Holy Sepulchre, near the Garden Tomb.

But as Kathleen Kenyon later pointed out, given the severe erosion of the hill due

[135] Robert L. Hohlfelder, "Caesarea beneath the Sea," *BAR* 8, no. 3 (1982): 42–47; Robert L. Hohlfelder et al., "Sebastos: Herod's Harbor at Caesarea Maritima," *BA* 46, no. 3 (1983): 133–43; R. Lindley Vann, "Herod's Harbor Construction Recovered Underwater," *BAR* 9, no. 3 (1983): 10–14.

[136] Taylor, "Pontius Pilate and the Imperial Cult in Roman Judaea," 567, 570; Warren Carter, *Pontius Pilate: Portraits of a Roman Governor*, Interfaces Series (Collegeville, Minn.: Liturgical, 2003), 115.

[137] Arnold H. M. Jones, "Procurators and Prefects in the Early Principate," in *Studies in Roman Government and Law*, ed. Arnold H. M. Jones (Oxford: Blackwell, 1960), 115–25.

[138] Brian C. McGing, "Pontius Pilate and the Sources," *CBQ* 53 (1991): 416–38; Craig A. Evans, "Excavating Caiaphas, Pilate, and Simon of Cyrene: Assessing the Literary and Archaeological Evidence," in *Jesus and Archaeology*, ed. James H. Charlesworth (Grand Rapids: Eerdmans, 2006), 334–38.

[139] http://www.shapell.org/manuscript/calvary-crucifixion-sites-identified#b-icn.

to modern quarrying, it is unlikely that it retained its present appearance over the previous 2000 years.[140] Also, the text does not state that it resembled a skull, or that it was on a hill. There is no archaeological evidence to connect the popular site of Gordon's Calvary to the crucifixion.

However, it is known from ancient sources that the crucifixions took place outside the city wall of Jerusalem (John 19:20; cf. Heb 13:12) in a public place, perhaps near a busy road (e.g., Mark 15:29, 40). Also, the text states "in the place where he was crucified there was a garden, and in the garden a new tomb in which no one had yet been laid" (John 19:41).

The Church of the Holy Sepulchre (see Fig. 116), located within the Old City of Jerusalem, is the traditional location (fourth cent. AD) of the place of crucifixion.[141] In the 1960's, archaeological research, in conjunction with Josephus's description of the city's walls, indicated that this site was indeed outside the city walls in the first century.[142]

THE GIVAT HAMIVTAR HEEL BONE (MATT 27:33–44)

Up until 1968 there was much debate over how crucifixion was actually carried out, particularly whether people were either tied to the crossbeam or nailed.[143] However, a Jewish tomb was discovered in 1968 in Giv'at ha-Mivtar (Ras el-Masaref, ossuary no. 4 in Tomb 1), just north of Jerusalem near Mt. Scopus, that dated to the first cent. AD (7 BC–AD 70),[144] containing the remains of a crucified man (see Fig. 126).

The site was excavated by a team of archaeologists led by Vassilios Tzaferis, who uncovered the remains of some thirty-five individuals, nine of whom were violently killed.[145] The name of the crucified man, Jehohanan ben Ha'galqol,[146] was etched on the outside of the ossuary. His remains were examined by the late Professor Nicu Haas, an anthropologist at the Anatomy School at the Hebrew University of Jerusalem-Hadassah Medical School. He determined that the remains belonged to a man in his twenties who was crucified sometime between AD 7 and 66 (start of the Jewish revolt).[147] The evidence for his crucifixion was based on an iron nail (11.5 cm., 7 in. long) that still remained in his right heel bone. The end of the nail was bent,

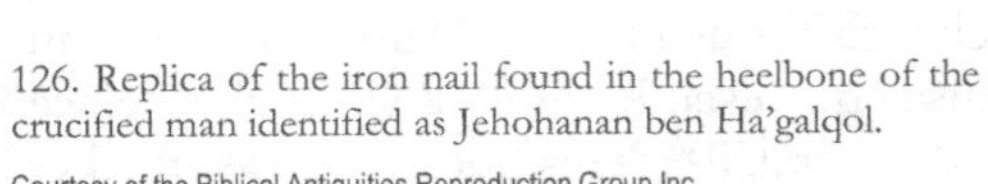

126. Replica of the iron nail found in the heelbone of the crucified man identified as Jehohanan ben Ha'galqol.
Courtesy of the Biblical Antiquities Reproduction Group Inc

[140] Joel B. Green, Scot McKnight, and I. Howard Marshall, eds., *Dictionary of Jesus and the Gospels* (Downers Grove, Ill.: InterVarsity, 1992), 150.

[141] Charles Cohasnon, *The Church of the Holy Sepulchre in Jerusalem*, trans. J. P. B. Ross and Claude Ross, The Schweich Lectures of the British Academy, 1972 (Oxford: Oxford University Press, 1974), 29.

[142] Kathleen M Kenyon, *Jerusalem Excavating 3000 Years of History* (London: Thames & Hudson, 1967), 153–54; Bruce Schein, "The Second Wall of Jerusalem," *BA* 44, no. 1 (1981): 21–26.

[143] J. W. Hewitt, "The Use of Nails in Crucifixion," *HTR* 25 (1932): 29–45.

[144] David W. Chapman, *Ancient Jewish and Christian Perceptions of Crucifixion*, WUNT 244 (Tübingen: Siebeck, 2008), 4–5.

[145] Vassilios Tzaferis, "Jewish Tombs at and near Giv'at Ha-Mivtar, Jerusalem," *IEJ* 20, no. 1 (1970): 18–32; "Crucifixion: The Archaeological Evidence," *BAR* 11 (1985): 44–53.

[146] Joseph Naveh, "The Ossuary Inscriptions from Giv'at Ha-Mivtar," *IEJ* 20, no. 1 (1970): 33–37.

[147] Nico Haas, "Anthropological Observations on the Skeletal Remains from Giv'at Ha-Mivtar," *IEJ* 20, no. 1 (1970): 38–59.

making it difficult to remove from the olive wood, which may explain why it was still in his heel. Furthermore, nails were driven through his wrists, between the radius and cubitus and not the palms, which scholars had speculated was the common practice and has been proven to be unable to support the weight of a human body.[148] Ancient writers considered the wrist to be part of the hand.

In addition, there was a piece of acacia wood between the head of the nail and his foot; perhaps a piece of wood was placed over the foot before nailing to prevent the foot from slipping over the head of the nail. According to the custom mentioned in John 19:31–32, Yehohanan's legs were broken (Lat. *crucifragium*).

More recently Zias and Sekeles have re-examined the skeletal remains and altered some of the initial conclusions. They concluded that the iron nail still lodged in the right heel bone had passed from the right to the left of only that heal, and that the legs had not been nailed together since the nail was too short. The crucified man's legs had straddled the upright beam and were nailed on either side. They also concluded that the man was tied to the crossbeam since there were no traumatic injuries to his arms or forearms and questioned whether the man's legs were broken prior to his death.[149]

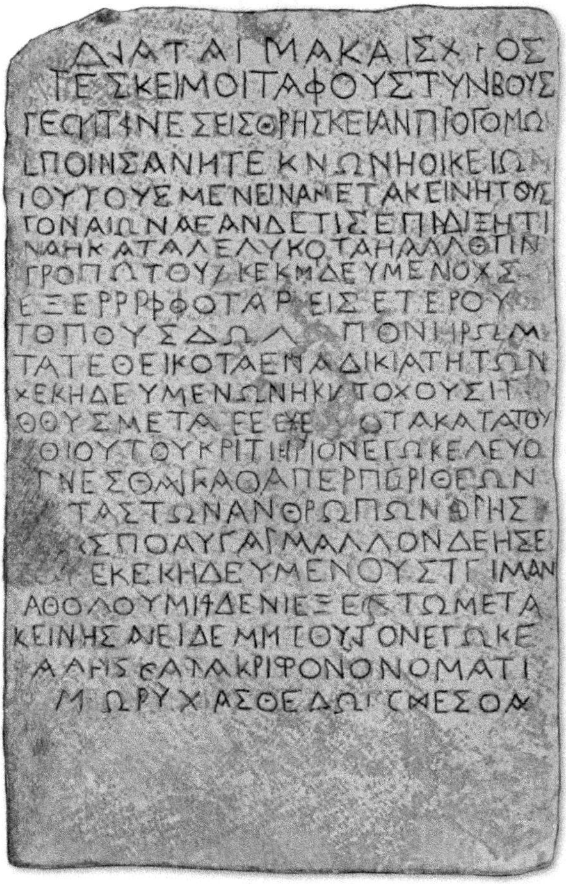

While this find does help to support the literary descriptions of crucifixion in the NT period (Matt 27:33–44; Luke 23:33–43; John19:17–30), the conclusions drawn are only based on just one archaeological discovery and are therefore limited.

127. Drawing of the Nazareth Inscription .

The Bibliothèque nationale, Paris, displayed in the Cabinet des Médailles

THE NAZARETH INSCRIPTION (MATT 28:11–15)

The "Nazareth Inscription" (*SEG* 8:13; see Fig. 127) [150] is a marble table (24" x 15" or 6 cm x 38 cm), containing a 22 line inscription of an "Edict of Caesar." It was acquired by Wilhelm Frohner, in Paris, in 1878, having been sent from Nazareth.[151] It is now displayed in the Bibliothèque nationale, Paris and was published

[148] Arthur C. Aufderheide and Conrado Rodriguez-Martin, *The Cambridge Encyclopedia of Human Paleopathology* (Cambridge, U.K.: Cambridge University Press, 1998), 38.

[149] Joseph Zias and Eliezer Sekeles, "The Crucified Man from Giv'at Ha-Mivtar: A Reappraisal," *IEJ* 35, no. 1 (1985): 22–27.

[150] Louis Robert, *Collection Froehner: I. Inscriptions grecques* (Paris: Éditions des Bibliothèques nationales, 1936), 114, 70.

[151] Bruce M. Metzger, *New Testament Studies: Philological, Versional, and Patristic* (Leiden: Brill, 1980), 75–92.

Quotes from Antiquity

The Nazareth Inscription

Edict of Caesar It is my decision [concerning] graves and tombs—whoever has made them for the religious observances of parents, or children, or household members—that these remain undisturbed forever. But if anyone legally charges that another person has destroyed, or has in any manner extracted those who have been buried, or has moved with wicked intent those who have been buried to other places, committing a crime against them, or has moved sepulcher-sealing stones, against such a person, I order that a judicial tribunal be created, just as [is done] concerning the gods in human religious observances, even more so will it be obligatory to treat with honor those who have been entombed. You are absolutely not to allow anyone to move [those who have been entombed]. But if [someone does], I wish that [violator] to suffer capital punishment under the title of tomb-breaker.

Billington, "The Nazareth Inscription," op. cit.

by Cumont in 1930.[152] It prescribes capital punishment for anyone caught stealing bodies and is considered by some to be an implicit reference to the resurrection.

The inscription (*SEG* 8:13), which dates to the reign of Emperor Caesar Augustus, (31 BC–AD 14)[153] or Emperor Claudius (AD 41–54),[154] translates from the Greek as follows in the *Quotes from Antiquity*.[155]

The value of this text is connected with it being a possible Roman reaction to the Jewish response to the resurrection of Jesus, who reported that his body was taken by the disciples (Matt 28:11–15). While the text does not refer to the resurrection, it would appear that the news of the empty tomb reached the Roman elite back in Rome through Pontius Pilate, and this was the imperial reaction. To date, the Nazareth Inscription remains one of the most significant extra-biblical texts verifying the resurrection of Jesus and the circulation of the story in the first century.

[152] Franz Cumont, "Un Réscrit Impérial Sur La Violation de Sépulture," *Revue Historique* 163 (1930): 341–66.

[153] Cumont, "Un Réscrit Impérial Sur La Violation de Sépulture," 365; F. de Zulueta, "Violation of Sepulture in Palestine at the Beginning of the Christian Era," *JRS*, 1932, 186.

[154] M. P. Charlesworth, *Documents Illustrating the Reigns of Claudius and Nero* (Cambridge: Cambridge University Press, 1952), 3.

[155] Clyde E. Billington, "The Nazareth Inscription: Proof of the Resurrection of Christ?," *Artifax* 20, no. 2 (Spring 2005): n.p.

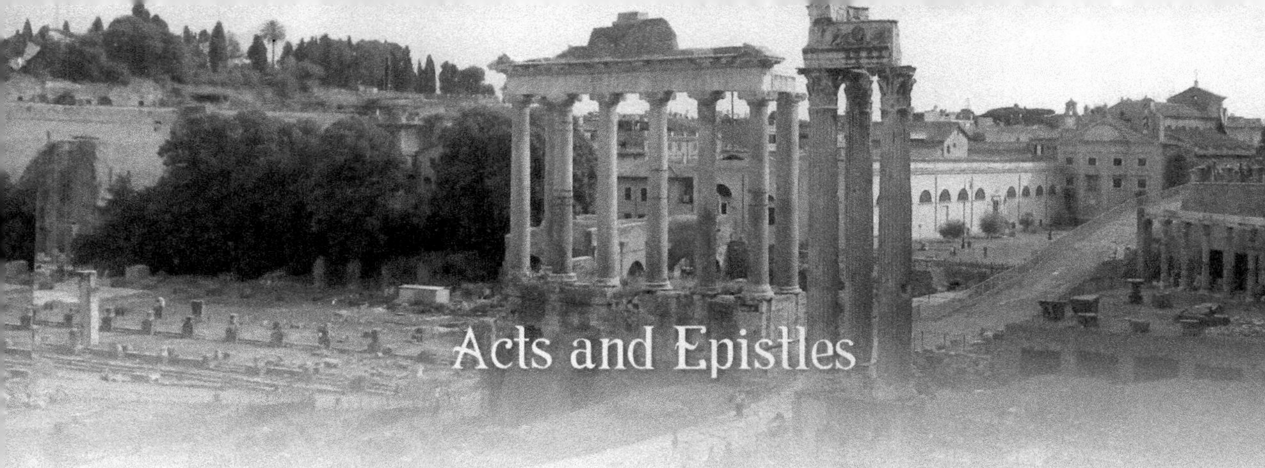

Acts and Epistles

128. Temple of Saturn (8 columns, built in 42 BC and reconstructed in 283 AD) and Temple of Vespasian dn Titus (3 columns built in 79 AD) at the Roman Forum seen from the Capitol, anient Roman ruins, Rome, Italy.

© David E. Graves

The Book of Acts is overflowing with historical and geographical details that contribute to the investigation of archaeology. The majority of the archaeology pertaining to the book of Acts and the Epistles of Paul deals with the cities that he visited on his missionary trips to Syria, Asia Minor (modern Turkey), Macedonia (modern Bulgaria and Greece), Greece, and Italy. Surprisingly, about two- thirds of the NT takes place in the countries of Turkey and Greece. While most of the cities Paul visited have been excavated,[1] there still many that have not been fully uncovered, such as Colossae, Iconium, Lystra, and Derbe.

Although there have been a number of significant inscriptions discovered, the inscriptions of Sergius Paulus (Acts 13), Politarch (Acts 17), Gallio (Acts 18), Miletus (Acts 20), Caesarean Mosaic (Rom 13), Erastus (Rom 16), and the Megiddo Church have all been examined in Graves *Biblical Archaeology,* Volume One and will not be considered here.[2]

MASADA (ACTS 5:38–39)

In Acts 5:38–39 Gamaliel gave advice that proved true with the fall of Masada[3]: "keep away from these men and let them alone, for if this plan or this undertaking is of man, it will fail; but if it is of God, you will not be able to overthrow them. You

129. Ostracon from Masada bearing the name "ben Yair" which could be short for Eleazar ben Ya'ir, the leader of the Zealots who led the revolt against the Romans from Masada in AD 70–73.

© David E. Graves

[1] Edward M. Blaiklock, *Cities of the New Testament* (New York, N.Y.: Revell, 1965); John McRay, *Archaeology and the New Testament* (Grand Rapids: Baker, 1991), 225–350; Edwin M. Yamauchi, *The Archaeology of New Testament Cities in Western Asia Minor* (Grand Rapids: Baker, 1980); Colin J. Hemer, "Seven Cities of Asia Minor," in *Major Cities of the Biblical World*, ed. R.K. Harrison (Nashville, Tenn.: Nelson, 1985), 234–48; Hemer and Gempf, *The Book of Acts in the Setting of Hellenistic History*; *New Testament Cities in Western Asia Minor: Light from Archaeology on Cities of Paul and the Seven Churches of Revelation* (Eugene, Oreg.: Wipf & Stock, 2003); Roland H. Worth, Jr., *The Seven Cities of Apocalypse and Greco-Asian Culture* (New York, N.Y.: Paulist, 2002); *The Seven Cities of the Apocalypse and Roman Culture* (New York, N.Y.: Paulist, 2002); LaMoine F. DeVries, *Cities of the Biblical World: An Introduction to the Archaeology, Geography, and History of Biblical Sites* (Eugene, Oreg.: Wipf & Stock, 2006); William M. Ramsay, *The Cities of St. Paul: Their Influence on His Life and Thought, The Cities of Eastern Asia Minor* (Whitefish, Mont.: Kessinger, 2004); *The Historical Geography of Asia Minor* (Cambridge, Mass.: Cambridge University Press, 2010); Mark W. Wilson, *Biblical Turkey: A Guide to Jewish and Christian Sites of Asia Minor* (Istanbul: Ege Yayinlari, 2010); Jack Finegan, *The Archeology of the New Testament: The Life of Jesus and the Beginning of the Early Church*, Revised (Princeton, NJ: Princeton University Press, 2014).

[2] Graves, *Biblical Archaeology Vol 1: An Introduction* 2nd ed 1:234–46.

[3] Ehud Netzer, "The Last Days and Hours at Masada," *BAR* 17, no. 6 (1991): 20–32; Robin Ngo, ed., *Masada: The Dead Sea's Desert Fortress* (Washington, D.C.: Biblical Archaeology Society, 2014).

130. The fortress of Masada.

© David E. Graves

might even be found opposing God!". The archaeological evidence from Masada includes OT scripture (8), apocryphal texts (6), Greek and Latin papyri (29), ostracon (700 Greek and Aramaic; see Fig. 129), and coins (18 Ptolemaic and Seleucid, 90 Hasmonian, and 400 Herodian).[4] Of most importance to NT studies is the discovery of scriptural texts including fragments from Genesis (MasGen = Gen 46:7–11), Leviticus (MasLev[a,b] = Lev 4:3–9 + 8:31–11:40), Deuteronomy (MasDeut = Deut 32:46–47; 33:17–24; 34:2–6), Ezekiel (MasEzek = Ezek 35:11–38:14), Psalms (MasPs[a,b] = Pss 81:2–85:6 + 150:1–6), and Sirach (MasSir = Sir 37:27–43:30).[5]

Two texts, Deuteronomy and Ezekiel (*ca.* AD 73), were buried in the ground under the floor of the Zealot synagogue[6]

131. Aerial view of Masada (Heb. מצדה), in the Judaean Desert (Hebrew: מִדְבַּר יְהוּדָה), with the Dead Sea in the distance. Jewish zealots on Masada revolted against the Romans in AD 70–73.

© Andrew Shiva / Wikimedia Commons

[4] Evans, *Ancient Texts for New Testament Studies*, 136–38.

[5] Shemaryahu Talmon, "Hebrew Written Fragments from Masada," *Dead Sea Discoveries* 3, no. 2 (1996): 168–77; Evans, *Ancient Texts for New Testament Studies*, 136; Yigael Yadin, "The Excavation of Masada—1963/64: Preliminary Report," *IEJ* 15, no. 1/2 (January 1, 1965): 79–82; "The Excavations of Masada-the Inscribed Scrolls," *Yediot* 29 (1965): 115–17 [Hebrew].

[6] Ehud Netzer, *The Buildings, Stratigraphy and Architecture (Masada 3)* (Jerusalem: Israel Exploration Society, 1991).

at Masada,[7] perhaps to hide them from the approaching Romans or perhaps as evidence of the practice of *genizah* (preserving corrupt texts).[8] Since several of the scriptural text were found in the synagogue and living quarters, it has been argued that this indicates that the reading and study of scripture also took place outside the temple setting.

THE PORTRAIT OF CLAUDIUS (ACTS 11:28; 18:1)

Luke is one of the only NT writers to mention Roman emperors, which places his writing in the context of world history. While he mentions Augustus (Luke 2:1) and Tiberius (Luke 3:1) only once, he mentions Claudius[9] (Lat. *Tiberius Claudius Nero Germanicus*, r. AD 41–54. See Fig. 132) twice, once in Acts 11:28 and again in Acts 18:1.[10]

However, externally to the Bible, Claudius is mentioned in several inscriptions that have been found attesting to his deification. They state: "Tiberius Claudius lord" (*SB* no. 4331; P.Oxy. 37); "Claudius god" (*SB* no. 8245, 8444; P.Oxy. 713); and "God Claudius Caesar Augustus Germanicus, emperor" (*OGIS* no. 668).

Acts eleven speaks of prophets coming down from Jerusalem to Antioch (Acts 27–28), and that one of them named Agabus prophesied that there would be a great famine, which Luke states happened during the time of Claudius (*ca.* AD 46), resulting in a gift of money being sent to Jerusalem from the Christians in Antioch (Acts 11:28).

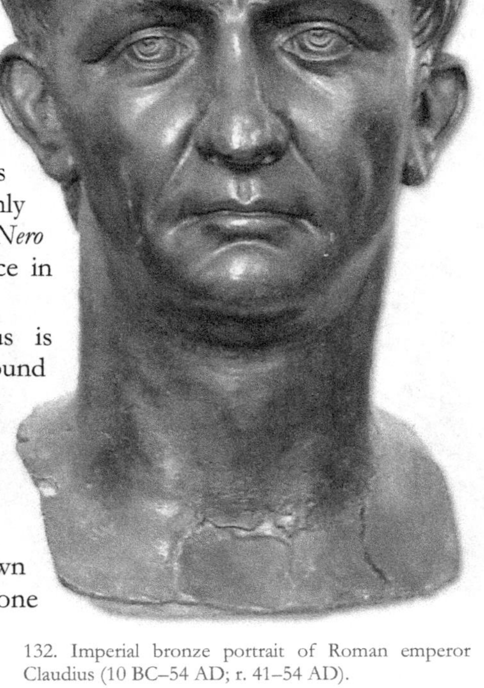

132. Imperial bronze portrait of Roman emperor Claudius (10 BC–54 AD; r. 41–54 AD).

National Archaeological Museum of Spain, Madrid. © Luis García / Wikimedia Commons

Several ancient writers recount a shortage of food in the Roman Empire during his reign (Suetonius *Claud.* 18; Tacitus *Ann.* 12.43; Cassius Dio *Hist. Rom.* 60.11; Josephus *Ant.* 3.320–321; 20.2.5; 20.5.2). Also, papyri, dating from *ca.* AD 46, show high grain prices during Claudius' reign, and Queen Helena of Adiabene is recorded as helping famine-stricken Palestinian Jews with Egyptian grain (*ca.* AD 45–46).[11]

The second account in Acts (18:1–2), where Luke refers to Claudius, involves the expulsion of Jews from Rome. Luke recounts how two of Paul's companions, Aquila and Priscilla, had recently come from Italy because of an edict of Claudius which "had commanded

---

[7] Foerster, "Synagogues at Masada and Herodium." 224–28.

[8] Emanuel Tov, *Hebrew Bible, Greek Bible and Qumran: Collected Essays* (Mohr Siebeck, 2008), 172.

[9] Not to be confused with Claudius Lysias, the Roman Tribune and military commander in Jerusalem (Acts 21:31-24:22).

[10] Frederick Fyvie Bruce, "Christianity Under Claudius," *BJRL* 44 (1962): 309.

[11] Craig S. Keener, *The IVP Bible Background Commentary: New Testament* (Downers Grove, Ill.: InterVarsity, 1994), 354.

all the Jews to leave Rome" (Acts 18:1–2).

Although Josephus stated that Claudius was somewhat more tolerant to Jews than previous emperors and was responsible for an edict that guaranteed Jews the right to practice their religion in the empire without interference (*Ant.* 19.5.2–3), the statement in Acts is supported by a statement of Suetonius (*ca.* AD 69/75—after 130), who claims that the Jews were expelled from Rome (*ca.* AD 49)[12] because of the continual disturbances created by one called *Chrestus* (Christ?).[13] Suetonius states: "Since the Jews constantly made disturbances at the instigation of *Chrestus*, he [Emperor Claudius in AD 49] expelled them from Rome." (*Claud.* 5.25.4 [Rolfe])

133. The Areopagus Hill (Mars Hill or Hill of Ares), as seen from the Acropolis, Athens, Greece.

© Jebulon / Wikimedia Commons

MARS HILL, ATHENS (ACTS 17:22)

The Bible states that, "Paul, standing in the midst of the Areopagus, said: 'Men of Athens, I perceive that in every way you are very religious….'" (Acts 17:22).[14] The Areopagus (Gr. *Areios Pagos*, translated as "Ares[15] Rock" or ""hill of Ares"")[16] is identified with a limestone hill (115 m. or 377 ft. high) NW of the Acropolis in the center of Athens (see Fig. 133). Originally there was a structure on the top of the hill where the Areopagus council met. Still evident today are the benches carved into the rock and steps that led to the summit of the hill.

The term Areopagus can be identified with both the location on Mars Hill and the council which was the "chief court of imperial Athens."[17]

---

[12] This date is further confirmed by Paul's encounter with Gallio (Lat. Lucius Junius Gallio Annaeus; Pliny *Nat.* 31.33), the proconsul (governor) of Corinth in either AD 51 or 52 (Cassius Dio *Hist. Rom.* 57.14.5). The arrival of Aquila and Priscilla had to have happened prior to this date. Craig A. Evans and Stanley E. Porter, eds., *Dictionary of New Testament Background: A Compendium of Contemporary Biblical Scholarship* (Downers Grove, Ill.: InterVarsity, 2000), 206–207; Rainer Riesner, *Paul's Early Period: Chronology, Mission Strategy, Theology*, trans. Douglas W. Stott (Grand Rapids: Eerdmans, 1998), 202–11; Andreas J. Köstenberger, L. Scott Kellum, and Charles L Quarles, *The Cradle, the Cross, and the Crown: An Introduction to the New Testament* (Nashville, Tenn.: Broadman & Holman Academic, 2009), 400; H. Dixon Slingerland, "Acts 18:1-18, the Gallio Inscription, and Absolute Pauline Chronology," *JBL* 110, no. 3 (1991): 439–49.

[13] While some scholars believe this to a particular Jew who was an agitant to the Romans (Slingerland), most scholars agree that this is a conflict between Christians and Jews and that *Chrestus* can be identified with Christ. Stephen Benko, "The Edict of Claudius of A.D. 49 and the Instigator Chrestus," *Theologische Zeitschrift* 25 (1969): 406–18; H. Dixon Slingerland, "Chrestus: Christus?," in *The Literature of Early Rabbinic Judaism: Issues in Talmudic Redaction and Interpretation*, ed. Alan J. Avery-Peck, New Perspectives on Ancient Judaism 4 (Lanham, Md.: University Press of America, 1989), 439–49; Robert E. Van Voorst, *Jesus Outside the New Testament: An Introduction to the Ancient Evidence* (Grand Rapids: Eerdmans, 2000), 30–39; Craig S. Keener, *The Historical Jesus of the Gospels* (Grand Rapids: Eerdmans, 2012), 66.

[14] Bertil Edgar Gärtner, *The Areopagus Speech and Natural Revelation* (Lund, Sweden: Gleerup, 1955); Ned Bernard Stonehouse, *Paul Before the Areopagus: And Other New Testament Studies* (Wheaton, Ill.: Tyndale, 1957).

[15] Ares was the Greek god of war, and Mars Hill was the location for the aetiological myth of the trial of Ares for the murder of Poseidon's son Alirrothios (Pausanias, *Descr.* 1.21.4; 1.28.5).

[16] H. M. Martin Jr., "Areopagus (Place)," ed. David Noel Freedman et al., *ABD* (New York, N.Y.: Doubleday, 1996), 370.

[17] Timothy David Barnes, "An Apostle on Trial," *JTS* 20, no. 2 (1969): 412.

134. Synagogue inscription, Corinth

Archaeological Museum of Ancient Corinth (ID 123). © Ferrell Jenkins, BiblicalStudies.info

F. F. Bruce and others suggest that: "In NT times, except for investigating cases of homicide, it [The Council of the Areopagus] met in the 'Royal Porch' (*stoa basileios*) in the Athenian market-place (*agora*), and it was probably here that Paul was brought before the Areopagus (Acts 17:19) and not, as AV puts it, 'in the midst of Mars' hill' (v. 22)."[18]

THE SYNAGOGUE INSCRIPTION AT CORINTH (ACTS 18:4)

Following Paul's arrival from Athens (AD 51),[19] he stayed in Corinth for eighteen months. His custom was to seek out a synagogue to reason the case for Jesus being the Messiah. Acts states that "he reasoned in the synagogue every Sabbath, and tried to persuade Jews and Greeks" (Acts 18:4). Two individuals are mentioned as converts of Paul's ministry in the synagogue: Crispus (official of the synagogue; Gr. *archisynagogos*; Acts 18:8; 1 Cor 1:14) and Sosthenes (ruler of the synagogue; Gr. *archisynagogos*; Acts 18:17; 1 Cor 1:1).[20]

In 1898 evidence of at least one of the synagogues in Corinth was uncovered by Rufus Richardson of the American School of Classical Studies in Athens, who found an inscriptions that stated: "[Syna]gogue of the Hebr[ews]" (see Fig. 134).[21] It was located on the Lechaion Road near the *Agora* (marketplace), and although initially it was dated to the first cent. AD, most scholars now date it to somewhere between the second and fourth cent. AD based on the style of the letters.[22]

The use of the term "Hebrews" to identify the Jews and not the Greek term *Ioudaioi* is unusual, although a synagogue in Rome also used the same name "Hebrews" to identify their synagogue.[23] Some speculate that the members in Corinth may have moved from Rome to form the synagogue in Corinth in response to the persecution unleashed under Claudius.[24]

THE BEMA SEAT AT CORINTH (ACTS 18:12–17)

The apostle Paul was brought before the proconsul Gallio, in Corinth, to judge his case at a

---

[18] Frederick Fyvie Bruce, "Areopagus," ed. I. Howard Marshall et al., *NBD* (Downers Grove, Ill.: InterVarsity, 1996), 79; Colin J. Hemer, "Paul at Athens: A Topographical Note," *NTS* 20, no. 3 (1974): 341–50.

[19] This date is based on Luke's mention of the proconsul Gallio (Acts 18:12), who only ruled for two years beginning on July 1, AD 51. See footnote 6 for further details.

[20] On the office of synagogue ruler see Schürer, *The History of the Jewish People,* 433-36.

[21] Benjamin Powell, "Greek Inscription from Corinth," *AJA* 7, no. 1 (1903): 60–61; Benjamin D. Meritt, *Greek Inscriptions, 1896-1927,* Part 1, Corinth vol. 8 (Athens: American School of Classical Studies, 1931), no. 111 .

[22] John Harvey Kent, *The Inscriptions, 1926 to 1950*, Corinth 8.3 (Princeton, NJ: American School of Classical Studies at Athens, 1966), 79; McRay, *Archaeology and the New Testament*, 319.

[23] Fant and Reddish, *Lost Treasures of the Bible*, 362.

[24] Keener, *The IVP Bible Background Commentary*, 379.

135. The *bema* or platform in the agora of Corinth. It is mentioned in Acts 18 and dates to AD 44.

© Photo courtesy of Ferrell Jenkins, BiblicalStudies.info

location called the *bema* (Gk *bēma;* Lat. *rostra*; Acts 18:12–17). The *bema*, also known as the tribunal or judgement seat, was a public platform used by officials to make proclamations or where citizens could appeal their case before civil authorities.

In 1935, Oscar Broneer of the University of Chicago discovered just such a *bema* (see Fig. 135).[25] Its identification is verified by a broken inscription which Kent reconstructed and translated from the Latin as: "He revetted the Bema (Lat. *rostra*, Gr. *bēma*) and paid personally the expense of making all its marble."[26]

Based on the style of the letters, Kent and Wiseman date the inscription to AD 25–50, the time of Claudius.[27] The Gallio inscription (*SIG* 2:801d),[28] dating to AD 52, was found nearby at Delphi (it is also called the Delphi inscription). It too confirms the identification of the *bema* at Corinth. Gallio began his reign in AD 51, and is an important marker in determining Paul's visit to Corinth.

---

[25] Charles H. Morgan II, "Excavations at Corinth, 1935-1936," *AJA* 40, no. 4 (1936): 471–74; Oscar Broneer, "Studies in the Topography of Corinth at the Time of St. Paul," *Arkhaiologike Ephemeris* 105 (1937): 125–28; Robert L. Scranton, *Corinth*, Corinth 1.3 (Princeton, NJ: American School of Classical Studies at Athens, 1951), 91ff; Oscar Broneer, "Corinth: Center of St. Paul's Missionary Work in Greece," *BA* 14, no. 4 (1951): 91–92.

[26] Kent, *The Inscriptions*, 128–29 #322.

[27] Ibid.; James Wiseman, "Corinth and Rome I: 228 B.C. – 267 A.D.," in *Aufstieg Und Niedergang Der Romischen Welt*, ed. Hildegard Temporini and Wolfgang Haase, vol. 7.1, II (New York, N.Y.: Gruyter, 1979), 516 n.308.

[28] Jerome Murphy-O'Connor, *St. Paul's Corinth: Text and Archaeology*, Good News Studies 6 (Minneapolis: Liturgical, 2002), 161–69; Graves, *Biblical Archaeology Vol 1: An Introduction* 2nd ed 1:236–38.

THE TYRANNUS INSCRIPTION (ACTS 19:9)

According to Acts, for two years Paul spoke daily at the hall of Tyrannus, preaching the gospel to all who would attend (Acts 19:9–10). Unfortunately, no "Hall of Tyrannus" has yet been discovered in Ephesus,[29] although an inscription describing an *audeitorion* (Lat. *Auditorium; I.Eph.* 3009; *ca.* 230 AD), near the Library of Celsus, has been uncovered.[30] Hemer has suggested that this was a "lecture hall", though Engleman has argued against this theory.[31]

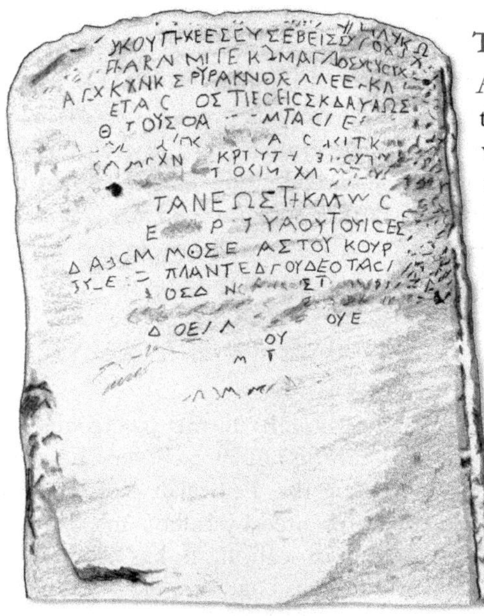

137. Drawing of a pillar in Ephesus with the name Tyrannius inscribed on it, dating from the first century AD.

However, several first cent. AD inscriptions have been discovered, some on stone pillars in Ephesus (see Fig. 137), which contain the name of *Tyrannus* (*I.Eph.* 1001.5 [14–37 AD]; *I.Eph.* 20B.40 [54–59 AD];[32] *I.Eph.* 1012.4 [92–93 AD]).[33] The name *Tyrannus* is also known in other places and periods,[34] leading Trebilco to speculate that: "in the 1st–2nd century CE it may have been used as a *cognomen* [third name] in successive generations of a small group of interrelated leading families in Ephesus."[35]

There seems no reason to not accept Luke's account of Paul speaking in a hall that was connected with Tyrannus, especially since Tyrannus was a name well known in Ephesus and elsewhere in the first cent. AD.

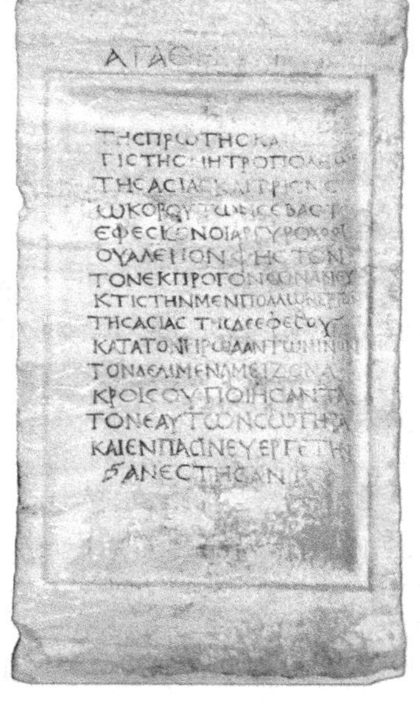

136. The Silversmith's Inscription from Ephesus.

© Photo courtesy of Mark Wilson

THE SILVERSMITH'S INSCRIPTION (ACTS 19:24)

In 1984, an honorary monument was discovered near the theater in Ephesus, beside the commercial agora, with an

[29] Yamauchi, *NT Cities*, 99–100.

[30] Rudolf Heberdey, "Vorläufiger Bericht über Die Grabungen in Ephesus 1902/3," *JÖAI* 7 (1904): 52; Helmut Engelmann, "Celsusbibliothek Und Auditorium in Ephesus (IK 17, 3009)," *JÖAI* 62 (1993): 105–11.

[31] Colin J. Hemer, "Audeitorion," *TynBul* 24 (1973): 128; Engelmann, "Celsusbibliothek Und Auditorium in Ephesus (IK 17, 3009)," 106.

[32] Michael Fieger, *Im Schatten der Artemis: Glaube und Ungehorsam in Ephesus* (Bern: Lang, 1998), 83–6.

[33] Hemer and Gempf, *The Book of Acts in the Setting of Hellenistic History*, 120, 234; Peter Lampe, "Acta 19 Im Spiegel Der Ephesischen Inschriften," *Biblische Zeitschrift* 36 (1992): 70.

[34] Walter Dennison, "The Latest Dated Inscription from Lavinium," *Classical Philology* 5, no. 3 (July 1, 1910): 286; Wilhelm Pape and Gustav Eduard Benseler, *Wörterbuch Der Griechischen Eigennamen* (Braunschweig: Vieweg & Sohn, 1911), 1565; Paul R. Trebilco, *The Early Christians in Ephesus from Paul to Ignatius*, WUNT 166 (Grand Rapids: Eerdmans, 2007), 144 n.173.

[35] Trebilco, *Early Christians in Ephesus*, 144 n.173.

inscription paid for by the silversmiths (ἀργυροκόπος *argyrokopos)*[36] from the "greatest metropolis of Asia, [and] the thrice-honored temple guardian (νεωκόρος *neōkoros*) of the venerable Ephesians" (*I.Eph.* 2.547.1; *SEG* 34-1094; second half of the thrid cent. AD).[37] Acts 19:24 states "For a man named Demetrius, a silversmith (ἀργυροκόπος *argyrokopos* v. 24), who made silver shrines of Artemis, brought no little business to the craftsmen. . . the city of the Ephesians is temple keeper of the great Artemis, and of the sacred stone that fell from the sky?" This confirms the Bible's claim of the presence of both *silversmiths* and *temple wardens* (νεωκόρος *neōkoros*) in the city of Ephesus in the first century.

138. The Asiarch inscription from a pillar at the theater of Miletus, 30 miles from Ephesus. The term Asiarch is highlighted in red. It includes the name "M(arcus) Antonius Apollodorus, the Asiarch." In other inscriptions Asiarchs are associated with "philanthropists," "benefactors" and "orators."

© Photo courtesy of Mark Wilson

ASIARCH INSCRIPTION (ACTS 19:31)

Although in the late ninteenth century many scholars believed that the Ephesian riot account presented by Luke (Acts 19) was a fabrication, it has now been shown that no less than 18 historical references or terms that occur in Acts 19:23–40, have been verified by archaeological inscriptions. Among the terms are "silversmith" (ἀργυροκόπος *argyrokopos* v. 24; see Fig. 138); "Temple of the Great goddess Artemis" (μεγάλης θεᾶς Ἀρτέμιδος ἱερὸν *megalēs theas Artemidos hieron* v. 27); "temple guardian" (νεωκόρος *neōkoros* v. 35); "fallen from heaven" (διοπετης *diopetēs* v. 35); "town clerk" (γραμματεὺς *grammateus* v. 35); "assembly," (ἐκκλησία *ekklēsia* v. 32, 39, 40); "standing courts" (ἀγοραῖοι *agoraioi* v. 38); and the "proconsul" or "governor" (ἀνθύπατος *anthupatos* v. 38).

Luke uses the title Asiarch (Ἀσιαρχῶν, *Asiarchōn* v. 31) for some of Paul's friends who sent him a message pleading with him not to enter the theater. This is the only place in the Bible that Asiarch is used and not commonly found in ancient literature leading some to be skeptical of Luke. However, it has now been identified in more than a dozen inscriptions (see Fig. 138).[38] The sacred games for the various festivals were arranged by the "*Asiarch* of the temples in Ephesos" (*I.Eph.* 7.1.3017; Acts 19:31) who coordinated the gladiators, "procuring the proper sacrifices, and often" led the "ritual sacrifices",[39] along with arranging the agenda for the games. The prevailing view that *asiarch* was a title for the priesthood of the imperial cult,[40]

[36] Erol Atalay, "Die Kurudağ-Höhle [Bei Ephesos] Mit Archäologischen Funden," *JÖAI* 52 (1980 1978): 40, no. 56a; G. H. R. Horsley, "The Silversmiths at Ephesos," in *New Documents Illustrating Early Christianity*, vol. 4 (Grand Rapids, Mich.: Eerdmans, 2001), 7–10

[37] Dieter Knibbe and Bülent Iplikçioğlu, "Neue Inschriften Aus Ephesos IX," *JÖAI* 55 (1984): 130–31.

[38] Magie, *Roman Rule in Asia Minor*, 2:198–99 n.61; Steven J. Friesen, "Asiarch," *ZPE* 126 (1999): 275–90; Rosalinde A. Kearsley, "Asiarchs," in *The Book of Acts in Its Graeco-Roman Setting*, ed. David W. Gill and Conrad H. Gempf, vol. 2, BAFCS 2 (Grand Rapids: Eerdmans, 1994), 362–76; "Asiarchs," ed. David Noel Freedman et al., *ABD* (New York, N.Y.: Doubleday, 1996), 1:495–97.

[39] Friesen, "Asiarchs," 286.

[40] James R. Edwards, "Archaeology Gives New Reality to Paul's Ephesus Riot," *BAR* 42, no. 4 (August 2016): 24–33.

has been disproven by Friesen.[41]

There is great confidence in the accuracy of Luke's descriptions of the events described in both his works.

THE GOD-FEARERS INSCRIPTION AT MILETUS (ACTS 20:17–38)

During Paul's Third Missionary Journey (*ca.* AD 56–57), he stopped at the port of Miletus (modern Balat, Turkey) for three days, and called the Ephesian elders together to say farewell and exhort them in the faith, in what must have been a sorrowful departure (Acts 20:17–38). He stated: "I am going to Jerusalem, constrained by the Spirit, not knowing what will happen to me there, except that the Holy Spirit testifies to me in every city that imprisonment and afflictions await me" (Acts 20:22–23).

139. The theatre in Miletus. An inscription referring to the "Jews and god-fearers" can be found inscribed into one of the seats.

Paul departed for Jerusalem, knowing that he would not see their faces again. Paul hinted at future persecution and possible imprisonment in his address to the Ephesian elders.[42] Despite knowing that he may face possible persecution in Jerusalem because of his Gentile ministry, he was determined to report to the Jerusalem church with an offering to assist those suffering from a famine (see the portrait of Claudius above; Acts 11:28; 18:1). It was here in Miletus that Paul left Trophimus because he was ill (2 Tim 4:20), although some speculate that this may have been during another visit to the city.

140. An inscription (*CIJ* 748) on a theatre seat in the Miletus theatre that states "Place of the Jews, who are also called God-fearing."

[41] Friesen, "Asiarchs," 286.

[42] Colin J. Hemer, "The Speeches of Acts: I. The Ephesian Elders at Miletus," *TynBul* 40, no. 1 (1989): 77–85; C. K. Barrett, "Paul's Address to the Ephesian Elders," in *God's Christ and His Peopl E, Studies in Honour of Nils Alstrup Dahl*, ed. J. Jervell and W. A. Meeks (Oslo: Univer sitetsforlaget, 1977), 107–21.

During Paul's visit many of the buildings were already standing, including the temple of Athena, the sanctuary of Apollo, the harbour gate, and the Graeco-Roman theatre (see Fig. 139).[43] The theatre (built in *ca.* 250–225 BC and newly renovated again in AD 68–96), which faced the harbour, was excavated by the Royal Berlin Museum (Königliche Museen zu Berlin), under the direction of Theodor Wiegand and Hubert Knackfuss, between 1903 and 1905.[44] The theatre could seat some 15,000 people and was one of the largest theaters in Asia Minor.

Some of the seats in the theatre were marked for special guests from guilds, as well as those from political and religious groups.[45] On one of the seats, in the fifth row from the bottom, and in the second section (Gr. *kerkides*) from the right (southeast), is an inscription written "Τοπος Ειουδεων των και Θεοσεβεων," (see Fig. 140) which when translated means "Place of the Jews, who are also called God-fearing (Gr. *theosebion*)."[46]

In the NT "those among you who fear God" (Gr. *sebomenai)* are usually understood as Gentiles (Acts 13:16, 26), and were equivalent to Jewish proselytes (converts), but uncircumcised.[47] However, while Deissmann argues that this inscription seems to indicate "reserved seating," rather than segregated seating for Jews and Gentiles,[48] a new inscription from Aphrodisias[49] demonstrates that there was a distinct group called "god-fearer," that was distinct to the Jews.[50] Van der Horst points out that:

> The dispute during the last decade over whether or not such a thing as a distinct class of "God-fearers" had ever existed at all, has now been settled – thanks to the discovery of a new and revealing inscription – in favour of the traditional point of view: the new inscription from Aphrodisias makes a clear-cut distinction between Jews, proselytes, and God-fearers, the third (large) category obviously being pagan sympathizers, no doubt with varying degrees of adherence to Judaism.[51]

Whether the inscription indicates a separate group or not, it does indicate that there were Jews in Miletus in Roman times, and they held prominent places in the city deserving of honoured seating in the theatre.

THE SOREG INSCRIPTION (ACTS 21:28–29)

The Gentile court of the Jewish Temple in Jerusalem had a 1.5 m (5 ft.) fence (Heb. *soreg*) or barricade (Fr. *balustrade*) wall which contained notices in Greek, Hebrew, and Latin warning

---

[43] Wilson, *Biblical Turkey: A Guide to Jewish and Christian Sites of Asia Minor*, 269.

[44] Ioannis Andreas Panteleon, *Eine Archäologie der Direktoren. Die Erforschung Milets im Namen der Berliner Museen 1899–1914*, Mittelmeerstudien 5 (Schöningh: Paderborn, 2015).

[45] Bernard McDonagh, *Blue Guide: Turkey*, 3rd ed. (London: A & C Black, 2001), 245.

[46] Gustav Adolf Deissmann, *Light from the Ancient East*, trans. Lionel R. M. Strachan (New York, N.Y.: Harper & Brothers, 1927), 451.

[47] F. F Bruce, *Paul, Apostle of the Heart Set Free* (Grand Rapids: Eerdmans, 2000), 128.

[48] Deissmann, *Light from the Ancient East*, 451.

[49] Schürer, *History of the Jewish People*, 150–76; Robert F. Tannenbaum, "The God-Fearers: Did They Exist? Jews and God-Fearers in the Holy City of Aphrodite," *BAR* 12, no. 5 (1986): 54–57; Joyce Maire Reynolds and Robert F. Tannenbaum, *Jews and God-Fearers at Aphrodisias: Greek Inscriptions with Commentary: Texts from the Excavations at Aphrodisias Conducted by Kenan T. Erim*, Proceedings of the Cambridge Philological Association Supplement 12 (Cambridge, U.K.: Cambridge Philological Society, 1987); Louis H. Feldman, "Proselytes and 'Sympathizers' in the Light of the New Inscription from Aphrodisias," *Revue Des études Juives* 148 (1989): 265–305; Irina A. Levinskaya, "The Inscription From Aphrodisias and the Problem of God-Fearers," *TynBul* 41, no. 2 (1990): 312–18; Louis H. Feldman, *Jewish Life and Thought Among Greeks and Romans: Primary Readings* (New York, N.Y.: Continuum International, 1996).

[50] For an extended bibliography and current research on God-fearers, including inscriptions, see Feldman's work, chapter seven "sympathizers" ("God-fearers"). Feldman, *Jewish Life and Thought Among Greeks and Romans*, 137–46.

[51] Pieter Wilhelm van der Horst, *Ancient Jewish Epitaphs: An Introductory Survey of a Millennium of Jewish Funerary Epigraphy (300 BCE-700 CE)* (Louvain, Belgium: Peeters, 1991), 71.

foreigners not to enter.[52] This wall was erected in the Gentile court, which came between the beautiful *stoa basileia* and the sacred space of the Temple itself (*Mid.* 2:3).[53] Josephus described it in two of his works as:

> In the midst of which, and not far from it [the temple], was the second [enclosure], to be gone up to by a few steps: this was surrounded by a stone wall [*soreg*] for a partition, with an inscription, which forbade any foreigner to go in under pain of death. (*Ant.* 15.417 [Whiston])
>
> When you go through these [first] cloisters, to the second [court of the] temple, there was a partition made of stone [*soreg*] all around, whose height was three cubits: its construction was very elegant; upon it stood pillars, at equal distances from one another, declaring the law of purity, some in Greek, and some in Roman letters, that "no foreigner should go within that sanctuary;" for that second [court of the] temple was called "the Sanctuary." (*J.W.* 5.193–194 [Whiston])

141. The Temple Warning or Soreg inscription, discovered by Clermont-Ganneau in Jerusalem in 1871. It forebade the entry of Gentiles into the sacred space of the Jewish Temple.

The Archaeological Museum, Istanbul, Turkey. Courtesy of Greg Gulbrandson

In 1871 Charles Simon Clermont-Ganneau discovered the only complete soreg inscripton near the St. Stephen's gate in northeatern corner of the Temple Mount (see Fig. 141). It dates to before the destruction of the Temple in AD 70, and reads: "No foreigner is to enter within the balustrade around the temple and (its) enclosed area. Whoever is caught, will have himself to blame because the incurred (penalty is) death." (*CIJ* 2.1400 = *OGIS* II 598)[54]

The sign was intended to keep foreigners/Gentiles (Gr. *allethne*) from entering the Temple area with the punishment being death for any who disobeyed (Num 1:51; 3:10, 38; 18:7; *Sifra* Num 116; *m. Sanh.* 9:6; *Mid.* 2:1ff; Philo *Legat.* 31.212; Josephus *J.W.* 6.124–126).[55]

In Acts 21:28, Paul was accused of allowing Gentiles into the Temple and defiling the holy place. This barricade may also have been the "the dividing wall of hostility" that Paul refers to when he stated: "For he himself is our peace, who has made us both one and has broken down in his flesh the dividing wall of hostility" (Eph 2:14)

A DIPLOMA GRANTING ROMAN CITIZENSHIP (ACTS 22:23–29; 25:10–12)

Roman citizenship (Lat. *civitas*), in its various forms, was a sought-after badge of personal honour. An increase in the granting of citizenship in the second cent. AD was regarded by some with disdain as devaluing the privilege (Tacitus *Ann.* 3.40.2). However, Roman citizenship held many advantages and was sought by all, slave and free. Although there were more Jews than Roman citizens in the Roman Empire, the Roman citizens were *the* members

---

[52] Charles S. Clermont-Ganneau, "The Discovery of a Tablet from Herod's Temple," *PEQ* 3 (1871): 132–33; Walter A. Elwell and Robert W. Yarbrough, *Readings from the First-Century World: Primary Sources for New Testament Study*, Encountering Biblical Studies (Grand Rapids: Baker Academic, 1998), 83.

[53] Stephen R. Llewelyn and Dionysia van Beek, "Reading the Temple Warning as a Greek Visitor," *Journal for the Study of Judaism* 42, no. 1 (2011): 1–22.

[54] Stephen R. Llewelyn and J. R. Harrison, *New Documents Illustrating Early Christianity: A Review of the Greek and Other Inscriptions and Papyri Published Between 1988 and 1992*, ed. E. J. Bridge, vol. 10 (Grand Rapids: Eerdmans, 2012), 136.

[55] S. Zeitlin, "The Warning Inscription of the Temple," *JQR* 38, no. 1 (1947): 111–16; Elias J. Bickerman, "The Warning Inscriptions of Herod's Temple," *JQR* 37, no. 4 (1947): 387–405; Peretz Segal, "The Penalty of the Warning Inscription from the Temple of Jerusalem," *IEJ* 39, no. 1/2 (1989): 79–84; Leen Ritmeyer, *The Quest: Revealing the Temple Mount in Jerusalem* (Jerusalem: Carta, 2006), 346–47; Price, *Rose Guide to the Temple*, 78.

of the Empire.[56]

As is illustrated in Acts 22, Roman Citizens were protected by Roman law and could not be flogged without a trial. Note the amazing transformation of the commander's attitude when he learns of Paul's free-born citizenship.

142. Fragment of a Roman military diploma, or certificate of successful military service, granting citizenship to a retiring soldier and the dependents he had with him at the time. The key phrase is "*est civitas eis data*" where *civitas* means citizenship (*CIL* XVI 26 tabula II).

Museum Carnuntum, Austria. © Matthias Kabel / Wikimedia Commons

Obtaining Roman Citizenship

Roman citizenship could be obtained in a number of ways.

1. One might be born into the privilege through parents who were Roman citizens (Lat. *ingenuus*), as the apostle Paul was (Acts 22:28; cf. 22:3).

2. A slave could be granted citizenship by his master (Lat. *manumissio*; Pliny *Ep.* 10.104–5) after long service or out of kindness.

3. A soldier who had completed his compulsory military service could be granted citizenship. If you worked for the government, upon discharge you would receive a document making you a Roman citizen (see Fig. 142). Many Italian soldiers by the time of the *Pax Romana* (6 BC) had been granted this type of citizenship, and so by Paul's time there were a great number of this type of Roman citizen. However, for a religious Jew, acquiring citizenship through military service was out of the question, as military service required involvement in the imperial cult and breaking the Sabbath (Josephus *Ant.* 14.10.12–19).

> *Quotes from Antiquity*
>
> **Paul the Roman citizen**
>
> I am a Jew, born in Tarsus in Cilicia, but brought up in this city, educated at the feet of Gamaliel according to the strict manner of the law of our fathers, being zealous for God as all of you are this day. . . But when they had stretched him out for the whips, Paul said to the centurion who was standing by, "Is it lawful for you to flog a man who is a Roman citizen and uncondemned?" When the centurion heard this, he went to the tribune and said to him, "What are you about to do? For this man is a Roman citizen." So the tribune came and said to him, "Tell me, are you a Roman citizen?" And he said, "Yes." The tribune answered, "I bought this citizenship for a large sum." Paul said, "But I am a citizen by birth." So those who were about to examine him withdrew from him immediately, and the tribune also was afraid, for he realized that Paul was a Roman citizen and that he had bound him. (Acts 22:3, 25–29).

4. If someone performed an exceptional deed for the state or a government official, then citizenship might be decreed as an appropriate reward by the state for this valuable act of service (Cicero *Balb.* 8.19).

5. Large groups of people could be made citizens through colonization or by assimilation through Roman law (Strabo *Geogr.* 5.1.6; Suetonius *Jul.* 28).[57]

6. A final means was through some form of financial consideration provided in the form

---

[56] Adrian N. Sherwin-White, "The Roman Citizenship: A Survey of Its Development into a World Franchise," in *ANRW*, ed. Hildegard Temporini and Wolfgang Haase, Part 1, Principat 2 (Berlin: De Gruyter, 1974), 23–58; *The Roman Citizenship* (Oxford: Clarendon, 1980).

[57] Shimon Applebaum, "The Legal Status of the Jewish Communities in the Diaspora," in *The Jewish People in the First Century*, ed. Shemuel Safrai, vol. 2, Compendia Rerum Iudaicarum Ad Novum Testamentum 1 (Philadelphia, Pa.: Fortress, 1974), 420–63; A. M. Rabello, "The Legal Condition of the Jews in the Roman Empire," in *ANRW*, ed. Hildegard Temporini and Wolfgang Haase, Part 2, Principat 13.1 (Berlin: De Gruyter, 1989), 662–762.

of either money, supplies or products, and allowing the giver to purchase their citizenship (Acts 22:28; Cicero *Phil.* 2.92; 5.11–12; Cassius Dio *Hist. Rom.* 10.17.4–8; Tacitus *Ann.* 14.50.1).

7. While dual citizenship was not permitted during the Republic (Cicero *Balb.* 28–30; *Caecin.* 100; *Leg.* 2.2.5), it was allowed by the time of Claudius (AD 41–54), as is evident in the life of the apostle Paul, who claimed Roman and Tarsian citizenship (Acts 16:37–38; 21:39; 22:25).

Identification of Roman Citizens

Every Roman citizen was identified by three names (Lat. *tria nomina*) and a birth certificate (Lat. *testatio*). Their names comprised of a personal name (Lat. *praenomen*), the name of their relatives (surname – Lat. *nomen* or *nomen gentilicium*) and their common name (Lat. *cognomen*). Acts 13:9 suggests that Paul was the apostle's common name while Saul was his Jewish personal name. Rapske indicates that "there were severe penalties for the false use of Roman names" (Suetonius *Claud.* 25.3; Arrian *Epict. diss.* 3.24.41).[58] Thus, both Paul and Saul are believed to be legitimate names for the apostle.

Rapske recounts how Hemer speculates that "Favorable relations between the city of Tarsus, where Paul was born, and Pompey, Julius Caesar, Mark Antony and Augustus, who had the power of conferral, allow that Paul might have been born Cn. Pompeius Paulus, C. Julius Paulus or M. Antonius Paulus."[59]

Roman citizens were given birth certificates (Lat. *testatio*), and Roman officials in legal situations could take a Roman citizen at their word. Their birth certificate was a waxed plate made of metal or wood carried on their person.[60] They were also registered in their place of birth. Bruce points out that during the first century AD all children born to Roman citizens had to have been registered (Lat. *professio*) within thirty days.[61] For travel, retired soldiers would receive a certificate in bronze (Lat. *diploma militaris* or *instrumentum*). Civilians would also have a similar set of travel documents (Lat. *diploma,* Suetonius *Nero* 12).[62]

In Paul's hometown, his citizenship would have been easy to confirm and he likely carried similar documents with him when he traveled, to back up his verbal declaration of his citizenship.

Privileges of Roman Citizens

The privileges of Roman citizenship affected every area of life from business to the domestic sphere.[63] Rapske states that: "In the realms of business (holding property, making contracts and paying taxes), domestic affairs (getting married, having legitimate children and making wills) and litigation (courts, custody and punishments), the citizen was accorded better treatment than was the imperial subject who did not possess the franchise."[64]

---

[58] Brian M. Rapske, "Citizenship, Roman," ed. Craig A. Evans and Stanley E. Porter, *DNTB* (Downers Grove, Ill.: InterVarsity, 2000), 216.

[59] Ibid.; Colin J. Hemer, "The Name of Paul," *TynBul* 36 (1985): 179.

[60] Henry A. Sanders, "The Birth Certificate of a Roman Citizen," *Classical Philology* 22, no. 4 (1927): 409–13.

[61] Bruce, *Paul, Apostle of the Heart Set Free*, 39–40.

[62] Fritz Schulz, "Roman Registers of Births and Birth-Certificates, Part I," *JRS* 32, no. 1–2 (1943): 55–64; "Roman Registers of Births and Birth Certificates. Part II," *JRS* 33, no. 1–2 (1943): 78–91.

[63] Peter Garnsey, *Social Status and Legal Privilege in the Roman Empire* (Oxford: Oxford University Press, 1970); E. A. Judge, *Rank and Status in the World of the Caesars and St Paul*, Broadhead Memorial Lecure 1981/University of Canterbury Publications 29 (Christchurch, N.Z.: University of Canterbury, 1982).

[64] Rapske, "Citizenship, Roman," 215.

A Roman citizen could hold a government office, conduct business unhindered, and travel freely throughout the empire.

Special privileges in the realm of justice were also afforded Roman citizens. They could not be flogged or detained if they had not been tried in court (Acts 16:37–39; 22:25–29; Livy *Hist. Rome* 10.9.4; Cicero *Rab. Post.* 4.12–13; *Verr.* 2.5.66; Appian *Bell. civ.* 2.26.98). In addition they could not be executed without a legal trial and only the emperor could declare the sentence of crucifixion for a Roman citizen. They had the right to appeal to a magistrate (Lat. *provocatio* later replaced by *appellation;* Livy *Hist. Rome* 3.13, 56; Cicero *De or.* 2.48) in Rome[65] and governors, such as Festus, had no right to block this (Acts 25:7–12; 26:32). Paul used these privileges of citizenship when facing opposition (Acts 16:37; 25:11).

THE PRAETORIAN GUARD, ROME (ACTS 28:16; PHIL 1:13)

The praetorian guard (Lat. *Praetoriani*) were the Imperial bodyguard of Rome (see Fig. 143), whose primary responsibility was to guard the Roman emperor and his family. Augustus created them and gave them the name praetorian cohorts (Lat. *praetoriae cohortes*), as they were to guard the Roman general (Lat. *Praetor*), along with, as Bingham points out, "policing the games, assisting in fighting fires, protection (and often surveillance) of the imperial family, and the confinement of criminals"[66] (Tacitus *Ann.* 1.77.1; 6.13.1; Suetonius *Tib.* 37.2). However, over time, Augustus discovered that having such a large body of soldiers in the capital could be useful for ensuring general safety and so he broadened their responsibilities.

143. Marble relief of a soldier from the Praetorian Guard from Puteoli, Italy.

Pergamum Museum, Berlin (Sk 887). © Albert Krantz / Wikimedia Commons

Originally the praetorian guard consisted of nine to twelve cohorts, with five hundred soldiers to each cohort, later to be increased to one thousand guards. Initially, only three thousand soldiers (three cohorts) were posted in Rome, while the remaining six cohorts were posted in areas around Italy. With the arrival of Tiberius (AD 14–37; Tacitus *Ann.* 1.5.3–4), Aelius Sejanus convinced Tiberus (AD 23) to unify the guard in Rome and built the fort of the praetorians (Lat. *Castra Praetoria*) outside Rome (Tacitus *Ann.* 4.2.1; Suetonius *Tib.* 37.1) for nine cohorts of soldiers (Tacitus *Ann.* 4.5.3). Under Domitian the guard was standardized to ten cohorts. They originally served for twelve

[65] William Smith, *Dictionary of Greek and Roman Antiquities* (London: Murray, 1875), 107–108.

[66] Sandra J. Bingham, "The Praetorian Guard in the Political and Social Life of Julio-Claudian Rome" (Ph. D. diss., The University of British Columbia, 1997), 39.

years, but this was later increased to sixteen years, and they also had the privilege of receiving pay-and-a-half (Lat. *sesquiplex stipendum*) when compared with other soldiers. They reported to two commanders called "prefects for the headquarters" (Lat. *praefectus praetorio*).

Their power at times even exceeded that of the emperors, and they were subsequently disbanded by Emperor Severus in AD 193, but then reinstated with even more power, until they were finally dissolved by Constantine in AD 312.

A marble relief that was part of an arch of the gate at Puteoli, Italy, was erected in AD 102 and depicts the soldiers of the praetorian guard. The soldier in Fig. 143 is holding a spear and shield with a sword in its sheath at his side. The shield of one of the other soldiers, not shown, but now in the University of Pennsylvania Museum (MS 4916), contains embossed flowers and a scorpion which identifies the soldiers as members of the praetorian guard.[67]

Paul possibly encountered the praetorian guard on his arrival in Rome (Phil 1:12–13). Luke records that "they delivered Paul and some other prisoners to a centurion of the Augustan Cohort named Julius" (Acts 27:1). While most translations of Acts 28:16 state that "when we came into Rome, Paul was allowed to stay by himself, with the soldier who guarded him," the Western text (*Codex Bezae*) adds "the centurion delivered the prisoners to the captain of the guard [Gr. *stratopedarch*], but Paul was allowed to live by himself outside the camp" (Acts 28:16).[68] Sherwin-White argues that Paul was delivered to the *princeps castrorum*, a subordinate of the prefect or commander (Lat. *praefectus praetorii*) of the praetorian guard.[69]

The prefect during this time was Sextus Afranius Burrus (AD 51–62; Tacitus *Ann.* 12.42.2; Cassius Dio *Hist. Rom.* 60.32.6) and Julius was a subordinate given the responsibility of guarding Paul during his house arrest. Paul indicated in his letter to the Philippians that the gospel had even reached into the confines of the praetorian guard (Phil 1:13 Gr. *praitōrion, Lat. praetorium*).

THE MAMERTINE PRISON (ACTS 28:30)

Paul arrived in Rome in AD 60,[70] fulfilling his great desire to visit the capital of the empire (Rom 15:32). But he was still a prisoner under house arrest chained to a soldier. Paul's two year incarceration (Lat. *publica custodia* and *vincula publica)* in Rome (Acts 28:30) was the period of time prescribed by later Roman law as the limit a prisoner might be held after appeal to the emperor's court, if they were not prosecuted (Cassius Dio *Hist. Rom.* 60.28.6; Philo *Flacc.* 128–129). However Paul was free to receive visitors and carried on an effective ministry through messengers (Acts 28:17–31).

It is following his proposed visit to Spain (*1 Clem.* 5:7; Rom 15:24) that Paul was again arrested and held prisoner in Rome. Tradition holds that Paul was beheaded on the Ostian Way, along with Peter (Eusebius *Hist. eccl.* 2.25.7–8).[71]

The Mamertine Prison (Italian *Carcere Mamertino;* see Fig. 144), constructed in 64 BC in Rome, Italy, was a series of underground dungeons under the main sewer system of ancient

---

[67] Fant and Reddish, *Lost Treasures of the Bible*, 369.

[68] I. Howard Marshall, *Acts*, vol. 5, Tyndale New Testament Commentaries (Grand Rapids: IVP Academic, 2008), 440–41.

[69] Adrian N. Sherwin-White, *Roman Society and Roman Law in the New Testament: The Sarum Lectures 1960-1961*, Oxford University Press Academic Monograph Reprints (Oxford: Clarendon, 2004), 108–12.

[70] Karl Paul Donfried, "Chronology: New Testament," ed. David Noel Freedman et al., *ABD* (New York, N.Y.: Doubleday, 1996), 1016.

[71] M. Reasoner, "The City of Rome in the First Century A.D.," in *DNTB*, ed. Craig A. Evans and Stanley E. Porter (Downers Grove, Ill.: InterVarsity, 2000), 1016.

144. Mamertine Prison where tradition holds that Paul was imprisoned in Rome, Italy.

© David E. Graves

Rome, where prisoners were incarcerated (Lat. *publica custodia).*[72] It is believed, by eighth cent. tradition, to be the prison of Peter and Paul during the persecution of Nero (*ca.* A.D. 64–67. Tacitus *Ann.* 15.44; Suetonius *Nero* 35; *1 Clem.* 5:2–5).[73] The sign over the entrance in Italian reads: "*Prigione dei ss apostoli pietro e paolo*", which translates as "prison of the apostles, Peter and Paul." It is believed they were held prisoner here under the protection of the praetorian guard (see Praetorian Guard, Rome, page 195).

In ancient Rome, the Mamertine prison was located in the original open-air public meeting space, called the *Comitium* (Italian *Comizio*), on the northwest corner of the Roman forum. It was called the *Tullianum* and was the only state prison in Rome (Sallust *Bell. Cat.* 55; Calpurnius Flaccus *Declam.* 4.15).[74]

It was comprised of two chambers, one on top of the other, only granting access to the chamber below through a hole in the floor of the top chamber. Stairs to the lower chamber were added in modern times.

The top chamber was called the *Carcer,* (place where prisoners waited for their trial), while the bottom chamber was known as the *Tullianum* (place of execution), from which it derived its popular name. The *Tullianum* derived its name either from the name of the Roman king, Servius Tullius (578–535 BC), or the Latin term *tullius,* meaning "spring of water," from the spring that flowed through it. Watkin recounts that the tradition of the presence of Peter and Paul in the prison caused "the spring to rise miraculously so that they could baptise their fellow prisoners and gaolers."[75]

Today two churches share the property, the church of San Giuseppe dei Falegnami (The Guild of Carpenters) is located on the upper level, while the S. Pietro in Carcere is housed on the lower level.[76]

[72] Mitchel P. Roth, *Prisons and Prison Systems: A Global Encyclopedia* (Westport, Conn.: Greenwood, 2006), 171.

[73] Maurice Hassertt, "Mamertine Prison," ed. Condé Bénoist Pallen, Charles George Herbermann, and Edward Aloysius Pace, *CE* (New York, N.Y.: Appleton & Company, 1913), 579–80.

[74] Lewis A. Sussman, *The Declamations of Calpurnius Flaccus: Text, Translation, and Commentary* (Leiden: Brill, 1994), 106.

[75] David Watkin, *The Roman Forum,* Wonders of the World (Cambridge, Mass.: Harvard University Press, 2009), 128.

[76] Hassertt, "Mamertine Prison," 579–80.

Revelation

145. Acropolis of Pergamum, with the Hellenistic theater (ca. 225–200 BC) carved vertically out of the side of the mountain with a capacity of ca. 10,000 citizens. Visible on the top are the pillars of the Temple of Trajan (second cent. AD).

Archaeology is no less important in understanding the historical context of the Book of Revelation than the other books in the Bible, but sadly this area is often neglected. Revelation is perhaps the least understood and most misrepresented book in the NT. The title for Revelation comes from the first sentence which, as in many other ancient books, provides the title for the work along with the content and the name of the author. The book begins with the phrase "The revelation (Gr. *apokalypsis*) of Jesus Christ" (Rev 1:1) and "John" is simply stated as the author. *Apocalypse*[1] means "to disclose," "unveiling" or "revealing,"[2] but for most readers the book tends to hide rather than reveal its message, as much of it is disputed by scholars. Therefore, archaeology has an important role to play in unlocking the enigma of this fascinating book.

The Occasion of Revelation

The letter of Revelation was written to seven churches (Ephesus, Smyrna, Pergamum, Thyatira, Sardis, Philadelphia, and Laodicea) in Asia Minor that John knew well during[3] the late first century AD (Eusebius *Chron.* 19.551–52; *Hist. eccl.* 2.22.5; 3.3.43; 3.17–20; 3.23.3–4; *contra* Irenaeus *Haer.* 5.30.3; Victorinus *Comm. Apoc.* 10.11; 17.10; Jerome *Vir. ill.* 9; Irenaeus *Haer.* 2.22.5; 3.3.4; Epiphanius of Salamis *Pan.* 51.12.1–2).[4] Each church had their own set of problems and instructions.[5] The letter of Revelation, which presents the triumph of Christ over evil, was meant to be a source of encouragement to these suffering churches dealing with

[1] For the study of genre and apocalyptic literature and the book of Revelation, see E. Frank Tupper, "The Revival of Apocalyptic in Biblical and Theological Studies," *Review and Expositor* 72, no. 3 (1975): 279–303; Jan Lambrecht, "The Book of Revelation and Apocalyptic in the New Testament," in *L'Apocalypse Johannique et L' Apocalyptique Dans Le NouveauTestament*, ed. Jan lambrecht (Leuven: Leuven University Press, 1980), 18; David Hellholm and Kungl Vitterhets, *Apocalypticism in the Mediterranean World and the Near East: Proceedings of the International Colloquium on Apocalypticism, Uppsala, August 12-17, 1979* (Tübingen: Siebeck, 1989); David E. Aune, "The Apocalypse of John and the Problem of Genre," in *Early Christian Apocalypticism: Genre and Social Setting*, Semeia 36 (Atlanta, Ga.: Scholars Press, 1986), 65–69; John M. Court, *The Book of Revelation and the Johannine Apocalyptic Tradition* (Sheffield, U.K.: Sheffield Academic, 2000).

[2] Richard J. Bauckham, "Apocalyptic," ed. Sinclair B. Ferguson, David F. Wright, and James I. Packer, *NDT* (Downers Grove, Ill.: InterVarsity, 1988), 34.

[3] Scholars vigorously debate the date of Revelation's writing. There are three periods proposed: the reign of Nero (AD 54–68), the reign of Domitian (AD 81-96), and the reign of Trajan (AD 98–117). David E. Graves, *The Seven Messages of Revelation and Vassal Treaties: Literary Genre, Structure, and Function*, Gorgias Dissertations Biblical Studies 41 (Piscataway, N.J.: Gorgias, 2009), 41–42.

[4] For the arguments for the early date, during Nero's reign (pre-70 AD), see Kenneth L. Gentry Jr., *Before Jerusalem Fell: Dating the Book of Revelation* (Powder Springs, GA: American Vision, 1998).

[5] David E. Graves, "Jesus Speaks to Seven of His Churches, Part 1," *BS* 23, no. 2 (Spring 2010): 46–56; "Jesus Speaks to Seven of His Churches, Part 2," *BS* 23, no. 3 (Summer 2010): 66–74; "Local References in the Letter to Smyrna (Rev 2: 8–11), Part 1: Archaeological Background," *BS* 18, no. 4 (2005): 114–23; "Local References in the Letter to Smyrna (Rev 2: 8–11), Part 2: Historical Background," *BS* 19, no. 1 (2006): 23–31; "Local References in the Letter to Smyrna (Rev 2: 8–11), Part 3: Jewish Background," *BS* 19, no. 2 (2006): 41–47; "Local References in the Letter to Smyrna (Rev 2: 8–11), Part 4: Religious Background," *BS* 19, no. 3 (2007): 88–96.

persecution (Eusebius *Chron.* 19.551–52; *Hist. eccl.* 3.23.3–4) from Rome and the Jewish community. John addressed his message to the seven churches "using a prophetic oracle genre in the tradition of OT prophets."[6]

THE STATUE OF TITUS OR DOMITIAN (REV 1)

Domitian (Lat. *Titus Flavius Caesar Domitianus Augustus* AD 81–96), the son of Vespasian, succeeded his brother Titus in AD 81 and gradually acquired despotic powers, demanding that public worship should be given to him as "Lord and God" (Lat. *dominus et Deus*). Suetonius states that Domitian requested his correspondence sent out in the name of "Our Lord and God" (Lat. *dominus et dues noster*) and that "the custom arose of henceforth addressing him in no other way even in writing or in conversation" (Suetonius *Dom.* 13.2 [Rolfe], cf. Cassius Dio *Hist. Rom.* 67.4.7; 67.13.4).[7] This practice of worshiping the emperor was known as the Imperial Cult.

146. Bust of Roman emperor Domitian. Antique head, body added in the eighteenth century.

Musée du Louvre (Ma 1264), Paris. © Sailko / Wikimedia Commons

The city of Ephesus in Asia Minor was granted the prestigious privilege of "temple-keeper or warden" (Gr. *neōkoros*, cf. Acts 19:35) for its temples to the Imperial Cult.[8] In fact Ephesus had this distinction granted to her four times.[9] To commemorate this distinction, during the reign of Domitian (AD 81–96) the Ephesians built a Temple to Domitian, called the *Flavian Sebastoi.* The temple was dedicated to the worship of the emperors Domitian, Titus (his brother), and Vespasian (his father). The name of the temple, *Flavian Sebastoi*, is derived from *Flavius,* which was their "family name" and *sebastoi,* the Greek equivalent to "augustus".

Inside the temple stood a statue of Domitian to a height of over five meters (16.4 ft.). Parts of the statue including the head, arm, big toe and finger were discovered during excavations in the substructure (*cryptoporticus*) of the temple (see Fig. 147). Although it was

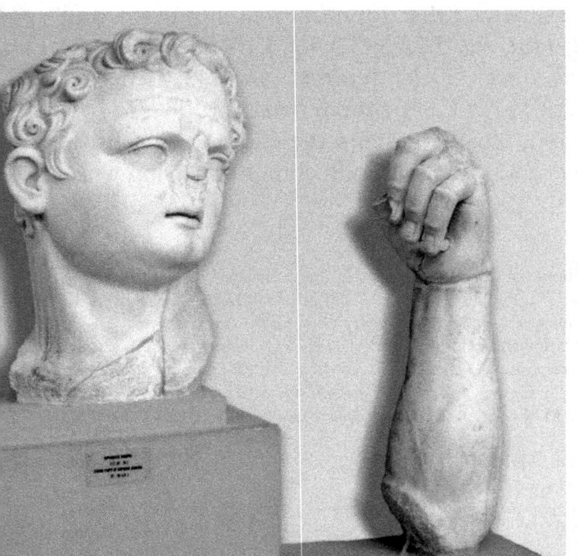

147. Parts of the colossal statue from the Temple of Sebastoi, Ephesus. The head is over 1.18 m high. Originally identified as Emperor Domitian (AD 81–96), it has since been identified as Emperor Titus (r. AD 79–81).

Ephesus Museum, Selçuk, Turkey (Head 1.76.92; Hand 2.76.92) © David E. Graves

---

[6] Graves, *Seven Messages of Revelation and Vassal Treaties*, 123.

[7] *Contra* Thompson, *Revelation*, 105.

[8] William M. Ramsay, *The Letters to Seven Churches: Updated,* ed. Mark W. Wilson (Peabody, Mass.: Hendrickson, 1994), 168–69.

[9] Ibid., 168.

once

identified as Emperor Domitian,[10] it has since been identified as Emperor Titus.[11] It would have stood inside the temple and Titus originally would have held a spear or javelin in his hand. Today it is on display in the Imperial Cult Room of the Ephesus Museum, Selçuk, Turkey.

THE COIN OF DEIFIED DOMITIAN (REV 1:13, 16)

148. Silver Denarius coin (AD 82–83) of Domitian.

The book of Revelation opens with John describing his vision of Christ as follows: "and in the midst of the seven lampstands One like the Son of Man, clothed with a garment down to His feet … He had in His right hand seven stars" (Rev 1:13, 16). Various interpretations of what these seven stars represented have been offered by commentators. Revelation interprets them as angels (Rev 1:20). Beale has suggested John had the OT in mind, deriving his allusion to seven stars from Daniel 12:3 and the seven lamps from Zechariah chapter four.[12] However, John may also have been aware of the early Jewish tradition that symbolically connected the seven lamps in the temple with seven planets (see Josephus *Ant.* 3.145; *J.W.* 5.217; Philo *Mos.* 2.102–5; *Her.* 45.221–25; *QE* 2.73–81; *Targ. Pal.* Exod. 40:4; *Midr. Rab.* Num 12:13; see also Clement of Alexandria *Strom.* 5.6).[13]

Beale and others have suggested that the reference in Revelation may be "a polemic against the imperial myth of an emperor's son who dies and becomes a divine ruler over the stars of heaven, since the title 'ruler of the kings of the earth' in [Rev] 1:5 likely also has such a polemical connotation."[14]

A silver denarius coin from AD 82–83 features Domitian's deified infant son, seated on a globe surrounded by seven stars (see Fig. 148). The child has been identified as the empress Domitia Longinas' son (AD 82–96 left), T. Flavius Caesar,[15] who was born in AD 73 and died young (Suetonius *Dom.* 3.1).[16] The inscription on the coin reads: *DIVVS CAESAR IMP*

---

[10] Josef Keil, E. Reisch, and F. Knoll, *Die Marienkirche in Ephesos*, FiE, 4.1 (Wien: ÖAI, 1932), 59–60; Jale Inan and Elisabeth Rosenbaum, *Roman and Early Byzantine Portrait Sculpture in Asia Minor* (Oxford: Oxford University Press, 1966), 67, 16 #1.

[11] The appearance of the statue resembles Titus. Georg Daltrop, Ulrich Hausmann, and Max Wegner, *Die Flavier: Vespasian, Titus, Domitian, Nerva, Julia Titi, Domitilla, Domitia* (Berlin: Mann, 1966), 26, 38, 86, and pl. 15b.

[12] Gregory K. Beale, *The Book of Revelation: A Commentary on the Greek Text*, New International Greek Testament Commentary 12 (Grand Rapids: Eerdmans, 1998), 211–13.

[13] David E. Aune, *Revelation 1-5,* WBC 52A (Nashville: Nelson, 1997), 97–98; Beale, *The Book of Revelation*, 212; Michael Wojciechowski, "Seven Churches and Seven Celestial Bodies (Rev 1,16; Rev 2-3)," *BN* 45 (1988): 48–50.

[14] Beale, *The Book of Revelation*, 211; G. B. Caird, *The Revelation of Saint John* (Peabody, MA: Hendrickson, 1993), 15; Ernst Lohmeyer, *Die Offenbarung Des Johannes,* Handbuch Zum Neuen Testament 16 (Tübingen: Siebeck, 1926), 18.

[15] Desnier believes that the child was probably called T. Flavius Caesar. Jean-Luc Desnier, "Divus Caesar Imp. Domitiani F.," *Revue Des études Anciennes* 81 (1979): 64.

[16] John Garthwaite, "Martial, Book 6, on Domitian's Moral Censorship," *Prudentia* 22 (1990): 16–17; Brian W. Jones, *The Emperor Domitian* (New York, N.Y.: Routledge, 1993), 37; Eric R. Varner, "Domitia Longina and the Politics of Portraiture," *AJA*

DOMITIANI, which translates as "The Deified Caesar, Son of the Emperor Domitian."[17] The seven stars symbolize the child's divine status, perhaps connected to the seven hills of Rome (Virgil *Aen.* 6.782; Martial *Epig.* 4.64; Cicero *Att.* 6.5; see also Rev 17:9).[18] The globe suggests the world-wide rule of the emperor over the kings of the earth.[19] It is very possible that John had this coin in mind when he wrote his polemic in Revelation where Christ is the one depicted as ruling over the kings of the earth and holding the seven stars in his hand.

THE PORTRAIT OF NERO (REV 13; 17)

Nero (Lat. *Domitius Ahenobarbus* and changed to *Nerō Claudius Caesar Germanicus* Tacitus, *Ann.* 12.25; see Fig. 138) was adopted by Claudius, his grand-uncle, to become the Roman emperor following Claudius' death (r. AD 54–68; Cassius Dio *Hist. Rom.* 62.3; Josephus *J.W.* 4). He was the last Roman emperor decended from Augustus and ended the Julio-Claudian dynasty.[20]

149. Marble portrait of Nero. This seventeenth cent. scupture is based on a first cent. portrait from the Palatine Hill, Antiquarium of the Palatine, Inv. 618.

The Palazzo Nuovo, Hall of the Emperors, Capitoline Museum Rome (Inv. MC0427). © Carole Raddato / Wikimedia Commons

Nero's mother, Agrippina, prepared her son for politics by training him in oratory at the feet of the distinguished orator and philosopher Lucius Annaeus Seneca. Although Claudius's son Britannicus was the expected political heir, Nero's mother saw to it that the Senate and praetorian guard (see Fig. 149) supported Nero, and following Claudius's death, on the 13th of October 54, Claudius was declared a god, Agrippina, his priestess (Suetonius *Nero* 9), and Nero was pronounced emperor at the young age of 17.

In Nero's early years he gave himself more to poetry, music, and chariot-racing, as well as building gymnasiums and theatres, leaving the bulk of the government to be run by his mother and Seneca. He promoted the arts in public games and contests, soon Nero himself began to participate – and win – even though his voice was known to be unbearable (Tacitus *Ann.* 14.20, 2; Suetonius *Nero* 12).

Although Nero indicated in his first speech to the Senate that he would bring and end to

99, no. 2 (1995): 188; Olivier Joram Hekster, *Emperors and Ancestors: Roman Rulers and the Constraints of Tradition* (Oxford: Oxford University Press, 2015), 57.

[17] Harold Mattingly and Edwars Sydenham, eds., *Roman Imperial Coinage: Vespasian to Hadrian (69–138)*, vol. 2 (London: Spink & Son, 1926), 209a.

[18] Grant Heiken, Renato Funiciello, and Donatella de Rita, *The Seven Hills of Rome: A Geological Tour of the Eternal City* (Princeton, NJ: Princeton University Press, 2013).

[19] The globe also indicates that the Romans believed the earth was a sphere, although Eratosthenes (276–194 BC) of Cyrene (modern Libya) was the first to discover that the earth was round. Mary Gow, *Measuring the Earth: Eratosthenes and His Celestial Geometry* (Berkeley Heights, N.J.: Enslow, 2009), 6.

[20] Miriam T. Griffin, "Nero (Emperor)," ed. David Noel Freedman et al., *ABD* (New York, N.Y.: Doubleday, 1996), 4:1076.

bribery, malicious prosecution, and corruption (Tacitus *Ann.* 13.4; Suetonius *Nero* 10), he went on to kill his brother (Britannicus [Tacitus *Ann.* 13.17]), two wives (Olympia and Poppaea [Tacitus *Ann.* 14.64; 16.6; Cassius Dio *Hist. Rom.* 62.27; Suetonius *Nero* 35; *Schol. ad Juv.* 6.462]), mother (Agrippina [Tacitus *Ann.* 15.67]), not to mention many of his rivals and opponents.[21]

His ultimate downfall was in how he depleted empire funds by lavishly spending on gifts, festivals, games and construction projects. He tried to compensate for the losses by increasing taxes, which led to public revolts, particularly in Britain (Tacitus *Ann.* 14.29–39) and Judea (Josephus *J.W.* 2.13.7; 3.1.3; 7.1.1). This led to further expenses incurred in putting down the revolts.

In AD 64, half of the city of Rome was destroyed by fire (Tacitus *Ann.* 15.38). Many citizens in Rome believed that Nero started the fire himself[22] to clear land for his planned construction of the *Domus Aurea* (Suetonius *Nero* 31),[23] and in order to shift blame from himself, Nero accused the Christians of causing the fire. Christians were rounded up, soaked in oil and set on fire to light Nero's garden at night in punishment (Tacitus *Ann.* 15.44).[24] Suetonius and Cassius Dio report that, when Rome originally caught fire, Nero sang as the flames took hold (Suetonius *Nero* 38; Cassius Dio *Hist. Rom.* 62.16).[25] However, while Suetonius does report that Nero persecuted Christians for being "a new and mischievous superstition" (Suetonius *Nero* 16.2), he does not attribute the fire of Rome to them.[26]

Nero's career and life ended in AD 68 when, faced with fabricated charges as an enemy of the state, he committed suicide (Suetonius *Nero* 49).

Several inscriptions testify to his deification, including "Nero Caesar the lord" (*SB* no. 9604; P.Oxy. 246); "Nero Claudius Caesar . . . the savior and benefactor of the inhabited world" (*OGIS* no. 668) and "the good god (*OGIS* no. 666) of the inhabited world, the beginning of all good things" (P.Oxy. 1021).

Nero Redivius and the Antichrist (Rev 13; 17)

Some biblical scholars discern the account of the wounding and healing of the beast in Revelation 13:3, and the reference to the eighth king, who is also one of the earlier seven kings in Revelation 17:8–11, as referring to the Nero *redivius*[27] legend. The myth stated that Nero would come back to life after death (68 AD).[28] The myth was supported by claims that Nero had not really died (68 AD), but instead fled to the Parthians, where he was assembling a large army and preparing to one day return and destroy Rome (Suetonius *Nero* 47; 57). Bousset believes that John "expects the return of Nero with the Parthians to take vengeance on Rome,

---

[21] Vasily Rudich, *Political Dissidence Under Nero: The Price of Dissimulation* (New York, N.Y.: Routledge, 1993), 134–36; Miriam T. Griffin, *Nero: The End of a Dynasty* (New York, N.Y.: Routledge, 2002), 73–77.

[22] Nero is famous for the quote that he "fiddled while Rome burned". However, as Gyles points out the instrument that Nero played was the lyre (Suetonius *Nero* 38), and Nero was reportedly away from Rome at the time. In addition, the fiddle would not be invented for another 1000 years! Mary Francis Gyles, "Nero Fiddled While Rome Burned," *CJ* 42, no. 4 (1947): 211–17.

[23] Leland M. Roth, *Understanding Architecture: Its Elements, History, And Meaning* (Boulder, Colo.: Westview, 1993), 227–28.

[24] F. W. Clayton, "Tacitus and Christian Persecution," *The Classical Quarterly* 41, no. 3–4 (1947): 81–85.

[25] Ibid.; William H. C. Frend, *Martyrdom and Persecution in the Early Church: A Study of a Conflict from the Maccabees to Donatus* (Oxford: Blackwell, 1965), 163.

[26] Clayton, "Tacitus and Christian Persecution," 81–85.

[27] The term *redivius* comes from the Latin meaning "renewed, renovated, living, restored to life; reborn; [and] reincarnated." Michael E. Agnes, *Webster's New World College Dictionary*, 4th ed. (Cleveland, Ohio: Webster's New World, 1999), ad loc.

[28] Lohmeyer, *Die Offenbarung Des Johannes*, 115; James Stuart Russell, *The Parousia. The New Testament Doctrine of Our Lord's Second Coming* (Grand Rapids: Baker, 1999), 462; Gentry, *Before Jerusalem Fell*, 128–31; Trebilco, *Early Christians in Ephesus*, 294.

because she had shed the blood of the saints."[29] Instead of becoming an adversary of Rome, this beastly figure of Nero becomes the enemy of God and Christ.

The belief was either the result or cause of several impostors (Otho or Galba [Tacitus *Ann.* 2.8; See also Cassius Dio *Hist. Rom.* 11.15; 64.9] and Terentius Maximus [Cassius Dio *Hist. Rom.* 11.12; Suetonius *Nero* 57] who had used the rumour to impersonate Nero for rebellious purposes and "therefore many people imagined and *believed that he was alive.*" (Tacitus *Ann.* 2.8 [Jackson]).

Dio Chrysostom (*ca.* AD 40 – *ca.* 115), a Greek philosopher and historian, described the general belief of the public in his day concerning the *redivius* of Nero: "...for so far as the rest of his subjects were concerned, there was nothing to prevent his continuing to be Emperor for all time, seeing that even now *everybody wishes he [Nero] were still alive.* And the great majority do believe that he is, although in a certain sense he has died not once but often along with those who had been firmly *convinced that he was still alive.*" (Dio Chrysostom *Or.* 21.10 [Cohoon])

The Nero *redivius* myth was also adopted by Jewish apocalyptic writers, particularly in the *Sibylline Oracles* (AD 79; *Sib. Or.* 4.119–24; 5.137–41; 5.214–27; 5.361–96).[30] However, Van Henten cautions against placing too much trust in the *Sibylline Oracles,* since they also mention Nero's return as a fact (*Sib. Or.* 5.137–154, 214–227, 361–38).[31]

Even as late as AD 100, many still believed that Nero was alive. For example, the OT Pseudepigrapha work, *Martydom and Ascension of Isaiah* (late first cent. AD),[32] identifies the reign of Beliar or the antichrist with Nero:

> and after it has been brought to completion, Beliar will descend, the great angel, the king of this world, which he has ruled ever since it existed. He will descend from his firmament in the *form of a man, a king of iniquity, a murderer of his mother* [Nero's matricide; Tacitus *Ann.* 14][33]–this is the king of this world–and will persecute the planet which the twelve of his Beloved will have planted; some of the twelve will be given into his hand. This angel, Beliar, will come in the form of that king, and with him will come all the powers of this world, and they will obey him in every wish. (*Mart. Isa.* 4.2b–5a [Knibb])

In addition, both Jewish and Christian writers identified the antichrist, mentioned in the Book of Revelation, as the Roman Emperor Nero (Commodianus *Inst.* 41;[34] Victorinus *Comm. Apoc.* 17:11, 16; Lactantius *Mort.* 2; Sulpicius Severus *Hist. Sac.* 2.28; Augustine *Civ.* 20.19.3).[35]

THE ISOPSEPHY INSCRIPTION (REV 13:18)

Nero's identification as the antichrist is further reinforced by the mysterious number 666 ascribed to the Antichrist in Revelation (13:18), which translates using the Hebrew practice of *gematria* (Heb. *gimatria*; Aramaic *gīmaṭrĕyā*, from Gr. *gēometria* or *grammateia*) into the name of Nero. *Gematria* is a traditional Jewish [Kabbalistic] numerical system used to assign values to

---

[29] Wilhelm Bousset, "Antichrist," in *Encylopaedia of Religion and Ethics*, ed. James Hastings, vol. 1 (T&T Clark, 1908), 580.

[30] John J. Collins, "Sibylline Oracles," in *DNTB*, ed. Craig A. Evans and Stanley E. Porter (Downers Grove, Ill.: InterVarsity, 2000), 1109.

[31] However, Van Henten does admit to one exception (*Sib. Or.* 5.367). Jan Willem van Henten, "Nero Redivivus Demolished: The Coherence of the Nero Traditions in the Sibylline Oracles," *Journal for the Study of the Pseudepigrapha* 11, no. 3 (2000): 17.

[32] Michael Anthony Knibb, "Martyrdom and Ascension of Isaiah: A New Translation and Introduction," in *The Old Testament Pseudepigrapha: Apocalyptic Literature and Testaments*, ed. James H. Charlesworth, vol. 1 (Peabody, Mass.: Hendrickson, 1983), 149.

[33] Nero ordered his mother, Agrippina, murdered in AD 59 (*Sib. Or.* 4.121; 5.29ff, 142, 363).

[34] Gazaeus Commodianus, "The Instructions of Commodianus in Favour of Christian Discipline, Against the Gods of the Heathens," in *Ante-Nicene Fathers: Fathers of the Third Century: Tertullian, Part Fourth: Minucius Felix; Commodian; Origen, Parts First and Second*, ed. Alexander Roberts et al., trans. Robert Ernest Wallis, New Ed, vol. 4 (Peabody, Mass.: Hendrickson, 1994), 385.

[35] Bousset, "Antichrist," 580.

words or phrases in the Hebrew scriptures, as it was believed that the numbers related in some way (age, year, etc.) to the word being represented.[36]

150. Example of isopsephy from the Sanctuary of Artemis Orthia, second cent. AD

Closely related to *gematria* is the Greek practice of *isopsephy* (Gr. *isos* meaning "equal" and *psephos* meaning "pebble").[37] *Isopsephia* ("numerical equality")[38] is derived from the practice of using pebbles to count and add up numbers, but the term refers to the art of assigning values to letters in a name and then adding up the numbers to give a single value.

Use of both the Greek and Hebrew numerical "cryptograms" was a fairly common practice in antiquity to conceal personal names as numbers. This practice of numerology[39] is verified by several archaeological discoveries.

A second cent. AD example of isopsephy was discovered on a headstone at the Sanctuary of Artemis Orthia (see Fig. 150). It reads: ΟΡΘΕΙΗ ΔΩΡΟΝ ΛΕΟΝΤΕΥΣ ΑΝΕΘΗΚΕ ΒΟΑΓΟΣ **ΒΨΛ** ΜΩΑΝ ΝΙΚΗΣΑΣ ΚΑΙ ΤΑΔΕ ΕΠΑΘΛΑ ΛΑΒΩΝ **ΒΨΛ** ΚΑΙ Μ ΕΣΤΕΨΕ ΠΑΤΗΡ ΕΙΣΑΡΙΘΜΟΙΣ ΕΠΕΣΙ **ΒΨΛ**. The votive stele is a isopsephic elegiac[40] poem about a boy who won a singing competition and each verse adds up to 2730 (ΒΨΛ).

Several Greek isopsephy inscriptions are found in graffiti on the walls at Pompeii (see Fig. 151), demonstrating that it was known and used in NT times. Antonio Sogliano has published wall-writing from Pompeii (AD 79)[41] that states:

VIIRVS HIC VBI STAT
NIHIL · VIIRI

151. Graffiti on the outside door of the house of Octavius that translates from the Latin as "Amerimnus thought upon his lady Harmonia for good. The number of her honorable name is 45."

Giuseppe Fiorelli, *Descrizione di Pompeii* (Napoli: Tipografia italiana, 1875), 312. Wikimedia Commons

[36] Angus Stevenson, *Oxford English Dictionary*, 3rd ed. (Oxford: Oxford University Press, 2010), 3297; Shmuel Sambursky, "On the Origin and Significance of the Term 'Gematria.,'" *JJS* 29, no. 1 (1978): 35–38.

[37] Lionel & Patricia Fanthorpe, *Mysteries and Secrets of Numerology* (Toronto, Can.: Dundurn, 2013), 289; Dimitris K. Psychoyos, "The Forgotten Art of Isopsephy and the Magic Number KZ," *Semiotica* 154, no. 1–4 (2005): 157–224.

[38] Kenneth L Gentry, *The Beast of Revelation* (Fort Worth, Tex.: Dominion, 1989), 31.

[39] For a detailed explanation of how gematria and isopsephy functions see Adam Clarke, *The Holy Bible Containing the Old and New Testaments with a Commentary and Critical Notes*, vol. 2 (London: Tegg & Son, 1836), 2081–2084.

[40] A form of ancient poetry, popular in Greek and Latin, using a form of couplets consisting of dactylic hexameter and a pentameter.

[41] Wilhelm Hirschfelder and Georg Andresen, eds., *Wochenschrift Für Klassische Philologie*, vol. 19 (Leipzig: Reisland, 1902), col. 52.

152. Smyrna graffiti discovered in the excavations of the commercial agora that included an isopsephic epigram of a female "whose number is 731" (T24.2).

"Amerimmus thought upon his lady Harmonia for good. The number of her honourable name is 45 (or 1035) [and another Φιλω ης αριθμος φμε,] I love her whose number is 545 [φμε]."[42]

The Roman historian Suetonius (AD 69–after 138), who also acted as Emperor Hadrian's secretary (AD 117–138) in his work *The Twelve Caesars,* reported that some of Nero's enemies wrote graffiti on the walls in Rome and used numbers to accuse him of killing his mother:

> Count the numerical values
> Of the letters in Nero's name,
> And in "murdered his own mother":
> You'll find their sum is the same. (Suetonius *Nero* 39.2 [Graves])[43]

In Rolfe's work–in the Loeb Classical Library series–the translation is more literal, and as Kraybill explains: "the gematrial allusion is more subtle "[Nero, Orestes, Alcmeon their mothers slew.] A calculation new. Nero his mother slew" [Suetonius *Nero* 39.2 (Rolf)]. The point in either case is that the Greek gematrial value for both "Nero" (Νερων) and "killed his

[42] Antonio Sogliano, "Isopsephia Pompeiana," *Rendiconti Della Reale Academia Dei Lincei* 10 (1901): 256–59; Erwin Rohde, *Der griechische Roman und seine Vorläufer* (Leipzig: Breitkopf & Härtel, 1914), 487 n. 1; Franz Dornseiff, *Das Alphabet in Mystik Und Magie*, 2. Aufl edition, Etoixeia, Studien Zur Geschichte Des Antiken Weltbildes Und Der Griechischen Wissenschaft, Hrsg. von F. Boll. Hft. VII (Leipzig: Teubner, 1925), 113; Deissmann, *Light from the Ancient East*, 277; Maurice H. Farbridge, *Studies in Biblical and Semitic Symbolism* (Hoboken, N.J.: Ktav, 1970), 95; Kieren Barry, *The Greek Qabalah: Alphabetical Mysticism and Numerology in the Ancient World* (York Beach, Maine: Weiser Books, 1999), 128; Nicholas Vinel, "Le Judaïsme Caché Du Carré Sator de Pompéi: The Hidden Judaism of the Pompeiian Sator Square," *Revue de L'histoire Des Religions* 2 (2006): 180; Georges Ifrah, *The Universal History of Numbers: From Prehistory to the Invention of the Computer*, trans. David Bellos (New York, N.Y.: Wiley, 2000), 256.

[43] Gaius Suetonius Tranquillus, *The Twelve Caesars*, ed. Michael Grant, trans. Robert Graves, Rev., Penguin Classics (Harmondsworth, U.K.: Penguin, 1987), 236; Ifrah, *The Universal History of Numbers*, 256.

own mother" (ιδιαν μητερ ααπεκτεινε) is 1,005."[44]

Deisman gets to the point that "the name 'Nero' is there numerically resolved into 'matricide.'"[45] This is referring to the well-known fact that Nero had arranged the assassination of his mother, Agrippina, in AD 59 (Tacitus *Ann.* 12).

Leonidas of Alexandria (first cent. AD) composed an isopsephic epigram (short satiristic poem) on Nero *(Gr. Anth.)*[46] with an equinumeral rhyming couplet (distichs); defined by Psychoyos as "epigrams of four lines, whose first hexameter and pentameter, if their letters' values were added, have the same arithmetical value with the next two verses."[47]

During the Imperial Roman period (27 BC–AD 476), many inscriptions have been discovered that use numerical isopsephy, including at Pergamum and Smyrna, which are two of the seven churches mentioned in Revelation (Rev 2.12ff.). During the second cent. a Greek architect from Pergamum, by the name of Aelius Nikon, was described by his son Galen, the famous physician, as having "mastered all there was to know of the science of geometry and numbers,"[48] and was proficient in the art of composing isopsephic works.[49] In Smyrna several graffiti included isopsephic epigrams. Three female names, in the same building, are identified representing 616. One reads "I love a woman whose number is 616" (T22.1).[50] Others read "whose number is 731" (T24.2; see Fig. 152) and "1308" (T27.3).[51] Another inscription from the agora Basilica, that was an example of isopsephism from Smyrna, states: "equal in value: lord, 800; faith 800" (TP100.3 = *SIG* 3.973).[52]

Also, Apollonius, a mathematician from Pergamum (AD third cent.), asked: "Given the verse: ΑΡΤΕΜΙΔΟΣ ΚΛΕΙΤΕ ΚΡΑΤΟΣ ΕΞΟΧΟΝ ΕΝΝΕΑ ΚΟΥΡΑΙ ["Nine maidens, praise the glorious power of Artemis"], what does the product of all its elements equal?"[53]

Driver points out possible examples of gematria in both the OT and NT[54] and Hvalvik finds it possibly being used in the apocryphal book of Barnabas (*Barn.* 9:8).[55] The practice of turning words or names into numbers is documented in other ancient texts (Lucian *Alex.* 11; *Anth. pal.* 14.20, 105 *Sib. Or.* 1.137–46; 1.324–30; 5.1–51). The later *Sibylline Oracles* (AD 235–265) often represented the names or initials of Roman emperors as numbers (*Sib. Or.* 11.29–30, 92, 114, 189–90, 208, 256, 266; 12.39, 49–50, 68, 78, 96, 101, 121, 125, 144, 148, 189, 207,

[44] J. Nelson Kraybill, *Apocalypse and Allegiance: Worship, Politics, and Devotion in the Book of Revelation* (Grand Rapids: Brazos Press, 2010), 67 n. 26; Gaius Suetonius Tranquillus, *Lives of the Caesars: Claudius. Nero. Galba, Otho, and Vitellius. Vespasian. Titus, Domitian. Lives of Illustrious Men: Grammarians and Rhetoricians. Poets (Terence. Virgil. Horace. Tibullus. Persius. Lucan). Lives of Pliny the Elder and Passienus Crispus*, trans. John C. Rolfe, vol. 2, LCL 38 (Cambridge, Mass.: Harvard University Press, 1914), 2:158–59.

[45] Deissmann, *Light from the Ancient East*, 278; Franz Bücheler, *Rheinisches Museum für Philologie*, vol. 61 (Berlin: Weber, 1906), 307 f.

[46] Michael A. Tueller, ed., *The Greek Anthology: Book 1: Christian Epigrams. Book 2: Description of the Statues in the Gymnasium of Zeuxippus. Book 3: Epigrams in the Temple of Apollonis at Cyzicus. Book 4: Prefaces to the Various Anthologies. Book 5: Erotic Epigrams*, trans. William R. Paton, vol. 1, Loeb Classical Library 67 (Cambridge, Mass.: Harvard University Press, 2014), 1:470; 2:294.

[47] Psychoyos, "Forgotten Art of Isopsephy," 179.

[48] Ifrah, *The Universal History of Numbers*, 256.

[49] Psychoyos, "Forgotten Art of Isopsephy," 179.

[50] Roger S. Bagnall, "Isopsephisms of Desire," in *Graffiti from the Basilica in the Agora of Smyrna*, ed. Roger S. Bagnall et al., Institute for the Study of the Ancient World (New York: New York University Press, 2016), 50, 226.

[51] Ibid. 48.

[52] Roger S. Bagnall, "Christianity," in *Graffiti from the Basilica in the Agora of Smyrna*, ed. Roger S. Bagnall et al., Institute for the Study of the Ancient World (New York: New York University Press, 2016), 46.

[53] Ibid., 178; Max Fränkel, Ernst Fabricius, and Carl Schuchhardt, *Die Inschriften von Pergamon*, vol. 8, Sonderausgabe Aus Den Altertümern von Pergamon (Berlin: Spemann, 1890), nos. 333, 339, 587.

[54] G. R. Driver, "The Number of the Beast," in *Bibel Und Qumran: Beitrage Zur Erforschung Der Beziehungen Wischen Bibel- Und Qumran- Wissenschaft*, ed. S. Wagner, Hans Bardtke Zum 22.9.1966 (Berlin: Evangelische Haupt-Bibelgesellschaft, 1968), 75–78.

[55] Reider Hvalvik, "Barnabas 9.7–9 and the Author's Supposed Use of Gematria," *New Testament Studies* 33 (1987): 276–82.

246, 250, 258; 13.83–84; 14.21, 28, 44, 59–60, 79, 95, 106, 126, 137, 150, 163, 227, 248).

John, in writing Revelation, is thus not alone in representing a Roman emperor as a number and referring to Nero (*Nerō Claudius Caesar Augustus Germanicus;* r. AD 54–68)[56] using gematria. One might argue that *Nerō(n) Kaisar* in Greek is not 666; however, John is writing a riddle to be solved, and seems to have expected some of the Jews in the seven churches to not only understand gematria but to be able to use it in Hebrew. John wrote "let the one who has understanding *calculate the number* of the beast, for it is the number of *a man*, and his number is *666*" (Rev 13:18). The table below shows the calculation:[57]

Gematria for Nero and Jesus

Hebrew	**Hebrew**	**Greek**
Neron Caesar	Nero Caesar	Jesus
nrwn qsr	*nrw qsr*	*Iesous*
Q=100	Q=100	I=10
S=60	S=60	E=8
R=200	R=200	S=200
N=50	N=50	O=70
R=200	R=200	U=400
W=6	W=6	S=200
N=50		
666[58]	**616**[59]	**888**[60]

Lawrence explains the manuscript evidence for the variant calculation of 616 (see Fig. 153),[61] which lends further evidence that the solution to the calculation of the number is Nero. He states:

> Some mss. of Revelation—13:18, however, have the number 616 instead of 666, e.g., Ephraemi Rescriptus, some mss. known to Irenaeus [Irenaeus *Haer.* 5:28:2], and Tyconius. Tischendorf mentions in his edition of the Greek New Testament that minuscules number 5 and 11 (now lost) also had the number 616. Though Irenaeus questioned the authenticity of the mss. with the number 616, it is interesting to note that the Latin form of 616 transliterated into Hebrew letters spells *"Nero Caesar"* too.[62]

Commenting on the textual variant 616, the distinguished textual scholar, Bruce M. Metzger, states that: "Perhaps the change was intentional, seeing that the Greek form *Neron Caesar* written in Hebrew characters (*nrwn qsr*) is equivalent to 666, whereas the Latin form *Nero Caesar* (*nrw qsr*) is equivalent to 616."[63] While *nrwn qsr* is an unusual spelling of Nero's name, it is found in this form in the Talmud[64] and a contemporary Aramaic scroll from a cave at Qumran (Mur 18).[65]

As Sanders points out, there are other names which, when

153. Fragment from Papyrus 115 (P115) of Revelation in the 66th vol. of the Oxyrhynchus series (P. Oxy. 4499). It has the number of the beast as XIC, 616.

[56] Epiphanius of Salamis states that John left Patmos during the reign of Claudius Caesar (AD 41–54) when John was over ninety years old (*Pan.* 51.12.1–2). Aune points out that there is some confusion over Claudius's name as he was also known as Nero Claudius Caesar. Aune, *Revelation 1-5*, 77–78.

[57] Kraybill, *Apocalypse and Allegiance*, 67; James Stuart Russell, *The Parousia. A Critical Inquiry into the New Testament Doctrine of Our Lord's Second Coming* (London: Dalby, Isbister & Co., 1878), 464.

[58] R. C. Sproul, *The Last Days According to Jesus* (Grand Rapids: Baker, 2000), 187–89; Adela Yarbro Collins, "Numerical Symbolism in Jewish and Early Christian Apocalyptic Literature," *ANRW* 21, no. 2 (1984): 1221–1287.

[59] *P.Oxy.* 66.4499.

[60] A probable Christian insertion into the *Sibylline Oracles* (1.324–30). Aune, *Revelation 6-16*, 772.

[61] Kraybill, *Apocalypse and Allegiance*, 66 n. 25.

[62] John M. Lawrence, "Nero Redivivus," *Fides et Historia* 11 (1974): 54–55.

[63] Bruce M. Metzger, *A Textual Commentary on the Greek New Testament*, 2nd ed. (Stuttgart, Germany: Deutsche Bibelgesellschaft, 2002), 750.

[64] Marcus Jastrow, *Dictionary of Targumim, Talmud and Midrashic Literature* (New York, N.Y.: Putnam's Sons, 1903), loc. cit.; Robert H. Charles, *A Critical and Exegetical Commentary on the Revelation of St John,* ICC (Edinburgh, U.K.: T&T Clark, 1963), 1:367.

[65] Delbert R. Hillers, "Revelation 13:18 and a Scroll from Murabba'ât," *BASOR* 170 (1963): 65.

154. The traditional tomb of the apostle John located in the ruins of the sixth cent. basilica of St. John in Selçuk near ancient Ephesus in Turkey.

put through the same process, equal 666. Irenaeus (*Haer.* 5.29–30) gave three names that total 666 (*Euanthas*, *Teitan*, *Lateinos*). Andreas of Caesarea in his *Commentary on Revelation* gave seven names which totalled 666 (see also Arethas' *Commentary* which gives 9 names; Primasius who gives 2 names; Victorinus who gives 4 names; Venerable Bede who gives 3 names; and Beatus who gives 8 names).[66] However, the contemporary evidence for the use of *nrwn qsr* as Nero's name seems compelling when taken with the variant 616 (*nrw qsr).*

The Tomb of St. John

Church tradition from Irenaeus, as quoted by Eusebius, stated that the apostle John returned to Ephesus after being released from prison with other political prisoners under the reign of Nerva (AD 96–98) following the death of Domitian (*Hist. eccl.* 3.17–20) and survived into the reign of Trajan (*Hist. eccl.* 2.22.5; 3.3.43; 23.1–3). However, Epiphanius of Salamis contradicts this tradition, stating that John left Patmos during the reign of Claudius Caesar (A.D. 41–54) when John was over ninety years old (*Pan.* 51.12.1–2). Aune points out that there is some confusion over Claudius's name, as he was also known as Nero Claudius Caesar,[67] and, according to the Syriac Apocrypha, John's exile took place under "Nero, the unclean and impure and wicked king."[68]

Despite the confusion of his release from captivity it is generally accepted that John lived to a very old age and died in Ephesus (Eusebius who appeals to Irenaeus [*Hist. eccl.* 3.18.1; 39, 3–4], Justin [*Hist. eccl* 4.18.6–8], Clement of Alexandria [*Hist. eccl.* 3.39.3–4], Apollonius [*Hist.*

---

[66] Henry A. Sanders, "The Number of the Beast in Revelation," *JBL*, 95-99, 37, no. 1 (1918): 95–96; Jöran Friberg, "Numbers and Counting," ed. David Noel Freedman et al., *ABD* (New York, N.Y.: Doubleday, 1996), 1145.

[67] Aune, *Revelation 1-5*, 77–78.

[68] William Wright, *Apocryphal Acts of the Apostles* (London: Williams & Norgate, 1871), 2:55.

eccl. 5.18.14] and Polycrates [*Hist. eccl.* 5.24.3]).[69]

In the sixth cent. AD (AD 548–565) a basilica was built by Justinian I, 3.5 km (2.2 mi) outside of Ephesus, over the believed burial site of the Apostle John (see Fig. 154).[70] It was constructed based on the Church of the Holy Apostles in Constantinople.[71]

One of the only sources suggesting that the basilica of St. John is build over the grave of the apostle John comes from a description by Procopius of Caesarea (*ca.* AD 500–?) in his work *Buildings*. (see *Quotes from Antiquity*)[72]

Quotes from Antiquity

Procopius of Caesarea

There chanced to be a certain place before the city of Ephesus, lying on a steep slope hilly and bare of soil and incapable of producing crops, even should one attempt to cultivate them, but altogether hard and rough. On that site the natives had set up a church in early times to the Apostle John; this Apostle has been named "the Theologian," because the nature of God was described by him in a manner beyond the unaided power of man. This church, which was small and in a ruined condition because of its great age, the Emperor Justinian tore down to the ground and replaced by a church so large and beautiful, that, to speak briefly, it resembles very closely in all respects, and is a rival to, the shrine which he dedicated to all the Apostles in the imperial city.

Procopius *Build.* 5.4–6.

The bishop of Ephesus at the time was Hypatius of Ephesus, who possibly convinced Justinian to build the church and restore the tomb of the apostle John. As Procopius reports, after its completion it was regarded as one of the "most holy one [church] there and held in very high honour" (Procopius *SH* 3.3). However, in the ninth cent. a new Church of John the Theologian was built on this location in honor of St. John, and it is these ruins which are visible today (see Fig. 154).[73] There is a plaque on this square which marks the believed tomb of John.

THE MADABA MAP

There are limited resources available to those looking to link sites mentioned in ancient sources with modern tells/talls in the Levant. The Byzantine Madaba Map, a masterpiece of Near Eastern geography, is often cited to lend weight to certain identifications. For Oswald Dilke, the mosaic map at Madaba is "probably the best known example of Byzantine cartography."[74] The Mosaic map was discovered in 1884 under the floor during restoration of a Byzantine church[75] in Madaba, Jordan (see Fig. 155, 156).[76] The mosaic was incorporated into the floor of the new, but smaller, St. George's church. The mosaic dates to AD 542–570 (middle of the sixth cent.) and displays cities and towns with their monasteries and religious

[69] T. Zahn, "John the Apostle," ed. Johann Jakob Herzog and Philip Schaff, *The New Schaff-Herzog Encyclopedia Of Religious Knowledge* (Grand Rapids: Baker, 1951), 6:205–206; Frederick Fyvie Bruce, "St John at Ephesus," *BJRL* 60 (August 1977): 339–61; F. Collins Raymond, "John (Disciple)," ed. David Noel Freedman et al., *ABD* (New York, N.Y.: Doubleday, 1996), 3:885–86.

[70] Richard Krautheimer and Slobodan Curcic, *Early Christian and Byzantine Architecture*, 4th ed., Pelican History of Art (New Haven, Conn.: Yale University Press, 1992), 242–44.

[71] Ken Dark and Ferudun Özgümüş, "New Evidence for the Byzantine Church of the Holy Apostles from Fatih Camii, Istanbul," *Oxford Journal of Archeology* 21, no. 4 (2002): 393–413.

[72] Procopius of Caesarea, *On Buildings. General Index*, trans. H. B. Dewing and Glanville Downey, vol. 7, LCL 343 (Cambridge, Mass.: Harvard University Press, 1940), 319.

[73] John F. Baldovin, *The Urban Character of Christian Worship: The Origins, Development, and Meaning of Stational Liturgy*, Orientalia Christiana Analecta 228 (Rome: Pontificium Institutum Studiorum Orientalium, 1987), 178.

[74] Oswald Dilke, *The History of Cartography: Cartography in Prehistoric, Ancient, and Medieval Europe and the Mediterranean*, ed. J. B. Harley and David Woodward, vol. 1 (Chicago, Ill.: University of Chicago Press, 1987), 264.

[75] Today the Greek Orthodox Parish Church of St. George has been built over the Byzantine Church preserving the mosaic.

[76] Herbert Donner, *The Mosaic Map of Madaba. An Introductory Guide*, Palaestina Antiqua 7 (Kampen: Kok Pharos, 1992), 11.

sites present during the Byzantine period (AD 325–638) depicted in mosaic tiles (*tesserae*).

The mosaic did not draw the interest of scholars until Father Cleopas M. Koikylides visited the church in 1896 and produced an accurate sketch of the map and published a small commentary in 1897.[77] It was restored by Henrich Brandt, under the direction of Herbert Donner, in 1965.[78]

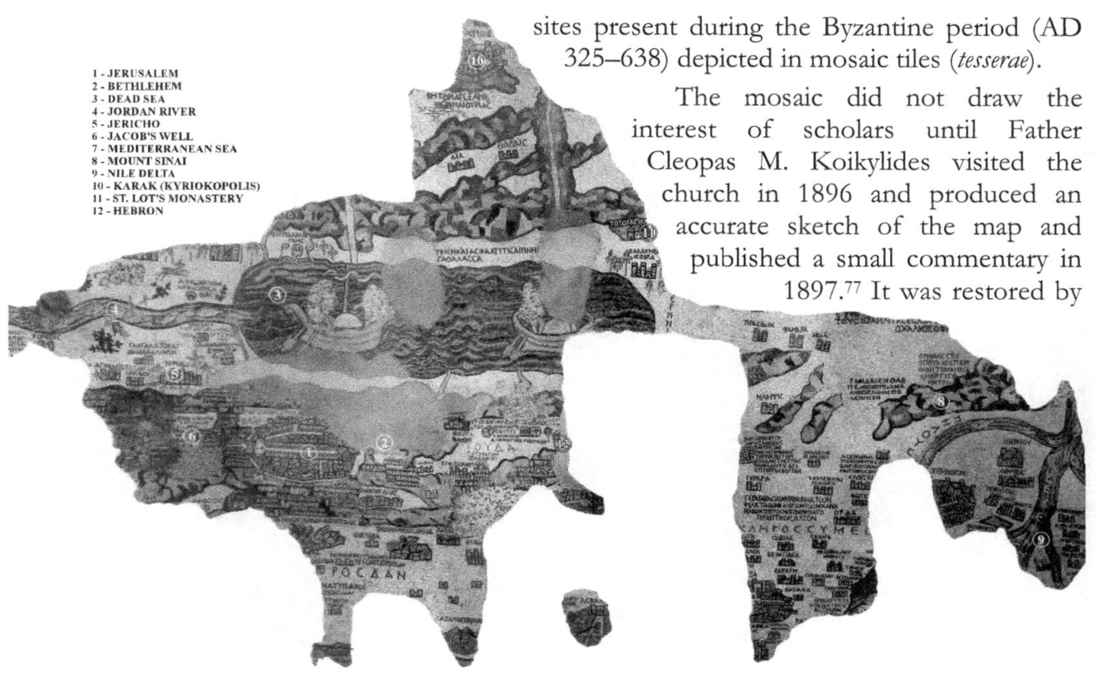

155. Photo of the Madaba Map displayed at the Greek Orthodox Church of St. George, Madaba Jordan.
© David E. Graves

It is one of the oldest extant maps of the Holy Land and Jerusalem, and preserves the location of holy sites from the biblical periods. It was used by early Christian pilgrims traveling in the region to locate sites of interest, as indicated by the Spanish pilgrim Egeria in the sixth century.[79] As Donner points out "it is a real geographical and topographical map"[80] and not simply pictures of Bible places.

There is little doubt that the map was constructed from the personal observations of the area by the original cartographers, who also relied on the Bible and Eusebius' *Onomasticon of*

[77] Cleopas M. Koikylides, *The Geographical Madaba Mosaic Map on Syria, Palestine and Egypt* (Jerusalem, Israel, 1897); "The Geographical Mosaic at Madaba," *RB*, April 1, 1897, 165–50; Caspar René Gregory, "The Mâdaba Map," *The Biblical World* 12, no. 4 (1898): 244–50.

[78] Herbert Donner, "The Uniqueness of the Madaba Map and Its Restoration in 1965," in *The Madaba Map Centenary: Travelling Through the Byzantine Umayyad Period. Proceedings of the International Conference Held in Amman 7–9 April 1997*, ed. Michele Piccirillo and Eugenio Alliata, Studium Biblicum Franciscannum Collectio Maior 40 (Jerusalem: Studium Biblicum Franciscannum, 1999), 37–40.

[79] John Wilkinson, ed., *Egeria's Travels: Translated with Supporting Documents and Notes*, trans. John Wilkinson, 3rd ed. (Warminster: Aris & Phillips, 1999); Eugenio Alliata, "The Legends of the Madaba Map," in *The Madaba Map Centenary: Travelling Through the Byzantine Umayyad Period. Proceedings of the International Conference Held in Amman 7–9 April 1997*, ed. Michele Piccirillo and Eugenio Alliata, Studium Biblicum Franciscannum Collectio Maior 40 (Jerusalem: Studium Biblicum Franciscannum, 1999), 47–101; Eugenio Alliata, "The Pilgrimage Routes during the Byzantine Period in Transjordan," in *The Madaba Map Centenary: Travelling Through the Byzantine Umayyad Period. Proceedings of the International Conference Held in Amman 7–9 April 1997*, ed. Michele Piccirillo and Eugenio Alliata, Studium Biblicum Franciscannum Collectio Maior 40 (Jerusalem: Studium Biblicum Franciscannum, 1999), 121–24.

[80] Donner, *Mosaic Map of Madaba*, 18.

Place Names (AD 320), to locate many of the biblical sites.[81] They also used other sources available in the Madaba Library, such as Josephus and the earlier road map called the Peutinger Plates (*Tabulae Peutingerinae*).[82]

Tall el-Hammam has recently been identified on the Madaba map as Livias, the capital of Perea. In addition, since Zoar was identified on the map (see Figs. 155 no. 11, 157) and pilgrims were always looking for holy sites to visit, Sodom and Gomorrah may have originally been identified on the map, as one of two sites that have the tessera of their Greek names damaged and missing (see Fig. 158).[83]

156. The author kneeling pointing to Zoar at the edge of the Madaba Map displayed at the Greek Orthodox Church of St. George, Madaba Jordan.

[81] G. S. P. Freeman-Grenville and Joan E. Taylor, eds., *The Onomasticon by Eusebius of Caesarea and the Liber Locorum of Jerome: Palestine in the Fourth Century AD*, trans. G. S. P. Freedman-Grenville (Jerusalem: Carta, 2003); Leah Di Segni, "The 'Onomasticon' of Eusebius and the Madaba Map," in *The Madaba Map Centenary: Travelling Through the Byzantine Umayyad Period. Proceedings of the International Conference Held in Amman 7–9 April 1997*, ed. Michele Piccirillo and Eugenio Alliata, Studium Biblicum Franciscannum Collectio Maior 40 (Jerusalem: Studium Biblicum Franciscannum, 1999), 115–20; Pamphilus Eusebius, The Onomasticon of Eusebius Pamphili: Compared with the Version of Jerome and Annotated, ed. Noel C. Wolf, trans. C. Umhau Wolf (Washington, D.C.: Catholic University of America Press, 1971).

[82] Donner, *Mosaic Map of Madaba*, 24–27.

[83] David E. Graves and D. Scott Stripling, "Identification of Tall El-Hammam on the Madaba Map," *BS* 20, no. 2 (2007): 35–45; "Re-Examination of the Location for the Ancient City of Livias," *Levant* 43, no. 2 (2011): 178–200.

CONCLUSION

Although there are still many archaeological discoveries waiting to be uncovered, what has been presented here, as a collection of the notable discoveries, clearly demonstrates that both the OT and NT are historically reliable sources of information. Even though there is much we still do not understand about the meaning of the biblical text, archaeology has assisted in explaining many passages that were previously unclear and improved our knowledge of the past. Biblical sceptics must now evaluate this large body of archaeological evidence, though students of the Bible can be assured that the details of this ancient text are reliable and trustworthy.

157. A section of the Madaba map marked as *Balak Zoora,* identied by the six palm trees indicating the location of Byzantine Zoar (*Segor* or *Es-Safi*) at the southern end of the Dead Sea. Lot's cave is also identified above Zoar. Madaba Map displayed at the Greek Orthodox Church of St. George, Madaba Jordan.

© David E. Graves

158. Segment of the Madaba map found on the floor of St. George, Madaba Jordan indicating the unidentified Site One and Two. The author has identified site Two with Tall el-Hammam, believed by some to be biblical Sodom and Abel Shittim. In the Roman period it was rebuilt as Livias.

© David E. Graves

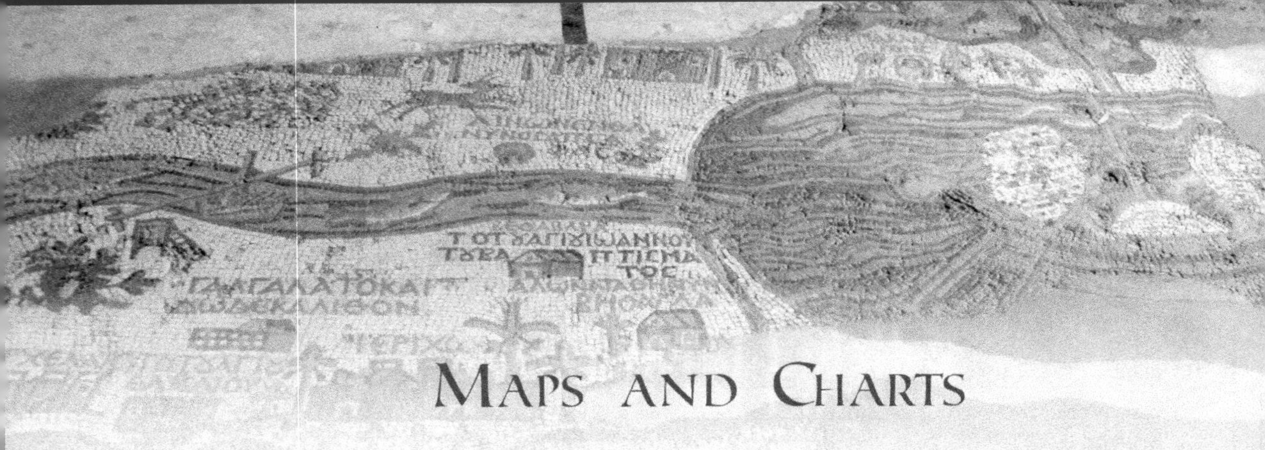

Maps and Charts

Map 1: Migration of Abraham from Babylon

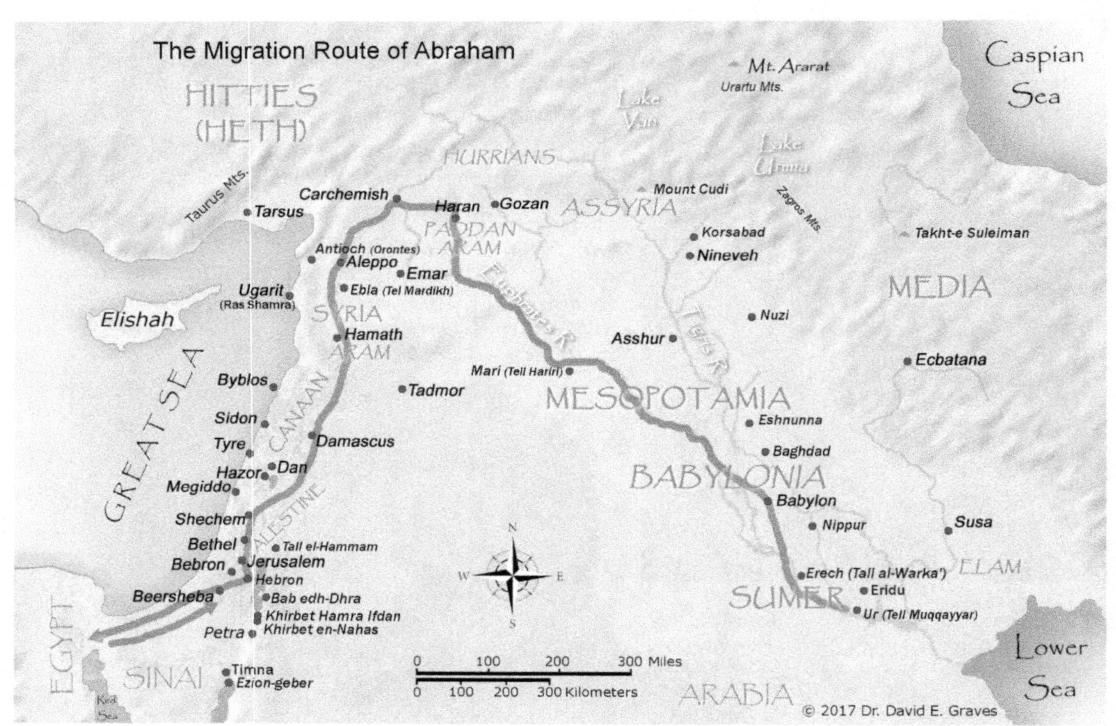

159. **MAP 1:** Migration of Abraham from Babylon.

MAP 2. TRIBAL ALLOTMENTS OF ISRAEL

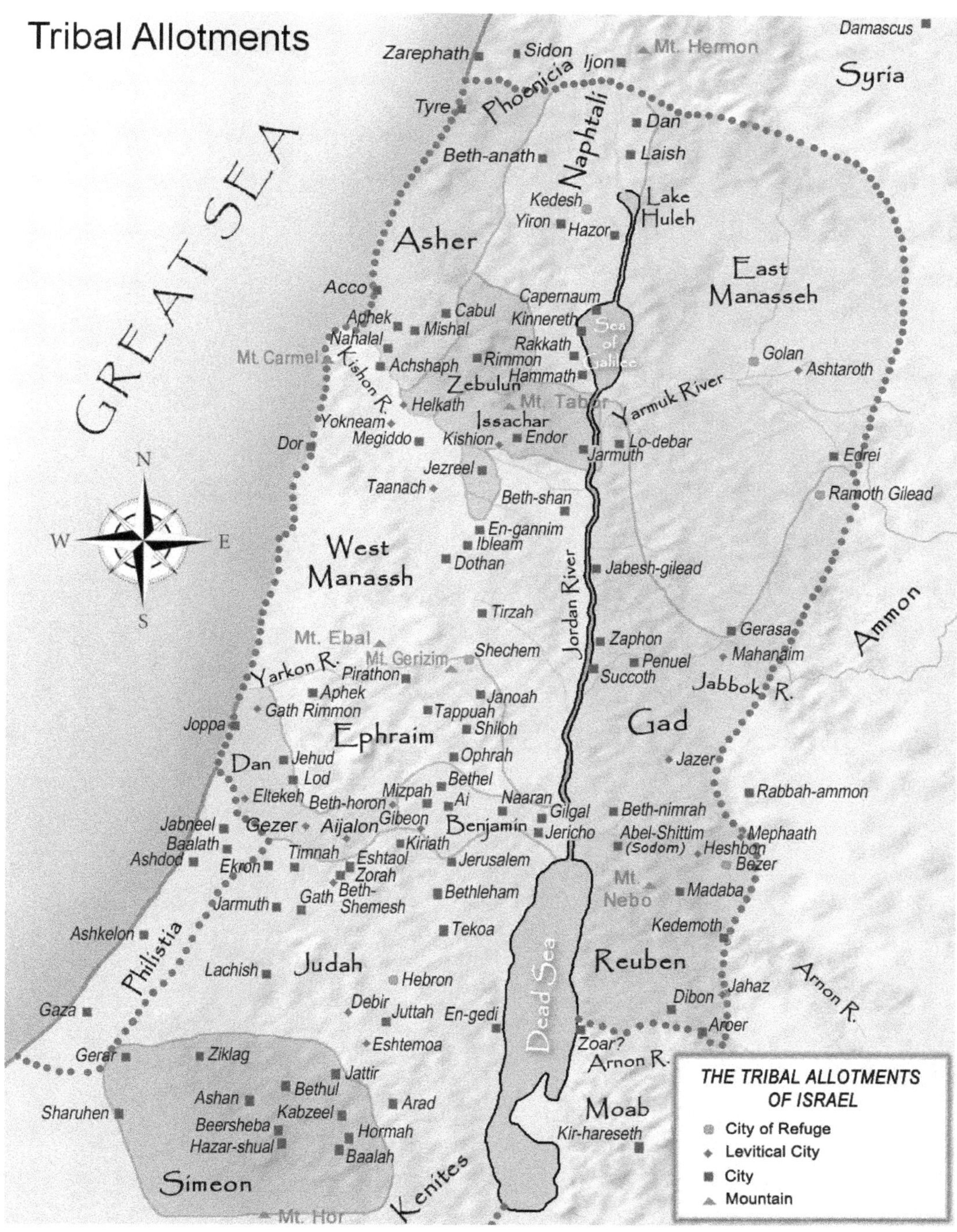

160. **MAP 2.** Map of the tribal allotments of Israel with Levitical cities and cities of refuge.

MAP 3: THE ROUTE OF THE EXODUS

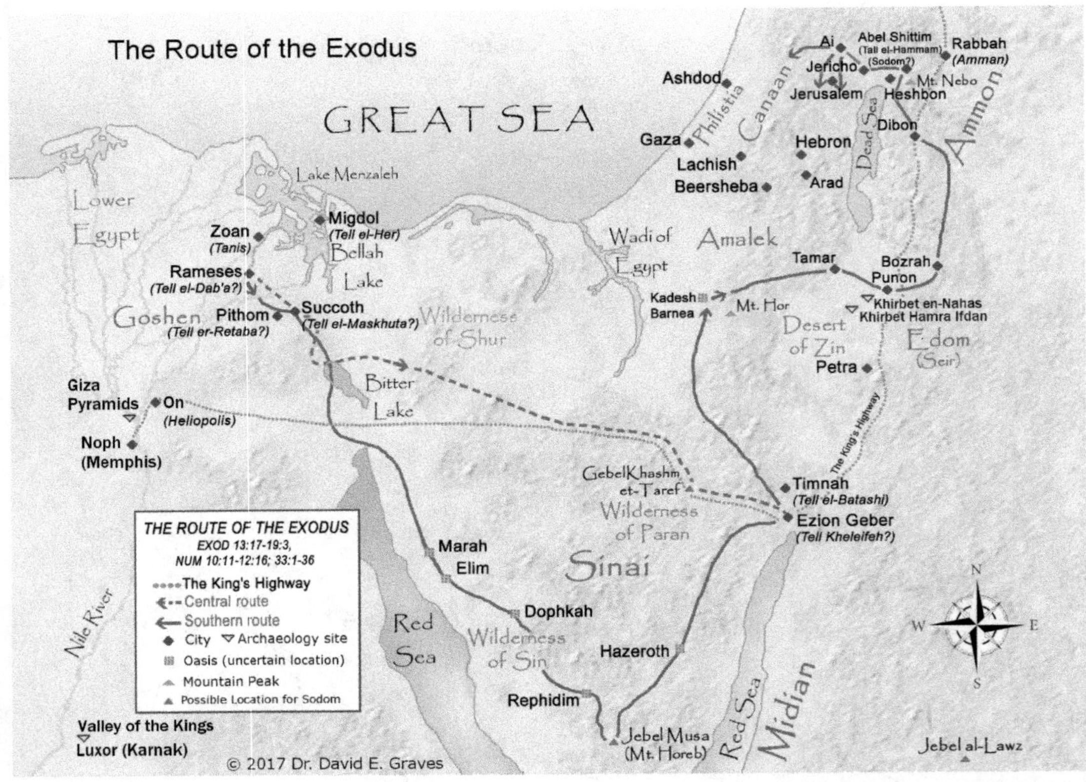

161. **MAP 3:** The route of the Exodus.

MAP 4: JUDEA IN THE TIME OF JESUS

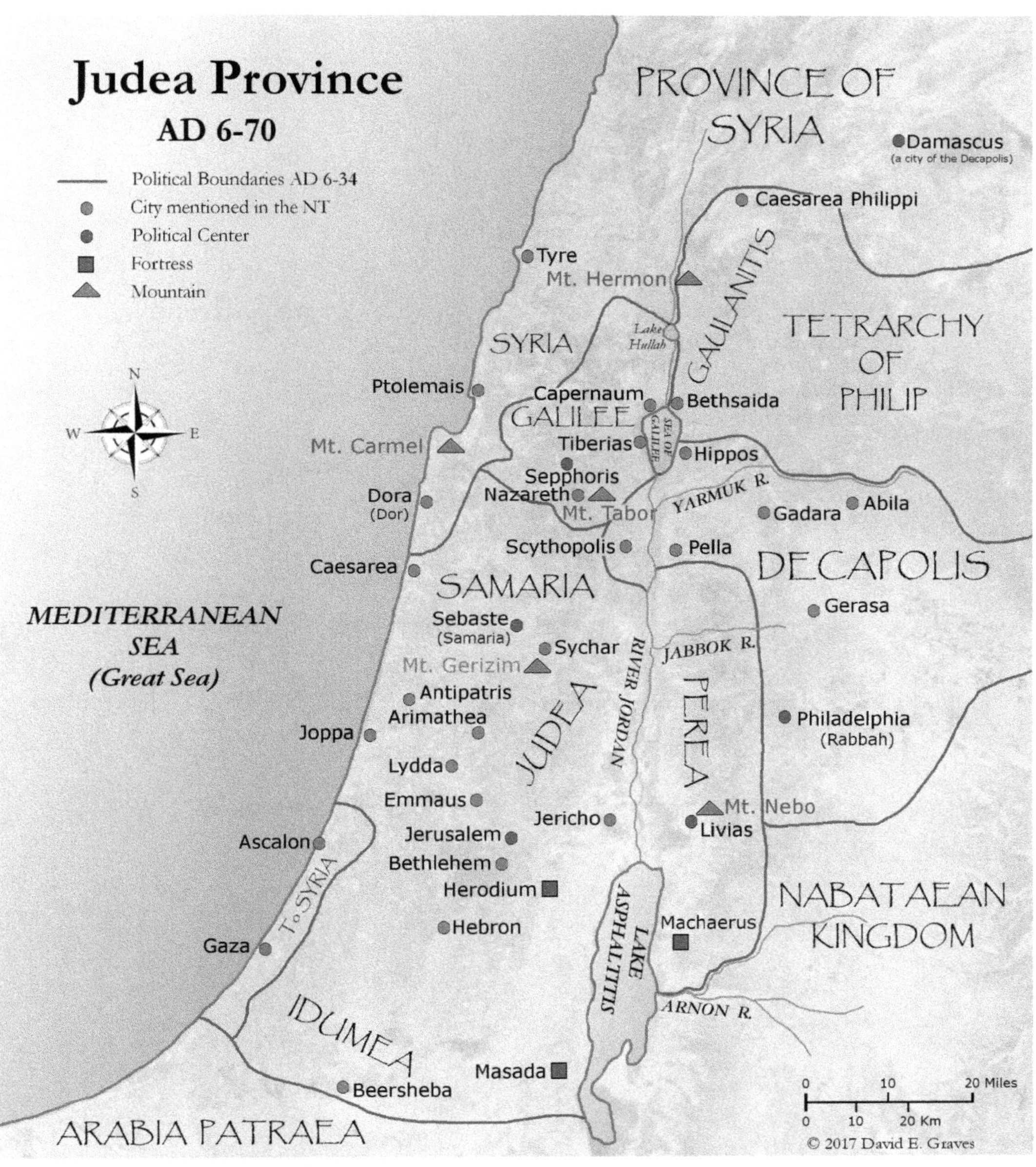

162. **MAP 4:** Judea in the time of Jesus.

MAP 5: THE FIRST MISSIONARY JOURNEY

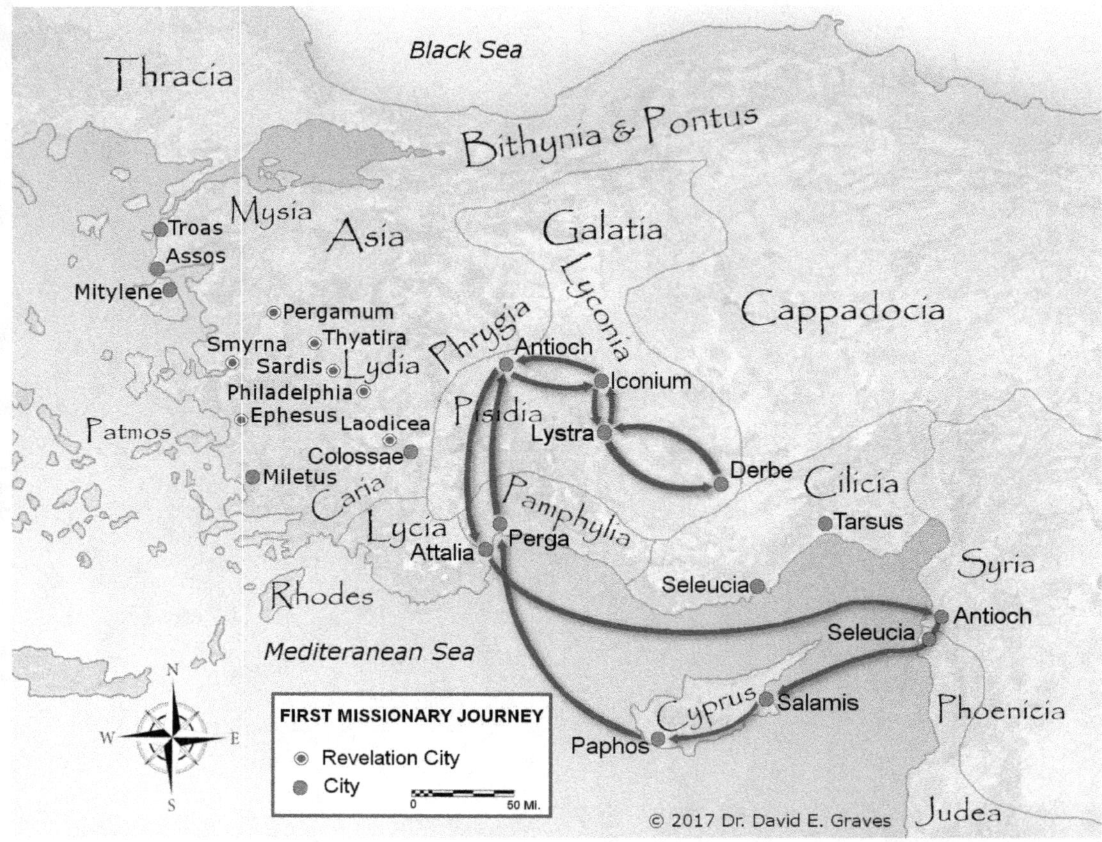

163. **MAP 5**: The First Missionary Journey.

MAP 6: THE SECOND MISSIONARY JOURNEY

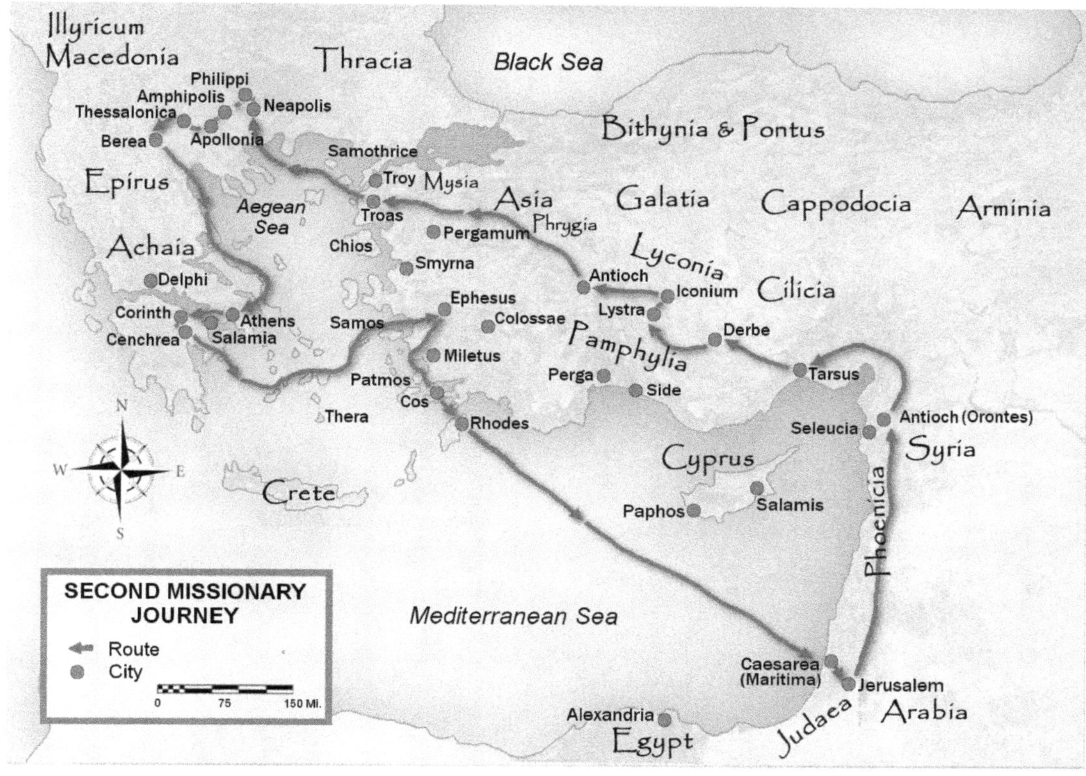

164. **MAP 6:** The Second Missionary Journey.

MAP 7: THE THIRD MISSIONARY JOURNEY AND TRIP TO ROME

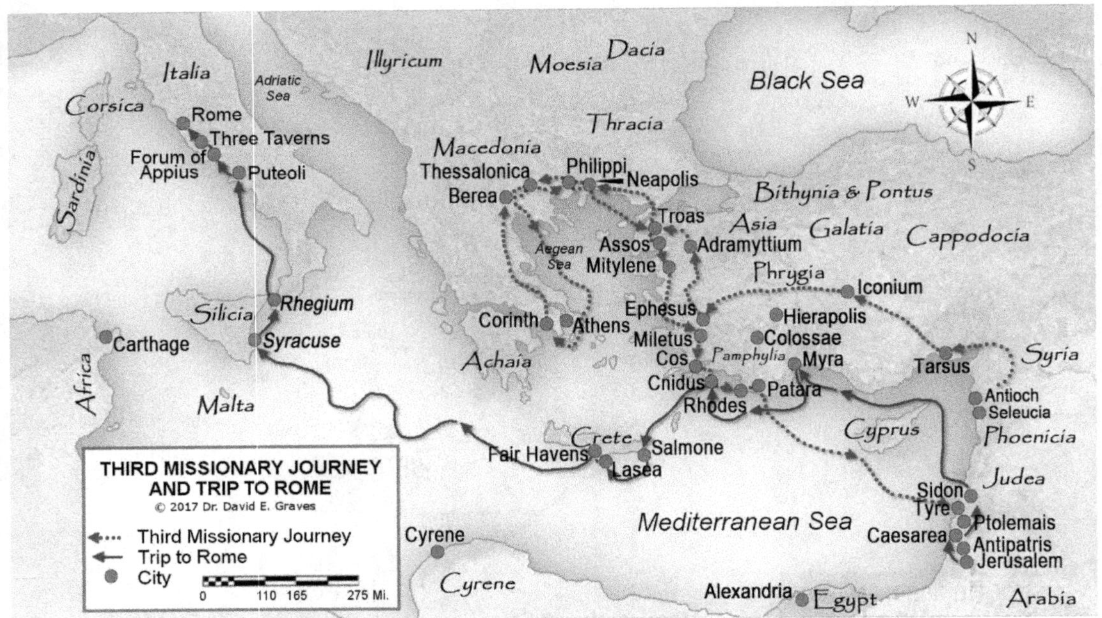

165. **MAP 7**: The Third Missionary Journey and trip to Rome.

CHART 8: ARCHAEOLOGICAL PERIODS (NEW CHRONOLOGY)[1]

Period	Abbreviation	Historical Period	Dates
PREHISTORIC PERIOD			
Pre-Pottery Neolithic A, B	PPNA, PPNB	Post Creation	8500–6000 BC
Pottery Neolithic A, B	PNA, PNB	Ubaid Period (Sumer)	6000–4300 BC
Chalcolithic Period	Cal.	Ubaid Uruk Period (Sumer)	4300–3600 BC
BIBLICAL PERIOD			
Early Bronze Age 1	EB 1	Uruk Period (Sumer) Writing	3600–3100 BC
Early Bronze Age 2	EB 2	Dynastic Period (flood?)	3100–2800 BC
Early Bronze Age 3	EB 3	Dynastic Period (flood?)	2800–2500 BC
Intermediate Bronze Age 1	IB 1 (formerly EB IV–MB I	Third Dynasty of Ur	2500–2200 BC
Intermediate Bronze Age 2	IB 2 (formerly EB IV–MB I	Third Dynasty of Ur	2200–1950 BC
Middle Bronze Age 1	MB 1 (formerly MB IIA)	Middle Kingdom Egypt	1950–1800 BC
Middle Bronze Age 2	MB 2 (formerly MB IIB)	Israel's Patriarchs	1800–1540 BC
Late Bronze Age 1	LB 1	Mosaic Period /New Kingdom Egypt	1540–1400 BC
Late Bronze Age 2	LB 2	Exodus & Conquest	1400–1200 BC
Iron Age 1	IA 1	Judges	1200–1000 BC
Iron Age 2	IA 2	United & Divided Monarchy / Babylonian Conquest	1000–586 BC
Persian Period	Pers.	Neo-Babylonian Period/ Exile	586–332 BC

[1] Johanna Regev et al., "Chronology of the Early Bronze Age in the Southern Levant: New Analysis for a High Chronology," *Radiocarbon* 3–4 (2012): 525–66.

Period	Abbreviation	Historical Period	Dates
CLASSICAL PERIOD			
Hellenistic Period	Hell.	Alexander the Great	332–63 BC
Maccabean / Hasmonean Period	Macc.	Maccabean Revolt	165–63 AD
Early Roman Period	ER or E. Rom.	Herodian/ NT Period	63 BC–70 AD
Middle Roman Period	MR or M. Rom.	Yavne Period	70–135 AD
Late Roman Period	LR or L. Rom.	Mishnaic Period	135–200 AD
Late Roman Period	LR or L. Rom.	Talmudic Period	200–330 AD
Byzantine Period	Byz.	Eastern Roman Empire	330–638 AD
ISLAMIC PERIOD			
Umayyad Period	Umay.	Arab Caliphate Period	638–750 AD
Abbasid Period	Abb.	Arab Caliphate Period	750–969 AD
Fatimid Period	Fat.	Caliphate Egyptians	969–1171 AD
Kingdom of Jerusalem Period	Crus.	Crusader Period	1099–1187 AD
Ayyubid Period	Ayy.	Crusader Period	1187–1244 AD
Mamluk Period	Mam.	Crusader Period	1244–1517 AD
Ottoman Period	Ott.	Ottoman Empire	1517–1917 AD
MODERN PERIOD			
British Mandate Period	Brit. Man.	British Occupation and Arab states	1917–1948 AD
Israeli Period	Isr.	Modern Israel	1948–Present

Glossary

Acropolis: (ἀκρόπολις from ἄκρος [*akros*] "highest, topmost, outermost" and πολις [*polis*] "city") Although technically this has referred to the citadel in Athens which housed the Parthenon it can refer to any high elevation of a city which is easily fortified. This is usually where cities placed their temples and palaces.

Agora: (Ἀγορά) The central market place or forum of a city where commerce, administration and even sacrifices were performed.

Amphora(e): (ἀμφιφορεύς *amphiphoreus* from ἀμφί *amphi* "on both sides" or "around" + φέρειν *pherein*, "to carry") Large storage jar with two handles and a pointed bottom; used for storing and transporting wine, oil, grapes, olive oil, olives, grain, fish, and other commodities.

Apocrypha: (ἀπόκρυφος *apókruphos* "hidden", "obscure", or "spurious") Non-canonical books that contain figures from Scripture. Some writings found a place in the Septuagint (LXX) and the Latin Vulgate version of the OT but not the Jewish or Protestant Bible.

Aqueduct: Water channel usually associated with high arches to traverse a ravine, though they can also run along the ground, as at Tall el-Ḥammâm.

Artifact: A man-made object made from stone, metal, clay or other substance (e.g., coins, flint, figurines, pottery, etc.)

Basilica: A rectangular building or hall with a central nave and two side aisles. The Romans used them for administrative buildings while the Christians converted them for churches.

Bedouin: Members of nomadic Arab tribes that still inhabit the desert regions of much of the Middle East.

Bema: (βῆμα, *bēma* "a step" Lat. *rostra*) A raised platform around the altar of a church or synagogue for the clergy and choir that is associated with a place of judgment (2 Cor 5:10; Acts 18:12–17).

Body sherds: Unrecognizable pieces of broken pottery that cannot be used as diagnostic sherds.

Bulla: (pl. *bullae*) A seal impression in the clay of an ancient pot or jar.

Canon: (κανών *kanōn* "rule, measuring stick, or pattern". Heb. *qaneh* reed) It conveys the idea of meeting a standard or being complete. The authoritative list of books accepted by the church and regarded as Scripture; generally understood as the OT and NT.

Ceramic typology: The careful observation of changing pottery (ceramic) forms to determine the chronological dating sequence.

Cartonnage: A type of material simlar to *papier-mâché*, where scraps of linen or papyrus were stuck together with plaster or resin to make Ancient Egyptian painted funerary masks and used from the First Intermediate Period to the Roman era.

Chalcolithic: (χαλκός *chalkos* "copper" + λίθος *lithos* "stone"). The first archaeological period to use copper.

Codex: (pl. *codices,* Lat. *caudex,* "tree trunk", "book", or "notebook") An ancient bound manuscript (distinguished from a scroll) comprising a collection of single pages stitched together with a binding to form a book.

Coptic: The religious writing of the Egyptian Coptic Church replacing demotic and uses the Greek alphabet.

Covenant: A covenant is an agreement between two parties. In the OT it means to fetter, bondage, to bind, an intensified oath, making an oath part of a covenant, or a contract. In the NT the term signifies an agreement, testament, or will.

Cuneiform Script: (Lat. *cuneus,* "wedge") Cursive wedge-shaped writing created by using a cut reed or stylus on set clay, dating to 3000 BC. The method is attested in Sumerian, Hittite, Ugaritic, Elamite, and Akkadian texts.

damnatio memoriae: (Lat. "condemnation of memory") Judgment by the Roman Senate, as a form of dishonour upon a person or emperor, who has discredited the Roman State. Their names were often chiselled out of monuments and removed from official documents. A modern designation not used by the Romans.

Demotic: (δημοτική *dēmotikē* "people of the town") An abbreviated and simplified form of the Egyptian Hieratic character invented to more quickly write hieroglyphics for literary and commercial purposes.

Diagnostic sherds: Pieces of pottery, such as rims, handles, bases and painted sherds, which identify the structure of the whole vessel.

Elegiac: A form of ancient poetry, popular in Greek and Latin, using a form of couplets consisting of dactylic hexameter and a pentameter.

Epigraphy: (ἐπιγραφή *epigraphē*; from ἐπι, *epi* "on" + γράφειν *graphein* "to write") The study of ancient languages and writing.

Essenes: ('Εσσαῖου *essaiou*, the "silent" or "reticent" ones) A Jewish sect identified by Josephus and Pliny (*Nat.* 5.17) residing around the Dead Sea and who are generally identified by scholars as the residents of Qumran and the custodians of the Dead Sea Scrolls.

Execration Texts: Egyptian texts (MB2) inscribed with curses upon cities, towns, and people from Palestine and Syria.

Field: The area of excavation on a tel composed of a unit of one or more squares.

First Temple Period: (*ca.* 965–586 BC) The period from the building of Solomon's temple until its destruction.

Flavius Josephus: First-century Jewish historian who wrote for the Romans an account of Jewish history including the Roman assault and conquest of Jerusalem and the Temple Mount.

Gematria: (Heb. *gimatria*; Aramaic *gīmatrěyā*; γεωμετρία *geōmetria*). A traditional Jewish numerical system used to assign values to words or phrases in the Hebrew language. Many commentators believe that 666 represents Emperor Nero's name.

Genizah: (Heb. גניזה "storage"; plural: *genizot* or *genizoth* or *genizahs*) A temporary repository or archive storage area in a Jewish synagogue or cemetery designated for the storage of worn-out or copies of Hebrew texts with mistakes.

Gnostic: (γνωστικός *gnōstikos*, "having knowledge") A sect in the early church that believed that the cosmos emanated from a transcendent god and salvation is achieved through acquiring secret knowledge (γνῶσις *gnōsis*). Gnostics also believe in a dualism between good and evil where there is not a salvation from sin, but rather a deliverance from the ignorance of which caused sin.

Heresy: Teachings and beliefs condemned by the Church as not orthodox and corrupting the dogma.

Herodian: The time period or architectural structures connected with Herod the Great or his family.

Hieroglyphics: (ἱερογλυφικός *hieroglyphikos* from ἱερός *hieros* "sacred" + γλύφω *glyphō* "to carve, write or engrave") Ancient Egyptian script (4th millennium BC) using the form of over 600 pictures or symbols that represent sounds, syllables and words. Nearly all Egyptian state and ceremonial documents that were to be seen by the public were written in this script. Also, funerary and religious texts were copied using the script.

Hoard: A group of coins or other small artifacts discovered together.

Hyksos: (Ὑκσώς, Ὑξώς *Hyxōs* or Ὑκουσσώς *Hykussōs*, Egyptian *heqa khaseshet,* "ruler(s) of the foreign countries") An ethnically mixed group of Western Asiatic Semitc (originating in the Levant i.e., Canaan or Syria) people who overthrew the Egyptian Thirteenth Dynasty and formed the Fifteenth and Sixteenth Dynasties in Egypt (ca. 1674–1548 BC). The Hyksos are known for introducing new tools of warfare into Egypt including the composite bow and the horse-drawn chariot.

***in situ*:** (Lat. "in position" or "on site.") The precise location of an artifact and indicates that it has not been moved from its original location. This is critical for the dating and interpretation of the strata.

Khirbet: (Arabic خربة "ruin" or "ruin on a hill") Arabic equivalent of the Hebrew *tel* (mound). While a tel is genearlly buried underground, the Khirbet is partly exposed above ground.

Koine: (ἡ κοινὴ διάλεκτος *he koinē dialektos* "the common dialect") The Greek language of the Septuagint, the New Testament, and other commercial and private documents.

Lapis Lazuli: A blue stone prize by the ancients for use in artistic creations, such as jewelry and settings for the eyes of idols.

Levant: The eastern Mediterranean countries of Israel, Jordan, Palestine, Syria, Lebanon, Turkey, Cyprus, Egypt and Greece.

Masoretic: (also Massoretic) The oldest accepted Hebrew text of the Bible based on a vowel system with a critical apparatus developed for the Hebrew Bible to make it possible to read the verbal Hebrew language. AD 1st–7th century.

Mastaba: (Egyptian "eternal house") The earliest form of pyramid building by the Egyptians.

Maximalist: In the context of archaeology, maximalists are those who do not limit the historicity of biblical accounts and hold to the view that they contain a *maximum* amount of history. A maximalist is one who finds that the Bible contributes significantly (or prioritize) to our understanding of the historicity of the biblical accounts (See Chapter One).

Minimalist: A minimalist is one who limits the historicity of biblical accounts and believes they contain a *minimal* amount of history. In archaeology, a biblical minimalist is one who finds that the Bible contributes little or nothing at all to our understanding of the historicity of the biblical accounts before about 500 BC (before the return from exile. See Chapter One).

Mikveh: (pl. *miqva'ot*, Heb. *miqveh*, "ritual bath") Stepped immersion pool for Jews to perform their ritual cleansing (immersion) either at home or in public. Most *miqvaot* have a rock cut division (small wall) down the center of the steps to separate pre- and post-ritual immersion.

Mishnah: (מִשְׁנָה "study by repetition", or *Mishna*, pl.

Mishnayot) The first major written redaction of Jewish oral tradition (oral law; Heb. *halakhot*) and the first work of rabbinic literature (ca. AD 220). They are collected as part of the Jewish writing called the Talmud.

Monolith: (Lat. *monolithus*; μονόλιθος *monolithos*, from μόνος *monos* "one" or "single" + λίθος *lithos* "stone") A large single-cut stone.

Mosaic: (Ital. *mosaic, mosaicus;* μούσειος *mouseios*, "belonging to the Muses"). Pictures or inscriptions made from small cut pieces of coloured stone called *tessera* (pl. *tesserae*).

Neolithic: (νεῖος *neîos* "new" + λίθο *lithos* "stone") The new Stone Age period (ca. 10,200–4,500/2,000 BC).

Numismatic: (νόμισμα, *nomisma* "current coin, money, usage", Lat. *Numismatis*). The science and study of coins.

Obelisk: (ὀβελίσκος *obeliskos*; derived from ὀβελός *obelos* "spit, nail, pointed pillar") A four-sided stone pillar with a tapered pyramidal point.

Onomasticon: (ὀνομαστικόν *onomastikon* "belonging to names") An alphabetical list of geographical places mentioned in the Bible, most often identified with the one written by Eusebius and translated by Jerome.

Ossuary: (Lat. *ossuarium* from *ossuarius*, "for bones") A limestone box used to store the bones of the dead (secondary burial) after the flesh has decayed from the bones.

Ostracon: (ὄστρακον *ostracon*; pl. ὄστρακα *ostraka* "a shard of pottery") A piece of pottery or other substance with an inscription on it.

***Otzer*:** (Heb. "treasure") A small pool that feeds "living" water to a *mikveh*.

Palimpsest: (Lat. *palimpsestus* from παλίμψηστος *palimpsēstos* "again scraped") A manuscript that has been scraped clean of the writing or been washed off and made ready to be used again.

Paleography (παλαιός *palaiós* "old" + γράφω *graphō* "to write") The study of ancient writing and texts.

Patriarchs: (πατριάρχης *patriarchēs* from πατριά *patria* "lineage, family"; πατηρ *patēr* "father" + ἄρχειν *archein* "to rule"; Heb. אבות *Avot* or *Abot)* The father of a family. In the Bible it refers to Abraham, Isaac, and Jacob. The patriarchal age is the period during which they lived.

Papyrus: (Lat. pl. *papyri*; πάπυρος *papyros)* A type of paper made from the Egyptian papyrus reed which grows along the Nile River. Papyri was used as writing material during the Old and New Testament periods and the early church.

Parchment: (περγαμηνός *pergamenos* "of Pergamon") Writing material made from animal skins (vellum) that originated in the city of Pergamum, Asia Minor.

Pentateuch: (πεντάτευχος *pentateuchos* "five scrolls") The first five books of the OT: Genesis, Exodus, Leviticus, Numbers and Deuteronomy. Jewish and Christian tradition holds that they were written by Moses.

Period: A time of occupation in the history of a site or stratum (i.e., Early Bronze Age, Iron Age, etc.).

Phase: A subdivision of a period or stratum of occupation. It is sometimes used as a temporary designation during excavation before the stratigraphy is clear.

Potsherd: (sherd) Broken pieces of ancient clay pottery often used to date an archaeological strata.

Provenance: The original location for an artifact. It is sometimes used synonymously with *in-situ*.

Pseudepigrapha: (ψευδής *pseudēs* "false" + επιγραφή *epigraphē* "to inscribe or write") Commonly refers to works of Jewish religious literature written between 200 BC and AD 200. Many are lost and only mentioned by other writers (e.g., *1 En., 2 Bar., 3–4 Macc, As. Mos.,* and *Sib. Or.*).

Rabbah: (Abbr. *Rab.*) A Jewish collection of ancient rabbinical interpretations usually on one of the Books of the Pentateuch (i.e, Genesis Rabbah; *Rab.* Gen 3:15).

Qumran: An archaeological site and located on a plateau north northwest of the Dead Sea that hosted a Jewish community from the Iron Age II through the end of the Second Temple Period (until the destruction by the Romans in AD 68). The Jewish community of the Second Temple period produced and preserved the Dead Sea Scrolls discovered in 1947.

Sanhedrin: : (Heb. סַנְהֶדְרִין *sanhedrín*; συνέδριον *synedrion*, "sitting together," hence "assembly" or "council") Aramaic term designating the Jewish political assembly at Jerusalem that represented the highest magistracy of the country (Josephus *Ant.* 14.5.4). It was also an assembly of twenty to twenty-three men (*m. Sanh.* 1:1) appointed in every city in the biblical land of Israel.

Scarab: (κάραβος *karabos* "beetle") An Egyptian seal made in the shape of a scarab beetle.

Second Temple Period: (536 BC–AD 70) The period from the return of the Babylonian exiles to the destruction of Jerusalem and the Temple by the Romans.

Septuagint: (abbr. LXX, Lat. *septuginta* "The Seventy") The Koine Greek translation of the Hebrew textual tradition that included certain texts which were later included in the canonical Hebrew Bible (Old Testament) made in Alexandria, Egypt by Jewish scholars (ca. 280–150 BC).

Shaft tomb: A type of vertical underground burial chamber dug down into a deep rectangular burial structure. They are often built with a stone floor and lined with mudbrick, masonry or wood. They are deeper than cist graves. This type of tomb was found in the cemeteries on the southeastern side of the Dead Sea.

Sherd: (also *shard*) A fragile fragment of pottery or other artifact collected to determine the pottery assemblage present at a site.

Square: The basic area of excavation developed for precise documentation of the location of artifacts within a numbered grid system. The standard size that is excavated is 5 meters by 5 meters, leaving a 1-meter unexcavated baulk on the north and east side.

Squeeze: Process of pressing a soft substance (i.e., plaster, plastic, etc.) into an inscription to make a reliable reproduction for translating and preservation.

Stele or stela: (στήλη *stēlē* "pillar, upright rock; or column"; pl. στῆλαι *stelai* or *stelae)* Upright stone pillars often containing an inscription to commemorate a military victory, boundary or tombstone.

Stoa: (στοά; pl. *stoae* "base stand") A long, covered hallway to protect the public from the elements, supported with a colonnade of pillars, often with a portico (Lat. *porlicus* "porch") and wall on one side.

Stratum: (Lat. *stratum;* pl. *strata* "a spread for a bed, quilt, or blanket") A horizontal layer of soil containing artifacts and debris representing a particular time period and dated by using pottery and coins.

Tel (Heb. "mound or hill") or **Tell** (Arabic "mound or hill") An unnatural mound created by the repeated destruction and rebuilding of ancient cities on the same site.

Talmud: (לְמוּדָה *talmūd* "instruction, learning") The collection of rabbinic writings that form the authoritative body of Jewish tradition comprising Jewish civil and ceremonial law, including the Mishnah (abbr. m.). There are two versions of the Talmud: the Babylonian Talmud (ca. AD 550 but includes earlier material; abbr. b.) and the later Palestinian or Jerusalem Talmud (ca. AD 450; abbr. y.).

Targum: (תרגום "translation", or "interpretation") Aramaic translation of the Hebrew Bible *(Tanakh)*. Collected over a five-hundred-year period, it is difficult to date individual passages. Fragments were found at Qumran among the Dead Sea Scrolls

Terracotta: (also terra-cotta or terra cotta; Italian from *terra* "earth" + *cotta* "baked" i.e., "baked earth") Reddish clay or unglazed ceramic pottery.

Tessera: (τέσσερα "four"; pl. *tesserae)* Small, individual square stones, ivory, or wood used to create a picture or mosaic. Also, used as a ticket, or token.

Tetrarch: (Lat. *tetrarches)* A governor of the fourth part of a province in Ancient Rome first instituted by Diocletian (AD 292).

Tetragrammaton: (τετραγράμματον "having four letters") It has become a technical term for the name YHWH (יהוה) in the Bible. Ancient Hebrew words did not contain vowels. Because Jews would not say Yahweh occasionally this special name for God was represented by the old Paleo-Hebrew letters or four dots.

Tosefta: (Heb. "supplement") A large collection of writings, written in Mishnaic Hebrew, that are similar to the Mishnah but not as authoritative for religious Jews.

Typology: The study and comparison of the various shapes of artifacts for their classification.

Ugaritic: The Northwest Canaanite Semitic language of Ugarit, spoken by the people of Ugarit (Ras Shamra) and discovered in 1928.

Umayyad: The first Arab dynasty of caliphs who ruled the Muslim Empire (AD 661–750) whose capital was Damascus.

Uncial: A style of manuscript writing that used capital letters and was common for Greek and Latin manuscripts from the fourth to eithth centuries AD.

Vellum: (Fr. *vélin* from *vel,* "veal") A fine parchment prepared from the skin of the young skin of a calf or lamb used by scribes to write documents such as biblical manuscripts.

Votive: (Lat. *vōtīvus* from *vōtum* "vow") An object dedicated in fulfillment of a vow for a religious purpose.

Vulgate: (Lat. *versio vulgate,* "edition in vernacular language") The Latin translation of the Bible by St. Jerome (fourth cent. AD) and the official Bible used by the Roman Catholic Church.

Ziggurat: (Akkadian *ziqqurratu* from *zaqāru* "to build high") A Mesopotamian pyramid-like mound of mud brick constructed with a temple on top. Possible Tower of Babel story (Gen 11).

BIBLIOGRAPHY

PRIMARY SOURCES

Abegg, Jr., Martin G., Michael O. Wise, and Edward M. Cook. *The Dead Sea Scrolls: A New Translation.* San Francisco, Calf.: HarperCollins, 2005.

Aharoni, Yohanan. *Arad Inscriptions.* Jerusalem, Israel: Israel Exploration Society, 1981.

Aharoni, Yohanan, and Joseph Naveh. *Arad Inscriptions [Hebrew].* Jerusalem, Israel: Israel Exploration Society, 1975.

Ahituv, Shmuel. *Echoes from the Past: Hebrew and Cognate Inscriptions from the Biblical Period.* Jerusalem: Carta, 2008.

———. *Handbook of Ancient Hebrew Inscriptions: From the Period of the First Commonwealth and the Beginning of the Second Commonwealth (Hebrew, Philistine, Edomite, Moabite, Ammonite, and the Bileam Inscriptions).* Biblical Encyclopaedia Library 7. Jerusalem, Israel: Bialik, 1992.

Allegro, John M., and A. A. Anderson. *Qumrân Cave 4: I (4Q 158 – 4Q 186).* DJD 5. Oxford: Clarendon, 1968.

Albright, William F. "Palestinian Inscriptions: Moabite Stone." In *The Ancient Near East: An Anthology of Texts and Pictures*, edited by James B. Pritchard, 287. Princeton, N.J.: Princeton University Press, 2010.

———. "Palestinian Inscriptions: The Lachish Ostraca." In *The Ancient Near East: An Anthology of Texts and Pictures*, edited by James B. Pritchard, 292–93. Princeton, N.J.: Princeton University Press, 2010.

———. "Palestinian Inscriptions: The Siloam Inscription." In *The Ancient Near East: An Anthology of Texts and Pictures*, edited by James B. Pritchard. Princeton, N.J.: Princeton University Press, 2010.

Ampelius, Lucius. *Lucii Ampelii Liber Memorialis.* Translated by Edidit Erwin Assmann. Leipzig: Teubner, 1935.

Appian. *Roman History: The Civil Wars, Books 1–3.26.* Translated by Horace White. Vol. 3. LCL 4. Cambridge, Mass.: Harvard University Press, 1913.

Aristides, Aelius. *The Complete Works: Orations.* Translated by C. A. Behr. 2 vols. Leiden: Brill, 1981.

Arrian. *Epictetus Discourses, Books 3–4.* Fragments. The Encheiridion. Translated by W. A. Oldfather. Vol. 2. LCL 218. Cambridge, Mass.: Harvard University Press, 1928.

Baillet, M., Józef Tadeusz Milik, and Roland de Vaux, eds. *Les "petites grottes" de Qumrân.* DJD 3. Oxford: Clarendon, 1962.

Barns, John W. B., Gerald M. Browne, and John C. Shelton, eds. *Nag Hammadi Codices: Greek and Coptic Papyri from the Cartonnage of the Covers.* Leiden: Brill, 1981.

Beckman, Gary M. *Hittite Diplomatic Texts.* Edited by Harry A Hoffner. 2nd ed. Society of Biblical Literature Writings from the Ancient World 7. Atlanta, Ga.: Scholars Press, 1999.

Beld, Scott G., William W. Hallo, and Piotr Michalowski. *The Tablets of Ebla: Concordance and Bibliography.* Winona Lake, Ind.: Eisenbrauns, 1984.

Birdsall, James Neville. *The Bodmer Papyrus of the Gospel of John.* Wheaton, Ill.: Tyndale, 1960.

Böeckh, August, Johannes Franz, Ernst Curtius, and Adolf Kirchhoff. *Corpus inscriptionum graecarum*. 4 vols. Berolini, Italy: Officina academica, 1877.

Budge, E. A. Wallis, and Carl Bezold. *The Tell El-Amarna Tablets in the British Museum with Autotype Facsimiles*. London: British Museum Press, 1892.

Caesar, Julius. *The Civil Wars*. Translated by A. G. Peskett. Vol. 2. LCL 39. Cambridge, Mass.: Harvard University Press, 1914.

Cassius Dio. *Roman History: Books 1–11*. Translated by Ernest Cary and Herbert B. Foster. Vol. 1. 9 vols. LCL 32. Cambridge, Mass.: Harvard University Press, 1914.

———. *Roman History: Books 56–60*. Translated by Ernest Cary and Herbert B. Foster. Vol. 7. 9 vols. LCL 175. Cambridge, Mass.: Harvard University Press, 1924.

———. *Roman History: Books 61–70*. Translated by Ernest Cary and Herbert B. Foster. Vol. 8. 9 vols. LCL 176. Cambridge, Mass.: Harvard University Press, 1924.

Chaniotis, Angelos, Thomas Corsten, N. Papazarkadas, and Rolf A. Tybout, eds. *Supplementum Epigraphicum Graecum*. Leiden: Gieben, 1923.

Charles, R. H., ed. *The Apocrypha and Pseudepigrapha of the Old Testament*. 2 vols. Oxford: Clarendon, 1913.

Charlesworth, James H. *The Dead Sea Scrolls: Hebrew, Aramaic, and Greek Texts With English Translations*. Louisville: Westminster/Knox, 2000.

Chrysostom, Dio. *Discourses 1–11*. Translated by J. W. Cohoon. Vol. 1. 5 vols. LCL 257. Cambridge, Mass.: Harvard University Press, 1939.

———. *Discourses 12-30*. Translated by J. W. Cohoon and H. Lamar Crosby. Vol. 2. 5 vols. LCL 339. Cambridge, Mass.: Harvard University Press, 1939.

———. *Discourses 31–36*. Translated by J. W. Cohoon and H. Lamar Crosby. Vol. 3. 5 vols. LCL 358. Cambridge, Mass.: Harvard University Press, 1940.

———. *Discourses 37–60*. Translated by H. Lamar Crosby. Vol. 4. 5 vols. LCL 376. Cambridge, Mass.: Harvard University Press, 1940.

Cicero, Marcus Tullius. *In Catilinam 1–4. Pro Murena. Pro Sulla. Pro Flacco*. Translated by C. Macdonald. Vol. 10. 29 vols. LCL 324. Cambridge, Mass.: Harvard University Press, 1976.

———. *Letters to Atticus*. Translated by D. R. Shackleton Bailey. Vol. 22. 29 vols. LCL 7. Cambridge, Mass.: Harvard University Press, 1999.

———. *Orations: Pro Lege Manilia. Pro Caecina. Pro Cluentio. Pro Rabirio. Perduellionis Reo*. Translated by H. Grose Hodge. Vol. 9. 29 vols. LCL 198. Cambridge, Mass.: Harvard University Press, 1990.

———. *Orations: Pro Caelio. De Provinciis Consularibus. Pro Balbo*. Translated by R. Gardner. Vol. 13. 29 vols. LCL 447. Cambridge, Mass.: Harvard University Press, 1958.

———. *On the Orator: Books 1–2*. Translated by E. W. Sutton and H Rackham. Vol. 3. 29 vols. LCL 348. Cambridge, Mass.: Harvard University Press, 1942.

———. *On the Republic. On the Laws*. Translated by Clinton W. Keyes. Vol. 16. 29 vols. LCL 213. Cambridge, Mass.: Harvard University Press, 1928.

———. *Philippics 1–6*. Edited by John T. Ramsey and Gesine Manuwald. Translated by D. R. Shackleton Bailey. Vol. 15a. 29 vols. LCL 189. Cambridge, Mass.: Harvard University Press, 2010.

———. *The Verrine Orations I: Against Caecilius. Against Verres, Part 1; Part 2, Books 1–2*. Translated by L. H. G. Greenwood. Vol. 7. 29 vols. LCL 221. Cambridge, Mass.: Harvard University Press, 1928.

Collins, John, Peter W. Flint, James C. VanderKam, George Brooke, Torleif Elgvin, Jonas C. Greenfield, Erik Larson, Carol A. Newsom, Émile Puech, and Lawrence H. Schiffman. *Qumran Cave 4: XVII, Parabiblical Texts, Part 3.* DJD 22. Oxford: Clarendon, 1997.

Commodianus, Gazaeus. "The Instructions of Commodianus in Favour of Christian Discipline, Against the Gods of the Heathens." In *Ante-Nicene Fathers: Fathers of the Third Century: Tertullian, Part Fourth: Minucius Felix; Commodian; Origen, Parts First and Second*, edited by Alexander Roberts, James Donaldson, Philip Schaff, and Henry Wace, translated by Robert Ernest Wallis, New Ed., 4:199–402. Peabody, Mass.: Hendrickson, 1994.

Comfort, Philip. *Encountering the Manuscripts: An Introduction to New Testament Paleography & Textual Criticism.* Nashville, Tenn.: Broadman & Holman Academic, 2005.

Comfort, Philip W., and David P. Barrett, eds. *The Text of the Earliest New Testament Greek Manuscripts.* Wheaton, Ill.: Tyndale, 2001.

Dalley, Stephanie. *Myths from Mesopotamia: Creation, the Flood, Gilgamesh, and Others.* Revised. Oxford World's Classics. Oxford: Oxford University Press, 2009.

Danby, Herbert. *The Mishnah: Translated from the Hebrew with Introduction and Brief Explanatory Notes.* Oxford: Oxford University Press, 1933.

Davies, Graham I., Markus N. A. Bockmuehl, Douglas R. De Lacey, and Andrew J. Poulter. *Ancient Hebrew Inscriptions: Corpus and Concordance.* Vol. 1. Cambridge University Press, 1991.

Davis, Malcolm C., and Ben Outhwaite. *Hebrew Bible Manuscripts in the Cambridge Genizah Collections.* 4 vols. Cambridge University Library Genizah. Cambridge, Mass.: Cambridge University Press, 2003.

DeConick, April D. *The Original Gospel of Thomas in Translation: With a Commentary and New English Translation of the Complete Gospel.* The Library of New Testament Studies. New York: Bloomsbury, 2006.

Dietrich, Manfried, Oswald Loretz, and Joaquín Sanmartín, eds. *The Cuneiform Alphabetic Texts: From Ugarit, Ras Ibn Hani and Other Places (KTU).* 2nd ed. Abhandlungen Zur Literatur Alt-Syrien-Palästinas Und Mesopotamiens 8. Münster: Ugarit, 1995.

Dittenberger, Carl Friedrich Wilhelm, Johann Friedrich Wilhelm Rudolf August Hiller Von Gaertringen, Johannes E. Kirchner, Joannes Pomtow, Georg Wissowa, and Erich Ziebarth, eds. *Sylloges insciptionum graecarum.* 3rd ed. 4 vols. Leipzig: Hirzel, 1915.

Dittenberger, Carl Friedrich Wilhelm, ed. *Orientis Graeci inscriptiones selectae.* 2 vols. Leipzig: Hirzel, 1905.

Dobbs-Allsopp, F. W., J. J. M. Roberts, Choon-Leong Seow, and G. H. Whitaker. *Hebrew Inscriptions: Texts from the Biblical Period of the Monarchy with Concordance.* New Haven, Conn.: Yale University Press, 2004.

Driver, G. R., and John C. Miles, eds. *The Babylonian Laws.* 2 vols. Ancient Texts and Translations. Eugene, Oreg.: Wipf & Stock, 2007.

Eisenman, Robert H., and James M. Robinson. *A Facsimile Edition of the Dead Sea Scrolls.* Washington, D.C.: Biblical Archaeology Society, 1992.

Eisenman, Robert H, and Michael Owen Wise. *The Dead Sea Scrolls Uncovered: The First Complete Translation and Interpretation of 50 Key Documents Withheld for Over 35 Years.* Rockport, Mass.: Element, 1992.

Ellige, K., and Rudolph, eds. *Biblia Hebraica Stuttgartensia.* Stuttgart, Germany: Deutsche Bibelstiftung, 1977.

Elliott, Keith, and Ian Moir. *Manuscripts and the Text of the New Testament: An Introduction for English Readers.* Edinburgh: T&T Clark, 1996.

Epiphanius of Salamis. *Panarion: Book II and III (Sects 47–80, De Fide).* Translated by Frank Williams. Leiden: Brill, 1993.

Eusebius, Pamphilus, and Jerome. *The Bodleian Manuscript of Jerome's Version of the Chronicles of Eusebius.* Edited by John Knight Fotheringham. Oxford: Clarendon, 2012.

Eusebius, Pamphilus. *Ecclesiastical History: Books 1–5.* Translated by Kirsopp Lake. Vol. 1. 2 vols. LCL 153. Cambridge, Mass.: Harvard University Press, 1926.

———. *The Onomasticon of Eusebius Pamphili: Compared with the Version of Jerome and Annotated.* Edited by Noel C. Wolf. Translated by C. Umhau Wolf. Washington, D.C.: Catholic University of America Press, 1971.

Felix, Marcus Minucius, and Tertullian. *Apology. De Spectaculis. Minucius Felix: Octavius.* Translated by T. R. Glover and Gerald H. Randall. LCL 250. Cambridge, Mass.: Harvard University Press, 1931.

Fisher, Loren R., M. C. Astour, and P. D. Miller. *The Claremont Ras Shamra Tablets.* Analecta Orientalia 48. Rome: Gregorian University Press, 1971.

Foster, Benjamin. *The "Epic of Gilgamesh."* Norton Critical Editions. New York: Norton & Company, 2001.

Fränkel, Max, Ernst Fabricius, and Carl Schuchhardt. *Die Inschriften von Pergamon.* Vol. 8. Sonderausgabe Aus Den Altertümern von Pergamon. Berlin: Spemann, 1890.

Freedman, H., and Maurice Simon, eds. *Midrash Rabbah.* 10 vols. London: Soncino, 1992.

Freeman-Grenville, G. S. P., and Joan E. Taylor, eds. *The Onomasticon by Eusebius of Caesarea and the Liber Locorum of Jerome: Palestine in the Fourth Century AD.* Translated by G. S. P. Freedman-Grenville. Jerusalem: Carta, 2003.

Freedman, David Noel, Astrid B. Beck, Bruce Zuckerman, and Marilyn J. Lundberg, eds. *The Leningrad Codex.* Facsimile edition. Grand Rapids: Eerdmans, 1998.

George, Andrew R. *The Babylonian Gilgamesh Epic: Introduction, Critical Edition and Cuneiform Texts HELP.* Vol. 1. 2 vols. Oxford: Oxford University Press, 2003.

———. *The Epic of Gilgamesh.* Rev Ed edition. New York: Penguin Classics, 2003.

Gibson, John C. L. *Textbook of Syrian Semitic Inscriptions: Hebrew and Moabite Inscriptions.* Vol. 1. Oxford: Oxford University Press, 1971.

Glassner, Jean-Jacques. *Mesopotamian Chronicles.* Edited by Benjamin R. Foster. Writings from the Ancient World 19. Atlanta, Ga.: SBL, 2004.

Goldwurm, Hersh, and Nosson Scherman, eds. *The Talmud: Schottenstein Edition.* 73 vols. Brooklyn, N.Y.: Mesorah, 1990.

Grayson, A. Kirk, and James Novotny. *The Royal Inscriptions of Sennacherib, King of Assyria: Part 1.* Royal Inscriptions of the Neo-Assyrian Period 3.1. Winona Lake, IN: Eisenbrauns, 2012.

———. *The Royal Inscriptions of Sennacherib, King of Assyria: Part 2.* Royal Inscriptions of the Neo-Assyrian Period 3.2. Winona Lake, IN: Eisenbrauns, 2014.

Grayson, Albert Kirk. *Assyrian and Babylonian Chronicles.* Texts from Cuneiform Sources 5. Locust Valley: Augustin, 1975.

———. *Assyrian Rulers of the Early First Millennium BC I (858-745 BC).* Vol. 1. The Royal Inscriptions of Mesopotamia: Assyrian Periods 2. Toronto, Can.: University of Toronto Press, 1991.

———. *Assyrian Rulers of the Early First Millennium BC II (858-745 BC).* Vol. 3. The Royal Inscriptions of Mesopotamia: Assyrian Periods 3. Toronto, Can.: University of Toronto Press, 1987.

Greenfield, Jonas C., and Bezalel Porten. *The Bisitun Inscription of Darius the Great: Aramaic Version.* Vol. 5 The Aramaic Versions of the Achaemenian Inscriptions, etc. 5 vols. Corpus Inscriptionum

Iranicarum, Part I Inscriptions of Ancient Iran. London: Corpus Inscriptionum Iranicarum, 1982.

Grenfell, Bernard Pyne, and Arthur Surridge Hunt. *The Oxyrhynchus Papyri.* 75 vols. London: Egypt Exploration Society, 2009.

Haase, Wolfgang, and Hildegard Temporini, eds. *Aufstieg und Niedergang der römischen Welt: Geschichte und Kultur Roms im Spiegel der neueren Forschung. Principat. Religion. 2. 26.* Berlin: de Gruyter, 1995.

Hallo, William W., and K. Lawson Younger, eds. *The Context of Scripture: Archival Documents from the Biblical World.* 3 vols. Leiden: Brill Academic, 2002.

Harold Mattingly, and Edwars Sydenham, eds. *Roman Imperial Coinage: Vespasian to Hadrian (69–138).* Vol. 2. 10 vols. London: Spink & Son, 1926.

Harper, Robert Francis. *Assyrian and Babylonian Literature: Selected Translations.* The World's Great Books. New York: Appleton & Company, 1901.

———. *The Code of Hammurabi.* Union, NJ: Lawbook Exchange, 2010.

Heimpel, Wolfgang. *Letters to the King of Mari: A New Translation, With Historical Introduction, Notes, and Commentary.* Mesopotamian Civilizations 12. Ann Arbor, Mich.: American Oriental Society, 2003.

Herodotus. Historia: *The Persian Wars: Books 1–2.* Translated by Alfred Denis Godley. Vol. 1. 4 vols. LCL 117. Cambridge, Mass.: Harvard University Press, 1920.

———. *Historia: The Persian Wars: Books 5–7.* Translated by Alfred Denis Godley. Vol. 3. 4 vols. LCL 119. Cambridge, Mass.: Harvard University Press, 1922.

Hoftijzer, Jacob, and G. Van der Kooij. *Aramaic Texts from Deir 'Alla.* Leiden: Brill, 1976.

Homer. *Iliad: Books 13–24.* Edited by William F. Wyatt. Translated by A. T. Murray. Vol. 2. 2 vols. LCL 171. Cambridge, Mass.: Harvard University Press, 1925.

Horsley, G. H. R, and Stephen R. Llewelyn. *New Documents Illustrating Early Christianity: A Review of the Greek Inscriptions and Papyri Published in 1976.* Vol. 1. Grand Rapids: Eerdmans, 2005.

Hughes, George R., and The Epigraphic Survey. *The Epigraphic Survey, Reliefs and Inscriptions at Karnak, Volume III: The Bubastite Portal.* Oriental Institute Publications 74. Chicago, Ill.: The University of Chicago Press, 1954.

Israeli, Yael, and Ruth Hestrin. *Inscriptions Reveal: Documents from the Time of the Bible, the Mishna and the Talmud.* Jerusalem, Israel: Israel Museum, 1973.

Izreʿel, Shlomo. *The Amarna Scholarly Tablets.* Cuneiform Monographs 9. Leiden: Brill, 1997.

Jerome. *On Illustrious Men.* Edited and translated by Thomas P. Halton. Washington, D.C.: Catholic University of America Press, 1999.

Josephus, Flavius. *Jewish Antiquities: Volume I, Book 1–3.* Translated by H. St. J. Thackeray. Vol. 5. 13 vols. LCL 242. Cambridge, Mass.: Harvard University Press, 1930.

———. *Jewish Antiquities: Volume IX, Book 20.* Translated by Louis H. Feldman. Vol. 13. 13 vols. LCL 456. Cambridge, Mass.: Harvard University Press, 1965.

———. *Jewish Antiquities: Volume VI, Books 14–15.* Translated by Ralph Marcus and Allen Wikgren. Vol. 10. 13 vols. LCL 489. Cambridge, Mass.: Harvard University Press, 1943.

———. *Jewish Antiquities: Volume VII, Books 16–17.* Translated by Ralph Marcus and Allen Wikgren. Vol. 11. 13 vols. LCL 410. Cambridge, Mass.: Harvard University Press, 1963.

———. *Jewish Antiquities: Volume VIII, Books 18–19.* Translated by Louis H. Feldman. Vol. 12. 13 vols. LCL 433. Cambridge, Mass.: Harvard University Press, 1965.

———. *The Jewish War: Volume I, Books 1–2.* Translated by H. St. J. Thackeray. Vol. 2. 13 vols. LCL 203. Cambridge, Mass.: Harvard University Press, 1927.

———. *The Jewish War: Volume II, Books 3–4.* Translated by H. St. J. Thackeray. Vol. 3. 13 vols. LCL 487. Cambridge, Mass.: Harvard University Press, 1927.

———. *The Jewish War: Volume III, Books 5–7.* Translated by H. St. J. Thackeray. Vol. 4. 13 vols. LCL 210. Cambridge, Mass.: Harvard University Press, 1928.

———. *The Life. Against Apion.* Translated by H. St. J. Thackeray. Vol. 1. 13 vols. LCL 186. Cambridge, Mass.: Harvard University Press, 1926.

———. *The Works of Josephus: Complete and Unabridged.* Translated by William Whiston. New Updated. Peabody, Mass.: Hendrickson, 1980.

Kahle, Paul Ernst. *The Cairo Geniza.* 2nd ed. Oxford: Blackwell, 1959.

Kelley, Page H., Timothy G. Crawford, and Daniel S. Mynatt. *The Masorah of Biblia Hebraica Stuttgartensia: Introduction and Annotated Glossary.* Grand Rapids: Eerdmans, 1998.

Kent, John Harvey. *The Inscriptions, 1926 to 1950: Corinth.* Vol. 8, Part 3. Athens: American School of Classical Studies at Athens, 1966.

Kenyon, Frederic G. *The Codex Alexandrinus.* Facsimile edition. 4 vols. London: Trustee of the British Museum, 1915.

King, Leonard W. *Enuma Elish: The Seven Tablets of Creation; the Babylonian and Assyrian Legends Concerning the Creation of the World and of Mankind.* 2 vols. London: Luzac, 1902.

———. *The Code of Hammurabi.* Calgary, Alberta: Theophania, 2012.

Kitchen, Kenneth A. *Ramesside Inscriptions: Merenptah and the Late Nineteenth Dynasty: Translated and Annotated, Translations.* Vol. 4. Oxford: Wiley-Blackwell, 2003.

Knibb, Michael Anthony. "Martyrdom and Ascension of Isaiah: A New Translation and Introduction." In *The Old Testament Pseudepigrapha: Apocalyptic Literature and Testaments,* edited by James H. Charlesworth, 1:143–76. Peabody, Mass.: Hendrickson, 1983.

Knudtzon, Jörgen A. *Die El-Amarna-Tafeln, mit Einleitung und Erläuterungen.* 2 vols. Leipzig: Hinrichs, 1915.

Lambert, Wilfred G., and Alan R. Millard. *Atra-Hasis: The Babylonian Story of the Flood.* Edited by Alan R. Millard and Miguel Civil. Winona Lake, Ind.: Eisenbrauns, 1999.

Leichty, Erie. *Royal Inscriptions of Esarhaddon, King of Assyria 680-699 BC.* The Royal Inscriptions of the Neo-Assyrian Period 4. Winona Lake, Ind.: Eisenbrauns, 2011.

LeMaire, André. *Inscriptions Hébraïques. I. Les Ostraca.* Vol. 1. Littératures Anciennes Du Proche-Orient 9. Paris: Les Éditions du Cerf, 1977.

Lichtheim, Miriam. *Ancient Egyptian Literature: Late Period.* 2nd ed. Vol. 3. 3 vols. Berkeley, Calf.: University of California Press, 2006.

———. *Ancient Egyptian Literature: The New Kingdom.* 2nd ed. Vol. 2. 3 vols. Berkeley, Calf.: University of California Press, 2006.

———. *Ancient Egyptian Literature: The Old and Middle Kingdoms.* 2nd ed. Vol. 1. 3 vols. Berkeley, Calf.: University of California Press, 2006.

Lindenberger, James M. *Ancient Aramaic and Hebrew Letters.* 2nd ed. Writings from the Ancient World 14. Atlanta, Ga.: SBL, 2003.

Lipman, Eugene J., ed. *The Mishnah: Oral Teachings of Judaism.* Berlin: Schocken, 1974.

Lightfoot, Joseph B. *The Apostolic Fathers: Greek Texts and English Translations.* Edited by Michael W. Holmes. Translated by J. R. Harmer. 2nd ed. Rev. Grand Rapids: Baker Academic, 1989.

Livy. *History of Rome: Books 3-4.* Translated by B. O. Foster. Vol. 2. 14 vols. LCL 133. Cambridge, Mass.: Harvard University Press, 1922.

———. *History of Rome: Books 8-10.* Translated by B. O. Foster. Vol. 4. 14 vols. LCL 191. Cambridge, Mass.: Harvard University Press, 1926.

Llewelyn, Stephen R., and Dionysia van Beek. "Reading the Temple Warning as a Greek Visitor." *Journal for the Study of Judaism* 42, no. 1 (2011): 1–22.

Llewelyn, Stephen R., and J. R. Harrison. *New Documents Illustrating Early Christianity: A Review of the Greek and Other Inscriptions and Papyri Published Between 1988 and 1992.* Edited by E. J. Bridge. Vol. 10. Grand Rapids: Eerdmans, 2012.

Loewinger, D. S., ed. *Codex Cairo of the Bible from the Karaite Synagogue at Abbasiya.* Facsimile Edition. Jerusalem, Israel: Makor, 1971.

Lubetski, Meir, and Edith Lubetski, eds. *New Inscriptions and Seals Relating to the Biblical World.* Atlanta, Ga.: SBL, 2012.

Lucian of Samosata. *Anacharsis or Athletics. Menippus or The Descent into Hades. On Funerals. A Professor of Public Speaking. Alexander the False Prophet. Essays in Portraiture. Essays in Portraiture Defended. The Goddesse of Surrye.* Translated by A. M. Harmon. Vol. 4. 8 vols. LCL 162. Cambridge, Mass.: Harvard University Press, 1925.

Luckenbill, Daniel David. *Ancient Records of Assyria and Babylon: Historical Records of Assyria from Sargon to the End.* Vol. 2. 2 vols. Chicago, Ill.: University Of Chicago Press, 1927.

———. *The Annals of Sennacherib.* Eugene, Oreg.: Wipf & Stock, 2005.

Macrobius. *Saturnalia: Books 1-2.* Translated by Robert A. Kaster. Vol. 1. 3 vols. LCL 510. Cambridge, Mass.: Harvard University Press, 2011

Martínez, Florentino García, and W. G. E. Watson. *The Dead Sea Scrolls Translated: The Qumran Texts in English.* 2nd ed. Leiden: Brill Academic, 1997.

Martial, Marcus Valerius. *Epigrams: Spectacles, Books 1–5.* Edited and translated by D. R. Shackleton Bailey. Vol. 1. 3 vols. LCL 94. Cambridge, Mass.: Harvard University Press, 1999.

Mattingly, Harold B. *Coins of the Roman Empire in the British Museum.* 6 vols. London: British Museum, 1965.

Mattingly, Harold B., Edward Allen Sydenham, and Carol Humphrey Vivian Sutherland, eds. *The Roman Imperial Coinage.* 13 vols. London, U.K.: Spink & Son, 1923.

Meritt, Benjamin D. *Greek Inscriptions, 1896-1927.* Part 1. Corinth Vol. 8. Athens: American School of Classical Studies, 1931.

Meshorer, Ya'aḳov. *Jewish Coins of the Second Temple Period.* Tel-Aviv, Israel: Am Hassefer and Masada, 1967.

Meyer, Marvin, and James M. Robinson, eds. *The Nag Hammadi Scriptures: The Revised and Updated Translation of Sacred Gnostic Texts Complete in One Volume.* New York: HarperCollins, 2009.

Millard, Alan R. "The Babylonian Chronicle." In *The Context of Scripture: Archival Documents from the Biblical World*, edited by William W. Hallo and K. Lawson Younger, 1:467–68. Leiden: Brill Academic, 2002.

———. "The Tell Dan Stele." In *The Context of Scripture: Canonical Compositions from the Biblical World*, edited by William W. Hallo and K. Lawson Younger, 2:161–62. Leiden: Brill Academic, 2002.

Mitchell, Stephen. *Gilgamesh: A New English Version.* New York: Free Press, 2006.

Moldenke, Charles E., ed. *Papyrus D'Orbiney (British Museum): The Hieroglyphic Transcription.* Watchung, N.J.: Elsinore, 1900.

Moran, William L. *The Amarna Letters.* Baltimore, Md.: Johns Hopkins University Press, 2000.

Musée du Louvre. *Textes cunéiformes.* Département des Antiquités Orientales. Paris, France: Geuthner, 1910.

Oppenheim, A. Leo. "Assyrian and Babylonian Historical Texts." In *The Ancient Near East: An Anthology of Texts and Pictures*, edited by James B. Pritchard, 247–86. Princeton, N.J.: Princeton University Press, 2010.

Orelli, Johann Caspar von, and Wilhelm Henzen, eds. *Inscriptionum Latinarum selectarum amplissima collectio ad illustrandam Romanae antiquitatis.* Vol. 2. Zürich: Fuesslini et Sociorum, 1828.

Ovid. *Metamorphoses: Books 1–8.* Edited by J. P. Goold. Translated by Frank Justus Miller. Vol. 1. 6 vols. Loeb Classical Library 42. Cambridge, Mass.: Harvard University Press, 1916.

Pagels, Elaine. *The Gnostic Gospels.* New York: Random House, 2004.

Parpola, Simo. *The Standard Babylonian Epic of Gilgamesh: Cuneiform Text, Transliteration, Glossary, Indices, and Sign List.* SAA Cuneiform Texts 1. Helsinki: Eisenbrauns, 1997.

Parsons, Peter John, and N. Gonis, eds. ***The Oxyrhynchus Papyri.*** Vol. 83. Graeco-Roman Memoirs. London, UK: Egypt Exploration Society, 2018.

Paton, William R., trans. *The Greek Anthology: Book 13: Epigrams in Various Metres. Book 14: Arithmetical Problems, Riddles, Oracles. Book 15: Miscellanea. Book 16: Epigrams of the Planudean Anthology Not in the Palatine Manuscript.* Vol. 5. Loeb Classical Library 86. Cambridge, Mass.: Harvard University Press, 1918.

Patterson, Stephen J., Hans-Gebhard Bethge, and James M. Robinson. *The Fifth Gospel: The Gospel of Thomas Comes of Age.* New York: Bloomsbury Academic, 1998.

Pausanias, *Description of Greece, Books 3–5: Laconia, Messenia, Elis 1.* Translated by W. H. S. Jones and Henry A Ormerod. Vol. 2. 5 vols. LCL 188. Cambridge, Mass.: Harvard University Press, 1926.

———. *Description of Greece, Books 6–8.21: Elis 2, Achaia, Arcadia.* Translated by W. H. S. Jones. Vol. 3. 5 vols. LCL 272. Cambridge, Mass.: Harvard University Press, 1933.

Pettinato, Giovanni, and A. Alberti. *Catalogo Dei Testi Cuneiformi Di Tell Mardikh-Ebla.* Materiali Epigrafici Di Ebla 1. Naples: Istituto Universitario Orientale di Napoli, 1979.

Pettinato, Giovanni. *Old Canaanite Cuneiform Texts of the Third Millennium.* Vol. 7. Sources and Monographs. Monographs on the Ancient Near East 1. Malibu, Calf.: Undena, 1979.

———. *The Archives of Ebla: An Empire Inscribed in Clay.* Translation of Ebla: Un Impero Inciso Nell'Argilla. Garden City, N.Y.: Doubleday, 1981.

Philo. *Every Good Man Is Free. On the Contemplative Life. On the Eternity of the World. Against Flaccus. Apology for the Jews. On Providence.* Translated by F. H. Colson. Vol. 9. 10 vols. LCL 363. Cambridge, Mass.: Harvard University Press, 1941.

———. *On Abraham. On Joseph. On Moses.* Translated by F. H. Colson. Vol. 6. 10 vols. LCL 289. Cambridge, Mass.: Harvard University Press, 1935.

———. *On the Confusion of Tongues. On the Migration of Abraham. Who Is the Heir of Divine Things? On Mating with the Preliminary Studies.* Translated by F. H. Colson and G. H. Whitaker. Vol. 4. 10 vols. LCL 261. Cambridge, Mass.: Harvard University Press, 1932.

———. *On the Embassy to Gaius. General Indexes.* Edited by J. W. Earp. Translated by F. H. Colson. Vol. 10. 10 vols. LCL 379. Cambridge, Mass.: Harvard University Press, 1962.

———. *Supplement II: Questions on Exodus.* Translated by Ralph Marcus. LCL 401. Cambridge, Mass.: Harvard University Press, 1953.

Philostratus, Flavius. *Life of Apollonius of Tyana: Books 1–4.* Translated by Christopher P. Jones. Vol. 1. 4 vols. LCL 16. Cambridge, Mass.: Harvard University Press, 2005.

Pliny the Elder. *Natural History: Books 3–7.* Translated by H. Rackham. Vol. 2. 10 vols. LCL 352. Cambridge, Mass.: Harvard University Press, 1942.

———. *Natural History: Books 12–16.* Translated by H. Rackham. Vol. 4. 10 vols. LCL 370. Cambridge, Mass.: Harvard University Press, 1945.

———. *Natural History: Books 36–37.* Translated by D. E. Eichholz. Vol. 10. 10 vols. LCL 419. Cambridge, Mass.: Harvard University Press, 1962.

Pliny the Younger. *Letters, Books 8–10: Panegyricus.* Translated by Betty Radice. Vol. 2. 2 vols. LCL 59. Cambridge, Mass.: Harvard University Press, 1969.

Poebel, Arno. *Historical and Grammatical Texts.* PBS 5. Philadelphia, Pa.: University of Pennsylvania Museum, 1914.

Pritchard, James Bennett. *Ancient Near Eastern Texts Relating to the Old Testament with Supplement.* 3rd ed. Princeton, N.J.: Princeton University Press, 1969.

———. , ed. *The Ancient Near East, Volume 1: An Anthology of Texts and Pictures.* Princeton, N.J.: Princeton University Press, 1973.

Procopius of Caesarea. *History of the Wars: Books 3-4. (Vandalic War).* Translated by H. B. Dewing. Vol. 2. 7 vols. LCL 81. Cambridge, Mass.: Harvard University Press, 1914.

———. *The Anecdota or Secret History.* Translated by H. B. Dewing. Vol. 6. 7 vols. LCL 290. Cambridge, Mass.: Harvard University Press, 1935.

———. *On Buildings. General Index.* Translated by H. B. Dewing and Glanville Downey. Vol. 7. 7 vols. LCL 343. Cambridge, Mass.: Harvard University Press, 1940.

Preisigke, Friedrich, ed. *Sammelbuch Griechischer Urkunden aus Ägypten.* 5 vols. Strassburg: Trübner, 1915.

Rainey, Anson F. *El Amarna Tablets 359-379: Supplement to J. A.. Knudtzon, Die El-Amarna-Tafeln.* Alter Orient Und Altes. Testament 8. Kevelaer, Germany: Butzon & Bercker, 1978.

Rawlinson, Henry C. *The Cuneiform Inscriptions of Western Asia. Vol. III. A Selection from the Miscellaneous Inscriptions of Assyria.* London: Bowler, 1870.

———. *The Persian Cuneiform Inscription at Behistun, Decyphered and Translated.* London: Parker, 1847.

———. *The Persian Cuneiform Inscription at Behistun, Decyphered and Translated; With a Memoir on Persian Cuneiform Inscriptions in General, and on That of Behistun in Particular.* Journal of the Royal Asiatic Society of Great Britain and Ireland, 1848.

Reed, Stephen A. *The Dead Sea Scrolls Catalogue: Documents, Photographs, and Museum Inventory Numbers.* Edited by Marilyn J. Lundberg and Michael B. Phelps. SBL Resources for Biblical Study 32. Atlanta, Ga.: Scholars Press, 1994.

Richardson, M. E. J. *Hammurabi's Laws: Text, Translation and Glossary.* Edinburgh: T&T Clark, 2005.

Robert, Louis. *Collection Froehner: I. Inscriptions grecques.* Paris: Éditions des Bibliothèques nationales, 1936.

Roberts, Alexander, James Donaldson, Philip Schaff, and Henry Wace, eds. *Ante-Nicene Fathers.* New Ed. 10 vols. Peabody, Mass.: Hendrickson, 1994.

———. *Nicene and Post-Nicene Fathers, Series II.* 14 vols. Peabody, Mass.: Hendrickson, 1994.

Robinson, James M. *From the Nag Hammadi Codices to the Gospel of Mary and the Gospel of Judas.* Institute for Antiquity and Christianity Occasional Papers 48. Claremont, Calf.: Institute for Antiquity & Christianity, 2006.

———., ed. *The Nag Hammadi Library: A Translation of the Gnostic Scriptures.* London: HarperCollins, 1990.

———. *The Story of the Bodmer Papyri, the First Christian Monastic Library The Story of the Bodmer Papyri: From the First Monaster's Library in Upper Egypt to Geneva and Dublin.* Nashville, Tenn.: James Clarke & Co., 2013.

Rodkinson, Michael L. *New Edition of the Babylonian Talmud: Original Text, Edited, Corrected, Formulated and Translated into English.* 20 vols. Boston, Mass.: The Talmud Society, 1918.

Rost, Paul. *Die Keilschrifttexte Tiglat-Pilesers III.* Leipzig: Pfeiffer, 1893.

Sallust, Gaius. *The War with Catiline. The War with Jugurtha.* Translated by John C. Rolfe and John T. Ramsey. Vol. 1. 2 vols. LCL 116. Cambridge, Mass.: Harvard University Press, 2013.

Sanders, J. A. *The Psalms Scroll of Qumran Cave 11.* DJD 4. Oxford: Oxford University Press, 1965.

Schmitt, Rüdiger. *The Bisitun Inscriptions of Darius the Great: Old Persian Text.* Vol. 1 The Old Persian Inscriptions Texts. 5 vols. Corpus Inscriptionum Iranicarum, Part I Inscriptions of Ancient Iran. London: Corpus Inscriptionum Iranicarum, 1991.

Seneca, Lucius Annaeus. *Moral Essays, Volume I De Providentia. De Constantia. De Ira. De Clementia.* Translated by John W. Basore. Vol. 1. 10 vols. LCL 214. Cambridge, Mass.: Harvard University Press, 1928.

Simpson, William Kelly, ed. *The Literature of Ancient Egypt: An Anthology of Stories, Instructions, Stelae, Autobiographies, and Poetry.* Translated by Robert K. Ritner, Vincent A. Tobin, and Edward F. Wente, Jr. New Haven, Conn.: Yale University Press, 2003.

Skeat, Theodore C., and H. J. M. Milne. *The Codex Sinaiticus and the Codex Alexandrinus.* London: Trustee of the British Museum, 1963.

Smelik, Klaas A. D. *Writings from Ancient Israel: A Handbook of Historical and Religious Documents.* Louisville: Westminster/Knox, 1991.

Smith, George E., and Andrew Dickson White. *The Chaldean Account of Genesis.* Elibron Classics. Charleston, SC: Nabu, 2010.

Smith, Sidney. *Assyrian Sculptures in the British Museum: From Shalmaneser III to Sennacherib.* London: The British Museum, 1938.

———. *Babylonian Historical Texts Relating to the Capture and Downfall of Babylon.* London: Methuen & Co, 1924.

Strabo. *Geography: Books 3–5.* Translated by Horace Leonard Jones. Vol. 2. 8 vols. LCL 50. Cambridge, Mass.: Harvard University Press, 1923.

———. *Geography: Books 13–14.* Translated by Horace Leonard Jones. Vol. 6. 8 vols. LCL 223. Cambridge, Mass.: Harvard University Press, 1929.

Suetonius Tranquillus, Gaius. *Lives of the Caesars: Claudius. Nero. Galba, Otho, and Vitellius. Vespasian. Titus, Domitian. Lives of Illustrious Men: Grammarians and Rhetoricians. Poets (Terence. Virgil. Horace. Tibullus.*

Persius. Lucan). *Lives of Pliny the Elder and Passienus Crispus.* Translated by J. C. Rolfe. Vol. 2. LCL 38. Cambridge, Mass.: Harvard University Press, 1914.

———. *The Lives of the Caesars: Julius. Augustus. Tiberius. Gaius. Caligula.* Translated by J. C. Rolfe. Vol. 1. LCL 31. Cambridge, Mass.: Harvard University Press, 1914.

———. *The Twelve Caesars.* Edited by Michael Grant. Translated by Robert Graves. Rev. Penguin Classics. Harmondsworth: Penguin, 1987.

Sukenik, Eleazar Lipa. *The Dead Sea Scrolls of the Hebrew University.* Jerusalem: Hebrew University Press Magnes, 1955.

Sussman, Lewis A. *The Declamations of Calpurnius Flaccus: Text, Translation, and Commentary.* Leiden: Brill, 1994.

Tacitus, Cornelius. *Annals: Books 13–16.* Translated by John Jackson. Vol. 5. 5 vols. LCL 322. Cambridge, Mass.: Harvard University Press, 1937.

———. *Annals: Books 4–6, 11–12.* Translated by John Jackson. Vol. 4. 5 vols. LCL 312. Cambridge, Mass.: Harvard University Press, 1937.

———. *Histories: Books 1-3.* Translated by Clifford H. Moore. Vol. 2. 5 vols. LCL 111. Cambridge, Mass.: Harvard University Press, 1925.

———. *Histories: Books 4-5. Annals: Books 1-3.* Translated by Clifford H. Moore and John E. Jackson. Vol. 3. 5 vols. LCL 249. Cambridge, Mass.: Harvard University Press, 1931.

Talmon, Shemaryahu, and Yigael Yadin, eds. *Masada VI:The Yigael Yadin Excavations 1963-1965: Hebrew Fragments from Masada.* The Masada Reports 6. Jerusalem, Israel: Israel Exploration Society and The Hebrew University of Jerusalem, 1999.

Testa, Emmanuele. *Cafarnao IV. I Graffiti Della Casa Di S. Pietro.* Studium Biblicum Franciscannum 19. Jerusalem, Israel: Franciscan Printing Press, 1972.

Theophanes. *Chronographia.* Edited by Carl de Boer. 2 vols. Leipzig, 1883.

Thomas, D. Winston, ed. *Documents from Old Testament Times.* Ancient Texts and Translations. Eugene, Oreg.: Wipf & Stock, 2005.

Tigchelaar, Eibert J. C., and Florentino García Martínez. *The Dead Sea Scrolls, Study Edition.* 2 vols. Grand Rapids: Eerdmans, 1999.

Tischendorf, Constantine. *Codex Ephraemi Syri Rescriptus, Sive Fragmenta Veteris Testamenti.* Lipsiae: Tauchnitz Jr., 1845.

———. *Novum Testamentum Vaticanum.* Lipsiae: Giesecke & Devrient, 1867.

Torczyner, Harry, J. Lankester Harding, Alkin Lewis, and J. L. Starkey. *Lachish I (Tell Ed Duweir): Lachish Letters.* Oxford: Oxford University Press, 1938.

Tueller, Michael A., ed. *The Greek Anthology: Book 1: Christian Epigrams. Book 2: Description of the Statues in the Gymnasium of Zeuxippus. Book 3: Epigrams in the Temple of Apollonis at Cyzicus. Book 4: Prefaces to the Various Anthologies. Book 5: Erotic Epigrams.* Translated by William R. Paton. Vol. 1. Loeb Classical Library 67. Cambridge, Mass.: Harvard University Press, 2014.

Ulmer, Rivka, ed. *A Synoptic Edition of Pesiqta Rabbati Based upon All Extant. Manuscripts and the Editio Princeps.* 3 vols. South Florida Studies in the History of Judaism 155. Lanham, Md.: University Press of America, 2002.

Ulrich, Eugene, Frank Moore Cross, and Sidnie White Crawford, eds. *Qumran Cave 4: IX. Deuteronomy, Joshua, Judges, Kings.* DJD 14. Oxford: Clarendon, 1999.

Victorinus, Apringius of Beja, Caesarius of Arles, and The Venerable Bede. *Latin Commentaries on Revelation: Victorinus of Petovium, Apringius of Beja, Caesarius of Arles and Bede the Venerable.* Edited and translated by William C. Weinrich. Ancient Christian Texts. Downers Grove, Ill.: IVP Academic, 2012.

Virgil. *Eclogues. Georgics. Aeneid: Books 1-6.* Edited by G. P. Goold. Translated by H. Rushton Fairclough. Vol. 1. 2 vols. LCL 63. Cambridge, Mass.: Harvard University Press, 1999.

von Voigtlander, Elizabeth. *The Bisitun Inscription of Darius the Great: Babylonian Version.* Vol. 2 The Babylonian Versions of the Achaemenian Inscriptions. 5 vols. Corpus inscriptionum iranicarum, Part I Inscriptions of Ancient Iran. London: Corpus Inscriptionum Iranicarum, 1978.

Wacholder, Ben Zion, and Martin G. Abegg. *A Preliminary Edition of the Unpublished Dead Sea Scrolls: The Hebrew and Aramaic Texts from Cave Four.* 4 vols. Washington, D.C.: Biblical Archaeology Society, 1996.

Waldstein, Michael, and Frederik Wisse, eds. *The Apocryphon of John: Synopsis of Nag Hammadi Codices II,1, III,1, and IV,1 with BG 8502,2.* Nag Hammadi and Manichaean Studies: The Coptic Gnostic Library 33. Leiden: Brill Academic, 1995.

Wankel, Hermann, ed. *Die Inschriften von Ephesos.* 8 vols. Inschrifien griechischer Stadte aus Kleinasien 11.1-17.4. Bonn: Habelt, 1979.

Wessner, Paul, ed. *Scholia in Juvenalem Uetustiora.* Leipzig: Teubner, 1931.

Westenholz, Joan Goodnick. *Legends of the Kings of Akkade: The Texts.* Winona Lake, Ind.: Eisenbrauns, 1997.

Wilkinson, John, ed. *Egeria's Travels: Translated with Supporting Documents and Notes.* Translated by John Wilkinson. 3rd ed. Warminster: Aris & Phillips, 1999.

Winckler, Hugo. *The Tell-El-Amarna Letters.* Translated by J. Metcalf. New York: Metcalf, 1896.

Wiseman, Donald J. *Chronicles of Chaldaean Kings (626-556 BC) in the British Museum.* London: Trustee of the British Museum, 1961.

Wright, David F., Sinclair B. Ferguson, and James I. Packer, eds. *New Dictionary of Theology.* Downers Grove, Ill.: InterVarsity, 1988.

Wright, William. *Apocryphal Acts of the Apostles.* 2 vols. London: Williams & Norgate, 1871.

SECONDARY SOURCES

Abel, F. M. "Notes Complemenaires Sur La Mer Morte." *RB* 38 (1929): 237–60.

Abusch, Tzvi. "The Development and Meaning of the Epic of Gilgamesh: An Interpretive Essay." *JAOS* 121, no. 4 (2001): 614–22.

Ackerman, Susan. "Assyria in the Bible." In *Assyrian Reliefs from the Palace of Ashurnasirpal II: A Cultural Biography*, edited by Ada Cohen and Steven E. Kangas, 124–42. Hanover, N.H.: University of New England, 2010.

Adams, Edward. "The Ancient Church at Megiddo: The Discovery and an Assessment of Its Significance." *ExpTim* 120, no. 2 (2008): 62–69.

Adey, John W. "Social and Historical Aspects of the Lachish Letters." MPhil, University of Cambridge, 2012.

Agnes, Michael E. *Webster's New World College Dictionary*. 4th ed. Cleveland, Ohio: Webster's New World, 1999.

Aharoni, Yohanan. "Arad: Its Inscriptions and Temple." *BA* 31, no. 1 (1968): 1–32.

———. *The Land of the Bible: A Historical Geography*. Translated by Anson F. Rainey. 2nd ed. Louisville: Westminster/Knox, 1981.

Ahlstrom, Gosta W. "The Seal of Shema." *SJOT* 7 (1993): 208–13.

Aland, Kurt, and Barbara Aland. *The Text of the New Testament an Introduction to the Critical Editions and to the Theory and Practice of Modern Textual Criticism*. Translated by Erroll F. Rhodes. 2nd ed. Grand Rapids: Eerdmans, 1995.

Albright, William F. "A Biblical Fragment from the Maccabean Age: The Nash Papyrus." *JBL* 56 (1937): 145–76.

———. "The Gezer Calendar." *BASOR* 92 (1943): 16–26.

Alexander, Patrick, John F. Kutsko, and Shirley Decker-Lucke. *The SBL Handbook of Style: For Ancient Near Eastern, Biblical, and Early Christian Studies*. Peabody, Mass.: Hendrickson, 1999.

Alföldy, Géza. "Pontius Pilatus Und Das Tiberieum von Caesarea Maritima Scripta." *Scripta Classica Israelica* 18 (1999): 85–108.

Alliata, Eugenio. "The Legends of the Madaba Map." In *The Madaba Map Centenary: Travelling Through the Byzantine Umayyad Period. Proceedings of the International Conference Held in Amman 7–9 April 1997*, edited by Michele Piccirillo and Eugenio Alliata, 47–101. Studium Biblicum Franciscannum Collectio Maior 40. Jerusalem: Studium Biblicum Franciscannum, 1999.

———. "The Pilgrimage Routes during the Byzantine Period in Transjordan." In *The Madaba Map Centenary: Travelling Through the Byzantine Umayyad Period. Proceedings of the International Conference Held in Amman 7–9 April 1997*, edited by Michele Piccirillo and Eugenio Alliata, 121–24. Studium Biblicum Franciscannum Collectio Maior 40. Jerusalem: Studium Biblicum Franciscannum, 1999.

Allinger-Csollich, W. "Birs Nimrud I. Die Baukörper Der Ziqqurat von Borsippa. Ein Vorbericht." *Baghdader Mitteilungen* 22 (1991): 383–499.

Altman, R. I. "Some Notes on Inscriptional Genres and the Siloam Tunnel Inscription." *Antiquo Oriente* 5 (2007): 35–88.

Amore, Giordano dell', Virginio Borroni, and Antonio Frova. *Scavi di Caesarea Maritima*. Milano: "L'Erma" di Bretschneider, 1966.

Andersen, Francis I. *Job*. TOTC. Downers Grove, Ill.: IVP Academic, 2008.

Applebaum, Shimon. "The Legal Status of the Jewish Communities in the Diaspora." In *The Jewish People in the First Century*, edited by Shemuel Safrai, 2:420–63. Compendia Rerum Iudaicarum Ad Novum Testamentum 1. Philadelphia, Pa.: Fortress, 1974.

Archi, Alfonso. "Ebla Texts." In *OEANE*, edited by Eric M. Meyers, 2:184–86. Oxford: Oxford University Press, 1997.

———. "The Archives of Ebla." In *Cuneiform Archives and Libraries*, edited by Klaas R. Veenhof, 72–86. Papers Read at the 30e Rencontre Assyriologique Internationale, Leiden, 4-8 July 1983. Leiden: Netherlands Institute for the Near East, 1986.

———. "The Epigraphic Evidence from Ebla and the Old Testament." *Biblica* 60, no. 4 (1979): 556–66.

Ariel, Donald T. "Coins From the Synagogue at 'En Nashut.'" *IEJ* 37 (1987): 147–57.

Artus, Paul. *Art and Architecture of the Roman Empire*. Bellona Books, 2006.

Assmann, Jan. *The Mind of Egypt: History and Meaning in the Time of the Pharaohs*. Cambridge, Mass.: Harvard University Press, 2003.

Astour, Michael C. "Ugarit and the Great Powers." In *Ugarit in Retrospect: Fifty Years of Ugarit and Ugaritic*, edited by Gordon Douglas Young, 3–30. Winona Lake, Ind.: Eisenbrauns, 1981.

Atalay, Erol. "Die Kurudağ-Höhle [Bei Ephesos] Mit Archäologischen Funden." *JÖAI* 52 (1980 1978): 33–44.

Athas, George. *The Tel Dan Inscription: A Reappraisal and a New Introduction*. JSOTSup 360. New York: Bloomsbury, 2006.

Aufderheide, Arthur C., and Conrado Rodriguez-Martin. *The Cambridge Encyclopedia of Human Paleopathology*. Cambridge: Cambridge University Press, 1998.

Aune, David E. *Revelation 1-5*. Word Biblical Commentary 52A. Dallas, Tex.: Word Books, 1997.

———. *Revelation 6-16*. Word Biblical Commentary 52B. Dallas, Tex.: Word Books, 1998.

———. "The Apocalypse of John and the Problem of Genre." In *Early Christian Apocalypticism: Genre and Social Setting*, 65–69. Semeia 36. Atlanta, Ga.: Scholars Press, 1986.

Avigad, Nahman. "An Inscribed Ivory Pomegranate from the 'House of the Lord' [Hebrew]." *Qadmoniot* 22, no. 3–4 (1989): 95–102.

———. "Archaeology." In *Sefer Yerushalayim*, edited by Michael Avi-Yonah, 1:145–55 [Hebrew]. Jerusalem, Israel: Bialik Institute and Dvir, 1956.

———. *Discovering Jerusalem*. Nashville, Tenn.: Nelson, 1983.

———. "How the Wealthy Lived in Herodian Jerusalem." *BAR* 2, no. 4 (1976): 23–35.

———. "It Is Indeed a Pomegranate from the 'Temple of Yahweh,' (in Hebrew)." *Qadmoniot* 24 (1991): 60.

———. "Jerahmeel & Baruch." *BAR* 42, no. 2 (1979): 114–18.

———. "The Epitaph of a Royal Steward from Siloam Village." *IEJ* 3, no. 3 (1953): 137–52.

———. "The Inscribed Pomegranate from the 'House of the Lord,.'" *The Israel Museum Journal* 8 (1989): 7–16.

———. "The Inscribed Pomegranate from the 'House of the Lord.'" *BA* 53 (1990): 157–66.

———. "The Inscribed Pomegranate from the 'House of the Lord.'" In *Ancient Jerusalem Revealed*, edited by Hillel Geva, 128–37. Jerusalem, Israel: Israel Exploration Society, 1994.

Avigad, Nahman, and Benjamin Sass. *Corpus of West Semitic Stamp Seals.* 2nd ed. Jerusalem: Israel Academy of Sciences & Humanities, 1997.

Avi-Yonah, Michael, and Ephraim Stern, eds. *Encyclopedia of Archaeological Excavations in the Holy Land.* 3rd ed. 4 vols. New York: Prentice Hall, 1996.

Babelon, Ernest. "Recent Archæological Discoveries in Persia." *The American Journal of Archaeology and of the History of the Fine Arts* 2, no. 1 (1886): 53–60.

Bae, Chul-Hyun. "Comparative Studies of King Darius's Bisitun Inscription." Ph.D. diss., Harvard University, 2001.

Bagnall, Roger S., Roberta Casagrande-Kim, Akin Ersoy, and Cumhur Tanriver, eds. *Graffiti from the Basilica in the Agora of Smyrna.* Institute for the Study of the Ancient World. New York: New York University Press, 2016.

Bahat, Dan. "Does the Holy Sepulchre Church Mark the Burial of Jesus." *BAR* 12, no. 3 (1986): 26–45.

Balch, David L., and Carolyn Osiek. *Early Christian Families in Context: An Interdisciplinary Dialogue.* Grand Rapids: Eerdmans, 2003.

Baldovin, John F. *The Urban Character of Christian Worship: The Origins, Development, and Meaning of Stational Liturgy.* Orientalia Christiana Analecta 228. Rome: Pontificium Institutum Studiorum Orientalium, 1987.

Baltzer, Klaus. *The Covenant Formulary in Old Testament, Jewish, and Early Christian Writings.* Translated by David E. Green. Oxford: Blackwell, 1971.

Barguet, Paul. *La stèle de la famine à Séhel.* Cairo: l'institut français d'archéologie orientale, 1953.

Barkay, Gabriele. *Ketef Hinnom: A Treasure Facing Jerusalem's Walls.* Jerusalem, Israel: The Israel Museum, 1986.

———. "News From the Field: The Divine Name Found in Jerusalem." *BAR* 9, no. 2 (1983): 14–19.

———. "The Priestly Benediction on Silver Plaques from Ketef Hinnon in Jerusalam." *Tel Aviv* 19 (1992): 139–92.

———. "The Riches of Ketef Hinnom: Jerusalem Tomb Yields Biblical Text Four Centuries Older than Dead Sea Scrolls." *BAR* 35, no. 4 (2009): 23–35.

Barkay, Gabriele, and Amos Kloner. "Burial Caves North of Damascus Gate, Jerusalem." *IEJ* 26 (1976): 55–57.

Barkay, Gabriele, Marilyn J. Lundberg, Andrew G. Vaughn, Bruce Zuckerman, and Kenneth Zuckerman. "The Challenges of Ketef Hinnom: Using Advanced Technologies to Reclaim the Earliest Biblical Texts and Their Context." *NEA* 66, no. 4 (2003): 162–71.

———. "Using Advanced Technologies to Recover the Earliest Biblical Texts and Their Context." *NEA*, Using Advanced Technologies, 66, no. 4 (2003): 162–71.

Barkay, Gabriele, Marilyn J. Lundberg, Bruce Zukerman, and Andrew G. Vaughn. "The Amulets from Ketef Hinnom: A New Edition and Evaluation." *BASOR* 334 (2004): 41–70.

Barnes, Timothy David. "An Apostle on Trial." *JTS* 20, no. 2 (1969): 407–19.

Barré, Michael L. "The Portrait of Balaam in Numbers 22-24." *Int* 51, no. 3 (1997): 254–66.

Barrett, Anthony. *Livia: First Lady of Imperial Rome.* New Haven, Conn.: Yale University Press, 2004.

Barrett, C. K. "Paul's Address to the Ephesian Elders." In *God's Christ and His Peopl E, Studies in Honour of Nils Alstrup Dahl*, edited by J. Jervell and W. A. Meeks, 107–21. Oslo: Univer sitetsforlaget, 1977.

Barry, Kieren. *The Greek Qabalah: Alphabetical Mysticism and Numerology in the Ancient World.* York Beach, Maine: Weiser Books, 1999.

Bar, Shaul. *A Letter That Has Not Been Read: Dreams in the Hebrew Bible.* Jerusalem, Israel: Hebrew Union College Press, 2001.

Barton, George Aaron. *Archaeology and the Bible.* 7th ed. Philadelphia, Pa.: American Sunday School Union, 1937.

———. "Temple of Solomon." In *The Jewish Encyclopedia*, edited by Isidore Singer, Cyrus Adler, Gotthard Deutsch, Kaufmann Kohler, and Emil G. Hirsch, 98–101. New York: Funk & Wagnalls, 1906.

Batto, Bernard F. "Creation Theology in Geneis." In *Creation in the Biblical Traditions*, edited by Richard J. Clifford and John Joseph Collins, 16–38. Washington, D.C.: Catholic Biblical Association of America, 1992.

Bauckham, Richard J. "Apocalyptic." Edited by Sinclair B. Ferguson, David F. Wright, and James I. Packer. *NDT*. Downers Grove, Ill.: InterVarsity, 1988.

Bauer, Walter, William F. Arndt, and F. Wilbur Gingrich, eds. *A Greek-English Lexicon of the New Testament, and Other Early Christian Literature.* 3rd ed. Chicago, Ill.: University of Chicago Press, 1957.

Beale, Gregory K. *The Book of Revelation: A Commentary on the Greek Text.* New International Greek Testament Commentary 12. Grand Rapids: Eerdmans, 1998.

Becking, Bob. "Does a Recently Published Paleo-Hebrew Inscription Refer to the Solomonic Temple?" *BN* 92 (1998): 5–11.

———. *The Fall of Samaria: An Historical and Archaeological Study*. Studies in the History of the Ancient Near East 2. Leiden: Brill, 1992.

———. "The Identity of Nabu-Sharrussu-Ukin, the Chamberlain: An Epigraphic Note on Jeremiah 39,3. With an Appendix on the Nebu(!)sarsekim Tablet by Henry Stadhouders." *BN* 140 (2009): 35–46.

Berenbaum, Michael, and Fred Skolnik, eds. *Encyclopedia Judaica.* 2nd ed. 22 vols. New York: MacMillan, 2006.

Beckman, Gary M. "Mesopotamians and Mesopotamian Learning at Ḫattuša." *JCS* 35, no. 1/2 (1983): 97–114.

———. "Hittite Treaties and the Development of Cuneiform Treaty Tradition." In *Die Deuteronomistischen Geschichtswerke: Redaktions– Und Religionsgeschichtliche Perspektiven Zur "Deuteronomismus"–Diskussion in Tora Und Vorderen Propheten*, edited by Marku Witte, Konrad Schmid, Doris Prechel, and Jan Christian Gertz, 279–301. Beihefte Zur Zeitschrift Für Die Alttestamentliche Wissenschaft 365. Berlin: de Gruyter, 2006.

Beek, Martin A., and Harold Henry Rowley. *Atlas of Mesopotamia.* London: Nelson, 1962.

Ben Arieh, S. "A Burial Cave on Mount Scopus." *Atiqôt* 8 (1982): 59–60.

Benko, Stephen. "The Edict of Claudius of A.D. 49 and the Instigator Chrestus." *Theologische Zeitschrift* 25 (1969): 406–18.

Bentzen, Aage. "The Ritual Background of Amos 1.2-2.16." *OtSt* 8 (1950): 85–99.

Ben-Zvi, Izhak. "The Codex of Ben Asher." *Textus* 1 (1960): 1–16.

Berdowski, Piotr. "Garum Of Herod The Great (Latin-Greek Inscription On The Amphora From Masada)." *Analecta Archaeologica Ressoviensia* 1 (2006): 239–57.

———. "Garum Of Herod The Great (Latin-Greek Inscription On The Amphora From Masada)." *The Qumran Chronicle* 16, no. 3–4 (December 2008): 107–22.

Berlin, Adele. *Enmerkar and Ensuhkesdanna: A Sumerian Narrative Poem.* Occasional Publications of the Babylonian Fund 2. Philadelphia, Pa.: University Museum, University of Pennsylvania, 1979.

Best, Robert M. *Noah's Ark and the Ziusudra Epic: Sumerian Origins of the Flood Myth.* Winona Lake, Ind.: Eisenbrauns, 1999.

Bickerman, Elias J. "The Edict of Cyrus in Ezra 1." *JBL* 65, no. 3 (1946): 249–75.

———. "The Warning Inscriptions of Herod's Temple." *JQR* 37, no. 4 (1947): 387–405.

Biddle, Martin. *The Tomb of Christ.* Stroud: Sutton, 1999.

Bierling, Neal. *Tel Miqne-Ekron: Report on the 1995–1996 Excavations in Field XNW: Areas 77, 78, 79, 89, 90, 101, 102—Iron Age I.* Edited by Seymour Gitin. Tel Miqne-Ekron Limited Edition Series 7. Jerusalem, Israel: W. F. Albright Institute of Archaeological Research, 1998.

Billington, Clyde E. "Christian Century Attacks Document Seekers." *Artifax* 33, no. 2 (Spring 2018): 12–13.

———. "The Nazareth Inscription: Proof of the Resurrection of Christ?" *Artifax* 20, no. 2 (Spring 2005): n.p.

Bimson, John J. "Archaeological Data and the Dating of the Patriarchs." In *Essays on the Patriarchal Narratives*, edited by Alan R. Millard and Donald J. Wiseman, 59–92. Downers Grove, Ill.: InterVarsity, 1980.

———. "Merenptah's Israel and Recent Theories of Israelite Origins." *Journal for the Study of the Old Testament*, no. 49 (1991): 3–29.

Bingham, Sandra J. "The Praetorian Guard in the Political and Social Life of Julio-Claudian Rome." Ph. D. diss., The University of British Columbia, 1997.

Biran, Avraham. "An Israelite Horned Altar at Dan." *BA* 37, no. 4 (1974): 106–7.

———. "Sacred Spaces: Of Standing Stones, High Places and Cult Objects at Tel Dan." *BAR* 24, no. 5 (1998): 38–41, 44–45, 70.

———. "Tel Dan." *BA* 37, no. 2 (1974): 26–51.

———. "Two Discoveries at Tel Dan." *IEJ* 30, no. 1–2 (1980): 89–98.

Biran, Avraham, and Joseph Naveh. "An Aramaic Stele Fragment from Tel Dan." *IEJ* 43, no. 2/3 (January 1, 1993): 81–98.

———. "The Tel Dan Inscription: A New Fragment." *IEJ* 45, no. 1 (January 1, 1995): 1–18.

Blaiklock, Edward M. *Cities of the New Testament.* New York: Revell, 1965.

Boardman, John. *Persia and the West: An Archaeological Investigation of the Genesis of Achaemenid Art.* London: Thames & Hudson, 2000.

Bock, Darrell L. *The Missing Gospels: Unearthing the Truth Behind Alternative Christianities.* Nashville, Tenn.: Nelson, 2006.

Boecker, Hans Jochen. *Law and the Administration of Justice in the Old Testament and Ancient East.* Translated by J. Moiser. Minneapolis, Minn.: Augsburg, 1980.

Bonani, Georges, Magen Broshi, Israel Carmi, J. Stugnell, and W. Woelfli. "Radiocarbon Dating of the Dead Sea Scrolls." *Tigot* 20 (1991): 27–32.

Bonani, Georges, Susan Ivy, Willy Wolfli, Magen Broshi, Israel Carmi, and John Strugnell. "Radiocarbon Dating of Fourteen Dead Sea Scrolls." *Radiocarbon* 34, no. 3 (2006): 843–49.

Bond, Helen K. *Caiaphas: Friend of Rome and Judge of Jesus.* Louisville: Westminster John Knox Press, 2004.

Booth, Arthur John. *The Discovery and Decipherment of the Trilingual Cuneiform Inscriptions.* London: Longmans, Green & Company, 1902.

Bordreuil, Pierre, Felice Israel, and Dennis Pardee. "Deux Ostraca Paléo-Hébreux de La Collection Sh. Moussaieff." *Semitica* 46 (1996): 49–76.

———. "King's Command and Widow's Plea: Two New Hebrew Ostraca of the Biblical Period." *NEA* 61 (1998): 2–13.

Borowski, Oded. *Agriculture in Iron Age Israel.* Winona Lake, Ind.: Eisenbrauns, 2009.

———. "Scholars' Corner: Yadin Presents New Interpretation of the Famous Lachish Letters." *BAR* 10, no. 2 (1984): 74–77.

Botta, Paul-Émile, and Eugène Flandin. *Les Monuments de Ninive.* 5 vols. Paris, France: Imprimerie Nationale, 1859.

Bousset, Wilhelm. "Antichrist." In *Encylopaedia of Religion and Ethics*, edited by James Hastings, 1:578–81. T&T Clark, 1908.

Bowman, Alan K., Edward Champlin, and Andrew Lintott, eds. *The Cambridge Ancient History: The Augustan Empire, 44 BC–AD 70.* Vol. 10. Cambridge: Cambridge University Press, 1996.

Brand, Chad, Charles Draper, Archie England, C. Bond, E. R. Clendenen, and Trent C. Butler, eds. *Holman Illustrated Bible Dictionary.* Nashville, Tenn.: Broadman & Holman, 2003.

Bridger, David, and Samuel Wolk. *The New Jewish Encyclopedia.* Springfield, NJ: Behrman, 1962.

Brinkman, J. A. "Neo-Babylonian Texts in the Archeological Museum at Florence." *JNES* 25, no. 3 (July 1, 1966): 202–9.

Bromiley, Geoffrey W., ed. *The International Standard Bible Encyclopedia.* Revised. 4 vols. Grand Rapids: Eerdmans, 1995.

Broneer, Oscar. "Corinth: Center of St. Paul's Missionary Work in Greece." *BA* 14, no. 4 (1951): 77–96.

———. "Studies in the Topography of Corinth at the Time of St. Paul." *Arkhaiologike Ephemeris* 105 (1937): 125–33.

Browning, W. R. F. *A Dictionary of the Bible.* 2nd ed. Oxford Paperback Reference. Oxford: Oxford University Press, 2011.

Bruce, F. F. *Paul, Apostle of the Heart Set Free.* Grand Rapids: Eerdmans, 2000.

Bruce, F. F., Philip W. Comfort, and James I. Packer. *The Origin of the Bible.* Wheaton, Ill.: Tyndale, 2003.

Bruce, Frederick Fyvie. "Areopagus." Edited by I. Howard Marshall, Alan R. Millard, James I. Packer, and Donald J. Wiseman. *NBD.* Downers Grove, Ill.: InterVarsity, 1996.

———. "Christianity Under Claudius." *BJRL* 44 (1962): 309–26.

———. "Lysanias." Edited by I. Howard Marshall, Alan R. Millard, James I. Packer, and Donald J. Wiseman. *NBD.* Downers Grove, Ill.: InterVarsity, 1996.

———. "St John at Ephesus." *BJRL* 60 (August 1977): 339–61.

Bryce, Trevor. *Life and Society in the Hittite World.* Oxford: Oxford University Press, 2004.

———. *The Kingdom of the Hittites.* Oxford: Oxford University Press, 1999.

———. *The Major Historical Texts of Early Hittite History.* Sydney, Australia: University of Queensland, 1982.

Bücheler, Franz. *Rheinisches Museum für Philologie.* Vol. 61. Berlin: Weber, 1906.

Budge, E. A. Wallis. *Legends of the Gods The Egyptian Texts, Edited with Translations.* London: Kegan Paul, Trench, Trubner & Co., 1912.

———. *The Rise and Progress of Assyriology.* New York: Hopkinson & Co., 1925.

Bull, Robert J. "Caesarea Maritima: The Search for Herod's City." *BAR* 8, no. 3 (1982): 24–40.

———. "Pontius Pilate Inscription." *BAR* 8, no. 5 (1982).

Burkitt, F. C. "The Hebrew Papyrus of the Ten Commandments." *JQR* 15 (1903): 392–408.

Buttrick, George A., and Keith R. Crim, eds. *The Interpreter's Dictionary of the Bible.* 5 vols. Nashville, Tenn.: Abingdon, 1976.

Byers, Gary A. "The Bible According To Karnak." *BS* 17, no. 4 (2004): 98–107.

Cahill, Jane M. "A Rejoinder to 'Was the Siloam Tunnel Built by Hezekiah?'" *BA* 60, no. 3 (1997): 184–85.

Caird, G. B. *The Revelation of Saint John.* Peabody, Mass.: Hendrickson, 1993.

Campbell, Edward F. "The Amarna Letters and the Amarna Period." *BA* 23 (1960): 2–22.

Carmi, Israel. "Radiocarbon Dating of the Boat." In *The Excavations of an Ancient Boat in the Sea of Galilee (Lake Kinneret)*, edited by Shelley Wachsmann, 127–28. 'Atiquot (English Series) 19. Jerusalem, Israel: Israel Antiquities Authority, 1990.

Carter, Warren. *Pontius Pilate: Portraits of a Roman Governor.* Interfaces Series. Collegeville, Minn.: Liturgical, 2003.

Castro, Federico Pérez. *El Codice de Profetas de El Cairo.* 9 vols. Madrid: Instituto Arias Montano, 1979.

Caubet, Annie, and Daucé. "The Fired Arts." In *The Palace of Darius at Susa: The Great Royal Residence of Achaemenid Persia*, edited by Jean Perrot, 311–58. London: Tauris, 2013.

Ceram, C. W. *Gods, Graves & Scholars: The Story of Archaeology.* Translated by E. B. Garside and Sophie Wilkins. 2d Revised Edition. New York: Vintage, 1986.

———. *The March of Archaeology.* Translated by Richard Winston and Clara Winston. New York: Random House, 1970.

Chancey, Mark A. *The Myth of a Gentile Galilee.* Cambridge, Mass.: Cambridge University Press, 2002.

Chapman, David W. *Ancient Jewish and Christian Perceptions of Crucifixion.* WUNT 244. Tübingen: Siebeck, 2008.

Charles, Robert H. *A Critical and Exegetical Commentary on the Book of Daniel.* Eugene, Oreg.: Wipf & Stock, 2006.

———. *A Critical and Exegetical Commentary on the Revelation of St John.* 2 vols. The International Critical Commentary. Edinburgh: T&T Clark, 1963.

Charlesworth, James H. "The Dead Sea Scrolls and the Gospel according to John." In *Exploring the Gospel of John: In Honor of D. Moody Smith*, edited by R. Alan Culpepper and C. Clifton Black, 65–97. Louisville, Ky: Westminster/Knox, 1996.

Charlesworth, M. P. *Documents Illustrating the Reigns of Claudius and Nero*. Cambridge: Cambridge University Press, 1952.

Chavalas, Mark W., and K. Lawson Younger, eds. *Mesopotamia and the Bible: Comparative Explorations*. JSOTSup 341. London: T&T Clark, 2003.

Cherniss, Eric, Tim Crockett, Neva Ayn Rovner, and Kelli Vail. "The Incirli Stela Unveiling the Past: The Incirli Trilingual Inscription," 1993. http://www.usc.edu/dept/LAS/arc /incirli/.

Childs, Brevard S. "The Birth of Moses." *JBL* 84, no. 2 (June 1, 1965): 109–22.

Civil, Miguel. *The Farmer's Instructions: A Sumerian Agricultural Manual*. AuOrSup 5. Barcelona, Spain: Editorial Ausa, 1994.

Clarke, Adam. *The Holy Bible Containing the Old and New Testaments with a Commentary and Critical Notes*. Vol. 2. London: Tegg & Son, 1836.

Clayton, F. W. "Tacitus and Christian Persecution." *The Classical Quarterly* 41, no. 3–4 (1947): 81–85.

Clements, R. E. *Isaiah and the Deliverance of Jerusalem: Study of the Interpretation of Prophecy in the Old Testament*. New edition. JSOT Supplements 13. New York: Continuum International, 1980.

Clermont-Ganneau, Charles S. *Archaeological Researches in Palestine*. Translated by John MacFarlane. Vol. 1. 2 vols. London: Palestine Exploration Fund, 1899.

———. "The Discovery of a Tablet from Herod's Temple." *PEQ* 3, no. 1 (1871): 132–33.

Cline, Eric H. *Biblical Archaeology: A Very Short Introduction*. Oxford: Oxford University Press, 2009.

Codlla, Kim, and David Stronach. "Persepolis." In *OEANE*, edited by Eric M. Meyers, 4:4:273–77. Oxford: Oxford University Press, 1997.

Cogan, Mordechai. "Cyrus Cylinder." In *The Context of Scripture: Archival Documents from the Biblical World*, edited by William W. Hallo, K. Lawson Younger, and Leo G. Perdue, 2.124:314–16. Leiden: Brill Academic, 2002.

Cohasnon, Charles. *The Church of the Holy Sepulchre in Jerusalem*. Translated by J. P. B. Ross and Claude Ross. The Schweich Lectures of the British Academy, 1972. Oxford: Oxford University Press, 1974.

Cohen, Ada. *Art in the Era of Alexander the Great: Paradigms of Manhood and Their Cultural Traditions*. Cambridge: Cambridge University Press, 2010.

Cohen, Ada, and Steven E. Kangas, eds. *Assyrian Reliefs from the Palace of Ashurnasirpal II: A Cultural Biography*. Hanover, N.H.: University of New England, 2010.

Cohen, Chaim. "Biblical Hebrew Philology in the Light of the Last Three Lines of the Yeho'ash Royal Building Inscription (YI: Lines 14-16)." In *New Inscriptions and Seals Relating to the Biblical World*, edited by Meir Lubetski and Edith Lubetski, 243–76. Atlanta, Ga.: SBL, 2012.

Cohen, Oma. "Conservation of the Boat." In *The Excavations of an Ancient Boat in the Sea of Galilee (Lake Kinneret)*, edited by Shelley Wachsmann, 15–22. 'Atiquot (English Series) 19. Jerusalem, Israel: Israel Antiquities Authority, 1990.

Cohen, Rudolf, and Yigal Yisraeli. "The Excavations of Rock Shelter XII/50 and in Caves XII/52-53." *'Atiqot* 41, no. 2 (2002): 207–13.

Collins, Adela Yarbro. "Numerical Symbolism in Jewish and Early Christian Apocalyptic Literature." *ANRW* 21, no. 2 (1984): 1221–87.

Collins, John J. "Sibylline Oracles." In *DNTB*, edited by Craig A. Evans and Stanley E. Porter, 1109. Downers Grove, Ill.: InterVarsity, 2000.

———. *The "Dead Sea Scrolls": A Biography*. Princeton: Princeton University Press, 2012.

Collon, Dominique. *First Impressions: Cylinder Seals in the Ancient Near East.* London: British Museum Press, 2006.

Cook, Stanley A. "A Pre-Massoretic Biblical Papyrus." *PSBA* 25 (1903): 34–56.

Cooper, Jerrold S., and Wolfgang Heimpel. "The Sumerian Sargon Legend." *JAOS* 103, no. 1 (1983): 67–82.

Corbo, Virgilio C. *Cafarnao I: Gli edifici della città.* Studium Biblicum Franciscannum 19. Jerusalem, Israel: Franciscan Printing Press, 1975.

———. *Il Santo Sepolcro Di Gerusalemme, Aspetti Arceologici Dalle Origini Al Periodo Crociato. Parts I–III.* Jerusalem: Franciscan, 1982.

Cornill, Carl Heinrich. *Introduction to the Canonical Books of the Old Testament.* Translated by G. H. Box. Theological Translation Library 23. London: Williams & Norgate, 1907.

Cotton, Hannah M., Joseph Geiger, and David J. Thomas. *Masada, II: The Yigael Yadin Excavations, 1963–1965. Final Reports; the Latin and Greek Documents.* The Masada Reports 2. Jerusalem, Israel: Israel Exploration Society and the Hebrew University of Jerusalem, 1989.

Cotton, Hannah M., Omri Lernau, and Yuval Goren. "Fish Sauces from Herodian Masada." *JRA* 9 (1996): 223–38.

Court, John M. *The Book of Revelation and the Johannine Apocalyptic Tradition.* Sheffield: Sheffield Academic, 2000.

Cross, Frank Leslie, and Elizabeth A. Livingstone, eds. *The Oxford Dictionary Of The Christian Church.* Oxford: Oxford University Press, 2005.

Cross, Frank Moore. "Fragments of the Prayer of Nabonidus." *IEJ* 34 (1984): 260–64.

———. "King Hezekiah's Seal Bears Phoenician Imagery." *BAR* 25, no. 2 (1999): 42–45.

———. "Notes on the Forged Plaque Recording Repairs to the Temple." *IEJ* 53 (2003): 119–22.

Cumont, Franz. "Un Réscrit Impérial Sur La Violation de Sépulture." *Revue Historique* 163 (1930): 341–66.

Curtis, J. E., M. R. Cowell, and C. B. F. Walker. "A Silver Bowl of Artaxerxes I." *Iran* 33 (January 1, 1995): 149–53.

Curtis, John. *Ancient Persia.* London: Harvard University Press, 1990.

D'Ancona, Matthew, and Carsten Thiede. *The Jesus Papyrus.* New York: Doubleday, 2000.

Daltrop, Georg, Ulrich Hausmann, and Max Wegner. *Die Flavier: Vespasian, Titus, Domitian, Nerva, Julia Titi, Domitilla, Domitia.* Berlin: Mann, 1966.

Dandamaev, M. A. *A Political History of the Achaemenid Empire.* Translated by W. J. Vogelsang. Leiden: Brill Academic, 1997.

Dark, Ken, and Ferudun Özgümüş. "New Evidence for the Byzantine Church of the Holy Apostles from Fatih Camii, Istanbul." *Oxford Journal of Archeology* 21, no. 4 (2002): 393–413.

Dart, John. *The Jesus of Heresy and History: The Discovery and Meaning of the Nag Hammadi Gnostic Library.* Rev Exp. New York: HarperOne, 1989.

Daviau, P. M. Michèle, and Paul-Eugène Dion. "Moab Comes to Life." *BAR* 28, no. 1 (2002): 38.

Davies, W. W. *Codes of Hammurabi and Moses.* Whitefish, Mont.: Kessinger, 2003.

Davis, Andrew R. *Tel Dan in Its Northern Cultic Context.* John Hopkins University: UMI Dissertations, 2010.

Davis, Ellen N. "A Storm in Egypt during the Reign of Ahmose." In *Thera and the Aegean World III*, edited by David A. Hardy and A. C. Renfrew, 3:232–35. Proceedings of the Third International Congress, Santorini, Greece, 3–9 September 1989. London: The Thera Foundation, 1990.

Dearman, John Andrew, ed. *Studies in the Mesha Inscription and Moab.* SBL Archaeology and Biblical Studies 2. Atlanta, Ga.: Scholars Press, 1989.

Deissmann, Gustav Adolf. *Light from the Ancient East.* Translated by Lionel R. M. Strachan. New York: Harper & Brothers, 1927.

Delitzsch, Friedrich. *Babel and Bible: A Lecture on the Significance of Assyriological Research for Religion.* Charleston, SC: BiblioBazaar, 2009.

Dennison, Walter. "The Latest Dated Inscription from Lavinium." *Classical Philology* 5, no. 3 (July 1, 1910): 285–90.

Desnier, Jean-Luc. "Divus Caesar Imp. Domitiani F." *Revue Des études Anciennes* 81 (1979): 54–65.

Deutsch, Robert. *Biblical Period Hebrew Bullae. The Josef Chaim Kaufman Collection (in Hebrew).* Tel Aviv, Israel: Archaeological Center Publications, 2003.

———. "First Impression: What We Learn from King Ahaz's Seal." *BAR* 24, no. 3 (1998): 54–56, 62.

———. "Lasting Impressions: New Bullae Reveal Egyptian-Style Emblems on Judah's Royal Seals." *BAR* 28, no. 4 (2002): 42–51, 60–62.

———. *Messages from the Past: Hebrew Bullea from the Time of Isaiah Through the Destruction of the First Temple-Shlomo Moussaieff Collection and an Up-To-Date Corpus (in Hebrew).* Tel Aviv, Israel: Archaeological Center Publications, 1997.

———. "Tracking Down Shebnayahu, Servant of the King: How an Antiquities Market Find Solved a 42-Year-Old Excavation Puzzle." *BAR* 35, no. 3 (2009): 45–49, 67.

Deutsch, Robert, Shlomo Moussaieff, and André LeMaire. *Biblical Period Personal Seals in the Shlomo Moussaieff Collection.* JNES 62. Tel Aviv, Israel: Archaeological Center Publications, 2003.

DeVries, LaMoine F. *Cities of the Biblical World: An Introduction to the Archaeology, Geography, and History of Biblical Sites.* Eugene, Oreg.: Wipf & Stock, 2006.

DeWitt, Dale S. "The Historical Background of Gen 11:1–9: Babel or Ur?" *Journal of the Evangelical Theological Society* 22, no. 1 (1979): 15–26.

Dieulafoy, Jane. *La Perse, La Chaldee and La Susiane.* Paris, France: Hachette, 1887.

Dilke, Oswald. *The History of Cartography: Cartography in Prehistoric, Ancient, and Medieval Europe and the Mediterranean.* Edited by J. B. Harley and David Woodward. Vol. 1. 3 vols. Chicago, Ill.: University of Chicago Press, 1987.

Dilk, Jacobus Van. "The Amarna Period and the Later New Kingdom." In *The Oxford History of Ancient Egypt*, edited by Ian Shaw. Oxford: Oxford University Press, 2000.

Dines, Jennifer Mary, and Michael Anthony Knibb. *The Septuagint.* New York: T&T Clark, 2004.

Diringer, David. *Le Iscrizioni Antico-Ebraiche Palestinesi.* Florence, Italy: Le Monnier, 1934.

———. "The Biblical Scripts." In *The Cambridge History of the Bible*, edited by Peter R. Ackroyd and Craig F. Evans, 1:, From the Beginnings to Jerome:11–29. Cambridge: Cambridge University Press, 1975.

Di Segni, Leah. "The 'Onomasticon' of Eusebius and the Madaba Map." In *The Madaba Map Centenary: Travelling Through the Byzantine Umayyad Period. Proceedings of the International Conference Held in Amman 7–9 April 1997*, edited by Michele Piccirillo and Eugenio Alliata, 115–20. Studium Biblicum Franciscannum Collectio Maior 40. Jerusalem: Studium Biblicum Franciscannum, 1999.

Domeris, W. R., and S. M. Long. "The Recently Excavated Tomb of Joseph Bar Caipha and the Biblical Caiaphas." *Journal of Theology for Southern Africa* 89 (1994): 50–58.

Donner, Herbert. *The Mosaic Map of Madaba. An Introductory Guide.* Palaestina Antiqua 7. Kampen: Kok Pharos, 1992.

———. "The Uniqueness of the Madaba Map and Its Restoration in 1965." In *The Madaba Map Centenary: Travelling Through the Byzantine Umayyad Period. Proceedings of the International Conference Held in Amman 7–9 April 1997*, edited by Michele Piccirillo and Eugenio Alliata, 37–40. Studium Biblicum Franciscannum Collectio Maior 40. Jerusalem: Studium Biblicum Franciscannum, 1999.

Dornseiff, Franz. *Das Alphabet in Mystik Und Magie.* 2. Aufl edition. Etoixeia, Studien Zur Geschichte Des Antiken Weltbildes Und Der Griechischen Wissenschaft, Hrsg. von F. Boll. Hft. VII. Leipzig: Teubner, 1925.

Dotan, Aron. "Ben-Asher, Moses." Edited by Fred Skolnik and Michael Berenbaum. *EJ*. New York: MacMillan, 2006.

———. "Reflections Towards a Critical Edition of Pentateuch Codex Or. 4445." In *Estudios Masoreticos: Proceedings of the 10th Congress of IOMS*, 39–51. Madrid: Instituto de Filogogia, CSIC, Departamento de Filologia Biblica y de Oriente Antiquo, 1993.

Doudna, G. "Dating the Scrolls on the Basis of Radiocarbon Analysis." In *Dead Sea Scrolls After Fifity Years*, edited by Peter W. Flint and James C. VanderKam, 1:430–71. Leiden: Brill Academic, 1999.

Dougherty, Raymond P. *Nabonidus and Belshazzar: A Study of the Closing Events of the Neo-Babylonian Empire.* Eugene, Oreg.: Wipf & Stock, 2008.

Drews, Robert. "The Babylonian Chronicles and Berossus." *IRAQ* 37, no. 1 (1975): 39–55.

Drinkard, Joel F. "North-West Semitic Inscriptions and Biblical Interpretation: Issues of Provenance." In *Israel: Ancient Kingdom or Late Invention?*, edited by Daniel I. Block, 56–77. Nashville, Tenn.: B&H, 2008.

Driver, G. R. "The Number of the Beast." In *Bibel Und Qumran: Beitrage Zur Erforschung Der Beziehungen Wischen Bibel- Und Qumran- Wissenschaft*, edited by S. Wagner, 75–81. Hans Bardtke Zum 22.9.1966. Berlin: Evangelische Haupt-Bibelgesellschaft, 1968.

Dundes, Alan. *The Flood Myth.* Berkeley: University of California Press, 1988.

Dunn, M. R. "An Examination of the Textual Character of Codex Ephraimi Syri Rescriptus (C 04) in the Four Gospels." Ph.D. diss., South Western Baptist Seminary, 1990.

Duprez, Antoine. *Jésus et les dieux guérisseurs: à propos de Jean.* Cahiers de la Revue biblique 12. Paris, France: Gabalda, 1970.

Edwards, Chilperic. *The Hammurabi Code and the Sinaitic Legislation.* London; New York: Watts, 1904.

Edwards, I. E. S., C. J. Gadd, and N. G. L. Hammond. *The Cambridge Ancient History: Early History of the Middle East.* Cambridge: Cambridge University Press, 1970.

Edwards, James R. "Archaeology Gives New Reality to Paul's Ephesus Riot." *BAR* 42, no. 4 (August 2016): 24–33.

Eichhorn, Johann G. *Einleitung in des Alte Testament.* 4th ed. Göttingen: Rosenbusch, 1924.

Eichrodt, Walther. *Theology of the Old Testament.* 2 vols. Old Testament Library. Louisville: Westminster/Knox, 1967.

Eisenberg, Aziel. *Voices from the Past: Stories of Great Biblical Discoveries.* London: Abelard-Schuman, 1962.

Elliott, J. K. "Review of the Jesus Papyrus by Carsten Peter Thiede; Matthew d'Ancona; Gospel Truth? New Light on Jesus and the Gospels by Graham Stanton." *NovT* 38, no. 4 (1996): 393–99.

Elwell, Walter A., and Robert W. Yarbrough. *Readings from the First-Century World: Primary Sources for New Testament Study*. Encountering Biblical Studies. Grand Rapids: Baker Academic, 1998.

Emerton, John A. "The Value of the Moabite Stone as an Historical Source." *VT* 52, no. 4 (2002): 483–92.

———. "Were the Lachish Letters Sent to or from Lachish?" *PEQ* 133 (2001): 2–15.

Engelmann, Helmut. "Celsusbibliothek Und Auditorium in Ephesus (IK 17, 3009)." *JÖAI* 62 (1993): 105–11.

Enmarch, Roland. *Dialogue of Ipuwer and the Lord of All*. Oxford: Griffith Institute, 2005.

Enmarch, Ronald. "The Reception of a Middle Egyptian Poem: The Dialogue of Ipuwer and the Lord of All in the Ramesside Period and beyond." In *Ramesside Studies in Honour of K. A. Kitchen*, edited by Mark Collier and Steven R. Snape, 169–75. Bolton: Rutherford, 2011.

Eph'al, Israel, and Joseph Naveh. "Remarks on the Recently Published Moussaieff Ostraca." *IEJ* 48, no. 3/4 (1998): 269–73.

Evans, Craig A. *Ancient Texts for New Testament Studies: A Guide to the Background Literature*. Grand Rapids: Baker Academic, 2005.

———. "Caiaphas Ossuary." Edited by Craig A. Evans and Stanley E. Porter. *DNTB*. Downers Grove, Ill.: InterVarsity, 2000.

———. "Excavating Caiaphas, Pilate, and Simon of Cyrene: Assessing the Literary and Archaeological Evidence." In *Jesus and Archaeology*, edited by James H. Charlesworth, 323–40. Grand Rapids: Eerdmans, 2006.

———. *Fabricating Jesus: How Modern Scholars Distort the Gospels*. Downers Grove, Ill.: InterVarsity, 2006.

———. Jesus and the Ossuaries: What Burial Practices Reveal about the Beginning of Christianity. Waco, TX: Baylor University Press, 2003.

Evans, Craig A., and Stanley E. Porter, eds. *Dictionary of New Testament Background: A Compendium of Contemporary Biblical Scholarship*. Downers Grove, Ill.: InterVarsity, 2000.

"Excavations Begin at the Temple of Artemis." *Archaeology*, August 11, 2014. http://archaeology.org/news/2420-140811-excavations-begin-at-temple-of-artemis.

Fagan, Brian M. *A Brief History of Archaeology: Classical Times to the Twenty-First Century*. Upper Saddle River, N.J.: Prentice Hall, 2004.

———. *Return to Babylon: Travelers, Archaeologists and Monuments in Mesopotamia*. Boulder, Colo.: University Press of Colorado, 2007.

Fales, F. M. "A List of Assyrian and West Semitic Women's Names." *Iraq* 41, no. 1 (1979): 55–73.

———. "West Semitic Names in the Šēḫ Ḥamad Texts." *State Archives of Assyria Bulletin* 7 (1993): 139–50.

Fant, Clyde E., and Mitchell Glenn Reddish. *Lost Treasures of the Bible: Understanding the Bible Through Archaeological Artifacts in World Museums*. Grand Rapids: Eerdmans, 2008.

Fanthorpe, Lionel & Patricia. *Mysteries and Secrets of Numerology*. Toronto, Can.: Dundurn, 2013.

Farbridge, Maurice H. *Studies in Biblical and Semitic Symbolism*. Hoboken, N.J.: Ktav, 1970.

Faulkner, R. O. "The Admonitions of an Egyptian Sage." *JEA* 51 (December 1, 1965): 53–62.

Fawkers, Ann. "The Behistun Relief." In *The Cambridge History of Iran: The Median and Achaemenian Periods*, edited by Ilya Gershevitch, 2:828–31. Cambridge, Mass.: Cambridge University Press, 1985.

Feinsilver, Goldie. "How the Silver Amulet Inscribed with the Divine Name Was Unrolled." *BAR* 9, no. 2 (1983): 19.

Feldman, Louis H. *Jewish Life and Thought Among Greeks and Romans: Primary Readings.* New York: Continuum International, 1996.

———. "Proselytes and 'Sympathizers' in the Light of the New Inscription from Aphrodisias." *Revue Des études Juives* 148 (1989): 265–305.

Feldman, Marian H. "Darius I and the Heroes of Akkad: Affect and Agency in the Bisitun Relief." In *Ancient Near Eastern Art in Context: Studies in Honor of Irene J. Winter by Her Students*, edited by Jack Cheng and Marian H. Feldman, 265–94. Culture and History of the Ancient Near East. Brill, 2007.

Ferguson, Everett. *Backgrounds of Early Christianity.* 3rd ed. Grand Rapids: Eerdmans, 2003.

Fieger, Michael. *Im Schatten der Artemis: Glaube und Ungehorsam in Ephesus.* Bern: Lang, 1998.

Finegan, Jack. *Encountering New Testament Manuscripts: A Working Introduction to Textual Criticism.* Grand Rapids: Eerdmans, 1974.

———. *The Archeology of the New Testament: The Life of Jesus and the Beginning of the Early Church.* Revised. Princeton, N.J.: Princeton University Press, 2014.

Fine, Steven. *Art and Judaism in the Greco-Roman World: Toward a New Jewish Archaeology.* Revised. Cambridge: Cambridge University Press, 2010.

Finkel, Irving. "Finkel Assistant Keeper Ancient Mesopotamian (i.e. Sumerian, Babylonian and Assyrian) Script, Languages and Cultures Department: Middle East." *The British Museum*, 2015. http://www.britishmuseum.org/about_us/departments/staff/middle_east/irving_finkel.aspx.

Finkel, Irving, and R. J. Van der Spek. *Babylonian Chronicles of the Hellenistic Period*, Forthcoming.

Finkelstein, Israel. "The Campaign of Shoshenq I to Palestine: A Guide to the 10th Century BCE Polity." *Zeitschrift Des Deutschen Palästina-Vereins* 118 (2002): 109–35.

Finkelstein, Israel, and Neil Asher Silberman. *The Bible Unearthed: Archaeology's New Vision of Ancient Israel.* New York: Touchstone, 2002.

Finkelstein, Isreal. "A Talmudic Note on the Word for Cutting Flax in He Gezer Calendar." *BASOR* 94 (1944): 28–29.

Fiorelli, Giuseppe. *Descrizione di Pompeii.* Napoli: Tipografia italiana, 1875.

Fisher, Loren R. *Ras Shamra Parallels: The Texts From Ugarit and the Hebrew Bible.* Vol. 1 & 2. Analecta Orientalia 49 & 50. Rome: Pontificium Institutum Biblicum, 1975.

Fleming, Daniel E. "Mari and the Possibilities of Biblical Memory." *RA* 92, no. 1 (January 1, 1998): 41–78.

Flemings, Hal. *Examining Criticisms of the Bible.* Bloomington, Ind.: AuthorHouse, 2008.

Flint, Peter W., and James C. VanderKam, eds. *The Dead Sea Scrolls After Fifty Years: A Comprehensive Assessment.* Vol. 2. Leiden: Brill, 1999.

Foerster, Gideon. "The Synagogues at Masada and Herodium (Hebrew)." *Eretz Israel* 2 (1973): 224–28.

Foster, Benjamin R. "The Birth Legend of Sargon of Akkad." In *Before the Muses: An Anthology of Akkadian Literature*, translated by Benjamin R. Foster, 2:819. Winona Lake, Ind.: Eisenbrauns, 2005.

Franklin, Norma. "A Room with a View: Images from Room V at Khorsabad, Samaria, Nubians, The Brooks of Egypt and Ashdod." In *Studies in the Archaeology of the Iron Age in Israel and Jordan*, edited by Amihai Mazar, 257–77. Library Hebrew Bible/Old Testament Studies. Edinburgh: T&T Clark, 2001.

———. "The Room V Reliefs at Dur-Sharrukin and Sargon II's Western Campaigns." *Tel Aviv* 21 (1994): 255–75.

Franzmann, Majella. *Jesus in the Nag Hammadi Writings*. Edinburgh: T&T Clark, 1996.

Freedman, David Noel. "Don't Rush to Judgment: Jehoash Inscription May Be Authentic." *BAR* 30, no. 2 (2004): 48–51.

Freedman, David Noel, Gary A. Herion, David F. Graf, and John David Pleins, eds. *The Anchor Yale Bible Dictionary*. 6 vols. New York: Doubleday, 1996.

Free, Joseph P., and Howard F. Vos. *Archaeology and Bible History*. Grand Rapids: Zondervan, 1992.

Frendo, Anthony J. "Two Long-Lost Phoenician Inscriptions and The Emergence of Ancient Israel." *PEQ* 134, no. 1 (January 2002): 37–43.

Frend, William H. C. *Martyrdom and Persecution in the Early Church: A Study of a Conflict from the Maccabees to Donatus*. Oxford: Blackwell, 1965.

Freyne, Seán. "A Galilean Messiah?" *ST* 55 (2001): 198–218.

Friedman, Matti. *The Aleppo Codex: In Pursuit of One of the World's Most Coveted, Sacred, and Mysterious Books*. Chapel Hill, N.C.: Algonquin, 2013.

Friesen, Steven J. "Asiarchs." *ZPE* 126 (1999): 275–90.

———. *Imperial Cults and the Apocalypse of John: Reading Revelation in the Ruins*. Oxford: Oxford University Press, 2001.

Frösén, Jaakko. "Conservation of Ancient Papyrus Materials." In *The Oxford Handbook of Papyrology*, edited by Roger S. Bagnall, 79–100. Oxford Handbooks. Oxford: Oxford University Press, 2011.

Frothingham, A. L. "A Lost Section of the Frieze of the Arch of Titus?" *AJA* 18, no. 4 (1914): 479–83.

Frova, Antonio. "L'Iscrizione Di Ponzio Pilato a Cesarea." *Rendiconti dell'Istitutio Lombardo* 95 (1961): 419–34.

Frumkin, Amos E., Aryeh E. Shimron, and Jeff Rosenbaum. "Radiometric Dating of the Siloam Tunnel, Jerusalem." *Nature* 425, no. 6954 (2003): 169–71.

Frumkin, Amos, Galit Kadan, Enzel Yehouda, and Yehuda Eyal. "Radiocarbon Chronology Of The Holocene Dead Sea: Attempting A Regional Correlation." *Radiocarbon* 43, no. 3 (2001): 1179–89.

Gadd, C. J. "Inscribed Prisms of Sargon II from Nimrud." *Iraq* 16, no. 2 (1954): 173–201.

Galil, Gershon. *The Chronology of the Kings of Israel and Judah*. Leiden: Brill, 1996.

Ganor, Nissim R. "The Lachish Letters." *PEQ* 99, no. 2 (74-77): 1967.

Garbini, Giovanni. *Myth and History in the Bible*. The Library of Hebrew Bible/OT Studies. London: Sheffield Academic Press, 2003.

Gardiner, Alan H. "Davies's Copy of the Great Speos Artemidos Inscription." *JEA* 32 (1946): 43–56.

———. *Late-Egyptian Stories*. Turnhout, Belgium: Brepols, 1981.

———. *The Admonitions of an Egyptian Sage from a Hieratic Papyrus in Leiden*. Hildesheim: Georg Olms Verlag, 1969.

Garnsey, Peter. *Social Status and Legal Privilege in the Roman Empire*. Oxford: Oxford University Press, 1970.

Garthwaite, John. "Martial, Book 6, on Domitian's Moral Censorship." *Prudentia* 22 (1990): 13–22.

Gärtner, Bertil Edgar. *The Areopagus Speech and Natural Revelation*. Lund, Sweden: Gleerup, 1955.

Gasche, Hermann, and Caroline Janssen. "Sippar." In *OEANE*, edited by Eric M. Meyers, 5:47–49. Oxford: Oxford University Press, 1997.

Geisler, Norman L., and Peter Bocchino. *Unshakeable Foundations*. Minneapolis, Minn.: Bethany House, 2001.

Geisler, Norman L., and Joseph M. Holden. *The Popular Handbook of Archaeology and the Bible*. Eugene, Oreg.: Harvest House, 2013.

Geisler, Norman L., and William E. Nix. *A General Introduction to the Bible*. New and Revised. Chicago, Ill.: Moody, 1986.

Gentry, Kenneth L. *The Beast of Revelation*. Fort Worth, Tex.: Dominion, 1989.

Gentry, Kenneth L., Jr. *Before Jerusalem Fell: Dating the Book of Revelation*. Powder Springs, GA: American Vision, 1998.

George, Andrew R. "The Tower of Babel: Archaeology, History and Cuneiform Texts, Review of Hansjörg Schmid, Der Tempelturm Etemenanki in Babylon 1995." *AfO* 51 (2007): 75–95.

Gethman, Charles Wesley. *The Code of Hammurabi and the Book of the Covenant*. Evanston, Ill.: Northwestern University, 1911.

Geva, Hillel, ed. *Jewish Quarter Excavations in the Old City of Jerusalem Conducted by Nahman Avigad: Architecture and Stratigraphy, Areas A, W, and X-2 - Final Report*. Vol. 1. Jerusalem: Israel Exploration Society, 2000.

———. "Western Jerusalem at the End of the First Temple Period in Light of the Excavations in the Jewish Quarter." In *Jerusalem in Bible and Archaeology: The First Temple Period*, edited by Andrew G. Vaughn and Ann E. Killebrew, 183–208. SBL Symposium Series 18. Atlanta, Ga.: SBL, 2003.

Gibbon, Edward. *Decline and Fall of the Roman Empire*. Wordsworth Classics of World Literature. Ware, Hertfordshire: Wordsworth, 1998.

Gibson, Shimon. "The Pool of Bethesda in Jerusalem and Jewish Purification Practices of the Second Temple Period." *Proche-Orient Chrétien* 55, no. 3–4 (2005): 270–93.

Gichon, M., and Benjamin H. Isaac. "A Flavian Inscription from Jerusalem." *IEJ* 24, no. 2 (January 1, 1974): 117–23.

———. "A Flavian Inscription from Jerusalem." In *The Near East under Roman Rule*, edited by Benjamin H. Isaac, 76–86. Leiden: Brill, 1998.

Gill, Dan. "How They Met: Geology Solves the Mystery of Hezekiah's Tunnelers." *BAR* 20, no. 4 (1994): 20–33, 64.

———. "Jerusalem's Underground Water Systems: How They Met: Geology Solves Long-Standing Mystery of Hezekiah's Tunnelers." *BAR* 20, no. 4 (1994): 20–33.

———. "The Geology of the City of David and its Ancient Subterranean Waterworks." In *Excavations at the City of David 1978-1985 Directed by Yigal Shiloh: Various Reports*, edited by Donald T. Ariel and Alon De Groot, 3:1–28. Qedem 35. Jerusalem, Israel: Institute of Archaeology, Hebrew University, 1992.

Ginsburg, Christian D. *Introduction to the Masoretico-Critical Edition of the Hebrew Bible*. Vol. 2. New York: KTAV, 1897.

Gitin, Seymour, Trude Dothan, and Joseph Naveh. "A Royal Dedicatory Inscription from Ekron." *IEJ* 47, no. 1/2 (1997): 1–16.

———. "Ekron Identity Confirmed: A Unique Royal Inscription Offers Clues to Early Philistine History." *Archaeology* 51, no. 1 (1998): 30–31.

Goedicke, Hans. "Hatshepsut's Temple Inscription at Speo Artemidos." *BAR* 7, no. 5 (1981): 42.

Golden, Jonathan M. *Ancient Canaan and Israel: New Perspectives.* Understanding Ancient Civilizations. Santa Barbara, Calf.: ABC-CLIO, 2004.

Goldsworthy, Adrian. *Augustus: First Emperor of Rome.* New Haven, Conn.: Yale University Press, 2014.

Gonen, Rivka. "The Late Bronze Age." In *The Archaeology of Ancient Israel,* edited by Amnon Ben-Tor, translated by R. Greenberg, 211–57. New Haven, Conn.: Yale University Press, 1994.

Goodman, Martin. *Rome and Jerusalem: The Clash of Ancient Civilizations.* Reprint. New York: Vintage, 2008.

Good, Robert M. "The Israelite Royal Steward in the Light of Ugaritic 'L Bt." *RB* 86 (1979): 580–82.

Gordon, Cyrus H. "The New Amarna Tablets." *Orientalia* 16 (1947): 1–21.

Goren, Yuval, Shmuel Ahituv, Avner Ayalon, Miryam Bar-Matthews, and Uzi Dahari. "A Re-Examination of the Inscribed Ivory Pomegranate from the Israel Museum." *IEJ* 55, no. 3 (2005): 3–20.

Goren, Yuval, Shmuel Ahituv, Avner Ayalon, Miryam Bar-Matthews, Uzi Dahari, Michal Dayagi-Mendels, Aaron Demsky, and Nadav Levin. "Authenticity Examination of the Ivory Pomegranate Bearing a Palaeo-Hebrew Dedication Inscription from the Israel Museum." *IEJ* 55, no. 1 (2005): 3–20.

Goren, Yuval, Shmuel Ahituv, Aaron Demsky, and André LeMaire. "The Inscribed Ivory Pomegranate from the Israel Museum Examined Again." *IEJ* 57 (2007): 87–95.

Goren, Yuval, Avner Ayalon, Miryam Bar-Matthews, and Bettina Schilman. "Authenticity Examination of Jehoash Inscription." *Journal of the Institute of Archaeology of Tel Aviv University* 31 (2004): 3–16.

Görg, Manfred, Peter van der Veen, and Christoffer Theis. "Israel in Canaan (Long) Before Pharaoh Merenptah? A Fresh Look at Berlin Statue Pedestal Relief 21687." *Journal of Ancient Egyptian Interconnections* 2, no. 4 (2010): 15–25.

Gow, Mary. *Measuring the Earth: Eratosthenes and His Celestial Geometry.* Berkeley Heights, N.J.: Enslow, 2009.

Grabbe, Lester L. *Ahab Agonistes: The Rise and Fall of the Omri Dynasty.* New York: Continuum International, 2007.

Gräbe, Petrus J. *New Covenant, New Community the Significance of Biblical and Patristic Covenant Theology for Contemporary Understanding.* Exeter: Paternoster, 2006.

Graves, David E. *Biblical Archaeology: An Introduction with Recent Discoveries That Support the Reliability of the Bible.* Vol. 1. Moncton, N.B.: Electronic Christian Media, 2014.

———. "Jesus Speaks to Seven of His Churches, Part 1." *BS* 23, no. 2 (Spring 2010): 46–56.

———. "Jesus Speaks to Seven of His Churches, Part 2." *BS* 23, no. 3 (Summer 2010): 66–74.

———. *Key Facts for the Location of Sodom Student Edition: Navigating the Maze of Arguments.* Moncton, N.B.: Electronic Christian Media, 2014.

———. "Local References in the Letter to Smyrna (Rev 2: 8–11), Part 1: Archaeological Background." *BS* 18, no. 4 (2005): 114–23.

———. "Local References in the Letter to Smyrna (Rev 2: 8–11), Part 2: Historical Background." *BS* 19, no. 1 (2006): 23–31.

———. "Local References in the Letter to Smyrna (Rev 2: 8–11), Part 3: Jewish Background." *BS* 19, no. 2 (2006): 41–47.

———. "Local References in the Letter to Smyrna (Rev 2: 8–11), Part 4: Religious Background." *BS* 19, no. 3 (2007): 88–96.

———. *The Seven Messages of Revelation and Vassal Treaties: Literary Genre, Structure, and Function.* Gorgias Dissertations Biblical Studies 41. Piscataway, N.J.: Gorgias, 2009.

Graves, David E., and D. Scott Stripling. "Identification of Tall El-Hammam on the Madaba Map." *BS* 20, no. 2 (2007): 35–45.

———. "Re-Examination of the Location for the Ancient City of Livias." *Levant* 43, no. 2 (2011): 178–200.

Greenhut, Zvi. "Burial Cave of the Caiaphas Family." *BAR* 18, no. 5 (1992): 28–44, 76.

———. "Caiaphas' Final Resting Place." *Israel Hilton Magazine*, 1993, 16, 23.

Green, Joel B., Scot McKnight, and I. Howard Marshall, eds. *Dictionary of Jesus and the Gospels.* Downers Grove, Ill.: InterVarsity, 1992.

Gregory, Caspar René. "The Mâdaba Map." *The Biblical World* 12, no. 4 (1898): 244–50.

Gressmann, Hugo. *Mose und seine Zeit: ein Kommentar zu den Mose-Sagen.* Göttingen: Vandenhoeck & Ruprecht, 1913.

Griffin, Miriam T. *Nero: The End of a Dynasty.* New York: Routledge, 2002.

Griffiths, J. Gwyn. "Review of Der ägyptische Mythos von Der Himmelskuh. Eine Ätiologie Des Unvollkommenen by Erik Hornung." *JEA* 74 (January 1, 1988): 275–77.

Guichard, Michaël. "Mari Texts." In *OEANE*, edited by Eric M. Meyers, 3:419–21. Oxford: Oxford University Press, 1997.

Gundry, Robert Horton. *Matthew, A Commentary on His Literary and Theological Art.* Grand Rapids: Eerdmans, 1982.

Gunkel, Hermann. *Creation And Chaos in the Primeval Era And the Eschaton: A Religio-Historical Study of Genesis 1 and Revelation 12.* Translated by K. William Whitney, Jr. Grand Rapids: Eerdmans, 2006.

Gunter, Ann C., and Paul Jett. *Ancient Iranian Metalwork in the Arthur M. Sackler Gallery and the Freer Gallery of Art.* Mainz: Sackler Art Gallery, 1992.

Güterbock, Hans Gustav. "Boğazköy." In *OEANE*, edited by Eric M. Meyers, 1:1:333–35. Oxford: Oxford University Press, 1997.

Gutfeld, Oren, and J. Randall Price. "Hebrew University Archaeologists Find 12th Dead Sea Scrolls Cave." *The Hebrew University of Jerusalem (blog)*, February 8, 2017. https://new.huji.ac.il/en/article/33424.

Gyles, Mary Francis. "Nero Fiddled While Rome Burned." *CJ* 42, no. 4 (1947): 211–17.

Haas, Nico. "Anthropological Observations on the Skeletal Remains from Giv'at Ha-Mivtar." *IEJ* 20, no. 1 (1970): 38–59.

Hackett, Jo Ann. *The Balaam Text from Deir 'Allā.* Harvard Semitic Monographs 31. Atlanta, Ga.: Scholars Press, 1980.

Hagelia, Hallvard. *Tel Dan Inscription: A Critical Investigation of Recent Research on Its Palaeography & Philology.* Studia Semitica Upsaliensia 22. Uppsala: Uppsala Universitet, 2006.

Hämmerly-Dupuy, Daniel. "Some Observations on the Assyro-Babylonian and Sumerian Flood Stories." In *The Flood Myth*, edited by Alan Dundes, 49–60. Berkeley: University of California Press, 1988.

Hammurabi. *The Oldest Code of Laws in the World: The Code of Laws Promulgated by Hammurabi, King of Babylon, BC 2285-2242.* Translated by Claude Hermann Walter Johns. Union, NJ: Lawbook Exchange, 2000.

Hare, Augustus John Cuthbert. *Walks in Rome.* Vol. 1. London: Allen, 1897.

Harrison, R. K., and Martin G. Abegg, Jr. "Dead Sea Scrolls." Edited by Merrill C. Tenney and Moises Silva. *ZPEB.* Grand Rapids: Zondervan, 2009.

Harrison, Timothy P. *Megiddo 3: Final Report on the Stratum VI Excavations.* Oriental Institute Publications 127. Chicago, Ill.: Oriental Institute of the University of Chicago, 2004.

Harris, Stephen L., and Robert Platzner. *The Old Testament: An Introduction to the Hebrew Bible.* New York: McGraw-Hill, 2002.

Hartley, John E. *The Book of Job.* NICOT. Grand Rapids: Eerdmans, 1988.

Hasel, Gerhard F. "The Polemic Nature of the Genesis Cosmology." *Evangelical Quarterly* 46 (1974): 81–102.

Hasel, Michael G. "Israel in the Merneptah Stela." *BASOR*, no. 296 (November 1, 1994): 45–61.

———. "Merenptah's Inscription and Reliefs and the Origin of Israel." In *The Near East in the Southwest: Essays in Honor of William G Dever*, edited by Beth Alpert Nakhai, 19–44. Annual of ASOR. Boston, Mass.: American Schools of Oriental Research, 2004.

———. "The Structure of the Final Hymnic-Poetic Unit of the Merenptah Stela." *ZAW* 116 (2004): 75–81.

Hassertt, Maurice. "Mamertine Prison." Edited by Condé Bénoist Pallen, Charles George Herbermann, and Edward Aloysius Pace. *CE.* New York: Appleton & Company, 1913.

Hastings, James, and John A. Selbie, eds. *A Dictionary of the Bible: Dealing with Its Language, Literature and Contents Including the Biblical Theology.* 5 vols. New York: Scribner's Sons, 1911.

Head, Peter M. "The Date Of The Magdalen Papyrus Of Matthew (P. Magd. Gr. 17 = P64): A Response To C. P. Thiede." *TynBul* 46 (1995): 251–85.

Heberdey, Rudolf. "Vorläufiger Bericht über Die Grabungen in Ephesus 1902/3." *JÖAI* 7 (1904): 38–55.

Heidel, Alexander. *Gilgamesh Epic and Old Testament Parallels.* 2nd ed. Chicago, Ill.: University Of Chicago Press, 1970.

———. *The Babylonian Genesis: The Story of Creation.* 2nd ed. Chicago, Ill.: University of Chicago Press, 1963.

Heiken, Grant, Renato Funiciello, and Donatella de Rita. *The Seven Hills of Rome: A Geological Tour of the Eternal City.* Princeton, N.J.: Princeton University Press, 2013.

Hekster, Olivier Joram. *Emperors and Ancestors: Roman Rulers and the Constraints of Tradition.* Oxford: Oxford University Press, 2015.

Hellholm, David, and Kungl Vitterhets. *Apocalypticism in the Mediterranean World and the Near East: Proceedings of the International Colloquium on Apocalypticism, Uppsala, August 12-17, 1979.* Tübingen: Siebeck, 1989.

Heltzer, Michael, and Robert Deutsch. *Forty New Ancient West Semitic Inscriptions.* Jerusalem, Israel: Israel Numismatic Society, 1994.

Hemer, Colin J. "Audeitorion." *TynBul* 24 (1973): 128.

———. "Paul at Athens: A Topographical Note." *NTS* 20, no. 3 (1974): 341–50.

———. "Seven Cities of Asia Minor." In *Major Cities of the Biblical World*, edited by R.K. Harrison, 234–48. Nashville, Tenn.: Nelson, 1985.

———. "The Name of Paul." *TynBul* 36 (1985): 179–83.

———. "The Speeches of Acts: I. The Ephesian Elders at Miletus." *TynBul* 40, no. 1 (1989): 77–85.

Hemer, Colin J., and Conrad H. Gempf, eds. *The Book of Acts in the Setting of Hellenistic History*. WUNT 49. Winona Lake, Ind.: Eisenbrauns, 1990.

Hendel, Ronald S. "The Date of the Siloam Inscription: A Rejoinder to Rogerson and Davies." *BA* 59, no. 4 (1996): 233–37.

Hernández, Juan. *Scribal Habits and Theological Influences in the Apocalypse: The Singular Readings of Sinaiticus, Alexandrinus, and Ephraemi*. Leiden: Mohr Siebeck, 2006.

Herr, Larry G. "The Palaeography of West Semitic Stamp Seals." *BASOR* 312 (1998): 45–77.

Herrmann, Siegfried. "Operationen Pharao Schoschenks I. Im Ostlichen Ephraim." *Zeitschrift Des Deutscher Palastina-Vereins* 80 (1964): 55–79.

Hess, Richard S. *Amarna Personal Names*. American Schools of Oriental Research Dissertation Series 9. Winona Lake, Ind.: Eisenbrauns, 1993.

———. "Amarna Proper Names (Egypt)." Ph.D. diss., Hebrew Union College - Jewish Institute of Religion (Ohio), 1984.

———. "Divine Names in the Amarna Correspondence." *UF* 18 (1986): 149–68.

Hewitt, J. W. "The Use of Nails in Crucifixion." *HTR* 25 (1932): 29–35.

Hillers, Delbert R. "Revelation 13:18 and a Scroll from Murabba'ât." *BASOR* 170 (1963): 65.

Hilprecht, H. V. *Explorations in Bible Lands During the 19th Century*. Piscataway, N.J.: Gorgias, 2004.

Hirschfelder, Wilhelm, and Georg Andresen, eds. *Wochenschrift Für Klassische Philologie*. Vol. 19. Leipzig: Reisland, 1902.

Hitzig, Ferdinand. *Das Buch Daniel*. Leipzig: Weidmann, 1850.

Hoerth, Alfred J. *Archaeology and the Old Testament*. Grand Rapids: Baker, 1999.

Hoerth, Alfred J., and John McRay. *Bible Archaeology: An Exploration of the History and Culture of Early Civilizations*. Grand Rapids: Baker, 2006.

Hoffman, Adina, and Peter Cole. *Sacred Trash: The Lost and Found World of the Cairo Geniza*. New York: Schocken, 2011.

Hoffmeier, James K. *Ancient Israel in Sinai: The Evidence for the Authenticity of the Wilderness Tradition*. Illustrated edition. Oxford: Oxford University Press, USA, 2005.

———. *Israel in Egypt: The Evidence for the Authenticity of the Exodus Tradition*. Oxford: Oxford University Press, 1999.

———. , ed. *The Archaeology of the Bible: Reassessing Methodologies and Assumptions*. Oxford: Lion Hudson, 2008.

———. "The Evangelical Contribution to Understanding the (Early) History of Ancient Israel in Recent Scholarship." *Bulletin for Biblical Research* 7 (1997): 77–90.

———. "The (Israel) Stela of Merneptah (2.6)." In *The Context of Scripture: Monumental Inscriptions from the Biblical World*, edited by William W. Hallo, K. Lawson Younger, Harry A. Hoffner, and Robert K. Ritner, 2:40–41. Leiden: Brill Academic, 2001.

Hoftijzer, Jacob. "The Prophet Balaam in a 6th Century Aramaic Inscription." *BA* 39, no. 1 (1976): 11–17.

Hoftijzer, Jacob, and G. Van der Kooij, eds. *The Balaam Text from Deir 'Alla Re-Evaluated: Proceedings of the International Symposium Held at Leiden, 21–24 August 1989.* Leiden: Brill, 1991.

Hogg, John. "On the City of Abila, and the District Called Abilene near Mount Lebanon, and on a Latin Inscription at the River Lycus, in the North of Syria." *Journal of the Royal Geographical Society of London* 20 (1850): 38–48.

Hohlfelder, Robert L. "Caesarea beneath the Sea." *BAR* 8, no. 3 (1982): 42–47.

Hohlfelder, Robert L., John P. Oleson, Avner Raban, and R. Lindley Vann. "Sebastos: Herod's Harbor at Caesarea Maritima." *BA* 46, no. 3 (1983): 133–43.

Hollis, Susan T. *The Ancient Egyptian "Tale of Two Brothers": A Mythological, Religious, Literary, and Historico-Political Study.* Oklahoma Series in Classical Culture. London: Bannerstone, 2008.

Holloway, Steven W. "The Quest for Sargon, Pul and Tiglath-Pileser in the Nineteenth Century." In *Mesopotamia and the Bible: Comparative Explorations,* edited by Mark W. Chavalas and K. Lawson Younger, 68–87. JSOTSup 341. London: T&T Clark, 2003.

Honour, Hugh, and John Fleming. *A World History of Art.* 7th ed. London: Laurence King, 2009.

Horbury, William. "The 'Caiaphas' Ossuaries and Joseph Caiaphas." *PEQ* 126, no. 1 (1994): 32–48.

Horn, Siegfried H. "Why the Moabite Stone Was Blown to Pieces: 9th Century B.C. Inscription Adds New Dimension to Biblical Account of Mesha's Rebellion." *BAR* 12, no. 3 (June 1986): 50–61.

Hornung, Erik. *Der ägyptische Mythos von der Himmelskuh: Eine Ätiologie des Unvollkommenen.* Orbis biblicus et orientalis 46. Göttingen: Vandenhoeck & Ruprecht, 1982.

———. *The Ancient Egyptian Books of the Afterlife.* Translated by David Lorton. Ithaca, N.Y.: Cornell University Press, 1999.

———. *The Tomb of Pharaoh Seti I.* Zürich: Artemis & Winkler, 1991.

Horsley, G. H. R. "The Inscriptions of Ephesos and the New Testament." *NovT* 34, no. 2 (1992): 105–68.

———. "The Silversmiths at Ephesos." In *New Documents Illustrating Early Christianity,* 4:7–10. Grand Rapids: Eerdmans, 2001.

Hvalvik, Reider. "Barnabas 9.7–9 and the Author's Supposed Use of Gematria." *New Testament Studies* 33 (1987): 276–82.

Ifrah, Georges. *The Universal History of Numbers: From Prehistory to the Invention of the Computer.* Translated by David Bellos. New York: Wiley, 2000.

Ilani, Shimon, Amnon Rosenfeld, and M. Dvorachek. "Archaeometry of a Stone Tablet with Hebrew Inscription Referring to Repair of the House." *Israel Geological Survey Current Research* 13 (2002): 109–16.

Inan, Jale, and Elisabeth Rosenbaum. Roman and Early Byzantine Portrait Sculpture in Asia Minor. Oxford, U.K.: Oxford University Press, 1966.

Israel Antiquities Authority. "Earliest Archaeological Evidence of the Existence of the City of Bethlehem Already in the First Temple Period." *Israel Antiquities Authority,* May 23, 2012. http://www.antiquities.org.il/article_eng.aspx?sec_id=25&subj_id=240&id=1938.

Jackson, Wayne. "The Ras Shamra Discovery." *Apologetics Press,* 2013, 1–10.

Jacobsen, Thorkild. "The Battle between Marduk and Tiamat." *JAOS* 88, no. 1 (1968): 104–8.

———. "The Eridu Genesis." *JBL* 100, no. 4 (1981): 513–29.

James, Peter. "The Date of the Ekron Temple Inscription: A Note." *IEJ* 55, no. 1 (January 1, 2005): 90–93.

Janzen, David. *Witch-Hunts, Purity, and Social Boundaries: The Expulsion of the Foreign Women in Ezra 9-10.* London: A&C Black, 2002.

Jarus, Owen. "Mummy Mask May Reveal Oldest Known Gospel." *Live Science*, January 18, 2015. http://www.livescience.com/49489-oldest-known-gospel-mummy-mask.html.

Jastrow, Marcus. *Dictionary of Targumim, Talmud and Midrashic Literature.* New York: Putnam's Sons, 1903.

Jastrow, Morris, and Albert T. Clay. *An Old Babylonian Version of the Gilgamesh Epic (Illustrated Edition).* Ill. Dodo Press, 2009.

Jefferson, Rebecca J. W., and Erica C. D. Hunter. *Published Material from the Cambridge Genizah Collections. A Bibliography 1980-1997.* 4 vols. Cambridge University Library Genizah 13. Cambridge, Mass.: Cambridge University Press, 2004.

Jensen, Robin Margaret. *Understanding Early Christian Art.* New York: Routledge, 2000.

Jeremias, Joachim. *The Rediscovery of Bethesda: John 5:2.* New Testament Archaeology Monographs 1. Louisville: Southern Baptist Theological Seminary, 1966.

Jones, Arnold H. M. "Procurators and Prefects in the Early Principate." In *Studies in Roman Government and Law*, edited by Arnold H. M. Jones, 115–25. Oxford: Blackwell, 1960.

Jones, Brian W. *The Emperor Domitian.* New York: Routledge, 1993.

Jongeling, Bastiaan, Casper J. Labuschagne, and Adam Simon Van Der Woude, trans. *Aramaic Texts from Qumran.* Vol. 1. Semitic Study Series 4. Leiden: Brill Academic, 1976.

Judge, E. A. *Rank and Status in the World of the Caesars and St Paul.* Broadhead Memorial Lecure 1981/University of Canterbury Publications 29. Christchurch, N.Z.: University of Canterbury, 1982.

Kaufman, Steven A. "The Phoenician Inscription of the Incirli Trilingual: A Tentative Reconstruction and Translation." *Maarav* 14, no. 2 (2007): 7–26.

Kearsley, Rosalinde A. "Asiarchs." In *The Book of Acts in Its Graeco-Roman Setting*, edited by David W. Gill and Conrad H. Gempf, 2:362–76. Book of Acts in Its First Century Setting 2. Grand Rapids, Mich.: Eerdmans, 1994.

Keener, Craig S. *The Historical Jesus of the Gospels.* Grand Rapids: Eerdmans, 2012.

———. *The IVP Bible Background Commentary: New Testament.* Downers Grove, Ill.: InterVarsity, 1994.

Keil, Josef, E. Reisch, and F. Knoll. *Die Marienkirche in Ephesos.* FiE, 4.1. Wien: ÖAI, 1932.

Kelle, Brad E. "What's in a Name? Neo-Assyrian Designations for the Northern Kingdom and Their Implications for Israelite History and Biblical Interpretation." *JBL* 121, no. 4 (Winter 2002): 639–66.

Kempinski, Aharon. "Is It Really a Pomegranate from the 'Temple of Yahweh?' (in Hebrew)." *Qadmoniot* 23, no. 3–4 (1991): 126.

Kenyon, Frederic G. *Our Bible and the Ancient Manuscripts.* New York: Harper, 1958.

Kenyon, Kathleen M. *Jerusalem Excavating 3000 Years of History.* London: Thames & Hudson, 1967.

Kikawada, Isaac M. "The Double Creation of Mankind in Enki and Ninmah, Atrahasis I 1–351, and Genesis 1–2." *Iraq* 45 (1983): 43–45.

Kilmer, Anne D. "A Music Tablet from Sippar(?): BM 65217 + 66616." *Iraq* 46 (1984): 69–80.

———. "The Musical Instruments from Ur and Ancient Mesopotamian Music." *Expedition* 402 (1998): 12–19.

———. "World's Oldest Musical Notation Deciphered on Cuneiform Tablet." *BAR* 6, no. 5 (1980): 14–25.

King, Philip J. *Jeremiah: An Archaeological Companion.* Louisville: Westminster/John Knox, 1993.

Kitchen, Kenneth A. "Ancient Egyptian Chronology for Aegeanists." *Mediterranean Archaeology and Archaeometry* 2, no. 2 (2002): 5–12.

———. "A Possible Mention of David in the Late Tenth Century BCE, and Deity *Dod as Dead as the Dodo." *JSOT*, no. 76 (1997): 29–44.

———. *On the Reliability of the Old Testament.* Grand Rapids: Eerdmans, 2003.

———. "The Joseph Narrative (Genesis 37, 39–50)." *BS* 15, no. 3 (2003): 4–10.

———. "The Physical Text of Merenptah's Victory Hymn (The 'Israel Stela')." *The Journal of the Society for the Study of Egyptian Antiquities* 24 (1994): 71–76.

———. "The Shoshenqs of Egypt and Palestine." *JSOT* 93 (2001): 3–12.

———. *The Third Intermediate Period in Egypt, 1100-650 BC.* 2nd ed. Egyptology. Warminster: Aris & Phillips, 1996.

———. "The Victories of Merenptah, and the Nature of Their Record." *JSOT* 28, no. 3 (March 1, 2004): 259–72.

Kitchen, Kenneth A., and T. C. Mitchell. "Chronology of the Old Testament." Edited by I. Howard Marshall, A. R. Millard, J. I. Packer, and Donald J. Wiseman. *NBD*. Downers Grove, Ill.: InterVarsity, 1996.

Kleiner, Fred S. *Gardner's Art Through the Ages: Backpack Edition, Book 1.* 13th ed. Vol. 1. 2 vols. Cengage Learning, 2009.

———. "Review of The Spoils of Jerusalem on the Arch of Titus: A Re-Investigation by Leon Yarden." *AJA* 96, no. 4 (October 1, 1992): 775–76.

Klein, Jacob. "The Origin and Development of Languages on Earth: The Sumerian versus the Biblical View." In *A History of Israel From the Bronze Age Through the Jewish Wars*, edited by Moshe Greenberg, Mordechai Cogan, Barry L. Eichler, and Jeffrey H. Tigay, 77–92. Winona Lake, Ind.: Eisenbrauns, 1998.

Knibbe, Dieter, and Bülent Iplikçioğlu. "Neue Inschriften Aus Ephesos IX." *JÖAI* 55 (1984): 107–35.

Knight, William. *The Arch of Titus and the Spoils of the Temple, an Historical Lecture.* Charleston, SC: BiblioBazaar, 2010.

Knoppers, Gary N. "The Vanishing Solomon: The Disappearance of the United Monarchy from Recent Histories of Ancient Israel." *JBL* 116, no. 1 (April 1, 1997): 19–44.

Koester, Helmut. *Ancient Christian Gospels: Their History and Development.* 2nd ed. New York: T&T Clark, 1992.

———. , ed. *Ephesos Metropolis of Asia: An Interdisciplinary Approach to Its Archaeology, Religion, and Culture.* Harvard Theological Studies 41. Cambridge, Mass.: Harvard Divinity School, 1995.

Koikylides, Cleopas M. *The Geographical Madaba Mosaic Map on Syria, Palestine and Egypt.* Jerusalem, Israel, 1897.

———. "The Geographical Mosaic at Madaba." *RB*, April 1, 1897, 165–84.

Koldewey, Robert. *The Excavations at Babylon.* Translated by Agnes S. Johns. New York: MacMillan & Co., 1914.

Königliche Museen zu Berlin. *Verzeichnis Der in Der Formerei Der Königl. Museen Käuflichen Gipsabgüsse.* Berlin: Herausgegeben von der General-Verwaltung, 1902.

Köstenberger, Andreas J., L. Scott Kellum, and Charles L Quarles. *The Cradle, the Cross, and the Crown: An Introduction to the New Testament.* Nashville, Tenn.: Broadman & Holman Academic, 2009.

Kraabel, A. Thomas. "Impact of the Discovery of the Sardis Synagogue." In *Sardis from Prehistoric to Roman Times: Results of the Archaeological Exploration of Sardis, 1958-1975*, edited by George M. A. Hanfmann, William E. Mierse, and Clive Foss, 178–90. Cambridge, Mass.: Harvard University Press, 1983.

Kraabel, A. Thomas, J. Andrew Overman, and Robert S. MacLennan, eds. *Diaspora Jews and Judaism: Essays in Honor Of, and in Dialogue With, A. Thomas Kraabel.* Scholars Press, 1992.

Kramer, Samuel Noah. *Enmerkar and the Lord of Aratta: A Sumerian Epic Tale of Iraq and Iran.* Philadelphia, Pa.: University Museum, University of Pennsylvania, 1952.

———. "Man's Golden Age: A Sumerian Parallel to Genesis 11:1." *JAOS* 63 (1943): 191–94.

———. "Reflections on the Mesopotamian Flood: The Cuneiform Data New and Old." *Expedition* 9, no. 4 (1967): 12–18.

———. "The 'Babel of Tongues': A Sumerian Version." *JAOS* 88, no. 1 (1968): 108–11.

Krautheimer, Richard, and Slobodan Curcic. *Early Christian and Byzantine Architecture.* 4th ed. Pelican History of Art. New Haven, Conn.: Yale University Press, 1992.

Kraybill, J. Nelson. *Apocalypse and Allegiance: Worship, Politics, and Devotion in the Book of Revelation.* Grand Rapids: Brazos Press, 2010.

Kuhrt, Amélie. "The Cyrus Cylinder and Achaemenid Imperial Policy." *JSOT* 25, no. 8 (1983): 83–97.

Kutsch, Ernst. *Verheißung Und Gesetz: Untersuchungen Zum Sogenannten Bund Im Alten Testament.* Beihefte Zur Zeitschrift Für Die Alttestamentliche Wissenschaft 13. Berlin: de Gruyter, 1973.

Laessoe, Jørgen. "The Atrahasis Epic, A Babylonian History of Mankind." *Biblioteca Orientalis* 13 (1956): 90–102.

Lambert, Wilfred G. "A New Look at the Babylonian Background of Genesis." *JTS* 16 (1965): 287–300.

———. "Babylonien Und Israel." *Theologische Realenzyklopädie* 5 (1980): 71–72.

Lambert, Wilfred G., and Miguel Civil. "The Sumerian Flood Story." In *Atra-Hasis: The Babylonian Story of the Flood*, edited by Alan R. Millard and Miguel Civil, 138–45. Winona Lake, Ind.: Eisenbrauns, 1999.

Lambrecht, Jan. "The Book of Revelation and Apocalyptic in the New Testament." In *L'Apocalypse Johannique et L' Apocalyptique Dans Le NouveauTestament*, edited by Jan lambrecht, 1–18. Leuven: Leuven University Press, 1980.

Lampe, Peter. "Acta 19 Im Spiegel Der Ephesischen Inschriften." *Biblische Zeitschrift* 36 (1992): 59–76.

Lanciani, Rodolfo Amedeo. *Ancient Rome in the Light of Recent Discoveries.* New York: Houghton, Mifflin & Compan, 1898.

Land, H. T., and G. Feucht. "Expertise, Sample No. PE 257-1, Sample No. PE 257-5." *Undated and Unpublished Report Submitted by Aventis Research & Technologies*, 2003, 1–15.

Langmead, Donald, and Christine Garnaut. *Encyclopedia of Architectural and Engineering Feats.* Santa Barbara, Calf.: ABC-CLIO, 2001.

La Sor, William Sanford. "Merodach-Baladan." In *ISBE2*, edited by Geoffrey W. Bromiley, Revised., 3:325–26. Grand Rapids: Eerdmans, 1995.

Laughlin, John Charles Hugh. "Capernaum: From Jesus' Time and After." *BAR* 19, no. 5 (1993): 54–61.

———. "The Remarkable Discoveries at Tel Dan." *BAR* 7, no. 5 (1981): 20–37.

Lawler, Andrew. "First Churches of the Jesus Cult." *Archaeology* 60, no. 5 (2007): 46.

Lawrence, John M. "Nero Redivivus." *Fides et Historia* 11 (1974): 54–66.

Leithart, Peter J. *A House for My Name: A Survey of the Old Testament.* Moscow, Idaho: Canon, 2000.

LeMaire, André. "A Re-Examination of the Inscribed Pomegranate: A Rejoinder." *IEJ* 56, no. 2 (2006): 167–74.

———. "Fragments from the Book of Balaam Found at Deir Alla: Text Foretells Cosmic Disaster." *BAR* 11, no. 5 (1985): 26–39.

———. "'House of David' Restored in Moabite Inscription." *BAR* 20, no. 3 (1994): 30–37.

———. "Mari, the Bible, and the Northwest Semitic World." *BA* 47, no. 2 (1984): 101–8.

———. "Ostraca and Incised Inscriptions." In *The Renewed Archaeological Excavations at Lachish (1973-1994): Introduction. The Bronze Age Stratigraphy and Architecture*, edited by David Ussishkin, 2099–2132. Tel Aviv, Israel: Emery and Claire Yass Publications in Archaeology, 2004.

———. "Probable Head of Priestly Scepter from Solomon's Temple Surfaces in Jerusalem." *BAR* 10, no. 2 (1984): 24–29.

———. "The Mesha Stele and the Omri Dynasty." In *Ahab Agonistes: The Rise and Fall of the Omri Dynasty*, edited by Lester L. Grabbe, 135–44. The Library of Hebrew Bible/Old Testament Studies 421. New York: Continuum International, 2007.

———. "Une Inscription Paléo-Hébraïque Sur Grenade En Ivoire." *RB* 88 (1981): 236–39.

Lemche, Niels Peter. *The Israelites in History and Tradition.* Library of Ancient Israel. Louisville: Westminster/Knox, 1998.

Lester, Meera. *Sacred Travels.* Fort Collins, Col.: Adams Media, 2011.

Levine, Baruch A. "The Deir 'Alla Plaster Inscriptions." *JAOS* 101 (1981): 195–205.

Levine, Lee I. *The Ancient Synagogue: The First Thousand Years.* 2nd ed. New Haven, Conn.: Yale University Press, 2005.

Levinskaya, Irina A. "The Inscription From Aphrodisias and the Problem of God-Fearers." *TynBul* 41, no. 2 (1990): 312–18.

Lewis, Brian. *The Sargon Legend: A Study of the Akkadian Text and the Tale of the Hero Who Was Exposed at Birth.* ASOR Dissertation Series 4. Cambridge, Mass.: ASOR, 1980.

Lichtheim, Miriam. "The Naucratis Stela Once Again." In *Studies in Honor of George R. Hughes*, edited by Janet H. Johnson, 139–46. Studies in Ancient Oriental Civilizations 39. Chicago, Ill.: Oriental Institute of the University of Chicago, 1977.

Ling-Israel, P. "The Sennacherib Prism in the Israel Museum—Jerusalem." In *Bar-Ilan: Studies in Assyriology Dedicated to Pinḥas Artzi*, edited by J. Klein and A. Skaist, 213–47. Jerusalem: Ramat-Gan: Bar-Ilan University Press, 1990.

Lipinski, Edward, and S. David Sperling. "Jeremiah." In *EJ*, edited by Michael Berenbaum and Fred Skolnik, 2nd ed., 11:124–33. New York: MacMillan, 2006.

Lofenfeld, Lea, and Ramit Frenkel. *The Boat and the Sea of Galilee.* Translated by Ora Cummings. Jerusalem: Gefen, 2007.

Loffreda, Stanislao. *A Visit to Capharnaum.* 3rd ed. Jerusalem: Franciscan, 1975.

———. *Cafarnao II: La Ceramica.* Studium Biblicum Franciscannum 19. Jerusalem, Israel: Franciscan Printing Press, 1975.

———. "Capernaum-Jesus' Own City." *BS* 10, no. 1 (1981): 1–17.

———. *Recovering Capharnaum.* Jerusalem, Israel: Edizioni Custodia Terra Santa, 1985.

———. "The Late Chronology of the Synagogue of Capernaum." *IEJ* 23 (1973): 37–42.

Lohmeyer, Ernst. *Die Offenbarung Des Johannes.* Handbuch Zum Neuen Testament 16. Tübingen: Siebeck, 1926.

Longman, Tremper. *Fictional Akkadian Autobiography: A Generic and Comparative Study.* Winona Lake, Ind.: Eisenbrauns, 1991.

López, René A. "Israelite Covenants in the Light of Ancient Near Eastern Covenants." *Chafer Theological Seminary Journal* 10 (2004): 72–106.

Loretz, Oswald. *Habiru-Hebräer. Eine Sozio-Linguistische Studie über Die Herkunft Des Gentiliziums ‹ibrî Vom Appellativum Habiru.* Beihefte Zur ZAW 160. Berlin: de Gruyter, 1984.

Lubetski, Meir, and Chaim Cohen, eds. "Biblical Hebrew Philology in the Light of Research on the New Yeho'ash Royal Building Inscription." In *New Seals and Inscriptions, Hebrew, Idumean and Cuneiform*, 222–86. Hebrew Bible Monographs 8. Sheffield: Phoenix, 2007.

Luckenbill, Daniel David. "Benhadad and Hadadezer." *The American Journal of Semitic Languages and Literatures* 27, no. 3 (1911): 267–83.

Lyon, R. W. A. "Re-Examination of Codex Ephraemi Rescriptus." *NTS* 5 (1959): 266–72.

Macalister, Robert Alexander Stewart. *The Excavation of Gezer, 1902-1905 and 1907-1909.* 3 vols. London: Murray, 1912.

Magie, David. *Roman Rule in Asia Minor to the End of the Third Century After Christ.* Edited by T. James Luce. 2 vols. Roman History. New York, N.Y.: Arno, 1975.

Magness, Jodi. *The Archaeology of Qumran and the Dead Sea Scrolls.* Grand Rapids: Eerdmans, 2003.

———. "The Arch of Titus at Rome and the Fate of the God of Israel." *JJS* 59, no. 2 (2008): 201–17.

Maier, Paul L. "Archaeology—Biblical Ally or Adversary?" *BS* 17, no. 3 (2004): 83–95.

Malamat, Abraham M. *Mari and the Bible: A Collection of Studies.* Jerusalem: Hebrew University Press, 1977.

———. *Mari and the Early Israelite Experience.* Oxford: Oxford University Press, 1989.

———. "The Ban in Mari and in the Bible." In *Biblical Essays*, 40–49. Proceedings of the Ninth Meeting of Die Ou-Testamentiese Werkgemeenskap in Suid-Afrika 1966. Potchefstroom, South Africa: Society for the Study of the Old Testament, 1967.

Marcos, Natalio Fernández, and Wilfred G. E. Watson. *The Septuagint in Context: Introduction to the Greek Version of the Bible.* Leiden: Brill, 2000.

Mare, W. Harold. *The Archaeology of the Jerusalem Area.* Eugene, Oreg.: Wipf & Stock, 2002.

———. "The Place of Christ's Crucifixion And Burial." *BS* 3, no. 2 (1974): 33–39.

Margueron, Jean-Claude. "Mari." In *OEANE*, edited by Eric M. Meyers, 3:413–16. Oxford: Oxford University Press, 1997.

Markschies, Christoph. *Gnosis: An Introduction*. New York: T&T Clark, 2003.

Marmorstein, A. "About the Inscription of Judah Ben Ishmael." *PEFSt.*, 1927, 101–2.

Marshall, I. Howard. *Acts*. Vol. 5. Tyndale New Testament Commentaries. Grand Rapids: IVP Academic, 2008.

Marshall, I. Howard, Alan R. Millard, James I. Packer, and Donald J. Wiseman, eds. *New Bible Dictionary*. 3rd ed. Downers Grove, Ill.: InterVarsity, 1996.

Marsh, John. *The Gospel of Saint John*. The Pelican New Testament Commentaries. Harmondsworth: Penguin Books, 1968.

Marston, Charles. "The Lachish Letters." *ExpTim* 46, no. 11 (1935): 502–4.

Marucchi, Orazio. "Archaeology of the Cross and Crucifix." Edited by Condé Bénoist Pallen, Charles George Herbermann, and Edward Aloysius Pace. *CE*. New York: Appleton & Company, 1913.

Mason, Steve. *Josephus and the New Testament*. 2nd ed. Peabody, Mass.: Hendrickson, 2003.

Masters, Peter. *Heritage of Evidence: In the British Museum*. London: Wakeman Trust, 2004.

Mathews, Thomas F. *The Clash of Gods: A Reinterpretation of Early Christian Art*. Princeton Paperbacks. Princeton, N.J.: Princeton University Press, 1999.

Matthews, Victor Harold. *Old Testament Parallels: Laws and Stories from the Ancient Near East*. 3 Rev Exp. New York: Paulist, 2007.

Matthiae, Paolo. "Ebla." In *OEANE*, edited by Eric M. Meyers, 2:180–82. Oxford: Oxford University Press, 1997.

———. "Ebla Recovered." In *Ebla to Damascus: Art and Archaeology of Ancient Syria: An Exhibition from the Directorate-General of Antiquities and Museums, Syrian Arab Republic*, edited by Harvey Weiss, 134–39. Washington, D.C.: Smithsonian Institution Traveling Exhibition Service, 1985.

———. "The Archives of the Royal Palace G of Ebla: Distribution and Arrangement of the Tablets according to the Archaeological Evidence." In *Cuneiform Archives and Libraries: Papers Read at the 30e Rencontre Assyriologique Internationale, Leiden, 4-8 1983*, edited by Klaas R. Veenhof, 53–71. Nederlands Historisch-Archaeologisch Instituut Te İstanbul 57. Leiden: Nederlands Historisch-Archaeologisch Instituut te İstanbul, 1986.

Mazar, Amihai. *Archaeology of the Land of the Bible: 10,000-586 B.C.E.* Vol. 1. The Anchor Yale Bible Reference Library. New Haven, Conn.: Yale University Press, 1992.

———. "The Divided Monarchy: Comments on Some Archaeological Issues." In *The Quest for the Historical Israel*, edited by Israel Finkelstein and Brian B. Schmidt, 159–80. Archaeology and Biblical Studies 17. Atlanta, Ga.: SBL, 2007.

Mazar, Benjamin. "Excavations Near the Temple Mount." *Qadmoniot* 5 (1973): 83–84 [in Hebrew].

———. *The Mountain of the Lord: Excavating in Jerusalem*. New York: Doubleday, 1975.

McCarter Jr., P. Kyle. *Ancient Inscriptions: Voices from the Biblical World*. Washington, D.C.: Biblical Archaeology Society, 1996.

———. "The Balaam Texts from Deir 'Alla: The First Combination." *BSOR* 239 (1980): 49–60.

———. "The Historical David." *Int* 40, no. 2 (1986): 117–29.

———. " 'Yaw, Son of 'Omri': A Philological Note on Israelite Chronology." *BASOR*, no. 216 (December 1974): 5–7.

McCarthy, Dennis J. *Treaty and Covenant: A Study in the Ancient Oriental Documents and in the Old Testament.* Analecta Biblica 21. Rome: Biblical Institute, 1981.

McDonagh, Bernard. *Blue Guide: Turkey.* 3rd ed. London: A & C Black, 2001.

McGing, Brian C. "Pontius Pilate and the Sources." *CBQ* 53 (1991): 416–38.

McGrath, Alister E. *Christian Theology: An Introduction.* Hoboken, N.J.: Wiley-Blackwell, 2006.

McKendrick, Scot. "The Codex Alexandrinus or The Dangers of Being A Named Manuscript." In *The Bible as Book: The Transmission of the Greek Text,* edited by Scot McKendrick and Orlaith A. O'Sullivan, 1–16. New Castle, Del.: Oak Knoll, 2003.

McLaren, James S. "Jews and the Imperial Cult: From Augustus to Domitian." *Antichthon* 47 (2013): 156–72.

McNutt, Paula. *The Forging of Israel: Iron Technology, Symbolism and Tradition in Ancient Society.* London: A&C Black, 1990.

McRay, John. *Archaeology and the New Testament.* Grand Rapids: Baker, 1991.

———. "Tomb Typology and the Tomb of Jesus." *Archaeology and the Biblical World* 2, no. 2 (1994): 34–44.

Mendenhall, George E. "Covenant." Edited by G. A. Buttrick and Keith R. Crim. *IDB.* Nashville, Tenn.: Abingdon, 1962.

Merrill, Elmer Truesdell. "The Expulsion of Jews from Rome under Tiberius." *Classical Philology* 14, no. 4 (1919): 365–72.

Metzger, Bruce M. *A Textual Commentary on the Greek New Testament.* 2nd ed. Stuttgart, Germany: Deutsche Bibelgesellschaft, 2002.

———. *Manuscripts of the Greek Bible: An Introduction to Greek Palaeography.* Oxford: Oxford University Press, 1981.

———. *New Testament Studies: Philological, Versional, and Patristic.* Leiden: Brill, 1980.

Metzger, Bruce M., and Bart D. Ehrman. *The Text of the New Testament: Its Transmission, Corruption, and Restoration.* 4th ed. Oxford: Oxford University Press, 2005.

Meyer, Marvin. *The Gnostic Discoveries: The Impact of the Nag Hammadi Library.* New York: HarperCollins, 2005.

Meyers, Eric M. "Ancient Synagogues in Galilee: Their Cultural and Religious Setting." *Biblical Archaeologist* 43 (1980): 97–108.

———. ed. *The Oxford Encyclopedia of Archaeology in the Near East.* 5 vols. Oxford: Oxford University Press, 1997.

Miano, David. *Shadow on the Steps: Time Measurement in Ancient Israel.* Resources for Biblical Study. Atlanta, Ga.: Society of Biblical Literature, 2010.

Miano, David, and Sarah Miano, eds. *Milk and Honey: Essays on Ancient Israel and the Bible in Appreciation of the Judaic Studies Program at the University of California.* Winona Lake, Ind.: Eisenbrauns, 2007.

Millard, Alan R. "An Assessment of the Evidence for Writing in Ancient Israel." In *Biblical Archaeology Today, Proceedings of the International Congress on Biblical Archaeology, Jerusalem,* edited by Avraham Biran, 301–12. Jerusalem: Israel Exploration Society, 1985.

———. "A New Babylonian 'Genesis' Story." *TynBul* 18 (1967): 3–18.

———. "A New Babylonian 'Genesis' Story." In *"I Studied Inscriptions from before the Flood": Ancient Newr Eastern, Literary, and Linguistic Approaches to Genesis 1-11*, edited by Richard S. Hess and D. T. Tsumura, 114–28. Winona Lake, Ind.: Eisenbrauns, 1994.

———. "Authors, Books and Readers in the Ancient World." In *The Oxford Handbook of Biblical Studies*, edited by J. W. Rogerson and Judith M. Lieu. Oxford Handbooks. Oxford: Oxford University Press, 2008.

———. *Discoveries from Bible Times: Archaeological Treasures Throw Light on the Bible.* Oxford: Lion Books, 1997.

Millar, Fergus. "Last Year in Jerusalem: Monuments of the Jewish War in Rome." In *Flavius Josephus and Flavian Rome*, edited by Jonathan Edmondson, Steve Mason, and James B. Rives, 101–28. Oxford: Oxford University Press, 2005.

———. "Local Cultures in the Roman Empire: Libyan, Punic and Latin in Roman Africa." *JRS* 58 (1968): 126–34.

———. *Rome, the Greek World, and the East: Volume 2: Government, Society, and Culture in the Roman Empire.* Studies in the History of Greece and Rome. Chapel Hill, N.C.: University of North Carolina Press, 2004.

Miller, James Maxwell. "The Moabite Stone as a Memorial Stela." *PEQ* 106 (1974): 9–18.

Miller, Patrick D. "Eridu, Dunu, and Babel: A Study in Comparative Mythology." *Hebrew Annual Review* 9 (1985): 227–51.

Mitchell, T. C. *Biblical Archaeology: Documents from the British Museum.* Cambridge: Cambridge University Press, 1988.

———. "Judah Until the Fall of Jerusalem." In *The Cambridge Ancient History: The Assyrian and Babylonian Empires and Other States of the Near East, from the Eighth to the Sixth Centuries BC*, edited by John Boardman, I. E. S. Edwards, Edmond Sollberger, and N. G. L. Hammond, 3:, Part 2:371–409. Cambridge: Cambridge University Press, 1992.

———. *The Bible in the British Museum: Interpreting the Evidence.* Mahwah, N.J.: Paulist, 2004.

Moeller, Nadine, and Robert K. Ritner. "The Ahmose 'Tempest Stela', Thera and Comparative Chronology." *JNES* 73, no. 1 (April 1, 2014): 1–19.

Mommsen, M., I. Perlman, and J. Yellin. "The Provenience of the 'Lmlk' Jars." *IEJ* 34, no. 2/3 (1984): 89–113.

Moran, William L. *Amarna Studies: Collected Writings.* Edited by John Huehnergard and Shlomo Izreʿel. Winona Lake, Ind.: Eisenbrauns, 2003.

Morgan, Charles H., II. "Excavations at Corinth, 1935-1936." *AJA* 40, no. 4 (1936): 466–84.

Morrey, P. R. S. "Where Did They Bury the Kings of the IIIrd Dynasty of Ur?" *Iraq* 46, no. 1 (1984): 1–18.

Moss, Candida R., and Joel S. Baden. "Why Did the Museum of the Bible's Scholars Destroy Ancient Egyptian Artifacts?" *The Christian Century*, November 29, 2017. https://www.christiancentury.org/article/features/why-did-museum-bible-s-scholars-destroy-ancient-egyptian-artifacts.

Murphy-O'Connor, Jerome. *St. Paul's Corinth: Text and Archaeology.* Good News Studies 6. Minneapolis, Minn.: Liturgical, 2002.

———. *The Holy Land: An Oxford Archaeological Guide From Earliest Times to 1700.* 5th ed. Oxford Archaeological Guides. Oxford: Oxford University Press, 2008.

———. "Where Was Jesus Born? Bethlehem… Of Course." *BR*, February 2000, 40–45, 50.

Mykytiuk, Lawrence J. "Corrections and Updates to 'Identifying Biblical Persons in Northwest Semitic Inscriptions of 1200-539 BC.'" *Maarav* 16 (2009): 49–132.

———. *Identifying Biblical Persons in Northwest Semitic Inscriptions of 1200-539 B.C.E.* SBL Academia Biblica 12. Atlanta, Ga.: Society of Biblical Literature, 2004.

Na'aman, Nadav. "Habiru and Hebrews: The Transfer of a Social Term to the Literary Sphere." *JNES* 45 (1986): 271–88.

———. "Israel, Edam and Egypt in the 10th Century B.C.E." *Tel Aviv* 19 (1992): 71–93, 81.

———. "Sennacherib's Campaign to Judah and the Date of the Lmlk Stamps." *VT* 29, no. 1 (1979): 61–86.

———. "Sennacherib's 'Letter to God' on His Campaign to Judah." *BASOR* 214 (1974): 25–39.

Naveh, Joseph. "The Date of the Deir 'Alla Inscription in Aramaic Script." *IEJ* 17 (1967): 236–38.

———. "The Ossuary Inscriptions from Giv'at Ha-Mivtar." *IEJ* 20, no. 1 (1970): 33–37.

Naʾaman, Nadav. "Hezekiah's Fortified Cities and the 'LMLK' Stamps." *BASOR*, no. 261 (February 1, 1986): 5–21.

Netzer, Ehud. "The Last Days and Hours at Masada." *BAR* 17, no. 6 (1991): 20–32.

———. *The Buildings, Stratigraphy and Architecture (Masada 3).* Jerusalem: Israel Exploration Society, 1991.

Newberry, Percy Edward. "Beni Hasan Part I." In *Archaeological Survey of Egypt*, edited by Fl Griffith, 41–79. London: Egypt Exploration Fund, 1893.

Newman, Francis William. *A History of the Hebrew Monarchy: From the Administration of Samuel to the Babylonish Captivity.* London: Chapman, 1853.

Newman, Murray. "Review of Meredith G. Kline, The Structure of Biblical Authority and Ernst Kutsch, Verheißung Und Gesetz: Untersuchungen Zum Sogenannten Bund Im Alten Testament." *JBL* 94, no. 1 (1975): 117–18, 120.

Newton, Homer Curtis. *The Epigraphical Evidence for the Reigns of Vespasian and Titus.* Edited by Charles Edwin Bennett, John Robert Sitlington Sterrett, and George Prentice Bristol. Ithaca, N.Y.: Cornell University Press, 1901.

Ngo, Robin, ed. *Masada: The Dead Sea's Desert Fortress.* Washington, D.C.: Biblical Archaeology Society, 2014.

Niccacci, Alviero. "The Stele of Mesha and the Bible: Verbal System and Narrativity." *Orientalia* 63, no. 3 (1994): 226–48.

Niehaus, Jeffrey J. *Ancient Near Eastern Themes in Biblical Theology.* Grand Rapids: Kregel, 2008.

Novotny, Jamie. "New Proposed Chronological Sequence and Dates of Composition of Esarhaddon's Babylon Inscriptions." *JCS* 67 (January 1, 2015): 145–68.

Oded, Bustanay. "Gezer Calendar." Edited by Fred Skolnik and Michael Berenbaum. *EJ.* New York: MacMillan, December 12, 2006.

Oden, Robert A. "Divine Aspirations in Atrahasis and in Genesis 1-11." *ZAW* 93 (1981): 197–216.

Oliver, Harold H. "A Textual Transposition in Codex C (Ephraemi Syri Rescriptus)." *JBL* 76, no. 3 (1957): 233–36.

Olmstead, Albert T. "The Text of Sargon's Annals." *The American Journal of Semitic Languages and Literatures* 47, no. 4 (1931): 259–80.

Orfali, Gaudence. *Capharnaum et Ses Ruines D'après Les Fouilles Accomplies Par La Custodie Franciscaine de Terre Sainte (1905-1921)*. Paris, France: Picard, 1922.

Orlinksy, Harry M. *Israel Exploration Journal Reader Selected with a Prolegomenon*. 2 vols. New York: Ktav, 1981.

Ortiz, Steven M. "The Archaeology of David and Solomon: Method or Madness?" In *Do Historical Matters Matter to Faith?: A Critical Appraisal of Modern and Postmodern Approaches to Scripture*, edited by James K. Hoffmeier and Graham A. Magary, 497–516. Wheaton, Ill.: Crossway Books, 2012.

Ory, J. "An Inscription Newly Found in the Synagogue of Kerazeh." *PEFSt.*, 1927, 51–52.

Ousterhout, Robert. "Rebuilding the Temple: Constantine Monomachus and the Holy Sepulchre." *The Journal of the Society of Architectural Historians* 48, no. 1 (1989): 66–78.

Packer, J. I., Merrill C. Tenney, and William White, eds. *Illustrated Manners and Customs of the Bible*. Nashville, Tenn.: Nelson, 1997.

Paget, James Carleton. "After 70 and All That: A Response to Martin Goodman's Rome and Jerusalem." *JSNT* 31, no. 3 (March 2009): 339–65.

Panteleon, Ioannis Andreas. *Eine Archäologie der Direktoren. Die Erforschung Milets im Namen der Berliner Museen 1899–1914*. Mittelmeerstudien 5. Schöningh: Paderborn, 2015.

Pape, Wilhelm, and Gustav Eduard Benseler. *Wörterbuch Der Griechischen Eigennamen*. Braunschweig: Vieweg & Sohn, 1911.

Pardee, Dennis. "Ugaritic." In *OEANE*, edited by Eric M. Meyers, 5:262–64. Oxford: Oxford Biblical Studies Online, 1997.

———. "Ugaritic Inscriptions." In *OEANE*, edited by Eric M. Meyers, 5:264–66. Oxford: Oxford Biblical Studies Online, 1997.

Pardee, Dennis, and J. T. Glass. "The Mari Archives." *BA* 47 (1984): 88–100.

Parker, David C. "Was Matthew Written Before 50 CE? The Magdalen Papyrus Of Matthew." *ExpTim* 107 (1996): 40–43.

Parkinson, R. B., trans. *The Tale of Sinuhe and Other Ancient Egyptian Poems*. Oxford: Oxford World's Classics, 1999.

Parrot, André. *Abraham and His Times*. Minneapolis, Minn.: Fortress, 1968.

———. *The Tower of Babel*. Translated by Edwin Hudson. Studies in Biblical Archaeology. London: SCM, 1955.

Pearse, Roger. "The Nag Hammadi Discovery of Manuscripts." *A Survey of the Manuscripts of Some Ancient Authors*, July 31, 2003. http://www.tertullian.org/rpearse/manuscripts/nag_hammadi.htm.

Pedersen, Olof. *Archives and Libraries in the Ancient Near East 1500-300 B.C.* Bethesda, Md.: CDL, 1998.

Perrot, Jean, ed. *The Palace of Darius at Susa: The Great Royal Residence of Achaemenid Persia*. London: Tauris, 2013.

Peters, John P. "Excavations in Persia." *HTR* 8, no. 1 (1915): 82–93.

Petrie, William M. Flinders. *Six Temples at Thebes in 1896*. London: Quaritch, 1897.

Pettinato, Giovanni. "Ebla and the Bible." *BA* 43 (1980): 203–16.

———. *Ebla, A New Look at History.* Translated by C. Faith Richardson. Near Eastern Studies. Baltimore, Md.: Johns Hopkins University Press, 1991.

———. "Gli archivi reali di Tell Mardikh-Ebla: riflessioni e prospettive." *Rivista Biblica Italiana* 25, no. 1 (1977): 225–43.

Pfanner, Michael. *Der Titusbogen.* Beitrage Zur Erschliessung Hellenistischer Und Kaiserzeitlicher Skulptur Und Architektur 2. Mainz am Rhein: von Zabern, 1983.

Pfeiffer, Charles F. "Habiru, Hapiru." *WDBA.* Peabody, Mass.: Hendrickson, 2000.

———. *Ras Shamra and the Bible.* Grand Rapids: Baker, 1962.

———. , ed. *Wycliffe Dictionary of Biblical Archaeology.* Peabody, Mass.: Hendrickson, 2000.

Pinch, Geraldine. *Magic in Ancient Egypt.* Austin, Tex.: University of Texas Press, 1995.

Pitard, Wayne T. *Ancient Damascus: A Historical Study of the Syrian City-State from Earliest Times Until Its Fall to the Assyrians in 732 B.C.E.* New edition edition. Winona Lake, Ind.: Eisenbrauns, 1987.

———. "Voices from the Dust: The Tablets from Ugarit and the Bible." In *Mesopotamia and the Bible: Comparative Explorations*, edited by Mark W. Chavalas and K. Lawson Younger, 251–75. JSOTSup 341. London: T&T Clark, 2003.

Pococke, Richard. *A Description of the East and Some Other Countries.* Vol. 2, Part 1. London: Bowyer, 1745.

Pollock, Susan. "Ur." In *OEANE*, edited by Eric M. Meyers, 5:5:288–91. Oxford: Oxford Biblical Studies Online, 1997.

Porter, H. "Money." Edited by James Orr and Melvin Grove Kyle. *ISBE2*, 1915.

Porter, Stanley E. *How We Got the New Testament: Text, Transmission, Translation.* Edited by Craig Evans and Lee McDonald. Acadia Studies in Bible and Theology. Grand Rapids: Baker Academic, 2013.

Postgate, J. Nicholas. "The Four 'Neo-Assyrian' Tablets from Šēẖ Ḥamad." *State Archives of Assyria Bulletin* 7 (1993): 109–24.

Powell, Benjamin. "Greek Inscription from Corinth." *AJA* 7, No. 1 (1903): 60–61.

Price, J. Randall. *Rose Guide to the Temple.* Torrance, Calif.: Rose, 2012.

———. *The Dead Sea Scrolls Pamphlet: The Discovery Heard around the World.* Torrance, Calif.: Rose, 2005.

———. *The Stones Cry Out: What Archaeology Reveals About the Truth of the Bible.* Eugene, Oreg.: Harvest House, 1997.

Price, J. Randall, and H. Wayne House. *Zondervan Handbook of Biblical Archaeology: A Book by Book Guide to Archaeological Discoveries Related to the Bible.* Grand Rapids: Zondervan, 2018.

Pringle, Dennis. *The Defence of Byzantine Africa from Justinian to the Arab Conquest: An Account Of The Military History And Archaeology Of The African Provinces In The Sixth And Seventh Centuries.* 2 vols. BAR. International Series. Oxford: British Archaeological Reports, 1981.

Provan, Iain W., V. Philips Long, Tremper Longman III, and Philips V. Long. *A Biblical History of Israel.* 1st ed. Louisville: Westminster/Knox, 2003.

Psychoyos, Dimitris K. "The Forgotten Art of Isopsephy and the Magic Number KZ." *Semiotica* 154, no. 1–4 (2005): 157–224.

Quirke, Stephen. *Egyptian Literature 1800 BC: Questions and Readings.* Revised. GHP Egyptology 2. Golden House, 2004.

Rabello, A. M. "The Legal Condition of the Jews in the Roman Empire." In *ANRW*, edited by Hildegard Temporini and Wolfgang Haase, 662–762. Part 2, Principat 13.1. Berlin: De Gruyter, 1989.

Ragozin, Zénaïde Alexeïevna. *The Story of Assyria from the Rise of the Empire to the Fall of Nineveh.* New York: Putnam's Sons, 1893.

Rainey, Anson F. "Rainey's Challenge: Can You Name the Panel with the Israelites?" *BAR* 17, no. 6 (1991): 56–60, 93.

———. "The 'House of David' and the House of the Deconstructionists." *BAR* 20, no. 6 (1994): 47.

———. "Watching for the Signal Fires of Lachish." *PEQ* 119 (1987): 149–51.

Ramsay, William M. *The Cities of St. Paul: Their Influence on His Life and Thought, The Cities of Eastern Asia Minor.* Whitefish, Mont.: Kessinger, 2004.

———. *The Letters to Seven Churches: Updated Edition.* Edited by Mark W. Wilson. Peabody, Mass.: Hendrickson, 1994.

Rapaport, Izaak. *Tablet XI of the Gilgamesh Epic and the Biblical Flood Story: A Refutation of the Generally Held View That Genesis Chapters 6-9 Is Based upon a Babylonian Prototype.* Tel Aviv, Israel: Tel Aviv University Press, 1981.

Rapske, Brian M. "Citizenship, Roman." Edited by Craig A. Evans and Stanley E. Porter. *DNTB.* Downers Grove, Ill.: InterVarsity, 2000.

Rassam, Hormuzd. *Asshur and the Land of Nimrod.* New York: Eaton & Mains, 1807.

Reasoner, M. "The City of Rome in the First Century A.D." In *DNTB*, edited by Craig A. Evans and Stanley E. Porter, 1016. Downers Grove, Ill.: InterVarsity, 2000.

Redford, Donald B. "Textual Sources for the Hyksos Period." In *The Hyksos: New Historical and Archaeological Perspectives*, edited by Eliezer D. Oren, 1–44. Philadelphia, Pa.: University of Pennsylvania Museum, 1997.

———. "The Ashkelon Reliefs at Karnak and the Israel Stela." *IEJ* 36 (1986): 188–200.

Regev, Johanna, Pierre de Miroschedji, Raphael Greenberg, Eliot Braun, Zvi Greenhut, and Elisabetta Boaretto. "Chronology of the Early Bronze Age in the Southern Levant: New Analysis for a High Chronology." *Radiocarbon* 3–4 (2012): 525–66.

Reich, Ronny. "Caiaphas Name Inscribed on Bone Boxes." *BAR* 18 (1992): 38–44.

Reich, Ronny, and Eli Shukron. "The Siloam Pool in the Wake of Recent Discoveries." In *New Studies on Jerusalem*, edited by Eyal Baruch, Ayelet Levy-Reifer, and Avraham Faust, 137–39. 10. Jerusalem, Israel: Bar-Ilan University, 2004.

Reider, Joseph. "The Lachish Letters." *JQR* 29, no. 3 (1939): 225–39.

Reif, Stefan C., Shulamit Reif, Salomon Marcus Schiller-Szinessy, Herbert M. J. Loewe, and Jacob Leveen. *Hebrew Manuscripts at Cambridge University Library: A Description and Introduction.* University of Cambridge Oriental Publications 52. New York: Cambridge University Press, 1997.

Rendsburg, Gary A. "A Reconstruction of Moabite and Israelite History." *Journal of the Ancient Near Eastern Society of Columbia University* 13 (1981): 67–73.

———. "Israel Without the Bible." In *The Hebrew Bible: New Insights and Scholarship*, edited by Frederick E. Greenspahn, 3–23. Jewish Studies in the Twenty-First Century. New York: New York University Press, 2007.

Reynolds, Joyce Maire, and Robert F. Tannenbaum. *Jews and God-Fearers at Aphrodisias: Greek Inscriptions with Commentary: Texts from the Excavations at Aphrodisias Conducted by Kenan T. Erim.* Proceedings of the

Cambridge Philological Association Supplement 12. Cambridge: Cambridge Philological Society, 1987.

Riesner, Rainer. *Paul's Early Period: Chronology, Mission Strategy, Theology.* Translated by Douglas W. Stott. Grand Rapids: Eerdmans, 1998.

Ritmeyer, Leen. *The Quest: Revealing the Temple Mount in Jerusalem.* Jerusalem: Carta, 2006.

Rives, James B. "Flavian Religious Policy and the Destruction of the Jerusalem Temple." In *Flavius Josephus and Flavian Rome*, edited by Jonathan Edmondson, Steve Mason, and James B. Rives, 145–66. Oxford: Oxford University Press, 2005.

Roberts, Bleddyn J. "Recent Discoveries of Hebrew Manuscripts." *ExpTim* 60, no. 11 (1949): 305–8.

Roberts, C. H. "An Early Papyrus of the First Gospel." *Harvard Theological Review* 46 (1953): 233.

Robinson, Edward. *Biblical Researches in Palestine and in the Adjacent Regions.* 2nd ed. Vol. 1. Boston, Mass.: Crocker & Brewster, 1860.

Robinson, James M. "The Discovery of the Nag Hammadi Codices." *BA* 42, no. 4 (October 1, 1979): 206–24.

Rogers, Jr., Cleon L. "The Covenant with Abraham and Its Historical Setting." *BSac* 127 (1970): 241–56.

Rogerson, John W., and Philip R. Davies. "Was the Siloam Tunnel Built by Hezekiah?" *BA* 59, no. 3 (1996): 138–49.

Rohde, Erwin. *Der griechische Roman und seine Vorläufer.* Leipzig: Breitkopf & Härtel, 1914.

Rohl, David M. *Pharaohs and Kings: A Biblical Quest.* New York: Three Rivers, 1997.

Rollston, Christopher A. "Non-Provenanced Epigraphs I: Pillaged Antiquities, Northwest Semitic Forgeries, and Protocols for Laboratory Tests." *Maarav* 10 (2003): 135–93.

Rollston, Christopher A., and Andrew G. Vaughn. "The Antiquities Market, Sensationalized Textual Data, and Modern Forgeries." *NEA* 68, no. 1–2 (2005): 61–68.

Rosenfeld, Amnon, Shimon Ilani, H. R. Feldman, W. E. Krumbein, and J. Kronfeld. "Archaeometric Analysis of the 'Jehoash Inscription.'" *Journal of Archaeological Science* 35 (2008): 2966–72.

Rosenfeld, Amnon, Shimon Ilani, Yoel Kronfeld, Howard R. Feldman, and Elan M. Telem. "Archaeometric Analysis of the "'Jehoash Inscription'" Stone Describing the Renovation of the First Temple of Jerusalem." In *Geological Society of America Abstracts with Programs*, 7:278. Annual Meeting: Salt Lake City 37. Boulder, Colo.: GSA, 2005.

Roth, Leland M. *Understanding Architecture: Its Elements, History, And Meaning.* Boulder, Colo.: Westview, 1993.

Roth, Martha T. *Law Collections from Mesopotamia and Asia Minor.* 2nd ed. Atlanta, Ga.: Society of Biblical Literature, 1997.

Roth, Mitchel P. *Prisons and Prison Systems: A Global Encyclopedia.* Westport, Conn.: Greenwood, 2006.

Rousée, J. -M. "Chroniques Archéologiques." *RB* 69 (1962): 107–9.

Rousée, J. -M., and M. -J. Pierre. "Sainte-Marie de La Probatique, état et Orientation Des Recherches." *Proche-Orient Chrétien* 33 (1981): 23–42.

Rousée, J. -M., and Roland de Vaux. "Chroniques Archéologiques." *RB* 64 (1957): 226–28.

Rousseau, John J., and Rami Arav. *Jesus and His World: An Archaeological and Cultural Dictionary.* Minneapolis, Minn.: Fortress, 1995.

Roux, Georges. "The Great Enigma of the Cemetery at Ur." In *Everyday Life in Ancient Mesopotamia*, edited by Jean Bottéro, translated by Antonia Nevill, 24–40. Baltimore, Md.: Johns Hopkins University Press, 2001.

Rowley, Harold Henry. *Darius, the Mede and the Four Empires in the Book of Daniel: A Historical Study of Contemporary Theories*. Cardiff: University of Wales Press, 1935.

Rudich, Vasily. *Political Dissidence Under Nero: The Price of Dissimulation*. New York: Routledge, 1993.

Rummel, Stan, A. Cooper, F. B. Knutson, M. H. Pope, and R. E. Whitaker. *Ras Shamra Parallels: The Texts from Ugarit and the Hebrew Bible*. Analecta Orientalia 51. Rome: Gregorian University Press, 1981.

Rupprecht, Arthur A. "The House of Annas-Caiaphas." *Archaeology in the Biblical World* 1, no. 1 (1991): 4–17.

Russell, James Stuart. *The Parousia. A Critical Inquiry into the New Testament Doctrine of Our Lord's Second Coming*. London: Dalby, Isbister & Co., 1878.

———. *The Parousia. The New Testament Doctrine of Our Lord's Second Coming*. Grand Rapids: Baker, 1999.

Sáenz-Badillos, Angel. *A History of the Hebrew Language*. Translated by John Elwolde. Cambridge: Cambridge University Press, 1996.

Salmenkivi, Erja. *Cartonnage Papyri in Context: New Ptolemaic Documents from Abū Ṣīr Al-Malaq*. Helsinki: The Finish Society of Sciences and Letters, 2002.

Sambursky, Shmuel. "On the Origin and Significance of the Term 'Gematria.'" *JJS* 29, no. 1 (1978): 35–38.

Sanders, Henry A. "The Birth Certificate of a Roman Citizen." *Classical Philology* 22, no. 4 (1927): 409–13.

———. "The Number of the Beast in Revelation." *JBL*, 95-99, 37, no. 1 (1918).

Sass, Benjamin. "The Pre-Exilic Hebrew Seals: Iconism vs. Aniconism." In *Studies in the Iconography of Northwest Semitic Inscribed Seals: Proceedings of a Symposium Held in Fribourg on April 17-20, 1991*, edited by Benjamin Sass and Christoph Uehlinger, 194–256. Orbis Biblicus et Orientalis 125. Gottingen: Vandenhoeck & Ruprecht, 1993.

Sass, Benjamin, and Christoph Uehlinger, eds. *Studies in the Iconography of Northwest Semitic Inscribed Seals: Proceedings of a Symposium Held in Fribourg on April 17-20, 1991*. Orbis Biblicus et Orientalis 125. Gottingen: Vandenhoeck & Ruprecht, 1993.

Sasson, Victor. "Philological and Textural Observations on the Controversial Jehoash Inscription." *UF* 35 (2004): 573–87.

———. "The Siloam Tunnel Inscription." *PEQ* 114 (1982): 111–17.

Sayce, A. H. *The Hittites the Story of a Forgotten Empire*. Classic Reprint. Charleston, SC: Forgotten Books, 2012.

Schaeffer, Claude F. A. *The Cuneiform Texts of Ras Shamra-Ugarit: The Schweich Lectures of the British Academy 1937*. Munich: Periodicals Service Co, 1986.

Schein, Bruce. "The Second Wall of Jerusalem." *BA* 44, no. 1 (1981): 21–26.

Schiffman, Lawrence H., ed. *Archaeology and History in the Dead Sea Scrolls: The New York University Conference in Memory of Yigael Yadin*. Vol. JSOT/ASOR Monographs 2. Journal for the Study of the Pseudepigrapha Supplement Series 8. Sheffield: JSOT Press, 1990.

Schmidt, Brian B. "Neo-Assyrian and Syro-Palestinian Texts I: The Moabite Stone." In *Ancient Near East: Historical Sources in Translation*, edited by Mark W. Chavalas, 311–12. Blackwell Sourcebooks in Ancient History. Oxford: Wiley & Sons, 2006.

Schmidt, Erich F. *Persepolis II: Contents of the Treasury and Other Discoveries.* Oriental Institute Publications 69. Chicago, Ill.: University Of Chicago Press, 1957.

———. *The Persepolis Expedition.* Aerial Survey Expedition. Chicago, Ill.: University Of Chicago Press, 1941.

Schmitz, Philip C. "Procopius' Phoenician Inscriptions: Never Lost, Not Found." *PEQ* 139, no. 2 (2007): 99–104.

Schneider, Tammi. "Did King Jehu Kill His Own Family?" *BAR* 21, no. 1 (1995): 26–33, 80–82.

Schneider, Tsvi. "Six Biblical Signatures: Seals and Seal Impressions of Six Biblical Personages Recovered." *BAR* 17, no. 4 (1991): 26–33.

Schoville, Keith N. "Top Ten Archaeological Discoveries of the Twentieth Century Relating to the Biblical World." *Stone Campbell Journal* 4, no. 1 (2001): 29–34.

Schulz, Fritz. "Roman Registers of Births and Birth-Certificates, Part I." *JRS* 32, no. 1–2 (1943): 55–64.

———. "Roman Registers of Births and Birth Certificates. Part II." *JRS* 33, no. 1–2 (1943): 78–91.

Schumacher, Gottlieb, and C. Steuernagel. *Tell El-Mutesellim: Text.* Vol. 1, A. Leipzig: Haupt, 1908.

Schürer, Emil. *The History of the Jewish People in the Age of Jesus Christ (175 BC–AD 135).* Edited by G. Vermes, F. Miller, and M. Black. Rev. 2 vols. Edinburgh: T&T Clark, 1979.

Scranton, Robert L. *Corinth.* Corinth 1.3. Princeton, N.J.: American School of Classical Studies at Athens, 1951.

Seager, Robin. *Tiberius.* Oxford: Blackwell, 2008.

Seely, Jo Ann H. "The Fruit of the Vine: Wine at Masada and in the New Testament." In *Masada & the World of the New Testament*, edited by John W. Welch and John F. Hall, 207–27. Byu Studies Monographs. Provo, Utah: Friends of the Library, 1997.

Segal, Peretz. "The Penalty of the Warning Inscription from the Temple of Jerusalem." *IEJ* 39, no. 1/2 (1989): 79–84.

Seligmann, M. "Nimrod." In *JE*, edited by Isidore Singer, Cyrus Adler, Gotthard Deutsch, Kaufmann Kohler, and Emil G. Hirsch, 9:309–11. New York: Funk & Wagnalls, 1906.

Seow, Choon-Leong. "Deir 'Alla Plaster Texts." In *Prophets and Prophecy in the Ancient Near East*, edited by Peter Machinist and Martti Nissinen. Atlanta, GA: Society of Biblical Literature, 2003.

Shanks, Hershel. "Fingerprint of Jeremiah's Scribe." *BAR* 22, no. 2 (1996): 36–38.

———. "First Person: A New Target." *BAR* 40, no. 6 (2014).

———. "History of Bethlehem Documented by First Temple Period Bulla from the City of David: Jesus' Birthplace in Ancient Bethlehem Confirmed as an Israelite City Centuries Earlier." *BAR*, May 23, 2012, n.p.

———. "Is Oded Golan a Forger?" *BAR* 29, no. 5 (2003): 34–37.

———. "Jeremiah's Scribe and Confidant Speaks from a Hoard of Clay Bullae." *BAR* 13, no. 5 (1987): 58–65.

———. "Messages from the Past: Hebrew Bullae from the Time of Isaiah Through the Destruction of the First Temple." *Biblical Archaeology Review* 26, no. 2 (April 2000): 64–67.

———. "The Exodus and the Crossing of the Red Sea, According to Hans Goedicke." *BAR* 7, no. 5 (1981): 42–50.

———. "The Pomegranate Scepter Head—From the Temple of the Lord or from a Temple of Asherah?" *BAR* 18, no. 3 (1992): 42–45.

———. "The Siloam Pool: Where Jesus Cured the Blind Man." *BAR* 31, no. 5 (2005): 17–23.

———. "The Three Shekels and Widow's Plea Ostraca: Real or Fake?" *BAR* 29, no. 3 (June 2003): 40–45.

———. "Three Shekels for the Lord, Ancient Inscription Records Gift to Solomon's Temple." *BAR* 23, no. 6 (1997): 28–32.

———. "Will King Hezekiah Be Dislodged from His Tunnel?" *BAR* 39, no. 5 (2013): 52–54.

Shanks, Hershel, Niels Peter Lemche, Thomas L. Thompson, William G. Dever, and P. Kyle McCarter Jr. "Face to Face: Biblical Minimalists Meet Their Challenge." *BAR* 23, no. 4 (1997): 26–42, 66.

Shanks, Hershel, and James F. Strange. "Has the House Where Jesus Stayed in Capernaum Been Found?" In *Archaeology in the World of Herod, Jesus, and Paul*, edited by Hershel Shanks and Dan P. Cole, 188–99. Washington, D.C.: Biblical Archaeology Society, 1990.

Shea, William H. "Artistic Balance Among the Beni Hasan Asiatics." *BA* 44 (1981): 219–28.

———. "Esther and History." *AUSS* 14 (1976): 227–46.

———. "Nabonidus, Belshazzar, and the Book of Daniel: An Update." *AUSS* 20, no. 2 (1982): 133–49.

———. "Sennacherib's Description of Lachish and of Its Conquest." *AUSS* 26, no. 2 (1988): 171–80.

———. "Sennacherib's Second Palestinian Campaign." *JBL* 104, no. 3 (1985): 401–18.

———. "The Inscribed Tablets From Tell Deir ʿAlla." *AUSS* 27 (1989): 21–37; 97–119.

Sherwin-White, Adrian N. *Roman Society and Roman Law in the New Testament: The Sarum Lectures 1960-1961.* Oxford University Press Academic Monograph Reprints. Oxford: Clarendon, 2004.

———. *The Roman Citizenship.* Oxford: Clarendon, 1980.

———. "The Roman Citizenship: A Survey of Its Development into a World Franchise." In *ANRW*, edited by Hildegard Temporini and Wolfgang Haase, 23–58. Part 1, Principat 2. Berlin: De Gruyter, 1974.

Siddall, Luis Robert. "Tiglath-Pileser III's Aid to Ahaz: A New Look at the Problems of the Biblical Accounts in the Light of the Assyrian Sources." *ANES* 46 (2009): 93–106.

Sigrist, M., Zadok, R., and Walker, C. B. F., ***Catalogue of the Babylonian Tablets in the British Museum, III,*** London, BMP, 2006.

Silva, Moisés, and Karen Jobes. *Invitation to the Septuagint.* Grand Rapids: Baker Academic & Brazos, 2005.

Singer, Isidore, Cyrus Adler, Gotthard Deutsch, Kaufmann Kohler, and Emil G. Hirsch, eds. *The Jewish Encyclopedia.* 12 vols. New York: Funk & Wagnalls, 1906.

Sivan, Daniel. "The Gezer Calendar and Northwest Semitic Linguistics." *IEJ* 48, no. 1–2 (1998): 101–5.

Sivertsen, Barbara J. *The Parting of the Sea: How Volcanoes, Earthquakes, and Plagues Shaped the Story of Exodus.* Princeton, N.J.: Princeton University Press, 2011.

Skeat, Theodore C. "The Codex Sinaiticus, the Codex Vaticanus and Constantine." *JTS* 50, no. 2 (1999): 583–625.

———. "The Codex Vaticanus in the Fifteenth Century." *JTS* 35, no. 2 (n.d.): 454–65.

———. "The Oldest Manuscript Of The Four Gospels?" *NTS* 43 (1997): 1–34.

Skinner, Christopher W. *What Are They Saying About the Gospel of Thomas?* New York: Paulist, 2012.

Slingerland, H. Dixon. "Acts 18:1-18, the Gallio Inscription, and Absolute Pauline Chronology." *JBL* 110, no. 3 (1991): 439–49.

———. "Chrestus: Christus?" In *The Literature of Early Rabbinic Judaism: Issues in Talmudic Redaction and Interpretation*, edited by Alan J. Avery-Peck, 133–44. New Perspectives on Ancient Judaism 4. Lanham, Md.: University Press of America, 1989.

Smith, George. "Early History of Babylonia." In *Transactions of the Society of Biblical Archaeology*, 1:28–92. London: Longmans, Green, Reader & Dyer, 1872.

Smith, George E. *Assyrian Discoveries: An Account of Explorations and Discoveries on the Site on Nineveh, During 1878 and 1874*. New York: Scribner, Armstrong & Co., 1875.

———. "The Chaldean Account of the Deluge." *PSBA* 2 (1872): 213–34.

Smith, Henry B. "Bethlehem: Seal Uncovered in the City of David." *Associate for Biblical Research*, May 25, 2012.

Smith, William. *Dictionary of Greek and Roman Antiquities*. London: Murray, 1875.

Smoak, Jeremy Daniel. *The Priestly Blessing in Inscription and Scripture: The Early History of Numbers 6:24-26*. Oxford: Oxford University Press, 2015.

Snyder, Graydon F. *Ante Pacem: Archaeological Evidence of Church Life Before Constantine*. Macon, Ga.: Mercer University Press, 2003.

Sogliano, Antonio. "Isopsephia Pompeiana." *Rendiconti Della Reale Academia Dei Lincei* 10 (1901): 256–59.

Sparks, Brad C. "Egyptian Text Parallels to the Exodus: The Egyptology Literature." In *Out of Egypt: Israel's Exodus Between Text and Memory, History and Imagination Conference*, edited by Thomas E. Levy. University of California, San Diego, 2013. https://www.youtube.com/watch?v=F-Aomm4O794.

Sparks, Kenton L. *Ancient Texts for the Study of the Hebrew Bible: A Guide to the Background Literature*. Grand Rapids: Hendrickson, 2005.

Spence, Lewis. *An Introduction to Mythology*. Hardpress, 2013.

Spijkerman, Augusto. *Cafarnao III: Catalogo della monete della città*. Studium Biblicum Franciscannum 19. Jerusalem, Israel: Franciscan Printing Press, 1975.

Spinka, Matthew. "Acquisition of the Codex Alexandrinus by England." *The Journal of Religion* 16, no. 1 (1936): 10–29.

Sproul, R. C. *The Last Days According to Jesus*. Grand Rapids: Baker, 2000.

Stager, Lawrence E. "Merneptah, Israel and Sea Peoples: New Light on an Old Relief." *Eretz Isreal* 18 (1985): 56–64.

Steffy, J. Richard. "The Boat: A Preliminary Study of Its Construction." In *The Excavations of an Ancient Boat in the Sea of Galilee (Lake Kinneret)*, edited by Shelley Wachsmann, 29–47. 'Atiquot (English Series) 19. Jerusalem, Israel: Israel Antiquities Authority, 1990.

Steiner, Margreet L. "It's Not There: Archaeology Proves a Negative." *BAR* 24, no. 4 (1998): 26–33, 62–63.

Stern, Ephraim, Ayelet Levinson-Gilboa, and Joseph Aviram, eds. *The New Encyclopedia of Archaeological Excavations in the Holy Land*. 4 vols. New York: MacMillan, 1993.

Stern, Philip D. "Of Kings and Moabites: History and Theology in 2 Kings 3 and the Mesha Inscription." *Hebrew Union College Annual* 64 (1993): 1–14.

Stevenson, Angus. *Oxford English Dictionary*. 3rd ed. Oxford: Oxford University Press, 2010.

Stiebing, Jr., William H. *Out of the Desert?: Archaeology and the Exodus/Conquest Narratives*. Buffalo, N.Y: Prometheus, 1989.

Stonehouse, Ned Bernard. *Paul Before the Areopagus: And Other New Testament Studies*. Wheaton, Ill.: Tyndale, 1957.

Stone, R. B. "The Life and Hard Times of Ephraimi Rescriptus." *The Bible Today* 24 (1986): 112–18.

Strack, Hermann Leberecht. *Prophetarum posteriorum codex Babylonicus petropolitanus*. Petropoli: Editio Bibliothecae Publicae Imperialis, 1876.

Strange, James F., and Hershel Shanks. "Synagogue Where Jesus Preached Found at Capernaum." *BAR* 9, no. 6 (1983): 24–31.

Studevant-Hickman, Benjamin, Sarah C. Melville, and Scott Noegel. "Neo-Babylonian Period Texts from Babylonia and Syro-Palestine." In *Ancient Near East: Historical Sources in Translation*, edited by Mark W. Chavalas, 382–406. Blackwell Sourcebooks in Ancient History. Oxford: Wiley & Sons, 2006.

Süel, Aygül. "Ortaköy: Eine hethitische Stadt mit hethitischen und hurritischen Tontafelentdeckungen." In *Hittite and Other Anatolian and Near Eastern Studies in Honour of Sedat Alp: Sedat Alp'a Armağan*, edited by Heinrich Otten and Sedat Alp, 487–92. Ankara: Türk Tarih Kurumu Basımevi, 1992.

Sukenik, Eleazar Lipa. "Funerary Tablet of Uzziah, King of Judah." *PEFSt.* 63, no. 4 (1931): 217–21.

Suriano, Matthew J. "The Apology of Hazael: A Literary and Historical Analysis of the Tel Dan Inscription." *JNES* 66, no. 3 (2007): 163–76.

Swiggers, Pierre. "Babel and the Confusion of Languages (Genesis 1:1-9)." In *Mythos im Alten Testament und seiner Umwelt: Festschrift für Hans-Peter Müller zum 65. Geburtstag*, edited by Armin Lange, Hermann Lichtenberger, and Diethard Römheld, 182–95. BZAW 278. Berlin: de Gruyter, 1999.

Syme, Ronald. "Antonius Saturninus." *JRS* 68 (1978): 12–21.

Tadmor, Hayim. "The Campaigns of Sargon II of Assur: A Chronological-Historical Study (Conclusion)." *JCS* 12, no. 3 (1958): 80–84.

Talmon, Shemaryahu. "Hebrew Written Fragments from Masada." *Dead Sea Discoveries* 3, no. 2 (1996): 168–77.

———. "The Gezer Calendar and the Seasonal Cycle of Ancient Canaan." *JAOS* 83, no. 2 (1963): 177–87.

Tannenbaum, Robert F. "The God-Fearers: Did They Exist? Jews and God-Fearers in the Holy City of Aphrodite." *BAR* 12, no. 5 (1986): 54–57.

Tappy, Ron E. *The Archaeology of Israelite Samaria, Vol. 2: The Eighth Century BCE*. Harvard Semitic Studies 50. Winona Lake, Ind.: Eisenbrauns, 2007.

Tawil, Hayim, and Bernard Schneider. *Crown of Aleppo: The Mystery of the Oldest Hebrew Bible Codex*. Philadelphia, Pa.: Jewish Publication Society, 2010.

Taylor, Joan E. "Pontius Pilate and the Imperial Cult in Roman Judaea." *NTS* 52 (2006): 555–82.

Taylor, John George. "Travels in Kurdistan, with Notices of the Sources of the Eastern and Western Tigris, and Ancient Ruins in Their Neighbourhood." *Journal of the Royal Geographical Society of London* 35 (1865): 21–58.

Tenney, Merrill C., and Moisés Silva, eds. *Zondervan Pictorial Encyclopedia of the Bible*. Revised, Full-Color Edition. 5 vols. Grand Rapids: Zondervan, 2009.

Tepper, Yotam, and Leah Di Segni. *A Christian Prayer Hall of the Third Century CE at Kefar 'Othnay (Legio): Excavations at the Megiddo Prison 2005.* Jerusalem: Israel Antiquities Authority, 2006.

Thiede, Carsten P. "Papyrus Magdalen Greek 17 (Gregory-Aland P64): A Reappraisal." *TynBul* 46 (1995): 29–42.

Thomas, D. Winton. "The Lachish Letters." *JTS* 40 (1939): 1–15.

Thompson, Henry O. *Biblical Archaeology: The World, the Mediterranean, the Bible.* New York: Paragon, 1987.

Thompson, Leonard L. *The Book of Revelation: Apocalypse and Empire.* New York: Oxford University Press, USA, 1997.

Thompson, R. Campbell. "The Rock of Behistun." In *Wonders of the Past: A World-Wide Survey of the Marvellous Works of Man in Ancient Times*, edited by John Alexander Hammerton, 2:760–67. New York: Wise & Co., 1952.

Thompson, Thomas L. *The Historicity of the Patriarchal Narratives: The Quest for the Historical Abraham.* Valley Forge, PA: Trinity Press International, 2002.

———. *The Mythic Past: Biblical Archaeology And The Myth Of Israel.* New York: Basic Books, 2000.

Tigay, Jeffrey H. *The Evolution of the Gilgamesh Epic.* Philadelphia, Pa.: University of Pennsylvania Press, 1982.

Tomei, Maria Antonietta. *Museo Palatino.* Rome: Electa, 1997.

Tov, Emanuel. "A List of the Texts from the Judean Desert." In *The Dead Sea Scrolls After Fifty Years: A Comprehensive Assessment*, edited by Peter W. Flint and James C. VanderKam, 2:669–717. Leiden: Brill, 1999.

———. *Hebrew Bible, Greek Bible and Qumran: Collected Essays.* Mohr Siebeck, 2008.

———. *Textual Criticism of the Hebrew Bible.* Minneapolis, Minn.: Augsburg Fortress, 2001.

Trebilco, Paul R. *The Early Christians in Ephesus from Paul to Ignatius.* WUNT 166. Grand Rapids: Eerdmans, 2007.

Trümper, Monika. "The Oldest Original Synagogue Building in the Diaspora: The Delos Synagogue Reconsidered." *Hesperia* 73, no. 4 (2004): 513–98.

Tucker, Gene M. "The Legal Background of Genesis 23." *JBL* 85, no. 1 (1966): 77–84.

Tuckett, Christopher. "Thomas and the Synoptics." *NovT* 30, no. 2 (April 1, 1988): 132–57.

Tuckett, Christopher M. *Nag Hammadi and the Gospel Tradition: Synoptic Tradition in the Nag Hammadi Library.* Edinburgh: T&T Clark, 1986.

Tupper, E. Frank. "The Revival of Apocalyptic in Biblical and Theological Studies." *Review and Expositor* 72, no. 3 (1975): 279–303.

Tzaferis, Vassilios. "Crucifixion: The Archaeological Evidence." *BAR* 11 (1985): 44–53.

———., ed. *Excavations at Capernaum 1978–1982.* Vol. 1. Winona Lake, Ind.: Eisenbrauns, 1989.

———. "Jewish Tombs at and near Giv'at Ha-Mivtar, Jerusalem." *IEJ* 20, no. 1 (1970): 18–32.

———. "Oldest Church Found? Inscribed 'To God Jesus Christ' Early Christian Prayer Hall Found in Megiddo Prison." *BAR*, 2006. http://www.bib-arch.org/online-exclusives/ oldest-church-02.asp.

Urman, D., and Paul Virgil McCracken Flesher. *Ancient Synagogues: Historical Analysis and Archaeological Discovery.* SPB 47. Leiden: Brill, 1998.

Ussishkin, David. *Biblical Lachish: A Tale of Construction, Destruction, Excavation and Restoration.* Translated by Miriam Feinberg Vamosh. Jerusalem, Israel: Israel Exploration Society and Biblical Archaeology Society, 2014.

———. "Gate 1567 at Megiddo and the Seal of Shema, Servant of Jeroboam." In *Scripture and Other Artifacts: Essays on the Bible and Archaeology in Honor of Philip J. King*, edited by Philip J. King, Michael David Coogan, J. Cheryl Exum, and Lawrence E. Stager, 410–28. Louisville: Westminster/Knox, 1994.

———. "Jezreel—Where Jezebel Was Thrown to the Dogs." *BAR* 36, no. 4 (2010): 32–42.

———. "Royal Judean Storage Jars and Private Seal Impressions." *BASOR*, no. 223 (1976): 1–13.

———. "Solomon's Jerusalem: The Text and the Facts on the Ground." In *Jerusalem in Bible and Archaeology: The First Temple Period*, edited by Andrew G. Vaughn and Ann E. Killebrew, 103–16. Atlanta, Ga.: SBL, 2003.

———. *The Conquest of Lachish by Sennacherib.* Tel Aviv, Israel: Tel Aviv University/Institute of Archaeology, 1983.

———. "The 'Lachish Reliefs' and the City of Lachish." *IEJ* 30, no. 3/4 (1980): 174–95.

van der Horst, Pieter Wilhelm. *Ancient Jewish Epitaphs: An Introductory Survey of a Millennium of Jewish Funerary Epigraphy (300 BCE-700 CE).* Louvain, Belgium: Peeters, 1991.

VanderKam, James C. *The Dead Sea Scrolls Today.* 2nd ed. Grand Rapids: Eerdmans, 2010.

VanderKam, James C., and Peter W. Flint. *The Meaning of the Dead Sea Scrolls: Their Significance for Understanding the Bible, Judaism, Jesus, and Christianity.* San Francisco, Calf.: Harper, 2002.

Vander Laan, Ray. *Faith Lessons on the Promised Land: Crossroads of the World.* Grand Rapids: Zondervan, 1999.

van Henten, Jan Willem. "Nero Redivivus Demolished: The Coherence of the Nero Traditions in the Sibylline Oracles." *Journal for the Study of the Pseudepigrapha* 11, no. 3 (2000): 3–17.

Vann, R. Lindley. "Herod's Harbor Construction Recovered Underwater." *BAR* 9, no. 3 (1983): 10–14.

Van Seters, John. *Abraham in History and Tradition.* New Haven, Conn.: Yale University Press, 1975.

———. "A Date for the 'Admonitions' in the Second Intermediate Period." *JEA* 50 (1964): 13–23.

———. *The Life of Moses: The Yahwist as Historian in Exodus-Numbers.* Louvain, Belgium: Peeters, 1994.

Vardaman, Jerry. "A New Inscription Which Mentions Pilate as 'Prefect.'" *JBL* 81, no. 1 (1962): 70–71.

Varner, Eric R. "Domitia Longina and the Politics of Portraiture." *AJA* 99, no. 2 (1995): 187–206.

Vaughn, Andrew G. "Palaeographic Dating of Judaean Seals and Its Significance for Biblical Research." *BASOR*, no. 313 (1999): 43–64.

Velikovsky, Immanuel. *Ages in Chaos: From the Exodus to King Akhnaton.* New York: Doubleday, 1952.

Vinel, Nicholas. "Le Judaïsme Caché Du Carré Sator de Pompéi: The Hidden Judaism of the Pompeiian Sator Square." *Revue de L'histoire Des Religions* 2 (2006): 173–94.

Voelz, James W. "The Greek of Codex Vaticanus in the Second Gospel and Marcan Greek." *NovT* 47, no. 3 (2005): 209–49.

von Wahlde, Urban C. "Archaeology and John's Gospel." In *Jesus and Archaeology*, edited by James H. Charlesworth, 523–86. Grand Rapids: Eerdmans, 2006.

———. "The Great Public Miqvaot at Bethesda and Siloam, the Development of Jewish Attitudes toward Ritual Purity in Late Second Temple Judaism, and Their Implications for the Gospel of John." In *Rediscovering John: Essays on the Fourth Gospel in Honour of Frederic Manns*, edited by Leslaw Daniel Chrupcala, Mul., 267–81. Milano, Italy: Edizioni Terra Santa, 2013.

———. "The Nature and History of the Birkat Isra'il and Its Relation to the Pool 'With the Expanse of the Sea' (Sir 50:3): Rereading Charles Warren." *PEQ* 142, no. 3 (2010): 159–81.

———. "The Pool of Siloam: The Importance of the New Discoveries For Our Understanding of Ritual Immersion in Late Second Temple Judaism and the Gospel of John." In *John, Jesus, and History: Aspects of Historicity in the Fourth Gospel*, edited by Paul N. Anderson, Felix Just, and Tom Thatcher, 155–73. Atlanta, Ga.: SBL, 2009.

———. "The Puzzling Pool of Bethesda Where Jesus Cured the Crippled Man." *BAR* 37, no. 5 (2011): 40–47, 65.

———. "The 'Upper Pool,' Its 'Conduit,' and 'the Road of the Fuller's Field' in Eighth Century BC Jerusalem and Their Significance for the Pools of Bethesda and Siloam." *RB* 113, no. 2 (2006): 242–62.

Voorst, Robert E. Van. *Jesus Outside the New Testament: An Introduction to the Ancient Evidence.* Grand Rapids: Eerdmans, 2000.

Waaler, Erik. "A Reconstruction of Ketef Hinnom I." *Maarav* 16, no. 2 (2011): 225–63.

Wachsmann, Shelley. *The Sea of Galilee Boat: An Extraordinary 2000 Year Old Discovery.* New York: Springer, 2013.

Wachsmann, Shelley, and Kurt Raveh. "The Discovery." In *The Excavations of an Ancient Boat in the Sea of Galilee (Lake Kinneret)*, edited by Shelley Wachsmann, 1–7. 'Atiquot (English Series) 19. Jerusalem, Israel: Israel Antiquities Authority, 1990.

Waerzeggers, Caroline. "The Babylonian Chronicles: Classification and Provenance." *JNES* 71, no. 2 (2012): 285–98.

Walker, C. B. F. "A Recently Identified Fragment of the Cyrus Cylinder." *Iran* 10 (January 1, 1972): 158–59.

Walker, Larry L. "Babel." Edited by Merrill C. Tenney and Moisés Silva. *ZPEB.* Grand Rapids: Zondervan, 1975.

Wallace, Daniel B. "Earliest Manuscript of the New Testament Discovered?" *The Center for the Study of New Testament Manuscripts*, February 10, 2012. http://www.csntm.org/.

Walton, John H., Victor H. Matthews, and Mark W. Chavalas. *The IVP Bible Background Commentary: Old Testament.* Downers Grove, Ill.: InterVarsity, 2000.

Wargo, Eric. "Everything You Always Wanted to Know About Kemosh (But Were Afraid to Ask)." *BAR* 28, no. 1 (2002): 44–45.

Warren, Charles. "The Moabite Stone." *PEFSt.* 1, no. 4 (1869): 169–82.

Waterhouse, S. Douglas. "Who Were the Habiru of the Amarna Letters?" *Journal of the Adventist Theological Society* 12 (2001): 31–42.

Watkin, David. *The Roman Forum.* Wonders of the World. Cambridge, Mass.: Harvard University Press, 2009.

Watson, Wilfred G. E., and Nicolas Wyatt, eds. *Handbook of Ugaritic Studies.* Atlanta, Ga.: SBL, 2015.

Watzinger, Carl. *Tell El-Mutesellim: Die Funde.* Vol. 2. Leipzig, 1929.

Weidner, Ernst F. "Johachin, König von Jud, in Babylonischen Keischrifttexten." In *Mélanges syriens: offerts à monsieur René Dussaud, secrétaire perpétuel de l'Académie des Inscriptions et Belles-Lettres*, edited by René Dussaud, 2:923–35. Paris, France: P. Geuthner, 1939.

Weiss, Meir. "The Pattern of the 'Execration Texts' in the Prophetic Literature." *IEJ* 19, no. 3 (1969): 150–57.

Wenham, Gordon J. "Grace and Law in the Old Testament." In *Law, Morality and the Bible*, edited by Bruce Kaye and Gordon J. Wenham, 1–24. Downers Grove, Ill.: InterVarsity, 1978.

———. "The Coherence of the Flood Narrative." *VT* 28, no. 3 (1978): 336–48.

Wente, Jr., Edward F. "The Israel Stela." In *The Literature of Ancient Egypt: An Anthology of Stories, Instructions, Stelae, Autobiographies, and Poetry*, edited by William Kelly Simpson, translated by Robert K. Ritner, Vincent A. Tobin, and Edward F. Wente, Jr., 356–60. New Haven, Conn.: Yale University Press, 2003.

Werker, E. "Identification of the Wood." In *The Excavations of an Ancient Boat in the Sea of Galilee (Lake Kinneret)*, edited by Shelley Wachsmann, 65–75. 'Atiquot (English Series) 19. Jerusalem, Israel: Israel Antiquities Authority, 1990.

White, L. Michael. "Synagogue and Society in Imperial Ostia: Archaeological and Epigraphic Evidence." *HTR* 90, no. 1 (1997): 23–58.

Williams, C. L. R. "A Model of the Mastaba-Tomb of Userkaf-Ankh." *The Metropolitan Museum of Art Bulletin* 8, no. 6 (1913): 125–30.

Williamson, H. G. M. "The Accession of Solomon in the Books of Chronicles." *VT* 26, no. 3 (1976): 351–61.

Wilson, Alister I., and Jamie A. Grant. "Introduction." In *The God of Covenant: Biblical, Theological and Contemporary Perspectives*, edited by Alister I. Wilson and Jamie A. Grant, 12–20. Leicester: Apollos, 2005.

Wilson, Kevin A. *The Campaign of Pharaoh Shoshenq I into Palestine*. Forschungen Zum AltenTestament, 2. Reihe 9. Tübingen: Mohr Siebeck, 2005.

Wilson, Mark W. *Biblical Turkey: A Guide to Jewish and Christian Sites of Asia Minor*. Istanbul: Ege Yayinlari, 2010.

———. "Letter from the Field: An Ancient Synagogue Comes to Light." *BAR*, 2009.

Wilson, Robert Dick. "The Papyrus of Elephantine." *The Princeton Theological Review* 12, no. 3 (1914): 411–26.

Winckler, Hugo. *Altorientalische Forschungen*. 3 vols. Leipzig: Pfeiffer, 1902.

———. *Untersuchungen Zur Altorientalischen Geschichte*. Leipzig: Pfeiffer, 1889.

Wiseman, Donald J. *1 and 2 Kings: An Introduction and Commentary*. TOTC. Downers Grove, Ill.: IVP Academic, 2008.

———. "Hammurabi." Edited by Merrill C. Tenney and Moises Silva. *ZPEB*. Grand Rapids: Zondervan, September 19, 2009.

———. *Nebuchadnezzar and Babylon*. Schweich Lectures 1983. Oxford: Oxford University Press, 1985.

Wiseman, James. "Corinth and Rome I: 228 B.C. – 267 A.D." In *Aufstieg Und Niedergang Der Romischen Welt*, edited by Hildegard Temporini and Wolfgang Haase, 7.1:438–548. II. New York: Gruyter, 1979.

Wojciechowski, Michael. "Seven Churches and Seven Celestial Bodies (Rev 1,16; Rev 2-3)." *BN* 45 (1988): 48–50.

Wood, Bryant G. "Balaam Son of Beor." *BS* 8, no. 4 (1995): 115–17.

———. "Extra-Biblical Evidence for the Conquest." *BS* 18, no. 4 (2005): 98–100.

———. "Jerusalem Report: Israeli Scholars Date Garden Tomb to the Israelite Monarchy." *BS* 11, no. 1 (1982): 30–32.

———. "Pharaoh Merneptah Meets Israel." *BS* 18, no. 3 (2005): 65–82.

Woolley, C. Leonard. *Discovering the Royal Tombs at Ur: Joint Expedition of the British Museum and of the Museum of the University of Pennsylvania to Mesopotamia.* New York: Macmillan, 1969.

Woolley, C. Leonard, and Peter R. S. Moorey. *Ur "of the Chaldees."* Revised and Updated. Ithaca, N.Y.: Cornell University Press, 1982.

Worth, Jr., Roland H. *The Seven Cities of Apocalypse and Greco-Asian Culture.* New York: Paulist, 2002.

———. *The Seven Cities of the Apocalypse and Roman Culture.* New York: Paulist, 2002.

Wright, David P. *Inventing God's Law: How the Covenant Code of the Bible Used and Revised the Laws of Hammurabi.* Oxford: Oxford University Press, 2013.

———. "The Laws of Hammurabi as a Source for the Covenant Collection." *Maarav* 20 (2003): 11–88.

Wright, G. Ernest. *Biblical Archaeology.* Abridged. Philadelphia, Pa.: Westminster, 1960.

———. "Judean Lachish." *BA* 18, no. 1 (February 1, 1955): 9–17.

Würthwein, Ernst, and Alexander Achilles Fischer. *The Text of the Old Testament: An Introduction to the Biblia Hebraica.* Translated by Erroll F. Rhodes. 2nd ed. Grand Rapids: Eerdmans, 2014.

Yadin, Yigael. "The Excavation of Masada—1963/64: Preliminary Report." *IEJ* 15, no. 1/2 (January 1, 1965): 1–120.

———. "The Excavations of Masada-the Inscribed Scrolls." *Yediot* 29 (1965): 115–17 (Hebrew).

———. "The Lachish Letters—Originals or Copies and Drafts?" In *Recent Archaeology in the Land of Israel*, edited by Hershel Shanks and Benjamin Mazar, 2nd ed., 179–86. Washington, D.C.: Biblical Archaeology Society, 1985.

Yamada, Shigeo. *The Construction of the Assyrian Empire: A Historical Study of the Inscriptions of Shalmaneser III (859-824 BC) Relating to His Campaigns to the West.* Leiden: Brill, 2000.

Yamauchi, Edwin M. "Archaeology of Palestine and Syria." Edited by Geoffrey W. Bromiley. *ISBE2.* Grand Rapids: Eerdmans, 1995.

———. *New Testament Cities in Western Asia Minor: Light from Archaeology on Cities of Paul and the Seven Churches of Revelation.* Eugene, Oreg.: Wipf & Stock, 2003.

———. "Pre-Christian Gnosticism in the Nag Hammadi Texts?" *Church History* 48, no. 2 (June 1, 1979): 129–41.

———. *The Archaeology of New Testament Cities in Western Asia Minor.* Grand Rapids: Baker, 1980.

Yardeni, Ada. "Remarks on the Priestly Blessing on Two Ancient Amulets from Jerusalem." *VT* 41, no. 2 (1991): 176–85.

Yarden, Leon. *The Spoils of Jerusalem on the Arch of Titus: A Re-Investigation.* Skrifter Utgivna Av Svenska Institutet I Rom 8. Göteborg: Astroms, 1991.

Yeivin, S. "The Date of the Seal 'Belonging to Shemaʿ (The) Servant (Of) Jeroboam.'" *JNES* 19, no. 3 (1960): 205–12.

Yeivin, Ze'ev. "Ancient Chorazin Comes Back to Life: A Galilee Town Is Reconstructed from Fragments." *BAR* 13, no. 5 (October 1987): 22–36.

———. "Has Another Ark Been Found?" *BAR* 9, no. 1 (February 1983): 75–76.

Youngblood, Ronald F., F. F. Bruce, and R. K. Harrison, eds. *Unlock the Bible: Keys to Exploring the Culture and Times.* The Best of Nelson's New Illustrated Bible Dictionary to Enrich Your Bible Study. Nashville, Tenn.: Nelson, 2012.

Younger, K. Lawson. "Yahweh at Ashkelon and Calaḫ? Yahwistic Names in Neo-Assyrian." *VT* 52, no. 2 (2002): 207–18.

Young, Ian. "The Style of the Gezer Calendar and Some 'Archaic Biblical Hebrew' Passages." *VT* 42, no. 3 (July 1, 1992): 362–75.

Yurco, Frank J. "3,200-Year-Old Picture of Israelites Found in Egypt." *BAR* 16, no. 5 (1990): 20–38.

———. "Merenptah's Canaanite Campaign." *Journal of the American Research Center in Egypt* 23 (January 1, 1986): 189–215.

———. "Mernephtah's Canaanite Campaign and Israel's Origins." In *Exodus: The Egyptian Evidence*, edited by Ernest S. Frerichs, Leonard H. Lesko, and William G. Dever, 27–41. Winona Lake, Ind.: Eisenbrauns, 1997.

———. "Yurco's Response." *BAR* 17, no. 6 (1991): 61.

Zahn, T. "John the Apostle." Edited by Johann Jakob Herzog and Philip Schaff. *The New Schaff-Herzog Encyclopedia Of Religious Knowledge.* Grand Rapids: Baker, 1951.

Zanker, Paul. *The Power of Images in the Age of Augustus.* Translated by Alan Shapiro. Ann Arbor, Mich.: University of Michigan Press, 1990.

Zecher, Henry. "The Papyrus Ipuwer, Egyptian Version of the Plagues - A New Perspective." *The Velikovskian, A Journal of Myth, History and Science* 3, no. 1 (1997): 91–126.

Zeitlin, Solomon. "The Warning Inscription of the Temple." *JQR* 38, no. 1 (1947): 111–16.

Zettler, Richard L., and Lee Horne, eds. *Treasures from the Royal Tombs of Ur.* Philadelphia, Pa.: University of Pennsylvania Museum of Archaeology and Anthropology, 1998.

Zevit, Ziony. "Implicit Population Figures and Historical Sense: What Happened to 200,150 Judahites in 701 BCE?" In *Confronting the Past: Archaeological and Historical Essays on Ancient Israel in Honor of William G. Dever*, edited by Seymour Gitin, J. Edward Wright, and J. P. Dessel, 357–65. Winona Lake, Ind.: Eisenbrauns, 2006.

Zias, Joseph. "Human Skeletal Remains from the 'Caiaphas' Tomb." *Atiqot* 21 (1992): 78–80.

Zias, Joseph, and Eliezer Sekeles. "The Crucified Man from Giv'at Ha-Mivtar: A Reappraisal." *IEJ* 35, no. 1 (1985): 22–27.

Zulueta, F. de. "Violation of Sepulture in Palestine at the Beginning of the Christian Era." *JRS*, 1932, 184–97.

Index of Subjects

A

B

E

I

J

K

L

M

N

O

P

Q

R

T

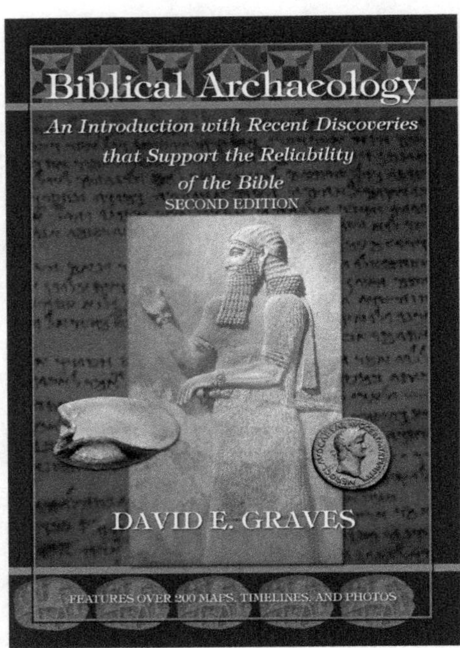

Also by David E. Graves

***Biblical Archaeology Second Edition Vol. 1: An Introduction with Recent Discoveries That Support the Reliability of the Bible*, 2017. B&W ISBN: 978-1502467072; Color ISBN: 978-1983978364; Digital E-ISBN: 978-1535929813**

Each year archaeologists discover many new finds at sites throughout the lands of the Bible, but few of them make the news headlines. Revisionist scholars often seek to undermine and downplay the relevance of many of the discoveries, believing that Sodom never existed, the Exodus never happened, Jericho never fell to the Israelites, and David was never a great king. This work challenges the minimalist views by bringing together many of the new discoveries from the last 20 years highlighting the recent finds that are relevant to the claims of the Bible. Experienced archaeologist David Graves has assembled a helpful collection of discoveries that will take you on a journey to:

- Confirm the historicity of the biblical events and people of the past
- Explore the full range of new archaeological discoveries, from pottery, inscriptions, seals, ossuaries, through to coins, manuscripts, and other artifacts
- Present a short history of archaeology, outlining its characteristics and role in Christian apologetics
- Lay out the limitations of archaeology and its methodological fallacies
- Explain the meticulous method of excavation
- Explore the significance of manuscripts for the transmission of the Bible
- Navigate the maze of arguments between the minimalists and maximalists controversy

This insightful book will:

- Illustrate archaeological finds with more than 140 pertinent photographs
- Provide numerous detailed maps, carefully crafted charts and tables of previous discoveries
- Include helpful breakout panes, dealing with "Quotes from Antiquity," and "Moments in History"
- Include a glossary defining technical archaeological terms
- Provide extensive footnotes and bibliography for future study

This invaluable resource provides an interesting and informative understanding of the cultural and historical background of the Bible illustrated from archaeology. This is an accessible resource intended for laypeople who want to know more about archaeology and the Bible, whether in seminary courses, college classrooms, church groups or personal study.

CPSIA information can be obtained
at www.ICGtesting.com
Printed in the USA
LVHW101911290719
625731LV00007B/225/P

9 781987 754049